PAGE
40

ON THE
ROAD

YOUR COMPLETE DESTINATION GUIDE
In-depth reviews, detailed listings
and insider tips

W9-CAE-054

★ Helsinki
(FINLAND)
p171

Estonia
p42

Latvia
p183

Lithuania
p276

Kaliningrad
(RUSSIA)
p386

THIS EDITION WRITTEN AND RESEARCHED BY

Brandon Presser,

Mark Baker, Peter Dragicevich, Simon Richmond,

Andy Symington

welcome to Estonia, Latvia & Lithuania

Li'l Nations; Big Attitude

From a foreign perspective it seems rather easy to group Estonia, Latvia and Lithuania into one Baltic bundle. They are, after all, three little countries in a tiny continental corner where Northern and Eastern Europe meet. Upon closer inspection, however, it becomes rapidly apparent that these three nations are hardly alike. Beyond the basics like language, you'll find wildly different worlds as you pass across borders. From religion to more modern propensities, such as design aesthetics and popular music, each Baltic sibling has a significantly different set of fundamentals that helps make it unique.

A Limitless History

The Baltic countries shouldn't merely be measured against each other: these three nations sit at the crossroads of some of the fiercest powers the world has even known, where, over a thousand years ago, warring pagan tribes battled each other. Christian subjugation soon followed with the arrival of the Hanseatic League and Teutonic Knights. Sweden, Poland and Russia each had their turn to incorporate the land into their expanding empires. Then modern powers, eg the Soviet Union and the Nazis, had a go, too.

Every power that's held claim over the Baltic has left an indelible mark of its rule, from the haunting tribal mounds of

A land of crumbling castles, soaring dunes, pagan rituals, towering pine forests, quaking lakelands and churning northern seas – a trip to the Baltic proves that fairy tales do come true...

(left) Old Town Rīga, Latvia (p185)
(below) Teashop, Vilnius, Lithuania (p280)

the ancient pagans, to the soaring stone castles and cathedral spires of medieval kingdoms, to the opulent manor houses of 18th- and 19th-century feudal lands, and the space station–like bases and efficiently boxy structures, of the Soviet era.

Welcome to the Party

On any trip, one gets a certain excitement – almost giddiness – when discovering a new destination, so consider for a minute that the Baltic nations are just as elated to get to know you (and to find out what has drawn you to their country). This newfound openness starkly contrasts with the terse qualities of the former Russian influence (not to mention the bleak winter weather) and shows that the Balts are primed for tourists and seem genuinely invested in ensuring that visitors have a good time.

There's eagerness in the air; it permeates the borders of all three countries featured in this book. Estonia, Latvia and Lithuania are ready to shed any remaining fetters from their history of Soviet oppression. These Baltic brothers are globalising, glamorising, stylising, and you've been officially invited to the party as they leapfrog over the other emerging European nations to firmly take their place on the world's stage as three distinct nations.

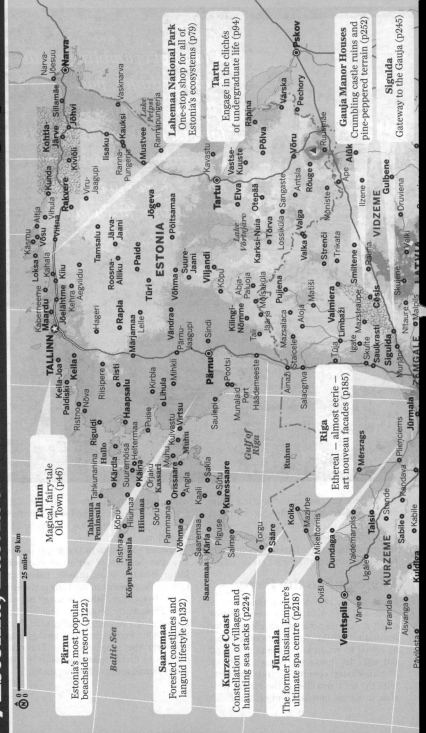

Lahemaa National Park
One-stop shop for all of Estonia's ecosystems (p79)

Tartu
Engage in the clichés of undergraduate life (p94)

Gauja Manor Houses
Crumbling castle ruins and pine-peppered terrain (p252)

Sigulda
Gateway to the Gauja (p245)

Tallinn
Magical, fairy-tale Old Town (p46)

Pärnu
Estonia's most popular beachside resort (p122)

Saaremaa
Forested coastlines and languid lifestyle (p132)

Kurzeme Coast
Constellation of villages and haunting sea stacks (p224)

Jūrmala
The former Russian Empire's ultimate spa centre (p218)

Riga
Ethereal – almost eerie – art nouveau facades (p185)

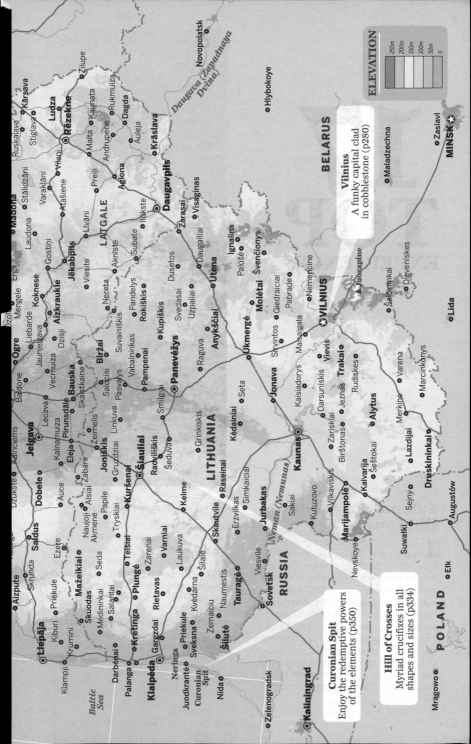

Baltic Sea

ELEVATION

250m
200m
150m
100m
50m
0

LATVIA

Daugava (Zapadnaya Dvina)

LATGALE

Vilnius
A funky capital clad
in cobblestone (p280)

Curonian Spit
Enjoy the redemptive powers
of the elements (p350)

Hill of Crosses
Myriad crucifixes in all
shapes and sizes (p334)

LITHUANIA

RUSSIA

Neman (Nemunas)

BELARUS

POLAND

MINSK ☆

VILNIUS ✪

17
TOP
EXPERIENCES

Tallinn's Fairy-tale Old Town

1 There was a time when sturdy walls and turreted towers enclosed most of Europe's cities but wartime bombing and the coming of the car put paid to most of them. In Estonia, Tallinn's Old Town (p47) is a magical window into that bygone world, inducing visions of knights, cads, ladies and wenches – not least due to the locals' proclivity for period dress. Rambling lanes lined with medieval dwellings open onto squares once covered in the filth of every-day commerce but now lined with cafes and altogether less gory markets selling handicrafts.

Midsummer's Eve

2 Although church affiliations are wide-spread throughout the Baltic, ancient pagan rituals are still deeply woven into the fabric of all three countries and their people. Storks are revered, even-numbered flowers are superstitiously rebuffed, and the summer solstice is held in the highest regard (p32). The religious element of midsummer's eve has largely disappeared; it's the spirit of togetherness that remains – family and friends gather at their forest cottages for a bright night of beer and bonfires. Jūrmala, Latvia

Latvia's Castles & Manor Houses

3 A quick glance at a map reveals Latvia's key position along the ancient trade routes between Western Europe and Russia. Crumbling castle ruins abound throughout the pine-peppered terrain, each a testament to a forgotten kingdom. For many years, the country was divided into feudal puzzle pieces, and thus you'll find dozens of manor houses throughout the landscape. Spending the night at one of these elegantly restored mansions (*muižas*; p252) is truly an unforgettable experience. Rundāle Palace (p239)

Curonian Spit

4 There's something elemental – even slightly old-fashioned – about Lithuania's loveliest seaside retreat: a long, thin strip of rare and majestic sand dunes that lines the southeastern corner of the Baltic Sea. Maybe it's the pine scent, or the sea breezes, or the relative isolation that so vividly recalls German writer Thomas Mann's sojourns here in the early 1930s. Come to Curonian Spit (p350) to recharge your batteries and renew your faith in the redemptive powers of wind, water, earth and sky.

Vilnius's Baroque Old Town

5 Tempting hideaways, inviting courtyards, big baroque churches and tiny cellar beer joints, Vilnius's Old Town (Lithuania; p283) is one of the funkiest places to get lost in all the Baltic. Old and new seem to coexist seamlessly and, whether you're looking for that thrift-shop boutique, an organic bakery, a cosy little bookshop or just a quiet spot to have a coffee, they're all likely to be standing side-by-side down some as yet unexplored, cobblestoned alleyway. Vilnius is yours for the taking.

Saaremaa

6 There's something about heading out to an island that lifts the experience out of the ordinary and, while Saaremaa in Estonia is no tropical paradise, the languid pace of this forested place weaves a magic all of its own. The highlight is Kuressaare Castle (p134), the Baltic's best-preserved medieval fortress, looming proudly behind its moat by the harbour. Yet it's the island's windmills, particularly the photogenic quintet at Angla (p140), that provide the iconic Saaremaa image that you'll see on bottles of beer, vodka and water throughout Estonia.

Rīga's Art Nouveau Architecture

7 If you ask any Rīgan where to find the city's world-famous art nouveau architecture (p202), you will always get the same answer: 'Look up!' Over 750 buildings in Latvia's capital (more than any other city in Europe) boast this flamboyant and haunting style of decor. Spend a breezy afternoon snapping your camera at the imaginative facades in the city's Quiet Centre district to find an ethereal – and almost eerie – melange of screaming demons, enraptured deities, overgrown flora and bizarre geometrical patterns.

STÉPHANE VICTOR/LONELY PLANET IMAGES © KISSING STUDENTS: MATI KARMIN & TIIT TRUMMAL

Tartu

8 Tartu (p94) is to Estonia what Oxford and Cambridge are to England. Like those towns, it's the presence of an esteemed ancient university and its attendant student population (with associated high japes and insobriety) that gives it its special character. There's a museum on nearly every corner of Tartu's elegant streets and, it seems, a grungy bar in every other cellar. When the sun shines, the verdant hill in the centre of town is the place to observe those eternal clichés of undergraduate life: earnest prattling, hopeless romancing and enthusiastic drinking.

Saunas & Spas

9 Although the Turks and the Russians may be more famous for their baths, the Baltic brethren love to hop into their birthday suits for a good soak and steam. There are plenty of spa centres around the Baltic – especially in Estonia and Latvia – where you can purr like a kitten while being pummelled by experts, but most prefer to go native, so to speak, and indulge in a traditional sauna experience: getting whipped by dried birch branches while sweating it out in temperatures beyond 60°C. Sounds relaxing...

Mushrooms!

10 Cast away your preconceived notions about potatoes and pork tongue – the Baltic table no longer feels like a Soviet cafeteria. The locavore movement isn't just up-and-coming, it has arrived with much ado and its mascot is the mushroom. The damp climate makes it one of the finest areas in the world for growing all sorts of scrumptious fungi, and plucking them from the wet earth is even more fun than devouring them. In fact, mushrooming isn't simply a pastime; it's a national obsession!

Sigulda & Gauja National Park

11 With a name that sounds like a mythical ogress, it comes as no surprise that Sigulda – the gateway to the Gauja, in Latvia – captures the hearts and minds of those who visit. The tower of Turaida Castle (p246) rises majestically over the huddling pines – a glorious reminder of the fairy-tale kingdoms that once ruled the land. And after you've had your history lesson, it's time to spice things up with a bevy of adrenalin sports, such as bungee jumping from a moving cable car or careening down a frozen bobsled track (p247).

Hill of Crosses

12 Your first thought as you traverse the flat Lithuanian landscape in search of this landmark is likely to be something along the lines of, 'Where did they ever find a hill?' And then you glimpse it in the distance, more a mound than a mountain, covered in crosses by the tens of thousands. The hill (p334) takes on even more significance when you realise that the crosses planted here represent not just religious faith but an affirmation of the country's very identity.

11

TRISH PUNCH/LONELY PLANET IMAGES ©

12

CRAIG PERSHOUSE/LONELY PLANET IMAGES ©

Jūrmala

13 Though it may not be obvious at first, Jūrmala (Latvia; p218) is *the* spa centre for all of the former Russian Empire. And while the sanatorium craze has come and gone, it's still an uberpopular place to pamper oneself silly with the unending menus of bizarre services (chocolate massages?). Even if you're not particularly keen to swim at the chilly Blue Flag beaches nearby, it's well worth the day trip from Rīga to check out the vacationing celebrities and witness the ostentatious presentations of the nouveau riche men and their trophy-wife arm candy.

Kurzeme Coast

14 While Lithuanians relish the dune-riddled Curonian Spit, and Estonians embrace island life on Saaremaa and Hiiumaa, Latvia's Kurzeme coastline in between is a rather desolate place, with but a small constellation of towns betwixt haunting sea stacks and crumbling Soviet watchtowers. There's punky Liepāja in the south, the cream-coloured beaches of wealthy Ventspils further along, and things come to a crashing climax in the north at Kolka (p225) where the Baltic Sea meets the Bay of Riga in a most dramatic fashion.

Pärnu

15 Chances are you're not visiting the Baltic with images of golden sand beaches hovering before your eyes, but Pärnu (p122) offers exactly that. When the quirky notion of sea-bathing became fashionable within a whisper of the 20th century, Pärnu became Estonia's most popular seaside resort – and it's hardly less so today. Architectural gems of that period combine with relics of the Hanseatic past to create very pleasant streets to explore, with interesting eateries and bars lurking within them.

Soviet Relics

16 It's been just over 20 years since the Baltic brothers ripped the iron curtain to shreds and, while these newborn nations soar towards globalisation with alacrity, there are still plenty of dour tenements and crumbling coastal watchtowers that remind us of harder times. Many of the other Soviet relics, however, allow visitors to explore the past à la James Bond: newly unearthed bunkers and re-furbished KGB headquarters offer mirth and wonderment for even the mildest of history buffs. Vilnius

Lahemaa National Park

17 Providing a one-stop shop of all of Estonia's major habitats (coast, forests, plains, peat bogs, lakes and rivers) within a very convenient 80km of the capital, Lahemaa (p79) is the slice of rural Estonia that travellers on a tight schedule really shouldn't miss. On top of the natural attractions, there are graceful baroque manors to peruse, dinky villages to visit and country taverns to take refuge in whenever the weather turns and the stomach growls.

need to know

Currency

» Estonia: euro (€)

» Latvia: lats (Ls)

» Lithuania: litas (Lt)

Language

» Estonia: Estonian

» Latvia: Latvian (Russian also commonly spoken)

» Lithuania: Lithuanian

When to Go?

Tallinn
GO May–Sep

Riga
GO Dec–Jan, Jun

Vilnius
GO Jun–Sep

Warm to Hot Summers, Cold Winters

High Season
(Jun–Aug)

» Beds in the capitals are usually booked out – plan ahead!

» Endless daylight and warm weather encourage alfresco dining.

» Midsummer festivities during the summer solstice are not to be missed.

Shoulder
(May & Sep)

» Airfare drops significantly outside of the summer rush, but the weather is still mild.

» Many attractions reduce their hours of operation.

Low Season
(Oct–Apr)

» Expect frigid temperatures and limited daylight.

» Coastal towns are almost completely shut down.

» Crowds often converge on the capitals and meagre ski hills during the holiday season.

Your Daily Budget

Budget less than
€60

» Hostel or guesthouse: €10–35

» Two meals: €15

» Walking around town: free

» Museum entry: €3

» Drinks at a beer garden: €7

Midrange
€60–120

» Hotel room: €50

» Two meals: €28

» Public transport: €2

» Entry to a couple of top museums: €5

» Drinks at a posh lounge: €15

Top end over
€120

» Luxury hotel room: €75

» Two meals: €55

» Taxis: €8

» A day spent at museums: €7

» Pub crawl: €20

Money

» ATMs are widely available throughout. Credit cards are commonly accepted at most restaurants and hotels.

Visas

» Citizens from the EU, Australia, Canada, Japan, New Zealand and the US do not require visas for entry into Estonia, Latvia or Lithuania.

Mobile Phones

» Pre-paid SIM cards available throughout; compatible with most foreign phones.

Driving/ Transport

» Drive on the right. Buses and trains are a common means of transport between cities, though private vehicles are easier.

Websites

» **Baltic Times** (www .baltictimes.com) English-language newspaper covering all three Baltic countries

» **Visit Estonia** (www .visitestonia.com) Estonia's official tourism portal

» **Latvia** (www.latvia .travel) Latvia's official tourism website

» **Lithuanian Travel Information** (www .travel.lt) Lithuania's leading tourism portal

» **Baltic Country Holidays** (www .traveller.lv) Extensive booking network for rural accommodation throughout all three countries

» **Lonely Planet** (www .lonelyplanet.com)

Exchange Rates

		Est	Lith	Lat
Australia	A$1	€0.73	2.58Lt	0.54Ls
Canada	C$1	€0.71	2.55Lt	0.52Ls
Euro zone	€1	€1	3.45Lt	0.71Ls
Japan	¥100	€0.96	3.51Lt	0.69Ls
UK	£1	€1.16	3.97Lt	0.83Ls
US	US$1	€0.74	2.53Lt	0.53Ls

For current exchange rates see www.xe.com.

Important Numbers

Estonia country code	372
Latvia country code	371
Lithuania country code	370
International access code	00

Arriving in the Region

» **Rīga Airport**
Lime-green taxis – (the most reliable option) flat rate 10Ls to the city (7km)
Bus 22 – 0.70Ls to city
Lime-green shared vans – 3Ls

» **Tallinn Airport**
Public bus – €1.60 to city (4km)
Hansabuss –blue, €2
Hotel shuttles – €5
Taxi – usually under €10 to city

» **Vilnius Airport**
Bus – 2.50Lt to city centre (5km)
Train – Train, or bus 1 connects to the train station
Minibus – 3Lt (faster)
Taxi – prebooked 30Lt; hailed at airport 50-60Lt

Getting There & Around

Besides the three international airports of the nations' capitals, it is also quite common to access the Baltic countries via the ferry from Helsinki that docks in Tallinn. Rapid bus services connect Tallinn, Rīga and Vilnius, though if you plan on travelling through rural areas it is best to hire your own vehicle. Rental cars can be driven in any of the three Baltic countries, but not beyond. Prices spike during the summer months. Both manual and automatic cars are commonly available. Dull wheels and uneven terrain may cause flat tyres – roads in Latvia are the worst of the bunch.

Within Estonia there are flights from Tallinn to Tartu and Kuressaare. There are no commercial flights within Latvia or Lithuania.

what's new

For this new edition of Estonia, Latvia & Lithuania, our authors have hunted down the fresh, the transformed, the hot and the happening. These are some of our favourites. For up-to-the-minute recommendations, see lonelyplanet.com.

Biking the Baltic

1 With a recent explosion of guide maps and brochures – enough to wallpaper your den – it is now easier than ever to navigate the Baltic by bike. In Lithuania dozens of urban bike paths have been added to the country's major cities, and further north in Latvia and Estonia you'll find over 1200km of signposted track as part of the new 'Tour de LatEst' project. (p29)

Cold War Museum

2 The much-anticipated Museum to the Cold War sits on the site of a former Soviet nuclear-missile base that once packed enough power to destroy the European continent. Situated deep in the heart of the Žemaitija National Park, it was kept secret from the Lithuanian people for decades. (p367)

Rotermann Quarter

3 Gentrification at its finest can be found at this former factory complex. Today it bustles with shops, offices, apartments and some of Tallinn's finest restaurants. In summer stop by for the weekly farmers market. (p56)

Piens

4 Party like a local at Piens ('Milk'), Rīga's premiere romp house located in the trendy Miera district just up from the city centre. A new branch of Deli-snack has opened on the premises, so you no longer have to make the trek out to Liepāja to taste-test this burger institution. (p212)

Rumene Manor

5 Rescued from a fate of perpetual disrepair, Rumene Manor has been fully restored to its former glory and transformed into an opulent hotel with the help of the owners of Hotel Bergs, Zaiga Gaile – famed local architect – and a small infusion of EU funds. This is, without a doubt, one of the most elegant stays in all of the Baltic. (p227)

Kastani 38

6 Opened in 1910 as a bread factory, this huge brick warehouse has become a crucible of creative activity. Expect to find ateliers for Tartu's up-and-coming fashion designers and photographers, in addition to several new museums and a promising hostel. (p100)

Latvian fashion design

7 After losing their jobs during the recent global economic crisis, many Latvians turned towards their hobbies for financial gain, and suddenly a mighty brigade of local designers emerged, who capitalised on low rents to peddle their unique retail wares. (p215)

Hotel Viru KGB Museum

8 When the Hotel Viru was built in 1972 it was not only Estonia's first skyscraper, it was, quite literally, the only place for tourists to stay in Tallinn. At the top of the tower was a KGB spy base, and today the now-privatised hotel offers guided tours of the facility in a multitude of languages. (p56)

if you like...

Castles

As the nexus of trading routes between Western Europe and Russia, the Baltic was once a veritable jigsaw puzzle of feudal territories – the scatter of castle ruins is a testament to the region's geographical importance.

Trakai This fairy-tale-worthy red-brick castle atop a tiny island provides a scenic backdrop for paddling around the pretty lakes of the Trakai Historical National Park (p308)

Rundāle Palace Latvia's primo palatial gem is a flawless tribute to opulence designed by Rastrelli, the architect responsible for St Petersburg's sumptuous Winter Palace (p239)

Kuressaare Castle The Baltic's best preserved medieval castle, moat and all (p134)

Muižas of the Gauja Go one better than visiting Latvia's feudal castles by spending the night at one of the striking *muižas* (manor houses) dotting the pine-studded countryside (p252)

Beaches

Surprise! Betcha didn't know the Baltic was top dog when it came to endless stretches of flaxen shoreline. The summers are short, of course, but beach bums will be handsomely rewarded with golden tresses of sand during the warmer months.

Nida Something completely different for a seaside resort: peace and quiet and unrivalled natural beauty amid sand dunes and pine trees (p354)

Jūrmala The Baltic's original flavour of posh beachside spa resort still teems with Russian oil tycoons and their model-esque trophy wives (p218)

Pärnu Synonymous in these parts with fun in the sun, the resort town of Pärnu has golden sand and bronzed bods aplenty (p122)

Tahkuna Accessed by a forest path on the island of Saaremaa, Tahkuna's sandy shore offers comparative peace and quiet (p140)

Museums

There's a lot of history to document here, but many of the region's museums pay tribute to a bevy of quirkier interests in addition to the region's war-torn past.

Museum of Occupations Five decades of WWII and Cold War occupation are brought to life through the personal stories of the victims and survivors (p49)

Pedvāle Open-Air Art Museum Deep in the heart of Latvia's Abava River Valley you'll find an unusual farmstead dotted with over 100 large-scale sculptures – art enthusiasts can even camp here for the night (p228)

Museum of Devils You'll find Lucifer in all of his (or her) various guises at this unusual three-floor exhibition in Kaunas's New Town (p329)

Tallinn's City Museum The tale of Tallinn is told across 10 different sites but this museum's main branch, in a 14th-century merchant's house, is particularly riveting (p49)

» Art nouveau facade in Rīga (p185)

Architecture

The architecture in all three of the Baltic's capitals is truly a sight for sore eyes, be it baroque flourishes, medieval gables or dazzling art nouveau – you'll need a back massage after days of craning your neck towards the heavens.

Rīga's Art Nouveau Architecture A feast of architectural eye-candy is yours for the taking in Latvia's bustling capital – overly adorned facades cloak the hundreds of imposing structures that radiate beyond the city's castle core (p202)

Vilnius' Old Town All steeples, domes and pillars, the capital's wonderfully preserved Old Town looks as if it were curated with a museum director with more than a penchant for baroque (p283)

Tallinn's Old Town A treasure trove of medieval battlements, dwellings and public buildings (p47)

Kumu Seven stories of limestone, glass and copper, Tallinn's spectacular art museum has set the standard for Estonia's new millennium (p57)

Quaint Villages

You want charming farmsteads and whisper-quiet villages? The Baltic's got them in spades, especially as locals trade in their bucolic lifestyles for life in the big city.

Koguva Trapped in a picturesque time rift in a corner of the island of Muhu, this fishing village offers places to stay and eat, and a window to the past (p131)

Labanoras An achingly pretty wooded village smack dab in the middle of a protected region of forests and ponds, and home to one of the country's most inviting old-school inns p316)

Kuldīga Whimsically known as the 'city where salmon fly', crumbly Kuldīga is a pleasant reward for more intrepid travellers; it's frequently used as the backdrop for local period films (p229)

Rõuge Set in valley punctuated by seven small lakes and surrounded by hills, Rõuge is the Estonian rural idyll personified (p110)

Wartime Relics

From Soviet strife and Nazi rule to ancient tribal battles and invading medieval forces, the Baltic has seen its fair share of bloodshed.

Līgatne Bunker Concealed under a rehabilitation centre for decades, this high-security bunker is now a delightful tribute to the Soviet spy game. Everything's perfectly intact – James Bond, eat your heart out! (p253)

Paneriai The Nazis murdered as many as 100,000 people, including some 70,000 Jews, in the woods here during WWII. A respectful memorial and museum helps to tell this tragic story (p308)

Karosta Prison Constructed as a hospital but used as a punishment facility for disobedient Russian soldiers, Karosta offers visitors the unique opportunity to experience life as a detainee – midnight bed checks and horrid latrines included (p235)

Žemaitija National Park This bucolic national park hides one of the great Soviet secrets of the Cold War: an underground nuclear missile base. Tour one of the former bunkers at the 'Cold War' museum (p366)

month by month

Top Events

1 **Midsummer's Eve**, June

2 **Song & Dance Festival**, July (every five years)

3 **Positivus Festival**, July

4 **Black Night's Film Festival**, November

5 **Christmas**, December

January

New Year's celebrations and continued festive cheer warm the hearts of locals as they weather what already feels like an endless winter with limited daylight.

New Year's Day

Festivities from the night before continue during this public holiday as locals incorporate pagan practices at family gatherings to ensure a happy and healthy year.

February

The cold and snowy winter continues, but locals make the most of it as they flock to their bunny slopes for some skiing.

Ski Marathon

Held in the countryside surrounding Estonia's second city, the Tartu Ski Marathon is a 63km cross-country race that draws about 4000 competitors, the winners completing the course in less than three hours. Participants slide off in sports-mad Otepää.

Fish & Dips

The three-day Palangos *ruoniai* (Palanga 'Seals' Festival), held in the Lithuanian seaside resort of Palanga in mid-February, lures hungry fish lovers to try the city's beloved smelts. There's also the annual polar bear event, at which hardy swimmers frolic in the freezing waters of the Baltic Sea.

March

Locals pull the curtains to check the weather outside and, yup, it's still winter out there.

Lithuanian Folk Art

The annual St Casimir's Fair (Kaziuko *mugė*), a festival of folk arts and crafts (www.kaziukomuge.lt in Lithuanian), is held at the beginning of March in both Vilnius and Kaunas.

Horror Show

Zombies take over the streets and screens of Haapsalu, on Estonia's west coast, during the Horror & Fantasy Film Festival, usually held in late March. This showcase of creepy and kooky films is timed to coincide with the full moon.

April

Frosty nights officially come to an end as the mean temperature stabilises well above zero. Hope of spring has arrived; locals burst forth from their shuttered houses to inhale the fickle spring air.

Jazz in Tallinn

Jazz greats from around the world converge on Tallinn, Estonia, in mid-April during the two-week Jazzkaar festival. Musicians play not just at concert halls but on the streets, in squares and parks, and even at the airport.

Tartu Student Days

Tartu's students let their hair down in this wild pagan celebration marking the end of term and the dawn of spring in Estonia. A second, smaller version occurs in mid-October.

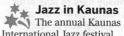
Jazz in Kaunas

The annual Kaunas International Jazz festival (www.kaunasjazz.lt), held in late April, is arguably Lithuania's most prestigious and popular jazz event.

May

The days are noticeably longer now as weather conditions dramatically improve. Tourist-focused businesses start revving their engines, and excitement fills the air in anticipation of a fruitful summer.

Tallinn Goes Medieval

Held in Tallinn's cinematic 14th-century streets, Old Town Days is a week of themed days involving dancing, concerts, costumed performers, sports and plenty of medieval merrymaking.

Modern Dance

The annual New Baltic Dance Festival (www.dance.lt), featuring contemporary and modern dance, draws companies from around Lithuania and the world to Vilnius for a week of performances in early May.

Baltic Ballet

The International Baltic Ballet Festival (www.ballet-festival.lv) features stirring performances by Latvian and international companies over three weeks in Rīga.

June

The warm weather is finally here to stay after several fits and bursts of spring sun in April and May. The region-wide Midsummer's Eve festivities officially announce the arrival of summer.

Midsummer's Eve

The region's biggest annual night out is a celebration of the Midsummer's Night, best experienced out in the countryside, where huge bonfires flare for all-night revellers.

Folk Fun

The annual International Folklore Festival (www.visitneringa.com) held in the town of Nida on Curonian Spit draws folk musicians and dance troupes from the various Lithuanian regions and from around Europe. It is held over the weekend in late June.

Opera in Rīga

The Latvian National Opera's showcase event (www.opera.lv), the Rīga Opera Festival takes place over 10 days and includes performances by world-renowned talent.

July

Summer is in full swing as locals gather on terraces and verandas during the week to sip mugs of beer alfresco; on the weekends everyone flees the cities for their countryside abodes.

Beer & Bands

The Estonian island of Saaremaa's long tradition of home brewing is celebrated at the Õlletoober beer festival, alongside live rock music and festivities. It's held in the village of Lilbi, 5km northeast of Kuressaare.

Folk fo(u)r Days

The Estonian town of Viljandi is overrun with folk-music aficionados during its hugely popular four-day festival featuring musicians from Estonia and abroad. Over 100 concerts are held, attended by more than 20,000 people.

Serious Cinema

Pärnu International Film Festival, coordinated by the city's Museum of New Art, showcases documentary and anthropological films from all over the world. It's held early in the month in the museum and other venues around Estonia's premier beach resort.

Rock-a-Beery

An extremely popular ale-guzzling and rock-music extravaganza, Õllesummer (Beer Summer) is held over three days at the historic Song Festival Grounds in Estonia's capital, Tallinn, in early July.

Sea Festival

The annual five-day Klaipėda Sea Festival (www.jurossvente.lt) is held over the third weekend in July and celebrates the Lithuanian seaport's rich nautical heritage.

Devil's Stone Music

Just a few years old, this rock and metal music festival (Velnio akmuo; www.devilstone.net) is held in the central Lithuanian town of Anykščiai in mid-July. Acts perform hard rock, heavy metal, Goth, electronica and speed metal. If you've got the hair, you know where to be.

All That Jazz
Jazz comes to the sand dunes of a Lithuanian Baltic Sea resort at the annual Nida Jazz Marathon (www.nidajazz.lt). Expect several days of concerts with jam sessions afterwards at various venues around the Curonian Spit in late July and early August.

Võru Folklore
Mid-July in Võru is a whir of dancers, singers and musicians decked out in the colourful folk costumes of Estonia and a dozen other nations, celebrating their respective ethnic traditions and cultures.

Medieval Mayhem
The Hansa Days Festival celebrates the Hanseatic past of Estonia's spiritual and intellectual capital, Tartu, with three days of costumed peasants, ladies, jesters, knights, crafts demonstrations, markets, family-friendly performances and more in mid-July.

Rīgas Ritmi
'Rīga's Rhythms' is the Latvian capital's international music festival (www.rigasritmi.lv).

New Singers
The New Wave Song Festival (www.newwavestars.com, in Russian), a soloist song contest held in Jūrmala, Latvia, attracts competitors from around the world. It has recently grown to phenomenal

heights in the Russian-speaking world.

Wine Festival
The village of Sabile, Latvia, is famed for its vineyard – the world's most northern open-air grape grower. The only chance to taste local wine is at this festival (www.sabile.lv).

Open-air Opera
An outdoor opera festival (www.sigulda.lv) is held in Sigulda's castle ruins, Latvia.

Song & Dance
Held separately in each Baltic country over several days, the massive Song & Dance Festival attracts people with Baltic roots from all over the world to perform in mammoth choirs or large-scale dance routines that give North Koreans a run for their money.

Positively Musical
Taking place amid the quiet pines of northern Vidzeme, Positivus has become an annual pilgrimage for many Latvians, who flock here for several days of music-filled revelry (www.positivusfestival.lv).

Summer Sound
Liepāja holds the title as Latvia's haven for punk garage-band players, so any of its local music festivals are well worth checking out – especially Summer Sound (www.summersound.lv), which draws up to 40,000 people each year.

August

Long live cloudless afternoons spent at the beach and extended holidays from work, as locals savour every drop of golden sun – despite the occasional rainstorm.

Film Alfresco
The week-long tARTuFF open-air film festival has free screenings of art-house features and documentaries in the atmospheric Raekoja plats (Town Hall Sq), in the heart of Tartu, Estonia. Poetry readings and concerts round out the program.

Ghost stories
Held in the grounds of Haapsalu's castle in western Estonia, the White Lady Festival culminates in the appearance of a ghostly apparition in the church window, caused by the reflection of the full moon in the glass.

Classical Concerts
The Christopher Summer Festival is two months of classical music concerts (www.kristupofestivaliai.lt) held around the Lithuanian capital, Vilnius.

Pagan Music
The popular MJR Alternative Music Festival (mėnuo Juodaragis; www.mjr.lt) celebrates – nominally – Lithuania's pagan roots; it's really just a chance to hear music rarely heard anywhere else. Held over the last weekend in August on an island near the eastern Lithuanian city of Zarasai.

Maritime Merriment

Early in the month, Kuressaare on the Estonian island of Saaremaa celebrates its maritime credentials with its Maritime Festival, a weekend of sea-related activities including regatta, fair, herring-cooking demonstrations, bands and a strong naval presence.

Classical Songbirds

The atmospheric ruins of St Bridget's Convent in Pirita, Tallinn's most popular beach suburb, offer an excellent backdrop to experience Estonia's vibrant singing tradition in the Birgitta Festival, comprising choral, opera and classical concerts.

Art by Night

Baltā Nakts (White Night; www.baltanakts.lv), sponsored by the Contemporary Art Forum, mirrors Paris' night-long showcase of artists and culture around the city of Rīga (Latvia).

Piens Fest

A hipster's dream festival, Piens Fest feels like an almost-accidental gathering of local artists (music and otherwise) in the industrial Miera iela area of Rīga. Devour fried food, peruse vintage attire and listen to indie beats while sitting on the grass.

September

The last days of summer quickly turn into the mild beginning of autumn; rain is more frequent by the end of the month, while leaves turn brilliant colours and tumble off the trees.

World Theatre

Sirenos (sirens) International Theatre Festival (www.okt.lt) is a popular annual drama festival held in Vilnius, Lithuania, from mid-September to mid-October and draws people from around the world for a lively program of live theatre.

Film Forum

Arsenāls (www.arsenals.lv) is an international film festival showcasing over 100 movies relating to experiential and interactive themes in Rīga, Latvia.

October

Days are noticeably shorter and afternoons on the beach are but a memory now; tourist-focused businesses start shuttering their windows as everyone prepares to hibernate.

Gaida Music Festival

One of the highlights of the Vilnius musical calendar is this annual celebration of classical and new music from Central and Eastern Europe held in Lithuania's capital, Vilnius, every October.

November

Autumn turns to winter as rainy days blend into snowy ones. This is perhaps one of the quietest months of the year – summer is long gone, yet winter holiday festivities have yet to begin.

Mama Jazz

Vilnius's biggest jazz event, Mamma Jazz (www.vilniusmamajazz.lt) is held every November and usually draws a banner list of top performers from around Europe and the world.

Black Nights Film Festival

Estonia's biggest film festival, Tallinn's Black Nights (http://2011.poff.ee) showcases films from all over the world, in the nation's capital over two weeks from mid-November. Subfestivals focus on animated films, children's films and student-made films.

Future Shorts

Kino Rīga hosts several film festivals, including the international Future Shorts (www.futureshorts.lv), celebrating short films (Rīga, Latvia).

New Music

The contemporary music festival Arēna New Music Festival (www.arenafest.lv) showcases various genres held at venues throughout Rīga, Latvia.

December

Yuletide festivities provide the perfect distraction from freezing temperatures

as decorations cheer the streets and families gather from all over to celebrate.

Christmas Markets

Festive decorations, arts and crafts, traditional

foods and entertainment brighten the dark days in the lead-up to Christmas, in each capital's Old Town (and many other towns around the region).

New Year's Eve

Fireworks and revelry on the main squares of Tallinn, Rīga and Vilnius in the countdown to midnight.

itineraries

Whether you've got three days or 30, these itineraries provide a starting point for the trip of a lifetime. Want more inspiration? Head online to lonelyplanet. com/thorntree to chat with other travellers.

Two Weeks
Best of the Baltic

Inaugurate your tour in **Tallinn** amid the Estonian capital's Old Town parade of polished medieval abodes. Don't miss the city's treasure trove of gastronomic delights before trekking out to **Lahemaa National Park**. The electric university town of **Tartu** awaits, then skip south into Latvia to take in the duo of crumbling castles in **Sigulda** and **Cēsis**. Spend the night at one of the posh **manor houses** *(muižas)* nearby, then plough through **Gauja National Park** to reach **Rīga**, home to a dizzying array of decorated facades. Next, head south to **Rundāle** to visit its opulent palace – the Baltic's version of Versailles, built by the architect responsible for St Petersburg's Winter Palace. From Rundāle, hop the border into Lithuania and stop at the **Hill of Crosses** in Šiauliai. Shoot west to **Curonian Spit** and spend a few days amid quaint cottages, shifting sand dunes and roving boar. End your trip in **Vilnius**, with its flamboyant baroque style.

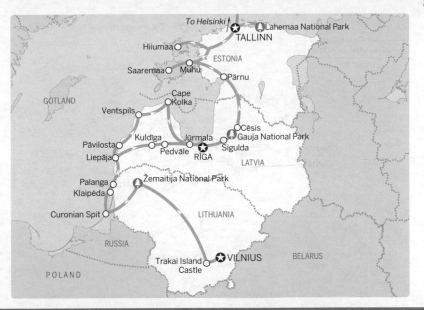

Three Weeks
The Grand Tour

> Start your journey in Lithuania's beautifully baroque **Vilnius**, spending a couple of days wandering the cobblestone streets, checking out **Gediminas Hill** and taking in the city's historical charms. Make a stop at **Trakai Island Castle** before heading west towards the sea. Stop at **Žemaitija National Park** for a quick lesson in Soviet missile tactics, then reward yourself with several days of uninterrupted relaxation along the dune-filled shores of the **Curonian Spit**. Follow the black Baltic Sea up through the Lithuanian port city of **Klaipėda** and family-friendly **Palanga** to reach the Latvian border. Over the border the first stop is **Liepāja**, famous for its gilded cathedrals and rectangular Soviet tenements that scar the landscape. Don't miss a tour of the red-brick Karosta Prison. From Liepāja you can either follow the desolate coast as it traces a snaking line past quiet villages and haunting sea stacks, or you can venture inland for a more direct route to the capital. Those who choose the seaside route will pass surfside **Pāvilosta**, oil-rich **Ventspils**, silent **Cape Kolka** and the spa retreat of **Jūrmala** – a hotspot for Russian tycoons. Inland treasures include the picturesque village of **Kuldīga** and the engaging open-air art museum at **Pedvāle** in the Abava River Valley. In **Rīga**, devote a day to exploring the ancient Old Town, then wander the grand boulevards just beyond while taking in the gorgeous **art nouveau facades** and bustling **Central Market**. After several days in Rīga, cruise through **Gauja National Park**, stopping in **Sigulda** for a side of bobsledding and bungee jumping, and **Cēsis** to wander among the fortress ruins. Then jump the border into Estonia for a few days of beach bliss in **Pärnu**. Move west to play hopscotch among the forested islands of **Muhu**, **Saaremaa** and **Hiiumaa** before returning to the mainland to take in **Tallinn**'s treasures, including the **City Museum**, the **Estonian History Museum** and any of the city's trendy corners, such as the **Rotermann Quarter**. Before completing the Baltic trifecta, hit up **Lahemaa National Park** nearby and – if time permits – jump on one of the ferries bound for **Helsinki**.

One week
Absolute Latvia

A full week in Latvia offers plenty of time to explore the nation's treasures beyond the stunning capital. After a few days in **Rīga** you can spend the latter half of the journey taking in the castle-clad forests of the east, or the desolate shorelines to the west. Those who are bound for the woods should start at Turaida Castle in **Sigulda** before moving onwards to the secret Soviet bunker at **Līgatne** and the stone fortress of **Cēsis**. Swing through the silent lakelands of **Latgale** to visit **Aglona**'s coveted basilica before looping back to **Rundāle** to take in the opulence of the palace. Those who venture west can follow the dramatic coastline through the constellation of lonely seaside villages. Depart Rīga for **Jūrmala**, the Baltic's original flavour of resort town. Then it's on to **Kolka** where the Bay of Rīga meets the Baltic Sea in a very dramatic fashion. Follow the crashing waves down the coast through wealthy **Ventspils**, **Pāvilosta** – a windsurfer's paradise – and **Liepāja**, home to Latvia's garage-band scene and the strikingly dour **Karosta district**. Swing back towards the capital through **Kuldīga**, one of the country's quaintest towns.

10 Days
Capital Drop-in

Ten days in the Baltic is just the right amount of time to get a feel for each of the region's capitals. Start your journey in **Vilnius** (Lithuania) to appreciate the sumptuous baroque architecture amid the curving cobbled streets. Two days will give you plenty of time to snap photos of **Gediminas Hill** and take in the city's rich **Jewish history**. A side trip to the castle at **Trakai** is a must before making tracks to Latvia's capital, **Rīga**: the Baltic's largest city. Haggle for your huckleberries at the **Central Market** and crane your neck to take in the glorious **art nouveau architecture** soaring above. You'll be spoilt for choice when it comes to day-tripping detours – cavort with the Russian elite in **Jūrmala**, Latvia's spa centre; or crank up the adrenalin in **Sigulda** with its clutch of adventure sports. Next it's on to Estonia and **Tallinn**, where you'll be treated to a fairy-tale kingdom of gingerbread trim and quaint medieval houses. Snoop around the city's world-class **culinary scene** and finish off the journey with a day at quiet **Lahemaa National Park**. If you have the time it's well worth hopping over to **Helsinki**, just a short boat ride away.

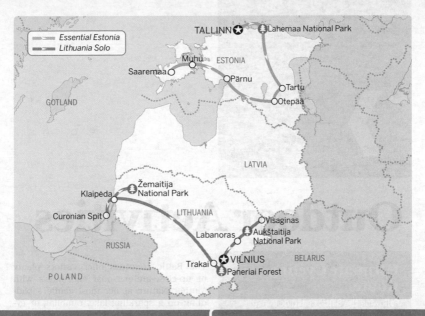

One Week
Lithuanian Solo

Compact Lithuania quickly rewards those with the luxury of time. A week's visit is best begun in **Vilnius**, followed by a few days along the jaw-dropping coastline or tucked away betwixt the towering pines of the inland forest. After taking in Vilnius' cathedral and museums, either head to **Trakai** to see the castle or, if your interests tilt toward Jewish heritage, visit the horrific **Paneriai** forest. Beach bums should then head to the Baltic coast, spending one day in the port of **Klaipėda** and the rest on **Curonian Spit**, particularly in the enchanting town of Nida. On your way, consider a stopover at **Žemaitija National Park** to see an abandoned Soviet missile base at the Museum of the Cold War. If it's woods you seek, head east to the **Aukštaitija National Park**, with its lakes and hiking paths. Plan your route via **Labanoras** for an overnight stay. Get your Soviet fix with a visit to **Visaginas**, built in the '70s to house workers at the now-shuttered **Ignalina Nuclear Power Station**.

One Week
Essential Estonia

On a week's journey through Estonia, it's best to give **Tallinn** at least half of your time, to be able to fully explore each crooked nook in the charming medieval core while sampling the spoils of the nation's 'new food' movements. **Lahemaa National Park** makes for a lovely day trip, while the university town of **Tartu** awaits those looking for more city life away from the capital. Swing through **Otepää**, Estonia's self-proclaimed 'winter capital', then switch seasons in **Pärnu** where sun worshippers come in droves for a bit of beach-lazing. Round off the week with a few days on one (or more) of Estonia's western islands that languidly float in the Baltic Sea. Try **Muhu** to enjoy time-warped Koguva village, or try **Saaremaa**'s forested expanse of whooshing windmills, quiet castle ruins, lonely churches and soaring sea cliffs.

Outdoor Activities

Ultimate Cycling Route

Following the Baltic coastline from the Curonian Spit, up through the Kurzeme Coast and onto the quiet western islands.

Best Authentic Sauna Experience

Try a **pirts**, a traditional Latvian cleanse involving extreme temperatures, a birch branch beating and jumping into a pond.

Top Forest Hikes

Estonia's **Lahemaa National Park**
Latvia's **Gauja National Park**
Lithuania's **Žemaitija National Park**

Excellent Spots to Paddle a Canoe

Estonia's **Soomaa National Park**
Latvia's **Latgale Lakelands**
Lithuania's **Aukštaitija National Park**

Must-See Wildlife

Blue cows in Latvia's Kurzeme region
Wild boar on Lithuania's Curonian Spit
Bears in Estonia's northeast

Best Resource for Outdoor Enthusiasts

Country Holidays (www.traveller.lv) Pan-Baltic website offering details on cycling routes, hiking trails and landmarks

The Baltic countries offer visitors plenty of up-close-and-personal encounters with Mother Nature at her most gentle – paddling on a sparkling lake, rambling or cycling through pretty birch or pine forest. Instead of craning your neck at sky-reaching peaks, here you can marvel over accessible nature – tame and neat – and superbly pretty scenery. Still, while the region lacks the drama of mountains and cliffs, there are places where you're left in no doubt that it's Mother Nature calling the shots, and she can sometimes be tempestuous – witness the shifting sands of the awesome Curonian Spit, or windswept, desolate Cape Kolka.

There's plenty of breathing space in Estonia, Latvia and Lithuania, too. Check those population figures and you'll be in little doubt that open space abounds here. Factor in the relatively low tourist numbers (compared with southern European destinations, for example) and you'll understand the appeal of some of the continent's best opportunities to ditch the crowds and simply frolic in the wilderness.

A smorgasbord of active endeavours awaits anyone with an appetite for the great outdoors. You can whet your appetite with berry picking before feeding on an alfresco meal of brisk, salty air, pristine white-sand beaches and icy-blue Baltic Sea vistas. Want seconds? Try cycling through dense, pine-scented forests, canoeing down a lazy river, or checking out the flora and fauna in a quiet nature reserve. Those craving an adrenalin fix can find some surprising options too; from bobsledding to bungee jumping. If you still have room for dessert, try baby-gentle downhill or cross-country skiing, or just get hot and sweaty in a sauna. In fact, whatever you're craving, the Baltic countries can usually deliver.

Cycling

The Baltic offers superb cycling territory. The region's flatness makes tooling around the countryside on a bicycle an option for anyone: casual cyclists can get the hang of things on gentle paved paths, while hard-core fanatics can rack up the kilometres on more challenging multiday treks. Although there's not much along the lines of steep single-track trails, dirt tracks through forests and (mini)hills abound, and the varied but always peaceful scenery ensures you'll never tire of the view.

The capital cities of the Baltic are also doing their share to increase the usability of bicycles in the city centres and surrounding areas. Cycling paths are multiplying each year as bike share and easy-access rental programs proliferate.

Among the most popular places to cycle are Lithuania's spectacular Curonian Spit, the islands of Muhu, Saaremaa and Hiiumaa in Estonia, and the Kurzeme coastline and 'Baltic Riviera' Jūrmala, in Latvia. The forested surrounds of the region's national parks offer superb two-wheeled adventures – top picks include lake-studded Dzūkija National Park in Lithuania, the bay-fringed Lahemaa National Park in Estonia, or castle-clad Gauja National Park in Latvia.

Plan Your Trip

If you want someone to help with planning, a growing band of cycling operators offer everything from itinerary-planning services to fully guided treks. Also, some tour operators (p414) offer guided cycling treks. For DIY planning, check out the info-laden sites www.bicycle.ee, www.bicycle.lv (in Latvian; use Google Translator) and www.bicycle.lt.

BalticBike (www.balticbike.lv; Latvia)

BalticCycle (www.bicycle.lt; Lithuania)

Bikerent.lv (www.bikerent.lv; Latvia)

City Bike (www.citybike.ee; Estonia)

Spas & Saunas

See p30 for more information about spas and saunas.

Latvia

Latvia's seaside town of Jūrmala (p218) is undoubtedly the spa capital of the Baltic. In its heyday it was the holiday centre of the entire Russian Empire – thousands of aristocrats would travel here in droves to slather themselves in curative mud, rinse in sulphur water, and enjoy the glorious views of the bay. Today, much of Jūrmala's allure remains, and it is still a popular spot for Russian tycoons to build a holiday home and get massage treatments. For an authentic cleansing experience, however, you'll have to venture far away from the crowds of Rīga or Jūrmala and head to the countryside where locals have constructed their own private *pirts* close to the water's edge (pond, river, lake or sea). Several private *pirts* can be booked by travellers, like the one shared by several hotels in Sigulda (boxed text p248); otherwise you'll have to befriend a bunch of locals to gain access.

Estonia

Spa-ing is also quite popular among Estonians, who draw their sauna habits from the Finns next door. You'll find traditional smoke saunas at Setomaa Tourist Farm (p108) in the southeastern part of the country, as well as at Mihkli Farm Museum (p150) on Hiiumaa island. Many Estonians refer to Saaremaa island as 'Spa-remaa' for its proliferation of spa resorts, particularly in Kuressaare. You'll find plenty of spa spots in Tallinn as well.

Lithuania

Lithuania has a less-developed spa and sauna scene than its Baltic brothers, but there are nonetheless a few places to indulge. The two most popular spa destinations include the fabled 19th-century spa town of Druskininkai on the Nemunas River and Birštonas. Of the two, Druskininkai is the destination of choice for serious spa-seekers. The town, which has been in the healing business for more than 200 years, boasts mineral spas for sipping (with a reputedly recuperative effect on everything from the stomach to the heart), mud baths, a relatively mild climate, and miles and miles of surrounding forest that keep the air fresh and clean. Added to that are a number of modern diversions, such as a huge water park, that make the town a perfect respite for the healthy as well as the ailing. We list the best Druskininkai spas on p320.

SWEAT IT OUT

Given that it's cold, dark and snowy for many months of the year in the Baltic, it's little surprise that the sauna is an integral part of local culture. Most hotels have one, and some cities have public bathhouses with saunas. But it's those that silently smoulder next to a lake or river, by the sea or deep in the forest that provide the most authentic experience.

There are three main types of sauna in the Baltic:

» In Finnish-style saunas an electric stove keeps the air temperature high (between 70°C and 95°C) and humidity is kept low. These are found in plenty of private homes, most hotels, all spas and water parks etc. Some hotel suites have a private sauna attached to the bathroom. Public or hotel saunas charge an hourly fee and there are plenty of small private saunas that can be rented by the hour.

» The smoke sauna is the most archaic type, where a fire is lit directly under rocks in the chimneyless sauna (generally a one-room wooden hut) and heating can take up to five hours. After the fire is put out in the hearth, the heat comes from the warmed rocks. The smoke is let out just before participants enter; the soot-blackened walls are part of the experience. Smoke saunas are rare but have become more popular in recent times.

» The 'Russian sauna' or steam sauna/steam bath is not as popular in the Baltic region as the Finnish style of sauna, but is found mainly in spas or water parks. In these, the air temperature is medium (about 50°C) and air humidity is high.

Locals use a bunch of birch twigs to lightly slap or flick the body, stimulating circulation, irrespective of which sauna type they're sweating in. Cooling down is an equally integral part of the experience: most Finnish-style saunas have showers or pools attached, while the more authentic smoke saunas are usually next to a lake or river. In the depths of winter, rolling in snow or cutting out a square metre of ice from a frozen lake, in order to take a quick dip, is not unheard of.

Hiking

While the Baltic countries lack the craggy grandeur or wild expanses of some of their neighbours, a day or two hiking in one of the forested national parks is rewarding all the same. All that forest (it covers 51% of Estonia, 45% of Latvia and 33% of Lithuania) just begs to be explored, especially if there are beavers to spot, berries to pick or resident witches and fairies to hear tales of along the way.

Grab your hiking boots, breathe deeply of the pine-fresh air, and hit the trails in the likes of Žemaitija National Park in Lithuania, Gauja National Park in Latvia, and Lahemaa National Park in Estonia. Pretty villages that make good bases for exploration include: Estonia's Otepää and Rõuge (p110); Valmiera and Cēsis in Latvia; and Nida in Lithuania. If ordinary walking doesn't float your boat, make a beeline for Estonia's Soomaa National Park, where you can go on a guided walk through the park's wetlands using special bog shoes (don't

laugh), which give you access to otherwise hard-to-reach areas.

Water Sports

Having been cooped up for most of the winter, the region comes alive in summer, with locals and visitors taking any opportunity to soak up some vitamin D during the gloriously long days. You're never far from the sea or a lake offering fishing, sailing, windsurfing and swimming. And when the weather doesn't favour outdoor frolicking, there's no shortage of wet 'n' wild water parks (with indoor pools, slides, saunas etc) in big cities and holiday areas (these guys know from experience that a Baltic summer is no guarantee for beach-going weather).

Great Baltic beachy spots are Pärnu, Narva-Jõesuu, Pirita (Tallinn) and Saaremaa in Estonia; Jūrmala, Ventspils, Pāvilosta and Liepāja in Latvia; and Palanga, Klaipėda and Nida in Lithuania. More heart-pounding water sports, such as kite surfing, can be attempted at the western end of Hiiumaa island in Estonia and Pāvilosta in Latvia.

Canoeing & Rafting

Watching the landscape slide slowly by while paddling down a lazy river is a fabulous way to experience the natural world from a different angle. As the region's rivers are not known for their wild rapids, this is a great place for beginners to hone their skills or for families to entertain the kids. Even if you're usually more into wild than mild, the region's scenic beauty and tranquillity create such a Zen experience you'll quickly forget you haven't hit a single rapid.

In Latvia, the Gauja and Abava Rivers offer uninterrupted routes stretching for several days, and you can join an organised tour or rent gear and run the routes on your own – the best places to start are Sigulda (p249), for the Gauja, and Kandava (p227) for the Abava. In Lithuania, Labanoras Regional Park, Dzūkija National Park, Trakai and Nemunas Loops Regional Park (p333) all offer the opportunity for great canoeing. Canoes or traditional *haabjas* (Finno-Ugric boats carved from a single log) serve as the primary vehicles for exploring Soomaa National Park in southwest Estonia – you can even learn to build your own *haabjas*. Otepää (p113) is another good Estonian spot to organise and access canoe trips, including ones that combine canoeing with hiking and cycling.

Fishing

Abundant lakes and miles of rivers and streams provide ample fishing opportunities in all three countries. Visit a regional tourist office for the scoop on the best angling spots and information pertaining to permits.

In the dark depths of the Baltic winter there is no finer experience than dabbling in a touch of ice-fishing with vodka-warmed local fishing folk on the frozen Curonian Lagoon (p350), off the west coast of Lithuania, or at Trakai. The Nemunas Delta Regional Park is another good western Lithuanian fishing spot. In Latvia, the Latgale Lakelands (p262) is packed with hundreds of deep-blue lakes offering fishing opportunities galore. In northern Kurzeme, Lake Engure (p226) is another favourite angling spot. Huge Lake Peipsi is popular in Estonia.

Berrying & Mushrooming

The Balts' deep-rooted attachment to the land is reflected in their obsession with berrying and mushrooming – national pastimes in all three countries. Accompanying a local friend into the forest on a summer berrying trip or autumn mushrooming expedition is an enchanting way to appreciate this traditional rural pastime.

If you're keen on picking but lack a local invitation, join an organised tour (locals closely guard the location of their favourite spots, so just asking around probably won't reap any useful information). For info on berrying and mushrooming tours, check out www.countryside.lt (Lithuania), www.maaturism.ee (Estonia) and www.traveller.lv (Latvia), and ask at local tourist offices. You can't go wrong at Lithuania's Dzūkija (p322) or Aukštaitija National Parks (p313). Failing that, head to any market and check out the freshly picked produce. The crinkle-topped, yellow chanterelle and stubby boletus are among the best. Of the more than a thousand types of mushroom found in the region, around 400 are edible and about 100 are poisonous (picker beware!). You can also peruse menus for in-season treasures from local forests, and pat yourself on the back for the low food miles your meal has travelled.

For mushroom aficionados, there's Varėna's mushroom festival (www.varena.lt/en/events) held every year on 24 September.

Birdwatching

Thanks to a key position on north–south migration routes, the Baltic countries are a twitcher's paradise. Each year hundreds of bird species descend upon the region, attracted by fish-packed wetlands and wide-open spaces relatively devoid of people. White storks arrive by the thousands each spring, nesting on rooftops and telegraph poles throughout the region. Other annual visitors include corncrakes, bitterns, cranes, mute swans, black storks and all types of geese.

Estonia

In Estonia, some of the best birdwatching in the Baltic is found in the Matsalu National Park, where 280 different species (many migratory) can be spotted, and where regular tours are run. Spring migration peaks in April/May, but some species arrive as early

MIDSUMMER MADNESS

In pagan times it was a night of magic and sorcery, when witches ran naked and wild, bewitching flowers and ferns, people and animals. In the agricultural calendar, it marked the end of the spring sowing and the start of the summer harvest. In Soviet times it became a political celebration: a torch of independence was lit in each capital and its flame used to light bonfires throughout the country.

Today Midsummer Day, aka summer solstice or St John's Day, falling on 24 June, is the Balts' biggest party of the year. On this night darkness barely falls – reason alone to celebrate in a part of the world with such short summers and such long, dark winters. In Estonia it is known as Jaanipäev, in Latvia Jāņi, Jāņu Diena or Līgo and in Lithuania Joninės or Rasos (the old pagan name).

Celebrations start on 23 June, particularly in Latvia, where the festival is generally met with the most gusto. Traditionally, people flock to the countryside to celebrate this special night amid lakes and pine forests. Special beers, cheeses and pies are prepared, wreaths are strung together from grasses, while flowers and herbs are hung around the home to bring good luck and keep families safe from evil spirits. Men adorn themselves with crowns made from oak leaves; women wear crowns of flowers.

Come Midsummer's Eve bonfires are lit and the music and drinking begins. No one is allowed to sleep until the sun has sunk and risen again – anyone who does will be cursed with bad luck for the coming year. Traditional folk songs are sung, dances danced and those special beers, cheeses and pies eaten! To ensure good luck, you have to leap back and forth over the bonfire. In Lithuania, clearing a burning wheel of fire as it is rolled down the nearest hill brings you even better fortune. In Estonia, revellers swing on special double-sided Jaanipäev swings, strung from trees in forest clearings or in village squares.

Midsummer's night is a night for lovers. In Estonia the mythical Koit (dawn) and Hämarik (dusk) meet but once a year for an embrace lasting as long as the shortest night of the year. Throughout the Baltic region, lovers seek the mythical fern flower, which blooms only on this night. The dew coating flowers and ferns on midsummer's night is held to be a purifying force, a magical healer and a much sought-after cure for wrinkles! Bathe your face in it and you will instantly become more beautiful and more youthful. However, beware the witches of Jaanipäev/Jāņi/Joninės, who are known to use it for less enchanting means.

as March. Autumn migration begins in July and can last until November. Vilsandi National Park (boxed text p141), off Saaremaa, is another prime spot for feathery friends, and the park's headquarters can help arrange birdwatching tours.

Lithuania

Some 270 of the 330 bird species found in Lithuania frequent the Nemunas Delta Regional Park (p360), making it a 'must' visit for serious birders. Park authorities can help organise birdwatching expeditions during the peak migratory seasons. The nearby Curonian Spit National Park offers opportunities for spotting up to 200 different species of birds amid dramatic coastal scenery.

Latvia

In Latvia, keep an eye out for some of Europe's rarest birds in splendid Gauja National Park. With thick forests and numerous wetlands, Ķemeri National Park (p223), in northern Kurzeme, is another great birdwatching spot. The boggy Teiči Nature Reserve (p258), in the Vidzeme Upland, is an important feeding and nesting ground for many bird species. Lake Engure, in northern Kurzeme, is a major bird reservation with 186 species (44 endangered) nesting around the lake and its seven islets.

Horse Riding

The gentle pace of horseback exploration is definitely in keeping with the yesteryear feel of parts of the Baltic countries. Some of the best and most bucolic places to get saddle-sore include Lahemaa National Park (p83) and the islands of Hiiumaa (p147) and Saaremaa (p132) in Estonia – operators here will usually combine rural and coastal rides, and can arrange multiday treks. In Latvia, head to Plosti, between Kandava and Sabile in the picturesque Abava River Valley; Untumi country ranch (p262), 7km northwest of Rēzekne; or the well-established Klajumi stables (p264), outside Krāslava in the Latgale Lakelands. Lithuanian visitors hankering for some four-legged fun can head to Trakai or the horse museum (p340) in the village of Niūronys, outside Anykščiai.

Skiing & Snowboarding

They might not have anything closely resembling a mountain, but Estonia and Latvia haven't let this geographic hurdle hinder their ski-resort efforts. Instead these countries have become masters at working with what they've got – and that means constructing lifts and runs on the tiniest of hills, and using rooftops and dirt mounds to create vertical drops. At least they've got the climate working for them, with cold temperatures ensuring snow cover for at least four months of the year. Don't expect much in the way of technical terrain or long powder runs – but you've got to admit that saying you've skied or snowboarded the Baltic is pretty damn cool!

Otepää in southeast Estonia is probably the best of the Baltic winter resorts. It offers a variety of downhill-skiing and snowboarding areas, myriad cross-country trails, a ski jump and plenty of outlets from which to hire gear. Lively nightlife and a ski-town vibe heighten the appeal for skiers and boarders. Kicksledding, cross-country skiing and snow-shoe excursions are available at Soomaa National Park.

The Gauja Valley is the centre of Latvia's winter-sports scene. Sigulda, Cēsis and Valmiera all offer short-but-sweet downhill runs as well as loads of cross-country trails. Adrenalin junkies disappointed by Sigulda's gentle slopes can get their fix swishing down the town's 1200m-long artificial bobsled run – the five-person contraptions reach speeds of 80kmh! The Vidzeme Upland, centred on the whopping 312m Gaiziņkalns (p258), is adored as the country's top spot for skiers and snowboarders.

Lithuania hasn't really joined the downhill game, but you can cross-country ski amid deep, whispering forests and frozen blue lakes in beautiful Aukštaitija National Park.

Travel with Children

Best Regions for Kids

Gauja National Park, Latvia

An enchanted forest of towering pines, fairy-tale castles, hidden ogres, secreted Soviet bunkers and myriad adventure activities such as ropes courses, Tarzan swings and canoeing.

Curonian Spit, Lithuania

Shifting sand dunes and miles of wind-swept beaches make Curonian Spit the best place in the Baltic to build the ultimate sandcastle, and roving wild boar provide endless mirth. Palanga, up the coast, welcomes families to its amusement parks.

Tallinn, Estonia

Estonia's beautiful capital looks as though it was ripped straight out of the pages of a fairy tale. Soaring spires and quaint gingerbread trim will provoke Disneyesque *oohs* and *aahs*.

Estonia, Latvia & Lithuania for Kids

Travelling through this region with children in tow isn't as daunting as it used to be. Hotels do their best to help make kids feel at home; many have family rooms designed for parents travelling with children; if not, most will gladly place an extra bed in the room for a small fee. A number of restaurants have kids' menus. Nappies (diapers) and known-brand baby foods, including some organic ones, are widely available in big supermarkets in the capitals. Unfortunately, you won't find many high chairs and restaurant changing rooms are yet to be invented here.

Bringing History to Life

The Baltic countries have some of the most fascinating history in all of Europe. This might be of keen interest to most adult visitors, but a tour through an occupation museum can be lost on toddlers and teens. Fortunately, there are tons of opportunities for younger travellers to engage with their surroundings in a fun and meaningful manner.

Estonia

» Rakvere Castle, in like-named Rakvere

» Hermann Castle in Narva, which has a mock-up of a 17th-century town during the summer months

» Ilon's Wonderland in Haapsalu

» Toy Museum in Tartu

Latvia
» Ludza Craftsmen Centre in Latgale
» Ventspils' House of Crafts, Kurzeme Coast
» Turaida Museum Reserve in Sigulda

Lithuania
» Narrow-gauge Railway Museum in Anykščiai
» Horse Museum (in Niūronys, near Anykščiai)

Activities for All Ages

Throughout the Baltic you'll find tours – particularly day trips from the capital cities – that shuttle visitors to the various attrations of note orbiting the region's major centres. These trips are, in general, not suited for youngsters, as most of them cater more for adults, checklist travellers and stags. If you have the little ones in tow, it's best to tailor-make your own adventure.

Of Estonia's spread of cities, the most kid-friendly destination is definitely Pärnu, sitting along the coast in the southwest of the country. It's a veritable magnet for families with its leafy parks, water park and lovely sandy beach. For fun any time of year, head to Otepää, Estonia's self-proclaimed 'winter capital', which actually has a bevy of nature-related activities throughout the year.

In Latvia, Sigulda has long established itself as the go-to spot for anyone seeking a bit of adrenalin. Heart-pounding bungee jumps and bobsled tracks are the main attraction, but there are plenty of more subdued options. In the nearby village of Līgatne you'll find a hidden Soviet bunker innocuously called 'The Pension'. This underground base is stocked with heaps of relics from the bygone Soviet era – it's truly fun for all ages, especially young boys. Latvia's western coastline is a delightful jumble of water parks and sandy strips of beach. Jūrmala is particularly family-friendly.

Lithuania's entire coastline is a veritable playground for kids, be it the funfair amusements and in-house restaurant entertainers in Palanga and Šventoji, the marine shows of Klaipėda's Sea Museum or the bikes and boats to rent on the Curonian Spit. Further inland there are plenty of forested landscapes to be explored by foot or canoe. Vilnius can be a bit more difficult as the city's architecture and history is most noteworthy, but kids will enjoy a climb up the TV Tower, a ride on the funicular up Gediminas Hill or a dip at the local water park.

Planning

The long days and mild weather make summer the perfect time to travel around the Baltic with children. Outdoor tourist amenities are in full swing – beach towns come alive and myriad rentable cottages dot the interior. The summer is, however, very popular with all types of holidaymakers, so it is crucial that you book accommodation (and car rental, if you're so inclined).

WHAT TO PACK

All Ages
The usual suspects:
» Sunscreen and insect repellent for the warmer months
» Weather-appropriate gear for winter
» Light raincoat is useful year-round
» Bathing suit – kids of any age will love taking a dip at the hotel's pool

Babies & Toddlers
» Folding pushchair – practical for most areas and useful in restaurants
» Small mat or towel for nappy (diaper) changes – appropriate facilities are a rarity

Ages 4–12
» Binoculars – for young explorers to zoom in on wildlife and fairy-tale-like architectural motifs
» Camera – to inject newfound fun into more grown-up-oriented walks or tours

Road Trips

Two Weeks with Your own Wheels

Toss your driving map out the window – you won't need it as you follow the smell of salt and smoked fish up the Baltic Sea's dramatic coastline.

Best Day Trip from Tallinn by Car

Enjoy Estonia's natural beauty and head east early in the morning to watch the forest come to life at Lahemaa National Park. If time permits, swing down to Tartu to check out the thriving university town before looping back to the capital.

Best Day Trip from Rīga by Car

While tour operators carry passengers to the castles of Gauja National Park or the palace at Rundāle, western Latvia remains largely untouched by the masses. Consider a stop at Pedvāle to peruse tower sculptures at the open-air art museum, then venture on to quaint Kuldīga, a charming village frozen in time.

Best Day Trip from Vilnius by Car

Most visitors head west to the castle at Trakai, so buck the trend and venture northeast to check out the quiet lakes and hiking paths of Aukštaitija National Park, stopping at Labanoras along the way.

Planning Essentials

When to Go

For fairly obvious reasons, the best time of year to travel with a vehicle is during the summer months (June to August), which are blissfully free from snow, sleet and any other weather that could negatively impact on your driving. The summer months are not, however, completely free of rain. The days are long, which means that driving is relatively safe even in the late evening.

Why Drive?

Signs are clearly marked, roads are kept in reasonable condition, and traffic doesn't exist beyond the largest cities – driving is not only an easy way to explore the Baltic, it's also a pleasure! Although buses and trains may be in line with efforts to stay 'green', they'll often have you seeing red – changing timetables and limited service can be frustrating. A car gives you the flexibility to explore the countries' quiet hinterlands, from the towering dunes of Lithuania's Curonian Spit to Estonia's windswept western islands to Latvia's pine-studded inner forests. Take your car off the main roads and stumble upon tiny villages locked away in time, or curious relics from the Soviet era when the Russians used space-station technology to spy on the West.

Where to Start/End

You'll be pleased to know that all car-hire companies allow mobility throughout all three Baltic countries, but you'll be hard-pressed to find a service that will allow you to take a vehicle to any countries beyond. If you hire a car from a smaller local service, you will be expected to return the vehicle to the location in which you picked it up. Some franchise operators will allow you to drop the car off in a different town, for an additional fee. If you are planning a pan-Baltic route and want to start and end at the same point, you could leave from Rīga and complete a figure-eight circuit up into Estonia and down through Lithuania. Those who are less concerned about starting and finishing their tour in the same place can consult the Itineraries section for tailor-made suggestions: all those routes can be followed in a private vehicle, which would allow for a more flexible schedule.

On the Road

Road Rules

Traffic drives on the right-hand side of the road. In older towns and villages, you will find a proliferation of one-way streets and roundabouts.

Although the Baltic nations have a fairly poor reputation when it comes to road etiquette and collisions, this is mostly unfounded. In the big cities you'll find that most drivers are forgiving of wrong turns and lane changing. You should, however, avoid inner-city driving during the workday rush hour – especially on Friday afternoons in the warmer months, when locals make a beeline to their countryside cottages. Driving in the region's rural parts is rarely a laborious task as populations are sparse. Do, however, be careful of passing vehicles, which tend to speed by unannounced and at surprisingly inopportune moments.

Petrol & Servicing

Although the Baltic countryside can feel desolate and unpopulated, there is a healthy proliferation of service stations in all three countries – it'll take some serious talent to run out of petrol. Before taking your vehicle off the lot, make sure to arm yourself with a service phone number for each of the Baltic countries, just in case your car should require any service while on the road. Tyres have been known to get punctures – especially in Latvia, where the road-maintenance infrastructure isn't as solid as it is in Lithuania or Estonia.

Driving vs Public Transport

Private vehicles far outweigh public transport when it comes to convenience. Over the last few years, all three countries have reduced their networks of buses and trains as locals flock to the capitals for job opportunities. If you are, however, simply travelling between capitals, we recommend using the bus system, which is geared towards commuting professionals and is thus very comfortable. Those wanting to explore the Baltic's rural treasures – especially in small groups and families – will quickly become amenable to the rather high petrol prices when zipping across the terrain from one highlight to the next.

regions at a glance

A quick glance at any Mercator map shows Western Europe's convenient positioning – primed to take on the rest of the world; at the other end of the continent is Russia, which stretches like a flying banner over the rest of the globe. And the flat, easily navigable borderlands in between? That's Estonia, Latvia and Lithuania. Relatively speaking, the Baltic is but the size of a pinprick, but for centuries the region was the gateway between megapowers, as thousands of castles and ruins can attest.

Although the region's history and topography may be the ties that bind, these Baltic nations could not be more different from one another in every other respect.

Estonia

Historic Towns ✓✓✓
Castles ✓✓✓
Nature ✓

Historic Towns
From Tallinn's magnificent medieval Old Town to the genteel lanes and parks of Pärnu to the university precinct of Tartu, Estonia has a wealth of streets that time seemingly forgot.

Castles
There has to be a bright side to being precariously positioned on the edge of civilisations and, in Estonia's case, the legacy of a millennium of warfare is a spectacular crop of fortresses scattered throughout the country.

Nature
Estonia's countryside may be flat and low key compared with much of Europe, but its low population density and extensive forests, bogs and wetlands make it an important habitat for a multitude of mammals, large and small, as well as a biannual seasonal influx of feathered visitors.

p42

Latvia

Architecture ✓✓✓
Castles ✓✓✓
Nature ✓

Architecture

No one mastered art nouveau like Rīga's coterie of architects at the turn of the 20th century. They covered the city's myriad facades with screaming goblins, praying goddesses, creeping vines and geometric emblems.

Castles

Once the feudal playground for dozens of German nobles, Latvia is riddled with crumbling reminders of a sumptuous bygone era. Many of these castles and manor houses have been lovingly restored and transformed into memorable inns – the perfect place to live out your fairy-tale fantasies.

Nature

Beyond Rīga's clutch of twisting spires and towering housing blocks you'll find miles and miles of quiet forests, intimate lakelands and flaxen shores that beckon the crashing Baltic tides.

p183

Lithuania

Nature ✓✓✓
Architecture ✓✓
Nightlife ✓✓

Nature

The Baltic seacoast, the dunes of the Curonian Spit and the long stretches of forest, broken up by meadows and lakes: Lithuania's landscape is blissfully unspoiled. Good tourist infrastructure allows you to hike it, bike it or boat it at your own pace.

Architecture

It's hard to imagine a more attractive Old Town than in the capital, Vilnius, with its unspoiled Renaissance, baroque and neoclassical architecture. Outside the city the simple wooden structures of the countryside will wow you with vivid colours and intricate carving work.

Nightlife

Vilnius and Kaunas are home to thousands of students, which translates into hundreds of cafes, bars, trendy restaurants and clubs. The centre of the Vilnius action is the Old Town, particularly around the university, but there are plenty of places all around the city.

p276

Every listing is recommended by our authors, and their favourite places are listed first

Look out for these icons:

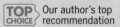 **TOP CHOICE** Our author's top recommendation

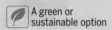 A green or sustainable option

 FREE No payment required

ESTONIA 42
TALLINN. 46
NORTHEASTERN ESTONIA 79
Lahemaa National Park . . .79
Rakvere 85
Ontika Landscape Reserve 87
Sillamäe. 87
Narva 88
Narva-Jõesuu 90
SOUTHEASTERN ESTONIA 91
Lake Peipsi 91
Tartu. 94
Setomaa 105
Võru 108
Haanja Nature Park 110
Valga. 111
Otepää 112
SOUTHWESTERN ESTONIA 116
Viljandi 117
Soomaa National Park . . .120
Pärnu 122
Kihnu 128
Ruhnu. 129
WESTERN ESTONIA & THE ISLANDS 129
Muhu 130
Saaremaa 132
Matsalu National Park. . . .143
Haapsalu 143
Hiiumaa 147
Vormsi 154

UNDERSTAND ESTONIA . . 155
Estonia Today 155
History 156
The People. 160
The Arts. 161
Food & Drink. 164
SURVIVAL GUIDE 167
Directory A–Z 167
Getting There & Away 169
Getting Around. 170

HELSINKI EXCURSION. 171
UNDERSTAND HELSINKI. 180
Helsinki Today. 180
History 180
SURVIVAL GUIDE 181
Getting There & Away 181
Getting Around. 181

LATVIA. 183
RĪGA 185
AROUND RĪGA 218
Jūrmala 218
Ķemeri National Park . . . 223
WESTERN LATVIA (KURZEME). 224
Tukums. 224
Talsi. 224
Cape Kolka (Kolkasrags) 225
Abava River Valley 227
Kuldīga 229
Ventspils 231

See the Index for a full list of destinations covered in this book.

On the Road

Pāvilosta 234

Liepāja 235

SOUTHERN LATVIA (ZEMGALE) 238

Bauska 238

Rundāle Palace 239

Jelgava 242

Dobele & Around 242

NORTHEASTERN LATVIA (VIDZEME) 242

Vidzeme Coast 244

Gauja National Park 245

Alūksne & Gulbene 258

Vidzeme Uplands 258

SOUTHEASTERN LATVIA (LATGALE) 259

Daugava River Valley 259

Daugavpils 259

Latgale Lakelands 262

UNDERSTAND LATVIA 265

Latvia Today 265

History 265

The People 268

The Arts 268

Food & Drink 269

SURVIVAL GUIDE 272

Directory A–Z 272

Getting There & Away 274

Getting Around 274

LITHUANIA 276

VILNIUS 280

AROUND VILNIUS 308

Paneriai 308

Trakai 308

Centre of Europe 310

Kernavė 311

EASTERN & SOUTHERN LITHUANIA 311

Aukštaitija National Park 312

Visaginas & Ignalina Nuclear Power Station ...315

Labanoras Regional Park 316

Molėtai 316

Utena 316

Around Utena 317

Druskininkai 318

Dzūkija National Park ... 322

CENTRAL LITHUANIA 323

Kaunas 323

Birštonas 333

Šiauliai 334

Radviliškis & Around 338

Panevėžys 338

Anykščiai 340

WESTERN LITHUANIA 341

Klaipėda 341

Curonian Spit National Park 350

Nemunas Delta 359

Palanga 361

Around Palanga 365

Žemaitija National Park 365

UNDERSTAND LITHUANIA 368

Lithuania Today 368

History 369

The People 373

The Arts 374

Food & Drink 377

SURVIVAL GUIDE 380

Directory A–Z 380

Getting There & Away ... 384

Getting Around 385

KALININGRAD EXCURSION 386

UNDERSTAND KALININGRAD 393

Kaliningrad Today 393

History 393

SURVIVAL GUIDE 394

Getting There & Away ... 394

Getting Around 394

Estonia

Includes »

Tallinn 46
Lahemaa National
Park 79
Lake Peipsi 91
Tartu 94
Setomaa 105
Otepää 112
Viljandi 117
Pärnu 122
Muhu 130
Saaremaa 132
Haapsalu 143
Hiiumaa 147
Vormsi 154

Best Places to Stay

» Pädaste Manor (p131)

» Old House Apartments (p64)

» Antonius (p101)

» Viru Inn (p64)

» Hostel Ingeri (p119)

Best Places to Eat

» Alexander (p132)

» Tchaikovsky (p67)

» Sfäär (p70)

» Ö (p70)

» NOP (p71)

Why Go?

Estonia doesn't have to struggle to find a point of difference; it's completely unique. It shares a similar geography and history with Latvia and Lithuania, but it's culturally very different. Its closest ethnic and linguistic buddy is Finland, and although they may love to get naked together in the sauna, fifty years of Soviet rule in Estonia have separated the two. For the last 300 years Estonia's been linked to Russia, but the two states have as much in common as a barn swallow and a bear (their respective national symbols).

With a newfound confidence, singular Estonia has crept from under the Soviet blanket and leapt into the arms of Europe. The love affair is mutual. Europe has fallen head-over-heels for the charms of Tallinn and its Unesco-protected Old Town. Put simply, Tallinn is now one of the continent's most captivating cities. And in overcrowded Europe, Estonia's sparsely populated countryside and extensive swathes of forest provide spiritual sustenance for nature-lovers.

When to Go

The most clement weather is from May to September, and while it can get a little crazy in Tallinn and Pärnu (especially in July and August), it's still the best time to visit. Almost all festivals are scheduled for summer, with the biggest celebrations saved for midsummer's eve.

Fans of cross-country skiing should make for Otepää, the unofficial winter capital from December to March. Yuletide in the real capital is unforgettable, with Christmas markets and a 570-year-old tradition of raising a Christmas tree on Tallinn's main square.

Arriving in Estonia

Most visitors to Estonia arrive in Tallinn, either at the airport or (in the case of ferries from Helsinki) the harbour. Both are close to the centre of town (the ferry terminals are within walking distance); taxis to the centre should cost less than €10 or you can catch a bus for around €2. Crossing from Latvia by car, motorbike or bus is a breeze as both countries are part of the Schengen Area, so there are no border checks. The main border checkpoint from Russia is at Narva. Buses connect Estonia with both countries. Trains from St Petersburg stop in Narva and Tallinn, while trains from Rīga stop in Valga; the stations are near the centre of each city.

LANGUAGE

Hello	te-rre	Tere
Goodbye	head ae-gah	Head aega
Yes	yah	Jah
No	ay	Ei
Thank you	ta-nahn	Tänan
You're welcome	pah-lun	Palun
Excuse me/I'm sorry	vah-bahn-dah-ge	Vabandage
Cheers!	Ter-vi-seks	Terviseks!
(literally 'to your health')		

Essential Food & Drink

» **Rukkileib** Rye bread, an Estonian staple, served with most meals and usually free at restaurants.

» **Kama** Light meal or drink made from buttermilk combined with a mixture of boiled, roasted and ground peas, rye, barley and wheat.

» **Suitsukala** Smoked fish; usually trout or salmon.

» **Sealiha ja kartul** Pork and potatoes, prepared in a hundred different ways.

» **Kana ja kartul** Chicken and potatoes, for when you're porked out.

» **Kasukas** Layered salad of Russian origin containing beetroot, potato, carrots, salted herring, boiled egg and yoghurt.

» **Vana Tallinn** A syrupy, sweet liqueur of indeterminate origin, best served over ice, in coffee or to disguise bad Russian sparkling wine. There's also a cream version.

RESOURCES

VisitEstonia.com (www.visitestonia.com)

Tallinn Tourism (www.tourism.tallinn.ee)

Estonia Public Broadcasting News (http://news.err.ee)

Estonica (www.estonica.org)

Fast Facts

» **Area** 45,227 sq km
» **Capital** Tallinn
» **Population** 1.3 million
» **Telephone country code** ☎372
» **Emergency** ☎112

Exchange Rates

Australia	A$1	€0.73
Canada	C$1	€0.71
Japan	¥100	€0.96
Latvia	1Ls	€1.42
Lithuania	1Lt	€0.29
New Zealand	NZ$1	€0.55
Russia	R100	€2.38
UK	£1	€1.16
USA	US$1	€0.74

For current exchange rates see www.xe.com.

Set Your Budget

» **Budget hotel room** €20-45
» **Two-course evening meal** €10-35
» **Museum entrance** €1-5
» **Beer** €3
» **Tallinn transport ticket** €1

Baltic Sea

Naissaar

Aegn

Keila-
Joa

Tallinn ①

Paldiski

Keila

Nõva

Hageri

Riisipere

Riguldi

Rapla

Vormsi

Tahkuna
peninsula

Ristna

Hullo

Risti

Kõpu
Peninsula

Kärdla

Hiiumaa

Haapsalu

Märjamaa

Suuremõisa

Heltermaa

Käina

E67

Kassari

Puise

Sõru

Lihula

Pärnu-
Jaagupi

⑤ Muhu

Mihkli

Võhma

Angla   Orissaare

Kuivastu   Virtsu

④ Saaremaa

Pärnu

Vilsandi
National
Park

Kärla

Kaali   Sakla

⑥

Sindi

Kuressaare

Salme

Munalaid   Pootsi
Port

E67

Kihnu

Häädemeeste   Tali

Torgu

Sääre

*Gulf of
Riga*

Ruhnu

Ainaži

Aloja

Kolka

Salacgrīva

Mazirbe

Miķeltornis

Estonia Highlights

① Embark on a medieval quest for atmospheric restaurants and hidden bars in the history-saturated lanes of **Tallinn** (p46)

② Wander the forest paths, bog boardwalks, abandoned beaches and manor-house halls of **Lahemaa National Park** (p79)

③ Further your education among the museums and student bars of **Tartu** (p94), Estonia's second city

④ Unwind among the windmills on **Saaremaa**

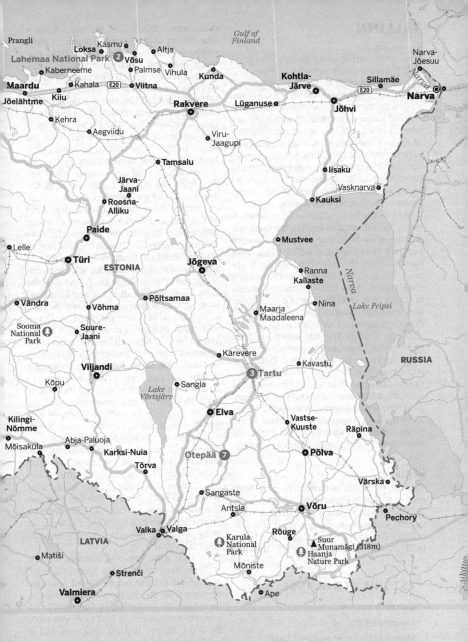

(p132) and explore the island's castles, churches, cliffs, coast and crater

5 Hop over to **Muhu** (p130) for frozen-in-island-time Koguva village and the gastronomic delights of Pädaste Manor

6 Stroll the golden sands and genteel streets of Estonia's 'summer capital', **Pärnu** (p122)

7 Get back to nature, even if the snow's a no-show, at the 'winter capital' **Otepää** (p112)

TALLINN

ESTONIA TALLINN

POP 400,300

If you're labouring under the misconception that 'former Soviet' means dull and grey and that all tourist traps are soulless, Tallinn will delight in proving you wrong. This city has charm by the bucketload, fusing the modern and medieval to come up with a vibrant vibe all of its own. It's an intoxicating mix of ancient church spires, glass skyscrapers, baroque palaces, appealing eateries, brooding battlements, shiny shopping malls, run-down wooden houses, and cafes set on sunny squares – with a few Soviet throwbacks in the mix, for added spice.

Despite the boom of 21st-century development, Tallinn remains loyal to the fairy-tale charms of its two-tiered Old Town – one of Europe's most beguiling walled cities. That wasn't always the case. For a while, it appeared to be willing to sell its soul to become the Bangkok of the Baltic: attracting groups of young men with the lure of cheap booze and rampant prostitution. That's calmed down somewhat and although sleazy elements remain, the city seems to have realised that there's more money to be made from being classy than brassy. Hence an ever-expanding roster of first-rate restaurants, atmospheric hotels and a well-oiled tourist machine that makes visiting a breeze, no matter which language you speak.

Increasingly sophisticated without being overly sanitised, forward-focused while embracing the past, Tallinn is a truly fascinating city.

History

The site of Tallinn is thought to have been settled by Finno-Ugric people around 2500 BC. There was probably an Estonian trading settlement here from around the 9th century AD and a wooden stronghold was built on Toompea (*tawm*-pe-ah; the hill dominating Tallinn) in the 11th century. The Danes under King Waldemar II (who conquered northern Estonia in 1219) met tough resistance at Tallinn and were on the verge of retreat when it's said that a red flag with a white cross fell from the sky into their bishop's hands. Taking this as a sign of God's support, they went on to win the battle and gain a national flag. The Danes built their own castle on Toompea. The origin of the name Tallinn is thought to be from *Taani linn*, Estonian for 'Danish town'.

The Knights of the Sword took Tallinn from the Danes in 1227 and built the first stone fort on Toompea. German traders arrived from Visby on the Baltic island of Gotland and founded a colony of about 200 people beneath the fortress. In 1238 Tallinn returned to Danish control but in 1285 it joined the German-dominated Hanseatic League as a channel for trade between Novgorod, Pihkva (Russian: Pskov) and the West. Furs, honey, leather and seal fat moved west; salt, cloth, herring and wine went east.

By the mid-14th century, when the Danes sold northern Estonia to the Teutonic Order, Tallinn was a major Hanseatic town with about 4000 people. Conflict with the knights and bishop on the hill led the mainly German artisans and merchants in the Lower Town to build a fortified wall to separate themselves from Toompea. Tallinn prospered regardless and became one of northern Europe's biggest towns. Tallinn's German name, Reval, coexisted with the local name until 1918.

Prosperity faded in the 16th century. The Hanseatic League had weakened, and Russians, Swedes, Danes, Poles and Lithuanians fought over the Baltic region. Tallinn survived a 29-week siege by Russia's Ivan the Terrible between 1570 and 1571. It was held by Sweden from 1561 to 1710, when, decimated by plague, Tallinn surrendered to Russia's Peter the Great.

In 1870 a railway was completed from St Petersburg, and Tallinn became a chief port of the Russian empire. Freed peasants converged on the city from the countryside, increasing the percentage of Estonians in its population from 52% in 1867 to 89% in 1897. By WWI, Tallinn had big shipyards and a working class of over 100,000.

Tallinn suffered badly in WWII, with thousands of buildings destroyed during Soviet bombing in 1944. After the war, under Soviet control, large-scale industry was developed – including the USSR's biggest

---

ESTONIA AT A GLANCE

Currency euro (€)

Language Estonian

Money ATMs are widespread. Cash preferred to credit cards for small purchases.

Visas Not required for citizens of the EU, USA, Canada, Japan, New Zealand and Australia.

TALLINN IN...

Two Days

Spend your first day exploring the **Old Town**. Tackle our **walking tour** in the morning and then stop for lunch in one of the many excellent eateries (if it's mid-week, the lunch special at **MEKK** is a great deal). Spend your afternoon exploring one or two of the museums – perhaps the **City Museum** and **Estonian History Museum**. That evening, put on your glad rags and head to **Tchaikovsky** for dinner, finishing up in the hidden depths of **Gloria Wine Cellar**.

The following day, do what most tourists don't do – step out of the Old Town. Breakfast at **NOP** before strolling to **Kadriorg Park** for a greenery and art fix. Between galleries, stop at **Park Cafe**, overlooking the pretty lake. That evening, hit the **Rotermann Quarter**.

Four Days

Four days is enough to cover the city's main highlights, with more nights of eating and partying chucked in. Round out your days with trips to the **Museum of Occupations** and the **Open Air Museum** (especially if you're not visiting the Estonian countryside). If it's summer, head to **Pirita Beach**. In winter, hit the **Harju Ice Rink** then warm up in a **sauna**.

---

grain-handling port – and the city expanded, its population growing to nearly 500,000 from a 1937 level of 175,000. Much of the new population came from Russia and new high-rise suburbs were built on the outskirts to house the workers.

The explosion of Soviet-style settlements in the suburbs meant a loss of cultural life in the centre. By the 1980s the Old Town was run down, with most people preferring to live in the new housing developments. It began to be renovated late in the decade, with the fight for independence largely playing out on the streets of Tallinn.

The 1990s saw the city transformed into a contemporary midsized city, with a restored Old Town and a modern business district. Today a look around the centre and the skyline of the business district indicates a city that is booming. Tallinn shows a taste for all things new, extending to IT-driven business at the fore of the new economy and an e-savvy, wi-fi–connected populace embracing a brighter future. Meanwhile, the outskirts of the city have yet to get the facelift that the centre has received. In those parts that few tourists see, poverty and unemployment is more evident.

⊙ Sights

While most of the city's sights are conveniently located within the medieval Old Town's walls, it's worth venturing out to the further-flung attractions – and given Tallinn's relatively compact size, there's really no excuse not to. Kadriorg, in particular, should not be missed.

OLD TOWN

The medieval jewel of Estonia, Tallinn's Old Town (Vanalinn) is without a doubt the country's most fascinating locality. Picking your way along the narrow, cobbled streets is like strolling into the 15th century – not least due to the tendency of local businesses to dress their staff up in peasant garb. You'll pass old merchant houses, hidden medieval courtyards, looming spires and winding staircases leading to sweeping views over the city. It's everyone's favourite tourist trap but carries this burden remarkably well. While almost every building has a helpful historical plaque (in Estonian and in English), they haven't all been excessively gentrified. Part of the Old Town's charm is that the chic sits comfortably alongside the déshabillé.

Of course, being so popular comes with its downsides. In summer, sometimes as many as six giant cruise ships descend at a time, disgorging their human cargo in slow-moving, flag-following phalanxes. If you're travelling on such a ship, it's worth noting that the Old Town is within walking distance of the harbour; you'll have a much better time if you dodge the organised tours and follow your own path. For everyone else, rest assured that most of the boats steam off

Tallinn

NORTH
TALLINN

KELMIKÜLA

OLD TOWN

TOOMPEA

KASSISABA

LASNAMÄE

Kadriorg
Park

See Kadriorg Map (p57)

See Central Tallinn Map (p52)

To Pirita (1.6km) / 4

Maarjamäe
Manor

Pirita tee

Narva mnt

Tallinna Laht

Passenger
Port

Terminal D

Linnahall

Baltic
Train Station

To Tallinn Zoological
Gardens (1km);
Saku Suurhall (1.3km);
Estonian Open Air
Museum (2km)

Toompuiestee

Kaarli puiestee

Rävala puiestee

Gonsiori

Tartu mnt

Liivalaia

Endla

Paldiski mnt

0   0.5 miles
0   1 km

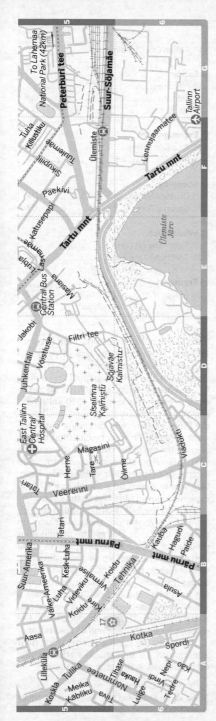

again in the afternoon, leaving the streets relatively clear by 5pm.

For a more general description of how the Old Town fits together, we'd recommend that you start with our walking tour (p62). This section focuses on sights that you can actually visit rather than those that you're more likely to walk past.

LOWER TOWN

City Museum   MUSEUM

(Linnamuuseum; Map p52; www.linnamuuseum .ee; Vene 17; adult/concession €3.20/1.92; ⊙10.30am-5.30pm Wed-Mon) Tallinn's City Museum is actually split over 10 different sites. This, its main branch, is set in a 14th-century merchant's house and traces the city's development from its earliest days. The displays are engrossing and very well laid out, with plenty of information in English, making the hire of the audio guide (€4.75) quite unnecessary. The top floor presents an insightful (and quite politicised) portrait of life under Soviet rule and there's a fascinating video of the events surrounding the collapse of the regime. Information about pro-Soviet protests at the time is included, albeit with a woefully dismissive commentary.

Estonian History Museum   MUSEUM

(Eesti Ajaloomuuseum; Map p52; www.ajaloo muuseum.ee; Pikk 17; adult/child €5/3; ⊙10am-6pm daily May-Aug, Thu-Tue Sep-Apr) Also occupying multiple locations, the Estonian History Museum has filled the striking 1410 Great Guild building with a series of ruminations on the Estonian psyche, presented through interactive and unusual displays. The major exhibition, *Spirit of Survival – 11,000 years of Estonian History,* poses such questions as 'Is Estonia the most secular country in the world?' and 'Have Estonians been happy in their own land?' (The answer to the latter is no, apparently, backed up with statistics suggesting that they're one of the least happy peoples of Europe.)

Coin collectors shouldn't miss the display in the old treasury, while military nuts should head downstairs. The basement also covers the history of the Great Guild itself.

Museum of Occupations   MUSEUM

(Okupatsioonide Muuseum; Map p52; www.oku patsioon.ee; Toompea 8; adult/child €2/1; ⊙10am-6pm Tue-Sun) Photos and artefacts illustrate the hardships and horrors of five decades of occupation, under both the Nazis, briefly, and the Soviets. The photos and artefacts are interesting but it's the videos (lengthy

Tallinn

◉ **Top Sights**
  Maarjamäe Manor G1

◉ **Sights**
  1 Estonian Maritime Museum
    - Museum Ships...................................B1
  2 Estonian National Library B4
  3 Linnahall..C2
  4 Maarjamäe War Memorial G1
  5 Tallinn Song Festival
    Grounds...G2

➕ **Activities, Courses & Tours**
  6 Club 26 ....C4
  7 Kalma Saun..B2

💤 **Sleeping**
  8 City Hotel Tallinn A3
  9 Euphoria..B4
  10 GIDIC Backpackers D4
  11 Kreutzwald Hotel Tallinn.....................B4
  12 L'Ermitage...B4

  13 Tallinn City Camping............................G2

🍴 **Eating**
  14 F-hoone..A3
  15 Moon C2
  16 Neh D3

🎭 **Entertainment**
  17 A Le Coq Arena....................................A5
  18 Club 69..C4

🛍 **Shopping**
  19 Central Market D4
  20 Sadama Turg..C2

ℹ **Information**
  21 Tallinn Dental Clinic B4
  22 Tõnismäe Apteek B4

ℹ **Transport**
  23 Europcar D3
  24 Hertz...D3

but enthralling) that leave the greatest impression – and the joy of a happy ending. It's fitting that a greater proportion of the displays are focused on the lengthy Soviet period, yet it's disappointing that Nazi crimes (particularly the murder of nearly 1000 Estonian Jews) aren't covered in more detail.

St Nicholas' Church Museum   MUSEUM
(Niguliste Muuseum; Map p52; www.ekm.ee/niguliste; Niguliste 3; adult/child €3.20/2; ☺10am-5pm Wed-Sun) Dating from the 13th century, St Nicholas' houses the Estonian Art Museum's collection of medieval religious art. Its most famous work is Berndt Notke's 15th-century masterpiece *Dance Macabre*. The gist of this eerie skeletal conga line is that whether you're a king, pope or young slacker, we're all dancing with death. Other artefacts here include painted altarpieces, carved tombstones and a chamber overflowing with silverware. The church was badly damaged by Soviet bombers in 1944 and a fire in the 1980s but today stands restored to its Gothic glory. The acoustics are first-rate and regular organ recitals are held here.

Town Hall   HISTORIC BUILDING
(Raekoda; Map p52; www.tallinn.ee/raekoda; Raekoja plats; adult/child €4/2; ☺10am-4pm Mon-Sat Jul & Aug) Rising over the Old Town's main square, this is the only surviving Gothic town hall in northern Europe. Built between 1371 and 1404, it was the seat of power in the medieval Lower Town. **Old Thomas** (Vana Toomas), Tallinn's symbol and guardian, has been keeping watch from his perch on the weathervane since 1530 (although his previous incarnation now resides in the City Museum). You can enjoy much the same views as Thomas by climbing the 115 steps to the top of the **tower** (adult/concession €3/1; ☺11am-6pm May–mid-Sep). According to legend, this elegant 64m minaret-like structure was modelled on a sketch made by an explorer following his visit to the Orient.

Entry to the hall itself is through the cellar. From here you can make your way up through the **Trade Hall** on the ground floor (housing a visitor book dripping in royal signatures) and then up to the main floor, where there's the **Council Chamber** (featuring Estonia's oldest woodcarvings, dating from 1374), the vaulted **Citizens' Hall**, a yellow-and-black-tiled councillor's office and a small kitchen. The steeply sloped attic has displays on the building and its restoration.

If the kids are getting restive, draw their attention to the iron shackles still hanging on the exterior wall facing the square.

Holy Spirit Church   CHURCH
(Püha Vaimu Kirik; Map p52; Pühavaimu 2; adult/child €1/50c; ☺9am-5pm Mon-Sat May-Sep, 10am-

3pm Mon-Sat Oct-Apr) The luminous blue-and-gold clock on the facade of this striking 14th-century Gothic church is the oldest in Tallinn, dating from 1684. Inside there are exquisite woodcarvings and painted panels including an altarpiece dating to 1483 and a 17th-century baroque pulpit. Johann Koell, a former pastor here, is considered the author of the first Estonian book, a catechism published in 1535. The church hosts regular classical music concerts.

St Olaf's Church   CHURCH, VIEWPOINT

(Oleviste Kirik; Map p52; Lai 50; tower €2/1; ☉10am-8pm Jul & Aug, 10am-6pm Sep-Jun) From 1549 to 1625, when its 159m steeple was struck by lightning and burnt down, this (now Baptist) church was the tallest building in the world. The current spire reaches a still respectable 124m and you can take a tight, confined, 258-step staircase up the tower for wonderful views of Toompea over the Lower Town's rooftops.

The church itself has been around since at least the 13th century, although it's been substantially added to over the years. The interior is typically stark, although a small section of stone carvings on the rear exterior wall escaped the Reformation's iconoclasts. Although dedicated to the 11th-century King Olaf II of Norway, the church is linked in local lore with another Olaf – its architect, who ignored the prophecies of doom to befall the one who completed the church's construction. Accordingly, Olaf fell to his death from the tower, and it's said that a toad and snake then crawled out of his mouth.

Estonian Maritime Museum   MUSEUM

(Eesti Meremuuseum; www.meremuuseum.ee; ☉10am-6pm Wed-Sun) The Great Coast Gate is joined to Fat Margaret (Paks Margareeta; Map p52; Pikk 70; adult/child €3.20/1.60), a rotund 16th-century bastion with 4m-thick walls that protected the port entrance to the Old Town. The Maritime Museum resides inside this corpulent lady, with displays of old charts, model ships (both huge and tiny), antiquated diving equipment and other artefacts from Estonia's seafaring history.

On Fat Margaret's other flank, in a 1748 gunpowder depot, is the associated Mine Museum (Miinimuuseum; Map p52; Uus 37; adult/child €3/1), a whimsical collection of cupboards, seats, toilets and BBQs created from old Soviet mines. The museum's ships (Muuseumilaevad; Map p48; Küti 15A/17; adult/child €3.20/1.60), including an icebreaker and

a submarine, are displayed at the Seaplane Harbour (Lennusadam), where, at the time of research, a major redevelopment was taking place.

St Catherine's Church & Cloister   CHURCH

(Map p52; www.kloostri.ee; Vene 16; adult/child €2/1; ☉10am-6pm mid-May–Aug) One of Tallinn's oldest buildings, the ruined St Catherine's was part of a Dominican monastery founded by Scandinavian monks in 1246. In its glory days the monastery had its own brewery and hospital. A mob of angry Lutherans torched the place in 1524, during the Reformation, and the monks fled town. The monastery languished for the next 400 years until its partial restoration in 1954. Today the complex, strewn with carved tombstones, includes the gloomy shell of the barren church and a peaceful cloister.

Sts Peter & Paul's Cathedral   CHURCH

(Peeter-Paul Katedraal; Map p52; ☎644 6367; Vene 16; ☉5-7pm daily, plus 7-10am Mon, Wed, Fri & Sat) Next to the monastery is the handsome 1844 Catholic cathedral, looking like it was beamed in from Spain. It was designed by the famed architect Carlo Rossi, who left his mark on the neoclassical shape of St Petersburg. It still functions as one of Tallinn's only Catholic churches, largely serving the Polish and Lithuanian communities.

St Nicholas Orthodox Church   CHURCH

(Map p52; Vene 24; ☉10am-6pm) Built in 1827 on the site of an earlier church, St Nicholas was the focal point for the Russian traders that Vene street was named for. It's known for its treasured iconostasis.

FREE Draakoni Gallery   GALLERY

(Map p52; www.eaa.ee/draakon; Pikk 18; ☉11am-6pm Mon-Sat) In among the guilds, behind a fabulous sculpted facade, this gallery hosts small, sometimes stimulating, exhibitions of contemporary art.

Photo Museum   MUSEUM

(Fotomuuseum; Map p52; www.linnamuuseum.ee; Raekoja 6; adult/child €2/1; ☉10.30am-5.30pm Thu-Tue) Only enthusiasts are likely to find much of interest in this little museum housed in the former town jail. Exhibits include old cameras and prints from photography's earliest days in Estonia.

Town Wall Walkway   FORTRESS

(Linnamüür; Map p52; Gümnaasiumi 3; adult/child €1.30/65c; ☉11am-7pm Jun-Aug, 11am-5pm

Central Tallinn

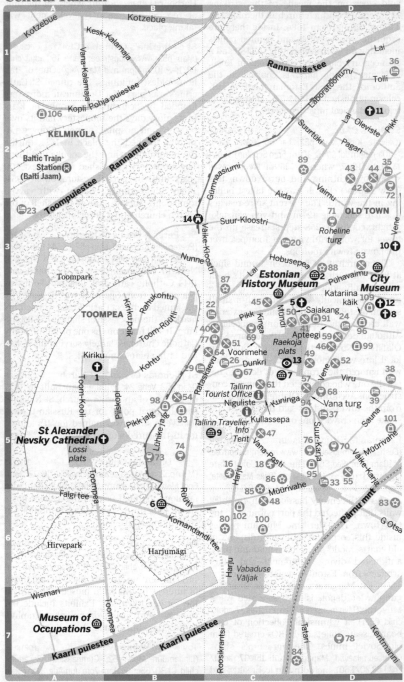

Kotzebue
Kotzebue
Kesk-Kalamaja
Vana-Kalamaja
Kopli Põhja puiestee
Lai
36
Tolli
KELMIKÜLA
Rannamäe tee
Laboratooriumi
11
Oleviste
Pikk
106
Suurtüki
Pagari
Baltic Train Station (Balti Jaam)
89
43
44
35
Vaimu
42
72
23
Rannamäe tee
Aida
71
OLD TOWN
Gümnaasiumi
14
Suur-Kloostri
Roheline turg
10
Väike-Kloostri
20
Vene
Nunne
Hobusepea
63
87
Lai
88
Pühavaimu
City Museum
Estonian History Museum **2**
Katariina käik
109
22
45
Pikk
5
Saiakang
50
12
8
Toom-Rüütli
40
Kinga
Mündi
91
24
96
77
51
69
Apteegi
59
46
99
Kiriku põik
64 Voorimehe
Raekoja plats
41
49
Rataskaevu
26
Dunkri
13
52
38
29
67
7
57
Viru
1
54
61
Vene
68
39
Tallinn Tourist Office
Kuninga
94 **Vana turg**
98
Niguliste
37
101
Pikk jalg
Kullassepa
76
Suur-Karja
70
Lühike jalg
Tallinn Traveller Info Tent **9**
47
95
Vana-Posti
74
16
18
Harju
86
85
33 55
St Alexander Nevsky Cathedral
73
Müürivahe
48
Lossi plats
83
Falgi tee
6
Rüütli
80
102
100
G Otsa
Komandandi tee
Pärnu mnt
Hirvepark
Harjumägi
Vabaduse Väljak
Museum of Occupations
Harju
78
Kaarli puiestee
Kaarli puiestee
84
Wismari
Toompea
Tatari
Kentmanni
Roosikrantsi

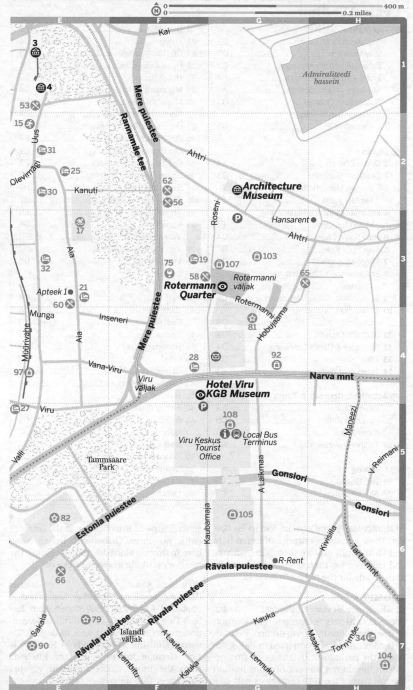

ESTONIA TALLINN

0 — 400 m
0 — 0.2 miles

Kai

Admiraliteedi
bassein

3
4
53
15
Uus
31
Olevimägi
25
30
Kanuti
17
Aia
32
Apteek 1
21
60
Munga
Müürivahe
97
27
Viru
Valli
Tammsaare
Park

Mere puiestee
Rannamäe tee

Ahtri

62
56

Roseni

Architecture
Museum

Hansarent

Ahtri

75
19
107
103
58
Rotermann
Quarter
Rotermanni
väljak
65
Rotermanni
81
Hobujaama
Mere puiestee
Inseneri
Vana-Viru
28
92
Viru
väljak
Narva mnt

Hotel Viru
KGB Museum

108
Viru Keskus
Tourist
Office
Local Bus
Terminus

Viru
A Laikmaa
Gonsiori
Maneezi
V Reimani
Gonsiori
82
Estonia puiestee
Kaubamaja
105
Tartu mnt
Kivisilla
Rävala puiestee
R-Rent
66
Rävala puiestee
79
Rävala puiestee
Islandi
väljak
A Lauteri
Kauka
Sakala
90
Lembitu
Kauka
Lennuki
Maakri
Tornimäe
34
104

Central Tallinn

◎ **Top Sights**
Architecture Museum G2
City Museum D3
Estonian History Museum C3
Hotel Viru KGB Museum F4
Museum of Occupations A7
Rotermann Quarter G3
St Alexander Nevsky
Cathedral B5

◎ **Sights**
1 Dome Church A4
2 Draakoni Gallery D3
3 Estonian Maritime Museum -
Fat Margaret E1
4 Estonian Maritime Museum -
Mine Museum E1
5 Holy Spirit Church C4
6 Kiek in de Kök B6
7 Photo Museum C4
8 St Catherine's Church &
Cloister D4
9 St Nicholas' Church Museum C5
10 St Nicholas Orthodox
Church D3
11 St Olaf's Church D2
12 Sts Peter & Paul's Cathedral D4
13 Town Hall C4
14 Town Wall Walkway B3

◎ **Activities, Courses & Tours**
15 City Bike E2
16 Harju Ice Rink C5
17 Kalev Spa E3
18 Tallinn Traveller Info C5

◎ **Sleeping**
19 16€ Hostel F3
20 Alur Hostel C3

21 Bern Hotel E3
22 Flying Kiwi C4
23 Go Hotel Shnelli A3
24 Hotel Telegraaf D4
25 Hotell Braavo E2
26 Merchant's House Hotel C4
27 Monk's Bunk E5
28 Nordic Hotel Forum F4
29 Old House Apartments B4
30 Old House Guesthouse E2
31 Old House Hostel E2
32 Old Town Backpackers E3
33 Savoy Boutique Hotel D5
34 Swissôtel Tallinn H7
35 Tallinn Backpackers D2
36 Three Sisters Hotel D1
37 Vana Tom D5
Villa Hortensia .... (see 99)
38 Viru Backpackers D4
39 Viru Inn D5

◎ **Eating**
40 Aed C4
41 Balthasar D4
Bestseller .... (see 108)
42 Bocca D2
43 Bonaparte Deli D2
44 Chedi D2
Chocolats de Pierre .... (see 99)
45 Clayhills Gastropub C4
46 Elevant D4
47 Fish & Wine C5
48 Gloria C6
Horisont .... (see 34)
49 Kaerajaan D4
50 Kehrwieder C4
51 Kompressor C4
52 La Bottega D4
53 Leib E1

Fri-Wed Apr-May & Sep-Oct, 11am-4pm Fri-Tue Nov-Mar) Three empty towers are connected here and visitors can explore their barren nooks and crannies for themselves, with cameras at the ready for the red-rooftop views.

TOOMPEA

St Alexander Nevsky Cathedral CHURCH
(Map p52; Lossi plats; ☉8am-8pm) The location of the magnificent, onion-domed Russian Orthodox cathedral (completed in 1900), opposite the parliament buildings, was no accident: the church was one of many built in the last part of the 19th century as part of a general wave of Russification in the empire's Baltic provinces. Orthodox believers come here in droves, alongside tourists ogling the interior's striking icons and frescoes.

Kiek in de Kök MUSEUM
(Map p52; www.linnamuuseum.ee; Komandandi 2; adult/child €4.50/2.60; ☉10.30am-5.30pm Tue-Sun) One of Tallinn's most formidable cannon towers is tall, stout Kiek in de Kök. Its name (amusing as it sounds in English) is Low German for 'Peep into the Kitchen'; from the upper floors medieval voyeurs could peer into the houses below.

54 Matilda Cafe B5
   MEKK ....(see 33)
55 Must Puudel D5
56 Ö F2
57 Olde Hansa D4
58 Platz F3
59 Ribe D4
60 Rimi E3
   Sfäär ....(see 56)
61 Silk C4
62 Spirit F2
63 Stenhus D3
   Tchaikovsky ....(see 24)
   Tristan ja Isolde ....(see 13)
64 Vanaema Juures C4
65 Vapiano G3
66 Vapiano E6

⊜ Drinking
67 Beer House C4
68 Clazz D5
69 DM Baar C4
70 Drink D5
   Gloria Wine Cellar ....(see 48)
71 Hell Hunt D3
72 Levist Väljas D2
73 Neitsitorn B5
74 Põrgu B5
75 Scotland Yard F3
76 St Patrick's D5
77 Von Krahli Baar C4
78 X-Baar D7

☺ Entertainment
79 Artis E7
   BonBon ....(see 62)
   Club Hollywood ....(see 86)
80 Club Privé C6

81 Coca-Cola Plaza G4
82 Estonia Concert Hall & National
   Opera E6
83 Estonian Drama Theatre D6
84 G-Punkt C7
85 Kapp C5
   Katusekino ....(see 108)
86 Kino Sõprus C5
87 Nuku C3
   Piletilevi ....(see 108)
88 St Canute's Guild Hall D3
89 Tallinn City Theatre........................ D2
90 Teater No99 .... E7
   Von Krahli Theatre ....(see 77)

⊜ Shopping
91 Antiik D4
92 Foorum G4
93 Galerii Kaks.................................. B5
94 IIDA D5
95 Ivo Nikkolo D5
96 Katariina Gild D4
97 Knit Market E4
98 Lühikese Jala Galerii B5
99 Masters' Courtyard......................... D4
100 Nu Nordik C6
101 Reet Aus D5
102 Reval Antique C6
103 Rotermanni Kaubamaja G3
104 Stockmann Kaubamaja H7
105 Tallinna Kaubamaja G6
106 Train Station Market......................A2
107 US Art Gallery G3
108 Viru Keskus...................................G5
109 Zizi D4
   Zizi ....(see 94)

Built around 1475, it was badly damaged during the Livonian War, but it never collapsed (nine of Ivan the Terrible's cannonballs remain embedded in the walls). Today it houses a branch of the City Museum, focusing mainly on the development of the town's elaborate defences. If you're interested in military paraphernalia, you'll find a treasure trove on the upper floors.

Staff here also arrange two-hour tours of the **Bastion Passages** (☑644 6686; adult/child €5.75/3.20), 17th-century tunnels connecting the towers, built by the Swedes to help protect the city; bookings required.

Dome Church CHURCH
(Toomkirik; Map p52; ☑644 4140; Toom-Kooli 6; ☺9.30am-5.30pm) Toompea is named after the cathedral (now Lutheran, originally Catholic), founded by at least 1233. The exterior dates mainly from the 15th century, with the tower added in 1779 (there is actually no dome – the nickname is a corruption of the Estonian word *toom,* itself borrowed from the German word *Dom,* meaning cathedral). The impressive, austere building was a burial ground for the rich and noble, and the whitewashed walls are decorated with the coats-of-arms of Estonia's noble families. Fit viewseekers can climb the **tower** (adult/child €5/3).

CITY CENTRE

Rotermann Quarter
NEIGHBOURHOOD

(Rotermanni Kvartal; Map p52; www.rotermanni kvartal.ee) One of Tallinn's recent developments has seen the restoration and reinvigoration of this former factory complex that sits between the city centre and the passenger port. It's now home to offices, apartments, shops, some of Tallinn's best restaurants and a quirky collection of studios and galleries. In summer, Rotermanni väljak – the square behind the cinema – hosts a farmers market (Wednesday to Saturday) and a craft market (Sunday).

Hotel Viru KGB Museum
MUSEUM

(Map p52; ☑680 9300; www.sokoshotels.fi; Viru väljak 4; tour €7) When the Hotel Viru was built in 1972 it was not only Estonia's first skyscraper, it was the only place for tourists to stay in Tallinn – and we mean that literally. Having all the foreigners in one place made it much easier to keep tabs on them and the locals they had contact with (including the hotel staff), which is exactly what the KGB did from their 23rd-floor spy base. The now-privatised hotel offers guided tours of the facility in Estonian, English, Finnish and Russian; call ahead for times and to book a place.

Architecture Museum
MUSEUM

(Arhitektuurimuuseum; Map p52; www.arhi tektuurimuuseum.ee; Ahtri 2; adult/child €3/1.50; ☺11am-6pm Wed-Sun) A restored limestone warehouse – the former Rotermann Salt Store – houses this modest museum, displaying building and town models, and regular temporary exhibitions.

KADRIORG

About 2km east of the Old Town, this beautiful park's ample acreage is Tallinn's favourite patch of green. Together with the baroque Kadriorg Palace, it was commissioned by the Russian tsar Peter the Great for his wife Catherine I soon after his conquest of Estonia (Kadriorg means Catherine's Valley in Estonian). Nowadays the oak, lilac and horse chestnut trees provide shade for strollers and picnickers, the formal pond and gardens provide a genteel backdrop for romantic promenades and wedding photos, and the children's playground (Map p57) is a favourite off-leash area for the city's youngsters.

Trams 1 and 3 stop right by Kadriorg Park. Buses 1A and 34A (among others) stop on Narva mnt, near the foot of the park, while 67 and 68 head to the Kumu end.

[TOP CHOICE] Kadriorg Art Museum
PALACE, GALLERY

(Kadrioru Kunstimuuseum; Map p57; www .ekm.ee; Weizenbergi 37; adult/child €4.20/2.70; ☺10am-5pm Tue & Thu-Sun, 10am-8pm Wed May-Sep, shorter hours Oct-Apr) Kadriorg Palace, built between 1718 and 1736 with the help of Peter himself, who laid no fewer than three sturdy bricks, now houses a branch of the Estonian Art Museum devoted to Dutch, German and Italian paintings from the 16th to the 18th centuries, and Russian works from the 18th to early 20th centuries (check out the decorative porcelain with communist imagery upstairs). The building is exactly as frilly and fabulous as a palace ought to be and there's a handsome French-style flower garden at the back.

WHEN BIGGER IS JUST BIGGER

Nothing says 'former Soviet' quite like a gigantic public building and Tallinn has two that are quite difficult to miss, both designed by local architect Raine Karp. Perhaps the more baffling of the two is the Linnahall (City Hall; Map p48; www.linnahall.ee; Mere pst 20), which stands as a colossal barricade, cutting off the Old Town from the harbour. Built for the 1980 Moscow Olympics and originally christened the Lenin Palace of Culture and Sport, it contains within its crumbling, much-graffitied concrete hulk a vast concert hall. It's fair to say that the city doesn't know quite what to do with it. Some support its preservation as part of Tallinn's history but it has decayed considerably since closing its doors in 2009.

In much better nick is the Estonian National Library (Map p48; www.nlib.ee; Tõnismägi 2; day pass 30c), built from local dolomite limestone. Construction commenced in 1985 but it wasn't completed until 1993, making this prime example of Soviet Monumentalism one of independent Estonia's first new public buildings. It's worth calling into the foyer if only to check out the pointy red chairs. Frequent exhibitions take place on the upper floors.

Kadriorg

In the 1930s the palace was the private domain of the president of independent Estonia. In 1938 a purpose-built residence was erected nearby and since Estonia's re-independence it is again the home of the country's president. It's not open to the public, but you'll see the honour guards out front.

Mikkel Museum

(Map p57; Weizenbergi 28; adult/concession €2.20/1.30; ⏰10am-8pm Wed, 10am-5pm Thu-Sun) The collection spills over to this former kitchen building, which displays a small but interesting assortment of paintings and porcelain, along with temporary exhibitions. Joint admission with the palace is €4.80.

Kumu   GALLERY

(Map p57; www.kumu.ee; Weizenbergi 34; adult/child €4.20/2.60, permanent collection only €4.20/2.60; ⏰11am-6pm Tue & Thu-Sun, 11am-8pm Wed, closed Mon & Tue Oct-Apr) Opened to rave reviews in 2006, this futuristic, Finnish-designed, seven-storey building is a spectacular structure of limestone, glass and copper, nicely integrated into the landscape. Kumu (the name is short for *kunstimuuseum* or art museum) contains the largest repository of Estonian art as well as constantly changing contemporary exhibits. The permanent collection is split into 'Treasury' (on the 3rd floor, featuring works from the beginning of the 18th century until the end of WWII) and 'Difficult Choices' (on the 4th floor, showcasing art during the Soviet era). Current and cutting-edge exhibitions fill the 5th floor. The complex is wheelchair accessible and houses an excellent shop and cafe.

Kadriorg

◎ **Top Sights**

Kadriorg Art Museum	C1
Kumu	D2

◎ **Sights**

1	House of Peter I	D2
2	Mikkel Museum	C2
3	Presidential Palace	D2

◉ **Activities, Courses & Tours**

4	Children's Playground	C2

⊗ **Eating**

5	NOP	A1
6	Park Cafe	B1

House of Peter I   MUSEUM

(Peeter I Majamuuseum; Map p57; www.linnamuuseum.ee; Mäekalda 2; adult/concession €2/1; ⏰10am-6pm Wed-Sun May-Aug, 10am-4pm Wed-Sun Sep-Apr) This is the humble cottage Peter the Great occupied on visits to Tallinn while the palace was under construction. The museum is filled with portraits, furniture and artefacts from the era.

Tallinn Song Festival Grounds   BUILDING

(Lauluväljak; Map p48; www.lauluvaljak.ee; Narva mnt) The site of the main gatherings of Estonia's national song festivals (and assorted rock concerts and festivals) is an open-air amphitheatre with an official capacity of 75,000 people and a stage that fits 15,000. Built in 1959, it's an elegant and surprisingly curvaceous piece of Soviet-era architecture.

In September 1988, 300,000 squeezed in for one songfest and publicly demanded independence in what became known as the 'Singing Revolution'. Approximately half a million people, including a large number of Estonian émigrés, were believed to have been present at the 21st Song Festival in 1990, the last major fest before the restoration of independence. An Estonian repertoire was reinstated and around 29,000 performers sang under the national flag for the first time in 50 years.

MAARJAMÄE

Pirita tee, the coastal road curving northwards alongside Tallinn Bay through Maarjamäe, is a popular route for joggers, cyclists and skaters, offering particularly fine sunset views over the Old Town. Buses 1A, 8, 34A and 38 all stop here.

Maarjamäe Manor   MUSEUM
(Maarjamäe loss; Map p48; Pirita tee 56; adult/child €3/1.50; ☺10am-5pm Wed-Sun) A kilometre north of Kadriorg Park, Maarjamäe is a neo-Gothic limestone manor house built in the 1870s as a summer cottage for the Russian general Anatoly Orlov-Davydov. It's now home to a less-visited branch of the Estonian History Museum and a particularly beautiful Socialist Realist mural in the banqueting hall, featuring triumphant factory workers, peasants, cosmonauts and an apparition of Lenin's face among the red flags. When this was unveiled in 1987, it's clear that nobody foresaw the dramatic events of the following few years.

Those events are covered by the major exhibition *A Will to Be Free,* marking the years from when Estonia won independence in 1918 until it was restored in 1991. The captions are entirely in Estonian and, while translation booklets are available, they're a little hard to follow. Once again, Nazi atrocities are glossed over while Soviet ones are highlighted, although there is a brief mention of Estonian resistance to the Nazi occupation. Still, there are some interesting photos and displays, and the video clips from the 'Singing Revolution' are fascinating.

Maarjamäe War Memorial   MEMORIAL
(Pirita tee) Perched on the headland next to the manor is this large Soviet-era monument consisting of an elegant bowed obelisk set amid a large crumbling concrete plaza. The obelisk was erected in 1960 to commemorate the Soviet troops killed in 1918 – hardly a popular edifice, as the war was against Estonia and all of the Estonian monuments to their dead were destroyed

shortly after the Soviet takeover (many have now been re-erected).

The remainder of the complex – broad concrete avenues, pointy protrusions and all – was built in 1975 as a memorial to Red Army soldiers killed fighting the Nazis. It was built partly over a war cemetery housing 2300 German dead, dating from 1941. The cemetery was rededicated in 1998 and is now delineated by sets of triple granite crosses in the style common to German WWII military cemeteries throughout Europe.

PIRITA

Just past Maarjamäe the Pirita River enters Tallinn Bay and Pirita Beach begins. Although it's no Bondi (or Pärnu, for that matter), it's easily Tallinn's largest and most popular beach and it has the advantage of being only 6km from the city. In summer, young, bronzed sun-lovers fill the sands and hang out in the laid-back cafes nearby. It's a bleak and windswept place if the weather's not good, but if the conditions are right there are plenty of wind- and kite-surfers providing visual entertainment.

Pirita's other claim to fame was as the base for the sailing events of the 1980 Moscow Olympics; international regattas are still held here. The Yacht Club by the river mouth is a relaxing spot for an alfresco drink.

Buses 1A, 8, 34A and 38 all run between the city centre and Pirita. Bus 34A and 38 go on to the Botanic Gardens (Kloostrimetsa stop).

St Bridget's Convent   RUIN
(Pirita kloostri varemed; www.piritaklooster.ee; Kloostri tee 9; adult/child €2/1; ☺10am-6pm Apr-Oct, noon-4pm Nov-Mar) Only the walls remain of this 1407 convent, located just behind the main Pirita bus stop. The rest was destroyed courtesy of Ivan the Terrible during the Livonian War in 1577. In 1996 Bridgettine nuns were granted the right to return and reactivate the convent. The convent's new headquarters are adjacent to the ruins. Atmospheric concerts are held here in summer.

Tallinn Botanic Gardens   GARDENS
(Tallinna Botaanikaaed; www.tba.ee; Kloostrimetsa tee 52; park free, glasshouses adult/child €3.50/1.60; ☺park 11am-8pm, glasshouses 11am-6pm May-Sep) Set on 1.2 sq km fronting the Pirita River and surrounded by lush woodlands, the gardens boast 8000 species of

plants scattered in a series of greenhouses and along a 4km nature trail. The gardens lie 2.5km east of Pirita.

TV Tower   VIEWPOINT
(Kloostrimetsa tee 58a) The 314m TV Tower is 400m east of the Botanic Gardens and once had a panoramic viewing platform at the 170m point. At the base there are still a few bullet holes from events during the August 1991 attempted Estonian breakaway (it was as violent as things became in Estonia's bid for independence). Due to safety concerns, the tower was closed to the public in late 2007. It's scheduled to be reopened to the public in spring 2012; double-check with the tourist office before heading all the way out here.

WEST TALLINN

Estonian Open Air Museum   MUSEUM, PARK
(Eesti Vabaõhumuuseum; ☎654 9100; www.evm.ee; Vabaõhumuuseumi tee 12, Rocca Al Mare; adult/child €6/3 May-Sep, €3/1.50 Oct-Apr; ⊙buildings 10am-6pm, grounds 10am-8pm May-Sep, grounds only 10am-5pm Oct-Apr) If tourists won't go to the countryside, let's bring the countryside to them. That seems to be the modus operandi of this excellent, sprawling complex, where historic buildings have been plucked and transplanted among the tall trees. In summer the time-warping effect is highlighted by staff in period costume performing traditional activities among the wooden farmhouses and windmills. There's also a chapel dating from 1699 and an old wooden tavern, Kolu Kõrts (open year-round), serving traditional Estonian cuisine (mains €4 to €6).

Kids love the horse-and-carriage rides (adult/child €3/1) and bikes can be hired (per hour €3). At 11am on weekends from June to August there are folk song-and-dance

shows. If you find yourself in Tallinn on Midsummer Eve (23 June), come here to witness the traditional celebrations, bonfire and all.

To get here from the centre, take Paldiski mnt. When the road nears the water, veer right onto Vabaõhumuuseumi tee. Bus 21 from the railway station stops right out front. Note that you can purchase a family combo ticket that takes in the open-air museum and the nearby zoo for €18.

Tallinn Zoological Gardens   ZOO
(Tallinna Loomaaed; www.tallinnzoo.ee; Paldiski mnt 145, Veskimetsa; adult/child €5.80/2.90; ⊙9am-9pm May-Aug, 9am-7pm Sep-Oct & Mar-Apr, 9am-5pm Nov-Feb, last entry 2hr before close) Boasting the world's largest collection of mountain goats and sheep, plus around 350 other species of feathered, furry and four-legged friends (including lions, leopards and elephants), this large, spread-out zoo is gradually upgrading its enclosures into modern, animal-friendly spaces as funds allow. It poses a bit of a dilemma for the animal-lover: while some of the older enclosures are certainly unsatisfactory (we felt particularly sorry for the poor old polar bear), things are clearly improving and if people don't visit they'll never have enough funds to complete the work. It's the best place to see all of the natives (bears, lynx, owls, eagles) you're unlikely to spot in the wild.

The zoo is best reached by bus 21 or trolleybus 7, which both depart from the train station, or by trolleybus 6 from Freedom Sq.

Stroomi beach   BEACH
About 3km due west of the Old Town (or a 20-minute ride on bus 40 or 48 from Viru Keskus or Freedom Sq), Stroomi beach is in Pelguranna, a neighbourhood favoured by Tallinn's Russian community. While the backdrop of ports and apartment blocks isn't as pleasant as Pirita, sun-lovers swarm to the long stretch of sand. There's a distinct local buzz in summer.

🏃 **Activities**

Locals attribute all kinds of health benefits to a good old-fashioned sweat and, truth be told, a trip to Estonia just won't be complete until you've paid a visit to the sauna. You won't have to look far: most places listed in the Sleeping section have one, but we've listed some public options here alongside other more active pursuits. For active tours, see p60.

TALLINN FOR CHILDREN

If you're travelling with kids, Tallinn's Old Town, with its lively medieval street scene and battlements, is pure eye candy for the under-12 crowd – although those cobblestones can play havoc with pushchair wheels. Kids are welcome almost everywhere; many restaurants have separate children's menus; and most larger hotels have play areas and child-minding services.

As well as the sights listed here, children will particularly enjoy the Estonian Open Air Museum, the zoo, the beaches, Kalev Spa and the Harju Ice Rink. There's a large playground in Kadriorg Park and others in Hirvepark, downhill from Toompea.

» **Nuku** (Map p52; ☑667 9555; www.nukuteater.ee; Lai 1; admission €4.80; ☺10am-6pm Tue-Sun) The state puppet museum and theatre. Before paying your admission, check to see whether there's a show on; they're included in the price but they're not held every day. Performances are in Estonian, but the visual fun is multilingual.

» **Thomas the Train** (Rong Toomas; ☑525 6490; departs from Kullassepa; adult/child €5/2.50; ☺noon-5pm daily Jun-Sep, Sat & Sun May & Sep) Departs from a point between Raekoja plats and the tourist office on a 20-minute loop through the Old Town; a favourite of little nippers and footsore adults.

Club 26
SAUNA, GYM

(Map p48; ☑631 5585; www.club26.ee; 26th fl, Liivalaia 33; per hr before/after 3pm €20/40; ☺7am-10pm) On the top floor of the Reval Hotel Olümpia, with correspondingly outstanding views, this is one of the most luxurious sauna choices in town. There are two private saunas, each with plunge pool and tiny balcony. Food and drink can be ordered to complete the experience; prices cover up to 10 people. There's also a small gym and 16m swimming pool.

Kalev Spa
WATER PARK, SAUNA

(Map p52; www.kalevspa.ee; Aia 18; per 2½hr €10.50; ☺6.45am-9.30pm Mon-Fri, 8am-9.30pm Sat & Sun) For serious swimmers there's an indoor pool of Olympic proportions but there are plenty of other ways to wrinkle your skin here, including waterslides, spa baths, saunas and a kids' pool. There's also a gym, day spa and three private saunas, with the largest holding up to 20 of your closest hot-and-sweaty mates.

Pirita River Boat Rental
BOATING

(Paadilaenutus Pirita jõel; ☑621 2175; www.bell marine.ee; Kloostri tee 6a; per hr kayak/rowboat €5/10; ☺10am-10pm Jun-Aug) The Pirita River is an idyllic place for a leisurely paddle, with thick forest edging the water. Rowboats and kayaks are rented from beside the road bridge, close to the convent ruins.

Harju Ice Rink
ICE SKATING

(Harju tänava Uisuplats; Map p52; ☑610 1035; www.uisuplats.ee; Harju; per hr adult/child/skate rental €4.50/2.50/1.50; ☺10am-10pm Nov-Mar) Wrap up warmly to join the locals at the Old Town's outdoor ice rink. You'll have earned a *hõõgvein* (mulled wine) by the end of it.

Kalma Saun
SAUNA

(Map p48; ☑627 1811; www.bma.ee/kalma; Vana-Kalamaja 9a; admission €8-9; ☺11am-11pm) In a grand building behind the train station, Tallinn's oldest public bath still has the aura of an old-fashioned, Russian-style *banya* (bathhouse). Private saunas are available (per hour €20).

☞ Tours

The tourist office and most travel agencies can arrange tours in English or other languages with a private guide; advance booking is required.

Tallinn Traveller Info
WALKING, CYCLING

(Map p52; ☑5837 4800; www.traveller.ee; Vana-Posti 2) Entertaining, good-value tours – including a free, two-hour walking tour of the capital, departing at noon daily. Bike tours (€13 to €20) take in the town's well-known eastern attractions (Kadriorg, Tallinn Song Festival Grounds etc), or more offbeat areas to the west. There's also a pub crawl (€16, including drinks) and day trips to Aegna Island (€35). From June to August, the tours run daily from the tent at the corner of Harju and Niguliste; the rest of the year they need to be booked in advance (minimum three participants) and are weather dependent.

City Bike WALKING, CYCLING
(Map p52; ☑511 1819; www.citybike.ee; Uus 33)
Has a great range of Tallinn tours, by bike or
on foot, as well as trips to Lahemaa National
Park (€49). Two-hour cycling tours (€13 to
€16) of Tallinn run year-round and include
Kadriorg and Pirita. A two-hour walking
tour (€16) of the Old Town includes passages
under the bastions. City Bike also arranges
multiday cycling tours through Estonia,
Latvia and Lithuania.

Tallinn City Tour BUS
(☑627 9080; www.citytour.ee; 24/48/72hr pass
€16/20/23; ☺10am-6.30pm May-Oct) Runs red
double-decker buses that give you quick,
easy, hop-on, hop-off access to the city's
top sights. The red line covers the city centre and Kadriorg; the green line travels to
Pirita and the Tallinn Botanic Gardens;
and the blue line heads west to the zoo and
Estonian Open Air Museum. A recorded
audio tour accompanies the ride. Buses leave
from Mere pst, just outside the Old Town.

Old Town Audioguide WALKING
(www.audioguide.ee; audioguide €9.50) On this
self-guided tour you follow a 41-stop route,
listening to historical details and anecdotes
along the way. It's available from the tourist
office and must be returned before its close
of business.

Euro Audio Guide WALKING
(www.euroaudioguide.com; iPod €19) Pre-loaded
iPods are available from the tourist office for
24-hour hire, meaning you can start the tour
of the Old Town sights at midnight if you so
choose. If you've got your own iPod, iPhone
or iPad you can download the tour for €6.90.

EstAdventures WALKING, MINIBUS
(☑5308 8373; www.estadventures.ee) Offers
themed three- to four-hour walking tours of
Tallinn (Soviet Tallinn, Legends of Tallinn;
from €23). Full-day excursions further afield
include Lahemaa National Park, Tartu,
Haapsalu and Communist Estonia.

360° Adventures KAYAKING, BOG-WALKING
(☑5622 2996; www.360.ee) Runs four-hour
guided kayaking tours on Tallinn Bay, departing twice-weekly from June through to
August. Also offers multiday kayaking, bog-
walking and snowshoeing excursions.

Reimann Retked KAYAKING, RAFTING
(☑511 4099; www.retked.ee) Offers sea-kayaking
excursions, including a four-hour paddle
out to Aegna Island (€29). Other interesting

possibilities include diving, rafting, bog-
walking and beaver watching.

Super Segway Tours SEGWAY
(www.supersegway.com; Vene 3; ☺10am-7pm Mon-
Fri, midday-9pm Sat Apr-Oct) Motor yourself
around town on a two-wheeled platform;
one hour's rental €32.

🎇 Festivals & Events
It seems like there's always something going
on in the city in summer. For a complete list
of Tallinn's festivals, visit www.culture.ee and
the events pages of www.tourism.tallinn.ee.

Jazzkaar MUSIC
(www.jazzkaar.ee) Jazz greats from around
the world converge on Tallinn in mid-April
during this excellent two-week festival; it
also hosts smaller events in autumn and
around Christmas.

Old Town Days MEDIEVAL
(www.vanalinnapaevad.ee) This weeklong fest
in late May/early June features themed days
(Music Day, Sports Day, Children's Day etc),
with dancing, concerts, costumed performers and plenty of medieval merrymaking
on nearly every corner of the Old Town.

Õllesummer MUSIC
(Beer Summer; www.ollesummer.ee) This extremely popular ale-guzzling, rock music
extravaganza takes place over three days
in early July at the Tallinn Song Festival
Grounds.

Medieval Festival HANDICRAFTS
(www.folkart.ee) A parade, carnival, long-bow
tournament and Raekoja plats covered in
craft stalls for four days in early July.

**Baltica International
Folklore Festival** FOLKLORE
(www.cioff.org) Music, dance and displays
focusing on Baltic and other folk traditions.
This festival is shared between Rīga, Vilnius
and Tallinn; it's Tallinn's turn to play host
again in July 2013.

**Estonian Song & Dance
Celebration** MUSIC, DANCE
(www.laulupidu.ee) Convenes every five years
in July (roll on 2014) and culminates in a
34,000-strong traditional choir.

Tallinn International Organ Festival MUSIC
(www.hot.ee/eoy/orelifestival.html) Ten days of
pulling out the stops in the city's churches,
starting late July.

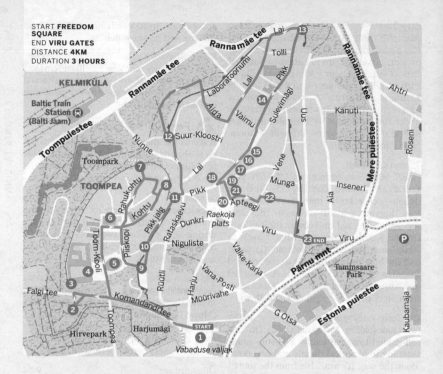

Walking Tour
Tallinn's Old Town

> We've designed this walking tour as an introduction to Tallinn's meandering medieval streets. Start at ❶ **Freedom Sq** (Vabaduse väljak), a large paved plaza that's used for summer concerts, skateboarding, impromptu ball games and watching heats of *Estonian Idol* (*Eesti Otsib Superstaari*) on the big screen at the southern end. The square sits just outside one of the former town gates, the remains of which are preserved under glass near the northwestern corner. A gigantic glass cross at the square's western end commemorates the Estonian War of Independence.

Take the stairs to the right of the cross and head along Komandandi tee into Toompea, the upper part of the Old Town. In German times this was the preserve of the feudal nobility, literally looking down on the traders and lesser beings of the Lower Town. According to Estonian legend, Toompea is the burial mound of Kalev, the heroic first leader of the Estonians, and was built by his widow Linda. Continue on a path running to the left of Falgi tee and you'll come to a ❷ **statue of Linda**, Kalev's grieving widow, surrounded by 250-year-old linden trees. During the Soviet years this became the unofficial memorial to victims of Stalin's deportations and executions.

Head back onto Falgi tee where there's a wonderful view of ❸ **Pikk Hermann**. Dating from 1371, it's the finest of the three surviving towers of Toompea Castle. Nothing remains of the earlier Danish castle, built here in 1219, or the Estonian stronghold which preceded it. In the 18th century the building underwent an extreme makeover at the hands of Russian empress Catherine the Great, converting it into the pretty-in-pink baroque palace that's now Estonia's parliament building, ❹ **Riigikogu**. Backtrack and turn left onto Lossi plats (Castle Sq) for a better view. Directly across the square is onion-domed ❺ **Alexander Nevsky Cathedral**.

Take Toom-Kooli to Toompea's other cathedral, the Lutheran ❻ **Dome Church**. After leaving the church, turn left and cut across Kiriku plats (Church Sq) onto

Rahukohtu, where a lane leads to the **7** **Patkul lookout** (Patkuli vaateplats), offering terrific views across the Lower Town to the sea. Continue winding around the lanes to the **8** **Court Sq lookout** (Kohtuotsa vaateplats).

Continue past the rear of both cathedrals and head through the opening in the wall to the **9** **Danish King's Courtyard**, where artists set up their easels in summer to capture the view over the rooftops. Take a left through the **10** **Short Leg Gate Tower**, which is thought to be the most haunted building in Tallinn. Ghostly apparitions have been reported inside this tower, including a crucified monk and a black dog with burning eyes. Turn right and take the long sloping path known as Long Leg (Pikk jalg) through the red-roofed **11** **Long Leg Gate Tower** (1380) and into the Lower Town.

Turn left along Nunne and then veer right into Väilke-Kloostri to Suur-Kloostri, where you'll come to the best-preserved section of the **12** **Lower Town Walls**, linking nine of the 26 remaining towers; there were once 45. Pass through the gate and turn right for a good view of the battlements that used to encircle the entire town. Head back through the next small gap in the walls onto Aida and at the end of the street, turn left onto Lai (Wide St), which is lined with German merchant's houses. Many of these were built in the 15th century and contain three or four storeys, with the lower two used as living and reception quarters and the upper ones for storage.

At the end of Lai, follow the small path to the right alongside the wall to the **13** **Great Coast Gate**, the most impressive of the remaining medieval gates. Note the crest on the outside wall and the religious statue in a niche on the town side.

Head up Pikk (Long St), where there are more merchant's houses. You can only imagine the horrors that went on at number 59, the **14** **former KGB headquarters**. The building's basement windows were bricked up to prevent the sounds being heard by those passing by on the street. A small memorial on the wall translates as: 'This building housed the headquarters of the organ of repression of the Soviet occupational power. Here began the road to suffering for thousands of Estonians.' Locals joked, with typically black humour, that the building had the best views in Estonia – from here you could see all the way to Siberia.

Further along the street are buildings belonging to the town's guilds, associations of traders or artisans, nearly all German dominated. First up, at number 26, is the unfortunately named **15** **Brotherhood of the Blackheads** (Mustpeade Maja). The Blackheads were unmarried young men who took their name not from poor dermatology but from their patron, St Maurice (Mauritius), a legendary African-born Roman soldier whose likeness is found between two lions on the building facade (dating from 1597), above an ornate, colourful door. Its neighbour, **16** **St Olaf's Guildhall** (Olevi Gildi Hoone), was the headquarters for what was probably the first guild in Tallinn, dating from the 13th century. Its membership comprised more humble non-German artisans and traders.

Next up is the 1860-built **17** **St Canute's Guildhall** (Kanuti Gildi Hoone), topped with zinc statues of Martin Luther and its patron saint. Across the road is the 1410 headquarters of the **18** **Great Guild**, to which the most eminent merchants belonged. It now houses an outpost of the Estonian History Museum.

Cross the small square to the left, past the photogenic **19** **Holy Spirit Church** and take the charming, narrow Saiakang (White Bread Passage – named after a historic bakery) to **20** **Raekoja Plats** (Town Hall Sq), which has been the pulsing heart of Tallinn since markets began here in the 11th century. All through summer, outdoor cafes implore you to sit and people-watch. Come Christmas time, a huge pine tree stands in the middle of the square, as it has since 1441 when it was the world's first publicly displayed Christmas tree. On the square, immediately to the left of Saiakang, is the **21** **Town Council Pharmacy** (Raeapteek), which has been dispensing medicines since at least 1422 (although the current facade is a mere 400 years old).

Take Apteegi, the lane to the left, down to Vene (the Estonian word for Russian, named for the Russian merchants who once resided and traded here) and turn left. This is one of the city's favourite restaurant precincts, home to several lovely passageways and courtyards. Look for **22** **St Catherine's Passage** (Katariina Käik) to the right, lined with artisans' studios and with old stone tombstones from the neighbouring Dominican monastery. At the far end, turn right and follow the town walls to Viru, one of the Old Town's busiest streets. Finish at the **23** **Viru Gates**, which connect the Old Town with the commercial centre of the modern city.

TALLINN SUMMER SCHOOL

Fancy spending some of the summer learning more about Estonian culture, or making sense of the local language? Tallinn University's **summer school** (☑619 9599; www.tlu.ee) is a good place to start. You can study the Estonian, Russian, English, Spanish, Italian or Mandarin language, and sample various cultural programs. A three-week Estonian-language course costs €420 and includes a cultural component that involves lectures and discussions delving into aspects of Estonian culture, history, art, music and traditions. Check out the details online. Creative writing, film-making, digital photography, painting and new media courses are also available.

Birgitta Festival　　MUSIC
(www.birgitta.ee) An excellent chance to enjoy some of Estonia's vibrant singing tradition, with choral, opera and classical concerts held at the atmospheric convent ruins in Pirita over a week in mid-August.

Black Nights Film Festival　　FILM
(www.poff.ee) Featuring films and animations from all over the world, Estonia's biggest film festival brings life to cold winter nights for two weeks from mid-November.

🛏 Sleeping

Tallinn's medieval charm is no longer a state secret, so be sure to book well in advance in summer. Prices rise considerably in high season (peaking in July and August) and, irrespective of budget category, it can be extremely difficult to find a bed on the weekend without a couple of weeks' notice.

Tallinn has a good range of accommodation to suit every budget. Most of it is congregated in the Old Town and its immediate surrounds, where even backpackers might find themselves waking up in an atmospheric historic building. If you're travelling with a car, you're more likely to find free parking a little further out.

OLD TOWN

🔲**TOP**
CHOICE **Old House Apartments**　APARTMENTS €€
(Map p52; ☑641 1464; www.oldhouse.ee; Rataskaevu 16; 1-/2-/3-bedroom apt €89/125/229; ☎)
Old House is an understatement for this wonderful 14th-century merchant's house. It's been split into eight beautifully furnished apartments (including a spacious two-bedroom one with traces of a medieval painted ceiling) and there are a further 12 scattered around the Old Town in similar buildings. Many of them have their own private saunas and laundry facilities.

Viru Inn　　HOTEL €€
(Map p52; ☑611 7600; www.viruinn.ee; Viru 8; s €70, d €84-125; ☎) Behind its pretty powder-blue facade this boutique 14th-century offering has richly furnished rooms with plenty of original features (timber beams, stone walls) scattered along a rabbit warren of corridors. Some can be snug (especially rooms 5 and 7), so check out the photos on the hotel's website. And note the sauna and spa area, and on-site pizzeria too.

Hotel Telegraaf　　HOTEL €€€
(Map p52; ☑600 0600; www.telegraafhotel .com; Vene 9; s €149-179, d €169-199, ste €299-750; ⓟ🐾☎) This upmarket hotel, in a converted 19th-century former telegraph station, delivers style in spades. It boasts a spa, gorgeous black-and-white decor, a pretty courtyard, an acclaimed restaurant and smart, efficient service. 'Superior' rooms are at the front of the house, with a little more historical detail (high ceilings, parquetry floors), but we prefer the marginally cheaper executive rooms for their bigger proportions and sharp decor.

Three Sisters Hotel　　HOTEL €€€
(Map p52; ☑630 6300; www.threesistershotel .com; Pikk 71; r €300-395, ste €425-975; ☎) Offering sumptuous luxury in three conjoined merchant houses dating from the 14th century, Three Sisters has 23 spacious rooms, each unique but with uniformly gorgeous details, including old-fashioned freestanding bathtubs, original wooden beams, tiny balconies and canopy beds. Outside of the rooms, there are plenty of romantic nooks to hide away in on chilly nights. If you've got regal aspirations, the piano suite is the usual choice of visiting royalty.

Tallinn Backpackers　　HOSTEL €
(Map p52; ☑644 0298; www.tallinnbackpackers .com; Olevimägi 11; dm €11-14; @☎) Staffed by young Aussies who are more than happy to go drinking with guests, and in a perfect Old Town location, this place has a good global feel and a roll-call of traveller-happy features: lockers, free sauna and spa, snazzy bathrooms (including some en-suites), big-screen

movies in the common room, a foosball table and day trips to nearby attractions.

Old House Hostel & Guesthouse HOSTEL €
(Map p52; ☑641 1281; www.oldhouse.ee; Uus 22 & 26; dm/s/tw €15/30/44; P@☎) Although one is called a hostel and one a guesthouse, these twin establishments both combine a cosy guesthouse feel with hostel facilities (dorm rooms, shared bathrooms, guest kitchens and lounges). The homey, old-world decor (think antiques, wacky wallpaper, plants, lamps and bedspreads, with minimal bunks) and the relatively quiet Old Town location will appeal to budget travellers who like things to be nice and comfortable.

Villa Hortensia APARTMENTS €€
(Map p52; ☑504 6113; www.hoov.ee/villa-hortensia.html; Masters' Courtyard, Vene 6; s €40-80, d €55-105; ☎) Villa Hortensia is a small collection of studio apartments in the sweet, cobblestoned Masters' Courtyard (p74). There are four split-level studios, featuring private bathrooms, kitchenettes and access to a shared communal lounge, but the two larger apartments are the real treats, with balconies and loads of character. This place offers unbelievable value in a superb location – book ahead.

Flying Kiwi HOSTEL €
(Map p52; ☑5821 3292; www.flyingkiwitallinn.com; Nunne 1; dm €13, r €36-42; @☎) The Flying Kiwi is a relaxed, friendly hostel run by a New Zealander, poised in the crotch of the 'short leg' and 'long leg' approaches to Toompea. The hostel occupies the two top floors of an old building, with dorms (single beds, not bunks) and a communal lounge at the top, and spacious private rooms and a kitchen below.

Savoy Boutique Hotel HOTEL €€€
(Map p52; ☑680 6688; www.tallinnhotels.ee; Suur-Karja 17/19; s €125-194, d €135-204; ☎) Soft cream and caramel tones make these rooms an oasis of double-glazed calm off one of the Old Town's busy intersections (request a room on a higher floor for the rooftop views). Nice boutiquey touches include robes and slippers in every room. Downstairs in the art deco–styled building are a cosy bar, popular alfresco terrace and excellent restaurant.

Merchant's House Hotel HOTEL €€€
(Map p52; ☑697 7500; www.merchantshouse hotel.com; Dunkri 4/6; s €130, d €160-175; @☎)

Set around a central courtyard, this 37-room boutique hotel combines medieval atmosphere with a modern design sensibility (Buddha paintings and feature walls), only a few metres from the Old Town's main square. The rooms are all quite different, as you'd expect from such an old building.

Viru Backpackers HOSTEL €
(Map p52; ☑644 0298; www.tallinnbackpackers.com; 3rd fl, Viru 5; s €25-29, d €42-48; ☎) A small offshoot of Tallinn Backpackers that offers cosy, brightly painted private rooms with shared bathrooms. It's a quieter environment than the main hostel, albeit in a noisier part of town.

Vana Tom HOSTEL €
(Map p52; ☑527 8409; www.vanatom.ee; Väike-Karja 1; dm €10-13, tw/tr/q €35/45/56; @☎) In a prime pub-visiting location (pack earplugs if you're sensitive to late-night revelry), this hostel is modern, clean and well set up: dorms of varying sizes on one floor, private rooms on another – all with shared bathrooms.

Bern Hotel HOTEL €€
(Map p52; ☑680 6630; www.tallinnhotels.com; Aia 10; s €67-86, d €76-91; P☎) One of a rash of newer hotels on the outskirts of the Old Town, Bern is named after the Swiss city to indicate 'hospitality and high quality'. It's nothing special from the outside, but rooms are petite and modern, with great attention to detail for the price – nice extras include robes and slippers, minibar, hairdryer, air-con and toiletries.

Hotell Braavo MOTEL €€
(Map p52; ☑699 9777; www.braavo.ee; Aia 20; s/d/apt €80/86/100; P☎) For such a place of beauty the extraordinary ugliness of this complex, seemingly built into the Old Town's earthen ramparts, is quite confronting. Still, this strange place has presentable apartments in bright citrus colours and offers free access to a large gym and car park. We particularly like the family suites – mini-apartments with a kitchenette and fold-out couch downstairs, plus an upstairs bedroom.

Alur Hostel HOSTEL €
(Map p52; ☑646 6210; www.alur.ee; Lai 20; dm €12-16, r €30; @☎) In a quieter location than most of the other Old Town hostels, Alur has dorms in spacious old rooms that still retain echoes of their former grandeur, as well as airy private rooms. The basement kitchen/lounge is small but perfectly adequate.

PRIVATE APARTMENTS & ROOMS

Apartment agencies can be an excellent option, especially for midrange travellers who prefer privacy and self-sufficiency. True, you're unlikely to meet other travellers but you'll usually get much more space than a hotel room, plus a fully equipped kitchen, lounge and often a washing machine. Prices for apartments drop substantially in the low season, and with longer stays. See also Old House Apartments (p64).

» **Erel International** (☑610 8780; www.erel.ee; apt €119-272; ☎) Offers dozens of handsomely furnished apartments, including some on Raekoja plats and others in Pärnu.

» **Ites Apartments** (☑631 0637; www.ites.ee; apt €80-200) Offers several apartments in the Old Town and its surrounds. Car rental can be arranged.

» **Rasastra** (☑661 6291; www.bedbreakfast.ee; s/d/tr €20/35/45, apt €40-165) Arranges central apartment rental or rooms in private homes (with shared bathrooms).

» **Red Group** (☑666 1650; www.redgroup.ee; apt €81-217) From modern studios to three-bedroom apartments in excellent locations (some overlook Raekoja plats); there's a two-night minimum. Airport pick-up included.

Monk's Bunk HOSTEL €
(Map p52; ☑656 1120; www.themonksbunk .com; Viru 22; dm €11-14, r €38) Marketed by the good folks at Tallinn Backpackers as their party branch (under the euphemism 'social hostel'), the only monk we can imagine fitting in here is, perhaps, Friar Tuck. Dorms are light-filled and pub crawls are encouraged.

Old Town Backpackers HOSTEL €
(Map p52; ☑517 1337; www.balticbackpachers .wordpress.com; Uus 14; dm €10; @☎) Enter this baroque house and the whole hostel is laid out before you: a large room with about a dozen beds that also serves as the kitchen and living room. Given the tightness, late-night partying isn't encouraged but you'll certainly get to know your fellow guests. Especially as there's a sauna and spa.

CITY CENTRE
Swissôtel Tallinn HOTEL €€€
(Map p52; ☑624 0000; www.swissotel.com; Tornimäe 3; r €116-225; ☎▤) Raising the standards at the big end of town while stretching up 30 floors, this 238-room hotel offers elegant, sumptuous rooms with superlative views. The bathroom design is ultra-cool (bronze and black tiles; separate freestanding bathtubs and shower stalls) and, if further indulgence is required, there's an in-house spa. Friendly staff, too.

Euphoria HOSTEL €
(Map p48; ☑5837 3602; www.euphoria.ee; Roosikrantsi 4; Mon-Fri dm/d €11/32, Sat & Sun dm/d €14/36; P@☎) So laid-back it's almost horizontal, this hostel, just south of the Old

Town, has created an entertaining place to stay with a sense of traveller community – especially if you like hookah pipes, bongo drums, juggling and impromptu late-night jam sessions (pack earplugs if you don't). Light breakfast is included, and there are plenty of kitchens and the expected chill-out areas and communal bathrooms.

Nordic Hotel Forum HOTEL €€€
(Map p52; ☑622 2900; www.nordichotels.eu; Viru väljak 3; r €100-240; P@☎▤) The Forum shows surprising style and personality for a large, business-style hotel – witness the rambling stencil of birds and winged elephants on the pink glass facade, the trees on the roof and the garden path carpet in the corridors. Facilities include saunas and an indoor pool with an 8th-floor view.

16€ Hostel HOSTEL €
(Map p52; ☑501 3046; www.16eur.ee; Roseni 9; Mon-Fri dm/s/d €10/25/32, Sat & Sun €13/28/38; P☎) The name no longer matches the rates and aside from the fact that there are dorms, there's not much of a hostel feel either. That said, private rooms are surprisingly nice: spacious, with their own bathrooms. There's only a small communal kitchen but there is access to a pool, sauna, foosball table and pinball machine.

GIDIC Backpackers HOSTEL €
(Map p48; ☑646 6016; www.gidic.ee; Tartu mnt 31; dm €12-14, r €36-40; @☎) Occupying an old wooden house surrounded by massage parlours, this Aussie-run hostel has an appealing selection of newly renovated rooms along with some cheapies awaiting

a spruce-up. Nice touches include big lockers and a giant TV that plays DVDs and satellite channels.

KASSISABA & KELMIKÜLA

Immediately west of the Old Town, at the base of Toompea hill, these small neighbourhoods have a good crop of modern, mid-rise, midprice hotels, handy for the train station. Kassisaba is Estonian for Cat's Tail, referring to the path through the ramparts into Toompea, while Kelmiküla means Rogue's Village, which remains apt as the area around the train station still has a roguish feel.

L'Ermitage   HOTEL €€
(Map p48; ☎699 6400; www.lermitagehotel.ee; Toompuiestee 19; s €60-130, d €70-165; P@☎) Built in 2004 but looking very 1970s, this love-it-or-hate-it metal-clad building contains unassuming but comfortable rooms. The interior design has a more contemporary feel and each floor has a different colour scheme. Rear rooms are quieter.

Go Hotel Shnelli   HOTEL €€
(Map p52; ☎631 0100; www.gohotels.ee; Toompuiestee 37; r €55-67; P@☎) Right next to the train station, this modern block has fresh and functional rooms a short walk from the Old Town. Rooms facing the tracks are actually quieter as trains don't run at night. On the other hand, some street-facing rooms have Old Town views. Rates include a buffet breakfast.

City Hotel Tallinn   HOTEL €€
(Map p48; ☎660 0700; www.uniquestay.com; Paldiski 3; s/d €60/65; ☎) An interesting concept this: smart, modern rooms offered at midrange prices without the usual hotel services. There's no reception (that's handled by their sister hotel, the more upmarket Von Stackelberg, a few doors away); daily room cleaning is €10 extra; and breakfast comes in a prepacked paper bag left in the basement kitchen/dining area.

Kreutzwald Hotel Tallinn   HOTEL €€
(Map p48; ☎666 48000; www.uniquestay.com; Endla 23; r €65-145; @☎) Here Scandinavian chic merges with Japanese minimalism to create an excellent midrange place to lay your head. The pricier 'Zen' doubles have spa baths, flatscreen computers and soothing mood lighting. It's a 15-minute walk from the Old Town.

OUTSIDE THE CENTRE

Valge Villa   GUESTHOUSE €€
(☎654 2302; www.white-villa.com; Kännu 26/2; s €30, d €35-90; P☎) Homely and welcoming, this three-storey, 10-room guesthouse in a quiet residential area, 3km south of the centre, is a great option, particularly if you've got your own wheels. All rooms have fridges and kettles and some have fireplaces, balconies, kitchenettes and bathtubs. Breakfast at the communal table costs €5.80 but it's a great way to meet fellow travellers. It's well connected to the Old Town by trolleybuses 2, 3 and 4 from the Tedre stop.

Tallinn City Camping   CAMPING €
(Map p48; ☎613 7322; www.tallinn-city-camping.ee; Pirita tee 28; per site/car/adult/child €14/7/4/2; ☺late May–mid-Sep; P@) By the Song Festival Grounds, this well-equipped site is an amble away from Pirita beach and Kadriorg Park, and just a short bus ride into town.

Eating

If your expectations of food in the former Soviet Bloc are low, prepare to be blown away by what's on offer in Tallinn these days. While it can, admittedly, be hard to find much to get excited about in the rest of Estonia, Tallinnites are spoilt for choice with an array of interesting, varied eateries, charging a fraction of what you'd pay for similar quality in other Western European capitals and tourist traps. The service can still be hit and miss, but most places have at least taught their staff to smile as they rush by.

While tourist-saturated neighbourhoods worldwide struggle to offer good-quality, good-value restaurants, Tallinn's Old Town has plenty. Plus, the atmosphere is hard to beat; winters are all about snuggling into cosy vaulted cellars, while in summer the streets are covered with temporary terraces garlanded in flowers or herb boxes.

The Old Town has the lion's share of good restaurants but on a scale of inventive-cuisine-in-hip-surrounds-per-square-metre, you can't beat the Rotermann Quarter. If you want to get even better gastronomic bang for your buck, we've nominated some wonderful locals' favourites within walking distance of the Old Town in North Tallinn.

OLD TOWN

TOP CHOICE Tchaikovsky   RUSSIAN €€€
(Map p52; ☎600 0610; www.telegraafhotel.com; Vene 9; mains €21-27) Few embrace glitz as enthusiastically as the Russians, as this,

Tallinn's best restaurant, demonstrates. Located in a glassed-in pavilion at the heart of the Telegraaf Hotel, Tchaikovsky offers a dazzling tableau of blinged-up chandeliers, gilt frames and greenery. Service is formal and faultless, as is the classic Franco-Russian menu, all accompanied on the weekends by live chamber music.

Bocca ITALIAN €€

(Map p52; ☑611 7290; www.bocca.ee; Olevimägi 9; mains €12-26) Sophistication and style don't detract from the fresh, delectable cuisine served at this much-lauded Italian restaurant. Creative dishes are matched to a strong wine list. Bocca also has a cosy lounge and bar where Tallinn's A-list gathers over evening cocktails.

Balthasar ESTONIAN €€€

(Map p52; www.balthasar.ee; Raekoja plats 11; mains €13-20) There's something oddly fitting about a garlic restaurant occupying the ancient pharmacy building, given the legendary health benefits of the pungent crop. Yet no one could accuse the hearty, meaty fare served here of being especially healthy. Duck is sozzled with cider, lamb with red wine and steaks are delivered sizzling to the table. Delicious? Yes. Atmospheric? Absolutely. Healthy? Who cares?

MEKK ESTONIAN €€€

(Map p52; ☑680 6688; www.mekk.ee; Suur-Karja 17/19; mains €16-25; ☺Mon-Sat) The name of the Savoy Boutique Hotel's ground-floor restaurant is a contraction of *Moodne Eesti Köök* (modern Estonian cuisine), which pretty much says it all. Best of all, this extremely upmarket eatery offers an extraordinarily affordable weekday lunch special: a choice from five simple but beautifully executed mains for €5.

Chocolats de Pierre CAFE €

(Map p52; ☑641 8061; www.pierre.ee; Vene 6; snacks €2.60-5; ☺9am-10pm) Nestled inside the picturesque Masters' Courtyard and offering respite from the Old Town hubbub, this snug cafe is renowned for its delectable handmade chocolates but it also sells pastries and quiches, making it a great choice for a light breakfast or lunch.

Stenhus EUROPEAN €€€

(Map p52; ☑699 7780; www.stenhus.ee; Schlössle Hotel, Pühavaimu 13/15; mains €19-25, chef's choice 4/5/6 courses €55/65/75) It's hard to pick which is the most romantic setting: the

13th-century vaulted cellar restaurant or the summery tables in the flower-strewn courtyard. The menu is modern European with Asian accents and while the servings aren't huge, the flavours are excellent. If you really want to splash the cash, oligarch-style, there are over a dozen wines costing more than €1000 on the list.

Olde Hansa ESTONIAN €€€

(Map p52; www.oldehansa.ee; Vana Turg 1; mains €14-21; ☺10am-midnight) Amid candlelit rooms with peasant-garbed servers labouring beneath laden plates of wild game, medieval-themed Olde Hansa is the place to indulge in a gluttonous feast. Juniper cheese, forest mushroom soup and exotic meats (wild boar, elk and even bear) are among the delicacies available. If it all sounds a bit cheesy, take heart – the chefs have done their research in producing historically authentic fare and even the locals rate this place.

Fish & Wine SEAFOOD €€

(Map p52; www.fw.ee; Harju 1; breakfast €2-5, mains €8-14; ☺8am-midnight Mon-Sat, 9am-9pm Sun) Over three design-driven floors, this hip restaurant delivers what it says on the tin: quality seafood dishes and a good wine list, including selections by the glass. Plus, it's one of the best spots in the Old Town for a proper cooked breakfast.

La Bottega ITALIAN €€

(Map p52; ☑627 7733; www.labottega.ee; Vene 4; mains €7-20) Ancient wooden beams and stone pillars contrast with a sweeping pine staircase in the high-ceilinged dining room, providing an atmospheric setting for hearty Sardinian food. Naturally, there's plenty of seafood on the menu (including traditional treats such as stuffed squid) alongside local game meats such as wild boar and rabbit.

Chedi PAN-ASIAN €€€

(Map p52; ☑646 1676; www.chedi.ee; Sulevimägi 1; mains €13-28) If you can't get a booking at London's top Chinese restaurants, console yourself at sleek, sexy Chedi. UK-based chef Alan Yau (of London's Michelin-starred Hakkasan and Yauatcha) consulted on the menu, and some of his trademark dishes are featured here. The food is exemplary (try the delicious crispy duck salad) and the surrounds suitably sleek.

Leib ESTONIAN €€

(Map p52; www.leibresto.ee; Uus 31; mains €8-14) An inconspicuous gate opens onto a large lawn guarded by busts of Sean Connery and Robbie Burns. Welcome to the home of Tallinn's Scottish club (really!), where 'simple, soulful food' (Estonian, not Scottish) is served along with homemade *leib* (bread) under a sky-blue St Andrew's flag. In summer, when the outdoor grill is fired up and folksy musicians strum on the terrace, it's a great spot for a wee dram.

Must Puudel CAFE €
(Map p52; Müürivahe 20; mains €4-6; ☺9am-2am) Mismatched 1970s furniture, an eclectic soundtrack, courtyard seating, excellent coffee, cooked breakfasts, tasty light meals, long opening hours and a name translating as 'black poodle' – yep, this is the Old Town's coolest cafe. It even has its own Facebook page.

Ribe ESTONIAN €€€
(Map p52; ☎631 3084; www.ribe.ee; Vene 7; mains €14-20) Occupying a corner position on the Old Town's main eat street, with tables spilling outdoors in summer, Ribe's ambience is as fresh and appealing as the seasonal, Estonian produce that fills its menu.

Matilda Cafe CAFE €
(Map p52; www.matilda.ee; Lühike jalg 4; snacks €2-5; ☺9am-7pm) There's a dearth of cafes in Toompea, so fuel up en route. This pretty pit stop offers old-world charm to go with its delectable home-baked quiches, cakes, pastries and truffles.

Kompressor PANCAKES €
(Map p52; Rataskaevu 3; pancakes €3-4) Under an industrial ceiling you can plug any holes in your stomach with cheap pancakes of the sweet or savoury persuasion. Don't go thinking you'll have room for dessert. By night, this is a decent detour for a drink.

🖉**Aed** ESTONIAN €€
(Map p52; ☎626 9088; www.vonkrahl.ee; Rataskaevu 8; mains €9-12; ☺noon-midnight Mon-Sat, noon-6pm Sun) From the pots of herbs framing the doorway to the artwork on the walls, a lot of care has gone into creating this beautiful, plant-filled restaurant (the name means 'garden'). Dubbing itself the 'Embassy of Pure Food' and flying its own green flag, Aed offers a fresh and healthy take on Estonian cuisine. The menu notes gluten-, lactose- and egg-free options; the weekday lunchtime special is great value at €4.

Vanaema Juures ESTONIAN €€
(Map p52; ☎626 9080; www.vonkrahl.ee; Rataskaevu 10/12; mains €12-17; ☺noon-10pm Mon-Sat, noon-6pm Sun) Food just like your grandma used to make, if she was a) Estonian, and b) a really good cook. 'Grandma's Place' was one of Tallinn's most stylish restaurants in the 1930s, and still rates as a top choice for traditional, home-style Estonian fare. The antique-furnished, photograph-filled dining room has a formal air, although the street terrace is a better choice in summer.

Tristan ja Isolde CAFE €
(Map p52; Raekoja plats 1; snacks €1; ☺10am-10pm Oct-Apr, 9am-midnight May-Sep) This Lilliputian cafe below the Town Hall plays on its historic setting with costumed wenches dishing out victuals in ceramic bowls. All that's on offer is soup, pies, beer and bucketloads of atmosphere (actually there's coffee too, but the medieval peasants aren't too skilled in that department).

Clayhills Gastropub PUB €€
(Map p52; www.clayhills.ee; Pikk 13; mains €8-16) As well as being our favourite Old Town pub – for its live bands, comfy couches, stone-walled upstairs room and sunny summer terrace – Clayhills serves up quality grub. Chow down on pub classics such as (Estonian pork-and-apple) bangers and mash, gourmet burgers and snack platters.

Gloria FRENCH €€€
(Map p52; ☎640 6800; www.gloria.ee; Müürivahe 2; mains €21-25; ☺noon-11.30pm) Serving the *crème de la crème* of Estonian society since the 1930s, Gloria offers a sumptuous pre-war dining room and deluxe dishes in the classic French tradition. It's probably Tallinn's most expensive restaurant but certainly not its most innovative.

Kehrwieder CAFE €
(Map p52; www.kohvik.ee; Saiakang 1; snacks €2-5; ☺8am-midnight; 🛜) Sure, there's seating on Raekoja plats, but inside the city's cosiest cafe is where the real ambience is found – you can stretch out on a couch, read by lamplight and bump your head on the arched ceilings. Foodwise, it offers only pastries, cakes, chocolates and pre-prepared wraps and salads.

Bonaparte Deli DELICATESSEN €
(Map p52; www.bonaparte.ee; Pikk 47; pastries €1; ☺10am-7pm) According to Napoleon, an

army marches on its stomach. Arm yourself with first-rate pastries, baguettes and other Gallic-style goodies at this deli before commencing your assault on Tallinn's Old Town.

Elevant
INDIAN €€

(Map p52; www.elevant.ee; Vene 5; mains €7-9) Aromas assault your senses as you ascend the wrought-iron staircase to the large, warm room where diners linger over expertly prepared Indian cuisine. There's a wide selection of vegetarian dishes and some curiosities (moose korma, wild boar curry, crocodile in mango sauce).

Kaerajaan
ESTONIAN €€

(Map p52; www.kaerajaan.ee; Raekoja plats 17; mains €13-19; ☺11am-midnight) Named after a traditional song and dance, this place has quirky decor and an intriguing menu of modern Estonian cuisine, taking traditional dishes and giving them an international, 21st-century twist.

Silk
JAPANESE €€

(Map p52; www.silk.ee; Kullassepa 4; mains €10-14) This sleek Japanese restaurant has a sparkly charcoal-tinted interior that wouldn't look out of place in a nightclub. The lengthy menu hits all the right sushi notes and throws in some *gyoza* (dumplings), *ramen* (noodle dishes) and more substantial Japanese meals for good measure. We can't decide if the sweet *gyoza* (with banana and honey or cherries and cinnamon) are gimmicky or genius.

Rimi
SUPERMARKET

(Map p52; Aia 7; ☺8am-10pm) The Old Town doesn't have convenience stores, making this small but well-stocked supermarket particularly handy.

CITY CENTRE

🏆 Sfäär
ESTONIAN €€

(Map p52; ☑5699 2200; www.sfaar.ee; Mere pst 6e; mains €8-17; ☺8am-11pm Mon-Fri, 11.30am-1am Sat, 11.30am-11pm Sun) Extremely chic but still informal, Sfäär delivers an inventive menu highlighting the best Estonian produce (Otepää lamb, Saaremaa beef and plenty of seafood). The setting is like something out of a Nordic design catalogue: a wall of yellow glass suffuses the whitewashed interior with a warm glow, while origami cranes dangle between space-age light fixtures. If you just fancy a tipple, the cocktail and wine list won't disappoint.

Ö
ESTONIAN €€€

(Map p52; ☑661 6150; www.restoran-o.ee; Mere pst 6e; mains €18-30) No, we can't pronounce it either, but award-winning Ö has certainly carved a unique space in Tallinn's culinary world. The dining room, with its angelic chandeliers, is understated and elegant – no less so than the dishes coming out of the kitchen. Seasonal Estonian produce is to the fore, with sorbets made from collected berries, and a choice of meats; fish is smoked in-house. The result is quite special.

Horisont
EUROPEAN €€€

(Map p52; ☑624 3000; www.horisont-restoran .com; 30th fl Swissôtel, Tornimäe 3; mains €21-29; ☺7-10.30pm Tue-Sat) Combining excellent service, a creative meat-focused menu, stylish decor and magnificent views (over most of the city except, sadly, the Old Town), Horisont offers a wonderful dining experience at the swishier end of the scale. Bread and dips, appetisers and palate-cleansing sorbets are liberally scheduled around the courses.

Neh
ESTONIAN €€

(Map p48; ☑602 2222; www.neh.ee; Lootsi 4; mains €9-16; ☺lunch Tue-Sun, dinner Tue-Sat Sep-Feb) Taking seasonal cooking to the extreme, Neh closes completely in summer and heads to the beach – well, Pädaste Manor on Muhu island – where they run Estonia's best restaurant. In the low season they decamp back to the city, bringing island flavours with them in the form of preserves and whatever's in season. Neh offers a simpler style of cooking than Pädaste's award-winning Alexander restaurant; it's best enjoyed over a lingering three-course Sunday lunch (€17).

Spirit
CAFE €€

(Map p52; www.kohvikspirit.ee; Mere pst 6e; mains €9-13) Blessed with model good looks and rich textures (stonework walls, marble tabletops, a fireplace and some poor creature's antlers on the wall), Spirit draws a stylish crowd, who hold court over coffee or cocktails. The eclectic and engaging menu veers from wild boar stew to antipasti to sushi to cake. Like all genuine hipster hang-outs, the entry is from the back alley.

Vapiano
ITALIAN €

(Map p52; www.vapiano.ee; mains €4-8) Foorum (Hobujaama 10); Solaris (Estonia pst 9) Choose your pasta or salad from the appropriate counter and watch as it's prepared in front of you. If it's pizza you're after, you'll receive a pager to notify you when it's ready. This is 'fast' food but it's healthy, fresh and cheap. The restaurant itself is big, bright and buzzing, with expansive windows, high tables and shelves of potted herbs.

Platz ESTONIAN €€
(Map p52; www.platz.ee; Roseni 7; mains €8-15) Exposed stone walls and a vaulted ceiling provide the backdrop at this elegant restaurant. While the techniques may drift around the Mediterranean, ingredients such as local whitefish and sea buckthorn keep the menu firmly anchored in the Baltic.

Bestseller CAFE €
(Map p52; 3rd fl Viru Keskus, Viru väljak; mains €5-7; 🛜) Located inside the city's best bookstore (Rahva Raamat), this is more than just a place where beautiful people come to pop open their laptops. Some very fine food (in delicate, French portions) is served here, including fresh, tangy salads, noodles, pasta and decadent sweets.

NORTH TALLINN (PÕHJA-TALLINN)
Moon ESTONIAN, RUSSIAN €€
(Map p48; ✆631 4575; www.kohvikmoon.ee; Võrgu 3; mains €7-15; ☺Tue-Sun) File this one under 'don't judge a book by its cover'. First, the name actually means 'poppy' and is pronounced 'mawn'. Secondly, despite its location in an uninspiring block in an unlikely lane in a slightly desolate part of town, the food here is excellent – combining Estonian, Russian and broader European styles into a harmonious whole. Plus it's priced for locals; few tourists make their way down here.

F-hoone CAFE, BAR €
(Map p48; Telliskivi 60A; mains €5-7) If you suspected that there was probably a cool, casual eatery hidden away somewhere – where in-the-know locals head for a quality, cheap feed – you were right. Hidden in an old warehouse on the wrong side of the tracks, this cavernous place embraces industrial chic, with mismatched furniture and oversized light fixtures. The menu is an unfussy mix of pasta, chicken, fish and vegetarian dishes. Service can be slow.

KADRIORG
TOP CHOICE **NOP** CAFE €
(Map p48; www.nop.ee; J Köleri 1; mains €4-6; ☺8am-8pm) Well off the tourist trail and a favourite with Tallinn's hipsters, NOP is the kind of neighbourhood deli-cafe that drives up real-estate prices. To your right as you

enter is a deli stocked with organic groceries and hard-to-find produce; to your left is a charming cafe. White walls, wooden floors and a kids' corner set the scene, while a menu highlights cooked breakfasts, soups, salads and wraps. It's not far from Kadriorg Park.

Park Cafe CAFE €
(Map p48; www.park-cafe.ee; Weizenbergi 22; pastries €1-2; ☺10am-8pm Tue-Sun) At the western entrance to Kadriorg Park is this sweet slice of Viennese cafe culture. If the sun's shining, the alfresco tables by the pond might just be our favourite place in town; in poor weather retreat upstairs to enjoy your cuppa. The pastries are irresistible.

🍷 Drinking

Since independence, Tallinn has established a reputation as a party town and while things have cooled off a little, marauding troops of British stag groups and Finnish booze-boys still descend, especially on summer weekends. Given that they tend to congregate around a small nexus of Irish and British pubs in the southeast corner of the Old Town (roughly the triangle formed by Viru, Suur-Karja and the city walls), they are easily avoided – or located, if you'd prefer. Elsewhere you'll find a diverse selection of bars where it's quite possible to have a quiet, unmolested drink.

OLD TOWN
See also Bocca (p68) for cocktails; Leib (p68) for a beer on the lawn; Clayhills Gastropub (p69) for live music and a cosy pub atmosphere; and Fish & Wine (p68) for, well, wine and fish.

TOP CHOICE **Gloria Wine Cellar** WINE BAR
(Gloria Veinikelder; Map p52; www.gloria.ee; Müürivahe 2; ☺11am-11pm Mon-Sat, noon-6pm Sun) At first glance, this is just a wine shop. But take the nondescript entrance at the far end, turn left down the passage and a magical wine bar comes into view, hidden within the subterranean nooks and crannies. The dark wood, antique furnishings and flickering candles add to the allure, but the best part is that you can avail yourself of any of the bottles in the shop for a modest corkage rate. It's like Narnia for grown-ups.

DM Baar BAR
(Map p52; www.depechemode.ee; Voorimehe 4; ☺noon-4am) For fans of Depeche Mode,

this is liable to be the holy grail of drinking establishments. Staying true to the band's aesthetics, the decor is mainly red and black, while the walls are covered with all manner of memorabilia, including pictures of the actual band partying here. And the soundtrack? Do you really need to ask?

Hell Hunt   PUB

(Map p52; www.hellhunt.ee; Pikk 39) See if you can't score a few of the comfy armchairs out the back of this trouper on the pub circuit, beloved of discerning locals of all ages. It boasts an amiable air and reasonable prices for local-brewed beer and cider – plus decent pub grub. Don't let the menacing-sounding name put you off – it actually means 'gentle wolf'. In summer, it spills onto the little square across the road.

Clazz   BAR

(Map p52; www.clazz.ee; Vana turg 2) Behind the cheesy name (a contraction of 'classy jazz') is a popular restaurant-bar, featuring live music every night of the week (the cover charge varies). Classy? Compared to the raucous boozers of the surrounding streets, certainly.

Von Krahli Baar   PUB

(Map p52; www.vonkrahl.ee; Rataskaevu 12) Comfortably grungy Von Krahli has courtyard tables and a barn-like interior which hosts the occasional live band or DJ. It's a great spot for an inexpensive meal or beer in an indie ambience.

Levist Väljas   BAR

(Map p52; Olevimägi 12; ⊘3pm-3am Sun-Thu, 3pm-6am Fri & Sat) Inside this cellar bar (usually the last pit stop of the night) you'll find broken furniture, cheap booze and a refreshingly motley crew of friendly punks, grunge kids and anyone else who strays from the well-trodden tourist path.

Drink   PUB

(Map p52; Väike-Karja 8) You know a bar means business when it calls itself Drink. The best of Tallinn's British-style pubs, it takes its beer seriously (serving drops from all over the world). There are plenty of beer-friendly accompaniments: traditional pub grub, happy hours, big-screen sports and quiz nights.

Pôrgu   PUB

(Map p52; www.facebook.com/porgu; Rüütli 4) While the name may mean 'hell', the descent to this particular underworld is too brightly lit to be devilishly atmospheric. For beer-lovers, the selection of local and imported beers is nothing short of heavenly.

Neitsitorn   CAFE

(Map p52; Lühike jalg 9a; entry €2; ⊘9am-midnight) Said to have been a prison for medieval prostitutes, the Virgin's Tower (Neitsitorn) now houses a small cafe where you can relax with a beer within the galleried town walls and gaze on the virtuous below.

Beer House   MICROBREWERY

(Map p52; www.beerhouse.ee; Dunkri 5) Tallinn's only microbrewery offers up the good stuff (seven house brews) in a huge, tavernlike space where, come evening, the German oompah-pah music can rattle the brain into oblivion. Sometimes raucous, it's for those who have had an overdose of cosy at other venues.

St Patrick's   PUB

(Map p52; www.patricks.ee; Suur-Karja 8; ⊘11am-2am Sun-Thu, 11am-4am Fri & Sat) One of a chain of four dotted around town, this lively, good-looking bar has plenty of beer to go round, and attracts a surprising number of Estonians. Expect plenty of tourists in the warmer months, decent-value meals and a regular roll-call of deals, including four beers for the price of three.

CITY CENTRE

Sfäär (p70) and Spirit (p70) are both sophisticated options, or head up to Horisont (p70) for a cocktail in the clouds.

Scotland Yard   BAR

(Map p52; www.scotlandyard.ee; Mere pst 6e; ⊘9am-midnight Sun-Thu, 9am-2am Fri & Sat) As themed bars go, this is very well done, right down to the prison-cell toilets and staff dressed as English bobbies. There's a big menu of all-day pub grub, a small outdoor terrace and clubby leather banquettes. The large fish tank and electric-chair loos may not quite fit the theme but neither do the live bands, and they all add to the fun.

☆ Entertainment

It's a small capital as capitals go, and the pace is accordingly slower than in bigger cities, but there's still plenty to keep you stimulated in Tallinn. Events are posted on walls, advertised on flyers found in shops and cafes, and listed in newspapers. During July and August pick up the free *Tallinn This Week* magazine, available from the tourist office and venues around town. Tallinn's best year-round listings guide is bi-monthly *Tallinn In Your Pocket* (www.inyourpocket.com); buy it at bookshops or the tourist office (€2.20), or download it for free from the website. For performing arts listings, see www.culture.ee, www.concert.ee and www.teater.ee.

Buy tickets for concerts and big events at **Piletilevi** (www.piletilevi.ee), either online or inside the Viru Keskus shopping centre.

Nightclubs

Club Privé   CLUB
(Map p52; www.clubprive.ee; Harju 6) Ranked by DJ magazine as the 23rd best club in the world in 2011, Privé occupies an old vaudeville theatre decked out with ornate chandeliers and baroque mirrors. Prices are high (admission around €14 on the weekends) and the door policy exacting (scour the suitcase for your coolest clean threads), but a discerning roster of international and local DJs make this Estonia's most progressive and glamorous clubbing option.

BonBon   CLUB
(Map p52; www.bonbon.ee; Mere pst 6e; ⊘11pm-5am Fri & Sat) With enormous chandeliers and a portrait of Bacchus overlooking the dance floor, BonBon is renowned for its chi-chi attitude. It attracts a 25- to 30-something A-list clientele who want to party in style. Frock up to fit in.

Club Hollywood   CLUB
(Map p52; www.club-hollywood.ee; Vana-Posti 8; admission €3-8; ⊘from 11pm Wed-Sat) A multi-level emporium of mayhem, this is the nightclub that draws the largest crowds. Plenty of tourists and Tallinn's young party crowd mix it up to international and local DJs. Wednesday night is ladies' night (free entry for women), so expect to see loads of guys looking to get lucky.

Cinemas

Films are shown in their original language, subtitled in Estonian and Russian. Tickets range from €4 to €7, depending on day and session time.

Katusekino   OUTDOOR CINEMA
(Map p52; www.katusekino.ee; Viru Keskus, Viru väljak 4; ⊘May-Sep) In the warmer months, an eclectic programme of films (cult classics, as well as interesting new releases) play on the rooftop of the Viru Keskus shopping centre. Screen times depend on sunset – anything from 9pm (September) to 11.30pm (late

---

GAY & LESBIAN TALLINN

Tallinn holds the monopoly on visible gay life in Estonia, with a small cluster of venues towards the south of the Old Town. Tallinn hosted Baltic Pride for the first time in June 2011, with support from the government and various foreign embassies, and plans to do so again every three years.

For more information, pick up a free copy of the excellent *Gay Map* (www.tallinn .gaymap.ee), available from gay and lesbian venues, or visit www.gay.ee.

» **X-Baar** (Map p52; www.xbaar.ee; Tatari 1; ⊘4pm-1am Sun-Thu, 4pm-3am Fri & Sat) Entered from Estonia pst, this long-standing bar sprawls over two floors and out into the car park. It's a relaxed kind of place, entertaining a mixed crowd of gays and lesbians with the usual trashy pop soundtrack.

» **Kapp** (Map p52; www.kapp.ee; Vana-Posti 8; ⊘10pm-3am Wed & Thu, 10pm-5am Fri & Sat) The name means 'closet' but this slick 'hetero-friendly' club presents a bold terrace to the street (open from midday). Inside, there's stiff competition for the podium whenever Lady Gaga hits the decks. On Wednesday the €7 charge includes as much beer and cider as you can drink.

» **G-Punkt** (Map p52; www.gpunkt.ee; Pärnu mnt 23; admission free; ⊘6pm-1am Tue-Thu, 8pm-6am Fri & Sat) To see what Eastern European gay clubs were like 15 years ago, head to this friendly venue, mainly attracting Russian-speaking lesbians. With no sign advertising itself, it's tricky to locate – as the *g-punkt* (g-spot) is wont to be. It's accessed across a parking lot from Tatari.

» **Club 69** (Map p48; www.club69.ee; Sakala 24; admission €5-14; ⊘4pm-2am Sun-Thu, 4pm-7am Fri & Sat) Gay men's sauna; push the buzzer by the discretely located sign at the gate for admittance.

June) – but food and drinks are available from 5pm.

Artis
CINEMA

(Map p52; www.kino.ee; Estonia pst 9) Inside the new Solaris Centre but somewhat tricky to find, this art-house cinema shows European, local and independent productions.

Kino Sõprus
CINEMA

(Map p52; www.kinosoprus.ee; Vana-Posti 8) Set in a magnificent Stalin-era theatre, this art-house cinema has an excellent repertoire of European, local and independent productions.

Coca-Cola Plaza
CINEMA

(Map p52; www.forumcinemas.ee; Hobujaama 5) Modern 11-screen cinema, playing the latest Hollywood releases. Located behind the post office.

Theatre & Dance

Most theatre performances are in Estonian, or occasionally in Russian.

Estonia Concert Hall & National Opera
CONCERT HALL

(Map p52; ☑683 1210; www.opera.ee; Estonia pst 4) The city's biggest classical concerts are held in this double-barrelled venue. It's Tallinn's main theatre and houses the Estonian national opera and ballet.

Tallinn City Theatre
THEATRE

(Tallinna Linnateater; Map p52; ☑665 0800; www .linnateater.ee; Lai 23) The most beloved theatre in town always stages something memorable. Watch for its summer plays on the outdoor stage or in various Old Town venues.

Estonian Drama Theatre
THEATRE

(Eesti Draamateater; Map p52; ☑680 5555; www .draamateater.ee; Pärnu mnt 5) Flagship company staging mainly classic plays.

Teater No99
THEATRE

(Map p52; ☑660 5051; www.no99.ee; Sakala 3) More experimental productions happen here.

Von Krahli Theatre
THEATRE

(Map p52; ☑626 9090; www.vonkrahl.ee; Rataskaevu 10) Known for its experimental and fringe productions.

St Canute's Guild Hall
DANCE

(Map p52; ☑646 4704; www.saal.ee; Pikk 20) Tallinn's temple of modern dance also hosts the occasional classical dance performance.

Live Music

Clazz (p72), Clayhills Gastropub (p69) and Scotland Yard (p72) all host regular live music, while Teater No99 has a weekly jazz club. Touring international acts usually perform at Tallinn Song Festival Grounds (p57), A Le Coq Arena or Saku Suurhall.

For major classical concerts, check out what's on at the Estonia Concert Hall. Chamber, organ and smaller-scale concerts are held at various halls and churches around town.

Sport

A Le Coq Arena
FOOTBALL

(Map p48; ☑627 9940; Asula 4c) About 1.5km southwest of town, this arena is home to the national squad and Tallinn's football team FC Flora (www.fcflora.ee).

Saku Suurhall
BASKETBALL

(www.sakusuurhall.ee; Paldiski mnt 104b) Basketball ranks as one of Estonia's most passionately watched games, and the big games are held in this arena, west of the centre.

🛍 Shopping

You'll be tripping over *käsitöö* (handicraft) stores in the Old Town. Dozens of small shops sell traditional Estonian-made souvenirs, such as linen, knitwear, leatherbound books, ceramics, jewellery (particularly amber), stained glass and objects carved from limestone or from juniper wood. There are plenty of antique stores selling everything from *objets d'art* to Soviet-era nostalgia. Arguably, the best place for the latter is the Train Station Market (boxed text), although there are likely to be as many cheap reproductions as actual relics.

If you're stuck for gift ideas, you can't go wrong with a bottle of Vana Tallinn liqueur.

OLD TOWN

TOP CHOICE Masters' Courtyard
HANDICRAFTS

(Meistrite Hoov; Map p52; Vene 6) Rich pickings here, with the cobblestoned courtyard not only home to a cosy cafe but also small stores and artisans' workshops selling quality ceramics, glass, jewellery, knitwear, woodwork and candles.

Katariina Gild
HANDICRAFTS

(Map p52; Katariina käik, at Vene 12) This lovely laneway is home to several artisans' studios where you can happily browse and

THE MARKET ECONOMY

If you're looking for picnic supplies or a knock-off Lenin alarm clock, Tallinn's markets provide fertile hunting grounds and excellent people-watching.

» **Sadama Turg** (Map p48; www.sadamaturg.ee; Sadama 25-4) Handy to the ferries and cruise ships, this new market aims to showcase the best of Estonian produce: fish, meat, cheese, berries (in season), traditional sweets and pastries. There's also a branch of GoodKaarma here (see p139) and an excellent handicrafts store.

» **Train Station Market** (Jaama Turg; Map p52; Kopli; ☺8am-5pm) A taste of old-school Russia, behind the train station. It's a bit seedy in parts (watch your bag) but there are lots of fascinating junk shops to delve through.

» **Knit Market** (Map p52; Müürivahe, near Viru) Along the Old Town wall, there are a dozen or so vendors praying for cool weather and selling their handmade linens, scarves, sweaters, mittens, beanies and socks.

» **Central Market** (Keskturg; Map p48; Keldrimäe 9; ☺8am-6pm) Popular food market. Take tram 2 or 4 to the Keskturg stop.

potentially pick up some beautiful pieces – stained glass, ceramics, textiles, patchwork quilts, hats, jewellery and beautiful leather-bound books.

Lühike jalg   HANDICRAFTS
(Map p52; ☺10am-6pm) Leading up to Toompea, this alley has a good selection of craft galleries. **Galerii Kaks** (www.galeriikaks.ee; Lühike jalg 1) has striking ceramics, jewellery and glassworks, while **Lühikese Jala Galerii** (Lühike jalg 6) also has paintings, floaty textiles and a natural waterfall that cascades down the back wall.

Ivo Nikkolo   FASHION
(Map p52; www.ivonikkolo.ee; Suur-Karja 14) Classic-with-a-twist women's fashion that's a mix of floaty and fun, or muted and professional, but all made with natural, high-quality fabrics. This Old Town address has two floors of womenswear and accessories, or you can find it in the Viru Keskus shopping centre.

IIDA   FASHION
(Map p52; www.iidadesign.eu; Suur-Karja 2) A worthy browsing stop, with intriguing Estonian fabrics and designs. There's a small range of jewellery, homewares and accessories too.

Reet Aus   FASHION
(Map p52; www.reetaus.com; Müürivahe 19) Quirky one-off pieces (dresses, shirts, coats), handmade by a popular local designer with a conscience – most are made from recycled fabrics.

Antiik   ANTIQUES
(Map p52; www.oldtimes.ee; Raekoja plats 11) There are plenty of treasures waiting to be unearthed in this crowded shop, in the same building as the Town Council Pharmacy. You just have to dive in – or shop online.

Reval Antique   ANTIQUES
(Map p52; Harju 13, entrance Müürivahe 2) Whether you're looking for icons religious or political, you'll find plenty of nostalgia buried here.

Nu Nordik   DESIGN
(Map p52; www.nunordik.ee; Vabaduse väljak 8) Lots of funky stuff, ranging from homeware to bags and jewellery.

Zizi   HANDICRAFTS
(Map p52; www.zizi.ee; Vene 12) Stocks a range of well-priced linen napkins, place mats, tablecloths and cushion covers. There's another branch at Suur-Karja 2.

CITY CENTRE
US Art Gallery   ART
(Map p52; www.usart.ee; Roseni 8; ☺11am-7pm Tue-Sat) Despite the name, this commercial gallery specialises in Estonian fine art from the 19th century onwards. Prices range mainly from four to five digits but it's fun to look.

Viru Keskus   SHOPPING CENTRE
(Map p52; www.virukeskus.com; Viru väljak 4; ☺9am-9pm) Tallinn's showpiece shopping mall, aka Viru Centre, is home to mainstream fashion boutiques, a great bookstore (Rahva Raamat; www.rahvaraamat .ee), and a tourist information desk. The bus

terminal for local buses is in the basement and in summer there's a rooftop cinema.

Stockmann Kaubamaja DEPARTMENT STORE
(Map p52; www.stockmann.ee; Liivalaia 53; ⊙9am-9pm Mon-Fri, 9am-8pm Sat & Sun) One of the first foreign stores to open after independence, this upmarket Finnish department store helped relegate Soviet shortages to the pages of textbooks and usher in a new era of Western-style rampant consumerism.

Tallinna Kaubamaja DEPARTMENT STORE
(Map p52; www.kaubamaja.ee; Gonsiori 2; ⊙9am-9pm) Established in 1960, this large store spills into the connected Viru Keskus shopping mall.

Foorum SHOPPING CENTRE
(Map p52; www.foorumkeskus.ee; Narva mnt 5; ⊙10am-8pm) Glitzy new shopping centre, chock full of fashion and accessories.

Rotermanni Kaubamaja SHOPPING CENTRE
(Map p52; www.rotermannikaubamaja.ee; Rotermanni 5; ⊙10am-8pm Mon-Sat, 11am-6pm Sun) A shiny monument to capitalism, opened in 2007, with 5000 sq m of shopping in three interconnected buildings.

 Information

Medical Services

You'll find English-speaking staff at all of these places.

Apteek 1 (Map p52; ☑627 3607; www.apteek1.ee; Aia 7; ⊙9am-8.30pm Mon-Fri, 9am-8pm Sat, 9am-6pm Sun) One of many well-stocked *apteek* (pharmacies) in town.

East Tallinn Central Hospital (Map p48; ☑620 7070, emergency 620 7040; www.itk.ee; Ravi 18) Offers a full range of services, including a 24-hour emergency room.

First-Aid Hotline (☑697 1145) English-language advice on treatment, hospitals and pharmacies.

Tallinn Dental Clinic (Tallinna Hambapolikliinik; Map p48; ☑611 9230; www.hambapol.ee; Toompuiestee 4)

Tõnismäe Apteek (Map p48; ☑644 2282; www.farmacia.ee; Tõnismägi 5; ⊙24hr) Pharmacy south of Old Town, open 24 hours.

Money

Currency exchange is available at any large bank, post office, transport terminal, exchange bureau or major hotel, but check the rate of exchange and ask for a receipt. For better rates, steer clear of the small Old Town exchanges. Banks and ATMs are widespread.

Post

Central post office (Map p52; Narva mnt 1; ⊙8am-8pm Mon-Fri, 9am-5pm Sat) Stamps can be purchased from any kiosk.

Tourist Information

Kadriorg Park Info Point (Map p57; Weizenbergi 33; ⊙10am-5pm Wed-Sun) Directly opposite Park Cafe. Call in to see a scale model of the palace and grounds.

Tallinn Tourist Office (Tallinna Turismiinfokeskus; Map p52;☑645 7777; www.tourism.tallinn.ee; Kullassepa 4; ⊙9am-5pm Mon-Fri, 10am-3pm Sat Oct-Apr, 9am-7pm Mon-Fri, 10am-5pm Sat & Sun May-Sep) A block south of Raekoja plats, the main tourist office has loads of brochures, maps, event schedules and other info.

Tallinn Traveller Info (Map p52; ☑5837 4800; www.traveller.ee; Vana-Posti 2; ⊙10am-6pm; @🛜) Be sure to stop by this fabulous source of information for independent travellers, set up by young locals. They produce two excellent free maps of Tallinn (www.likealocalguide.com), one for backpackers and one that's more general (along with similar maps of Tartu and Pärnu); dispense lots of local tips; offer free internet access; book transport, commission-

---

🛈 TALLINN CARD

Flash a **Tallinn Card** (www.tallinncard.ee; 1/2/3 days €24/32/40) to get free entry to most of the city's sights; discounts on shopping, dining and entertainment; free travel on Tallinn's buses, trolleys and trams; and your choice of one free sightseeing tour (the €12 six-hour card doesn't include the tour or some of the entertainment offers). Cards are sold at tourist offices, hotels and travel agencies, and children's cards (ages six to 14) are half-price.

The cards work out to be good value if you were already planning to take a tour. Otherwise, you'd need to cram a lot of sights into each day to make it worthwhile. If you're planning on spending a day visiting all the Kadriorg galleries or all the Old Town museums, the six-hour card is a good option.

free; and operate entertaining, well-priced walking and cycling tours. From June to August they operate an **info tent** in the park opposite the official tourist office with a 'what's on' board that's updated daily. Free walking tours leave from here daily at midday.

Viru Keskus Tourist Office (Map p52; 610 1557; Viru väljak 4; ⊙9am-9pm) Inside Viru Keskus shopping centre.

ℹ Getting There & Away

This section concentrates on transport between Tallinn and places covered in this book. For travel from further-flung destinations, see p404.

Air

Tallinn Airport (TLL; Tallinna lennujaam; 605 8888; www.tallinn-airport.ee; Tartu mnt) is 4km southeast of the Old Town. The following airlines all fly to Tallinn from within the region:

airBaltic (BT; 17107; www.airbaltic.com) Flies to/from Rīga seven times daily and to/from Vilnius most days.

Avies (U3; 680 3501; www.avies.ee) Flies to/from Kärdla (Hiiumaa) at least daily.

Estonian Air (OV; 640 1160; www.estonian-air.ee) Flies to/from Tartu and Kuressaare most days and to/from Vilnius twice on weekdays.

Finnair (AY; 626 6309; www.finnair.ee) Flies to/from Helsinki six times daily.

Flybe (FC; 44-1392-268 529; www.flybe.com) Flies to/from Helsinki, with fares starting at €39.

Boat

Ferries to Helsinki are covered on p181.

Bus

Regional and international buses depart from the **Central Bus Station** (Autobussijaam; Map p52; 12550; Lastekodu 46), about 2km southeast of the Old Town; tram 2 or 4 will get you there. These are major coach lines connecting the Baltic countries, and the destinations they serve:

Ecolines (606 2217; www.ecolines.net) Salacgrīva (€13.20, 2¾ hours, two daily) and Rīga (€16.80, four hours, three daily).

Hansabuss Business Line (627 9080; www.businessline.ee) Free wi-fi and the most comfortable ride, heading to Pärnu (€14 to €18, two hours, three daily) and Rīga (€23 to €31, 4½ hours, four daily); book online.

Lux Express (680 0909; www.luxexpress.eu) Pärnu (€10, 1¾ hours, daily), Rīga (€14 to €29, 4½ hours, nine daily) and Vilnius (€25, nine hours, twice daily).

The national bus network is extensive, linking Tallinn to pretty much everywhere you might care to go. All services are summarised on the extremely handy **BussiReisid** (www.bussi

reisid.ee) site. Some of the main routes, with numerous departures throughout the day:

» Narva (€9 to €12, three to four hours)

» Rakvere (€5 to €6.20, 1½ hours)

» Tartu (€8 to €12, 2½ hours)

» Viljandi (€8 to €9.40, 2½ hours)

» Pärnu (€6 to €8.50, two hours)

Car & Motorcycle

Like accommodation, cars book up quickly in summer, so it pays to reserve ahead. The large international companies are all represented, with hire starting from around €40 for a short rental. All the major players have desks at Tallinn airport. Smaller local companies usually offer cheaper rates and you find you get a better deal catching a bus to Tartu or Pärnu and picking up a car there – the tourist offices in both cities have extensive lists of rental agencies.

If you prefer to rent in Tallinn, try one of the following (or ask at your accommodation for recommendations):

Advantec (520 3003; www.advantage.ee; Tallinn Airport)

Bulvar (503 0222; www.bulvar.ee; Regati pst 1)

Europcar (www.europcar.ee) city centre (Map p48; 611 6202; Jõe 9); Tallinn Airport (605 8031; Lennujaama tee 2)

Hansarent (Map p52; 655 7155; www.hansarent.eu; Ahtri 6)

Hertz (www.hertz.ee) city centre (Map p48; 611 6333; Ahtri 12); Tallinn Airport (605 8923; Lennujaama tee 2)

R-Rent (www.rrent.ee) city centre (661 2400; Rävala pst 4-715); Tallinn Airport (605 8929)

Train

The **Baltic Train Station** (Balti Jaam; Map p52; 631 0023; www.baltijaam.ee; Toompuiestee 35) is on the northwestern edge of the Old Town. Despite the name, there are no direct services to the other Baltic states. **GoRail** (www.gorail.ee) runs a daily service stopping in Narva (from €27, 1½ hours, daily) en route to Moscow.

Local routes are operated by **Edelerautee** (www.edel.ee) and include the following destinations:

» Narva (€7.35, 3½ hours, one daily)

» Pärnu (€5.43, 2¾ hours, two daily)

» Rakvere (€4, 1¾ hours, two daily)

» Tartu (€6.71, three hours, three daily)

» Viljandi (€6.39, 2½ hours, one to three daily)

ℹ Getting Around

To/From the Airport

AIRPORT BUS If you're staying in the Old Town or on its periphery, the best option is to catch the big blue **Hansabuss** (www.hansabuss.ee; ticket €2, payable on board). It departs from the airport for a loop through the city centre and around the Old Town, stopping outside major hotels, every half hour from 7.30am to 6.30pm. For your return journey, pick up a timetable from the tourist office.

PUBLIC BUS Bus 2 runs every 20 to 30 minutes (6am to around 11pm) from the A Laikmaa stop, opposite the Tallink Hotel, next to Viru Keskus. From the airport, bus 2 will take you via five bus stops to the centre and on to the passenger port. Tickets are €1.60 from the driver (€1 from a kiosk); journey time depends on traffic but rarely exceeds 20 minutes.

SHUTTLE Look for the shuttle desk in the terminal. Charges €5 door-to-door for central hotel drop-offs.

TAXI A taxi between the airport and the city centre should cost less than €10. Ask the driver in advance about the likely fare and ask for a receipt if you feel like you've been overcharged.

To/From the Ferry Terminals

There are three main places where passenger services dock, all a short, 1km walk from the Old Town. Most ferries and cruise ships dock at the **Passenger Port** (Reisisadam; Sadama), with some pulling up at **Terminal D** (Lootsi), just across the water. Linda Line ferries dock a little further west at the hulking **Linnahall** (Kalasadama).

Bus 2 runs every 20 to 30 minutes from the bus stop by Terminal A, stopping at Terminal D, the city centre, central bus station and airport; if you're heading to the port from the centre, catch the bus from the A Laikmaa stop, out the front of the Tallink Hotel. Also from the heart of town, trams 1 and 2 and bus 3 go to the Linnahall stop (on Põja pst, near the start of Sadama), five minutes' walk from all of the terminals.

Linda Line has its own bus transfer service (€2), timed with boat arrivals, which loops right around the Old Town and city centre; buy your ticket on the boat or from the office at the port.

A taxi between the city centre and any of the terminals will cost about €5.

Bicycle

As well as offering tours, City Bike (p61) can take care of all you need to get around by bike within Tallinn, around Estonia or through the Baltic region (gearless city bikes per hour/day/week €1.60/10/42; other bikes €2.30/13/45). You can also rent panniers, GPS systems, and kids' bikes, seats and trailers. They also perform repairs and dispense maps and advice. For longer journeys, they offer one-way rentals, for a fee.

Car & Motorcycle

Driving in Tallinn provides a few unique challenges, not least as it means sharing the road with trams and trolleybuses. For those streets where the tram stop is in the centre of the road, cars are required to stop until the disembarking passengers have cleared the road.

The central city has a complicated system of one-way roads and turning restrictions, which can be frustrating to the newcomer. Surprisingly, you are allowed to drive in much of the Old Town – although it's slow going, parking is extremely limited and you can only enter via a few streets. Frankly, it's easier to park your car for the duration of your Tallinn stay and explore the city by foot or on public transport.

Parking is complicated, even for locals, and often involves paying via your mobile phone (which isn't easy if you don't have a local SIM). Look for signs (not that you'll necessarily make any sense of them) and expect a fine if you don't obey them. The first point for information is your accommodation provider – some will offer parking (rarely free), or will point you in the direction of the nearest parking lot. Two central 24-hour lots are at Viru Keskus (enter next to the Hotel Viru on Narva mnt; per hour €1.80), and below the Rotermanni complex (entry from Ahtri, just past Hotel Metropol; per hour/day €1.20/10).

Public Transport

Tallinn has an excellent network of buses, trams and trolleybuses that usually run from 6am to midnight. The major central bus terminal (*hobujaama*) is on the basement level of Viru Keskus shopping centre, although some buses terminate their routes on the surrounding streets. All local public transport timetables are online at **Tallinn** (www.tallinn.ee).

The three modes of transport all use the same ticket system. You can buy *piletid* (tickets) from street kiosks (€1, or a book of 10 single tickets for €8) or from the driver (€1.60). You'll then need to validate your ticket using the machine or hole puncher inside the vehicle – watch a local to see how this is done. Kiosks also sell day and multiday passes (one-/three-/five-day pass €4/6/7). The Tallinn Card (boxed text p176) includes free public transport. Travelling without a valid ticket runs the risk of a €40 fine – inspectors regularly board vehicles to check tickets, so keep yours at hand.

Taxi

Taxis are plentiful in Tallinn. Oddly, taxi companies set their own rates, so flagfall (the initial fee) and per-kilometre rates vary from cab to cab – prices should be posted in each taxi's right rear window. However, if you hail a taxi on the street, there's a chance you'll be overcharged. To save yourself the trouble, order a taxi by phone. Operators speak English; they'll tell you the car number (licence plate) and estimated arrival time (usually five to 10 minutes). If you're concerned you've been overcharged, ask for a receipt, which the driver is legally obliged to provide.

Reval Takso (☎601 4600; flagfall €2.24, per km 96c)

Tallink Takso (☎640 8921; flagfall €3.07, per km 6am-11pm 70c, 11pm-6am 86c)

Takso24 (☎640 8927; flagfall €2.30, per km 35c)

Tulika & Maksi Takso (☎612 0000) Tulika (flagfall €2.88, per km 6am-11pm 55c, 11pm-6am 70c); Maksi (flagfall €5.75, per km 96c) If you've got a bigger group, ask for a Maksi Takso maxi taxi (try saying that after a few).

Throughout central Tallinn, the ecologically sound **Velotakso** (☎5551 0095) offers rides in egg-shaped vehicles run by pedal power and enthusiasm. Rates are €2.23 for anywhere in the city centre; you'll generally find available vehicles lingering just inside the town walls on Viru.

NORTHEASTERN ESTONIA

The crowning glory of Estonia's national parks, Lahemaa occupies an enormous place – literally and figuratively – when talk of the northeast arises. Lahemaa, the 'land of bays', comprises a pristine coastline of rugged beauty, lush inland forests rich in wildlife, and sleepy villages scattered along its lakes, rivers and inlets.

The park lies about one third of the way between Tallinn and the Russian border. Travelling east of the park, the bucolic landscape transforms into an area of ragged, industrial blight. The scars left by Soviet industry are still visible in towns such as Kunda, home to a mammoth cement plant; Kohtla-Järve, the region's centre for ecologically destructive oil-shale extraction; and Sillamäe, once home to Estonia's very own uranium processing plant. Those willing to take the time will find some rewarding sites here, including the youthful city of Rakvere, the picturesque limestone cliffs around Ontika and the curious spectacle of the seaside city of Sillamäe, a living monument to Stalinist-era architecture. The most striking city of this region is Narva, with its majestic castle dating back to the 13th century.

For those seeking a taste of Russia without the hassle of visas and border crossings, northeastern Estonia makes an excellent alternative. The vast majority of residents here are native Russians, and you'll hear Russian spoken on the streets, in shops and in restaurants. You'll have plenty of opportunities to snap photos of lovely Orthodox churches, communist-bloc high-rises and other legacies left behind by Estonia's eastern neighbour.

Lahemaa National Park

Estonia's largest *rahvuspark* (national park), Lahemaa is 725 sq km of unspoiled, rural Estonia with picturesque coastal and inland scenery, making it the perfect country retreat from the nearby capital. A microcosm of Estonia's natural charms, the park takes in a stretch of deeply indented coast with several peninsulas and bays, plus 475 sq km of pine-fresh hinterland encompassing forest, lakes, rivers and peat

Northeastern Estonia

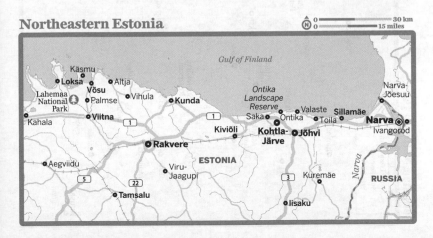

Lahemaa National Park

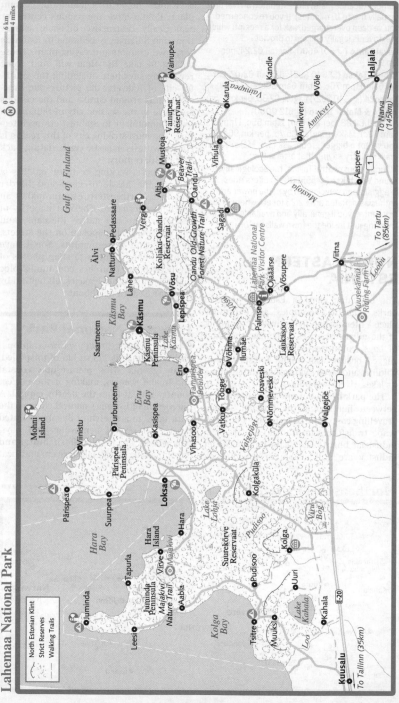

bogs, and areas of historical and cultural interest. Visitors are well looked after: there are cosy guesthouses, restored manors, remote camp sites and an extensive network of forest trails for walkers, cyclists and even neo-knights on horseback.

The landscape is mostly flat or gently rolling, with the highest point just 115m above sea level. Stone fields, areas of very thin topsoil called alvars and large rocks called erratic boulders (brought from Scandinavia by glacial action) are all typically Estonian.

Almost 840 plant species have been found in the park, including 34 rare ones. There are 50 mammal species, among them brown bear, lynx and wolf (none of which you're likely to see without specialist help). Some 222 types of birds nest here – including mute swans, black storks, black-throated divers and cranes – and 24 species of fish have been sighted. Salmon and trout spawn in the rivers.

In winter the park is transformed into a magical wonderland of snowy shores, frozen seas and sparkling black trees.

History

When it was founded in 1971, Lahemaa was the first national park in the Soviet Union. Though protected areas existed before that, the authorities believed that the idea of a national park would promote incendiary feelings of nationalism. Sly lobbying (including a reference to an obscure decree signed by Lenin which mentioned national parks as an acceptable form of nature protection) and years of preparation led to eventual permission. Latvia and Lithuania founded national parks in 1973 and 1974 respectively, but it wasn't until 1983 that the first one was founded in Russia.

◉ Sights

For ease of use, we've listed the following sights according to their location (roughly from west to east). However, we suggest that you start your explorations at the Lahemaa National Park visitor centre at Palmse Manor. Although technically outside the park, there are three lakes near Viitna that make lovely settings for a swim or hike along the pine-covered shorelines.

Kolga Museum   MUSEUM
(www.kuusalu.ee; adult/child €1.50/1; ⊙10am-6pm 15 May-15 Sep, 9am-4pm Mon-Fri 16 Sep-14 May) The photogenically tumbledown,

classical-style manor house at Kolga dates from 1642 but was largely rebuilt in 1768 and 1820. Attempts by the current owners to restore it have stalled, due to lack of finance. In a neighbouring building, this small local history museum has limited information in English but there's an interesting display on Bronze Age burials at nearby Lake Kahala.

Juminda Peninsula   PENINSULA
There's plenty to explore on the Juminda Peninsula, the park's westernmost protrusion. On its northern tip are a 1930s lighthouse and a monument to the several thousand civilians who were killed (by mines and German ships) trying to flee Estonia in 1941.

On the peninsula's eastern flank, the coastal village of Virve has a charmingly old-fashioned flavour. The 7km Majakivi Nature Trail starts nearby (on the Loksa–Leesi road), taking in 7m-high Majakivi (House Boulder); at 580 cubic metres, it's Lahemaa's largest erratic boulder.

Until 1992 Hara Island, south of Virve, was a Soviet submarine base and hence a closed area. Soviet-era maps of the park did not mark the island. During the 1860s, Hara enjoyed a successful sprat industry and about 100 people worked there. If you're interested in a trip over, the visitor centre can help find someone to take you. When the water's low enough, you can walk (check with the visitor centre for the best times).

Pärispea Peninsula   PENINSULA
Loksa, the main settlement within the park, sits at the western approach to the Pärispea Peninsula and has a popular sandy beach. The town's a bit down-at-heel but the 9km drive northeast to the village of Viinistu is pretty.

East of Vihasoo, at the foot of the peninsula, the 7.8m-high Tammispea boulder sits in a lovely stand of forest, just off the old coastal road. Over the years this gigantic erratic boulder has split into several pieces.

Viinistu Art Museum

(Kunstimuuseum; www.viinistu.ee; adult/child €2/1; ⊙11am-6pm daily Jun-Aug, Wed-Sun Sep-May) This museum houses the remarkable private art collection of Jaan Manitski, reputedly one of the country's richest men. He was born in the village but left when he was a baby and went on to make his fortune as the business manager for Swedish super-

FURRY & FEATHERY EESTI

Estonia has 64 recorded species of land mammals, and some animals that have disappeared elsewhere have survived within the country's extensive forests. The brown bear faced extinction at the turn of the 20th century but today there are more than 600 in Estonia. The European beaver, which was also hunted to near extinction, was successfully reintroduced in the 1950s and today the population is around 20,000. While roe deer and wild boar are present in their tens of thousands, numbers are dwindling, which some chalk up to predators – though these animals are hunted and appear on the menu in more expensive restaurants (along with elk and bear). Estonia still has grey wolves (thought to number around 135) and lynx (more than 700), handsome furry cats with large, impressive feet that act as snowshoes. Lynx, bears, wolves and beavers are just some of the animals that are hunted each year, although a system of quotas aims to keep numbers stable.

Estonia also has abundant birdlife, with 363 recorded species. Owing to the harsh winters, most birds here are migratory. Although it's found throughout much of the world, the barn swallow has an almost regal status in Estonia and is the 'national bird'; it reappears from its winter retreat in April or May. Another bird with pride of place in Estonia is the stork. While their numbers are declining elsewhere in Europe, white storks are on the increase – you'll often see them perched on the top of lamp posts in large round nests. Black storks, on the other hand, are in decline.

group ABBA. He has transformed this village with his art museum (displaying some 300 pieces, all Estonian artists, traditional and modern) and neighbouring hotel and restaurant (p85), housed in what was once a fish factory on the waterfront.

Käsmu & Võsu   VILLAGES

Known as the Captains' Village, from 1884 to 1931 tiny **Käsmu** was home to a marine school that churned out ship captains; at one stage it was said that every village family had at least one captain in their midst. In the 1920s a third of all boats in Estonia were registered to this village. Nowadays the main attraction is the beach, but from 1945 to 1991 the entire national park's coastline was a military-controlled frontier, with a 2m-high barbed-wire fence ensuring villagers couldn't access the sea.

Käsmu lies in a stone field which boasts the largest number of erratic boulders in Estonia. They can be viewed on the **Käsmu Nature & Culture Trail**, a 4.2km circuit, taking in the coast and pine forest. A longer hiking and cycling trail starts by the chapel and stretches 14km to Lake Käsmu (Käsmu järv).

With its long sandy beach, **Võsu** fills up with young revellers in peak season.

Sea Museum

(Meremuuseum; www.kasmu.ee; Merekooli tee 4; admission by donation; ☺9am-7pm) The former Soviet coastguard barracks at Käsmu now shelters this eclectic museum, displaying artfully arranged marine knick-knacks and charts.

Palmse Manor   HISTORIC BUILDING

(www.palmse.ee; adult/child €5/3.50; ☺10am-6pm) The wealth of the German land- and serf-owning class is aptly demonstrated by this manor complex, consisting of more than 20 buildings on a 52-hectare estate. In the 13th century there was a Cistercian convent here. From 1677 it was owned by a Baltic-German family (the von der Pahlens) who held it until 1923, when it was expropriated by the state – an event celebrated by the simple stone **Land Reform Monument**, gloating at the manor house from across the ornamental lake and French-style gardens.

Fully restored, Palmse Manor is now the showpiece of the national park, housing the visitor centre in the old stables. The pretty **manor house** (1720, rebuilt in the 1780s) is now a museum containing period furniture and clothing. Other estate buildings have also been restored and put to new use: the distillery houses a hotel; the steward's house is a guesthouse; the farm labourers' quarters became a tavern; the cavaliers' house, once a summer guesthouse, is now a souvenir shop; and the sweet lakeside bathhouse is now a restaurant. There are also working greenhouses and an orangery to explore.

TOP CHOICE **Sagadi Manor & Forest Museum** HISTORIC BUILDING
(Sagadi Mois & Metsamuuseum; www.sagadi.ee; adult/child €2.50/1.50; ⊙10am-6pm May-Sep, by appointment Oct-Apr) Quite possibly Estonia's prettiest manor, this striking pink-and-white baroque mansion was completed in 1753 and has been beautifully restored to its former splendour. The gardens are glorious (and free to visit), with the requisite lake, numerous modern sculptures, an arboretum and an endless view down a grand avenue of trees.

Sagadi was nationalised during Estonia's first period of independence, although the aristocratic von Fock's were permitted to live here until 1939. Like Palmse, Sagadi's buildings have a new lease of life, housing the State Forest Management Centre (Riigimetsa Majandamise Keskus; RMK), their Nature School, a hotel and hostel (see p84) and the Forest Museum (admission included with manor ticket), devoted to the forestry industry and the park's flora and fauna.

Altja VILLAGE
First mentioned in 1465, this fishing village has many restored or reconstructed traditional buildings, including a wonderfully ancient-looking tavern which was actually constructed in 1976. Altja's Swing Hill (Kiitemägi), complete with a traditional Estonian wooden swing, has long been the focus of Midsummer's Eve festivities in Lahemaa. The 3km circular **Altja Nature & Culture Trail** starts at Swing Hill and takes in traditional net sheds and fishing cottages, and the stone field known as the 'open-air museum of stones'.

There are some good beaches between Altja and Mustoja, to the east. A scenic hiking and biking route runs east along the old road from Altja to Vainupea. South of Altja, on the road to Oandu, is the **Beaver Trail**. This beautiful 1km walkway passes beaver dams on the Altja River, although you're unlikely to see the shy creatures.

🏃 Activities

Hiking
Some excellent hikes course through the park's diverse landscapes. Pick up maps and trail information from the visitor centre. Apart from the tracks mentioned within the Sights section, there are a couple more interesting trails.

The **Oandu Old-Growth Forest Nature Trail** is a 4.7km circular trail, 3km north of Sagadi, that is perhaps the park's most interesting. Note the trees that wild boars and bears have scratched, bark eaten by irascible elk and pines scarred from resin-tapping.

The **Viru Bog Nature Trail** is a 3.5km trail across the Viru Bog, starting at the first kilometre off the road to Loksa, off the Tallinn–Narva highway; look for the insectivorous sundew (Venus flytrap, Charles Darwin's favourite plant).

Horse Riding
Kuusekännu Riding Farm HORSE RIDING
(Kuusekännu Ratsatalu; ☑325 2942; www.kuusekannu.maaturism.ee) Just outside the national park, near Viitna, this riding farm arranges trail rides through Lahemaa including two-day, one-night treks to either Sagadi Manor (€230), Käsmu (€210) or Altja (€215); a three-day, two-night option taking in all three costs around €355 (including meals and accommodation). Call ahead and check the website for directions.

👉 Tours
Many tour operators offer excursions to Lahemaa out of Tallinn; these are a great option for those without their own wheels. City Bike (p61) runs a day-trip minibus tour of Lahemaa that takes in Palmse, Sagadi, Altja, Võsu and Käsmu villages (€49), with cycling or walking options while you're there.

🛏 Sleeping
Käsmu, set near a tiny beach, has plenty of low-key guesthouses. If you want rowdier beach action, head to Võsu, a popular summertime hang-out for Estonian students. Other guesthouses are sprinkled throughout the region. The visitor centre in Palmse keeps lists of options. Also, many small guesthouses have dogs (big ones). Keep that in mind before vaulting over fences.

The camping is fantastic in Lahemaa, with lots of free, basic RMK-administered camp sites. You will find them near Tsitre at Kolga Bay, at the northern tip of Juminda and Pärispea Peninsulas, and by the Sagadi–Altja road, 300m south of the Oandu trail. When looking for these sites, keep your eyes peeled for the small wooden signs with the letters 'RMK'. All camp sites (free RMK ones and private ones) are marked on the excellent *Lahemaa Rahvuspark* map available in the visitor centre (€1.90).

TOP CHOICE **Sagadi Manor** HOTEL, HOSTEL €€
(☏676 7888; www.sagadi.ee; dm €15, s €55, d €75-105; P🖧) Waking up within the rarefied confines of Sagadi Manor, with its gracious gardens at your disposal, is a downright lovely experience. There's a tidy 31-bed hostel in the former estate manager's house, while the hotel occupies the whitewashed stables block across the lawn. On the ground floor are fresh, modern rooms opening onto small decks and a cloister, while upstairs the rooms are more old-fashioned and marginally cheaper, under sloping roofs. The mezzanine restaurant (mains €7 to €16) offers substantial dishes, chock full of local game, fish, mushrooms and berries.

Toomarahva Turismitalu GUESTHOUSE €€
(☏505 0850; www.toomarahva.ee; Altja; caravan sites €10, d €40-60) Offering an unforgettable taste of rural Estonia, this farmstead comprises thatch-roofed wooden buildings and a garden full of flowers and sculptures. The converted stables contain four private rooms – two of which share bathrooms and one with kitchen facilities – or you can doss down in the hay in summer for €5. There's also a rustic sauna, and catering can be arranged. Signage is minimal – it's located opposite Swing Hill.

Vihula Manor HOTEL €€€
(☏326 4100; www.vihulamanor.com; Vihula; s €110-190, d €120-190; P🖧) As part of its transformation into a spiffy country club and spa, this estate has converted its peachy manor house and several historic outbuildings into guest rooms, eateries and a day spa. The rooms in the main house, particularly, are slick, elegant places to bed down, with tempting bathtubs. Hire a boat to row on the lake.

Palmse Guesthouse GUESTHOUSE €€
(☏5386 6266; www.palmse.ee; Palmse Manor; d/tr/q with shared bathroom €38/56/75, ste €77-96) Housed in Palmse estate's former steward's house (1820), this guesthouse is a more atmospheric option than the long-running Park Hotel Palmse. On offer is a variety of rooms for all budgets, from family rooms with shared facilities to plush suites with plasma TVs.

**Uustula B&B &
Campsite** GUESTHOUSE, CAMPGROUND €
(☏325 2965; www.uustalu.planet.ee; Neeme tee 78A, Käsmu; sites per person/car €2/1.50, s/d €26/42) At the end of the Käsmu road, this complex has simple, cheerful rooms on a waterfront property; breakfast is €4 extra. Campers are welcome to pitch a tent on the grassy lawn, and showers (€2), sauna (per hour €16) and bike rental are available.

Park Hotel Palmse HOTEL €€
(☏322 3626; www.phpalmse.ee; s/tw/d €51/64/70; 🖧) This hotel offers pine-fresh rooms under the enormous chimney of the Palmse Manor distillery – they're clean and comfy but looking a little dated compared with the newer offerings throughout the park.

Merekalda Guesthouse GUESTHOUSE €€
(☏323 8451; www.merekalda.ee; Neeme tee 2, Käsmu; r €45-52, apt €78; ☻mid-May–mid-Oct) In an idyllic waterfront setting, just on the right as you enter Käsmu, is this peaceful, adults-only retreat comprising rooms and apartments set around a lovely large garden. Ideally you'll plump for lodgings with a sea view and balcony, but you'll need to book ahead. If funds are running low, you can also stay in a super-basic cabin (€19) and still enjoy the surrounds. Boat and bike hire are available.

Viinistu Hotel HOTEL €€
(☏608 6422; www.viinistu.ee; s €45-70, tw €55, d €85; 🖧) More of Jaan Manitski's artworks are on display in this bright waterfront hotel, next door to his private art museum. There's a fresh nautical flavour to the decor, but the rooms are decidedly low on frills. Family rooms are considerably bigger, decked out with kitchenettes. Definitely opt for a sea-facing room with balcony.

Eesti Karavan CAMPGROUND €
(☏5370 5191; www.eestikaravan.eu; tent per person €5; ☻May-Oct) In Lepispea, 1km west of Võsu, this functional campground caters to campers and caravaners.

🍴 Eating & Drinking

You can load up on your provisions at **Meie** (Mere 67; ☻9am-9pm) in Võsu (which has an ATM inside) or at the much bigger **Loksa Kauplus** (Tallinna 36; ☻9am-10pm) in Loksa.

La Boheme FRENCH €€
(☏326 4100; www.vihulamanor.com; Vihula Manor; mains €13-17; P🖧) You can dine in the garden or on a balcony, but you'd be missing out on the grand ambience of Vihula Manor's ballroom. The menu features local fish and game but it's unmistakably French in its orientation. Make sure you save room for dessert.

Altja Kõrts
ESTONIAN €

(www.altja.ee; mains €5-8; ⊙May-Sep) Set in a thatched, wooden building with a large terrace, this charming place serves delicious plates of home cooking. Don't be deterred by the menu's first page, listing crisp pig's ears and black pudding as starters. Read on for more appetising options like juniper-grilled salmon, or pork roulade flavoured with horseradish and herbs.

Palmse Kõrts
ESTONIAN €

(Palmse; mains €4-8) Just a short walk south of the manor, housed in the 1831 farm labourers' quarters, this rustic tavern evokes yesteryear under heavy timber beams with a short, simple menu of traditional Estonian fare. The creamy, eggy potato salad is stodgy and delicious.

O Kõrts
PUB €€

(Jõe 3, Võsu; mains €9-10; ⊙11am-midnight Sun-Tue & Thu, 11am-3am Wed, Fri & Sat) This tavern has a flower-filled outdoor terrace, perfect for catching the late-afternoon sun, and a cosy wooden interior. The menu covers plenty of ground from beer-drinking snacks to predictable mains of pork, steak and salmon. There's live music and DJs some nights.

Restoran Peter Ludwig
EUROPEAN €€

(Palmse Manor; mains €7-13) Offering a fabulously formal setting in the Palmse estate's former bathhouse overlooking the swan-filled lake, this restaurant serves mainly fish and pasta dishes, with a few Asian flavours added to the mix.

Viinistu Restaurant & Bar
BAR €

(www.viinistu.ee; mains €5-11; ⊙noon-5pm Mon & Tue, noon-7pm Wed-Sun) You'll have plenty of time to enjoy the watery views from the deck or through the restaurant's big picture windows, as the service can be slack. The menu ranges from club sandwiches to pork cutlets by way of salads and salmon tagliatelle.

Viitna Kõrts
ESTONIAN €

(www.viitna.eu; Viitna; mains €4-12) Almost opposite the eastbound bus stop at Viitna (and a good pit stop if you're simply en route from Tallinn to Narva or beyond) is this reconstruction of an 18th-century tavern. The huge menu has some tempting traditional offerings such as honey-roasted pork or herring with cottage cheese. Next door is a basic cafe, open from 7am, serving up all the essentials (coffee, sandwiches, etc), and outside there's a 24-hour kiosk.

❶ Information

Lahemaa National Park visitor centre
(Lahemaa Rahvuspargi Külastuskeskus; ☎329 5555; www.rmk.ee; Palmse Manor; ⊙9am-7pm May-Aug, 9am-5pm Sep, 9am-5pm Mon-Fri Oct-Apr) Stocks the essential map of Lahemaa (€1.90), as well as information on hiking trails and accommodation possibilities. It's worth starting your park visit with the free 17-minute film entitled Lahemaa – Nature and Man.

❶ Getting There & Around

Lahemaa is best explored by car or bicycle as there are only limited bus connections within the park. You can rent bikes at Sagadi Manor's hotel, Toomarahva Turismitalu, Uustula B&B, Merekalda Guesthouse and Park Hotel Palmse (about €10 per day). Another option is to rent a bike and arrange transfers to/from the park with City Bike (p61) in Tallinn. The main bus routes through the park:

» Tallinn to Altja (€6, 1¾ hours, at least daily) via Loksa, Käsmu and Võsu

» Rakvere to Käsmu (€1.92 to €2.24, one to 1¾ hours, at least four daily) via Palmse and Võsu and either through Viitna or Sagadi

» Rakvere to Võsu (€1.73 to €2.25, 40 minutes to 1¾ hours, at least two daily) via either Vihula or Sagadi or Viitna, Palmse and Käsmu

Rakvere
POP 16,600

Roughly halfway between Tallinn and Narva, Rakvere is a thoroughly pleasant place for a pit stop or an overnight stay. The vibe here is upbeat, youthful and modern – quite unlike Narva. An interesting castle and a very large sculpture overlook the small town centre, which is grouped around the expansive Turuplats (market square). For a Soviet-era plaza, it's pretty cool – with big, orange, concrete lamps arching over pebble circles and fountains. Arvo Pärt, Estonia's most famous son, went to school here; look for the statue of the composer as a young boy on the square.

Rakvere's also known for a more unusual musical tradition, the **Estonian Punk Song Festival** (www.punklaulupidu.ee): you just haven't lived until you've heard Anarchy in the UK sung by a heavily accented mass choir sporting novelty technicolour mohawks. Started as a protest against the conservatism of the national festival, it's held every few years and was last staged in 2011.

◉ Sights & Activities

Rakvere Castle
CASTLE

(Rakvere Linnus; ☎507 6183; www.svm.ee; adult/child €4.50/3.50; ⊙11am-7pm May-Sep, by appointment Oct-Apr) Rakvere's star attraction was built by the Danes in the 14th century, though the hillside has served many masters, including Russians, Swedes and Poles. The fortress was badly damaged in the battle between the latter two powers in 1605 and was turned into an elaborate manor in the late 1600s.

Today the castle differentiates itself from other such mouldering ruins by offering hands-on, medieval-style amusements. While much is aimed towards children (candlemaking, animal feeding, pony rides), adults will get a kick out of handling the reproduction swords (blunted, thankfully), trying their hands at archery or jousting, and scoffing medieval beer and victuals in the inn.

Admission includes free multilingual tours of the torture chamber. Rest assured, it's not a real one, but there are plenty of red lights, fake skeletons and coffins to titillate the kids. Concerts and plays are held at the castle in summer; enquire at the tourist office.

Tarvas Statue
MONUMENT

In front of the castle is Rakvere's other icon – a massive seven-ton statue, which was completed by local artist Tauno Kangro to commemorate the town's 700th anniversary in 2002. You might be forgiven for thinking that's a lot of bull, but actually it's an aurochs – a large, long-horned wild ox that became extinct in the 17th century. The 1226 *Chronicle of Livonia* included a description of an ancient Estonian wooden castle on Rakvere hill, called Tarvanpea. In Estonian, Tarvanpea means 'the head of an aurochs' – hence the statue.

Rakvere Museum
MUSEUM

(www.svm.ee; Tallinna 3; adult/child €2.60/2; ⊙10am-5pm Tue-Fri, 10am-3pm Sat) Housed in a 1786 building which has served as a court and a revenue office, this museum contains modest expositions related to the town's history, including displays on spirit distillation, coins and bank notes, and weapons. More interesting is the edgy gallery upstairs.

Citizen's House Museum
MUSEUM

(Linnakodaniku Majamuuseum; Pikk 50; adult/child €1.60/80c; ⊙11am-5pm Tue-Sat) There are many historic wooden and stone buildings on Pikk, including this 18th-century home, kitted out mainly in early-20th-century garb. Displays include a cobbler's workshop, a collection of children's toys and a piano that once belonged to Arvo Pärt.

Trinity Church
CHURCH

(Pikk 17; tower adult/child €1/50c; ⊙11am-5pm Mon-Sat) Dating from the beginning of the 15th century, although it's been damaged and repaired several times since, this rather lovely Lutheran church has a 62m spire, a carved pulpit with painted panels and some impressive large canvasses. You can climb the steeple for views over the town.

⊨ Sleeping

Art Hotell
HOTEL €€

(☎323 2060; www.arthotell.ee; Lai 18; s/d €32/51; ☎) Under the same ownership as the smart cafe opposite, this little hotel has crisp, understated style – you'd never suspect that at the beginning of the 19th century it was a brothel. Rooms have sloping attic ceilings, frosted glass bathroom partitions and flatscreen TVs.

Aqva Hotel & Spa
HOTEL €€

(☎326 0000; www.aqvahotels.ee; Parkali 4; s €79-89, d €85-120, ste €190; ☎☒) This large complex includes a day spa and indoor water park, making it a predictable hit with Finnish families. The water theme is taken to the max here, from the fabulous swirly purple carpet to the aquarium and water wall in the lobby. Standard rooms are on the small size, but they're modern and stylish.

✗ Eating & Drinking

Art Café
CAFE €

(www.artcafe.ee; Lai 13; mains €4-9) With a big-city feel, an inviting rear garden and a diverse clientele, this cafe serves as a cool hang-out for food or late-night drinks. Friendly (but slow-moving) staff will help you select from a range of salads, soups, pancakes, pasta and other generally creative dishes.

Turuplatz
CAFE, BAR €

(Turuplats 3; mains €5-13) The huge wicker teapots hanging from the roof of this lounge bar-cafe on the main square may have you perusing the tea menu – but the cocktail list is also a winner, and the kitchen concocts a range of international meals, from *pelmeni* (Russian dumplings) to stir-fries, salads and pastas. The black velvet booths among mirrored walls and dwarf orange trees give the place an offbeat nightclub feel.

Old Victoria
PUB €€

(Inglise Pubi; www.inglisepubi.ee; Tallinna 27; mains €8-11) Amid antique wallpaper, dark timber and leather sofas, this place does a good impersonation of an English pub, and the beer garden is a great spot in which to sink a pint. The basic, no surprises menu of beef stew and spaghetti Bolognese lends authenticity.

ℹ Information

Tourist Office (☑324 2734; www.rakvere .ee; Laada 14; ⏱9am-5pm Mon-Fri, plus 9am-3pm Sat & Sun mid-May–mid-Sep) Your first stop should be here, where you can pick up a town map and walking-tour pamphlet from the affable staff.

ℹ Getting There & Away

BUS The bus station is on the corner of Laada and Vilde, one block south of the tourist office. Major routes:

» Tallinn (€3.50 to €6.20, 1½ hours, 19 daily) via Viitna

» Narva (€7 to €7.40, 2¼ to 2¾ hours, eight daily) via Sillamäe

» Tartu (€7 to €8.20, 2¼ to three hours, seven daily), some via Mustvee

» Viljandi (€8.50, 2½ hours, two weekly)

» Pärnu (€8.50 to €10, 3¼ to four hours, four daily)

TRAIN Rakvere has two trains daily to Tallinn (€4, 1¾ hours) and one to Narva (€4, 1¾ hours). The train station is on Jaama pst, 1.2km northeast of the main square.

Ontika Landscape Reserve

Squeezed between a narrow coastal road and the sea, roughly halfway between Rakvere and Narva, this slim reserve protects a section of the limestone escarpment known as the Baltic Klint, where the land falls suddenly into the sea, forming cliffs up to 54m high. The klint extends 1200km, from Sweden to Lake Ladoga in Russia, although 500km of this lies underwater.

At **Valaste** a viewing platform and metal stair faces Estonia's highest waterfall (varying from 26m to 32m), which, depending on the month, may be a mere trickle (or photogenically frozen in winter).

Continue 10km along the coastal road to reach the spa town of **Toila**, where once stood the majestic Oru Castle, built in the 19th century by notable St Petersburg businessman Yeliseev. It was used as President Konstantin Päts' summer residence between the world wars and was subsequently destroyed. Parts of the park have been reconstructed, including the old terrace, making it a pleasant place for a stroll or picnic.

🛏 Sleeping & Eating

Saka Cliff Hotel & Spa HOTEL, CAMPGROUND €€

(☑336 4900; www.saka.ee; Saka Manor; sites per person €4, s €60, d €80-100; [P][☎][⛽]) In a peaceful clifftop setting, signposted off the highway just east of Varja, is this manor estate, home to a low-key hotel, camping ground, spa and restaurant (mains €7 to €12). It's set among hiking trails and walking paths, with a metal stair leading from the cliff edge to the seashore below. Rooms aren't overly big, especially for the price.

Valaste Puhkemaja Hostel HOSTEL, CAMPGROUND €

(☑332 8200; info@copsmax.ee; Valaste; sites per person €3.20, s/d €20/30) Equally remote, this small, brightly painted hostel has a large communal kitchen, well-kept bathrooms and a large field for campers. Reception is handled by the cafe by the falls, where you can score artery-clogging snacks anytime of the day or night.

Toila Spa Hotell & Camping Männisalu HOTEL, CAMPGROUND €€

(☑334 2900; www.toilaspa.ee; Ranna 12, Toila; sites per person €3.20, cabins €39-64, s/d €52/78; [☎][⛽]) Despite its large water park and spa centre, Toila has achieved a look and feel perhaps best described as hospital-meets-1980s-motel. The camping area among the pines (open May to September) is a nicer option; simple wooden cabins are available.

Sillamäe

POP 16,100

Perhaps destined to be caught perpetually between the USSR (on a good day) and modern Estonia, the coastal town of Sillamäe is an intriguing place and a must for fans of Stalinist neoclassical architecture. Planned by Leningrad architects, its grand buildings include a town hall designed to resemble a Lutheran church. In the park opposite there's a **sculpture** of a muscle-bound worker holding aloft an atom.

The region's fate was sealed in the post-WWII years upon the discovery that oil shale contains small amounts of extractable

RUSSIANS IN ESTONIA

Estonia's citizenship laws (see the boxed text, p161) have caused conflict both within the country and in the country's dealings with Russia. While instances of overt hostility based on ethnicity or race are infrequent, they do occur. The tension, and ultimately violence, that was sparked by the government's decision in 2007 to move a Soviet-era war memorial from the centre of Tallinn demonstrated that fissures remain between the country's ethnic Russians and the rest of the population, and there are regular complaints (from the Russian media, in particular) that Russian-speaking minorities in Estonia are being discriminated against.

While the Council of Europe in its 2010 report noted that the Estonian government had made moves to improve the lot for minorities (of which Russians are by far the biggest group), they also noted that the unemployment rate for those minorities is double that of the general population. A drive through some of the crumbling towns of the northeast, where both work and hope are in short supply, gives some clue to the Russian plight. Russian speakers are over-represented in the prison population, HIV infection rates and drug-addiction statistics, and the greater social problems in the Russian community in turn feed the negative stereotypes that some Estonians have about ethnic Russians.

uranium. The infamous uranium processing and nuclear chemicals factory was quickly built by 5000 Russian political prisoners, and the town centre by 3800 Baltic prisoners of war who had previously served in the German army. By 1946 the city was strictly off limits to visitors; it was known by various spooky code names (Leningrad 1; Moscow 400) and was often omitted from Soviet-era maps. Yet life for the workers who lived here was generally better than in other parts of Estonia.

Only unfinished uranium was processed at the plant, though the eerily abandoned buildings on the city's western border are testament to Soviet plans to process pure, nuclear reactor–ready uranium. Only the disbanding of the USSR saved Estonia's ecology from this. The plant was closed in 1991 and today the radioactive waste is buried under concrete by the sea. Fears of leakage into the Baltic Sea have alarmed environmentalists; EU funding has been channelled towards ensuring the waste is stable and safe, at enormous cost.

The **Sillamäe Museum** (Kajaka 17a; adult/child €1.30/65c; ⊙10am-6pm Mon-Thu, 10am-4pm Fri) contains rusty tools, an excellent mineral display and a fascinating set of Soviet-era rooms, including uniforms, flags and large portraits of Lenin and Stalin. It's not well signed, set back between Kajaka and Majakovski streets, a block up from the water.

The only hotel in town is **Krunk** (☎392 9030; www.krunk.ee; Kesk 23; s/d/tr/ste €45/60/80/140), in an attractive yellow building on the main street. It has old-fashioned, agreeable rooms and a nicely positioned bar and grill facing the town hall.

❶ Getting There & Away

The major bus routes include the following:

» Tallinn (€7.50 to €11, 2½ to 3½ hours, 20 daily) via Viitna

» Rakvere (€6, 1¾ to 2¼ hours, eight daily)

» Narva (€1.47 to €2.40, 25 to 65 minutes, over 40 daily)

» Tartu (€5.40 to €9.20, 2¼ to three hours, seven daily), some via Kauksi and Mustvee

» Viljandi (€11.80, four hours, twice weekly) via Kauksi and Mustvee

Narva

POP 65,600

Estonia's easternmost city is separated from Ivangorod in Russia by the Narva River and is almost entirely populated by Russians. It's quite literally a border town: the bridge at the end of the main street is the country's principal link with Russia and no-man's-land protrudes right up to the edge of the town square. Aside from its magnificent castle and baroque Old Town Hall, most of Narva's outstanding architecture was destroyed in WWII. The reconstructed city has a melancholy, downtrodden air; the prosperity evident in other parts of the country is visibly lacking. Yet Estonia's third-largest city is an intriguing place for a (brief) visit – you'll find no other place in Estonia quite like it.

History

Inhabited since the Stone Age, Narva sits on an important trade route. After the Christian invasion, it found itself sitting on the edge of civilisations, on the divide between the Western (Catholic) and Eastern (Orthodox) Churches. Unsurprisingly, it has been embroiled in border disputes and wars throughout the centuries. Testimony to this is Hermann Castle's chess-piece face-off with the castle across the river at Ivangorod, built by Ivan III of Muscovy in 1492. In the 16th and 17th centuries Narva changed hands often from Russian to Swede, until falling to Russia in 1704.

During WWII, Narva was bombed by both the Germans and Russians and was almost completely destroyed in 1944 during its recapture by the Red Army. Afterwards it became part of the northeastern Estonian industrial zone and one of Europe's most polluted towns. Today emissions have been greatly reduced, with investment in cleaner technology well under way.

◎ Sights

Hermann Castle   CASTLE
(Peterburi 2) Built by the Danes at the end of the 13th century and strengthened over successive centuries, this imposing castle, along with Russia's matching Ivangorod Fortress across the river, creates an architectural ensemble unique in Europe. The outer walls enclose **Castle Yard**, a large expanse of lawn containing what must be one of Estonia's last remaining public statues of Lenin.

Restored after damage during WWII, Hermann Tower houses the **Narva Museum** (www.narvamuuseum.ee; adult/child €5/3.30; ☉10am-6pm). The pricey admission gives you the opportunity to ascend the tower to the wooden gallery and enjoy great views, while checking out exhibits on each level of your climb (of varying degrees of interest and relevance, not all with labelling in English).

In summer, the **Northern Yard** is set up like a 17th-century town, complete with an apothecary, blacksmith, potter and lace workshops. Admission is included in the museum

ticket and is also free if you just happen to have ventured out in period or folk costume.

The best view of the picturesque stand-off between the two castles is from the popular riverside **beach**, immediately south of the two.

Old Town   NEIGHBOURHOOD
The little that remains of Narva's war-pummelled Old Town is in the blocks north of the castle – although you'll have to circle the border fences to get to them. Most impressive is the baroque **Old Town Hall** (Raekoja plats 1), built between 1668 and 1671. As in Tallinn, the Swedes surrounded the town with a star-shaped set of bastions and most of the earthen ramparts are still visible. The **Dark Park** (Pimeaia) on the Victoria Bastion is a shady spot offering river views.

Kunstigalerii   GALLERY
(www.narvamuuseum.ee; Vestervalli 21; adult/child €1.50/1; ☉10am-6pm) Spread over three floors, the town's art gallery has an interesting collection, the highlight being the historic, pre-WWII items.

Cathedral of the Resurrection   CHURCH
(Voskresensky Sobor; Bastrakovi 4) Hidden, in typical Soviet atheist style, among dingy apartment blocks northwest of the train station, this 1898 Orthodox cathedral has an attractive red-brick exterior and a glittering core.

🛏 Sleeping & Eating

If the town's heavy mood has you longing for a bit of 21st-century modernity, your best bet is to head west along Tallinna mnt to malls such as Astri Keskus, where you'll find a few options for a quick bite.

King   HOTEL, RESTAURANT €€
(☏357 2404; www.hotelking.ee; Lavretsovi 9; s/d €44/57; P@) Not far north of Narva's town centre, King has snug modern rooms in a 1681 building and an excellent, atmospherically gloomy restaurant with a shady terrace (mains €6.60 to €18). Try the local speciality, lamprey fished from the Narva River.

Hotell Inger   HOTEL €€
(☏688 1100; www.inger.ee; Pushkini 28; s €50, d €65-100, ste €170-300) The modern exterior doesn't match the dated, scruffy but spacious rooms, and the reception was fabulously surly when we last visited. Still, Inger makes a handy backstop if King is full – as

it often is. Some rooms have a private sauna, and the themed suites are fun.

Castell
RESTAURANT €€

(Castle Yard; Peterburi 2; mains €10-20) Inside the castle grounds, this medieval-styled restaurant-bar offers up a big menu of dubiously titled dishes ('Mystery of the River Depths', 'Bravery of the Military Field' etc).

Salvadore
RESTAURANT €

(www.inger.ee; Pushkini 28; mains €5-12; ⊙6am-3pm & 5-10pm Mon-Fri, 7.30am-10pm Sat & Sun) The restaurant at Hotell Inger offers a surprisingly stylish, modern dining room with Dalí-esque murals on the wall. The menu gainfully plunders Russian, Estonian, German, French and Italian cuisines.

🛍 Shopping

Aleksandr Antiques
ANTIQUES

(www.narvantique.ee; Pushkini 13) Pop in for Russian memorabilia: Lenin busts, medals, jewellery and icons.

ℹ Information

Narva Central Library (www.narvalib.ee; 2nd fl, Malmi 8; ⊙11am-7pm Mon-Fri, plus 10am-5pm Sat Sep-May) Free internet access.

Tourist Office (☑359 9087; www.narva.ee; Peetri plats 3; ⊙10am-4pm) You can get maps and city information here from friendly and efficient English-speaking staff.

ℹ Getting There & Away

The train and bus stations are next to each other on Vaksali 2, at the southern end of the main street, Pushkini.

BUS Two daily buses to Rīga (€18 to €25, 6¾ hours) are run by **Lux Express** (☑680 0909; www.luxexpress.eu). Major domestic routes:

» Tallinn (€8.50 to €12, three to four hours, 20 daily) via Viitna

» Rakvere (€7 to €7.40, 2¼ to 2¾ hours, eight daily)

» Sillamäe (€1.47 to €2.40, 25 to 65 minutes, over 40 daily)

» Tartu (€6.40 to €11, 2¾ to 3½ hours, seven daily), some via Kauksi and Mustvee

» Viljandi (€12.10, 2½ hours, two weekly) via Kauksi and Mustvee

TRAIN Narva has one train to Rakvere (€4, 1¾ hours) and Tallinn (€7.35, 3½ hours) daily.

Narva-Jõesuu
POP 2600

About 13km north of Narva, the holiday resort of Narva-Jõesuu is a pretty but ramshackle town, popular since the 19th century for its long, golden-sand beach backed by pine forests. Impressive early-20th-century wooden houses and villas are scattered around, along with half a dozen hotels and spas – making this a good base for exploring Narva. There's plenty of new development going on, largely catering to holidaying Russians. The busiest area is centred on the new Meresuu hotel, 1.5km west from the turning to Narva.

🛏 Sleeping & Eating

Pansionaat Valentina
GUESTHOUSE €€

(☑357 7468; www.pansionaatvalentina.com; Aia 49; s €26, d €39-64, cabin €32; 🅿🛜) Behind the big Meresuu Spa & Hotel, metres from the beach, is this handsome, salmon-coloured guesthouse offering old-fashioned rooms and cabins in immaculate grounds. It's family friendly, with plenty of facilities, including bike rental, tennis courts, sauna, barbecue

---

DON'T MISS

PÜHTITSA CONVENT

Originally the site of ancient pagan worship, the hilltop village of Kuremäe, 20km southeast of Jõhvi, is home to the Orthodox **Pühtitsa Convent** (www.orthodox.ee; ⊙noon-6pm Mon-Fri). The name *pühtitsa* means 'blessed place' in Estonian and this certainly is a beautiful, peaceful place. Built between 1885 and 1895, the magnificent nunnery has five towers topped with green onion domes, visible for miles, and is a place of pilgrimage for believers. Murals by the convent gate depict the Virgin Mary, who, it is said, appeared to a 16th-century shepherd in an oak grove in these parts (echoing pre-Christian Estonian beliefs in divine beings living in holy groves). An icon was later found in the area and it is still in the main church of the convent. There is also a revered holy spring that never freezes. The nuns work the surrounding land and are self-sufficient; they will give tours to visitors for a small fee.

and cafe. Be sure to admire the alluring intricacy of the historic villa right next door.

Meresuu Spa & Hotel   HOTEL €€

(📞357 9600; www.meresuu.ee; Aia 48; r €70-120, ste €150-200; 🅿@🛜🐕) This shiny 11-storey hotel offers service with a smile, alongside a roll-call of extras: attractive rooms in browns and creams, sea views, an 'aqua centre' (seven pools!), saunas, wellness centre, kids' playroom, bike and even yacht rental, and the requisite restaurant, serving up buffets and à la carte dining.

ℹ️ Getting There & Away

Bus 31 runs about hourly to connect Narva with Narva-Jõesuu (€1.60, 20 minutes), as do numerous *marshrutkas* (minibuses), without set timetables. There are also four buses per day to and from Tallinn (€12, 4¼ hours), Rakvere (€8.20, three hours) and Sillamäe (€3.20, one hour).

SOUTHEASTERN ESTONIA

Set with rolling hills, picturesque lakes and vast woodlands, the southeast boasts some of Estonia's most attractive countryside. It also contains one of Estonia's most important cities, the vibrant university centre of Tartu.

Beyond the city – no matter which direction you head – you'll find resplendent natural settings. In the south lie the towns of Otepää and Võru, the gateway to outdoor adventuring: hiking and lake-swimming in summer and cross-country skiing in winter. Quaint towns set on wandering rivers or in picturesque valleys add to the allure. For a serious dose of woodland, head to the crisp lakes and gently rolling hills of Haanja Nature Park or Karula National Park.

To the east stretches Lake Peipsi, one of Europe's largest lakes. Along its shores are beautiful sandy beaches and a surprisingly undeveloped coastline. Aside from swimming, boating, fishing and soaking up the scenery, you can travel up its western rim stopping at roadside food stands and in tiny villages.

One of Estonia's most intriguing regions is also among its least visited. In the far southeast, clustered in villages near Lake Pihkva, live the Setos, descendents of Balto-Finnic tribes who settled here in the first millennium.

If you plan only to dip into the region, then you'll be fine getting around by bus. For more in-depth exploring – particularly around Haanja Nature Park, Setomaa and Lake Peipsi – services are infrequent and you'll save loads of time by renting a car.

Lake Peipsi

Straddling the Estonian-Russian border, Lake Peipsi (Chudskoe Ozero in Russian) is the fifth-largest lake in Europe (3555 sq km) – though its maximum depth is only 15m. Some of Estonia's finest (and least crowded) beaches are to be found on its sandy, 42km-long, northern coast. This area had popular resorts during Soviet times but many of them have been left to crumble. New development is very slowly arriving but it's largely in the shape of summer houses, rather than tourist accommodation.

In the 18th and 19th centuries Russian Old Believers – a breakaway Orthodox sect who were persecuted for refusing to accept liturgical reforms carried out in 1666 – took refuge on the western shores of the lake, particularly in Kallaste. This intriguing community survives in several coastal villages which they founded, such as Kolkja, Kasepää and Varnja, and on the island of Piirissaar.

◉ Sights & Activities

The following sights are listed geographically from north to south.

North Coast   VILLAGES, BEACH

On the northeastern corner of the lake is **Vasknarva**, an isolated fishing village with about 100 residents and an evocative Orthodox monastery that, according to some, once held a KGB radio surveillance centre. The Narva River starts here, draining the lake and forming the border with Russia as it rushes to the Baltic. Also in Vasknarva, scant ruins of a 1349 Teutonic Order castle stand by the shore of Lake Peipsi.

At **Alajõe** is the area's main Orthodox church and a shop. **Kauksi**, where the Narva-Jõhvi–Tartu road reaches the lake, is the area's most beautiful and popular beach.

Mustvee   TOWN

Mustvee may have only 1600 people but it has four churches (Old Believer, Lutheran, Orthodox and Unitarian) and there used to be seven. A forlorn WWII memorial, the **Mourning Virgin**, stands by the shore with

Southeastern Estonia

Southeastern Estonia map

her head bowed. You can take to the lake here on a rowboat (per one/six/12 hours €3/10/20) or motorboat (€3/20/30) from **Peipsirent** (☑504 1067; www.peipsirent.com; Narva 12).

Kallaste
TOWN

A settlement of Old Believers has existed here since 1720, when the area was known as Red Mountains (Krasniye Gori) because of the red sandstone cliffs, up to 11m high, that surround the town. Around 85% of its 1100 inhabitants are Russian-speaking. From June to August there's a **tourist**

office (☑745 2705; www.kallaste.ee; Oja 22; ⊙10am-6pm Mon-Fri, 10am-4pm Sat & Sun) dispensing local information. There's also a supermarket, an Old Believers' cemetery at the southern end of town, and a sandy beach with small caves.

TOP CHOICE Alatskivi Castle
HISTORIC BUILDING

(Alatskivi loss; www.alatskiviloss.ee; adult/child €3.50/2; ⊙11am-6pm daily Jun-Aug, Wed-Sun May & Sep) Signposted off the main Kallaste–Tartu road, Alatskivi Castle channels the Scottish Highlands into a particularly verdant slice of Estonia – its white turrets and stepped baronial-style roofline inspired by the British queen's favourite abode, Balmoral Castle. The surrounding estate encompasses 130 hectares of parkland (open to the public), filled with oaks, ashes, maples, alders and a linden-lined lane.

There's been a manor here for centuries, but the current neo-Gothic centrepiece dates from 1885. After nationalisation in 1919, the building was used as a school, cavalry barracks, state farm, council offices, cinema and library, but it's been recently restored to its former grandeur, based on old photos provided by descendents of the original aristocratic occupants.

Upstairs, five rooms are devoted to the life of Eduard Tubin (1905–82), an important Estonian composer and conductor; all signs are in Estonian. Downstairs there's a restaurant (see p94) and there are plans to open a set of suites for paying guests.

Liiv Museum MUSEUM
(www.muusa.ee; Rupsi; adult/child €1.60/70c; ⏰10am-6pm Jun-Aug, 10am-4pm Tue-Sat Sep-May) This museum is devoted to Juhan Liiv (1864–1913), a celebrated writer, poet and nationalist figure, of sorts. Even if you haven't heard of him (and let's face it, if you're not Estonian, you're not likely to have), it's a lovely rural setting and the 19th-century farm buildings where the Liiv family once lived are interesting in themselves. Occasional concerts and poetry competitions are held at the museum.

Kolkja TOWN
From Alatskivi, opposite the turn-off to the castle, a road heads 7km southeast to Kolkja, a village of Russian Old Believers with a dainty, green wooden church and a tiny **Old Believers' Museum** (admission €2;

⏰11am-6pm Wed-Sun) in what seems like a private house. There's not much here but it's interesting to read about the seemingly trivial liturgical changes that caused such conflict. The museum is tricky to find – turn left at the Estonian flag, continue past the blue-painted restaurant (see p94) and turn right at the lake.

🛏 Sleeping

Don't forget to pack the mosquito repellent if you're staying by the lake. At the time of research, there were plans to open a suite of luxurious rooms at Alatskivi Castle.

TOP CHOICE **Aarde Villa** B&B €€
(☎776 4290; www.aardevilla.ee; Sääritsa; sites per person €5, s/d €26/52; P🕏) Halfway between Mustvee and Kallaste, this lakeside estate offers comfy rooms (with TV and bathroom) in an old stone house set by its own beach. It's a wonderful, peaceful retreat with a plethora of activities on offer, including sauna, boat (with fishing equipment) and bike rental. Camping is possible within the leafy grounds.

Peipsi Lained Külalistemaja B&B €
(☎5569 0131; www.peipsi-lained.ee; per person €16-23; P) At Ninasi, about 5km north of Mustvee, this friendly guesthouse offers clean, cosy, pine-lined rooms with a mix of private and shared bathrooms. There's a kitchen for guest use, a restaurant, a sauna for hire, and the chance to hire boats (in summer) or snowmobiles (in winter). The lake is 50m from the door.

Kuru Puhkemajad CAMPGROUND €
(☎5690 6876; www.kurupuhkemajad.ee; Kuru; per person €10; P) At Kuru, just a couple of

---

RUSSIAN OLD BELIEVERS

In 1652 Patriarch Nikon introduced reforms to bring Russian Orthodox doctrine into line with the Greek Orthodox Church. Today, these liturgical reforms may seem trivial (including changes to the way the sign of the cross was made, the direction of a procession and the number of times that 'alleluia' should be said) but they were held to be vitally important by many believers. Those who rejected the reforms suffered torture or were executed, and many homes and churches were destroyed.

Over the next few centuries, thousands fled to the western shores of Lake Peipsi, where they erected new villages and worship houses. Although they escaped persecution, they were still governed by tsarist Russia and weren't allowed to openly practise their religion until Estonia gained its independence in 1918. Today there are around 2500 Russian Old Believers in Estonia, living in 11 congregations, primarily along the shore of Lake Peipsi.

kilometres east of Kauksi (off the road from the lake to Iisaku), this complex offers camping, rooms in barnlike buildings and wooden cabins – all sharing a communal kitchen and bathrooms. The pretty grounds have barbecues and kids' play equipment and you can rent a bike (per hour €1) or motorboat (per hour €85).

Hostel Laguun
HOSTEL €

(☑505 8551; www.hostel-laguun.ee; Liiva 1a, Kallaste; site/r per person €4/16) In a prime lakeside spot in Kallaste, the main town of the region, Laguun is a small (10-bed) guesthouse offering simple rooms with shared bathroom, plus space for campers. There's a large garden and barbecue area, plus a communal kitchen. Try for a room with lake views.

Kauksi Telklaager
CAMPGROUND €

(☑339 3840; www.tisler.ee; Kauksi; site/cabin per person €2/7, per car €2; ☺Jun-Aug; ℗) At Kauksi beach, this popular campsite gets packed with young partygoers on weekends. It has tiny two-person cabins among the pines and a very basic, A-frame cafe on the grounds. Ten-minute showers cost €2.

✕ Eating

Locally caught and smoked fish (trout or salmon) is a speciality of the area; some would say the delicious catch alone warrants the journey. Look for *suitsukala* (smoked fish) stands scattered all along the main road curving around the lake. There are supermarkets in Mustvee and Kallaste, and a *pood* (grocery store) in Kuru.

Alatskivi Castle
EUROPEAN €€

(☑5303 2485; www.lossirestoran.eu; Alatskivi; mains €9-15) The food served here is as traditional as the manor-house setting. The dining room is lined with dark wood and lit by sparkling chandeliers, while the kitchen prepares classic rustic dishes such as salmon with Béarnaise sauce, filet mignon, venison, pork chops, lamb and local fish.

Kivi Kõrts
ESTONIAN €

(www.kivikorts.ee; Tartu mnt 2, Alatskivi; mains €3-5; ☺10am-10pm Sun-Thu, 10am-2am Fri & Sat) Probably the most atmospheric place in the region for a cheap, hearty meal (the menu has patchy English translations and is *very* pork-heavy), this cosy, dimly lit tavern has taken an antique-shop-meets-junkyard approach to decor (much of what you see is for sale).

Fish & Onion Restaurant
OLD BELIEVERS €

(Kala-Sibula; ☑745 3445; www.hot.ee/kolkja restoran; Kolkja; ☺noon-6pm daily, by appointment in winter) This simple, blue-painted restaurant offers you the chance to try the Old Believer cuisine, largely based around locally caught fish and onions grown in the villagers' gardens. It's worth calling ahead to confirm opening hours.

❶ Getting There & Away

Getting to this area is tricky without your own wheels. From Mustvee there are buses to the following:

» Tallinn (€11, three hours, two daily) via Viitna

» Rakvere (€6, two hours, three daily)

» Narva (€4.80 to €7.40, 2½ hours, five daily) via Kauksi and Sillamäe

» Tartu (€4.50, one hour, seven daily)

» Viljandi (€7.60, 2¼ hours, daily)

From Kallaste there are buses to Tallinn (€12, 2¾ hours, two daily) via Mustvee and Viitna; Rakvere (€7, two hours, two daily) via Mustvee; and Tartu (€2.88, one to 2½ hours, 11 daily) via Alatskivi.

Tartu

POP 103,800

Tartu lays claim to being Estonia's spiritual capital, with locals talking about a special Tartu *vaim* (spirit), created by the time-stands-still feel of its wooden houses and stately buildings, and by the beauty of its parks and riverfront.

Small and provincial, with the tranquil Emajõgi River flowing through it, Tartu is Estonia's premier university town, with students making up nearly one fifth of the population. This injects a boisterous vitality into the leafy, historic setting and grants it a vibrant nightlife for a city of its size. On long summer nights, those students that haven't abandoned the city for the beach can be found on the hill behind the Town Hall, flirting and drinking.

Tartu was the cradle of Estonia's 19th-century national revival and it escaped Sovietisation to a greater degree than Tallinn. Its handsome centre is lined with classically designed 18th-century buildings, many of which have been put to innovative uses. Aside from its own attractions – including some interesting galleries and museums – Tartu is a convenient gateway to exploring southern Estonia.

History

By around the 6th century there was an Estonian stronghold on Toomemägi hill and in 1030 Yaroslav the Wise of Kyiv is said to have founded a fort here called Yuriev. The Estonians regained control, but in 1224 were defeated by the Knights of the Sword, who placed a castle, cathedral and bishop on Toomemägi. The town became known as Dorpat – its German name – until the end of the 19th century.

Throughout the 16th and 17th centuries Dorpat suffered repeated attacks and changes of ownership as Russia, Sweden and Poland-Lithuania fought for control of the Baltic region. Its most peaceful period was during the Swedish reign, which coincided with the university's founding in 1632 – an event that was to have an enormous impact on the city's future. This peace ended in 1704, during the Great Northern War, when Peter the Great took Tartu for Russia. In 1708 his forces wrecked the town and most of its population was deported to Russia.

In the mid-1800s Tartu became the focus of the Estonian national revival. The first Estonian Song Festival was held here in 1869, and the first Estonian-language newspaper was launched here – both important steps in the national awakening.

The peace treaty that granted independence to Estonia (for the first time in its history) was signed in Tartu between Soviet Russia and Estonia on 2 February 1920.

THE BLUE, BLACK & WHITE

Estonia's tricolour dates back to 1881, when a theology student named Jaan Bergmaan wrote a poem about a beautiful flag flying over Estonia. The only problem, for both Jaan and his countrymen, was that no flag in fact existed. Clearly, something had to be done about this. This was, after all, the time of the national awakening, when the idea of independent nationhood was on the lips of every young dreamer across the country.

In September of that year, at the Union of Estonian Students in Tartu, 20 students and one alumnus gathered to hash out ideas for a flag. All present agreed that the colours must express the character of the nation, reflect the Estonian landscape and connect to the colours of folk costumes. After long discussions, the students came up with blue, black and white. According to one interpretation, blue symbolised hope for Estonia's future; it also represented faithfulness. Black was a reminder of the dark past to which Estonia would not return; it also depicted the country's dark soil. White represented the attainment of enlightenment and education – an aspiration for all Estonians; it also symbolised snow in winter, light nights in summer and the Estonian birch tree.

After the colours were chosen, it took several years before the first flag was made. Three young activist women – Emilie, Paula and Miina Beermann – carried this out by sewing together a large flag made out of silk. In 1884 the students held a procession from Tartu to Otepää, a location far from the eyes of the Russian government. All members of the students' union were there as the flag was raised over the vicarage. Afterwards it was dipped in Pühajärv (a lake considered sacred to Estonians; see p112) and locked safely away in the student archive.

Although the inauguration of the flag was a tiny event, word of the flag's existence spread, and soon the combination of colours appeared in unions and choirs, and hung from farmhouses all across Estonia. By the end of the 19th century the blue, black and white was used in parties and at wedding ceremonies. Its first political appearance, however, didn't arrive until 1917, when thousands of Estonians marched in St Petersburg demanding independence. In 1918 Estonia was declared independent and the flag was raised on Pikk Hermann in Tallinn's Old Town. There it remained until the Soviet Union seized power in 1940.

During the occupation the Soviets banned the flag and once again it went underground. For Estonians, keeping the flag on the sly was a small but hopeful symbol of one day regaining nationhood. People hid flags under floorboards or unstitched the stripes and secreted them in bookcases. Those caught with the flag faced severe punishment – including a possible sentence in the Siberian Gulags. Needless to say, as the Soviet Union teetered on the brink of collapse, blue, black and white returned to the stage. In February 1989, the flag was raised again on Pikk Hermann. Independence had been regained.

Tartu

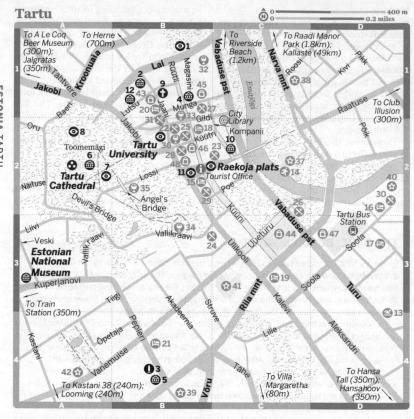

Tartu was severely damaged in 1941 when Soviet forces retreated, blowing up the grand 1784 Kivisild stone bridge over the river, and again in 1944 when they retook it from the Nazis. Both occupying forces committed many atrocities. A monument now stands on the Valga road where the Nazis massacred 12,000 people at Lemmatsi.

⊙ Sights & Activities

Tartu, as the major repository of Estonia's cultural heritage, has museums devoted to an eclectic array of subjects. We've covered most of them here, but the tourist office will be able to help you out if your interests extend to, say, metal farm machinery.

OLD TOWN

Raekoja plats SQUARE

Tartu's main square is deliciously impressive, lined with grand buildings and echoing with the chink of glasses and plates in summer. The centrepiece is the late-18th-century **Town Hall**, topped by a tower and weather vane, and fronted by a statue of lovers kissing under a spouting umbrella. The building's design came courtesy of the German architect JHB Walter, who modelled it on a typical Dutch town hall. A clock was added to encourage students to be punctual for classes. On the south side of the square, look out for the communist hammer-and-sickle relief that still remains on the facade of number 5.

Tartu University UNIVERSITY

(Tartu Ülikool; www.ut.ee; admission to hall, lock-up & museum €2.50; Ülikooli 18) Fronted by six Doric columns, the impressive main building of the university was built between 1803 and 1809. The university itself was founded in 1632 by the Swedish king Gustaf II Adolf (Gustavus Adolphus) to train Lutheran clergy and government officials. It was modelled on Uppsala University in Sweden.

Tartu

⊙ **Top Sights**
Estonian National Museum A3
Raekoja plats B2
Tartu Cathedral A2
Tartu University B2

⊙ **Sights**
1 Botanical Gardens B1
2 Citizen's Home Museum B1
3 Cornflower Monument B4
4 Estonian Sports Museum B1
5 KGB Cells Museum B4
6 Museum of University History A2
7 Rotunda A2
8 Sacrificial Stone A2
9 St John's Church B1
10 Tartu Art Museum C2
11 Town Hall B2
12 Toy Museum B1

⦿ **Activities, Courses & Tours**
13 Aura Keskus D4
14 Pegasus C2

🛏 **Sleeping**
Antonius .... (see 22)
15 Domus Dorpatensis B2
16 Dorpat D2
17 Hotell Tartu D3
18 London Hotell B2
19 Pallas Hotell C3
20 Tampere Maja B1
21 Tartu Student Village Hostel B4
Terviseks .... (see 23)
Wilde Guest Apartments .... (see 24)

🍴 **Eating**
22 Antonius B2

23 Chocolats de Pierre C2
Dorpat .... (see 16)
24 Eduard Vilde Restaurant &
Cafe B3
25 Gruusia Saatkond B2
26 Indoor Market C2
27 La Dolce Vita B1
28 Moka B2
29 Noir B2
30 Outdoor Market D2
31 University Cafe B2

🍷 **Drinking**
32 Genialistide Klubi B1
33 Möku B1
34 Nott B3
35 Püssirohukelder B2
36 Tsink Plekk Pang B2
Vein ja vine .... (see 25)

🎭 **Entertainment**
37 Atlantis C2
Cinamon .... (see 47)
38 Club Tallinn C1
39 Ekraan B4
40 Sadamateater D2
41 Vanemuine Theatre &
Concert Hall C3
42 Vanemuine Theatre (small
stage) A4

🛍 **Shopping**
43 Antoniuse Gild B1
44 Kaubamaja C3
45 Pille-Resa Nukumaja B1
46 Pits B2
47 Tasku D3
48 University Bookshop B2

The university closed during the Great Northern War around 1700 but reopened in 1802, later becoming one of the Russian empire's foremost centres of learning. Its early emphasis on science is evidenced by the great scholars who studied here in the 19th century, including physical chemistry pioneer and Nobel prize winner for chemistry, Wilhelm Ostwald; physicist Heinrich Lenz; and the founder of embryology, natural scientist Karl Ernst von Baer.

University Art Museum

(Ülikooli Kunstimuuseum; admission €1; ⊙11am-6pm Mon-Fri) The collection comprises mainly plaster casts of ancient Greek sculptures made in Europe in the 1860s and 1870s, along with an Egyptian mummy. The rest of the collection was evacuated to Russia during WWII and has never returned.

Students' Lock-Up

(admission €1; ⊙11am-6pm Mon-Fri) With its walls covered in its original graffiti, this is where 19th-century students were held in solitary confinement for various infractions. Back then, if you failed to return library books on time, you'd net two days in the attic; insulting a lady, four days; insulting a (more sensitive?) cloakroom attendant, five days; duelling, up to three weeks.

Tartu Art Museum
GALLERY

(Kunstimuuseum; www.tartmus.ee; Raekoja plats 18; adult/child €2.30/1; ☺noon-6pm Wed-Sun) If you're leaving one of the plaza's pubs and you're not sure whether you're seeing straight, don't use this building as your guide. Foundations laid partially over an old town wall have given a pronounced lean to this, the former home of Colonel Barclay de Tolly (1761–1818) – an exiled Scot who distinguished himself in the Russian army's 1812 campaign against Napoleon.

It now contains an engrossing gallery spread over three levels, the bottom of which is given over to temporary exhibitions. Paintings comprise the bulk of the permanent collection, along with some sculpture, photography, video art and mixed media work, including some truly wonderful 20th-century portraiture.

Estonian Sports Museum
MUSEUM

(Eesti Spordimuuseum; www.spordimuuseum.ee; Rüütli 15; admission €2.30; ☺11am-6pm Tue-Sun) Chronicling more than just Estonian Olympic excellence (although the glittering medal display serves that purpose admirably), this offbeat museum has a real sense of fun. While the photos of puffed-up early-20th-century bodybuilders in posing pouches suggest that they took themselves tremendously seriously, nobody's suggesting that you should. Estonia's more curious sports (wife-carrying, mosquito-swatting, underwater draughts *et al*) are given a plug, and there's an interactive tug-of-war on the 2nd floor.

The attached **postal museum** (ERMi Postimuuseum; www.erm.ee; admission free) is rather more staid but still quietly fascinating. The stamp displays lay bare Estonia's recent history, with the swastika appearing in 1941, giving way to the hammer and sickle in 1945.

Toy Museum
MUSEUM

(Mänguasjamuuseum; www.mm.ee; Lutsu 8; museum adult/child €2/1.60, museum & playroom €2.30/2; ☺11am-6pm Wed-Sun) A big hit with the under-eight crowd (and you won't see too many adults anxious to leave), this is a great place to while away a few rainy hours. Set in one of Tartu's oldest buildings (dating from the 1770s), this excellent museum showcases dolls, model trains, rocking horses, toy soldiers and tons of other desirables from over the centuries. If all those unobtainable toys have unearthed your inner child, there's a playroom upstairs for more hands-on activity. And be sure to wander through the adjacent TEFI House, home to a collection of theatre and animation puppets.

St John's Church
CHURCH

(Jaani Kirik; www.jaanikirik.ee; Jaani 5; ☺10am-7pm Mon-Sat) Dating to at least 1323, this imposing red-brick Lutheran church is unique for the rare terracotta sculptures placed in niches around its exterior and interior (look up). It lay in ruins and was left derelict following a Soviet bombing raid in 1944. In 2005 it reopened after 16 years of restoration. Climb the 135 steps of the 30m **observation tower** (adult/child €1.50/1) for a bird's-eye view of Tartu.

FREE Botanical Gardens
GARDENS

(Botaanikaaed; www.ut.ee/botaed; Lai 38; greenhouse adult/concession €2/1; ☺grounds 7am-7pm, greenhouses 10am-5pm) Founded in 1803, the university's gardens nurture 6500 species of plants and a large collection of palms in the giant greenhouse. A wander through the grounds is both pleasant and free (open until 9pm in summer).

Citizen's Home Museum
MUSEUM

(Linnakodaniku Muuseum; http://linnamuuseum.tartu.ee; Jaani 16; adult/child 64/32c; ☺11am-5pm

---

TARTU'S FROZEN PEOPLE

Hidden in parks, proudly displayed in squares and skulking in lanes, Tartu's sculptures are often surprising and sometimes plain bizarre. Here are some to look out for:

» **Everybody's favourite** The snogging students in front of the Town Hall.

» **Most whimsical** Oscar Wilde and Estonian writer Eduard Vilde, sharing both a surname and a park bench in front of Vallikraavi 4.

» **Creepiest** The man-sized naked baby holding hands with the baby-sized naked man on Küüni.

» **Most clever** The fountain at the corner of Vanemuise and Struve which at first glance looks like a tangle of steel tubes with water shooting out the back, but turns into a caricature of famed professor Yuri Lotman (1922–93) when viewed from certain angles.

Wed-Sat, 11am-3pm Sun Apr-Sep, 10am-3pm Wed-Sun Oct-Mar) In an old wooden house with period furnishings, this museum shows how a burgher from the 1830s lived. There are only a few rooms (what did you expect for less than a euro?) but it's still quite interesting.

TOOMEMÄGI

Toomemägi (Cathedral Hill), rising to the west of the town hall, is the original reason for Tartu's existence, functioning on and off as a stronghold from around the 5th or 6th century. It's now a tranquil park, with walking paths meandering through the trees and a pretty-as-a-picture rotunda which serves as a summertime cafe, perfect for an alfresco drink or ice cream.

Tartu Cathedral   RUIN, MUSEUM

Atop the hill, this imposing Gothic cathedral was built by German knights in the 13th century, rebuilt in the 15th century, despoiled during the Reformation in 1525, used as a barn, and partly rebuilt between 1804 and 1807 to house the university library, which is now the **Museum of University History** (Ülikooli Ajaloo Muuseum; ☑737 5674; www .ut.ee/ajaloomuuseum; Lossi 25; museum & tower/museum only €2.60/1.60; ☉11am-5pm Wed-Sun). Inside you'll find a range of exhibits, from a reconstructed autopsy chamber to displays chronicling student life. Start at the top and work your way down.

Sacrificial Stone   SHRINE

In pagan times, offerings used to be left in the cup-shaped depressions carved into this stone and the hundreds like it that are scattered throughout the country. Actually, offerings are still left; you'll often find coins or flowers, even on those stones that have made their way into museums, and on this particular stone, students leave burnt offerings of their lecture notes. Nearby is a natural parapet known as the Kissing Hill, where Russian newlyweds affix padlocks with their names scratched into them.

Angel's & Devil's Bridges   BRIDGES

The approach from Raekoja plats is along Lossi, which passes beneath the **Angel's Bridge** (Inglisild), which was built between 1836 and 1838 – follow local superstition and hold your breath and make a wish as you cross it for the first time. A bit further up the hill is **Devil's Bridge** (Kuradisild).

SUBURBS

Estonian National Museum   MUSEUM

(Eesti Rahva Muuseum; www.erm.ee; Kuperjanovi 9; permanent/all collections €1/2, free entry Fri; ☉11am-6pm Tue-Sun; ☏) Small, sweet and proud, much like the country itself, this museum's focus is less on history and more on Estonian life and traditions. The permanent displays are split into four main themes: Everyday Life, Holidays & Festivals, Regional Folk Culture and 'To be an Estonian'. Highlights include reproductions of living rooms from 1920, 1939 and 1978, plus the 'Red Corner' of a factory from 1951.

Other branches of the museum include the Post Museum and Raadi Manor Park. There are ambitious plans afoot to create a massive new home for the museum at Raadi Manor by around 2015.

Raadi Manor Park   PARK

(Raadi Mõisapark; www.erm.ee; Narva mnt 177; admission €1; ☉7am-10pm mid-May–mid-Sep) Part of the Estonian National Museum, this estate flanks the main road north out of town. The manor once housed the entire museum but wartime bombing has left only the shell of what was once a beautiful neo-renaissance baroque building. Displays in the water tower show what the house and gardens once looked like. In the 19th century it was considered one of Estonia's most beautiful parks and while it's well past its prime, locals still come to stroll around and swim in the lake.

Plans have been drawn up for an architecturally progressive new museum to be built here on the site of a Soviet airfield – although, at the time of writing, funding for the €38 million project had yet to be secured.

KGB Cells Museum   MUSEUM

(KGB Kongide Muuseum; ☑746 1717; http://linna muuseum.tartu.ee; Riia mnt 15b, entrance Pepleri; adult/child €1.30/70c; ☉11am-4pm Tue-Sat) What do you do when a formerly nationalised building is returned to you with cells in the basement and a fearsome reputation? In this case, the family donated the basement to the Tartu City Museum, which created this sombre and highly worthwhile exhibition. Chilling in parts, the displays give a fascinating rundown on deportations, life in the Gulags, the Estonian resistance movement and what went on in these former KGB headquarters, known as the 'Grey House'. In 1990 the **Cornflower Monument** was erected near the building in memory of the victims of Soviet repression; the blue cornflower is Estonia's national flower.

FREE **Kastani 38** MUSEUMS, WORKSHOPS
(Kastani 38; ⊙11am-6pm Fri-Sun) Opened in 1910 as a bread factory, this huge brick warehouse has become a crucible of creative activity. Aside from the museums listed here, and the Looming hostel (see p102), there are workshops for screen printers, fashion designers and photographers. It's an interesting place to poke about in.

Estonian Printing Museum
(Trükimuuseum; www.trykimuuseum.ee) From 1924, after its short stint as a bakery, the building housed a printing press right up until 2009 – making it a fitting home for this museum devoted to all things related to inky fingers, type blocks and machines that clank and spin. At the time of research the museum hadn't quite opened, so double-check opening times and prices on the website.

Paper Museum
(Paberi Muuseum; www.paberimuuseum.ee) Making a fine companion piece to the Printing Museum, this space is really part museum, part gallery devoted to paper as a 3D artistic medium – think origami on steroids. It too hadn't opened when we visited, so check details on the website.

A Le Coq Beer Museum MUSEUM
(☑744 9711; www.alecoq.ee/eng/activities/museum; Tähtvere 56, entry off Laulupeo; adult/child €1/50c; ⊙tours 2pm Thu, 10am, noon & 2pm Sat) Located at the brewery, the museum briefly covers the history of beer-making but focuses mainly on the machinery and brewing techniques, with free samples at the end. A Le Coq has churned out its trademark beverage since 1879.

 Activities

Pegasus RIVER CRUISE
(www.transcome.ee; adult/child €5/3; ⊙3pm & 5pm Tue-Sun, plus 11am & 1pm Sat & 1pm Sun) Hour-long riverboat cruises, departing from the quay by Atlantis nightclub.

Riverside Beach BEACH
(Ujula) If the sun's beating down and you can't make it to Pärnu, there's a pleasant beach along the northern bank of the Emajõgi, a 1km walk west of Kroonuaia bridge.

Aura Keskus WATER PARK
(www.aurakeskus.ee; Turu 10; admission pool €3-5, water park €5-7; ⊙6.30am-10pm Mon-Fri, 9am-10pm Sat & Sun, closed Jul) A 50m indoor pool and family-friendly water park with all the trimmings.

Festivals & Events

Tartu regularly dons its shiniest party gear and lets its hair down; check out www.kultuuriaken.tartu.ee for more. The lead-up to Christmas is full of cheer, with a market set up at Antoniuse Gild.

LOCAL KNOWLEDGE

MIKA KERÄNEN: CHILDREN'S BOOK AUTHOR

What's your favourite museum in Tartu? The Estonian Sports Museum. I don't have anything against the Estonian National Museum, but looking at history from the point of view of sport – I think that's great.

And your favourite places to hang out? The club of genialists (Genialistide Klubi, p103), for sure. Locals don't like to be in the main square so much, so my favourite places are just a few steps away. The University Cafe... that's where I wrote two of my last books. For regulars, they offer a personal kind of service that I love.

Where's a good place to take the kids? In Palamuse, about 35km north of Tartu, there's a school museum called **Palamuse O. Lutsu Kihelkonnakoolimuuseum** (www.palmuseum.ee; Köstr allee 3; admission €1; ⊙10am-6pm May-Sep, 10am-5pm Mon-Fri Oct-Apr) where a famous book called Spring (*Kevade*) was set – a story about schoolchildren in the 19th century. They made a film about the book in the 1960s and in this museum they have everything like it was in the film. One attraction, based on a scene in the book, is that you can fire a slingshot at the house of the priest. If someone actually breaks the window, they just change it.

Tartu Ski Marathon SPORTS
(www.tartumaraton.ee) Tartu hosts this 63km race every February, drawing around 4000 competitors to the region's cross-country tracks (it actually starts in Otepää and finishes in Elva). The same organisation hosts a range of sporting events (cycling road races, mountain-bike races, running races) in and around Tartu throughout the year.

Tartu Student Days STUDENT
(www.studentdays.ee) Catch a glimpse of modern-day student misdeeds at the end of April, when they take to the streets to celebrate term's end (and the dawn of spring) in every way imaginable. A second, smaller version occurs in mid-October.

Hansa Days Festival MEDIEVAL
(www.hansapaevad.ee) Crafts, markets, family-friendly performances and more commemorate Tartu's Hanseatic past over three days in mid-July.

tARTuFF FILM
(www.tartuff.ee) For one week in August, a big outdoor cinema takes over Raekoja plats. Screenings (with art-house leanings) are free, plus there are docos, poetry readings and concerts.

🛏 Sleeping
OLD TOWN

TOP CHOICE **Antonius** BOUTIQUE HOTEL €€€
(📞737 0377; www.hotelantonius.ee; Ülikooli 15; s €95, d €115-176, ste €219-275; @🛜) Sitting plumb opposite the main university building, this 18-room boutique hotel is loaded with antiques and period features, including heavy velvet drapes, floral wallpaper and chandeliers. Breakfast is served in the ancient vaulted cellar (which by night is a romantic restaurant). In summertime, guests gravitate to the internal courtyard, while in winter the library with its roaring fire is irresistible. Service is first class.

Domus Dorpatensis APARTMENTS €€
(📞733 1345; www.dorpatensis.ee; Raekoja plats 1; s €32-63, d €45-76; 🛜) Run by an academic foundation, this block of 10 apartments offers an unbeatable location and wonderful value for money. The units range in size but all have writing desks (it's run by scholars, after all) and almost all have kitchenettes. The staff are particularly helpful – dispensing parking advice, directing guests to the communal laundry, and even producing

drying racks and irons if required. The entrance is on Ülikooli.

Tampere Maja GUESTHOUSE €€
(📞738 6300; www.tamperemaja.ee; Jaani 4; s €40-66, d €59-87; @🛜) Maintained by the Finnish city of Tampere (Tartu's sister city), this cosy guesthouse, in one of Tartu's oldest wooden buildings, features six warm, light-filled guest rooms in a range of sizes. Breakfast is included and each room has access to cooking facilities. And it wouldn't be Finnish if it didn't offer an authentic sauna (open to non-guests).

Terviseks HOSTEL €
(📞565 5382; www.terviseksbbb.com; 4th fl, Raekoja plats 10; dm €15-18, r €30; @🛜) In a fully renovated historic building, smack in the heart of town, this 10-bed 'backpacker's bed and breakfast' (run by a Brit and a Canadian) offers great facilities and plentiful info about the happening places in town. It's really like staying at your rich mate's cool, inner-city pad. For snugglers there's a 'doubles dorm' with two double beds, charged at €25 per bed.

Wilde Guest Apartments APARTMENTS €€
(📞511 3876; www.wildeapartments.ee; Vallikraavi 4; apt €58-124) Rents three beautiful self-contained apartments on Ülikooli, within a short walk of Eduard Vilde Restaurant & Cafe. All can sleep up to four people.

London Hotell HOTEL €€€
(📞730 5555; www.londonhotel.ee; Rüütli 9; s €80-102, d €102-127; @🛜) After the serene refinement of the lobby, complete with a very Zen water feature, the rooms at this upmarket hotel are quite lacklustre. Still, you can't fault the prime location.

CITY CENTRE
Dorpat HOTEL €€
(📞733 7180; www.dorpat.ee; Soola 6; s/d from €45/65; P@🛜) With 200 rooms over six floors, the Dorpat is big, busy and shiny, complete with a riverside restaurant and spa. Rooms are crisp and smart (some are set up for allergy sufferers and the disabled), and the dotty carpet offers some fun among the clean, modern minimalism.

Hotell Tartu HOTEL €€
(📞731 4300; www.tartuhotell.ee; Soola 3; s €41-61, d €59-69; P@🛜) What was once an ugly Soviet-era block in a run-down part of the central city now finds itself in a glitzy new shopping precinct and has risen to the

occasion by smartening itself up. Artfully placed pine slats soften the brutalist exterior, while the rooms have graduated from the Ikea school of decoration – small and simple but clean and contemporary. Plus the staff are adorable and there's a sauna available.

Pallas Hotell
HOTEL €€

(📞730 1200; www.pallas.ee; Riia mnt 4; s €42, d €53-105; [P][@][🛜]) The Pallas occupies the site of a former art college and has attempted to channel some of that creativity into its decor. It's succeeded in the modern reception, but the rooms, while bright and airy, are a little dated. Request a city-facing room on the 3rd floor, for space, views and artworks.

SUBURBS

Villa Margaretha
BOUTIQUE HOTEL €€

(📞731 1820; www.margaretha.ee; Tähe 11/13; s €50-75, d €60-85, ste €70-155; [P][🛜]) Like something out of a fairy tale, this gorgeous, wooden, art nouveau house has a sweet wee turret and romantic rooms decked out with sleigh beds and artfully draped fabrics. It's a little away from the action but still within walking distance of the Old Town.

📷 Looming
HOSTEL €

(📞527 6370; www.loominghostel.ee; Kastani 38; dm €16-17, r €33-36; [@][🛜]) New to the scene in 2011, this promising hostel shares an old factory with a bunch of creative enterprises, some micro museums and a bar/nightclub. Run by urban greenies with a commitment to recycled materials and sustainable practices, Looming ('creation' in Estonian) offers smart bunk-free dorms and private rooms, an appealing roof terrace, bike rental (per day €10) and a sauna.

Tartu Student Village Hostel
HOSTEL €

(📞740 9955; www.tartuhostel.eu; Pepleri 14; s/tw €20/30; [🛜]) The university runs three hostels but only this one is open to nonstudents, year-round. Rooms are reasonably large and have private kitchenettes and bathrooms, and despite being a little institutional, they're excellent value for money. Advance reservations are a must.

Herne
GUESTHOUSE €

(📞744 1959; www.hot.ee/supilinn; Herne 59; sites per person €6.50, s/d €18/32) A 15-minute walk northwest of the city through a traditionally poor neighbourhood of atmospheric wooden houses brings you to this homey guesthouse with four simple rooms and clean shared bathrooms. There's a kitchen, outdoor grill and plenty of grass on which campers can pitch a tent. Campervans also welcome.

🍴 Eating

OLD TOWN

[TOP CHOICE] La Dolce Vita
ITALIAN €€

(www.ladolcevita.ee; Kompanii 10; mains €5-17) Thin-crust pizzas come straight from the wood-burning oven at this cheerful, family-friendly pizzeria. It's the real deal, with classic casual decor (checked tablecloths, Fellini posters – tick), friendly service and a lengthy menu of bruschetta, crudités, salads, pizza, pasta and gelato, plus heavier main courses.

Gruusia Saatkond
GEORGIAN €€

(www.gruusiasaatkond.ee; Rüütli 8; mains €7-13; ⏰noon-midnight Mon-Sat) The name means 'Georgian Embassy' and this place does a fine job representing its country on the food and wine front. A rustic, colourful dining room sets the scene for feasting on hearty Georgian cuisine: hatšapuri (cheese bread), trout and shashlik are among the favourites.

Moka
INTERNATIONAL €€

(www.moka.ee; Küütri 3; mains €5-16) Decor-wise, this restaurant is all over the place – we think it's aiming for African tribal chic – and in a way that suits the incredibly well-travelled menu, where pizza and pasta brush shoulders with tempura prawns, quesadillas, Cajun chicken and samosas. Surprisingly, the exuberant mishmash of flavours works well. In summer there's a special grill menu, which the chef sizzles up on a barbecue on the street.

Hansa Tall
ESTONIAN €

(www.hansahotell.ee; Alexandri 46; mains €5-9; 🛜) If you want to look at a menu and really know you're in Estonia, head to this super-rustic, barnlike tavern southeast of the centre. You need not try the smoked pig's ears or blood sausage to enjoy the diverse, hearty menu, live music and even livelier locals.

Antonius
ESTONIAN €€€

(📞737 0377; www.hotelantonius.ee; Ülikooli 15; mains €15-18; ⏰6-11pm) Tartu's most upmarket restaurant is within the romantic, candlelit nooks and crannies of the Antonius Hotel's vaulted cellar, which predates the 19th-century building above it by several centuries. Expect a concise menu of meaty dishes, prepared from the finest Estonian produce.

Noir
EUROPEAN €

(☎744 0055; www.cafenoir.ee; Ülikooli 7; mains €5-11; ⊙noon-11pm Mon-Sat, noon-6pm Sun) Definitely a place to impress a date, this sexy, black-walled restaurant-cum-*vinoteque* is a fine place for wining, dining and reclining. It's tucked away in a courtyard off Ülikooli, with outdoor tables and a sandpit for the tiddlers.

Chocolats de Pierre
CAFE €

(www.pierre.ee; Raekoja plats 12; snacks €2.60-5; ⊙8am-11pm Mon-Thu, 8am-1am Fri, 10am-1am Sat, 10am-11pm Sun) Tallinn's favourite chocmeister has set up on Tartu's main square, offering the same refined atmosphere, old-world decor and all-important truffles. This is a prime spot for coffee and a sugar fix at any time of day.

Eduard Vilde Restaurant & Cafe
INTERNATIONAL €€

(www.vilde.ee; Vallikraavi 4; mains €6-20) Choose grace and elegance in the cafe downstairs or head up to the restaurant for a pasta, curry, schnitzel or stone-grilled steak – or just for a tipple on the very pleasant terrace.

University Cafe
CAFE €

(Ülikooli Kohvik; www.kohvik.ut.ee; Ülikooli 20; mains €4-10; ⊙11am-11pm Mon-Sat) Some of the most economical meals in town are waiting for you at the ground-floor cafeteria, which serves up decent breakfasts and a simple daytime buffet. Upstairs is a labyrinth of elegantly decorated rooms, simultaneously grand and cosy, where artfully presented dishes are served.

CITY CENTRE

Dorpat
BUFFET €

(www.dorpat.ee; Soola 6; mains €5-12) The elegant restaurant at the Dorpat also has a reputable a la carte menu, but it's the weekday lunch buffet that we're particularly keen on. For €3 you'll get a bottomless bowl of your choice of soups, plus bread, water and a simple dessert. An extra 80c gives you access to the salad bar, while for a total of €6.80 you get the full bainmarie as well.

Outdoor Market
MARKET

(Soola; ⊙from 7am) Near the bus station, this is a fun place to browse for fresh produce, flowers and other goodies.

Indoor Market
MARKET

(Vabaduse pst; ⊙from 7.30am) By the river, in front of the Kaubamaja shopping centre (look for the pig statue).

🍸 Drinking

In summer the bars are quiet, unless they've got outside seating, and you'll find most of the students on the designated drinkers' hill behind the Town Hall. During term, Wednesday is the traditional scholars' party night.

TOP CHOICE Genialistide Klubi
CLUB

(www.genklubi.ee; rear Lai 37 or enter Magazini 5; admission free-€3; ⊙noon-3am Mon-Sat; 🛜) The Genialists' Club is an all-purpose, grungy 'subcultural establishment' that's simultaneously a bar, cafe, alternative nightclub, live-music venue, cinema, theatre, library and, just quietly, the coolest place in Tartu to hang out.

Püssirohukelder
PUB

(www.pyss.ee; Lossi 28; mains €6-15; ⊙noon-2am Mon-Sat, noon-midnight Sun) Set in a cavernous 1738 gunpowder cellar, built into the Toomemägi hillside, this boisterous pub serves lashings of beer and meaty meals under a soaring 10m-high vaulted ceiling. There's regular live music and a large beer garden out front.

Nott
BAR

(Vallikraavi 3; ⊙7pm-3am) Reasonably priced drinks ensure a steady stream of students, while the late hours mean that Nott is where everyone ends up, shattering the peace of a quiet location in the shadow of Toomemägi. It's small inside but everyone's content to spill outdoors anyway.

Tsink Plekk Pang
LOUNGE

(www.pang.ee; Küütri 6; mains €4-9) Behind Tartu's funkiest facade (look for the stripy paintwork) and set over three floors is this cool Asian-flavoured restaurant-lounge. The food's nothing special but it is a great place for cocktails or a beer on the roof terrace, with a DJ-spun soundtrack on weekends.

Vein ja vine
WINE BAR

(Rüütli 8; ⊙5-11pm Tue-Thu, 5pm-2am Fri & Sat) Serving wine and deli snacks, this little bar attracts a slightly older crowd (postgraduates, perhaps) but it still gets jammed and overflows onto the street in summer.

Möku
BAR

(www.pang.ee; Rüütli 18; ⊙6pm-3am) A popular student hang-out, this tiny cellar bar spills out onto the pedestrian-only street on summer nights.

☆ Entertainment

For information on classical performances, see www.concert.ee.

Vanemuine Theatre &
Concert Hall THEATRE
(☎744 0165; www.vanemuine.ee; Vanemuise 6) Named after the ancient Estonian song god, this venue hosts an array of theatrical and musical performances. It also stages performances at its small stage (Vanemuise 45) and Sadamateater (Harbour Theatre; Soola 5b). The latter has a prime location on the banks of the Emajõgi and tends to stage the most modern, alternative productions.

Club Tallinn CLUB
(www.clubtallinn.ee; Narva mnt 27; admission free-€6; ⊙Wed-Sat) Tartu's best dance club is a multifloored extravaganza with many nooks and crannies. Top-notch DJs spin here, drawing a fashionable, up-for-it crowd. It's open only during the school year; during the summer it relocates to Pärnu.

Club Illusion CLUB
(www.illusion.ee; Raatuse 97; admission €3-5; ⊙Wed, Fri & Sat) Occupying a Stalin-era movie theatre north of the river, Illusion has a lavish interior and draws a blinged-up crowd. Themed nights include retro, R&B, hip-hop and house; check the website for info.

Atlantis CLUB
(www.atlantis.ee; Narva mnt 2; admission €3-6; ⊙Tue-Sat) Overlooking the Emajõgi River, Atlantis is a popular, mainstream place that's pretty short on style; the riverside setting, however, is nice if you're in the mood for a cheesy good time.

Hansahoov THEATRE
(☎737 1800; www.hansahooviteater.ee, Aleksandri 46) Stages shows in the large rustic courtyard of the Hansa Tall tavern.

Cinamon CINEMA
(www.cinamon.ee; Turu 2; tickets €3.50-6) Multiplex above the Tasku shopping centre.

Ekraan CINEMA
(www.forumcinemas.ee; Riia 14; tickets €2-5) A smaller cinema, close to the KGB Cells Museum.

🛍 Shopping

Antoniuse Gild HANDICRAFTS
(www.antonius.ee; Lutsu 5; ⊙noon-6pm Tue-Fri) Here you'll find around 20 artisans' studios set around St Anthony's Courtyard, where local craftspeople make ceramics, stained glass, jewellery, textiles, woodcarvings, dolls etc. It's well worth a visit.

Tasku SHOPPING CENTRE
(www.tasku.ee; Turu 2; ⊙10am-9pm Mon-Sat, 10am-6pm Sun) A big, glitzy mall with a Rimi supermarket (⊙8am-11pm) on the bottom floor, a cinema multiplex on the top and a branch of the excellent Rahva Raamat (www.rahvaraamat.ee) bookstore chain in between.

Pille-Resa Nukumaja TOYS
(Munga 14; ⊙Tue-Sat) Behind a faded orange facade, this sweet, small store sells handmade dolls and toys for the young and young-at-heart.

Pits FASHION
(Rüütli 4) A small studio showcasing original clothing from young Estonian designers, plus jewellery, accessories and music. It's upstairs, at the rear of the courtyard.

University Bookshop BOOKS
(Ülikooli Raamatupood; www.ut.ee/raamatupood; Ülikooli 1) Great selection.

Kaubamaja DEPARTMENT STORE
(www.kaubamaja.ee; Riia 1; ⊙9am-9pm Mon-Sat, 10am-7pm Sun) Fashion and more.

ℹ Information

City Library (Linnaraamatukogu; www.luts.ee; Kompanii 3; ⊙9am-8pm Mon-Fri, 10am-4pm Sat Sep-Jun, 10am-6pm Mon-Fri Jul-Aug) Free internet upstairs with photo ID.

Raekoja Apteek (☎742 3560; Raekoja plats; ⊙24hr) Pharmacy within the town hall.

Tourist Office (☎744 2111; www.visittartu .com; Raekoja plats; ⊙9am-6pm) This friendly office inside the town hall has local maps and brochures (including an excellent walking-tour pamphlet), and loads of other city info. It can also book accommodation and tour guides, sell you parking passes and get you online (free internet access is available here). They stock the excellent *Tartu in Your Pocket* guide (€1.60), published twice a year and available free online (www.inyourpocket.com). Shorter hours winter Sundays.

ℹ Getting There & Away

Air

Tartu Airport (TAY; ☎605 8888; www.tartu -airport.ee) is 9km south of the city centre.
Estonian Air (OV; ☎640 1160; www.estonian -air.ee) flies to and from Tallinn most days.

VÕRO-SETO LANGUAGE

Visitors may notice a quite different, choppier-sounding language spoken in the south-eastern corner of this region. Võro-Seto, previously considered an Estonian dialect, was declared a separate language in 1998. Until the end of the 19th century, the northern and southern languages flourished quite independently of each other. Then, in the interests of nationalism, a one-country, one-language policy was adopted, and the dominant Northern Estonian became the country's main language. Today the southern language is once again enjoying a resurgence and Võro-Seto (more often called simply Võro) has more than 50,000 native speakers, most of whom live in Võrumaa and Setomaa. To learn more about this unique language, contact the **Võro Institute** (☑782 1960; www.wi.ee; Tartu 48, Võru).

Budget carrier **Flybe** (FC; ☑44-1392-268 529; www.flybe.com) flies to and from Helsinki daily, with fares starting at €39.

Bus

Regional and international buses depart from **Tartu bus station** (Autobussijaam; ☑733 1277; Turu 2), which is attached to the Tasku shopping centre. **Ecolines** (☑606 2217; www.ecolines.net) has a daily bus to Latvia, stopping in Valmiera (€7, two hours) and Rīga (€12, four hours); while **Lux Express** (☑12550; www.luxexpress.eu) has three buses to Rīga (€14 to €18, four hours).

Major domestic routes:

» Tallinn (€8 to €12, 2½ hours, numerous)

» Rakvere (€7 to €8.20, three hours, seven daily), some via Mustvee

» Narva (€6.40 to €11, three hours, seven daily), some via Kauksi and Mustvee

» Viljandi (€5, 1½ hours, 13 daily)

» Pärnu (€7.50 to €11, three hours, 10 daily)

Car & Motorcycle

The tourist office keeps up-to-date lists of car-hire agencies with prices.

Avis (☑744 0360; www.avis.ee; Tartu Airport)

Budget (☑605 8600; www.budget.ee; Tartu Airport)

City Car (☑523 9669; www.citycar.ee; Tartu Bus Station)

Europcar (www.europcar.ee) Hotell Tartu (☑511 0694; Soola 3); Tartu Airport (☑605 8031)

Hertz (☑506 9065; www.hertz.ee; Tartu Bus Station)

Train

The elegant but boarded-up old wooden **train station** (☑385 7123; Vaksali 6) is 750m southwest of Toomemägi. Timetables are posted outside and tickets are sold on the train.

Services are operated by **Edelerautee** (www.edel.ee), with three daily trains to Tallinn (€6.71, three hours) and to Valga (€3.20, 1½ hours).

ⓘ Getting Around

TO/FROM THE AIRPORT An airport shuttle is run by **Tartaline** (☑505 4342; www.tartaline.ee; ticket €3), departing the terminal 20 minutes after each flight and from Tartu Bus Station an hour before every flight. Hotel pick-ups can be prebooked in advance. Taxis cost around €10.

BICYCLE Bikes can be rented from **Jalgratas** (☑742 1731; Laulupeo 19; per day €15; ⊙10am-6pm Mon-Fri, 10am-2pm Sat) or from Looming hostel (see p102).

BUS Tartu is easily explored on foot but there is also a local bus service. You can buy a single-use ticket from any kiosk (83c) or from the bus driver (€1), and be sure to validate the ticket once on board or risk a fine. Kiosks also sell day passes (€2.50).

CAR Parking in the city is metered from 8am to 6pm Monday to Friday and through the weekends in July; buy a day ticket from the tourist office (€7.67) or pay by the hour at a machine (€1.60). There's a free lot by Atlantis nightclub at Narva mnt 2.

TAXI Local taxis include **Takso Üks** (☑742 0000; www.taksod.ee; flagfall €1.90, per km 55c) and **Tartu Taksopark** (☑1555; www.go taksopark.ee; flagfall €1.90, per km 70c).

Setomaa

In the far southeast of Estonia lies the (politically unrecognised) area of Setomaa (this is the spelling in the local language; non-Seto Estonians use Setumaa and Setu), stretching over into Russia. It's one of the most interesting and tragic areas of the country, politically and culturally. Its native people, the Setos, have a mixed Estonian-Russian culture. Like the Estonians they are of Finno-Ugric origin, but the people became Orthodox, not Lutheran, because this part of the country fell under the subjugation of Novgorod and later Pihkva (Russian: Pskov) and was not controlled by German

DAY OF THE SETOS

Peko, the pagan god of fertility, is as important to the Setos as the Orthodox religion they follow. The 8000-line Seto epic *Pekolanõ* tells the tale of this macho god, the rites of whom are known only to men. The epic dates back to 1927 when the Setos' most celebrated folk singer, Anne Vabarna, was told the plot and spontaneously burst into song, barely pausing to draw breath until she had sung the last (8000th) line.

According to folklore, Peko sleeps night and day in his cave of sand. So on the Day of the Seto Kingdom – proclaimed around 19 August each year – an *ülemtsootska* (representative) for the king has to be found. The Setos then gather around the statue of their 'Song Mother' in search of someone worthy of bearing the crown of the sleeping king's royal singer. Competitions are also held to find a strongman for the king.

The Seto king's dress, and the bread, cheese, wine and beer he consumes are also important. On the same day that his kingdom is declared for another year, people from the Seto stronghold are selected to serve the king as his mitten and belt knitters, and bread, beer, wine and cheese makers.

And so the royal throne is completed. Amid the day's celebrations, traditional Seto songs and dances are performed and customary good wishes exchanged. The women are adorned with traditional Seto lace and large silver breastplates and necklaces, said to weigh as much as 3kg each. Later in the day respects are paid to the dead.

barons, as was the rest of Estonia. They never fully assimilated into Russian culture and throughout the centuries retained their language (today known as Võro-Seto), many features of which are actually closer in structure to Old Estonian than the modern Estonian language. The same goes for certain cultural traditions, for instance leaving food on a relative's grave; this was practised by Estonian tribes before Lutheranism.

All of Setomaa was contained within independent Estonia between 1920 and 1940, but the greater part of it is now in Russia. The town of Pechory (Petseri in Estonian), 2km across the border in Russia and regarded as the 'capital' of Setomaa, is famed for its fabulous 15th-century monastery, considered one of the most breathtaking in Russia.

Today the Seto culture looks to be in a slow process of decline. There are approximately 4000 Setos in Estonia (and another 3000 in Russia), which is half the population of the early 20th century. While efforts are made to teach and preserve the language, and promote customs through organised feasts, the younger generation is being quickly assimilated into the Estonian mainstream. The impenetrable border with Russia that has split their community since 1991 has further crippled it.

A rough look at the Seto landscape illustrates how unique it is in the Estonian context. Notably, their villages are structured like castles, with houses facing each other in clusters, often surrounded by a fence. This is in stark contrast to the typical Estonian village where open farmhouses are separated from each other as far as possible. Here, the Orthodox tradition has fostered a tighter sense of community and sociability.

Aside from the large silver breastplate that is worn on the women's national costume, what sets the Seto aside is their singing style. Setomaa is particularly known for its women folk singers who improvise new words each time they chant their verses. Seto songs, known as *leelo,* are polyphonic and characterised by solo, spoken verses followed by a refrain chanted by a chorus. There is no musical accompaniment and the overall effect is archaic.

Information on the region can be found online at www.setomaa.ee.

◉ Sights & Activities

We've ordered the following sights geographically, roughly from north to southwest; in other words, the order you'd hit them if you were touring through the region from Tartu to Võru – and a very nice drive it makes too.

Võpolsova & Tonja   VILLAGES

A few kilometres north of Värska, on the west side of Värska Bay, are these classic Seto villages. There's not much to see here, but these back roads make for a very pleasant cycle. In Võpolsova there's a monument to folk singer Anne Vabarna, who knew 100,000 verses by heart. Võpolsova homesteads typically consist of a ring of outer buildings around an inner yard, while Tonja's houses face the lake from which its people get their livelihood.

Värska   TOWN
The town of Värska (population 1300) is known for its mineral water, sold throughout Estonia, and its healing mud. There's plenty of rural charm here, including a picturesque 1907 stone **church** and a leafy cemetery surrounding it.

Seto Farm Museum
(Seto Talumuuseum; www.setomuuseum.ee; Pikk 40; adult/child €2/1; ⏰10am-5pm Tue-Sun mid-May–mid-Sep, 10am-4pm Tue-Sat mid-Sep–mid-May) Presided over by a wooden carving of Peko, the museum comprises a re-created 19th-century farmhouse complex, with stables, granary and the former workshops for metalworking and ceramics. Don't bypass the charming restaurant here or the excellent gift shop – the region's best – selling handmade mittens, socks, hats, dolls, tapestries, books and recordings of traditional Seto music.

Podmotsa   TOWN
The tiny village of Podmotsa, northeast of Värska, was once closely linked to the village of Kulje, which stands just across the inlet in what is now Russia. Kulje's beautiful Orthodox church is clearly visible from the shoreline, as is the border-guard watchtower. The village cemetery contains three ancient stone crosses. In pagan times, a holy grove stood nearby.

Piusa Caves   MINE, WALKING
(Piusa Koopad; www.piusa.ee; ⏰11am-6pm daily mid-May–mid-Sep, 11am-5pm Sat & Sun mid-Sep–mid-May) Sitting on a band of sandstone nearly 500m thick, Piusa was the site of a major quarry from 1922 to 1966 when it was discovered that the stone contained 99% quartz and was perfect for glass production. The result is a 22km network of cathedral-like caves, forming the Baltic region's largest winter holiday resort for bats, including several rare species. About 3000 gather here from October to April, drawn from a 100km radius.

A flash new turf-roofed visitor centre screens films about the history and ecology of the site, allows you to explore the depths via an interactive computer simulation and lets you set in motion a large pendulum which carves graceful arcs in the sand laid on the floor. There's also a cafe and playground.

Cave tours (adult/child €3.90/2.60) depart from here, although they only lead you to the opening of the main cavern and not into the caves proper – both for safety reasons and to avoid bat-bothering. The subterranean temperatures remain at a steady four to five degrees even on the coldest or hottest days, so bring warm clothes.

This is also the starting point for the **Piusa Nature Trail**, a tranquil 1.5km loop through pine forests and past WWII trenches. A series of ponds have been created here to provide a home for the rare great crested newt.

If you're heading south from Piusa to Obinitsa, the road to the caves is signposted on the left, close to the railway bridge.

Obinitsa   VILLAGE
The village of Obinitsa, near a pristine lake, makes for a pleasant stop. The chief attraction is the one-room **Seto Museum House & Tourist Office** (Seto Muuseumitarõ; ☎785 4190; www.obinitsamuuseum.ee; adult/child €2/1; ⏰10am-5pm Mon-Fri year-round, plus 11am-5pm Sat & Sun mid-May–mid-Sep), which has a few folk costumes, tapestries, cookware and some old photos – but no explanations in English. There's also a **church** (built in 1897), a **cemetery** and a **sculpture** to the Seto 'Song Mother', which stares solemnly over Lake Obinitsa. There's a **swimming platform** by the lake.

Obinitsa has several big Seto celebrations, the most important being the 19 August **Feast of the Transfiguration**. Hundreds of

ⓘ RUSSIAN BORDER

The official crossing point with Russia in this area is at Koidula, immediately north of Pechory (Estonian: Petseri), but Setomaa is littered with abandoned control points, seemingly unguarded wooden fences and creepy dead ends with lonely plastic signs. One road, from Värska to Saatse, even crosses the zigzagging border into Russian territory for 2km; you're not allowed to stop on this stretch. Be aware that crossing the border at any unofficial point (even if you have a Russian visa) is illegal and could lead to your arrest.

Setos come for a procession from the church to the cemetery, which ends with a communal picnic and the leaving of food on graves for the departed souls.

Meremäe Hill
VIEWPOINT

In such a flat country, even a modest 204m hill can become a high point. This one, near Setomaa Tourist Farm, has a four-storey wooden viewing tower.

🛏 Sleeping & Eating

TOP CHOICE Setomaa

Tourist Farm
GUESTHOUSE, RESTAURANT €€

(Setomaa Turismitalu; 📞516 1941; www.setotalu .ee; s/d with shared bathroom €23/46) In idyllic surrounds by a lake, this tourist farm offers wonderfully rustic-looking but comfortable rooms in log cabins, as well as the opportunity to partake in traditional Seto arts and crafts and experience a smoke sauna. The lakeside restaurant serves excellent food (mains €7 to €11). It's well marked, on the road between Meremäe and Vana-Vastseliina.

Hirvemäe Holiday
Centre
GUESTHOUSE, CAMPGROUND €€

(Hirvemäe Puhkekeskus; 📞797 6105; www .hirvemae.ee; Silla 4; site per tent/car €4/2, s €30, d €44-60; P🛜) Set on a pretty lake on the main route into Värska, this attractive guesthouse has comfy, wood-floored rooms. The extensive grounds encompass a tiny beach, tennis courts, minigolf, a sauna and a playground. The on-site cafe's menu is short, simple and cheap (soup, salad, meat – you know the drill).

Seto Teahouse
SETO CUISINE €

(Seto Tsäimaja; www.setomuuseum.ee; Pikk 40, Värska; mains €4-5; ⏰11am-7pm Tue-Sun mid-May–mid-Sep, 11am-5pm Tue-Sat mid-Sep–mid-May; 🛜) Next door to the Seto Farm Museum, in an atmospheric log cabin, this makes an unbeatable setting for a traditional home-cooked meal. The fare is nothing fancy – cold Seto soup, smoked or stewed pork, herring with sour cream, fried chicken – but it's a real gem nonetheless.

Seto Seltsimaja
SETO CUISINE €

(Obinitsa; mains €1-2; 🛜) Doubling as Obinitsa's community centre, this private home serves traditional Seto dishes, such as milky cold soup with tomatoes, gherkins, lettuce and cucumber (it's surprisingly nice). Little English is spoken and hours

WORTH A TRIP

VASTSELIINA CASTLE

Vastseliina Castle (Vastseliina linnus; www.vastseliina.ee/linnus; adult/child €3/2; ⏰10am-6pm Wed-Sun May-Sep, 9am-4pm Mon-Fri Oct-Apr) was founded in 1342 by the German Livonian knights on the then border with Russia. It prospered from its position on the Pihkva–Rīga trade route until the mid-19th century but was also the scene of many battles. The evocative ruins stand on a high bluff above the Piusa River on the eastern edge of the settlement of Vana-Vastseliina (Old Vastseliina), near Meremäe Hill.

At the time of research, the castle was closed for restoration. By the time you're reading this, the northeastern tower, visitor centre, medieval museum, handicrafts store and 17th-century Piiri Tavern should all be open. Enquire at the visitor centre about the 15km hiking trail that loops around the estate.

About five buses run daily between Võru, Vana-Vastseliina and Meremäe.

are sporadic. Look for the sign reading 'Taarka Tarô Köökõnõ'.

ℹ Information

Värska Tourist Office (📞512 5075; www.verska .ee; Pikk 12; ⏰10am-6pm Tue-Fri, 10am-3pm Sat & Sun mid-May–mid-Sep, 10am-5pm Mon-Fri mid-Sep–mid-May)

ℹ Getting There & Away

This is another area that is much more profitably explored by car or bike. There are buses to Värska from Tartu (€5.80, 1½ hours, four daily) and Tallinn (€12, five hours, twice daily). From Võru there are three to seven buses per day to both Obinitsa (€2, one hour) and Meremäe (€2, one hour).

Võru
POP 14,300

Set on Lake Tamula, Võru has a mix of wooden 19th-century buildings (many of which are quite rundown) and some painfully ugly Soviet-era ones. The sandy shoreline is the town's best feature; it's been spruced up with a new promenade and attracts plenty of beachgoers in summer.

Võru was founded in 1784 by special decree from Catherine the Great, though archaeological finds here date back several thousand years. Its most famous resident, however, was neither a tribesman nor a tsarina, but the writer Friedrich Reinhold Kreutzwald (1803–82), known as the father of Estonian literature for his folk epic *Kalevipoeg*.

One of the biggest and brightest events in the local calendar is the mid-July **Võru Folklore Festival** (www.vorufolkloor.ee) – four days full of dancers, singers and musicians decked out in colourful traditional dress.

◉ Sights & Activities

St Catherine's Churches   CHURCHES
(Jekateriina kirik) Lutheran (Jüri 9); Orthodox (Tartu 26) The churches of the two major denominations are both dedicated to the early Christian martyr Catherine but named in honour of Tsarina Catherine the Great. Both date from the 18th century, both are painted yellow and white and both have a pyramid (symbolising the Holy Trinity) over their lintel. In front of the Lutheran church, overlooking the central square, is a granite **monument** to 17 locals who lost their lives in the 1994 *Estonia* ferry disaster. The Orthodox church contains the remains of Nikolai Bežanitski, a priest killed by the Bolsheviks, who is now honoured as a saint by the Russian Orthodox church.

Kreutzwald Memorial Museum   MUSEUM
(Kreutzwaldi Memoriaalmuuseum; www.hot.ee /muuseumvoru; Kreutzwaldi 31; adult/child €1.30/ 70c; ☉10am-5pm Wed-Sun) Võru's most interesting museum is set in the former house where the great man lived and worked as a doctor from 1833 to 1877. In addition to personal relics, there's a lovely garden at the back. There's also a **monument** to the writer in the park at the bottom of Katariina allee, near the lake.

Võrumaa Regional Museum   MUSEUM
(www.hot.ee/muuseumvoru/vorumaa_muuseum .html; Katariina allee 11; adult/child €1.30/70c; ☉10am-5pm Wed-Sun) Housed in one of the town's ugliest buildings, this museum has mildly interesting exhibits on regional history and culture.

🛏 Sleeping & Eating

Rändur   PUB, GUESTHOUSE €€
(☎786 8050; www.randur.ee; Jüri 36; s €25-30, d €38-50; [P]🛜) Rändur has handsomely set 2nd-floor rooms, each decorated around a different motif and colour scheme (Japanese, Egyptian, Russian etc). Third-floor rooms are pleasant but more basic, with shared bathrooms. Downstairs, the rustic, timber-lined pub serves fairly good food: you want pork, you've got it (mains €5 to €8).

Tamula Hotel   HOTEL €€
(☎783 0430; www.tamula.ee; Vee 4; s/d €48/57; 🛜) Right on the lakefront beach, this relatively new hotel is already looking a tad shabby but it does have bright rooms with water views. Save 10% by booking online.

TOP CHOICE Spring Cafe   CAFE €
(www.springcafe.ee; Petseri 20; mains €4-6; ☉11am-8pm Mon-Thu, 11am-9pm Fri & Sat) If you're longing for something a little less pubby, a little more cafe-bar, this slick lakeside spot should put a smile on your dial. It has a pretty terrace, brick-and-timber dining room, and loungey 2nd floor with big windows. There's a good, modern menu too, with plenty of salads and cooked mains. Ask about the sauna for hire.

Pub Õlle no 17   PUB €
(Jüri 17; mains €3-10) This convivial, Irish-style pub is a popular meeting place and drinking hole for locals, with a pool table, big-screen TV, back terrace and comprehensive pub-grub menu.

☆ Entertainment

Voru Kannel Cultural Centre THEATRE, CINEMA
(Voru Kultuurimaja Kannel; www.vorukannel.ee; Liiva 13) The garden behind the cultural centre hosts occasional concerts and folk festivals, while the centre itself acts as the town's cinema. Check with the tourist office to see if anything's on while you're in town.

🛍 Shopping

Karma   ANTIQUES
(www.antiques.ee; Koidula 14; ☉10.30am-6pm Tue-Fri, 10am-2pm Sat) One of Estonia's best antiques stores and a fun place to browse, even if you already have enough WWII helmets, scythes, sleigh bells, Soviet matchbooks and wooden beer steins.

❶ Information

Tourist office (☎782 1881; www.visitvoru.ee; Jüri 12, entrance Koidula; ☉10am-6pm Mon-Fri, 10am-3pm Sat & Sun, Mon-Fri only mid-Sep–mid-May) A good place to pick up a map and get information about festivals, attractions and tourist farms throughout Võru and Seto counties.

Võru Central Library (Võrumaa Keskraamatu-kogu; http://lib.werro.ee; Jüri 54; ☉10am-6pm Mon-Fri; 🛜) Free internet access; one-hour limit.

❶ Getting There & Away

Major bus routes stopping at Võru's **bus station** (☏782 1018; entrance on Vilja):

» Tallinn (€9 to €12, four hours, nine daily)

» Narva (€12, 4½ hours, daily) via Mustvee, Kauksi and Sillamäe

» Tartu (€2 to €5, 1¼ hours, 17 daily)

» Valga (€5.60, 1¾ hours, twice daily)

» Pärnu (€12, 4¼ hours, daily)

Haanja Nature Park

With 169 sq km of thick forests, rolling hills, picturesque villages, sparkling lakes and meandering rivers, this protected area south of Võru encompasses some of the nicest scenery in the country. Stock up on maps and information about the park's multifarious hiking and cross-country skiing opportunities from the park's visitor centres in Haanja and Rõuge or the tourist offices in Võru, Otepää or Tartu.

◎ Sights & Activities

Suur Munamägi   HILL
Suur Munamägi (literally Great Egg Hill), 17km south of Võru, is the highest peak in the Baltic at just over 318m. Still, the tree-covered 'summit' is easy to miss if you're not looking out for it. Crack the Great Egg with an ascent of its 29m observation tower (www.suurmu-namagi.ee; stairs adult/child €2.50/1.50, elevator €4; ☉10am-8pm daily Apr-Aug, 10am-5pm daily Sep-Oct, noon-3pm Sat & Sun Nov-Mar). On a clear day you can see Tartu's TV towers, the onion domes of the Russian town of Pihkva (Pskov) and lush forests stretching in every direction (binocular rental €1). There's a pleasant indoor-outdoor coffee shop on the ground floor, and a large cafe back on the main road.

The summit and tower are a 10-minute climb from the Võru–Ruusmäe road, start-ing about 1km south of the otherwise uninspiring village of Haanja.

Rõuge   VILLAGE
The charming village of Rõuge sits among gently rolling hills on the edge of the gent-ly sloping Ööbikuorg (Nightingale Valley), named for the nightingales that gather here in the spring for the avian version of the songfest. Seven small lakes are strung out along the ancient valley floor, including the pristine Suurjärv (Great Lake) in the middle of the village. Estonia's deepest lake (38m), it's said to have healing properties.

Opposite St Mary's (Maarja Kirik; tower adult/child €1.50/1; ☉11am-4pm Thu-Sat, 9am-3pm Sun Jun & Aug), Rõuge's whitewashed stone church (1730), stands a monument to the local dead of the 1918–20 independence war. The memorial was buried in someone's backyard throughout the Soviet period to save it from destruction.

Rõuge's Linnamägi (Castle Hill), by Lake Linnjärv, was an Estonian stronghold during the 8th to 11th centuries. In the 13th century the ailing travelled from afar to see a healer called Rougetaja, who lived here. There's a good view across the valley from the hill.

Luhasoo Nature Reserve   NATURE RESERVE
(Luhasoo Maastikukaitseala) Set in untouched swampland on the border with Latvia (actually outside the boundaries of Haanja Nature Park), this reserve provides a fascinat-ing glimpse into Estonia's primordial past. A well-marked 4.5km trail passes over varied bogs and along a velvety black lake, with Venus flytraps, water lilies and herbivorous shrubs among the scenery. You might spot elk and deer but the most you're likely to see of wolves, bears and lynx is their tracks.

To get there, take the Krabi road from Rõuge and, after the Pärlijõe bus stop, turn left towards Kellamäe, then continue another 5km.

Haanja Hikes   CANOEING, CYCLING
(Haanjamatkad; ☏511 4179; www.haanjamatkad.ee; per day bike/canoe €10/32) This Võru-based crew has canoes and bikes for rent and leads canoeing (three to six hours, adult/child €18/10) and rafting (four to six hours, 10-person raft €180) excursions, or two-day cycling and hiking adventures.

🛏 Sleeping

Rõuge Suurjärve Guesthouse GUESTHOUSE €€
(☏524 3028; www.hot.ee/maremajutus; Metsa 5, Rõuge; s/d/ste €26/45/77) The perfect place to unwind and enjoy the lovely surrounds, this big, yellow, family-run guesthouse has views over the valley and a range of fuss-free rooms (most with private bathroom, some with TV, a few with balcony). The

DON'T MISS

KARULA NATIONAL PARK

Fairies, ghosts and witches abound among the 111 sq km of wooded hills, small lakes and ancient stone burial mounds that form Karula National Park, at least according to local folklore. At its centre is Ähijärv, a beautiful lake ringed with trees and reeds which has been considered holy since pagan times. It takes about 90 minutes to circle the lake on foot via the 4km-long **Ähijärv Trail**. On the lakeside, the park's **visitor centre** (☑782 8350; www.karularahvuspark.ee; Ähijärve; ⊙10am-6pm daily mid-May–mid-Sep, 10am-4pm Wed-Fri mid-Sep–mid-May) distributes maps and information for this and other trails.

The park is accessed by a dirt road leading from Mõniste village in the south to the town of Antsla in the north.

---

gardens offer a pretty retreat and the breakfast will fuel your explorations. The turn-off to the guesthouse is opposite Rõuge's church. There's not much English spoken.

Ööbikuoru Puhkekeskus   CAMPGROUND €
(☑509 0372; www.visit.ee; Ööbikuoru 5, Rõuge; sites per adult/child €3/1.50, cabins per person €7-11, cottages per person €15-18) Set on a lovely spot overlooking Nightingale Valley, this outfit offers lodging in simple wooden cabins and cottages. Rowboat (per hour €4), canoe (€4) and bike (€2) rental is available. It's located 600m from the main road, signposted as you head south.

✗ Eating

Eating options within the park are limited. There's a small supermarket in Rõuge along with a weekend-only daytime cafe. Otherwise you'll have to head to Haanja.

❶ Information

Haanja Nature Park headquarters (☑782 9090; www.rmk.ee; Haanja village; ⊙10am-6pm mid-May–mid-Sep) Provides maps and detailed information about the area.

Ööbikuorg Keskus (☑785 9245; raugeinfo@ hot.ee; Rõuge; ⊙10am-6pm Tue-Sun mid-May–mid-Sep) Signposted about 1.5km east from Rõuge's church, on the road to Haanja. There's an information desk dispensing details on local walking trails and a handicraft shop. Behind the

centre is an observation tower you can climb for great views of the valley and lakes.

❶ Getting There & Away

There are buses from Võru to Haanja village (70c, 15 minutes, nine daily) and Rõuge (70c, 20 minutes, 13 daily).

Valga

POP 13,600

If you thought that Narva's central-city border crossing was odd, wait until you see Valga. This was the only area that was seriously contended between Estonia and Latvia after WWI. A British mediator had to be called in to settle the dispute and suggested the current border, splitting the town in two. As a result, as you wander around the town centre you'll find yourself passing in and out of Valga and Valka, as the Latvian side is known. Mercifully there are no longer checkpoints (cheers, Schengen!) and the local authorities co-operate on important stuff like tourist information.

Valga is enjoying a slow process of gentrification, but its old wooden houses and parks are still skirted by some grim industrial areas. Its bloody wartime history makes it an interesting place to explore before moving on.

◉ Sights

World War II remnants   HISTORIC SITES
An estimated 29,000 Russians died at the Nazi POW camp Stalag-351, which was located in converted stables at Priimetsa on Valga's outskirts. Nothing remains of the camp, but a simple, moving monument is located close by. The Soviets took over the camp and held German POWs here, 300 of whom are buried among the firs nearby. To find the site, take Kuperjanovi and turn left onto Roheline.

The Latvian side of town has large military **bunkers** (Tālavas 23), a **Soviet war cemetery** (Gaujas) and another **German war cemetery** (Varoņu).

St John's Church   CHURCH
(Jaani Kirik; Kesk 23) Close to the tourist office, this oddly shaped church was built in 1816 and holds the distinction of being the only oval church in Estonia.

Valga Museum   MUSEUM
(www.valgamuuseum.ee; Vabaduse 8; adult/child 64/32c; ⊙11am-6pm Wed-Fri, 10am-3pm Sat

SANGASTE

There are two good reasons to stop on the road between Valga and Otepää. In Lossiküla (castle village), 23km northeast of Valga, is majestic red-brick **Sangaste Castle** (Sangaste Loss, www.sangasteloss.ee; adult/child €2.30/1.30; ☺10am-6pm). It was completed in 1881, and the influence of England's Windsor Castle on the architecture is unmistakeable.

There's a summertime cafe here, but hold back until you get to the village of Sangaste, 4km further on, where you'll find **Sangaste Rye House** (Sangaste Rukki Maja; ☑766 9323; www.rukkimaja.ee; mains €5-6; ☎). Sangaste is the 'rye capital of Estonia' and this cosy restaurant celebrates the designation with a menu devoted to the grain. Alongside delicious rye bread there is a surprising array of traditional soups, pork, salmon and chicken dishes. If you feel like settling in for the night, there are fresh, modern rooms upstairs, available at a very reasonable price (single/double €24/36).

& Sun) Local history on display in an art nouveau-style building.

🛏 Sleeping & Eating

Metsis   HOTEL €€
(☑766 6050; www.hotellmetsis.com; Kuperjanovi 63; s €45, d €58-100; P☎) Set on large grounds, this 1912 hotel is the town's best option, with pleasant, well-priced rooms and a good restaurant decorated with hideous hunting trophies (mains €7 to €10).

Voorimehe Pubi   PUB €
(☑767 9627; Kuperjanovi 57; mains €5-8) An atmospheric dark-wood pub serving filling salmon, schnitzel, pork and the like. DJs spin on the weekend.

❶ Information

Tourist Office (☑766 1699; www.tourism .valgamaa.ee; Kesk 11; ☺10am-6pm Mon-Fri, 9am-3pm Sat & Sun, Mon-Fri only mid-Sep–mid-May) Town maps and information for both sides of the town divide.

❶ Getting There & Away

Valga Bus & Railway Station (Jaama pst 10) is a couple of blocks southeast of the town centre.

BUS Ecolines (☑606 2217; www.ecolines.net) has a daily bus to Valmiera (€4, 42 minutes) and Rīga (€7, 2¾ hours) in Latvia. **Lux Express** (☑680 0909; www.luxexpress.eu) has three daily buses to Rīga (€11 to €14, 2½ hours).

Major domestic routes:

» Tallinn (€12, four hours, seven daily)

» Narva (€12, 4¼ hours, daily) via Mustvee, Kauksi and Sillamäe

» Tartu (€5, 1½ hours, seven daily) via Otepää

» Viljandi (€6.20, 1¾ hours, seven daily)

» Pärnu (€8.60, 2½ hours, daily)

TRAIN Valga is the terminus for both the Estonian and Latvian rail systems; you'll have to change trains here if you're heading, say, between Tartu and Rīga. Estonian trains, operated by **Edelerautee** (www.edel.ee), head to Tartu (€3.20, 1½ hours, three daily). Latvian trains, operated by **Latvijas Dzelzceļš** (www.ldz.lv), head to Rīga (3.75Ls, 3¼ hours, three daily) via Valmiera, Cēsis and Sigulda.

Otepää
POP 2200

The small hilltop town of Otepää, 44km south of Tartu, is the centre of a picturesque area of forests, lakes and rivers. The district is beloved by Estonians for its natural beauty and its many possibilities for hiking, biking and swimming in summer, and cross-country skiing in winter. It's often referred to as Estonia's winter capital, and winter weekends here are busy and fun. Some have even dubbed the area (tongue firmly in cheek) the 'Estonian Alps' – a reference not to its peaks but to its excellent ski trails. The 63km Tartu Ski Marathon (p101) kicks off here every February but even in summer you'll see ski-bunnies hurtling around on roller skis.

The main part of Otepää is centred on the intersection of Tartu, Võru and Valga mnts, where you'll find the main square, shops and some patchy residential streets. A small swathe of forest separates it from a smaller settlement by the lakeshore, 2km southwest.

◉ Sights

Pühajärv   LAKE
(Holy Lake) According to legend, 3.5km-long Pühajärv was formed from the tears of the mothers who lost their sons in a battle of

the *Kalevipoeg* epic. Its islands are said to be their burial mounds. Pagan associations linger, with major midsummer festivities held here every year. The lake was blessed by the Dalai Lama when he came to Tartu in 1991; a **monument** near the sandy beach on the northeastern shore commemorates his visit. The popular beach has waterslides, a swimming pontoon, a cafe and lifeguards in summer. A blissful 12km nature trail and bike path encircles the lake.

Winter Sports Museum   MUSEUM
(Talispordimuuseum; Tehvandi Stadium House, Tehvandi; adult/child €1.50/1; ☺11am-4pm Wed-Sun) Big, flash Tehvandi Stadium, used for football and ski events, is a testimony to Otepää's obsession with sport. Within the bowels of the main stand, this two-room museum displays equipment, costumes and medals belonging to some of Estonia's most famous athletes.

St Mary's Lutheran Church   CHURCH
(Maarja Luteri Kirik; Võru mnt; ☺10am-4pm mid-May–Aug) Otepää's hilltop Gothic church dates from the late 19th century, although the belfry is much older. Inside there's intricate curly woodwork, low-hanging chandeliers and an impressive crucifixion scene above the altar. It was here in 1884 that the Estonian Students' Society consecrated its new blue, black and white flag (see the boxed text, p95), which later became the flag of independent Estonia. Bas reliefs on the outside wall on either side of the door remember the occasion; they were originally erected in 1934, destroyed during the Soviet era and re-erected in 1989.

Facing the church's main door is a small mound with a monument to those who died in the 1918–20 independence war. The memorial's top section was buried from 1950 to 1989 to prevent its destruction.

Linnamägi   RUINS
(Castle Hill) The pretty tree-covered hill south of the church was an ancient Estonian stronghold before it was topped by an episcopal castle in the 13th century. Remnants of the fortifications remain on the top along with wonderful views of the surrounding valleys.

Energy Column   MONUMENT
(Energiasammas; Mäe) If energy levels are low after the walk back from the lake, recharge at this odd bear-covered totem pole. It was erected in 1992 to mark the long-held belief of psychics that this area resounds with positive energy.

🏃 Activities
The tourist office has maps and information on trails in the park, which range from short and kid-focused to a 20km hiking/skiing track. Staff can also provide information on a raft of activities on offer in the region, including horse riding, golf, snowtubing, sleigh rides and snowmobile safaris.

For cross-country skiing, the closest trails start on the edge of town near Tehvandi Sports Centre. You can also find some good trails near Lake Kääriku.

If you're considering a canoeing or rafting trip, call at least a day or two ahead of time. Operators will pick you up from your hotel, take you to the river and drop you back afterwards.

Tehvandi Sports Centre   SPORTS CENTRE
(Tehvandi Spordikeskus; ☏766 9500; www.tehvandi.ee; Tehvandi) A former training centre for the Soviet Union's Winter Olympics team, Tehvandi is a hub for all manner of winter and summer activities, including Nordic skiing, ski jumping, running, cycling, roller skiing and skating. There's also a climbing wall and a 34m viewing platform; see the website for details.

Kuutsemäe Resort   SKIING
(Kuutsemäe Puhkekeskus; ☏766 9007; www.kuutsemae.ee; 1-day lift ticket Mon-Fri €14, Sat & Sun €19) While cross-country skiing is the area's drawcard, this resort operates seven modest downhill runs, ranging from 214m to 514m in length. It's the area's most developed ski centre, with a tavern, accommodation and a skiing and snowboarding school. It's located 14km west of Otepää at Kuutsemägi.

Veetee   CANOEING, RAFTING
(☏506 0987; www.veetee.ee) Offers a range of canoeing and rafting trips along the Ahja and Võhandu Rivers and around the small lakes of the Kooraste River valley (per person €20). It also rents skis and snowboards and offers lessons.

Toonus Pluss   CANOEING, SKIING
(☏505 5702; www.toonuspluss.ee) Specialises in canoeing trips in similar areas to those covered by Veetee; tailor-made trips can combine canoeing with hiking and mountain-biking. It also rents skis and offers instruction

Otepää & Around

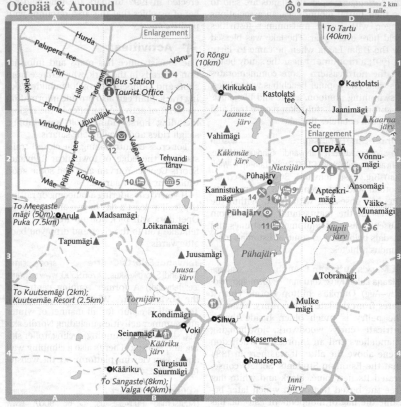

Fan-Sport   CANOEING, EQUIPMENT
(☎5077 537; www.fansport.ee) Rents bikes
(per hour/day €3.20/12.78), sleighs (per
hour/day €1.60/3.20), ice skates (three
hours €2.50), skis (per day €13) and snowboards (per day €13), runs canoeing trips
(per person €16 to €20) and ski lessons
(per hour €13).

Veesõidukite Laenutus   BOAT RENTAL
(☎5343 6359; ◷10am-7pm Jun-Aug) Rents rowboats (€7), canoes (€7), kayaks (€6) and
sailboats (€10) from the beach on the northeastern shore of Pühajärv; all prices per
hour.

Snowmobile Safari Park   SNOWMOBILE
(☎505 1015; www.paap.ee/eng/talvelehed/; Väike-
Munamägi; per hour €70; ◷Jan-Mar) Explore
the winter wonderland in a two-person
snowmobile; price includes training. It's
operated by the same adventurers who run
Surf Paradiis (p152) on Hiiumaa.

🛏 Sleeping

Low season here is April to May and September to November; at this time hotel prices are about 10 to 15% cheaper. Higher rates
are charged on weekends in high season.

TOP CHOICE **GMP Clubhotel**   APARTMENTS €€€
(☎766 7000; www.clubhotel.ee; Tennisevälja 1; apt
€105-135; ℗) Super slick, this new lakeside
block is decked out with funky furniture and
oversized photos. We're not convinced that
giving the studio apartments only sofa beds
was a good idea but rest assured, there are
proper comfy mattresses in all the others.
The icing on the cake is the luxurious pair of
single-sex saunas on the top level, open in the
evenings for those who fancy a sunset sweat.

Murakas   HOTEL €€
(☎731 1410; www.murakas.ee; Valga mnt 23A; s/d
€39/50; ℗🛜) With less than a dozen rooms,
Murakas is more like a large guesthouse than

Otepää & Around

◉ **Sights**
1 Beach................................C2
2 Energy Column........................D2
3 Linnamägi..........................B1
4 St Mary's Lutheran Church..........B1
5 Winter Sports Museum...............B2

➕ **Activities, Courses & Tours**
6 Snowmobile Safari Park.............D3
7 Tehvandi Sports Centre.............D2
  Veesõidukite Laenutus.........(see 1)

🛏 **Sleeping**
8 Edgar's............................A2
9 GMP Clubhotel......................C2
10 Murakas...........................B2
11 Nuustaku Villa....................C3

🍴 **Eating**
  Edgari Pood...................(see 8)
12 I.u.m.i...........................B2
  Nuustaku Pubi................(see 11)
13 Oti Pubi..........................B2
  Pühajärve Restaurant.........(see 9)
14 Pühajärve Spa Hotel Pub...........C2

a hotel. Stripey carpets, blonde wood and balconies give the rooms a fresh feel and there's a similarly breezy breakfast room downstairs.

Edgar's GUESTHOUSE €€
(Edgari Külalistemaja; ☏5343 4705; www.hot .ee/karnivoor; Lipuväljak 3; s/d/tr €20/40/60; 🅿) Edgar's bright little rooms and larger apartments occupy the upstairs levels of an attractive brick building, right in the centre of town, with a deli and cafe below. They may not be flash, but for the price they're a steal.

Nuustaku Villa GUESTHOUSE €
(☏5668 5888; www.nuustaku.ee; Nüpli; d €30-40) Better known for its cosy pub, Nuustaku has eight old-fashioned rooms in a building set on a small point overlooking the lake, 3km southwest of Otepää. The best is room 5, with a living area and its own terrace. The pub can be noisy but it closes at midnight.

Kuutsemäe Resort CABINS €€€
(Kuutsemäe Puhkekeskus; ☏766 9007; www.kuut semae.ee; Kuutsemägi; cabins €115) If you're serious about hitting the slopes, this ski resort rents seven cute wooden cabins with

mezzanines, each sleeping up to eight people. Each has its own kitchen and sauna. It's 14km out of town, so stock up on supplies before hunkering down.

🍴 Eating & Drinking

TOP CHOICE **Pühajärve Restaurant** FUSION €€
(www.clubhotel.ee; Tennisevälja 1; mains €7-17) From the 1960s to 1980s this was the area's most famous restaurant, but when the Soviet Union went down the gurgler it followed in its wake. Thankfully, the opening of the attached Clubhotel has given Pühajärve a new lease of life and it now offers an inventive menu on a terrace above its namesake, with enough thrills to rival those offered on the slopes.

I.u.m.i EUROPEAN €
(www.lumikohvik.ee; Mumamäe 8; mains €4-10) The hippy manifesto at the start of the menu informs us that *lumi* means snow, and among all the talk of good energy, there's a fairly traditional list of fish, pork, beef and chicken dishes, rounded out with some more creative items and an excellent tapas platter. The groovy vibe comes with the requisite mismatched furniture and some cool cutlery lampshades. An excellent choice.

Nuustaku Pubi PUB €€
(www.nuustaku.ee; Nüpli; mains €7-14; 🛜) This lively wooden pub has a popular outdoor terrace overlooking the lake, and the usual set of fish and pork grills. Live music on weekends brings in the punters.

Pühajärve Spa Hotel Pub PUB €
(☏766 5500; www.pyhajarve.com; Pühajärve tee; mains €5-10) The lakeside hotel's casual, all-day pub caters to everyone (kids, vegetarians, et al) with an extensive menu. The sunny outdoor terrace is the place to be, but the brick-lined interior, with pool tables and open fire, is not a bad wet-weather option.

Oti Pubi PUB €
(www.otipubi.ee; Lipuväljak 26; mains €5-8; 🛜) In an octagonal building draped in ski memorabilia in the centre of town, this casual pub has a loyal following and is a decent spot for a drink and a meal, so long as you're not expecting any surprises from the menu.

Edgari Pood DELICATESSEN €
(www.hot.ee/karnivoor; Lipuväljak 3; pastries 30c; ⏰8am-6pm Mon-Fri, 9am-3pm Sat) Stock up on sliced meat and vodka or grab some pastries for a cheap and tasty breakfast.

ℹ️ Information

Tourist Office (📞766 1200; www.otepaa.ee; Tartu mnt 1; ⊙10am-5pm, closed Sun & Mon mid-Sep–mid-May) Well-informed staff distribute maps and brochures, and make recommendations for activities, guide services and lodging in the area.

ℹ️ Getting There & Around

The **bus station** (Tartu mnt 1) is next to the tourist office.

» Tallinn (€12, 3½ hours, daily)

» Narva (€10, 4½ hours, twice weekly) via Mustvee, Kauksi and Sillamäe

» Tartu (€3, 40 minutes, 12 daily)

» Valga (€4, 55 minutes, twice daily) via Sangaste

SOUTHWESTERN ESTONIA

The big drawcard of this corner of the country is the beach. Set on a stretch of golden sand, Pärnu attracts legions of holidaymakers during the summer. Young partygoers appear from Tallinn and Tartu heading to the sands and nightclubs, just as busloads

Southwestern Estonia

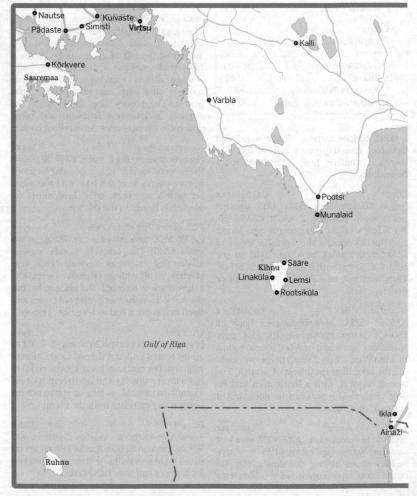

of elderly out-of-towners arrive seeking spa treatments and mud cures.

East of Pärnu stretches Soomaa National Park, a biodiverse region of meandering meadows and swamps. Viljandi lies just beyond Soomaa; it's a laidback regional centre and a focus for things folk, especially music.

Viljandi

POP 19,900

One of Estonia's most charming towns, Viljandi overlooks a picturesque valley with tranquil Lake Viljandi at its centre. The Knights of the Sword founded a castle at Viljandi in the 13th century. The town around it later joined the Hanseatic League, but subsequently was subject to the comings and goings of Swedes, Poles and Russians. It's now a relaxed kind of place, perfect for time-travelling ambles, with some evocative castle ruins, historic buildings and abundant greenery.

If you visit in late July, make sure your accommodation is sorted – the four-day Viljandi Folk Music Festival is the biggest annual music festival in Estonia.

◉ Sights & Activities

The old part of town in the blocks immediately surrounding the castle is lined with

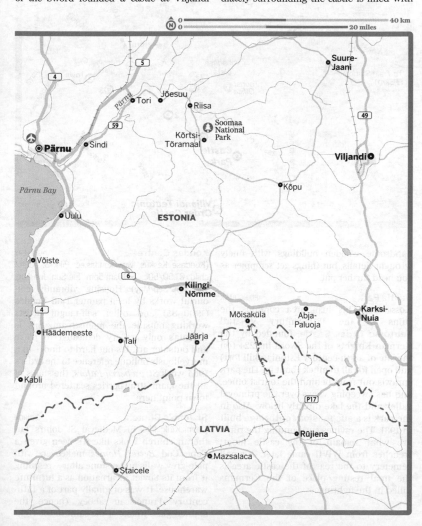

Viljandi

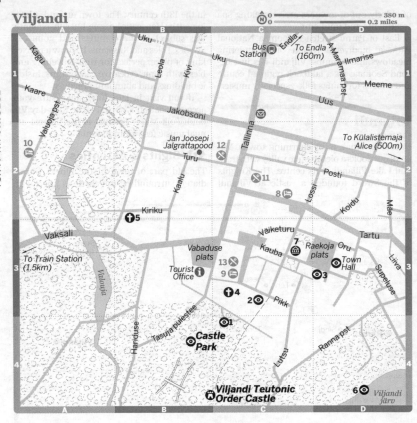

handsome wooden buildings with finely wrought details, but things get scrappier as you head further out.

Castle Park
RUINS, PARK

(Lossimäed) This lush area contains the ruins of the 13th-century **Viljandi Teutonic Order Castle**, founded by the German Knights of the Sword in 1224 (on the site of a 9th-century Estonian hill fort) and open for all to muck about in. The park sprawls out from behind the tourist office, and has sweeping views over the primeval valley and the lake directly below. Also in the park is a **suspension footbridge** built in 1931. The ravines surrounding the ruins are what remain of the castle moat; trenches from WWII came later. A small cemetery to the rear of the castle area is the final resting place of the Germans killed in the fighting.

Kondas Centre
GALLERY

(Kondase Keskus; www.kondas.ee; Pikk 8; adult/child €1.50/50c; ⊙10am-5pm Tue-Sun Jun-Aug, Wed-Sun Sep-May) Housing vibrantly colourful works by local painter Paul Kondas (1900–85) and other self-taught artists working outside the mainstream, this is Estonia's only gallery dedicated to naïve and outsider art. It's not hard to find – in a marvellously oblique reference to the artist's 1965 work *Strawberry Eaters*, the stalks of all the giant strawberries scattered around town point here.

St John's Church
CHURCH

(Jaani Kirik; Pikk 6) Medieval St John's Lutheran church looks like it's been given a Cape Cod *Better Homes* makeover, with pale-grey walls and a stone altar – rescuing it from its Soviet incarnation as a furniture warehouse. It was originally part of a 15th-century Franciscan abbey (hence the stained-glass image of the saint to the right

Viljandi

◎ Top Sights

Castle Park	B4
Viljandi Teutonic Order Castle	B4

◎ Sights

1	Estonian Traditional Music Centre	C4
2	Kondas Centre	C3
3	Old Water Tower	D3
4	St John's Church	C3
5	St Paul's Church	B2
6	Viljandi järv	D4
7	Viljandi Museum	C3

🛏 Sleeping

8	Grand Hotel Viljandi	C2
9	Hostel Ingeri	C3
10	Villa Hilda	A2

✖ Eating

	Aida	(see 1)
11	Soso Juures	C2
12	Suur Vend	C2
13	Tegelaste Tuba	C3

of the altar) and if you look closely you can spot the remains of pre-Reformation frescoes over the arch leading from the porch into the church proper.

Viljandi Museum   MUSEUM
(📞433 3316; www.muuseum.viljandimaa.ee; Laidoneri plats 10; adult/child €2/1; ⊙10am-5pm Tue-Sat) Facing the old market square stands this modest two-storey museum, which has displays tracing Viljandi's history from the Stone Age to the mid-20th century. There are folk costumes, stuffed animals, black-and-white photos of the city, and a mock-up of what the original castle probably looked like. English translations are limited.

Estonian Traditional Music Centre   FOLK MUSIC
(Eesti Pärimusmuusika Keskus; www.folk.ee; Tasuja pst 6; ⊙9am-9pm Mon-Fri, 11am-9pm Sat & Sun) Viljandi's reputation as Estonia's folk-music capital was cemented with the opening of this very un-folksy modern centre in 2007. As well as being a place for study, it has two state-of-the-art concert halls and an upmarket cafe; call in to see what's on the programme or enquire at the tourist office.

Viljandi järv   LAKE
Accessed by steps heading east along Kauba, the lake is a popular place for a swim on

warm summer days. All the usual hallmarks of the Estonian beach are here (volleyball court, cafes, boat rental) and there's a swimming platform just offshore.

St Paul's Church   CHURCH
(Pauluse Kirik; Kiriku 3) Built in the Tudor-Gothic style in 1866, this big, castlelike, stone-and-brick Lutheran church has a wooden pulpit and gallery, and a large crucifixion scene above its altar.

Old Water Tower   VIEWPOINT
(Vana Veetorn; Kauba; adult/child 62/32c; ⊙10am-5pm May-Sep) A 30m tower, near the museum, offering fine views over the countryside.

☞ Tours

From June to August a bargain-priced one-hour guided **walking tour** (adult/child €1/50c) of the town departs at 1pm from outside the tourist office. Tickets and information are from the tourist office; commentary is in English and Estonian.

✯ Festivals & Events

Hanseatic Days   MEDIEVAL
(Hansapäevad; www.viljandi.ee) In June, celebrates the town's past.

Old Music Festival   MUSIC
(Vanamuusika festival; www.kultuuri.net/muusika /vanamuusika) In mid-July, staged mainly in the town's churches, featuring archaic instruments and musical forms.

Viljandi Folk Music Festival   MUSIC
(Viljandi pärimusmuusika festival; www.folk.ee /festival) Easily the biggest event on the calendar is this hugely popular, four-day music festival held around the last weekend of July, renowned for its friendly relaxed vibe and impressive international line-up. It sees Viljandi's population double in size, with over 20,000 attendees at over 100 concerts.

🛏 Sleeping

Hostel Ingeri   GUESTHOUSE €
(📞433 4414; www.hostelingeri.ee; Pikk 2c; s/tw/d €23/32/40; 🅿🛜) On one of Viljandi's loveliest streets, this small six-room guesthouse offers seriously good value with its bright, comfortable rooms, all with TV and bathroom. Plant life and a kitchen for guest use make it a good home-from-home, while the parkside location couldn't be better.

Villa Hilda
GUESTHOUSE €€

(✆433 3710; www.hildavilla.ee; Valuoja pst 7; r €42-77; 🕾) While Hilda's a plain Jane from the outside, this homely guesthouse has plenty of 1930s period features inside, including polished wooden floors, antique stoves and some nana-fabulous furniture. There are only five rooms, with the three upstairs sharing a bathroom. Room 3 has a balcony overlooking the park.

Endla
GUESTHOUSE €

(✆433 5302; www.reinup.ee; Endla 9; s €26, d €32-40; @🕾) There's a vaguely Swiss feel to this altogether charming little guesthouse, set on a quiet backstreet north of the centre. The rooms are simple but smartly furnished and as spick and span as you could ask for.

Külalistemaja Alice
GUESTHOUSE €€

(✆434 7616; www.matti.ee/~alice; Jakobsoni 55; s €25, d €40-45; P🕾) In a peaceful neighbourhood 10 minutes' walk east of the centre, this small, friendly guesthouse is another excellent choice, with bright, neat rooms. Guests can use the kitchen, and there's a large garden. Breakfast is included.

Grand Hotel Viljandi
HOTEL €€

(✆435 5800; www.ghv.ee; Tartu 11; s/d €71/90, ste €167-275; 🕾) In the heart of the old part of town, this moderately chi-chi hotel has art deco–styled rooms with dark-wood trim, satiny chairs, large windows and wildly patterned carpets. There's a pleasant summertime cafe in front, as well as a smart à la carte restaurant. Look for the sign for 'EVE', the name of the 1938 building housing the hotel.

✕ Eating & Drinking

Dining options in Viljandi are quite limited for a town of its size and status, but there are some appealing pubs.

Aida
CAFE €€

(www.folk.ee; Tasuja pst 6; mains €7-10; ⏰11am-11pm Mon-Sat, 11am-7pm Sun) The cafe in the Estonian Traditional Music Centre has the best views of any eatery in town, looking over Castle Park through floor-to-ceiling windows and from its roof terrace. Hearty, skilfully cooked Estonian food is on offer but there's no English on the menu and little spoken by the staff.

Tegelaste Tuba
PUB €

(Pikk 2b; mains €3-6) The terrace overlooking the park is one drawcard of this tavern but so are the comfy interiors on cold, rainy days.

Estonian handicrafts enliven the walls, and a diverse crowd enjoys the wide-ranging menu of soups, salads and hearty mains.

Soso Juures
ARMENIAN €

(Posti 6; mains €5-10; ⏰11am-9pm Mon-Sat) Succulent Armenian cooking is found in this unassuming cafe with an outdoor terrace. Little English is spoken, but the photo board (with English translations) makes ordering easy; the *harcho* (spicy lamb and rice soup) and lamb dishes will have you purring with contentment.

Suur Vend
PUB €€

(www.suurvend.ee; Turu 4; mains €4-13) Friendly service, big portions, a pool table and boppy music from the jukebox create a cheerful mood at this cosy pub, with an outdoor deck and lots of dark-wood ambience inside. The wide-ranging menu offers few surprises and there are plenty of snacks perfect for beer-drinking.

❶ Information

Tourist Office (✆433 0442; www.viljandimaa .ee; Vabaduse plats 6; ⏰10am-6pm Mon-Fri, 10am-3pm Sat & Sun mid-May–mid-Sep, 10am-5pm Mon-Fri mid-Sep–mid-May; @) Local maps and information in loads of languages (catering to the huge festival crowd). It also has information on Soomaa National Park.

❶ Getting There & Around

BICYCLE Bike hire and service is available from **Jan Joosepi Jalgrattapood** (✆434 5757; Turu 6; per day €10; ⏰9am-6pm Mon-Fri, 9am-3pm Sat).

BUS The **bus station** (Bussijaam; ✆433 3680; www.bussireisid.ee; Ilmarise 1) is 500m north of the tourist office. Major routes:

» Tallinn (€8 to €9.40, 2½ hours, 14 daily)

» Rakvere (€8.50, 2½ hours, two weekly)

» Narva (€12.10, 2½ hours, two weekly) via Mustvee, Kauksi and Sillamäe

» Tartu (€5, 1½ hours, 13 daily)

» Pärnu (€6, two hours, nine daily)

TRAIN The **train station** (Raudteejaam; ✆434 9425; www.edel.ee; Vaksali 44) is 2km west of the centre. One to three trains run daily to and from Tallinn (€6.39, 2½ hours).

Soomaa National Park

Embracing Estonia's largest area of swamps, meadows and waterside forests, 390-sq-km Soomaa National Park (Soomaa literally means 'land of wetlands') is primarily made up of four bogs – Valgeraba, Öördi, Kikepera and Kuresoo – the peat layer of which measures 7m in places. The bogs are split by tributaries of the Pärnu River, the spring flooding creating a 'fifth season' in March and April for the inhabitants of this boggy land, when the waters can rise to 5m.

Up to 43 different mammal species inhabit the surrounding forests, among them the wolf, lynx, brown bear, elk, wild boar and otter. Thousands of birds migrate to Soomaa every year, with 180 observed species. The best time to visit for a wildlife encounter is from September to May, when you'll be able to see tracks in the snow at least – and avoid

THE FOREST BROTHERS

Today the sleepy marshes and quiet woodlands of Estonia are a haven only for wildlife, but between 1944 and 1956 much of what is now national park and nature reserve was a stronghold of the Metsavennad (or Metsavendlus; Forest Brothers) pro-independence movement. The Forest Brothers fiercely resisted the Soviet occupation. Many resorted to an underground existence in the woods and some remained there for years. They knew their terrain well and used this knowledge to their advantage both for their own survival and in the fight to restore the republic.

The Soviets claimed Estonia in the Molotov-Ribbentrop Pact of 1939 and, after the Germans retreated from a difficult three-year occupation, secured this claim by advancing on Tallinn in 1944. The early resistance, believing this latest occupation would not be recognised in accordance with the British-US Atlantic treaty of 1941 (which states that sovereignty and self-governance should be restored when forcibly removed), rallied support for what some thought would be a new war. As international assistance did not eventuate, the independence cause remained Estonia's own.

Resistance action began with isolated attacks on Red Army units that claimed the lives of around 3000 soldiers. Tactical expertise and secure intelligence networks resulted in damaging offensives on Soviet targets. At the height of the resistance there were more than 30,000 Forest Brothers and their supporters, which included women, the elderly, young people and a network of 'Urban Brothers'. The impact of resistance activity is found in Soviet records from the time, which detail incidents of sabotage on infrastructure such as railways and roads that hindered early attempts at moulding Estonia into a new Soviet state.

In the years that followed the Metsavennad suffered high casualties, with varied and increasing opposition. The NKVD (Soviet secret police) provided incentives to some of the local population who were able to infiltrate the resistance. The Soviets coordinated mass deportations of those suspected to be sympathetic to the resistance cause, and some Metsavennad supporters were coerced into acting against the resistance. By 1947 15,000 resistance fighters had been arrested or killed. The greatest blow to the Metsavennad came in 1949 with the deportation of 20,000 people – mainly women, children and the elderly – many of whom had provided the support base and cover for resistance activities.

The movement continued for some years but was greatly impeded by the strength of the Soviets and loss of local support due to ongoing deportations and the clearing of farmhouses for collectivisation. Some of the Forest Brothers who were not killed or imprisoned escaped to Scandinavia and Canada.

There are many heroes of the Metsavennad, most of whom came to a violent end. Kalev Arro and Ants Kaljurand (*hirmus*, or 'Ants the Terrible' to the Soviets) were famous for their deft disguises and the humour with which they persistently eluded the Soviets. It was only in 1980 that the final active Forest Brother, Oskar Lillenurm, was found – shot dead in Lääne county.

Much work has been done to compile a history of the movement by recording accounts of local witnesses. Surviving members are regarded as national heroes and are awarded some of the country's highest honours. For more details on the resistance, a good reference is former Estonian prime minister (and historian) Mart Laar's *War in the Woods: Estonia's Struggle for Survival, 1944–1956*.

the blitzkrieg of insects that comes with summer.

A good way to explore the national park and its numerous meandering waterways is by canoe or by *haabja,* a traditional Finno-Ugric single-tree boat that is carved from aspen wood and has been used for centuries for fishing, hunting, hauling hay and transportation.

Bogs have historically provided isolation and protection to Estonians. Witches were said to live there, although traditional healers were sometimes stuck with that label. According to folklore, it is the mischievous will-o'-the-wisp who leads people to the bog, where they are forced to stay until the bog gas catches fire, driving the grotesque bog inhabitants out for all to see. Closer to reality, bogs were also hiding places for partisans escaping from outside invaders who couldn't penetrate their murky depths as easily as they could the forests (perhaps they were scared of the gremlins).

Park information is available from the Soomaa National Park visitor centre (☑435 7164; www.soomaa.ee; ☉10am-6pm Apr-Sep, 10am-4pm Oct-Mar) in Kõrtsi-Tõramaal. It distributes hiking maps and can provide contacts for accommodation and guides (contact the centre in advance). There are 16 designated sites for free, basic camping in the park, including one near the centre. Each has a toilet, a fire ring and (usually) firewood, but no running water.

The 2km Beaver Trail starts here and leads past beavers' dams. Other walking trails in the park get you acquainted with forest, bog or wooded meadow, some via well-maintained boardwalks. Before hitting the paths, it's best to let the centre know what you plan to do, either by email or in person.

Soomaa.com (☑506 1896; www.soomaa .com) acts as a kind of umbrella organisation to help travellers access the wilderness, working in cooperation with local accommodation and service providers. There is an extensive range of activities on offer (with transfers available from Pärnu for €20), such as guided and self-guided canoe trips, beaver-watching by canoe, bog-shoeing and mushroom-picking tours, and in winter, kick-sledding, cross-country skiing and snowshoe excursions. The Wilderness Experience day trip includes bog-shoeing and canoeing (€50; runs from May to September).

❶ Getting There & Away

BUS There are four daily buses from Pärnu to Riisa (€2.30, one hour) and it's hoped that eventually the service will extend the 5km further to the visitor centre.

CAR & MOTORBIKE It's easiest to access the park from the Pärnu (western) side, heading through Tori and Jõesuu. Viljandi's actually closer, but the 23km road from the village of Kõpu to the visitor centre is largely unsealed.

Pärnu

POP 44,000

Local families, hormone-sozzled youths and Finnish holidaymakers join together in a collective prayer for sunny weather while strolling the golden-sand beaches, sprawling parks and picturesque historic centre of Pärnu (*pair*-nu), Estonia's premier seaside resort. In these parts, the name Pärnu is synonymous with fun in the sun; one hyperbolic local described it to us as 'Estonia's Miami' but it's usually called by its slightly more prosaic moniker, the nation's 'summer capital'.

In truth, most of Pärnu is quite docile, with leafy streets and expansive parks intermingling with turn-of-the-20th-century villas that reflect the town's fashionable, more decorous past. Older visitors from Finland and the former Soviet Union still visit, seeking rest, rejuvenation and Pärnu's vaunted mud treatments.

History

There was a trading settlement at Pärnu before the German crusaders arrived, but the place entered recorded history in 1234 when the Pärnu River was fixed as the border between the territories of the Ösel-Wiek bishop (west and north) and the Livonian knights (east and south). The town, joined by rivers to Viljandi, Tartu and Lake Peipsi, became the Hanseatic port of Pernau in the 14th century (sinking water levels have since cut this link). Pernau/Pärnu had a population of German merchants from Lübeck till at least the 18th century. It withstood wars, fires, plagues, and switches between German, Polish, Swedish and Russian rule, and prospered in the 17th century under Swedish rule until its trade was devastated by the Europe-wide blockades during the Napoleonic wars.

From 1838 it gradually became a popular resort, with mud baths as well as the beach proving a draw. Only the resort area was spared severe damage in 1944 as the Soviets drove out the Nazis, but many parts of the Old Town have since been restored.

◉ Sights & Activities

Pärnu straddles both sides of the Pärnu River at the point where it empties into Pärnu Bay. The south bank contains the major attractions, including the Old Town and the beach. The main thoroughfare of the historic centre is Rüütli, lined with splendid buildings dating back to the 17th century.

CENTRE

Museum of New Art GALLERY
(Uue Kunsti Muuseum; www.chaplin.ee; Esplanaadi 10; adult/child €1.60/1; ⊙9am-9pm) In the former Communist Party headquarters, this art museum has a cafe, bookshop and exhibitions that always push the cultural envelope. Founded by film-maker Mark Soosaar, it also hosts the annual Pärnu Film Festival.

Pärnu Museum MUSEUM
(www.pernau.ee; Aia 4; adult/child €2.60/1.30; ⊙10am-6pm Tue-Sat) Despite its modest size, this museum covers 11,000 years of regional history. Archaeological finds and relics from the city's Livonian, Russian and Soviet periods are on display.

Red Tower GALLERY
(Punane Torn; www.punanetorn.ee; Hommiku 11; ⊙10am-5pm Tue-Fri, 10am-3pm Sat) OK, so it's now white but the city's oldest building (dating from the 15th century) was once clad in red brick and was also bigger. This was the southeast corner of the medieval town wall, of which nothing more remains. The tower has been used as a prison but now it contains only artisans' workshops, a small gallery and a summertime craft market in the courtyard.

Tallinn Gate GATE
(Tallinna Värav) The typical star shape of the 17th-century Swedish ramparts that surrounded the old town can easily be spotted on a colour map as most of the pointy bits are now parks. The only intact section, complete with its moat, lies to the east of the centre. Where the rampart meets the western end of Kuninga it's pierced by this tunnel-like gate, that once defended the main road which headed to the river-ferry crossing and on to Tallinn.

St Elizabeth's Church CHURCH
(Eliisabeti Kirik; www.eelk.ee/parnu.eliisabeti; Nikolai 22) Named after Jesus' granny but also the Russian empress at the time it was built (1747), this baroque Lutheran church has low dangling chandeliers, a Gothic-style carved wooden pulpit and a wonderful altarpiece.

St Catherine's Church CHURCH
(Ekatarina Kirik; Vee 8) From 1768, this superb baroque Russian Orthodox church is named after another Russian empress, Catherine the Great, while also name-checking the early Christian martyr.

Mini Zoo ZOO
(Akadeemia tee 1; adult/child €4/2; ⊙10am-6pm Mon-Fri, 11am-4pm Sat & Sun) An eclectic collection of snakes, spiders, geckos and passive pythons awaits you in this strange basement.

Town Hall HISTORIC BUILDING
(Nikolai 3) This 1797 neoclassical building now houses the tourist office. Also note the half-timbered house, dating from 1740, across Nikolai.

BEACH

Pärnu Beach BEACH
Pärnu's long, wide, golden-sand beach – sprinkled with volleyball courts, cafes and tiny changing cubicles – is easily the city's main drawcard. A curving path stretches along the sand, lined with fountains and park benches perfect for people-watching. Early-20th-century buildings are strung along Ranna pst, the avenue that runs parallel to the beach, including the handsome 1927 neoclassical **Mudaravila** (Ranna pst 1). The legendary mud baths that once operated here have been closed for years, awaiting restoration. Across the road, the formal gardens of **Rannapark** are ideal for a summertime picnic.

Tervise Paradiis WATER PARK
(Veekeskus; www.terviseparadiis.ee; Side 14; day ticket €15-18, 3hr €8-13; ⊙11am-10pm) At the far end of the beach, Estonia's largest water park beckons with pools, slides, tubes and other slippery fun. It's a big family-focused draw, especially when bad weather ruins beach plans.

NORTH BANK

Lydia Koidula Memorial Museum MUSEUM
(www.pernau.ee; Jannseni 37; admission €1.30; ⊙10am-5pm) The memory of one of Estonia's poetic greats, Lydia Koidula (1843–86), is kept alive in this modest six-room museum

Pärnu

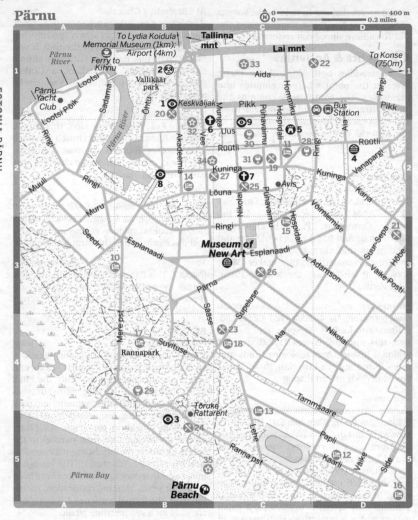

in her former home/schoolhouse. The old classroom and the antique-strewn living room and bedrooms are moderately interesting, even if you're not all that enthused about the Estonian cultural renaissance.

🎊 Festivals & Events

The biggest annual event is the increasingly prestigious **Pärnu International Film Festival** (www.chaplin.ee), showcasing documentary films since 1987. It's held at the Museum of New Art and other venues in town (and around Estonia) in early July.

The tourist office distributes *Pärnu This Week*, which lists events happening around town.

🛏 Sleeping

You'll need to book ahead in summer, especially if you're planning to stay on the weekend. Outside of high season you should be able to snare yourself a good deal – perhaps even half the rates we've listed here.

TOP CHOICE **Villa Johanna**   GUESTHOUSE €€
(☎443 8370; www.villa-johanna.ee; Suvituse 6; s/d/ste €45/75/95; P🖭) On a street lined with

Pärnu

◉ Top Sights
Museum of New Art...............................C3
Pärnu Beach...B5

◉ Sights
1 Central Library................................B1
2 Mini Zoo...B1
3 Mudaravila.....................................B5
4 Pärnu Museum...............................D2
5 Red Tower......................................C2
6 St Catherine's
   Church...B2
7 St Elizabeth's
   Church...C2
8 Tallinn Gate...................................B2
9 Town Hall.......................................C2

⬤ Sleeping
10 Ammende Villa.............................B3
11 Hommiku Hostel...........................C2
12 Inge Villa......................................D5
13 Legend...C5
14 Lõuna Hostel................................B2
15 Netti...C3
16 Tervise Paradiis...........................D5
17 Villa Johanna...............................B4
18 Villa Wesset.................................C4

✖ Eating
19 Mahedik.......................................C2
20 Mõnus Margarita..........................B1
21 Old Market...................................D3
22 Port Artur Toidukaubad.................D1
23 Si-si...C4
24 Steffani Pizzeria - Beach..............B5
25 Steffani Pizzeria - City..................C2
26 Supelsaksad................................C3
27 Trahter Postipoiss........................C2
   Villa Wesset..........................(see 18)

◯ Drinking
28 Citi..C2
29 Kuursaal.......................................B4
   Romantic Bar.........................(see 16)
30 Veerev Õlu...................................C2
31 Wine Piccadilly.............................C2

✪ Entertainment
   Beach Club.............................(see 29)
32 Endla Theatre...............................B2
33 Pärnu Concert Hall........................C1
34 Sugar...B2
35 Sunset Club..................................B5

family-run guesthouses, this pretty place stands out thanks to its hanging flowerpots and planter boxes. Many pine trees died in the making of the interior fit-out and furnishings, and the place is spotless. Low-season rates are a steal (single/double €17/34). Not much English is spoken.

Villa Wesset
HOTEL €€€
(☑697 2500; www.wesset.ee; Supeluse 26; s/d €79/101; 🖢) This elegant boutique hotel is kitted out in warm chocolate and vanilla tones (appropriately enough, given the 1928 villa was built by a sweet maker). It's in a great location just a short stroll from the beach and all the rooms have giant flat screens for any rainy days you might strike.

Inge Villa
GUESTHOUSE €€
(☑443 8510; www.ingevilla.ee; Kaarli 20; s/d/ste €72/90/105; ⊙Mar-Oct; 🖢) In a prime patch of real estate just back from the beach you'll find the low-key and lovely Inge Villa, a 'Swedish-Estonian villa hotel'. Its 11 rooms are simply decorated in muted tones with Nordic minimalism to the fore. The garden, lounge and sauna seal the deal.

Ammende Villa
HOTEL €€€
(☑447 3888; www.ammende.ee; Mere pst 7; r from €179; 🅿🖢) Class and luxury abound in this exquisitely refurbished 1904 art nouveau mansion, which lords it over a large lawn. The gorgeous exterior – looking like one of the cooler Paris metro stops writ large – is matched by an elegant lobby and individually antique-furnished rooms. Rooms in the gardener's house are more affordable but lack a little of the wow factor.

Tervise Paradiis
RESORT €€€
(☑445 1600; www.terviseparadiis.ee; Side 14; s/d/ste €132/165/247; ⊞) Big (120-odd rooms) and *busy* in summer, this hotel near the water has slick rooms, all with balconies and beach views (ask for a room on a higher floor). Here, happy-holiday facilities are laid on thick: bowling alley, kids' playroom, spa, fitness club, water park, restaurants, bar. It's very popular with Swedish and Finnish guests, so book ahead in high season.

Legend
HOTEL €€
(☑442 5606; www.legend.ee; Lehe 7; s/d €70/93; 🅿@🖢) The Tiffany-style lamps, model ships

and wooden panelling lend an old-world feel to the lobby which is neither reflective of the exterior or the rooms. However, for such tidy midrange accommodation with charming staff, right by the beach, we're prepared to overlook a few ugly bedspreads.

Netti
GUESTHOUSE €€

(✆516 7958; www.nettihotel.ee; Hospidali 11-1; ste €52-104; P🖳🎅) Anni, your host at Netti, is a ray of sunshine, and her three-storey guesthouse, comprising four two-room suites, positively gleams under her care. The suites sleep two to four, have some kitchen facilities and are bright and breezy, even if the decor's a little dated. The downstairs sauna area is a lovely place to unwind after a hard day at the beach.

Lõuna Hostel
HOSTEL €€

(✆443 0943; www.hostellouna.eu; Lõuna 2; dm €15-20, s/tw with shared bathroom €30/45, s/d with private bathroom €45/60) Overlooking Munamäe Park, this grand 1909 *Jugendstil* building offers quality budget digs in spacious, two- to seven-bed rooms with high ceilings. The shared kitchen doubles as a social room, where people compare suntans and travel tales. Entrance is on Akadeemia.

Hommiku Hostel
HOSTEL €€

(✆445 1122; www.hommikuhostel.ee; Hommiku 17; dm/s/d/tr/q €20/39/58/77/90; P🎅) Located in a prime central position, Hommiku is far more like a budget hotel than a hostel. Rooms have private bathrooms, TVs and kitchenettes; some also have old beamed ceilings.

Konse
CAMPGROUND €

(✆5343 5092; www.konse.ee; Suur-Jõe 44a; tent sites €4 plus €4 per person, r with shared/private bathroom €39/55) Perched on a spot by the river only 1km from the centre, Konse offers camp sites and a variety of rooms with kitchen access. It's not an especially charming spot but there is a sauna, and bike and rowboat rental.

✗ Eating & Drinking

TOP CHOICE Supelsaksad
CAFE €€

(www.supelsaksad.ee; Nikolai 32; mains €7-12) Looking like it was designed by Barbara Cartland on acid (bright pink and a riot of stripes and prints), this fabulous cafe serves an appealing mix of salads, pastas and a redoubtable Wiener schnitzel. If you eat all your veggies, make a beeline for the bountiful cake display. Drop by in the evening for a glass of wine on the terrace, served by the impeccably chirpy staff.

🌿 Mahedik
CAFE €

(www.mahedik.ee; Pühavaimu 20; mains €3-10; 🕘9am-7pm Mon-Thu, 9am-11pm Fri, 10am-11pm Sat, 10am-5pm Sun) The name roughly translates as 'organic-ish', which is a fair assessment of the food offered at this artsy but homey cafe. There's no English menu but the staff will happily explain the seasonal selection (the rhubarb pancakes were heavenly when we visited), while the home-cooked counter food is self-explanatory.

Villa Wesset
INTERNATIONAL €€

(www.wesset.ee; Supeluse 26; mains €6-10; 🕘noon-11pm) Both the glassed-in terrace and the more formal dining room at this boutique hotel hold great appeal. The fresh, modern menu features creative salads and soups, traditional herring and salmon dishes, and some tasty tricks from further-flung cuisines.

Trahter Postipoiss
RUSSIAN €€

(www.trahterpostipoiss.ee; Vee 12; mains €7-16) Housed in an 1834 postal building, this rustic tavern has excellent Russian cuisine, a convivial crowd (especially after a few vodka shots) and imperial portraits watching over the proceedings. The spacious courtyard opens during summer, and there's live music on weekends.

Steffani Pizzeria
ITALIAN €

(www.steffani.ee; mains €5-7; Nikolai 24) The queue out front should alert you – this is a top choice for thin-crust and pan pizzas, particularly in summer when you can dine alfresco on the big, flower-filled terrace. There's a complimentary self-service salad bar and the menu stretches to pasta and, oddly, burritos. There's a beach branch at Ranna pst 1 during summer.

Wine Piccadilly
CAFE €

(www.kohvila.ee; Pühavaimu 15; quiche €4) Piccadilly offers a plush, down-tempo haven for wine-lovers and an extensive range of coffee, tea and hot choc. Savoury food begins and ends with quiche – here it's all about the sweeties, including moreish cheesecake and handmade chocolates.

Mõnus Margarita
TEX-MEX €

(www.monusmargarita.ee; Akadeemia 5; mains €5-10) Big, colourful and decidedly upbeat, as all good Tex-Mex places should be, but if you're looking for heavy-duty spice you won't find it here. Fajitas, burritos and quesadillas all score goals, plus there are margaritas and tequilas for the grown-ups and a play area for the kids.

Si-si   ITALIAN €€
(www.si-si.ee; Supeluse 21; mains €6-12; ⊙1pm-midnight Mon-Sat) Beachside dining in Pärnu is disappointingly bland but a walk up Supeluse presents appealing options, including this Italian restaurant-lounge. Inside is smart white-linen dining, outside is a stylishly relaxed terrace. There's a good selection of gourmet-style pizzas, and the all-important tiramisu.

Veerev Õlu   PUB €
(www.rollingbeer.com; Uus 3a) Named after the Rolling Stones, the 'Rolling Beer' wins the award for friendliest and cosiest pub by a long shot. It's a tiny rustic space with good vibes, cheap beer and the occasional live folk-rock band (with compulsory dancing on tables, it would seem).

Kuursaal   PUB €
(www.kuur.ee; Mere pst 22; mains €4-5; ⊙noon-10pm Sun-Wed, noon-2am Thu, noon-4am Fri & Sat) This late-19th-century dance hall has been transformed into a spacious countrified beer hall with a large terrace at the back. An older mix of tourists and locals come for the draft beer and the occasional rock shows, and a menu that takes its meat and beer snacks seriously.

Citi   PUB €
(Hommiku 8; mains €5-10) When the sun's shining, the outdoor tables at this lively cafe-pub are jam-packed with a diverse crowd, while the rustic interior matches the simple menu of beery snacks and inexpensive meaty mains (salmon fillet, grilled chicken, pork roast). It's popular with visitors and locals, and the owner's a local character.

Romantic Bar   BAR
(8th fl Tervise Paradiis, Side 14; ⊙noon-midnight) Despite the cheesy name and bland hotel-bar vibe, the superb sea views from this venue make it the perfect setting for a sundowner cocktail or a nightcap, either inside on the white, podlike leather chairs, or on the small terrace.

Port Artur Toidukaubad   SUPERMARKET
(www.portartur.ee; Hommiku 2; ⊙9am-10pm) The most central supermarket is inside the Port Artur shopping centre.

Old Market   MARKET
(Vana Turg; Suur-Sepa 18; ⊙7am-4.30pm Tue-Sat, 7am-3pm Sun) Covered market; good for fruit and vegetables.

☆ Entertainment

In summer there are various concerts, held at traditional venues such as the concert hall and Kuursaal, as well as in parks, the town hall, churches and the grounds of the beautiful Ammende Villa.

Pärnu Concert Hall   CLASSICAL MUSIC
(Pärnu Konserdimaja; ☑445 5810; www.concert .ee; Aida 4) A striking riverside glass-and-steel auditorium with first-rate acoustics, considered the best concert venue in Estonia.

Endla Theatre   THEATRE
(☑442 0666; www.endla.ee; Keskväljak 1) Pärnu's best theatre, staging a wide range of performances (usually in Estonian). It also houses an art gallery and an open-air cafe.

Sunset Club   CLUB
(www.sunset.ee; Ranna pst 3; ⊙11pm-5am Fri & Sat Jun-Aug) Pärnu's biggest and most famous summertime nightclub has an outdoor beach terrace and a sleek multifloor interior with plenty of cosy nooks when the dance floor gets crowded. Imported DJs and bands plus a wild young crowd keep things cranked until the early hours.

Beach Club   CLUB
(www.beachclub.ee; Mere pst 22; admission €2-10; ⊙11pm-5am Fri & Sat year-round, plus Mon & Tue Aug, daily Jun & Jul) Attached to Kuursaal, this is one of the city's hot spots, with excellent DJs and an eager young crowd.

Sugar   CLUB
(www.sugarclub.ee; Vee 10; admission €3-10; ⊙11pm-4am Wed-Sat) Shiny Sugar offers you temptation in the form of the 'sweetest nightlife' and themed nights.

❶ Information

Central Library (Keskraamatukogu; www.pkr .ee; Akadeemia 3; ⊙10am-7pm Mon-Fri, 10am-5pm Sat; 🛜) Free internet at this spiffy new library.

Tourist Office (☑447 3000; www.visitparnu .com; Uus 4; ⊙9am-6pm mid-May–mid-Sep, 9am-5pm Mon-Fri, 10am-2pm Sat & Sun mid-Sep–mid-May) Stocks maps, a free walking-tour brochure and *Pärnu This Week* (free) and *Pärnu in Your Pocket* (€1.60). Helpful staff will book accommodation for a €2 fee.

❶ Getting There & Away

Air

Pärnu airport (Pärnu Lennujaam; EPU; ☑447 5001; www.parnu-airport.ee) lies on the northern edge of town, west of the Tallinn road, 4km from the town centre. Bus 23 runs from the bus station to the airport (20 minutes) or a taxi should cost no more than €3. In winter, when sea travel is impossible, Luftverkehr Friesland-Harle (LFH) flies to the islands of Kihnu and Ruhnu.

Boat

It's possible to take a ferry or private boat trip from Pärnu to Kihnu. **Pärnu Yacht Club** (Pärnu Jahtklubi; ☑447 1750; www.jahtklubi.ee; Lootsi 6) has a marina with a customs point, along with a restaurant and accommodation.

Bus

Buses stop at the corner of Pikk and Ringi, but the main **bus station ticket office** (www.bussipark.ee; Ringi 3; ⊙6.30am-7.30pm) is about 100m away, across Ringi. The following operators head to Latvia and Lithuania:

Ecolines (☑606 2217; www.ecolines.net) Salacgrīva (€6, one hour, three daily) and Rīga (€9.60, 2½ hours, three daily);

Hansabuss Business Line (☑627 9080; www.businessline.ee) Buses to Tallinn (€14 to €18, two hours, three daily) and Rīga (€14 to €18, 2½ hours, three daily).

Lux Express (☑680 0909; www.luxexpress.eu) Heads to Tallinn (€10, 1¾ hours, daily), Rīga (€9 to €13, 2½ hours, eight daily) and Vilnius (€20, seven hours, twice daily).

The main domestic routes:

» Tallinn (€6 to €8.50, two hours, numerous)

» Rakvere (€8.50 to €10, four hours, four daily)

» Tartu (€7.50 to €11, three hours, ten daily)

» Viljandi (€6, two hours, nine daily)

» Kuressaare (€12, three hours, four daily) via the ferry to Muhu Island

Car & Motorcycle

Rental options include **Avis** (☑447 3020; www.avis.ee; Kuninga 34), just behind Hotel Victoria.

Train

Two daily trains run between Tallinn and Pärnu (€5.43, 2¾ hours), but this isn't a great option given that **Pärnu station** (www.edel.ee; Riia mnt 116) is an inconvenient 5km east of the town centre along the Rīga road. There's no station office; buy tickets on the train.

❶ Getting Around

BICYCLE From June to August, **Tõruke Rattarent** (☑502 8269; www.torukebicycles.ee; bike per hr/day/week €2.70/10/43) rents bikes from a stand near the beach, on the corner of Ranna pst and Supeluse. Otherwise, you can get a bike delivered to you for an extra €1.

BUS There are local buses but given that all the sights are within walking distance of each other, you probably won't need to bother with them. Tickets for local journeys are 64c if pre-purchased or €1 from the driver.

TAXI Taxis line up near the bus station on Ringi. Both **E-Takso** (☑443 1111; www.etakso.ee) and **Pärnu Taksopark** (☑443 9222; www.parnutakso.ee) charge a €2.24 flagfall and then 77c per kilometre.

Kihnu

POP 494

Kihnu island, 40km southwest of Pärnu in the Gulf of Rīga, is almost a living museum of Estonian culture. Many of the island's women still wear the traditional, colourful striped skirts nearly every day. There are four villages on the 7km-long island, plus a school, church, lighthouse (shipped over from Britain), museum and combined library, internet point and council building in the centre of the island. Long, quiet beaches line the western coast.

The islanders are among the minority of ethnic Estonians who follow the Russian Orthodox religion. After WWII a fishery collective was established here, and fishing and cattle herding continue to be the mainstay of employment for Kihnu's inhabitants.

In December 2003 Unesco declared the Kihnu Cultural Space a masterpiece of the Oral and Intangible Heritage of Humanity. This honour is a tribute to the rich cultural traditions that are still practised, in song, dance, the celebration of traditional spiritual festivals and the making of handicrafts. In part, the customs of Kihnu have remained intact for so many centuries thanks to the island's isolation.

Many of the island's first inhabitants, centuries ago, were criminals and exiles from the mainland. Kihnu men made a living from fishing and seal hunting, while women effectively governed the island in their absence. The most famous Kihnuan was the sea captain Enn Uuetoa (better known as Kihnu Jõnn), who was said to have sailed on all the world's oceans. He drowned in 1913 when his ship sank off Denmark on what was to have been his last voyage before retirement. He was buried in the Danish town of Oksby but in 1992 his remains were brought home to Kihnu and reburied in the island's church.

⊙ Sights

Kihnu Museum   MUSEUM
(☑446 9983; www.kihnu.ee; Linaküla; adult/child €2/1; ⊗10am-4pm May-Aug, 10am-2pm Tue-Fri Sep-Apr) You can learn more about Kihnu Jõnn and life on Kihnu at this museum, near the picturesque Orthodox church in Linaküla.

Metsamaa   CULTURAL CENTRE
(☑507 1453; www.kultuuriruum.ee; Rootsiküla; adult/child €2/1) The Kihnu Cultural Space Foundation runs handicrafts workshops, music nights and performances from this traditional Kihnu homestead; call ahead to find out what's on.

🛏 Sleeping & Eating

Tolli Tourist Farm   GUESTHOUSE €
(☑527 7380; www.kihnukallas.ee; Sääre; sites per person €6, r €32-40) Located about 2km north of the port, Tolli offers rooms in the main farmhouse, the barn or in a rustic log cabin, and you can also pitch a tent. Other services include a sauna, bike rental and boating excursions, and guests can order meals. They can even arrange to sail you over from the mainland.

Rock City   GUESTHOUSE €
(☑446 9956; www.rockcity.ee; Sääre; d/tr €32/48; ⊗May-Aug) Even nearer to the port, this place offers simple, wood-floored rooms with shared bathroom. Services include bike rental, sauna, excursions and a restaurant serving hearty country fare.

ℹ Information

Kihnurand Travel Agency (☑525 5172; www.kihnurand.ee; Sääre) Arranges day trips and tours.

ℹ Getting There & Away

AIR In winter (usually from December or whenever the boats stop), **LFH** (☑512 4013; www.lendame.ee) flies to and from Pärnu (€8, 15 minutes, two daily).

BOAT As long as ice conditions allow (from at least mid-May to the end of October), there are ferries to Kihnu operated by **Veeteed** (☑443 1069; www.veeteed.com) from both Pärnu (adult/child/car/bike €4.50/2.20/12/1.60, 2¼ hours, no boats Monday or Tuesday) and from Munalaid (adult/child/car/bike €2.60/1.30/11/1, 50 minutes, two to three daily), 40km southwest of Pärnu (buses from Pärnu are theoretically timed to meet the ferries). Tickets can be purchased at both ports. The Pärnu tourist office keeps updated ferry timetables. The ferry dock is halfway between Sääre and Lemsi.

ℹ Getting Around

Bicycle is the best way to get around the island. You can rent bikes and pick up a map at **Jalgrattaläenutus** (☑527 3752; bikes per hr/day from €3.20/10), in a brick building 150m from the port.

Ruhnu
POP 72

Ruhnu, smaller than Kihnu at just 11 sq km and harder to reach, is 100km southwest of Pärnu and nearer to Latvia than the Estonian mainland. For several centuries Ruhnu had a mainly Swedish population of about 300, but they all fled in August 1944, abandoning homes and livestock, to avoid the advancing Red Army. Ruhnu has some sandy beaches, but the highlight is a very impressive **wooden church** (dating back to 1644), making it the oldest surviving wooden structure in Estonia. It has a wooden altar and pulpit dating from 1755 in its atmospheric interior. The island is flat but there's a forest of 200- to 300-year-old pines on its eastern dunes.

If you're thinking about visiting, the website www.ruhnu.ee has plenty of useful information.

ℹ Getting There & Away

AIR From mid-September, **LFH** (☑512 4013; www.lendame.ee) flies four times a week to and from both Pärnu (€29, 35 minutes) and Kuressaare on Saaremaa (€23, 25 minutes).

BOAT Three **SLK Ferries** (Saaremaa Laevakompanii; ☑452 4444; www.tuulelaevad.ee; adult/child/bike €16/8/10) a week from mid-May to mid-September run to Ruhnu from both Munalaid (three hours), near Pärnu, and Roomassaare on Saaremaa (2½ hours).

WESTERN ESTONIA & THE ISLANDS

One of the Baltic's most alluring regions, the west coast of Estonia encompasses forest-covered islands, verdant countryside and seaside villages slumbering beneath the shadows of picturesque medieval castles.

Pine forests and juniper groves cover Saaremaa and Hiiumaa, Estonia's largest islands. Dusty roads loop around them, passing desolate stretches of coastline, with few signs of development aside from

Western Estonia & the Islands

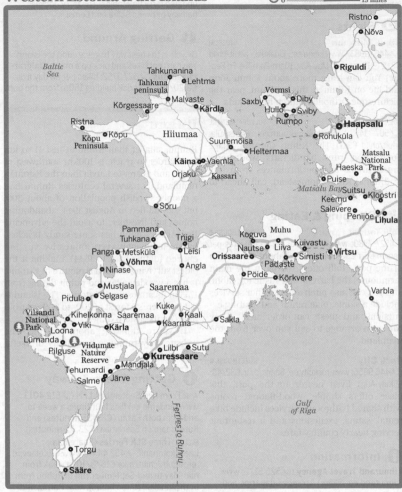

19th-century lighthouses and old wooden windmills – both icons of the islands. Here you'll find peaceful settings for hiking, horse riding or simply touring through the countryside in search of hidden stone churches and crumbling fortresses – ruins left behind by pagan Estonian warriors, German knights and Soviet military planners.

Saaremaa, the largest and most visited of the islands, boasts spa resorts, a magnificent castle and a pretty 'capital' that comes to life during the summer months. It's also the departure point for the wildlife-rich islands in Vilsandi National Park.

On the mainland, Haapsalu is an enchanting but ragged town that was once a resort for 19th-century Russian aristocrats. The jewel of its Old Town is a 14th-century bishop's castle, today the setting for open-air festivals and summer concerts.

Muhu

POP 1690

Connected to Saaremaa by a 2.5km causeway, the island of Muhu has the undeserved reputation as the 'doormat' for the bigger island – lots of people passing through on their way from the ferry, but few stopping. In fact, Estonia's third-biggest island offers plenty of excuses to hang around, not least the country's best restaurant and some excellent accommodation options. There's no tourist office on the island, but there's lots of good information online at www.muhu .info.

◉ Sights & Activities

Pädaste Manor
PARK
(www.padaste.ee; adult/child €3/1; ☉noon-9pm Jun-Aug) We've described the rarefied delights of Padaste in more detail under the Sleeping and Eating headings, but for those of more modest means, the seven-hectare landscaped waterfront park, surrounded by 22 hectares of forest and meadows, can be visited for a small fee (refunded if you dine at any of the manor's excellent eateries). The bones of the manor house date from the 14th century but its current makeover is 19th century.

Koguva
VILLAGE
On the western tip of Muhu, 6km off the main road, is an exceptionally well-preserved, fairy-tale fishing village which was first mentioned in written records in 1532. Its residents are still mainly descendents of the original inhabitants and it is now protected as an open-air museum (www.muhu muuseum.ee; adult/child €3/1.50; ☉10am-7pm mid-May–mid-Sep, 10am-5pm Wed-Sun mid-Sep–mid-May). One ticket allows you to wander through an old schoolhouse and two farm complexes, one displaying beautiful traditional textiles from the area, including painstakingly detailed folk costumes. The other is the ancestral home of author Juhan Smuul (1922–71) which contains, among other things, a collection of Singer sewing machines. Also in the village is the handsome modern-art gallery and cafe Koguva Kunstitall (www.koguva-art.ee; ☉11am-6pm Jun-Aug), a civilised spot for a glass of wine or coffee and cake.

Eemu Tuulik
WINDMILL
(adult/child 64/32c; ☉10am-6pm Wed-Sun mid-Apr–Sep) On the main road at Nautse, this working windmill has a display board and sells bread baked with its milled flour.

Muhu Stronghold
FORTRESS
Immediately southwest of the windmill, this earthen ring draped in greenery is where in 1227 the pagan Estonians made their last stand, holding off a 20,000-strong force led by the Knights of the Sword for six days before surrendering. A stone obelisk remembers the massacre that followed when all 2500 warriors were slaughtered by the Christians.

Muhu Ostrich Farm
FARM
(Muhu Jaanalinnufarm; www.jaanalind.ee; adult/child €3/2; ☉10am-6pm mid-May–mid-Sep) The quirky ostrich owners will give you an earful about these strange creatures and let you feed them (mind your fingers). There's also a mini-menagerie of kangaroos, wallabies, emus and ponies (for kids to ride). A small shop sells feathers, eggs, purses and shoes made from ostrich leather – it is a farm, after all. The signposted turn-off is 200m east of the Eemu windmill (to which it's no relation).

Courses

Nami Namaste
COOKING
(☎454 8890; www.naminamaste.com; Simisti; ☉Apr-Oct) Finnish TV personality Sikke Sumari offers bespoke cooking classes (€135 for a three-hour workshop and three-course meal), group dinners and B&B accommodation (€45 for course participants, €75 for others) in her rustic-chic farmhouse lodge in Muhu's south. Most ingredients are seasonal and local (many are home-grown); classes can be given in a number of languages, including English.

⌂ Sleeping

TOP CHOICE Pädaste Manor
RESORT €€€
(☎454 8800; www.padaste.ee; r €186-373, ste €423-676; ☉Mar-Oct; P@⊛) If money's no object, here's where to part with it – Pädaste is quite possibly Estonia's premier place to bed down and quite definitely its best place to pig out (see p132). In a manicured bayside estate, the boutique resort encompasses the exquisitely restored manor house (with 14 rooms and a fine-dining restaurant), a stone carriage house (with nine rooms, a private cinema and a spa centre) and a separate stone 'sea house' with a brasserie and terrace. The attention to detail is second-to-none, from the pop-up TVs, antique furnishings and Muhu embroidery, to the island's herbs, mud and honey used in the spa treatments.

Vanatoa Turismitalu GUESTHOUSE €€

(📞454 8884; www.vanatoa.ee; Koguva; sites per person €6, s/d €30/51) Within lost-in-time Koguva village, family-run Vanatoa has newly renovated rooms with slick little en suites (gotta love that underfloor heating) in a thatched-roof farm complex. Don't be fooled by the image on the website; it doesn't actually sit on a cliff. The attached restaurant serves up perfunctory Estonian stomach-fillers like pork fillet and herring (mains €8 to €12).

Eating

TOP CHOICE Alexander MODERN ESTONIAN €€€

(📞454 8800; www.padaste.ee; Pädaste Manor; 3/4/5 courses €48/52/63; ⊙lunch Mar-May, Sep & Oct, dinner Mar-Oct) If you're not interested in a culinary adventure, go elsewhere. Handsome local lad Peeter Pihel doesn't miss a trick with his 'chef's surprise' *table d'hôte*-style menu (you pick three to five courses from a list of seven), introducing elements of molecular gastronomy and a hefty dose of humour into his creations. Having all that fine island produce at his fingertips certainly helps. From June to August, a lighter lunch is served in the casual Sea House Terrace.

Muhu Fish Cafe SEAFOOD €

(Muhu Kalakohvik; 📞454 8551; www.kalakohvik.ee; Liiva; mains about €5; ⊙11am-6pm summer) Set slightly back from the main road at Liiva, this humble eatery serves up first-rate fish dishes in what is basically a family dining room. If we've been a bit vague about prices and opening hours, it's only because it's a very informal operation. Call ahead to ensure they're open or take your chances if you're passing through.

❶ Getting There & Away

BOAT Car ferries run by **SLK** (📞452 4444; www.tuulelaevad.ee; adult/child/car €2.24/1.12/6.39) make the 30-minute crossing between Virtsu on the mainland and Kuivastu on Muhu (roughly hourly from 5.30am to 10pm). You can reserve a place for your car for an extra couple of euros (online or by phone); you should consider this to avoid the queues heading to the island on Fridays and off on Sundays – but it won't necessarily help around midsummer, when the queues can stretch for kilometres and totally block the road. Some popular weekend sailings charge a 50% vehicle surcharge.

BUS Buses take the ferry from the mainland and continue through to Saaremaa via the causeway, stopping at Kuivastu and Liiva; sweet-talk the driver into stopping at other points along the main road. Major routes include:

» Tallinn (€11, three hours, 11 daily)

» Tartu (€14, five hours, two daily)

» Viljandi (€13, four hours, two daily)

» Pärnu (€8, two hours, three daily)

» Kuressaare (€4.79, one hour, 16 daily) via Orissaare

Saaremaa

POP 32,900

Saaremaa (literally 'island land') is synonymous to Estonians with space, spruce and fresh air – and killer beer. Estonia's largest island (roughly the size of Luxembourg) is still mainly covered in forests of pine, spruce and juniper, while its windmills, lighthouses and tiny villages seem largely unbothered by the passage of time.

During the Soviet era the entire island was off limits (due to an early-radar system and rocket base stationed there), even to 'mainland' Estonians, who needed a permit to visit. This resulted in a minimum of industrial build-up and the unwitting protection of the island's rural charm.

This unique old-time setting goes hand-in-hand with inextinguishable Saaremaan pride. Saaremaa has always had an independent streak and was usually the last part of Estonia to fall to invaders. Its people have their own customs, songs and costumes. They don't revere mainland Estonia's *Kalevipoeg* legend, for Saaremaa has its own hero, Suur Tõll, who fought many battles around the island against devils and fiends.

Kuressaare, the capital of Saaremaa, is on the south coast (75km from the Muhu ferry terminal) and is a natural base for visitors – it's here, among the upmarket hotels, that you'll understand where the island got its nickname, 'Spa-remaa'. When the long days arrive, so too do the Finns and Swedes, jostling for beach and sauna space with Estonian urban-escapees.

More information is online at www.saaremaa.ee and www.SaaremaaEstonia.com.

History

Saaremaa's earliest coastal settlements (dating from the 4th millennium BC) now lie inland because the land has risen about 15m over the last 5000 years. In the 10th to

13th centuries Saaremaa and Muhu were the most densely populated parts of Estonia. Denmark tried to conquer Saaremaa in the early 13th century; however, in 1227 it was the German Knights of the Sword who subjugated it. The island was then carved up between the knights, who took Muhu and the eastern and northwestern parts of Saaremaa, and the Haapsalu-based bishop of Ösel-Wiek, who made Kuressaare his stronghold.

Saaremaa rebelled against German rule many times between 1236 and 1343 (when the knights' castle was destroyed and the Germans were expelled), though their efforts were always short-lived (in 1345 the Germans reconquered the island).

In the 16th century Saaremaa became a Danish possession during the Livonian War, but by 1645 the Swedes had their turn, compliments of the Treaty of Brömsebro. Russia took over in 1710 during the Great Northern War and Saaremaa became part of the Russian province of Livonia, governed from Rīga.

☞ Tours

Pärimusmatkad Heritage Tours   ISLAND TOURS
(☎526 9974; www.parimusmatkad.ee) A recommended company that arranges a raft of year-round Saaremaa excursions and activities, including heritage tours, horse riding, seal-watching, ski trips and jeep safaris. Lots of Vilsandi options too.

Mere Travel Agency   ISLAND TOURS
(☎453 3610; www.rbmere.ee) Extremely knowledgeable about the islands, and can arrange boat trips to Vilsandi.

❶ Getting There & Away

Most travellers reach Saaremaa by taking the ferry from Virtsu to Muhu and then crossing the 2.5km causeway connecting the islands.

AIR The **Kuressaare Airport** (URE; Kuressaare Lennujaam; ☎453 0313; www.kuressaare-airport.ee; Roomassaare tee 1) is at Roomassaare, 3km southeast of the town centre. Buses 2 and 3 connect it with the bus station at Kuressaare. **Estonian Air** (☎640 1160; www.estonian-air.ee) flies to and from Tallinn (from €16, 45 minutes, 13 weekly). From mid-September, LFH flies four times a week to and from the island of Ruhnu (see p129).

BOAT Apart from the Muhu ferry, **SLK Ferries** (☎452 4444; www.tuulelaevad.ee) runs boats from Sõru on Hiiumaa to Triigi on the north coast of Saaremaa (adult/child/car €2.24/1.12/6.39, 65 minutes, two to three times daily). These

can also be prebooked online for a small fee, but bookings are rarely required. From mid-May to mid-September it also runs a boat to Ruhnu island (see p129).

Saaremaa is very popular with visiting yachties. The best **marina** (☎503 1953; www.kuressaare.ee/sadam/en; Tori 4) facilities are at Kuressaare, within a stone's throw of three spa hotels. Visit http://marinas.nautilus.ee for details of it and other harbours on Saaremaa.

BUS Buses from the mainland take the Muhu ferry and continue to Saaremaa via the causeway, terminating in Kuressaare. The major routes are Tallinn–Kuressaare (€14, four hours, 11 daily) and Tartu–Kuressaare (€15, six hours, two daily) via Viljandi (€15, five hours, two daily) and Pärnu (€12, three hours, four daily).

❶ Getting Around

There are over 400km of paved road on Saaremaa and many more dirt roads. Hitching is not uncommon on the main routes but you'll need time on your hands; there's not much traffic on minor roads.

BICYCLE Many accommodation providers rent bikes. In Kuressaare, **Bivarix** (☎/fax 455 7118; Tallinna mnt 26; bike per day €10; ⊙10am-6pm Mon-Fri) rents bicycles and touring gear such as trailers for kids or luggage.

BUS Local buses putter around the island, but not very frequently. The main terminus is **Kuressaare bus station** (☎453 1661; Pihtla tee 2) and there's a route planner online at www.bussipilet.ee.

CAR & MOTORCYCLE Cars and mopeds can be rented from **PolarRent** (☎513 3660; www.polarrent.ee; Tallinna mnt 9, Kuressaare), a Hertz associate. It's wise to book ahead in summer.

KURESSAARE
POP 15,000

What passes for the big smoke in these parts, Kuressaare has a picturesque town centre with leafy streets and a magnificent castle rising up in its midst, surrounded by the usual scrappy sprawl of housing and light industry. The town built a reputation as a health centre as early as the 19th century, when the ameliorative properties of its coastal mud were discovered and the first spas opened. Now they're a dime a dozen, ranging from Eastern Bloc sanatoriums to sleek and stylish resorts.

Kuressaare exists because of its castle, which was founded in the 13th century as the Haapsalu-based Bishop of Ösel-Wiek's stronghold in the island part of his diocese. The town became Saaremaa's main trading

Saaremaa & Muhu

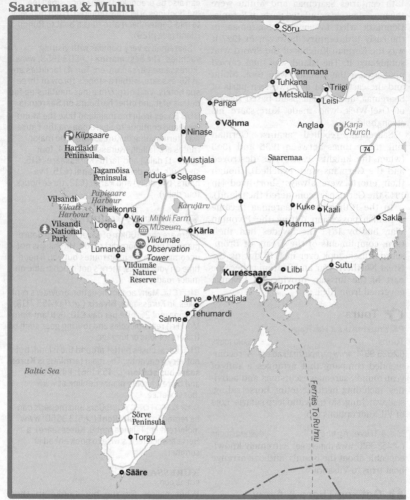

centre, developing quickly after passing into Swedish hands in 1645. In the Soviet era, Kuressaare was named Kingisseppa, after Viktor Kingissepp, an Estonian communist of the 1920s.

◉ Sights & Activities

Kuressaare Castle CASTLE
The majestic Kuressaare Castle stands facing the sea at the southern end of the town, on an artificial island ringed by a moat. It's the best-preserved castle in the Baltic and the region's only medieval stone castle that has remained intact.

A castle was founded in the 1260s, but the mighty dolomite fortress that stands today was not built until the 14th century, with some protective walls added between the 15th and 18th centuries. It was designed as an administrative centre as well as a stronghold. The more slender of its two tall corner towers, Pikk Hermann to the east, is separated from the rest of the castle by a shaft crossed only by a drawbridge, so it could function as a last refuge in times of attack.

Outdoor concerts are held in the castle yard throughout the summer and you can

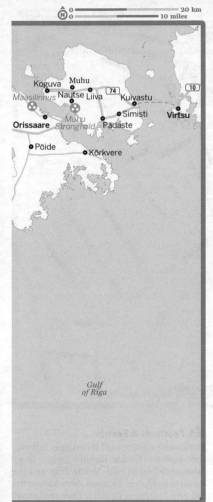

Gulf
of Riga

also hires ice skates when the moat freezes over.

Saaremaa Museum

(www.saaremaamuuseum.ee; adult/child €5/2.50, with audio guide €7; ☉10am-7pm daily May-Aug, 11am-6pm Wed-Sun Sep-Apr) Occupying the castle keep is the Saaremaa Museum, devoted to the island's nature and history. A large part of the fun is exploring the warren of chambers, halls, passages and stairways, apt to fuel anyone's Dungeons & Dragons fantasies. One room near the bishop's chamber looks down to a dungeon where, according to legend, condemned prisoners were dispatched to be devoured by hungry lions (recorded growls reinforce the mental image). Legend also tells of a knight's body found when a sealed room was opened in the 18th century, which has given rise to varying accounts of how he met his tragic fate. Upon discovery the knight's body dissolved into dust but don't worry, it's since been recreated to creepy effect.

In the museum proper, there's not a lot of signage in English until you hit the EU-sponsored post-WWII section, when suddenly the Estonian/Russian captions change to Estonian/English. There's some interesting coverage of daily life under the USSR, including the interior of a typical apartment, but some of the captions of more recent events are quite propagandist (you have to admire the irony of a photo labelled 'a prejudiced pro-Soviet crowd').

On the top floor, the museum has a cafe boasting fine views over the bay and surrounding countryside.

Town Centre   HISTORIC BUILDINGS

The best of Kuressaare's other old buildings are grouped around the central square, Keskväljak, notably the **town hall** (built in 1670), on the eastern side, with a pair of fine stone lions at the door, and the **weigh-house** (now Vaekoja pub) across from it, both 17th-century baroque. There's a handsome **Lutheran church** at the northeast end of Keskväljak and an **Orthodox church** (Lossi 8) further down the road.

Aaviks Museum   MUSEUM

(www.saaremaamuuseum.ee; Vallimaa 7; adult/child €1/50c; ☉11am-6pm Wed-Sun) The Aavik family home is now a small museum dedicated to the life and works of linguist Johannes

also try your hand at archery. There's a **memorial** on the eastern wall to 90 people killed within the castle grounds by the Red Army in 1941.

The shady park around the castle moat that extends to Kuressaare Bay was laid out in 1861 and there are some fine wooden resort buildings in and around it, notably the **Spa Hall** (Kuursaal), which is now a cafe.

If the weather's nice, you can hire rowboats or canoes and float idly along the castle's moat. Boat hire is available at **Lossikonn** (Allee 8; per hr €7); this pretty cafe

Kuressaare

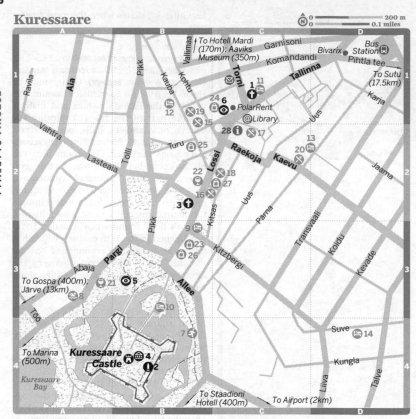

Aavik (1880–1973), who introduced major reforms to the Estonian language, and his musically talented cousin, Joosep Aavik (1899–1989).

Beaches & Water Park   SWIMMING
There's a small sandy beach behind the castle, but the best beach in the immediate area is **Järverand** at Järve, about 14km west. There's also a beach at **Sutu**, 17.5km east. Like many Estonian beaches, they are quite shallow for quite a way out. Buses go to Järve (83c, 20 minutes, about nine daily) but not Sutu.

If the weather means an indoor splash is best, head along to the water park attached to the **Spa Hotel Rüütli** (www.saare maaspahotels.eu; Pargi 12; adult/child €5/3.10; ⊙2-10pm).

Saare Golf   GOLF
(☎453 3502; www.saaregolf.ee; Merikotka 22; 9/18 holes €35/60) Immediately west of town; club hire €20.

✴ Festivals & Events
Kuressaare's dance card is certainly full over the summer. Events include **Opera Days** (www.concert.ee) in mid- to late July, and the **Chamber Music Festival** (www.kammerfest .ee) and **Maritime Festival** (www.merepaevad .ee) in early August. Rock music and beer fans should head to the village of Lilbi, 5km northeast of town, for **Õlletoober** (www .olletoober.ee), where lashings of the two are served over a weekend in mid-July. There are also regular summer concerts held in the castle grounds and park; find out what's up at the tourist office.

🛏 Sleeping
The tourist office can organise beds in private apartments and farms across the island. Hotel prices listed here are for summer – they're up to 50% cheaper from September through April. Spas are open to nonguests.

Kuressaare

◉ Top Sights
Kuressaare Castle B4

◉ Sights
1 Lutheran Church C1
2 Memorial B4
3 Orthodox Church B2
4 Saaremaa Museum B4
5 Spa Hall B3
Town Hall ....(see 28)
6 Weigh-house C1

◆ Activities, Courses & Tours
7 Lossikonn B4
8 Spa Hotel Rüütli A3

◎ Sleeping
9 Arensburg B3
10 Ekesparre Residents Hotell B3
11 Grand Rose Spa Hotel C1
12 Johan Spa Hotel B1
13 Karluti Hostel C2
14 Ovelia D4

◎ Eating
15 Chameleon B1
16 Classic Cafe B2
17 RAE Supermarket C2
18 Sadhu C2
19 Vanalinna B1
20 Veski Trahter C2

◎ Drinking
21 John Bull A3
22 Vinoteek Prelude B2

◎ Shopping
23 Antiigiaed B3
24 Central Market C1
25 GoodKaarma B2
26 Lossi Antiik B3
27 Saaremaa Kunstistuudio C2

ⓘ Information
28 Kuressaare Tourist Office C2

TOP CHOICE **Karluti Hostel** GUESTHOUSE €
(☑501 4390; www.karluti.ee; Pärna 23; s €13, tw €25-56; 🛜) A charming older couple run this cheerful mustard-coloured guesthouse, set on large lawns on a quiet residential street close to the centre. If you work up an appetite on the volleyball court, you can always sate it in the guest kitchen. There are only a handful of bright, spotless rooms available, so you'll need to

book ahead – especially in summer. For the price, it's excellent.

Gospa RESORT €€€
(☑455 0000; www.gospa.ee; Tori 2; s/d/ste from €70/108/191; 🅿🛜❄) Kuressaare's funkiest hotel, Gospa (formally the George Ots Spa Hotel, named after a renowned Estonian singer) has modern rooms with wildly striped carpet, enormous king-sized beds, CD players and a warm but minimalist design. Most rooms have balconies, and there's a pool, fitness centre and spa. Apartments are also available (see the website), and families are very well catered to.

Arensburg BOUTIQUE HOTEL €€€
(☑452 4700; www.arensburg.ee; Lossi 15; s €75-100, d €93-170, ste €247; 🅿🛜❄) Arensburg is almost two hotels in one, with a split personality and severe case of old versus new. Our vote goes to the bold and sexy charcoal-painted rooms in the slick 2007 extension to the historic hotel (standard rooms in the old wing are OK but unremarkable). A new spa and two restaurants round things out nicely.

Ekesparre Residents Hotell BOUTIQUE HOTEL €€€
(☑453 3633; www.ekesparre.ee; Lossi 27; s/d €160/166; 🅿🛜) Holding pole position on the castle grounds, this elegant 10-room hotel has been returned to its art nouveau glory. Exquisite period wallpaper, Tiffany lamps and a smattering of orchids add to the refined, clubby atmosphere, while the 3rd-floor guests' lounge is a gem. As you'd expect from the price, it's a polished operator. Prices rise by €19 on the weekend.

Grand Rose Spa Hotel HOTEL €€€
(☑666 7000; www.grandrose.ee; Tallinna 15; s €100, d €115-150, ste €190; 🅿🛜❄) Floral and frilly is the theme of this hotel, from the baroque black velvet chairs, chandeliers and water feature in the rose-filled lobby to the rose carpet throughout. Deluxe rooms have a balcony, separate bathtub and shower stall, and over-the-top beds, but feel more crammed than the standard rooms. The spa and restaurant have both garnered a reputation as among the town's best.

Staadioni Hotell HOTEL €€
(☑453 3556; www.staadionihotell.ee; Staadioni 4; s/d €40/51; ☼May-Sep; 🅿) Good-value

spacious and bright rooms are available at this pleasant, secluded spot, 1km south of the centre, surrounded by parkland and sports facilities. Bikes can be hired here.

Hotell Mardi
HOTEL €€

(📞452 4633; www.hotelmardi.eu; Vallimaa 5a; hostel dm/s/d/tr €13/20/26/39, hotel s €43, d €62-68; P🛜) Summer hostel and year-round hotel with simple, fuss-free rooms, attached to a college.

Ovelia
GUESTHOUSE €

(📞455 5732; www.ovelia.ee; Suve 8; d/tr €33/47; ⊙May-Sep; @) Friendly Ovelia is a budget guesthouse with small, basic rooms plus a garden area. Some rooms have private bathroom, some have TV – it's worth having a look before committing.

Johan Spa Hotel
HOTEL €€

(📞454 0000; www.johan.ee; Kauba 13; r old/new block €70/100; P🛜⚊) Johan has a split personality. The old wing is unconscionably ugly, with a facade that looks like it's about to fall off and rooms that are characterless and overpriced. The new wing is slick and minimalist, but still a little overpriced.

🍴 Eating & Drinking

To be honest, none of Kuressaare's restaurants knocked our socks off.

Veski Trahter
ESTONIAN €€

(www.veskitrahter.eu; Pärna 19; mains €7-11) How often can you say you've dined inside a windmill from 1899? Without being too touristy, this place keeps quality and ambience at a premium, with plenty of hearty local fare – including wild boar hotpot, cabbage soup, Saaremaa cheeses.

Sadhu
CAFE €

(Lossi 5; meals €5-11; ⊙8.30am-midnight Mon-Fri, 11am-1am Sat, 11am-10pm Sun; 🛜) With Indian fabrics billowing, Asian carvings and Gypsy music playing, Sadhu has certainly passed Hippy Chic 101. It's Kuressaare's best chill-out spot (perfect for a little night tipple), offering a belly-comforting blackboard menu of fish dishes, hearty hotpots and salads, along with a drool-inducing cake display. If it wasn't for the push-button coffee, we'd love it.

Vinoteek Prelude
WINE BAR €€

(www.prelude.ee; Lossi 4; mains €9-12; ⊙4pm-midnight) A cute bunch of grapes heralds the entrance to this cosy, dimly lit wine bar.

Climb the staircase to sofas under the eaves and choose from a menu of international wines (plenty by the glass), antipasti-style snacks and bistro meals.

Classic Cafe
CAFE €

(Lossi 9; mains €4-11) A laid-back menu (all-day breakfasts – a rarity in Estonia) and relaxed, stylish decor are the hallmarks of this, um, classic cafe. You can order meaty dishes from the grill, but better value are the fresh salads, soups and pasta dishes.

Vanalinna
CAFE €€

(📞455 5309; Kauba 8; mains €6-15; ⊙8am-7pm Mon-Sat, 8am-4pm Sun) There's an appealing vibe in this bakery cafe, with its timber-and-stone interior and black-and-white photos hanging from orange walls.

Gospa
EUROPEAN €€

(📞455 0000; Tori 2; mains €7-17; ⊙noon-11pm) Picture windows make the most of the marina views in Gospa hotel's bright and airy dining room. The food is light, fresh and creative, if not always perfectly executed, making good use of local produce.

Chameleon
CAFE-BAR €

(www.chameleon.ee; Kauba 2; mains €6-10) Chameleon is indeed a changeable creature, morphing from cafe to cocktail bar as the sun goes down, but it's the latter incarnation that suits it best. The sleek black and grey decor (with pink lighting) adds an air of city-slick, but it's not too cool to offer a kids' menu and playroom.

John Bull
PUB

(Pargi 4; ⊙11am-2am; 🛜) In the park surrounding the castle, this pub (not particularly English, despite its name) has a great moatside outdoor deck and a bar made from an old Russian bus.

RAE Supermarket
SUPERMARKET

(Raekoja 10; ⊙9am-10pm) Behind the tourist office.

🛍 Shopping

Lossi Antiik
ANTIQUES

(www.lossiantiik.ee; Lossi 19) Towards the castle, Lossi Antiik sells all sorts of antiques, from 19th-century farm tools to Soviet memorabilia. It's a fun place to browse.

Antiigiaed
ANTIQUES

(Lossi 17) Right next door to Lossi Antiik, this summer-only 'antiques garden' is a treasure-strewn shed opening onto a courtyard cafe.

Central Market   MARKET
(Tallinna) Next to Vaekoja pub you'll find dolomite vases, wool sweaters, honey, strawberries and other Saaremaa treats and tat.

Saaremaa Kunstistuudio   ART
(✆453 3748; Lossi 5) This bright gallery contains a variety of works by Estonian artists, including covetable textiles, ceramics, sculptures and paintings.

GoodKaarma   SOAP
(www.goodkaarma.com; Kauba 3) If you don't make it to the farm you can always buy GoodKaarma's organic soap here.

❶ Information

Kuressaare Tourist Office (✆453 3120; www.kuressaare.ee; Tallinna 2; ✇9am-6pm Mon-Fri, 10am-4pm Sat & Sun, Mon-Fri only mid-Sep–mid-May) Inside the old town hall, it sells maps and guides, arranges accommodation and has information on boat trips and island tours.

Library (Tallinna 6; ✇10am-7pm Mon-Fri, 10am-4pm Sat) Free internet access.

❶ Getting There & Around

See p133 for more Saaremaa travel information. Taxi services include **Kuressaare Takso** (✆453 0000; www.kuressaaretakso.ee) and **Saare Takso** (✆453 3333); there are ranks at the bus station, and opposite the Grand Rose Hotel.

AROUND SAAREMAA

Even in summer, it's relatively easy to beat the worst of the tourist hordes. Outside of Kuressaare there are sandy beaches, mystifying old ruins and windswept peninsulas with hardly a soul in sight, all waiting to be explored. The following Sights section is listed in the order you'd reach them if you were following an anticlockwise loop around the island from Kuressaare.

◎ Sights & Activities

GoodKaarma   FARM
(✆5348 4006; www.goodkaarma.com; Kuke; ✇10am-6pm Jun-Aug, other times by arrangement) Run by an English-Estonian couple from their farm outside the village of Kaarma, about 15km north of Kuressaare, GoodKaarma makes organic soaps from local ingredients such as juniper, pine and sea-buckthorn berries. If you're interested in getting your hands dirty (or should that be clean), you can book into a 75-minute soap-making workshop (adult/child €7.50/4; minimum four people). Also on site is a pretty garden

---

WWOOF-ING

If you don't mind getting your hands dirty, an economical and enlightening way of travelling around Estonia involves doing some voluntary work as a member of **Worldwide Opportunities on Organic Farms** (WWOOF; ✆505 5683; www.wwoof.ee) – also known as 'Willing Workers on Organic Farms'. Membership of this popular, well-established international organisation (which has representatives around the globe) provides you with access to the WWOOF Estonia website, which at the time of research listed 26 organic farms and other environmentally sound cottage industries throughout the country. In exchange for daily work at these farms, the owner will provide food, accommodation and some hands-on experience in organic farming. Check the website for more information.

---

terrace and cafe-bar, with homemade snacks, organic teas, local beers etc. Besides soap, the shop sells local arts and crafts.

Kaali Crater   METEORITE CRATER
Perhaps proof of its powers of attraction, Estonia has one of the world's highest concentrations of documented meteor craters. At Kaali, 18km north of Kuressaare, is a 100m-wide, 22m-deep, curiously round lake formed by a meteorite at least 4000 years ago. There are a further eight collateral craters in the vicinity, ranging from 12m to 40m in diameter, formed from the impact of fragments of the same meteorite. In Scandinavian mythology, the site was known as the sun's grave. A tourist village of sorts has sprung up here – there's a small **museum** (adult/child €1.30/65c), handicrafts stores (including a lace workshop) and a hotel, as well as an old-style tavern offering Estonian fare and locally brewed beer.

St Mary's Church   CHURCH
Pöide, 3km south of the main road, was the Saaremaa headquarters of the German Knights of the Sword and this church, built in the 13th and 14th centuries, remains an imposing symbol of their influence. During the St George's Night Uprising of 1343 the knights were besieged within the church for eight days. Their Estonian assailants

ISLAND BREW

Saaremaa has a long history of beer home-brewing and even its factory-produced brew has a great reputation. Tuulik, with its distinctive windmill branding, is the most popular, but don't mention that it's now brewed in Tartu (the popular Saaremaa vodka also has a windmill on its label and it's not distilled here either). The country's second-biggest beer festival takes place near Kuressaare in mid-July, showcasing both sophisticated and feral brews and with plenty of live music and festivities.

Beer-lovers should be sure to try any homemade beer wherever it's offered. A longtime island tradition, the brew features the traditional malt, yeast and hops, but comes off a bit sour on the palate. It's light and refreshing, best quaffed from a wooden tankard on a warm summer's day.

assured them that if they surrendered no swords would be raised against them. True to their word, and proving that pagans have a sense of humour, they stoned the Germans to death. Nowadays the church serves Lutheran, Methodist and Orthodox congregations and its crumbling exterior is offset by a perfect stained-glass window above the altar.

Tika Talu HORSE RIDING
(☑504 4169; www.tikatalu.ee; Kõrkvere: per hr €12) Offers simple B&B accommodation plus plenty of horseback action for adults and kids.

Maasilinnus CASTLE
The German knights built this castle, 4km north of Orissaare, during the 14th to 16th centuries. It was blown up by the Danes in 1578 to prevent the Swedes from taking it, leaving behind a jumble of stones by a pretty reed-lined shore. Indulge your inner archaeologist by exploring the restored underground chamber.

Angla Windmill Hill WINDMILLS
(Angla Tuulikumägi; adult/child €2/1; ⊙9am-9pm) Charge up those camera batteries; this is the site of the largest and most photogenic grouping of wooden windmills on the islands. By the early 16th century there

were already nine windmills on this hill. Now there are four small ones, mainly dating from the 19th century, and one large Dutch-style one, built in 1927. There are excellent (free) views from the road, but the modest admission charge allows you to poke around in their innards. There's also a collection of old tractors and ploughs, and an excellent tavern-style cafe where peasant-dressed staff dispense homemade bread, cakes and beer.

Karja Church CHURCH
(Karja Kirik; ⊙10am-5.30pm mid-May–mid-Sep) The pagan and Christian meet in this fortresslike 14th-century church. Outside there's an interesting panel about pre-Christian symbols with particular reference to some of the 13th- and 14th-century trapezoidal gravestones found here. Inside, oak leaves curl along the top of the columns. Also interesting is the unusual carved crucifixion scene above the exterior door on the right-hand side, showing Jesus between the two thieves. The good thief's soul (in mini-me form) is exiting through his mouth into the arms of an angel, ready to whisk him off to heaven. A similar-looking devil is awaiting the other.

Leisi VILLAGE
Leisi is a pretty village of old wooden houses, 3.5km from the harbour of Triigi. If you're arriving from Hiiumaa via the Sõru-Triigi ferry, pick up maps and get general Saaremaa information at the tiny **Leisi tourist office** (☑457 3073; ⊙noon-7pm Jun-Aug; 🐾), inside the pretty, vine-covered restaurant, Sassimaja.

Tahkuna BEACH
Tucked away within the forest, Tahkuna is one of Saaremaa's best sandy beaches, due in large part to its remoteness. Turn north at Metsküla (right if you're following the anticlockwise route) and after about 3km look out for the sign marked 'Puhkekoht' (resort) on your left. The beach is about 200m from the second car park.

Panga pank VIEWPOINT
Saaremaa's highest cliffs run along the northern coast near Panga for 3km. The highest point (21.3m) was a sacred place where sacrifices were made to the sea god; gifts of flowers, coins, vodka and beer are still sometimes left here. It's a pretty spot, looking down at the treacherous waters below.

Folk Windmills WINDMILLS

On the side of the road, some 7km north of Mustjala at Ninase (on the Ninase Peninsula), are two of Saaremaa's kitschier icons. This pair of clunky wooden windmills has been painted to resemble a giant mama and papa in traditional costume.

Pidula Trout FISHING

(www.saarepuhkus.ee; Pidula; trout per kg €12.90; ⊙10am-10pm) Set on a pretty lake about 1km west of Pidula, you can 'fish' for trout here in stocked ponds and then smoke or grill your catch. It's a lovely spot for a DIY meal on a sunny summer evening. Other activities on offer include canoeing, paintball and a sauna, and there's accommodation on site (see p142).

Tagamõisa Peninsula PENINSULA

Much of the beautiful and rarely visited western coast of the Tagamõisa Peninsula is protected as part of Vilsandi National Park, including the Harilaid Peninsula. At its northwestern tip (accessible only on foot),

is the striking Kiipsaare lighthouse, which began leaning at a steep angle towards the sea from the early 1990s. In a fortuitous twist, in recent times the lighthouse has righted itself again, largely thanks to beach erosion (the same thing that led it to lean in the first place), although now it sits about 30m out to sea.

St Michael's Church CHURCH

Kihelkonna village has a tall, austere, early-German church, dating from before 1280. It's dark and gloomy inside, partly due to the wooden supports holding up the roof.

Mihkli Farm Museum FARM

(Talumuuseum; www.saaremaamuuseum.ee; Viki; adult/child €1.50/1; ⊙10am-6pm Wed-Sun mid-Apr–mid-May & Sep–mid-Oct, daily mid-May–Aug) In a pretty setting southeast of Kihelkonna, this 18th-century farm has been preserved in its entirety, complete with thatched-roof wooden farmhouses, a sauna and a traditional village swing.

ESTONIA SAAREMAA

WORTH A TRIP

VILSANDI

Vilsandi, west of Kihelkonna, is the largest of 161 islands and islets off Saaremaa's western coast protected under the Vilsandi National Park (which also includes parts of Saaremaa itself, including the Harilaid Peninsula). The park covers 238 sq km (163 sq km of sea, 75 sq km of land) and is an area of extensive ecological study. The breeding patterns of the common eider and the migration of the barnacle goose have been monitored very closely here. Ringed seals can also be seen in their breeding season and 32 species of orchid thrive in the park.

Vilsandi, 6km long and in places up to 3km wide, is a low, wooded island. The small islets surrounding it are abundant with currant and juniper bushes. Around 250 bird species are observed here, and in spring and autumn there is a remarkable migration of waterfowl: up to 10,000 barnacle geese stop over on Vilsandi in mid-May, and the white-tailed eagle and osprey have even been known to drop by.

The National Park Visitor Centre (☑454 6880; www.vilsandi.info; ⊙9am-5pm) is on Saaremaa, at Loona Manor (p142), but there are no displays in English and no English-speaking staff (at least not when we last visited). If you're keen to visit, you're better off talking (in advance) to the staff at Loona Manor itself or the tour operators we've listed on p133.

One of few places to stay on the island is Tolli Turismitalu (☑5342 5318; www.tolli .vilsandi.info; sites per person €3, s €20-35, d €40-55), a tourist farm offering an idyllic setting amid the island's beauty. Its homestead is the oldest on the island and accommodation is available here, inside a summer house or in a windmill. Camping is possible, as is sauna rental, bike and boat hire, and nature trips. They're tied in with Vilsandi Line (☑520 2656; harri61@hot.ee), which from May to September makes semiregular trips between Papisaare and Vikati (five times a week); reservations are required. You can also book the boat (or snowmobile when the water's iced up) at nonscheduled times for a negotiated rate.

Islander (☑5667 1555; www.islander.ee; ⊙May-Sep; 🕸) offers speedboat trips to the island, diving, waterskiing, tubing and accommodation at Kusti Tourist Farm.

Viidumäe Nature Reserve FOREST

Founded in 1957, Viidumäe Nature Reserve covers an area of 19 sq km, with a 22m **observation tower** on Saaremaa's highest point (54m), about 25km west of Kuressaare. The tower (about 2km along a dirt road off the Kuressaare–Lümanda road at Viidu) offers a panoramic view of the reserve and the wonders of the island itself. The view is particularly memorable at sunset. There are two **nature trails** (2.2km and 1.5km), marked to highlight the different habitats of the area. Viidumäe is a botanical reserve, its favourable climate and conditions making it home to rare plant species. At the reserve's **headquarters** (☑457 6442; www.viidumae.ee; Audaku; ☺10am-6pm Jun-Aug), near the tower, you can see a small exhibition and book guided tours.

Sõrve Peninsula PENINSULA

Small cliffs, such as the **Kaugatoma pank** (bank) and **Ohessaare pank**, rear up along the west coast of the 32km-long southwestern Sõrve Peninsula. Legend has it that the cliffs were formed when the devil tried in vain to wrench this spit of land from the mainland to separate Suur Tõll, who was vacationing on Sõrve, from Saaremaa. This is where the island's magic can really be felt. A bike or car trip along the coastline will reveal fabulous views.

This sparsely populated strip of land saw heavy fighting during WWII, and the battle scars remain. By the **lighthouse** at Sääre, on the southern tip, you can walk around the ruins of an old **Soviet army base**. Other bases and the remnants of the Lõme-Kaimri anti-tank defence lines still stand. There's a large **monument** at Tehumardi, south of the beach at Järve, which was the site of a gruesome night battle in October 1944 between retreating German troops and an Estonian-Russian Rifle Division. The horror defies belief: both armies fought blindly, firing on intuition or finding the enemy by touch. Russian-Estonian dead lie buried in double graves in the cemetery nearby.

🛏 Sleeping & Eating

Loona Manor GUESTHOUSE €€

(☑454 6510; www.loonamanor.ee; Loona; sites per person €5, r/ste €83/103; ☺May-Oct; P🄿) Loona may be a 16th-century manor house but it's more homey than palatial, with simple, clean rooms and roomier suites. Vilsandi National Park's visitor centre is within the grounds, but you'll find the friendly staff at the manor a better bet for information in English. You can also hire bikes (per day €10), two-person canoes (€26), inflatable boats (four hours €32) and skis (€7).

Hotell Saaremaa HOTEL €€

(☑454 4100; www.saarehotell.ee; Mändjala; r €77-102; P🄿) It feels a little lost in time and space, but this low-key hotel has trim rooms and a pleasant outdoor terrace, plus a Thalasso spa. Best of all, it's right by Mändjala beach (see p136).

Värava Talu TOURIST FARM €

(☑5645 1606; www.varava.fie.ee; Selgase; sites per person €1.60, s/d €10/20; @) In a forested area along the idyllic northern coast, this pretty tourist farm offers rustic accommodation in wooden cabins and old barnhouses. Camping is possible, and the owners rent bicycles and offer hiking tours. It's located near Selgase, just off the Kihelkonna–Mustjala road.

Sõrve Turismitalu TOURIST FARM €

(☑452 3061; www.saaremaa.ee/sorve; Torgu; cabins €32, houses €87-130; P🄿) Near the village of Torgu on the Sõrve Peninsula, in rugged windswept surrounds, this complex offers rustic cabins and comfy, fully equipped holiday houses. It's 20 minutes' walk from the sea; boat trips can be arranged.

Kämping Karujärve CAMPGROUND €

(☑454 2181; www.karujarve.ee; sites per person €4, cabins €24; ☺mid-May–mid-Sep) Among the trees on the east side of Karujärv, a lake some 9km east of Kihelkonna (5.5km north from Kärla), this campground offers sheltered camp sites, windowless A-frame cabins and boat rental in a pretty locale.

Mändjala Kämping CAMPGROUND €

(☑454 4193; www.mandjala.ee; Mändjala; sites per person €3, cabins €55-170; ☺May-Sep; P@🄿) Heaving in high summer (with capacity for 1000 people), this camping ground 10km west of Kuressaare offers rustic wooden cabins and camp sites amid lots of pine-filled greenery. It's a short walk to the beach, and water sports are available, as are sauna and bike rental (per hour/day €3/13). There's a bar and restaurant.

Saare Puhkus CAMPGROUND €€

(☑680 6235; www.saarepuhkus.ee; Pidula; sites/ dm per person €5/7, s €26-29, d €39-45; P🄿) At the trout farm (p141), accommodation is available for campers in simple cabins or in rooms in the 'big house'. We particularly love the tiny hut on the island in the river.

Söögimaja SAAREMAAN RESTAURANT €
(☑457 6493; www.soogimaja.planet.ee; Lümanda; mains €4-9; ☺10am-10pm) This rustic farmhouse eatery is on the main road in Lümanda, right next door to the village church, and provides a unique snapshot into island life via its cuisine. The menu features the kind of food eaten by the island's forefathers – fish soup, boiled pork with turnips and carrots, and cabbage rolls.

Matsalu National Park

A twitcher's paradise, Matsalu National Park (Matsalu Rahvuspark) is a prime bird-migration and breeding ground, both for the Baltic and for Europe. Some 282 different bird species have been counted here. Encompassing 486 sq km of wetlands (including 20km-long Matsalu Bay, the deepest inlet along the west Estonian coast), it was first protected as a reserve in 1957 before being declared a national park in 2004.

Spring migration peaks in April/May, but swans arrive as early as March. Autumn migration begins in July and can last until November. Birdwatching towers, with extensive views of resting sites over various terrain, have been built at Keemu, Suitsu, Penijõe, Kloostri, Haeska and Puise. There are two marked **nature trails**, one at Penijõe (5km), another at Salevere (1.5km). Bring reliable footwear, as the ground is wet and muddy.

The reserve's headquarters is 3km north of the Tallinn–Virtsu road at Penijõe, an early-18th-century manor house near Lihula. Here you'll find a **nature centre** (☑472 4236; www.matsalu.ee; ☺9am-5pm daily mid-Apr–Sep, Mon-Fri Oct–mid-Apr) with a permanent exhibition and a free 20-minute film. With advance notice, the centre can hook you up with guides offering tours of the reserve, from two-hour canoe trips around the reed banks to several days of birdwatching. It can also recommend lodging in the area.

Estonian Nature Tours (☑5349 6695; www.naturetours.ee), based in nearby Lihula, employs naturalist guides who have a wealth of knowledge about Matsalu's avian riches. Every Saturday from May to September they offer bus and boat tours (per person €40) and guided canoe tours (per two-person

canoe €70), and rent bikes for a self-guided tour (per day €20).

Haapsalu
POP 11,600

Set on a fork-shaped peninsula that stretches into Haapsalu Bay, this quaint resort town (100km from Tallinn) makes a fine stopover en route to the islands. Haapsalu has a handful of museums and galleries, and a few rather modest spa hotels, but the town's biggest attraction is its striking castle. A bit rough around the edges, Haapsalu's Old Town is more rustic than urban, with old wooden houses set back from the narrow streets, a slender promenade skirting the bay and plenty of secret spots for watching the sunset.

Those seeking mud or spa treatments might opt for Haapsalu over Pärnu or Kuressaare, though the centres here are a bit more proletarian. Nevertheless, Haapsalu lays claim to superior mud, which is used by health centres throughout Estonia.

History
Like other Estonian towns, Haapsalu has changed hands many times since its founding. The German Knights of the Sword conquered this region in 1224, and Haapsalu became the bishop's residence, with a fortress and cathedral built soon afterwards. The Danes took control during the Livonian War (around 1559), then the Swedes had their turn in the 17th century, but they lost it to the Russians during the Great (but brutal) Northern War in the 18th century.

The city flourished under the tsars, mostly because of mud. Once the curative properties of its shoreline were discovered in the 19th century, Haapsalu transformed into a spa centre. The Russian composer Tchaikovsky and members of the Russian imperial family visited the city for mud baths. A railway that went all the way to St Petersburg was completed in 1907. In Soviet times, Haapsulu was closed to foreigners.

◉ Sights & Activities

Haapsalu Episcopal Castle CASTLE
(Piiskopilinnus; www.haapsalulinnus.ee; adult/child €3/2; ☺10am-6pm Jun-Aug, 10am-4pm May & Sep) Haapsalu's unpolished gem is its bishop's castle, which was western Estonia's centre of command from the 13th to 16th centuries but now stands in partial but very

Haapsalu

picturesque ruins. A turreted tower, most of the outer wall and some of the moat still remain. In summer, the park within the outer walls is used for concerts. There's a wonderful **children's playground**, complete with a pirate ship, and a **viewing platform** within one of the towers.

Entry to the grounds is free year-round, but a ticket is required to enter the castle proper, where there's a **museum** devoted to its history, including some creepy tunnels and dramatically displayed medieval weaponry. Accessed from within the museum is the striking **Dome Church** (or, more officially, St Nicholas' Cathedral), built in a mix of the Romanesque and Gothic styles, with three inner domes. It's the largest such structure in the Baltic and its acoustics are said to be phenomenal; concerts are regularly held here. Inside the church, keep your eyes peeled for the ghost of the White Lady (see the boxed text p146).

Promenaadi   WATERFRONT

Nineteenth-century Russian toffs, like their counterparts in Victorian England and Paris' *belle époque*, liked nothing more than a good see-and-be-seen promenade, and the premier strolling route was along the waterfront. The route passes by the magnificent pale-green-and-white **Haapsalu Kuursaal** (Spa Hall, 1897), which functions as a restaurant in summer. Sculptures dating from Haapsalu's fashionable era are scattered along the promenade, including a sundial commemorating mud-cure pioneer Dr Carl Abraham Hunnius and the symphony-playing **Tchaikovsky Bench**, erected in 1940 (sadly out of order on our last visit).

People still take to the waters at pint-sized **Africa Beach** (Aafrikarand), despite the water being murky and full of weeds. It earned its name from the statues of wild animals that used to grace the shoreline

Haapsalu

◎ **Top Sights**
    Haapsalu Episcopal Castle C2

◎ **Sights**
  1 Birdwatching tower D1
  2 Estonian Railway Museum
    Haapsalu C4
    Haapsalu Kuursaal .... (see 13)
  3 Ilon's Wonderland D2
  4 Läänemaa Museum D2
  5 St John's Church D2
  6 Tchaikovsky Bench C1

◎ **Activities, Courses & Tours**
  7 Fra Mare Thalasso Spa A4
  8 Rowboat Rental A3

◎ **Sleeping**
  9 Endla Hostel C3
  10 Kongo Hotell C3
  11 Suur-Lossi Guesthouse C2
  12 Vanalinna Hostel D2

◎ **Eating**
  13 Haapsalu Kuursaal C1
  14 Hermannuse Maja C2
  15 Konsum D4
  16 Market C4
  17 Müüriääre Kohvik C2

(and which were sadly used as firewood by Soviet soldiers in the 1940s). There's another excellent **children's playground** here.

Haapsalu Bay is one of the key habitats for migrating waterfowl in Estonia and is listed as a Ramsar Wetland of International Importance (www.ramsar.org). During their spring and autumn migrations as many as 20,000 birds descend. If you know your gadwalls from your grebes and fancy a gander at a goosander, head up the **birdwatching tower**, just south of the beach. Keep an eye out for circling white-tailed eagles.

Ilon's Wonderland   GALLERY
(Iloni Imedemaa; www.muuseum.haapsalu.ee; Kooli 5; admission €5; ⊙11am-6pm daily May-Aug, Wed-Sun Sep-Apr) Showcasing the works of Estonian-Swedish illustrator Ilon Wikland, who spent her childhood in Haapsalu and is best known for her illustrations of Pippi Longstocking books, this gallery is fabulously set up for kids, with many artworks hung at their viewing level.

Läänemaa Museum   MUSEUM
(www.muuseum.haapsalu.ee; Kooli 2; adult/child €2/50c; ⊙10am-6pm Wed-Sun May-Sep, 11am-4pm Wed-Sun Oct-Apr) The somewhat dry regional museum offers a glimpse of the region's history, with a recreated peasants' house, grocer's store and pharmacy, boating paraphernalia and early-20th-century dresses; there's very little signage in English. It's set in an 18th-century building that was at one time the town hall. Directly behind the museum is the 16th-century **St John's Church** (Jaani Kirik; Kooli).

Museum of the Estonian Swedes   MUSEUM
(Rannarootsi Muuseum; www.aiboland.ee; Sadama 32; adult/child €2/1.50; ⊙10am-6pm Tue-Sat May-Aug, 11am-4pm Tue-Sat Sep-Apr) This quaint museum has relics, photos, old fishing nets and a marvellous tapestry tracing the history of Swedes in Estonia from the 1200s to their escape back to Sweden on the *Triina* in 1944.

Estonian Railway Museum Haapsalu   MUSEUM
(Eesti Raudteemuuseum Haapsalus; www.jaam.ee; Raudtee 2; adult/child €2/1; ⊙10am-6pm Wed-Sun) Haapsalu's colourful former train station, with its wooden lace ornamentation and grand colonnade, was opened in 1907 to transport the Russian nobility to the spa resort. Designed to keep the royals dry, its 214m-long covered platform was said then to be the longest in the Russian empire. This boxcar-sized museum records the golden years of train travel and there are old locomotives to explore nearby.

Paralepa Forest Park   BEACH
On the western edge of town, beyond the train station, is this park with a popular beachfront. It's better than Afrika Beach and despite being a bit swampy it attracts plenty of sunseekers in the summer, with **rowboat rental** (☑5660 3144; per hr €7) nearby. If you want to experience Haapsalu's magic mud, the neighbouring **Fra Mare Thalasso Spa** (☑472 4600; www.framare.ee; Ranna tee 2) offers treatments (€29 to €48), along with a pool, sauna and gym.

★☆ Festivals & Events

Haapsalu has a packed calendar of concerts and festivals, with the action concentrated between June and August.

A GHOSTLY VIGIL

Haapsalu's biggest annual event, the **White Lady Festival**, coincides with the August full moon. The day begins with merriment – storytelling for the kids, theatre for the adults – and culminates with a ghastly apparition. During the full moon every August and February, moonlight at a precise angle casts a ghostly reflection across a cathedral window. According to legend, the shadow is cast by a young girl who, in the 14th century, was bricked up alive inside the walls. Back then, the castle was an all-male enclave, and the archbishop got pretty worked up when he heard that a young woman, disguised in monastic vestments, sneaked in to be close to her lover-monk. In August excited young crowds stay out late to see a play recounting the story in the castle grounds, after which everyone gathers around the wall to await the shadow.

Haapsalu Horror & Fantasy Film Festival CINEMA
(www.hoff.ee) The town is overtaken by zombies during this creepy, kooky weekend festival, held to coincide with the full moon (around April).

Early Music Festival MUSIC
(www.haapsalu.ee) Held in July and making full use of the magnificent acoustics of the Dome Church.

August Blues MUSIC
(www.augustibluus.ee) Over two days in early August, this is Estonia's biggest blues festival.

White Lady Festival CULTURAL
(Valge Daami Päevad) The biggest annual event, held in August; see the boxed text p145.

Sleeping

Kongo Hotell HOTEL €€
(☎472 4800; www.kongohotel.ee; Kalda 19; s/d/apt/ste €61/74/83/157; Wi-Fi) The unassuming exterior gives little indication of Kongo's stylish, Scandi-chic decor – all caramel-coloured walls, neutral linens and pale wooden floors. Rooms are on the small side but the double apartments, with kitchenette, have more cat-swinging room. And the name? A rough drinking den once stood on this spot, known for its brawling. The place was nicknamed 'Kongo' after the African country suffering through civil war at the time.

Suur-Lossi Guesthouse GUESTHOUSE €
(☎5568 4956; www.suurlossi.net; Suur-Lossi 6; s/d €13/32) There's loads of history in this rustically restored old home, full of quirky, artistic touches and blessed with a superb garden. Downstairs, a single and twin room share a bathroom; upstairs is a large room sleeping up to five. Guests share a lovely living space and sunroom. Hardly any English is spoken but it's a fabulous, character-filled option, and cheap to boot.

Vanalinna Hostel HOSTEL €
(☎473 4900; www.vanalinnabowling.ee; Janni 4; d without/with bathroom €33/42; Wi-Fi) Above a family-friendly bowling alley and right by the castle, this good-value option has neat, TV-free rooms on offer, plus a communal kitchen.

Endla Hostel HOSTEL €
(☎473 7999; www.endlahostel.ee; Endla 5; s/tw/tr €25/35/45; Wi-Fi) A decent budget option on a quiet street, with small, bright quarters and a guest kitchen. No dorms.

Eating & Drinking

Müüriääre Kohvik CAFE €
(www.muuriaare.ee; Karja 7; mains €3-6; ⏲10am-8pm Sun-Thu, 10am-10pm Fri & Sat) With more umlauts in its name than seems reasonable (the name means 'beside the walls'), this gorgeous cafe is clearly the town's favourite, if the crowds are anything to go by. And what's not to love in the warm interior, pretty rear terrace, cabinet full of cakes, and simple menu of fresh, tasty, light meals such as salads and quiche.

Haapsalu Kuursaal CAFE €€
(www.haapsalukuursaal.ee; Promenaadi 1; mains €7-12; ⏲noon-10pm May–mid-Sep) This fairytale confection sits plumb on the waterfront, surrounded by rose gardens. Stepping into the cavernous hall is like stepping back into a more genteel time, with cake cabinets at one end, a small stage at the other (used for summer concerts) and staff scuttling about in 1930s uniforms. The ambience trumps the food but it's certainly worth checking out.

Hermannuse Maja PUB €
(www.hermannus.ee; Karja 1a; mains €4-9; Wi-Fi) With a warm and inviting atmosphere, this

pub-restaurant serves hearty meals (pasta, schnitzel, pork chops, steaks etc) and it's a cosy spot just for a drink.

Market
MARKET

(Turg; Jaama; ◷7am-2pm Tue-Sun) For fresh fruits and vegetables visit the market, a few blocks east of the bus station. Don't miss fresh strawberries in summer.

Konsum
SUPERMARKET

(cnr Tallinna mnt & Posti) A large supermarket positioned in the middle of Haapsalu's main shopping precinct

ⓘ Information

Haapsalu Tourist Office (☏473 3248; www .haapsalu.ee; Karja 15; ◷9am-5pm daily mid-May–mid-Sep, Mon-Fri mid-Sep–mid-May) This friendly, well-staffed office has loads of info about Haapsalu and the surrounding area.
Library (Posti 3; ◷10am-6pm Tue-Fri, 10am-3pm Sat) This striking iron and limestone building offers free internet access. The town art gallery (Linnagalerii) is next door.

ⓘ Getting There & Away

The **bus station** (Jaama 1) is at the pretty but defunct train station. Major destinations include Tallinn (€7, two hours, 17 daily), Tartu (€12, 4½ hours, daily) and Pärnu (€8.30, 2½ hours, daily). For Hiiumaa, there are also two daily buses to Kärdla (2¾ hours) but only two per week to Käina (2½ hours).

Ferries to Hiiumaa and Vormsi leave from Rohuküla, 9km west of Haapsalu.

ⓘ Getting Around

You can rent bicycles at **Vaba Aeg Rattad** (☏521 2796; Karja 22; bikes per hr/day €2.30/12). Bus 1 runs regularly between Lossi plats, the train station and Rohuküla (the ferry wharf, 9km west); timetables are posted at Lossi plats and the bus station.

Hiiumaa
POP 11,100

Hiiumaa, Estonia's second-biggest island (1000 sq km), is a peaceful and sparsely populated place with some agreeable stretches of coast and a forest-covered interior. The island has less tourist development than Saaremaa, with considerably fewer options for lodging and dining. There's also less to do and see, but most visitors that come here are content simply to breathe in the fresh sea air and relax.

Scattered about Hiiumaa you'll find picturesque lighthouses, eerie old Soviet bunkers, empty beaches and a nature reserve with over 100 different bird species. Those seeking a bit more activity can hike, horse ride or indulge in various water sports. And the good news is that, thanks to the island's microclimate, the weather here is considerably warmer than on the mainland, 22km away.

Given their relative isolation from mainland Estonia, it's not surprising that the islanders have a unique take on things, and a rich folklore full of legendary heroes, such as Leiger, who had nothing to do with Kalevipoeg (the hero over on the mainland). People who move onto the island must carry the name *isehakanud hiidlane* (would-be islanders) for 10 years before being considered true residents. Hiiumaa is also said to be a haven for fairies and elves, ancestors of those born on the island. Modern-day Hiiumites rarely discuss this unique aspect of

---

HIIUMAA HANDICRAFTS

Handicraft hunters will find fertile ground in Hiiumaa, where traditional crafts are experiencing a minor resurgence. One of the best outlets is the museum shop in Kassari (see p153), which carries top-quality woven woollen rugs, among other things. The following are also worth checking out:

» **Heltermaa Crafts House** (Heltermaa Käsitöömaja; www.heltermaakasitoomaja.edicy pages.com; Heltermaa; ◷11am-6.30pm) If you've got time to kill before the ferry docks, stop in here for knitted socks, honey, wooden salad servers or the ubiquitous woven cloth rugs.

» **Wool Factory** (Hiiu Vill; www.hiiuvill.ee; Vaemla; ◷8am-6pm Mon-Fri, 10am-6pm Sat & Sun, closed Sun mid-Sep–mid-May) This small mill, 4km east of Käina, still uses 19th-century weaving and spinning machines to produce traditional knitwear. You can rug up in the sweaters and mittens for sale, or stock up on wool to knit your own. There's a sweet summer cafe on site.

Hiiumaa & Vormsi

20 km
10 miles

Rohuküla

Diby
Sviby
Vormsi
Hullo
Rumpo

Saxby

Saxby Lighthouse

Heltermaa

Suuremõisa

Airport

80

Kassari Chapel

Vaemla

Kassari

Kärdla

Hiiumaa Museum

Kassari

Lehtma

Käina

Tahkuna tuletorn

Orjaku

Säare Tirp

Tahkuna peninsula

Military Museum

Hill of Crosses

Malvaste

Minikh Farm Museum

Kõrgessaare

Hiiumaa

Sõru

Kõpu tuletorn

Kõpu

Kõpu Peninsula

Ristna tuletorn

Baltic Sea

their family tree, however, as this can anger their elusive relatives.

For further information about the island, see www.hiiumaa.ee.

ⓘ **Getting There & Away**

AIR There are **Avies** (U3; ✆680 3501; www.avies .ee) flights between Kärdla and Tallinn at least daily.

BOAT Most people arrive in Hiiumaa on the **SLK Ferries** (✆452 4444; www.tuulelaevad .ee) service from Rohuküla to Heltermaa (adult/ child/vehicle €2.56/1.28/7.68, 1½ hours, five to seven daily). There's usually no need to book ahead unless you're taking a car at popular times (ie leaving Friday evening/Saturday morning and returning on Sunday afternoon; some of these boats have a 50% surcharge for vehicles). Bookings cost about €2 extra and require your vehicle registration. Foot passengers can buy their tickets from vending machines inside the ferry terminal while drivers queue up in the vehicle lane and purchase their ticket at the booth. For ferry services between Hiiumaa (Sõru) and Saaremaa (Triigi), see p133.

BUS There are two daily buses between Kärdla and Tallinn (€12, 4½ hours, two daily) and one between Käina and Tallinn (€11, 4¼ hours, daily); both also stop in Suuremõisa, Heltermaa, Rohuküla and Haapsalu.

ⓘ **Getting Around**

Paved roads circle Hiiumaa and cover several side routes; the rest are dirt roads. There are petrol stations at Kärdla and Käina. Many accommodation providers can arrange car or bike hire, as can **Jaanus Jesmin** (✆511 2225; www.carrent.hiiumaa.ee) in Kärdla, which rents out cars from €20 per day.

Buses, nearly all radiating from Kärdla but some from Käina, get to most places on the island, though not very often. Schedules are posted inside the bus station in Kärdla and online at www.hiiumaa.eu.

SUUREMÕISA

Meaning 'large estate', Suuremõisa village is spread out around a blocky 18th-century manor house (Suuremõisa loss) which once belonged to the rich baronial Ungern-Sternberg family. It's certainly seen better days and is now looking very unkempt, with many of its windows painted over, but the leafy grounds are pleasant enough in an untidy kind of way.

More interesting is the nearby Pühalepa Church, the oldest building on Hiiumaa, dating from the 13th century. Twentieth-century stained glass enlivens the simple whitewashed structure and if you like poking around graveyards, there are some rare circular crosses to be spotted.

Allika Guesthouse (✆462 9026; www.allika .com; Suuremõisa; s €35, d €50-70) was originally the servants quarters of the manor house. The rooms are airy and country-style but vibrantly modern. The driveway entrance is opposite the small shop on the edge of the village.

KÄRDLA

POP 3700

Hiiumaa's 'capital' grew up around a cloth factory founded in 1829 and destroyed during WWII. It's a green town full of gardens and tree-lined streets, with a sleepy atmosphere and few diversions. Still, it's Hiiumaa's centre for services of all kinds and if you need to stock up on provisions, it has a couple of supermarkets.

The town sits on the edge of the world's 'best-preserved Palaeozoic meteorite crater', not that you'd know it as, despite being 4km in diameter, it's barely visible. It's fair to say that you wouldn't want to have been visiting here 455 million years ago when the impact occurred.

⊙ **Sights**

Pikk Maja MUSEUM
(www.muuseum.hiiumaa.ee; Vabrikuväljak 8; adult/child €2/1; ⊙10am-5pm Tue-Sat) The Long House was once home to the cloth-factory bigwigs but now has so-so displays related to the factory, along with work from local artists.

Beach BEACH
While not spectacular, Kärdla's beach is pleasant enough, with a sandy shoreline edged by Rannapark, an expanse of lawns and forest partly built on the site of a Swedish cemetery.

🛏 **Sleeping**

TOP CHOICE **Kivijüri Külalistemaja** B&B €€
(✆469 1002; www.hot.ee/kivijuri; Kõrgessaare mnt 1; s/d €30/40; 🅿🛜) This cosy, bright-red country house has only four pleasant rooms, each one pleasant and with TV and bath-room. Breakfast is excellent (one of the best we had in Estonia) and there's a backyard patio and a lawn to unwind on. Tenters are welcome, and the hospitable owner can help arrange bike and car rental. A fine choice.

Padu Hotell HOTEL €€
(✆463 3037; www.paduhotell.ee; Heltermaa mnt 22; s/tw €40/50, apt €60-75; 🅿@🛜🎱) If you're

staying here you may feel like you're sleeping inside a sauna, with the pleasant pine motif taken to extremes: walls, floors, ceilings, doors, furniture. The rooms are cosy and decently equipped, all with balconies, but the apartments are quite a bit bigger and some have their own saunas. There's also a communal sauna with a small pool, and an on-site cafe.

Nordtooder　　　　　　GUESTHOUSE €€
(☎509 2054; www.nordtooder.ee; Rookopli 20; s/d/tw €40/52/65) Very smart rooms are on offer at this central guesthouse, with antique furnishings, plasma TVs and black-and-white tiled bathrooms. You can also hire cars and bikes.

✗ Eating & Drinking

Linnumäe Puhkekeskus　　　　PUB €
(☎462 9244; Heltermaa mnt; mains €4-11; �11.30am-7pm Sun-Thu, 11.30am-9pm Fri & Sat; ☎) The outdoor deck at this restaurant-bar holds plenty of appeal for an afternoon beer, or you can opt to enjoy a meal inside. The menu holds few surprises but it's well priced and well executed, with big portions the name of the game. Try the tasty trout with Béarnaise sauce. It's on the outskirts of town, 500m past Padu Hotell.

Rannapaargu　　　　　　CLUB €
(www.rannapaargu.ee; Lubjaahju 3; mains €4-11; �noon-11pm Mon-Thu, noon-4am Fri & Sat, noon-9pm Sun) This pyramid-shaped restaurant has large windows overlooking the beach, plus an outdoor terrace. The food isn't up to much but come the weekend around 300 people descend to party along to the island's best DJs. It doesn't kick off until well after midnight.

Gahwa Cafe　　　　　　CAFE €
(Põllu 2a; �10am-6pm Mon-Fri, 10am-2pm Sat) A pretty pit stop, this cafe offers light meals such as soup or quiche, but is better for cake.

❶ Information

Kärdla Tourist Office (☎462 2232; www.hiiumaa.eu; Hiiu 1; �10am-6pm Mon-Fri, 10am-2pm Sat & Sun, Mon-Fri only mid-Sep—mid-May) This friendly centre distributes maps and can help arrange accommodation and guides. It also sells the Lighthouse Tour, a 40-page driving tour of the island in English (€1.60). The office is housed in an old fire tower.

Library (Rookopli 18; �10am-6pm Mon-Fri, 10am-2pm Sat) Internet access.

Tiit Reisid (☎463 2077; www.tiitreisid.ee; Sadama 13; �8am-5pm) Run by Hiiumaa experts, this travel agency inside the bus station arranges accommodation and tours.

WESTERN HIIUMAA

The western half of the island is sparsely populated, even for Estonia. Knobbly Tahkuna Peninsula was the scene of a vicious battle between German and Soviet troops during WWII. On the road leading to the lighthouse, and especially on the winding dirt road heading eastwards from here towards Lehtma, you'll see deserted Soviet military installations, including a complete underground bunker which you can wander through; bring a torch (flashlight).

The island ends at the narrow Kõpu Peninsula, stretching due west like an index finger pointing straight at Stockholm. If you've been to a few Estonian beaches and refuse to believe that anyone could surf here, be prepared to be proved wrong. At Ristna, where the peninsula protrudes out into the Baltic currents, waves of up to 10m have been seen. It's a dangerous stretch with rips that will do their darndest to deliver you on the doorstep of Finland, but for experienced surfers it's a blast.

Sõru, where the ferries leave for Saaremaa, is a beautiful spot, with a reed-lined forested shore stretching out in both directions.

◉ Sights

Hill of Crosses　　　　　MEMORIAL
(Ristimägi) Northern Hiiumaa had a population of free Swedish farmers until they were forced to leave on the orders of Catherine the Great, with many ending up in Ukraine on the false promise of a better life. This mound (only in flat Estonia could it be called a hill) beside the main road, 7km west of Kärdla, marks the spot where the last 1000 Swedish people living on Hiiumaa performed their final act of worship before leaving the island in 1781. It has become a tradition for first-time visitors to Hiiumaa to brave the mosquitoes to lay a homemade cross here.

Mihkli Farm Museum　　　　FARM
(Mihkli talumuuseum; www.muuseum.hiiumaa.ee; admission €1; �10am-6pm Wed-Sun Jun-Aug) At Malvaste, 2km north of the Kärdla–Kõrgessaare road, this (originally Swedish) farm complex gives an authentic taste of early rural life, including a working smoke sauna for hire, which can hold up to 10 people (€50 to heat, then €16 per hour). It's a unique,

old-fashioned experience – but not recommended for sensitive eyes.

Military Museum MUSEUM
(Militaarmuuseum; www.militaarmuuseum.ee; adult/child €2/1; ⏱10am-6pm Tue-Sun mid-May–mid-Sep) Despite a lack of English captions, this small museum is quite engrossing. There are big items of military hardware to peruse in the yard, while inside there are uniforms, photographs, posters and a room devoted to the Young Pioneers.

Tahkuna tuletorn LIGHTHOUSE
(adult/child €2/1; ⏱10am-7pm Tue-Sun May–mid-Sep) Dating from 1874, this 43m lighthouse watches over the peninsula's northwest tip. According to Soviet military lore concerning the battle that raged in this vicinity, the Red Army fought to the bitter end, their last man climbing to the top of the lighthouse and flinging himself off while still firing at the Germans. If you're planning on climbing all three of the island's lighthouses, a combined ticket is available for €5.

Beyond the lighthouse stands an eerie **memorial** to the victims of the *Estonia* ferry disaster. Facing out to sea, the 12m-tall metal frame encases a cross from the bottom of which a bell with sculpted children's faces is suspended; it only rings when the wind blows with the same speed and in the same direction as that fatal night in September 1994, when the *Estonia* went down.

Between the memorial and the lighthouse is a curious low **stone labyrinth**, a replica of an ancient one found on the island. The idea is that you follow the path between the stones as a form of meditation.

Kõpu tuletorn LIGHTHOUSE
(adult/child €2/1; ⏱10am-8pm May–mid-Sep) With its pyramid-like base and stout square tower, the inland Kõpu lighthouse is the best-known landmark on Hiiumaa and the third-oldest continuously operational lighthouse in the world. A lighthouse has stood on this raised bit of land since 1531, though the present white limestone tower was rebuilt in 1845. At 37m high, it can be seen 55km away. The neighbouring cafe shares the same hours as the lighthouse and concerts are staged on the lawns in summer.

MS ESTONIA: CONSIGNED TO MYSTERY

About 30 nautical miles northwest of Hiiumaa's Tahkuna Peninsula lies the wreck of the ferry *Estonia*, which sank during a storm just after midnight on 28 September 1994, en route from Tallinn to Stockholm. Only 137 people survived the tragedy, which claimed 852 lives in one of Europe's worst maritime disasters.

The cause of the tragedy remains the subject of contention and burgeoning conspiracy theory. In 1997 the final report of the Joint Accident Investigation Commission (JAIC), an official inquiry by the Estonian, Swedish and Finnish governments, concluded that the ferry's design was at fault and the crew were probably underskilled in emergency procedures. The report claimed the bow gate was engineered inadequately for rough sailing conditions and that during the storm the visor was torn from the bow, exposing the car deck to tonnes of seawater that sank the *Estonia* completely within one hour. Escape time for the 989 people on board was estimated at only 15 minutes and they were denied access to lifeboats due to the sudden list and sinking of the ferry. For those who did escape, the freezing conditions of the water that night reduced survival time to only minutes.

The integrity of the report was questioned after dissent within the JAIC became public. In 2000 a joint US-German diving expedition and new analyses of the *Estonia*'s recovered visor prompted theories of an explosion on board. Conspiracy theorists claim that the *Estonia* was transporting unregistered munitions cargo, as an illicit trade in weapons was to be curtailed with new export laws about to come into effect. Claims of a cover-up have been bolstered by the alleged disappearance of eight crew members, initially listed as survivors.

Unexplained interference with the wreck, along with the Swedish government's dumping of sand to stabilise it in 2000, further fuelled conspiracy claims and calls for a new inquiry. The governments of Estonia, Finland and Sweden are resolute that the ferry will remain where it sank as a memorial to the dead; an estimated 700 people are thought to be inside.

Ristna tuletorn
LIGHTHOUSE

(adult/child €2/1; ☉10am-7pm Tue-Sun May–mid-Sep) Kõpu Peninsula's second lighthouse stands in all its blazing red glory at the western tip of the peninsula (Stockholm is just over 200km west of here). It was brought to Hiiumaa by freighter from Paris where it was made, together with the lighthouse at Tahkuna. There's a small bar here serving drinks and snacks.

Surf Paradiis
WATER SPORTS

(☑505 1015; www.paap.ee/eng/suvi; ☉mid-May–Sep) Set on a stretch of sandy beach about 1km down a rough road from Ristna (the turn-off is just before you reach the lighthouse), this smooth operator is an unexpected treat. Here, you can undertake any number of activities: windsurfing, kite surfing, kayaking, tubing, jet-skiing, scuba diving, kayak-snorkelling (to a WWII wreck), ATV (all-terrain vehicle) safaris, waterskiing etc. Plus there are kid-friendly options such as banana boats and water trampolines. If the weather's good, there's no better place on the island to hang out – but it's a good idea to call ahead, as all activities are weather-dependent, and the place is sometimes booked solid by groups. A day pass for the 'water park' costs €30 and includes use of boogie boards, water trampoline, kayaks, skim boards, zip lines (from the roof of the sauna into the sea), snorkelling, sauna and sun lounges, often accompanied by live music.

For very experienced surfers, tow-in surfing is offered where you'll be taken out to the big breakers by jet ski and then released. Ristna is a surprisingly demanding surfing spot, so don't attempt to go it alone without first co-ordinating with the centre, which operates a professional rescue service.

🛏 Sleeping & Eating

Surf Paradiis
RESORT €

(☑505 1015; www.paap.ee/eng/suvi; Ristna; upturned boat/bungalow/villa €6/32/50; ☉mid-May–Sep) You can overnight here in various kooky options: hammocks, tepees, beach bungalows or on the sand in a surfboard bag or under an upturned boat. The log-built Paradise Villa sleeps up to 15 in three bedrooms and is fully self-contained, with its own sauna. The offers vary, so enquire directly about options; we've given only indicative prices above.

Randmäe Puhketalu
CAMPGROUND €

(☑5691 3883; www.puhketalu.ee; Tahkuna Peninsula; sites per 1/2 people €6/10, barn s/d €16/29, cottage s/d €65/115; ⓟ☎) Less than 1km north of Malvaste, this friendly, family-run place offers loads of space and rustic accommodation in its barn rooms – low on frills but rich in character. A small cottage, sleeping four, is also available. It's an excellent location 200m from a sandy beach (kayaks and boats are available for hire, as are bikes and cars).

Kalda Puhketalu
CAMPGROUND €

(☑462 2122; www.kaldapuhketalu.ee; Tahkuna Peninsula; sites €2.60 plus €2 per person, cabins €58, houses €160-205; ☎ⓟ☎) Just north of Randmäe Puhketalu and also close to the beach, you can rent simple wooden cabins (with shared bathrooms and communal kitchen) and larger holiday houses, sleeping up to eight people. A sauna (two hours €48), bikes (per day €10) and boats (per hour €3.20) are available.

Viinaköök
PUB, GUESTHOUSE €€

(☑517 8640; www.viinakook.com; Sadama 2, Kõrgessaare; s/d €60/80) Set in a photogenic 1880s stone building (once a distillery), Viinaköök offers reasonable rooms with shared bathrooms; some have two bedrooms sharing a bathroom and lounge (perfect for families). The rates include breakfast, dinner buffet and evening sauna; there's a two-night minimum stay. The pub below offers a reasonable all-you-can-eat buffet (€9.60) between noon and 8pm.

KÄINA
POP 2140

Hiiumaa's second-largest settlement is a nondescript place, apart from the ruins of a fine 15th-century stone church, which was wrecked by a WWII bomb. On the western edge of Käina is the Rudolf Tobias Museum (Rudolf Tobiase Majamuuseum; www.muuseum.hiiumaa.ee; Hiiu mnt; adult/child €2/1; ☉10am-6pm Wed-Sun mid-May–mid-Sep), housed in the humble 1840 wood-and-thatch home of Rudolf Tobias (1873–1918), composer of some of Estonia's first orchestral works. There's not much in English but the delightful staff do their best to explain everything. There's a windmill out the back.

🛏 Sleeping & Eating

Hotell Liilia
HOTEL, RESTAURANT €€

(☑463 6146; www.liiliahotell.ee; Hiiu mnt 22; s/d €36/41; ☎) Set in a two-storey building across from the church ruins in Käina, Liilia offers tasteful, well-kept rooms with pale wooden floors and ceilings. There's also a popular restaurant (mains €4 to €8), with a pleasant terrace for the summer months, serving simple but tasty local fare.

Tondilossi
GUESTHOUSE €€

(☎528 8405; www.tondiloss.ee; Hiiu mnt 11; r per adult/child €20/10) This is a comfortable wooden lodge fronting the supermarket car park, offering comfy, no-frills rooms with shared bathrooms. There's also a spacious garden with a sauna; bike rental is available.

KASSARI
POP 90

Thickly covered with mixed woodland and boasting some striking coastal scenery, this 8km-long island is linked to Hiiumaa by two causeways that virtually cut off Käina Bay from the open sea. The bay is an important bird reserve, serving as a breeding ground for about 70 different species. You can get a good view of the avian action from the **birdwatching tower** north of Orjaku, where you'll also find a short walking trail. During the hot summer months a large part of the bay dries up and becomes nothing more than a mud field.

◉ Sights & Activities

Hiiumaa Museum
MUSEUM

(www.muuseum.hiiumaa.ee; adult/child €2/1; ◷10am-6pm daily May-Oct, Mon-Fri Nov-Apr) Just inland of the main road, a short distance west of the Sääre Tirp fork, is this small museum with its collection of artefacts and exhibits on Hiiumaa's history and biodiversity. Among the curiosities: a 1955 Russian-made TV, the jewel-like prism of the 1874 Tahkuna lighthouse and the stuffed body of the wolf that allegedly terrorised the island until its 1971 demise. It also has excellent handicrafts for sale.

Sääre Tirp
SWIMMING, WALKING

Southern Kassari narrows to a promontory with some unusual vegetation and ends in a thin 3km spit of land, the tip of which juts out into the sea. Legend has it that it's the remains of an aborted bridge that local hero Leiger started to build to Saaremaa, to make it easier for his relative, Saaremaa's hero Suur Tõll, to visit and join in various heroic acts. It's a beautiful place for a walk and there's a small but surprisingly popular reedy beach on the way. As for Leiger, there's a statue of him at the Sääre Tirp fork, carrying a boulder on his shoulder.

Kassari Chapel
CHURCH

Another enjoyable walk, ride or drive is to the pretty, whitewashed, thatch-roofed, 18th-century chapel at the east end of Kassari. A sign 'Kassari Kabel' directs you down a dirt road from the easternmost point of the island's sealed road. A path continues nearly 2km to a small bay in Kassari's northeastern corner.

Kassari Ratsamatkad
HORSE RIDING

(☎518 9693; www.kassari.ee; per hr/day €10/40) On the road to the chapel, Hiiumaa's largest horse farm offers a range of excursions including multiday treks through forests and along untouched coastline.

🛏 Sleeping & Eating

TOP CHOICE Dagen Haus
GUESTHOUSE €€

(☎518 2555; www.dagen.ee; Orjaku; r €65-89; P🐾🛜) At the western end of Orjaku is one of Hiiumaa's most attractive options – an environmentally restored former granary with rough-hewn walls, timber beams and five stylish modern bedrooms, all set in big green grounds. The gorgeous communal lounge and kitchen will have you plotting to move in permanently. The owners have appealing holiday houses on offer too, sleeping up to 12 people (€99 to €199). Book well ahead.

Vetsi Tall
CAMPGROUND, TAVERN €

(☎462 2550; www.vetsitall.ee; sites/cabins per person €3.20/16, apt €96; P) On the main road between Orjaku and the fork to Sääre Tirp, Vetsi Tall is a campground set around a dark atmospheric tavern (mains €3 to €5), dating from 1843. Tiny barrel-shaped wooden cabins are set amid apple trees and there's a comfortable three-room apartment above the tavern (three-night minimum stay) and a sauna.

Kiigeplats Camping
CAMPGROUND €

(☎469 7169; sites €5) Sheltered basic camping (longdrop toilets, fire ring) is available near the swimming beach on the way to Sääre Tirp. Pay at Lest & Lammas, where there are also showers and nicer toilets.

Lest & Lammas
BARBECUE RESTAURANT €

(Kassari village; mains €5-12; 🛜) Abandoned factories are a dime a dozen in Estonia, but cool conversions like this one are scarce. The name means 'flounder and sheep' and the emphasis is on grilled fish and (beautifully marinated) lamb, along with barbecued beef and pasta dishes. Or you can just share a bottle of wine under a thatched shelter on one of the landscaped terraces.

Vormsi

POP 240

Vormsi, Estonia's fourth-biggest island (93 sq km), rose from the sea around 3000 years ago and continues to rise at a rate of 3mm per year (its highest point is a modest 13m above sea level and is apparently a hiding place for trolls). Except for its voracious mosquitoes, the island has only ever been sparsely inhabited and as a consequence its forests, coastal pastures and wooded meadows have remained relatively undisturbed. Swedes arrived in the 13th century and before WWII they formed the overwhelming majority of the island's then 2500 residents. They fled back to Sweden en masse during WWII and few have returned.

The island, 16km from east to west and averaging 6km from north to south, is a good place to tour by bicycle; there is about 10km of paved road. From the ferry, it's 1.5km to the village of Sviby. The cheerfully named Hullo, Vormsi's largest village, lies about 3km west of here. You'll spot ruins of a Russian Orthodox church within an old collective farm, right by the Hullo turn-off. Two kilometres south of here is the much smaller Rumpo (these people really do have a way with names!), sitting on an attractive juniper-covered peninsula jutting into Hullo Bay. Much of the island, including the 30 islets in Hullo Bay, is protected as part of the Vormsi Landscape Reserve (Vormsi Maastikukaitseala; http://vormsi.silma.ee). Wild critters include elk, roe deer, lynx and boar.

Sights

The island doesn't have a tourist office but there are information boards near the ferry wharf.

Pearsgarden Farmstead Museum   FARM
(Sviby; adult/child €2/50c; ⊙10am-4pm Wed-Sun) The island's Swedish heritage is kept alive in this restored farmstead, including the inhabitants' distinctive fashion sense (the women wore chunky red socks to emphasise their ankles as strong legs were a sex symbol; nobody wanted a wife who couldn't perform heavy manual work).

St Olaf's Church   CHURCH
There's a colourful little statue of the saint in the niche above the door of this blocky, whitewashed 14th-century church, just out of Hullo. It has a fine baroque painted pulpit and a collection of old Swedish

wheel-shaped crosses (they borrowed the idea from the Celts) in the graveyard, northwest of the church.

Saxby Lighthouse   LIGHTHOUSE
Built in 1864, this 24m lighthouse is a short walk from Saxby, the island's westernmost settlement, which is itself 7km from Hullo.

Church Rock   BOULDER
(Kirikukivi) This 5.8m-high erratic boulder stands near Diby in the northeast.

Sleeping & Eating

You can find more options online (www .vormsi.ee) or at the tourist office in Haapsalu. Both places listed here rent out bicycles and boats, have saunas, and include breakfast in the price.

Rumpo Mäe Farm   GUESTHOUSE €€
(Rumpo Mäe Talu; ☑472 9932; www.rumpomae.ee; sites per adult/child €3/2, d/tr €44/57; ☞) Just a few steps from the coast at Rumpo, this handsome thatched-roof farmhouse offers Vormsi's best accommodation. Rooms in the main house have an old-style ambience, and guests have access to a kitchen and grill. More basic accommodation is offered in a rustic sauna house (per person/whole house €25/182) and the eight-bed 'small house' (whole house €115 to €130). A single-night surcharge applies.

Elle-Malle Külalistemaja   GUESTHOUSE €€
(☑5467 2854; www.ellemalle.com; Hullo; s/d €24/40) In a peaceful location between Hullo and St Olaf's Church, this friendly guesthouse has tidy rooms in the main house, a romantic double inside a windmill or rooms inside a separate wooden cottage.

Hullo Kauplus   SELF-CATERING
(Hullo; ☞) Stock up on victuals in Hullo's small general store; there's an internet point attached.

Getting There & Around

Vormsi lies just 3km off the Estonian mainland. **Veeteed** (☑443 1069; www.veeteed.com) runs a ferry on the 10km route between Rohuküla and Sviby two to three times daily (return ticket per adult/child/car €6.40/3.20/14, 45 minutes). If you're taking a vehicle in the summer, reserve a place in advance.

By the ferry, **Sviby Bike & Boat Rental** (☑5695 5635; www.vormsi.ee/sviby; ⊙late May-Sep) doesn't just rent bikes (per 1½/8/24 hours €4/7/10) and rowboats (per hour €4), it also runs a water-taxi service (€40 to the mainland, daytime only) and tours around the island. Accommodation providers generally offer these services too.

UNDERSTAND ESTONIA

Estonia Today

The long, grey days of Soviet rule are well behind Estonia. Today, first-time visitors are astonished by the gusto with which the country has embraced the market economy. The new environment has created previously unimagined possibilities. Entrepreneurship is widespread (the developers of Kazaa, the peer-to-peer file-sharing software, and Skype, which allows free telephone calls over the internet, are Estonian), and the economy has diversified considerably since 1991.

Estonia has been lauded as the outstanding economic success story of the former Soviet Bloc. It has joined the EU, North Atlantic Treaty Organization (NATO), Organisation for Economic Co-operation and Development (OECD) and, in 2011, the Eurozone. Its large-scale privatisation, free-trade agreements and low corporate taxes have brought in enormous foreign investment, mainly in the finance, manufacturing and transport sectors. The effect on economic growth has been pronounced: from 2000 to 2007, real GDP growth averaged 8.8% per year – a remarkable achievement for such a tiny newcomer.

With capitalism's booms come the inevitable busts, and Estonia wasn't immune to the global economic crisis, falling into recession in 2008 and 2009. Growth has returned (with estimates hovering between 3.3% and 5.9% for 2011) but so has inflation, coming in at 5.1% per annum in March 2011, the second-highest in the EU. Estonia was, however, the only EU member to post a budget surplus in 2010 – a feat achieved partly through selling off its pollution quotas; it's expected to dip slightly into deficit again in 2011.

Economic improvements don't seem to have lifted the country's mood any; it ranks near the bottom of the OECD's *Better Life Initiative* results, with only 24% of Estonians saying they were satisfied with their life. Despite its gains, the average gross monthly wage is only €792 and Estonia still has the fifth-lowest GDP per capita in the EU (ahead of only Latvia, Lithuania, Bulgaria and Romania). Although the number of people living below the poverty line has fallen, wage disparities continue to grow, and the cost of goods continues to rise faster than salaries. Pensioners have been the hardest hit, as Estonia's social-welfare infrastructure struggles to keep up.

In the realm of education, Estonia has made enormous steps in ensuring students are prepared for the future, and today its schools and towns are among the most wired-up in the world. Internet and mobile-phone usage per capita is higher here than in many other parts of the EU; in 2005 Estonians even began voting online.

Having politically and economically shaken off the Soviet era, Estonia's gaze is very much to the West and the north. Its people view themselves as having more in common (linguistically and culturally) with their Finnish neighbours than they do with Latvia and Lithuania to their south, and see the 'Baltic countries' label as a handy geographic reference but not much more. There's even talk of further cementing ties with Finland by building a tunnel under the Gulf of Finland to connect the two countries, but the cost of such a venture is likely to be prohibitive.

Meanwhile, as Estonia looks to the West, its ongoing disputes with its large neighbour to the east have continued and tensions between the ethnic Estonian population and the ethnic Russian minority linger. These were brought to the fore in April 2007, when the Estonian government relocated the Bronze Soldier (a Soviet-era WWII memorial) from downtown Tallinn. Many ethnic Estonians considered the statue a symbol of Soviet occupation and repression. At the same time, the monument has significant value to Estonia's ethnic Russians as it remembers those killed battling Nazi Germany in the 'Great Patriotic War'. The

WAGE INEQUALITY & SALMON SANDWICHES

According to Eurostat, Estonian men earn an average of 31% more than Estonian women, which is the largest gender income gap in the EU. In a creatively obscure protest to highlight this gap (*lõhe*), participating cafes and restaurants sold sandwiches made from salmon (which is also *lõhe* in Estonian) at a 30% surcharge when served with dill (in Estonian *till,* which doubles as a childish word for penis).

disputes surrounding the relocation peaked with two nights of riots in Tallinn (including one death) and the besieging of the Estonian embassy in Moscow for a week.

Russian nationalists were widely blamed for a cyber attack on Estonia that same month, which took out much of the country's internet infrastructure. Websites for the country's government departments, banks, newspapers and other commercial operators were all forced offline. As a result, NATO set up an anti-cyberterrorism centre in Tallinn, which opened in May 2008. The centre, in an old military barracks, brings together experts from Western countries to analyse cyber threats and develop counterstrategies.

If Estonia hopes to further integrate with the West and improve relations with Russia, a series of public gatherings of Waffen-SS veterans and a small, unofficial commemoration of the 70th anniversary of the German invasion (held in Viljandi in 2011) will do little to help their cause. The latter was condemned by both the local Jewish community and the Simon Wiesenthal Centre. Says centre director Efraim Zuroff, 'No one is disputing that the Estonian population suffered under the Soviet Union. But to celebrate the Nazi invasion, in which 99.3 percent of Estonia's Jews ended up being murdered, is unacceptable.'

History

Beginnings

Estonia's oldest human settlements date back 10,000 years, with Stone Age tools found near present-day Pärnu. Finno-Ugric tribes from the east (probably around the Urals) came centuries later – most likely around 3500 BC – mingling with Neolithic peoples and settling in present-day Estonia, Finland and Hungary. They took a liking to their homeland and stayed put, spurning the nomadic ways that characterised most other European peoples over the next four millennia.

The Christian Invasion

By the 9th and 10th centuries AD, Estonians were well aware of the Vikings, who seemed more interested in trade routes to Kyiv (Kiev) and Istanbul than in conquering the land. The first real threat came from Christian invaders from the south.

Following papal calls for a crusade against the northern heathens, Danish troops and German knights invaded Estonia, conquering the southern Estonian castle of Otepää in 1208. The locals put up fierce resistance and it took well over 30 years before the entire territory was conquered. By the mid-13th century Estonia was carved up between the Danish in the north and the German Teutonic Order in the south. The Order, hungry to move eastward, was powerfully repelled by Alexander Nevsky of Novgorod on frozen Lake Peipsi (marvellously imagined in Sergei Eisenstein's film *Alexander Nevsky*).

The conquerors settled in at various newly established towns, handing over much power to the bishops. By the end of the 13th century cathedrals rose over Tallinn and Tartu, around the time that the Cistercian and Dominican religious orders set up monasteries to preach to the locals and (try to) baptise them. Meanwhile, the Estonians continued to rebel.

The most significant uprising began on St George's night (23 April) in 1343. It started in Danish-controlled northern Estonia when Estonians pillaged the Padise Cistercian monastery and killed all of the monks. They subsequently laid siege to Tallinn and the bishop's castle in Haapsalu and called for Swedish assistance to help them finish the job. The Swedes did indeed send naval reinforcements across the gulf, but they came too late and were forced to turn back. Despite Estonian resolve, by 1345 the rebellion was crushed. The Danes, however, decided they'd had enough and sold Estonia to the Livonian Order (a branch of the Teutonic Order).

The first guilds and merchant associations emerged in the 14th century, and many towns – Tallinn, Tartu, Viljandi and Pärnu – prospered as trade members of the Hanseatic League (a medieval merchant guild).

Estonians continued practising nature worship and pagan rites for weddings and funerals, though by the 15th century these rites became interlinked with Catholicism and they began using Christian names. Peasants' rights disappeared during the 15th century, so much so that by the early 16th century most Estonians became serfs (enslaved labourers bought and sold with the land).

The Reformation, which originated in Germany, reached Estonia in the 1520s, with Lutheran preachers representing the initial wave. By the mid-16th century the church had been reorganised, with churches now under Lutheran authority and monasteries closed down.

THE SOURCE OF EESTI

In the 1st century AD the Roman historian Tacitus described a people known as the 'Aestii'. In rather crude fashion he depicted them as worshipping goddess statues and chasing wild boars with wooden clubs and iron weaponry. These peoples collected and traded amber. Although Tacitus was describing the forerunners to the Lithuanians and Latvians, the name 'Aestii' was eventually applied specifically to Estonians.

The Livonian War

During the 16th century the greatest threat to Livonia (now northern Latvia and southern Estonia) came from the east. Ivan the Terrible, who crowned himself the first Russian tsar in 1547, had his sights clearly set on westward expansion. Russian troops, led by ferocious Tatar cavalry, attacked in 1558, around the region of Tartu. The fighting was extremely cruel, with the invaders leaving a trail of destruction in their wake. Poland, Denmark and Sweden joined the fray, and intermittent fighting raged throughout the 17th century. Sweden emerged the victor.

Like all wars, this one took a heavy toll on the inhabitants. During the two generations of warfare (roughly 1552 to 1629), half the rural population perished and about three-quarters of all farms were deserted, with disease (such as plague), crop failure and the ensuing famine adding to the war casualties. Except for Tallinn, every castle and fortified centre in the country was ransacked or destroyed – including Viljandi Castle, once among northern Europe's mightiest forts. Some towns were completely obliterated.

The Swedish Era

Following the war, Estonia entered a period of peace and prosperity under Swedish rule. Although the lot of the Estonian peasantry didn't improve much, cities, boosted by trade, grew and prospered, helping the economy speedily recover from the ravages of war. Under Swedish rule, Estonia was united for the first time in history under a single ruler; this period is regarded as an enlightened episode in the country's long history of foreign oppression.

The Swedish king granted the Baltic-German aristocracy a certain degree of self-government and even generously gave them lands that were deserted during the war. Although the first printed Estonian-language book dates from 1535, the publication of books didn't get under way until the 1630s, when Swedish clergy founded village schools and taught the peasants to read and write. Education received an enormous boost with the founding of Tartu University in 1632.

By the mid-17th century, however, things were going steadily downhill. An outbreak of plague, and later the Great Famine (1695–97), killed off 80,000 people – almost 20% of the population. Peasants, who for a time enjoyed more freedom of movement, soon lost their gains and entered the harder lot of serfdom. The Swedish king, Charles XI, for his part wanted to abolish serfdom in Estonian crown manors (peasants enjoyed freedom in Sweden), but the local Baltic-German aristocracy fought bitterly to preserve the legacy of enforced servitude.

The Great Northern War

Soon Sweden faced serious threats from an anti-Swedish alliance of Poland, Denmark and Russia – countries seeking to regain lands lost in the Livonian War. The Great Northern War began in 1700 and after a few successes (including the defeat of the Russians at Narva), the Swedes began to fold under the assaults on multiple fronts. By 1708 Tartu had been destroyed and all of its survivors shipped back to Russia. By 1710 Tallinn capitulated and Sweden had been routed.

The Enlightenment

Russian domination of Estonia was bad news for the peasants. War (and the 1710 plague) left tens of thousands dead. Swedish reforms were rolled back by Peter I, destroying any hope of freedom for the surviving serfs. Conservative attitudes towards Estonia's lower class didn't change until the Enlightenment, in the late 18th century.

Among those influenced by the Enlightenment was Catherine the Great (1762–96), who curbed the privileges of the elite while instituting quasi-democratic reforms. It wasn't until 1816, however, that the peasants were finally liberated from serfdom. They also gained surnames, greater freedom of movement and even limited access to self-government. By the second half of the 19th century, the peasants started buying farmsteads from the estates, and earning an income from crops such as potatoes and flax (the latter commanding particularly high prices during the US Civil War and the subsequent drop in American cotton export to Europe).

National Awakening

The late 19th century was the dawn of the national awakening. Led by a new Estonian elite, the country marched towards nationhood. The first Estonian-language newspaper, *Perno Postimees,* appeared in 1857. It was published by Johann Voldemar Jannsen, one of the first to use the term 'Estonians' rather than *maarahvas* (country people). Other influential thinkers included Carl Robert Jakobson, who fought for equal political rights for Estonians; he also founded *Sakala,* Estonia's first political newspaper.

Numerous Estonian societies emerged, and in 1869 the first song festival was held. Estonia's rich folklore also emerged from obscurity, particularly with the publication of *Kalevipoeg,* Friedrich Reinhold Kreutzwald's poetic epic that melded together hundreds of Estonian legends and folk tales. Other poems, particularly works by Lydia Koidula, helped shape the national consciousness – one imprinted with the memory of 700 years of slavery.

Rebellion & WWI

The late 19th century was also a period of rampant industrialisation, marked by the development of an extensive railway network linking Estonia with Russia and by the rise of large factories. Socialism and discontent accompanied those grim workplaces, with demonstrations and strikes led by newly formed worker parties. Events in Estonia mimicked those in Russia, and in January 1905, as armed insurrection flared across the border, Estonia's workers joined the fray. Tension mounted until autumn that year, when 20,000 workers went on strike. Tsarist troops responded brutally by killing and wounding 200.

Tsar Nicholas II's response incited the Estonian rebels, who continued to destroy the property of the old guard. Subsequently, thousands of soldiers arrived from Russia, quelling the rebellions; 600 Estonians were executed and hundreds were sent off to Siberia. Trade unions and progressive newspapers and organisations were closed down and political leaders fled the country.

More radical plans to bring Estonia to heel – such as sending thousands of Russian peasants to colonise the country – were never realised. Instead, Russia's tsar had another priority: WWI. Estonia paid a high price for Russia's involvement – 100,000 men were drafted, 10,000 of whom were killed in action. Many Estonians went off to fight under the notion that if they helped defeat Germany, Russia would grant them nationhood. Russia had no intention of doing so. But by 1917 the matter was no longer the tsar's to decide. In St Petersburg, Nicholas II was forced to abdicate and the Bolsheviks seized power. As chaos swept across Russia, Estonia seized the initiative and on 24 February 1918 it effectively declared its independence.

The War of Independence

Estonia faced threats from both Russia and Baltic-German reactionaries. War erupted as the Red Army quickly advanced, overrunning half the country by January 1919. Estonia fought back tenaciously, and with the help of British warships and Finnish, Danish and Swedish troops, it defeated its longtime enemy. In December Russia agreed to a truce and on 2 February 1920 it signed the Tartu Peace Treaty, which renounced forever Russia's rights of sovereignty over Estonian territory. For the first time in its history, Estonia was completely independent.

Fleeting Independence

In many ways, the independence period was a golden era. The largely German nobility were given a few years to sort their affairs before their manor houses were nationalised and their large estates broken up, with the land redistributed to the Estonian people. For the very first time many peasant farmers were able to own and work their own land.

The economy developed rapidly, with Estonia utilising its natural resources and attracting investments from abroad. Tartu University became a university for Estonians, and the Estonian language became the lingua franca for all aspects of public life, creating new opportunities in professional and academic spheres. Secondary education also improved (per capita the number of students surpassed most European nations) and an enormous book industry arose, with 25,000 titles published between 1918 and 1940 (again surpassing most European nations in books per capita).

On other fronts – notably the political one – independence was not so rosy. Fear of communist subversion (such as the failed 1924 coup d'état supported by the Bolsheviks) drove the government to the right. In 1934 Konstantin Päts, leader of the transitional government, along with Johan Laidoner, commander-in-chief of the Estonian army, violated the constitution and seized power, under the pretext of protecting democracy from extremist factions. Thus began the 'era of silence', a period of authoritarian rule that dogged the fledgling republic until WWII.

The Soviet Invasion & WWII

Estonia's fate was sealed when Nazi Germany and the USSR negotiated a secret pact in 1939, essentially handing Estonia over to Stalin. The Molotov-Ribbentrop Pact of 23 August 1939, a nonaggression pact between the USSR and Nazi Germany, secretly divided Eastern Europe into Soviet and German spheres of influence. Estonia fell into the Soviet sphere. At the outbreak of WWII, Estonia declared itself neutral, but Moscow forced Estonia to sign a mutual assistance pact. Thousands of Russian soldiers subsequently arrived, along with military, naval and air bases. Estonia's Communist Party orchestrated a sham rebellion whereby 'the people' demanded to be part of the USSR. President Päts, General Laidoner and other leaders were sacked and sent off to Russian prison camps, a puppet government was installed and on 6 August 1940 the Supreme Soviet accepted Estonia's 'request' to join the USSR.

Deportations and WWII devastated the country. Tens of thousands were conscripted and sent not to fight but to work (and usually die) in labour camps in northern Russia. Thousands of women and children were also sent to gulags.

When Russia fled the German advance, many Estonians welcomed the Nazis as liberators; 55,000 Estonians joined home-defence units and Wehrmacht Ost battalions. The Nazis, however, would not grant statehood to Estonia and viewed it merely as occupied territory of the Soviet Union. Hope was crushed when the Germans began executing communist collaborators (7000 Estonian citizens were shot) and those Estonian Jews who hadn't already fled the country (around 1000). To escape conscription into the German army (nearly 40,000 were conscripted), thousands fled to Finland and joined the Estonian regiment of the Finnish army.

In early 1944 the Soviet army bombed Tallinn, Narva, Tartu and other cities. Narva's baroque Old Town was almost completely destroyed. The Nazis retreated in September 1944. Fearing the advance of the Red Army, many Estonians also fled and around 70,000 reached the West. By the end of the war one in 10 Estonians lived abroad. All in all, Estonia had lost over 280,000 people in the war (a quarter of its population): in addition to those who emigrated, 30,000 were killed in action; others were executed, sent to gulags or exterminated in concentration camps.

The Soviet Era

After the war, Estonia was immediately incorporated back into the Soviet Union. This began the grim epoch of Stalinist repression, with many thousands sent to prison camps and 19,000 Estonians executed. Farmers were forced into collectivisation and thousands of immigrants entered the country from other regions of the Soviet Union. Between 1945 and 1989 the percentage of native Estonians fell from 97% to 62%.

As a result of the repression, beginning in 1944, Estonians formed a large guerrilla movement. Calling themselves the Metsavennad, or 'Forest Brothers', 14,000 Estonians armed themselves and went into hiding, operating in small groups throughout the country. The guerrillas had little success against the Soviet army, and by 1956 the movement had been effectively destroyed.

Although there were a few optimistic periods during the communist years (notably the 'thaw' under Khrushchev, where Stalin's crimes were officially exposed), it wasn't until the 1980s when Soviet leader Mikhail Gorbachev ushered in an era of *perestroika* (restructuring) and *glasnost* (openness) that real change seemed a possibility.

The dissident movement in Estonia gained momentum and on the 50th anniversary of the 1939 Molotov-Ribbentrop Pact, a major rally took place in Tallinn. Over the next few months, more and more protests were held, with Estonians demanding the restoration of statehood. The song festival was one of Estonia's most powerful vehicles for protest. The biggest took place in 1988 when 300,000 Estonians gathered on Tallinn's Song Festival Grounds (p57) and brought much international attention to the Baltic plight.

In November 1989 the Estonian Supreme Soviet declared the events of 1940 an act

TALLINN'S CHECHEN HERO

In January 1991 Soviet troops seized strategic buildings in Vilnius and Rīga, and soldiers were ordered to do the same in Tallinn. The commander of the troops at the time, however, disobeyed Moscow's orders, and refused to open fire upon the crowd. He even threatened to turn the artillery under his command against any attempted invasion from Russia. That leader was Dzhokhar Dudayev, who would go on to become the president of Chechnya and lead its independence movement. He was killed by the Russian military in 1995. In Estonia he is fondly remembered for his role in bringing about Estonian independence.

of military aggression and therefore illegal. Disobeying Moscow's orders, Estonia held free elections in 1990 and regained its independence in 1991.

Postindependence

In 1992 the first general election under the new constitution took place, with a proliferation of newly formed parties. The Pro Patria (Fatherland) Union won a narrow majority after campaigning under the slogan 'Cleaning House', which meant removing from power those associated with communist rule. Pro Patria's leader, 32-year-old historian Mart Laar, became prime minister.

Laar set to work transforming Estonia into a free-market economy, introducing the Estonian kroon as currency and negotiating the complete Russian troop withdrawal. (The latter was a source of particular anxiety for Estonians, and the country breathed a collective sigh of relief when the last garrisons departed in 1994.) Despite Laar's successes, he was considered a hothead, and in 1994 he was dismissed when his government received a vote of no confidence by the Riigikogu (National Council).

Following a referendum in September 2003, approximately 60% of Estonians voted in favour of joining the EU. The following spring, the country officially joined both the EU and NATO. This was followed by membership of the OECD in December 2010 and adoption of the euro in place of the short-lived kroon at the beginning of 2011.

Recurring post-EU-accession themes are the economy, increasing income inequality and strained relations with Russia, particularly with regards to Estonia's large Russian-speaking community.

The People

Despite (or perhaps because of) centuries of occupation by Danes, Swedes, Germans and Russians, Estonians have tenaciously held onto their national identity and are deeply, emotionally connected to their history, folklore and national song tradition. The Estonian Literary Museum in Tartu holds over 1.3 million pages of folk songs, the world's second-largest collection (Ireland has the largest), and Estonia produces films for one of the world's smallest audiences (only Iceland produces for a smaller audience).

According to the popular stereotype, Estonians (particularly Estonian men) are reserved and aloof. Some believe it has much to do with the weather – those long, dark nights breeding endless introspection. This reserve also extends to gross displays of public affection, brash behaviour and intoxication – all frowned upon. This is assuming that there isn't a festival under way, such as Jaanipäev, when friends, family and acquaintances gather in the countryside for drinking, dancing and revelry.

Estonians are known for their strong work ethic, but when they're not toiling in the fields, or putting in long hours at the office, they head to the countryside. Ideal weekends are spent at the family cottage, picking berries or mushrooms, walking through the woods, or sitting with friends soaking up the quiet beauty. Having a countryside sauna is one of the national aspirations.

Of Estonia's 1.3 million people, 69% are ethnic Estonians, 26% Russians, 2% Ukrainians, 1% Belarusians and 1% Finns. Ethnic Russians are concentrated in the industrial cities of the northeast, where in some places (such as Narva) they make up around 95% of the population. Russians also have a sizable presence in Tallinn (37%). These figures differ markedly from 1934, when native Estonians comprised over 90% of the population. Migration from other parts of the USSR occurred on a large scale from 1945 to 1955 and, over the next three decades, Estonia had the highest rate of migration of any of the Soviet republics.

One of the most overlooked indigenous ethnic groups in Estonia are the Seto people (called the Setu by non-Seto Estonians), who number 10,000, split between southeastern Estonia and neighbouring Russia.

According to a 2009 Gallup poll, Estonia is the least religious country in the world, although many consider themselves spiritual, with a nature-based ethos being popular. Since the early 17th century, Estonia's Christians have been predominantly Lutheran, although the Orthodox church gained a foothold under the Russian Empire. Today only a minority of Estonians profess religious beliefs, with 14% identifying as Lutheran and 13% as Orthodox; no other religion reaches over 1% of the population.

Jews arrived in Estonia as early as the 14th century and by the early 1930s the population numbered 4300. Three-quarters escaped before the German occupation and of those that remained, nearly all were killed. Today the Jewish population stands at around 2000 and in 2007 the Jewish community celebrated the opening of its first synagogue since the Holocaust, a striking modern structure at Karu 16, Tallinn.

The Arts

Music

On the international stage, the area in which Estonia has had the greatest artistic impact is in the field of classical music. Estonia's most celebrated composer is Arvo Pärt (b 1935), the intense and reclusive master of hauntingly austere music many have misleadingly termed minimalist. Pärt emigrated to Germany during Soviet rule and his *Miserere Litany, Te Deum* and *Tabula Rasa* are among an internationally acclaimed body of work characterised by dramatic bleakness, piercing majesty and nuanced silence.

The main Estonian composers of the 20th century remain popular today. Rudolf Tobias (1873–1918) wrote influential symphonic, choral and concerto works as well as fantasies on folk song melodies. Mart Saar (1882–1963) studied under Rimsky-Korsakov in St Petersburg but his music shows none of this influence. His songs and piano suites were among the most performed pieces of music in between-war concerts in Estonia. Eduard Tubin (1905–82) is another great Estonian composer whose body of work includes 10 symphonies. Contemporary composer Erkki-Sven Tüür (b 1959) takes inspiration from nature and the elements as experienced on his native Hiiumaa.

Hortus Musicus is Estonia's best-known ensemble, performing mainly medieval and Renaissance music. Bridging the gap between old and new is one of Estonia's more clever groups. Rondellus, an ensemble that has played in a number of early music festivals, performs on medieval period instruments and isn't afraid of experimentation. Its well-received album *Sabbatum* (2002) is

---

EESTI CITIZENSHIP

When Estonia regained independence in 1991, not every resident received citizenship. People who were citizens of the pre-1940 Estonian Republic and their descendants automatically became citizens. Those who moved to Estonia during the Soviet occupation (mostly Russian speakers, many of whom didn't learn the local language) could choose to be naturalised, an ongoing process that required applicants to demonstrate knowledge of Estonia's history and language to qualify. For these people, one alternative was to apply for Russian citizenship, as all citizens of the former USSR were eligible, and another was to remain in Estonia as noncitizen residents. However, only citizens may vote in parliamentary elections. Noncitizens can vote in local government elections providing they have legal residency.

The naturalisation process and the perceived difficulty of the initial language tests became a point of international contention as the Russian government, the EU and a number of human rights organisations (including Amnesty International) objected on the grounds that many Russian-speaking inhabitants were being denied their political and civil rights. As a result, the tests were somewhat altered and the number of stateless persons has steadily decreased. According to Estonian officials, 32% of residents lacked any form of citizenship in 1992 while today that figure is 8%.

One consequence of Estonia's citizenship policy is that 8% of the population holds the passport of another state, mostly the Russian Federation, Ukraine or Finland. Around 84% of the population of Estonia holds Estonian citizenship.

a tribute album of sorts to Black Sabbath – the only difference being the music is played on medieval instruments, and the songs are sung in Latin!

Rock and punk thrives in Estonia with groups like Vennaskond and the U2-style Mr Lawrence, which was very popular in the 1990s. Also popular (heavy, but timelessly Estonian) is Metsatöll, whose song titles and lyrics make heavy use of archaic Estonian language and imagery. The more approachable Ultima Thule and Smilers are among the country's longest-running and most beloved bands.

The pop and dance-music scene is strong in Estonia, exemplified by Estonia's performances in that revered indicator of true art, the Eurovision Song Contest (Tanel Padar won the competition for Estonia in 2001, making Estonia the first former-Soviet republic to win). The tough-girl band Vanilla Ninja became a hot ticket throughout central Europe (singing in English and Estonian) early in the millennium, while boy band Outloudz are making waves today. Koit Toome and Maarja-Liis Ilus are also popular pop singers.

See www.estmusic.com for detailed listings and streaming samples of Estonian musicians of all genres – it's a worthwhile site, despite not being particularly up to date.

Literature

Estonian was traditionally considered a mere 'peasants' language' rather than one with full literary potential, and as a result

CAN I BUY A VOWEL, PLEASE?

Intrigued by the national language? Fancy yourself a linguist? If you're keen to tackle the local language, bear in mind that Estonian has 14 cases, no future tense, and no articles. And then try wrapping your tongue around the following vowel-hungry words:

» *jäääär* – edge of the ice
» *töööö* – work night (can also be öötöö)
» *kuuuurija* – moon researcher
» *kuuüür* – monthly rent

And then give this a go: '*Kuuuurijate töööö jäääärel*', or 'a moon researcher's work night at the edge of the ice'!

the history of written Estonian is little more than 150 years old. Baltic Germans published an Estonian grammar book and a dictionary in 1637, but it wasn't until the national awakening movement of the late 19th century that the publication of books, poetry and newspapers began.

Estonian literature grew from the poems and diaries of a young graduate of Tartu University, Kristjan Jaak Peterson. Also a gifted linguist, he died when he was only 21 years old in 1822. His lines 'Can the language of this land/carried by the song of the wind/not rise up to heaven/and search for its place in eternity?' are engraved in stone in Tartu and his birthday is celebrated as Mother Tongue Day (14 March).

Until the mid-19th century Estonian culture was preserved only by way of an oral folk tradition among peasants. The national epic poem *Son of Kalev* (*Kalevipoeg*), written between 1857 and 1861 by Friedrich Reinhold Kreutzwald (1803–82), made use of Estonia's rich oral traditions; it was inspired by Finland's *Kalevala,* a similar epic created several decades earlier. Fusing hundreds of Estonian legends and folk tales, *Son of Kalev* relates the adventures of the mythical hero, which ends with his death and his land's conquest by foreigners, but also a promise to restore freedom. The epic played a major role in fostering the national awakening of the 19th century.

Lydia Koidula (1843–86) was the poet of Estonia's national awakening and first lady of literature. Anton Hansen Tammsaare (1878–1940) is considered the greatest Estonian novelist for *Truth and Justice* (*Tõde ja Õigus*), written between 1926 and 1933. A five-volume saga of village and town life, it explores Estonian social, political and philosophical issues.

Eduard Vilde (1865–1933) was an influential early-20th-century novelist and playwright who wrote *Unattainable Wonder* (*Tabamata Ime,* 1912). *Unattainable Wonder* was to be the first play performed at the opening of the Estonia Theatre in 1913 but was substituted with *Hamlet,* as Vilde's scathing critique of the intelligentsia was deemed too controversial. In most of his novels and plays, Vilde looked with great irony at what he saw as Estonia's mad, blind rush to become part of Europe. For Vilde, self-reliance was the truest form of independence.

Paul-Eerik Rummo (b 1942) is one of Estonia's leading poets and playwrights, dubbed the 'Estonian Dylan Thomas' for his patriotic pieces, which deal with contemporary problems of cultural identity. His contemporary, Mati Unt (1944–2005), played an important role in cementing the place of Estonian intellectuals in the modern world, and wrote, from the 1960s onwards, quite cynical novels (notably *Autumn Ball; Sügisball,* 1979), plays and articles about contemporary life in Estonia.

The novelist Jaan Kross (1920–2007) won great acclaim for his historical novels in which he tackled Soviet-era subjects. His most renowned book, *The Czar's Madman (Keisri hull,* 1978), relates the story of a 19th-century Estonian baron who falls in love with a peasant girl and later ends up in prison. It's loosely based on a true story, though the critique of past- and present-day authoritarianism is the crux of his work.

Estonia also has a number of outstanding contemporary poets. Jaan Kaplinski (b 1941) has had two collections, *The Same Sea In Us All* and *The Wandering Border,* published in English. His work expresses the feel of Estonian life superbly. Kross and Kaplinski have both been nominated for the Nobel Prize in Literature.

Tõnu Õnnepalu's *Border State (Piiri Riik,* 1993, published under the pseudonym Emil Tode) is about a young Estonian man who travels to Europe and becomes a kept boy for an older, rich gentleman. This leads him down a tortuous road of self-discovery. Not a mere confessional, *Border State* is a clever and absorbing critique of modern Estonian values. In popular fiction, Kaur Kender's *Independence Day (Iseseisvuspäev,* 1998) tells the misadventures of young and ambitious entrepreneurs in postindependence Estonia.

The most acclaimed Estonian novel of recent times is *Purge (Puhdistus,* 2008) by Sofi Oksanen, a harrowing tale weaving together Stalin's purges and modern-day people-trafficking and sex slavery. A bestseller in Estonia and Finland, it's won six major awards, has been published in 36 languages (including English) and at the time of writing was being made into a major feature film.

Cinema

The first moving pictures were screened in Tallinn in 1896, and the first theatre opened in 1908. Estonia's cinematographic output has not been prolific, but there are a few standouts. It's also worth noting that Estonia produces films for one of the world's smallest audiences – far more than the output of the neighbouring Baltic countries, and with domestic films capturing an impressive 14% of the filmgoing market share.

The nation's most beloved film is Arvo Kruusement's *Spring (Kevade,* 1969), an adaptation of Oskar Luts' country saga. Its sequel, *Summer (Suvi,* 1976), was also popular though regarded as inferior. Grigori Kromanov's *Last Relic (Viimne Reliikvia,* 1969) was a brave and unabashedly anti-Soviet film that has been screened in 60 countries.

More recently Sulev Keedus' lyrical *Georgica* (1998), about childhood, war, and life on the western islands, and Jaak Kilmi's *Pigs' Revolution (Sigade Revolutsioon,* 2004), about an anti-Soviet uprising at a teenagers' summer camp, have made the rounds at international film festivals.

One of Estonia's most popular locally made films is *Names in Marble (Nimed Marmortahvlil,* 2002), which tells the story of a group of young classmates and their decision to fight in the fledgling nation's War of Independence against the Red Army in 1918–20. It was directed by acclaimed Estonian stage director Elmo Nüganen and it's based on the book of the same name (by Albert Kivikas) that was banned during Soviet times.

Veiko Õunpuu's 2007 film *Autumn Ball (Sügisball),* based on the novel by Mati Unt, won awards at seven festivals from Brussels to Bratislava. His latest movie is the black comedy *The Temptation of St Tony (Püha Tõnu kiusamine,* 2009).

Theatre

Many of the country's theatres were built solely from donations by private citizens, which gives an indication of the role theatre has played in Estonian cultural life. The Estonian Drama Theatre in Tallinn, the Vanemuine Theatre in Tartu and the Drama Theatre in Rakvere (the last civic building erected in Estonia before WWII) were all built on proceeds from door-to-door collections.

The popularity of theatre is also evidenced in theatregoing statistics: in 2007 the Eurobarometer found 93% of Estonians go to concerts, the theatre and watch cultural content on TV (the EU average is 78%). Estonia is second to the Netherlands in theatre attendance, with 49% of the population attending plays or musicals.

KIIKING – WHAT THE...?

From the weird and wacky world of Estonian sport comes *kiiking*. Invented in 1997, it's the kind of extreme sport that, frankly, we're surprised the New Zealanders didn't think of first. *Kiiking* sees competitors stand on a swing and attempt to complete a 360-degree loop around the top bar, with their feet fastened to the swing base and their hands to the swing arms. The inventor of *kiiking*, Ado Kosk, observed that the longer the swing arms, the more difficult it is to complete a 360-degree loop. Kosk then designed swing arms that can gradually extend, for an increased challenge. In competition, the winner is the person who completes a loop with the longest swing arms – the current record stands at a fraction over 7m! If this concept has you scratching your head, go to www.kiiking.ee to get a more visual idea of the whole thing and to find out where you can see it in action (or even give it a try yourself).

Modern Estonian theatre is considered to have begun in 1870 in Tartu, where Lydia Koidula's *The Cousin from Saaremaa* became the first Estonian play to be performed in public. The Vanemuine Theatre (an outgrowth of the Vanemuine Society, an amateur troupe) launched professional theatre in 1906. Quickly thereafter the Estonia Theatre opened its doors in Tallinn, and the Endla Theatre in Pärnu followed suit in 1911. Within the first decade, theatre took off with talented directors and actors performing the works of August Kitzberg and Eduard Wilde.

During the country's independence days (1918–40) Estonian theatre thrived; however, by the 1930s there was a noticeable retreat from experimentation. Theatre, like the other arts, suffered heavily during Soviet rule, with heavy-handed censorship and a dumping of lifeless Soviet drama onto the stage. Things began to change after Stalin's death in 1953, as theatres gained more poetic freedom in stage productions. Although the '60s were still a time of repression in other spheres of life, on the stage the avant-garde emerged, with the staging of plays wild in subject matter and rich in symbolism. Paul-Eerik Rummo, perhaps Estonia's most famous poet of the time, wrote *The Cinderella Game,* a brilliant satire of Soviet-era repression that was performed in 1969. It was later performed at New York's La Mama theatre and in playhouses throughout Europe.

With the return to independence in 1991 and the disappearance of censorship, the stage once again held wide-open possibilities. Yet some critics contend that along with Estonia's new-found freedom, radicalism died in the theatre – for the very reason that the object of satire (Big Brother) had also died. Whatever the case, stage life continues to flourish, and today the halls are rarely empty. The most original directors currently on the theatre scene are Jaanus Rohumaa, Katri Aaslav-Tepand and Elmo Nüganen, who often work out of Tallinn's City Theatre (Linnateater); travellers, however, will have trouble tapping into the scene without any knowledge of the local language.

Food & Drink

Quite simply, Tallinn is a wonderful city for food lovers. Cuisines from all over the world are represented in its many atmospheric eateries and the prices are generally much lower than you'd pay for a similar meal in most other European capitals. There are some fantastic restaurants dotted around the rest of the country (most notably Alexander on Muhu island) but no other city comes close to the diversity and quality offered in the capital (we'd rate Pärnu ahead of Tartu on this front).

Many parts of Estonia offer visitors little variety beyond what type of meat they'd like with their potatoes. This owes much to Estonia's roots. For centuries Estonia was largely a farming country, and folks who worked the fields (serfs, prior to emancipation in the 1800s) sought heavy nourishment to fuel their long days. Food preparation was

EATING PRICE RANGES

For the purpose of this chapter we've based the Estonian budget breakdowns on the following price ranges, based on the cheapest main meal offered.

» **€**   less than €7
» **€€**   €7 to €14
» **€€€**   more than €14

simple and practical, using whatever could be raised, grown or gathered from the land. Daily fare was barley porridge, cheese curd and boiled potatoes. On feast days and special occasions, meat made its appearance. Coastal dwellers also garnered sustenance from the sea, mainly cod and herring. To make foods last through the winter, people dried, smoked and salted their fish.

Restaurants have turned humble traditions and historic locations to their advantage, offering table-straining feasts served by young folk in medieval peasant garb. The best example of this is Tallinn's Olde Hansa, but the trend has extended to historic taverns scattered throughout the countryside.

Eesti Specialities

Did someone say 'stodge'? Baltic gastronomy has its roots planted firmly in the land, with livestock and game forming the basis of a hearty diet. The Estonian diet relies on *sealiha* (pork), other red meat, *kana* (chicken), *vurst* (sausage) and *kapsa* (cabbage); potatoes add a generous dose of winter-warming carbs to a national cuisine often dismissed as bland, heavy and lacking in spice. Sour cream is served with everything but coffee, it seems. *Kala* (fish), most likely *heeringas* (herring), *forell* (trout) or *lõhe* (salmon), appears most often as a smoked or salted starter. Lake Peipsi is a particularly good place for tracking down *suitsukala* (smoked fish); look for roadside stands along the shore road.

At Christmas time *verivorst* (blood sausage) is made from fresh blood and wrapped in pig intestine (joy to the world indeed!). Those really in need of a culinary transfusion will find *verivorst, verileib* (blood bread) and *verikäkk* (balls of blood rolled in flour and eggs with bits of pig fat thrown in for taste) available in most traditional Estonian restaurants year-round. *Sült* (jellied meat) is likely to be served as a delicacy as well.

The seasons continue to play a large role in the Estonian diet. When spring arrives, wild leek, rhubarb, fresh sorrel and goat's cheese appear, and the spring lambs are slaughtered. During summer there are fresh vegetables and herbs, along with berries, nuts and mushrooms gathered from the forests – still a popular pastime for many Estonians. Be sure to take advantage of the local *turg* (market) and load up on superbly flavoured strawberries (check you're buying the local stuff, not imports).

Autumn was always the prime hunting season and although many species are now offered some protection through hunting quotas, you'll often see elk, boar, deer and even bear making their way onto menus, year-round. In winter, Estonians turn to hearty roasts, stews, soups and plenty of sauerkraut.

Given Estonia's rustic origins, it's not surprising that bread is a major staple in the diet, and that Estonians make a pretty good loaf. Rye is by far the top choice. Unlike other

ESTONIA FOOD & DRINK

LOCAL KNOWLEDGE

PILLE PETERSOO: FOOD BLOGGER

Pille Petersoo writes the Nami-Nami blog at http://nami-nami.blogspot.com (nami-nami basically means yum-yum).

Tell us about Estonian food. Traditional Estonian food is simple and hearty, a mixture of Nordic, Russian and German influences. Pork and potatoes feature heavily, though during the summer the diet is a lot lighter, with barbecued meats and salads. Surprisingly, there's not a strong fish culture here, and our food isn't very strongly seasoned.

What should visitors try? If they're brave, blood sausage (call it black pudding and it seems more palatable), or jellied pork. I'm a great fan of *kama* – a traditional dish made from a powdery mixture of boiled, roasted and ground peas, rye, barley and wheat. Traditionally, buttermilk or *kefir* (fermented milk) is added to it, and it's seasoned with salt and sugar. In its traditional form, it's a light meal or drink, especially in summer. But you can add, say, curd cheese, sugar, vanilla and chopped strawberries for a dessert dish.

And finally, what's a good edible Estonian souvenir? Vana Tallinn, especially the cream version (it has more flavour than Baileys, and isn't as sickly sweet). People might like to take home *kama* and make it themselves.

EAT YOUR WORDS

Don't know your *kana* from your *kala*? Your *maasikas* from your *marjad*? Get a head start on the cuisine scene by learning the words that make the dish. For pronunciation guidelines, see the Language chapter.

Useful Phrases

May I have a menu?	*kas* mah *saahk*-sin me*nüü*	*Kas ma saaksin menüü?*
I'd like ...	ma *saw*-vik-sin ...	*Ma sooviksin ...*
The bill, please.	*pah*-lun *ahrr*-ve	*Palun arve.*
I'm a vegetarian.	mah *o*-len *tai*-me-toyt-lah-ne	*Ma olen taimetoitlane.*
Bon appetit!	head *i*-su	*Head isu!*
To your health! (when toasting)	*ter*-vi-seks	*Terviseks!*
breakfast	*hom*-mi-ku-serrk	*hommikusöök*
lunch	*lyu*-na	*lõuna*
dinner	*er*-tu-serrk	*õhtusöök*

Food Glossary

berries	*mahrr*-yahd	*marjad*
cabbage	*kahp*-sahs	*kapsas*
caviar	*kaa*-vi-ah, ka-la-*mah*-rri	*kaaviar, kalamari*
cheese	yoost	*juust*
chicken	*kah*-nah	*kana*
fish	*kah*-lah	*kala*
fruit	*poo*-vil-yahd	*puuviljad*
grilled 'chop'	*kah*-bo-noahd	*karbonaad*
herring	rraim, *heh*-rrin-gahs	*räim, heeringas*
meat (red)	*li*-hah	*liha*
mushrooms	*seh*-ned	*seened*
pancake	*pahn*-kawk	*pannkook*
pork	*sea*-li-ha	*sealiha*
potato	*kahrr*-tul	*kartul*
rye bread	layb	*leib*
salmon	*ly*-he	*lõhe*
sausage	vorrst	*vorst*
sprats	*ki*-lud	*kilud*
vegetables	*kerrg*-vi-li	*köögivili*
white bread	sai	*sai*

ryes you may have eaten, here it's moist, dense and delicious (assuming it's fresh), and usually served as a free accompaniment to every restaurant meal.

Terviseks!

The traditional Estonian toast translates as 'your health' (it's much easier to remember if you think 'topsy-turvy sex'). Beer is the favourite tipple in Estonia and the local product is very much in evidence. The best brands are Saku and A Le Coq, which come in a range of brews. On Saaremaa and Hiiumaa you'll also find homemade beer, which is flatter than traditional beer but still the perfect refreshment on a hot day. In winter

Estonians drink mulled wine, the antidote to cold wintry nights.

Estonia's ties to Russia have led to vodka's enduring popularity. Viru Valge is the best brand, and it comes in a range of flavours, which some Estonians mix with fruit juices (try the vanilla-flavoured vodka mixed with apple juice).

Vana Tallinn is in a class of its own. No one quite knows what the syrupy liqueur is made from, but it's sweet and strong and has a pleasant aftertaste. It's best served neat, in coffee, over ice with milk, over ice cream, or in champagne or dry white wine.

Even without any vineyards to call their own, Estonia has a burgeoning wine culture. Wine bars are quite fashionable, especially in the larger cities, but few offer an extensive range served by the glass. The capital also boasts the largest wine cellars in the Baltic and plenty of medieval settings in which to imbibe.

Where, When & How

Meals are served in a *restoran* (restaurant) or a *kohvik* (cafe), *pubi* (pub), *kõrts* (inn) or *trahter* (tavern). Nearly every town has a *turg* (market), where you can buy fresh fruit and vegetables, as well as meats and fish.

Estonian eating habits are similar to other parts of northern Europe. Either lunch or dinner may be the biggest meal of the day. Cooked breakfasts aren't always easy to find but many cafes serve pastries and cakes throughout the day. Tipping is fairly commonplace, with 10% the norm. For standard opening times, see p397 and for reviews of the country's culinary best, see www.eesti maitsed.com.

If invited for a meal at an Estonian home you can expect abundant hospitality and generous portions. It's fairly common to bring flowers for the host. Just be sure to give an odd number (even-numbered flowers are reserved for the dead).

SURVIVAL GUIDE

Directory A–Z

The following contains practical information specifically related to travelling in Estonia. For regional information pertaining to all three countries, see p396.

SLEEPING PRICE RANGES

» €	up to €35 per night for the cheapest double room
» €€	cheapest double €35–100
» €€€	cheapest double over €100

Accommodation

If you like flying by the seat of your pants when you're travelling, you'll find July and August in Estonia very problematic. The best accommodation books up quickly and in Tallinn, especially on weekends, you might find yourself scraping for anywhere at all to lay your head. In fact, Tallinn gets busy most weekends, so try to book about a month ahead anytime from May through to September (midweek isn't anywhere near as bad).

For this book we've listed high-season prices, which in Estonia means summer. Prices drop off substantially at other times. The exception is Otepää, when there's also a corresponding peak in winter.

Customs Regulations

If arriving from outside the EU, there are the usual restrictions on what can be brought into the country; see www.emta.ee for full details, including alcohol and tobacco limits.

Embassies & Consulates

For up-to-date contact details of Estonian diplomatic organisations as well as foreign embassies and consulates in Estonia, check the website of the **Estonian Ministry of Foreign Affairs** (Välisministeerium; Map p52; ☑637 7000; www.vm.ee; Islandi Väljak 1, Tallinn). Most of the following embassies and consulates are in or near Tallinn's Old Town.

Australia (Map p48; ☑650 9308; www.sweden .embassy.gov.au; Marja 9) Honorary consulate; embassy in Stockholm.

Canada (Map p52; ☑627 3311; www.estonia.gc .ca; Toom-Kooli 13, 2nd fl) Office of embassy in Rīga.

Finland (Map p52; ☑610 3200; www.finland.ee; Kohtu 4)

France (Map p48; ☑631 1492; www.amba france-ee.org; Toom-Kuninga 20)

Germany (Map p48; ☑627 5300; www.tallinn .diplo.de; Toom-Kuninga 11)

Ireland (Map p52; ☑681 1888; www.embassy ofireland.ee; 2nd fl, Vene 2)

Latvia (Map p48; ☑627 7850; embassy .estonia@mfa.gov.lv; Tõnismägi 10)

Lithuania (http://ee.mfa.lt) Tallinn (Map p52; ☑616 4991; Uus 15); Tartu (Map p96; ☑737 5225; Ülikooli 18)

Netherlands (Map p52; ☑680 5500; www .netherlandsembassy.ee; Rahukohtu 4-I)

New Zealand (Map p48; ☑667 1470; www .nzembassy.com; Liivalaia 13) Honorary consulate; embassy in Berlin.

Russia (www.rusemb.ee) Tallinn (Map p52; ☑646 4175; Pikk 19); Narva (☑356 0652; Kiriku 8); Tartu (Map p96; ☑740 3024; Ülikooli 1)

Sweden (Map p52; ☑640 5600; www.sweden .ee; Pikk 28)

UK (Map p52; ☑667 4700; www.ukinestonia .fco.ee; Wismari 6)

USA (Map p52; ☑668 8100; http://estonia.us embassy.gov; Kentmanni 20)

Gay & Lesbian Travellers

Hand-in-hand with its relaxed attitude to religion, today's Estonia is a fairly tolerant and safe home to its gay and lesbian citizens – certainly much more so than its Baltic neighbours or Russia. Unfortunately, that ambivalence hasn't translated into a wildly exciting scene (only Tallinn has gay venues; see boxed text, p73), but it does mean that people can drink on a terrace in front of a Tallinn gay bar without passersby raising an eyebrow. Homosexuality was decriminalised in 1992 and since 2001 there has been an equal age of consent for everyone.

Internet Access

Wireless internet access (wi-fi) is ubiquitous in 'E-stonia' (you may find yourself wondering why our own country lags so far behind this tech-savvy place). You'll find over 1100 hotspots throughout the country, and at last count 350-plus hotspots in Tallinn (we're talking in hotels, hostels, restaurants, cafes, pubs, shopping centres, ports, petrol stations, even on long-distance buses and in the middle of national parks!). See www.wi-fi.ee for a complete list (and keep your eyes peeled for orange-and-black stickers indicating availability). In most places connection is free.

If you're not packing a laptop or smartphone, options for getting online are not as numerous as they once were (thanks to all that wi-fi and the abundance of laptop-toting locals, there is considerably less demand for internet cafes). Many accommodation providers will offer a computer for guest use. There are a few internet cafes with speedy connections, plus public libraries have web-connected computers that can usually be accessed free of charge. Most small communities will have a well-signed public internet point, often connected to the general store.

Maps

If you're just going to major cities and national parks, you'll find the maps in this book, coupled with those freely available in tourist offices and park centres, more than adequate. If, however, you're planning on driving around and exploring more out-of-the-way places, a good road atlas is worthwhile and easy to find. **EO Map** (www.eomap .ee) has fold-out sheet maps for every Estonian county and city, as well as a road atlas. **Regio** (www.regio.ee) also produces a good, easy-to-use road atlas, with enlargements for all major towns and cities.

Money

On 1 January 2011, Estonia joined the eurozone, bidding a very fond farewell to its short-lived kroon. ATMs are plentiful and credit cards are widely accepted. Most banks (but not stores and restaurants) accept travellers cheques, but commissions can be high. Tipping in restaurants has become the norm; round the bill up to something approaching 10% (or less).

Public Holidays

New Year's Day (Uusaasta) 1 January

Independence Day (Iseseisvuspäev) Anniversary of 1918 declaration on 24 February

Good Friday (Suur reede) March/April

Easter Sunday (Lihavõtted) March/April

Spring Day (Kevadpüha) 1 May

Pentecost (Nelipühade) Seventh Sunday after Easter (May/June)

Victory Day (Võidupüha) Commemorating the anniversary of the Battle of Võnnu (1919) on 23 June.

St John's Day (Jaanipäev, Midsummer's Day). Taken together, Victory Day and St John's Day on 24 June are the excuse for a week-long midsummer break for many people.

Day of Restoration of Independence
(Taasiseseisvumispäev) On 20 August, marking the country's return to independence in 1991.

Christmas Eve (Jõululaupäev)
24 December

Christmas Day (Jõulupüha) 25 December

Boxing Day (Teine jõulupüha)
26 December

Telephone

There are no area codes in Estonia; if you're calling anywhere within the country, just dial the number as it's listed in this book. All landline phone numbers have seven digits; mobile (cell) numbers have seven or eight digits and begin with ☑5. Estonia's country code is ☑372. To make a collect call dial ☑16116, followed by the desired number. To make an international call, dial 00 before the country code.

Almost all of Estonia is covered with digital mobile-phone networks, and every man and his dog has a mobile. To avoid the high roaming charges, you can get a starter kit (around €3), which will give you an Estonian number, a SIM card that you pop into your phone and around €3 of talk time (incoming calls are free with most providers). You can buy scratch-off cards for more minutes as you need them. SIM cards and starter kits are available from post offices, supermarkets and kiosks.

Public telephones accept chip cards, available at post offices, hotels and most kiosks. For placing calls outside Estonia, an international telephone card with PIN, available at many kiosks and supermarkets, is better value. Note that these cards can only be used from landlines, not mobile phones.

EMERGENCY NUMBERS

24-hour roadside assistance for drivers (☑1888)

Fire, ambulance and urgent medical advice (☑112)

Police (☑110)

Tallinn's First Aid hotline (☑697 1145) Can advise you in English about the nearest treatment centres.

Tourist Information

In addition to the info-laden, multilingual website of the **Estonian Tourist Board** (www.visitestonia.com), there are tourist offices in many towns and national parks throughout the country. At nearly every one you'll find English-speaking staff and lots of free material. See the Information section in each destination for details.

Getting There & Away

This section concentrates on travelling to Estonia from Latvia and Lithuania only. For details on connections outside of the region, see p404.

Air

air Baltic (BT; ☑17107; www.airbaltic.com) Flies to Tallinn from Rīga seven times daily and from Vilnius most days.

Estonian Air (OV; ☑640 1160; www.estonian -air.ee) Flies between Tallinn and Vilnius twice each weekday.

Bus

See each city's transport section for the frequency and cost of these services.

Ecolines (☑606 2217; www.ecolines.net) Three daily buses on the Rīga–Salacgrīva–Pärnu–Tallinn route and a daily Rīga–Valmeira–Valga–Tartu bus.

Hansabuss Business Line (☑627 9080; www.businessline.ee) Four daily buses between Rīga and Tallinn, three of which stop in Pärnu.

Lux Express (☑680 0909; www.luxexpress .eu) Nine daily buses between Tallinn and Rīga, some of which stop in Pärnu; two continue on to Vilnius. Also two to three daily buses on the St Petersburg–Narva–Tartu–Valga–Rīga route.

Car & Motorcycle

The three Baltic countries are all part of the Schengen agreement, so there are no border checks when driving between Estonia and Latvia. There's usually no problem taking hire cars across the border but it pays to let the rental company know at the time of hire if you intend to do so.

Train

Valga is the terminus for both the Estonian and Latvian rail systems, but the train services don't connect up (see p112). From Valga, Estonian trains head to Tartu, while Latvian trains head to Valmiera, Cēsis, Sigulda and Rīga.

Getting Around
Bicycle, Car & Motorcycle

Estonian roads are generally very good and driving is easy. Touring cyclists will find Estonia mercifully flat. In rural areas, particularly on the islands, some roads are unsealed but they're usually kept in good condition. Winter poses particular problems for those not used to driving in ice and snow. Car and bike hire is offered in all the major cities.

Bus

The national bus network is extensive, linking all the major cities to each other and the smaller towns to their regional hubs. All services are summarised on the extremely handy **BussiReisid** (www.bussireisid.ee) site.

Train

Most people prefer the buses to the trains, for convenience of services and for comfort. Local train services are operated by **Edelerautee** (www.edel.ee) and include the following routes:

» Tallinn–Rakvere–Narva (daily)
» Tallinn–Tartu (three daily)
» Tallinn–Viljandi (one to three daily)
» Tallinn–Pärnu (two daily)
» Tartu–Valga (two daily)

Helsinki Excursion

Includes »

Sights.............................173
Sleeping.........................175
Eating.............................177
Entertainment 179
Understand
Helsinki.........................180
Survival Guide...............181

Best Places to Stay

» Hotelli Helka (p175)

» Hotel GLO (p175)

» Hotel Finn (p175)

» Hotel Fabian (p175)

Best Places to Eat

» Olo (p178)

» Juuri (p178)

» Zucchini (p178)

Why Go?

It's fitting that harbour-side Helsinki, capital of a country with such a watery geography, melds so graciously into the Baltic. Half the city is liquid, and the writhing of the complex coastline includes any number of bays, inlets and a speckling of islands.

Though Helsinki can seem like a younger sibling to other Scandinavian capitals, it's the one that went to art school, scorns pop music, works in a cutting-edge design studio and wears black and plenty of piercings.

On the other hand, much of what is lovable in Helsinki is older. Its understated yet glorious art nouveau buildings; the spacious elegance of its centenarian cafes; the careful preservation of Finnish heritage in its dozens of museums; restaurants that have changed neither menu nor furnishings since the 1930s: all are part of the city's quirky charm. It makes a great trip across the Baltic for a couple of days or more.

When to Go?

Helsinki has year-round appeal; there's always something going on. The summer kicks off in June, when terraces sprout outside every cafe and bar, and the nights seem never to end. There's a bit of a lull in July when Finns head off to their summer cottages, but in August the capital is re-populated and plenty of activities are on offer. If you feel like seeing the wintry side of town, go in December, when you can ice-skate and absorb the Christmassy atmosphere before temperatures get too extreme.

Helsinki Highlights

1 Descend into the weekend maelstrom of Helsinki's **pubs and bars** (p178)

2 Grab a picnic and explore the fortress island of **Suomenlinna** (p173), which guarded Helsinki harbour

3 Browse the huge range of exciting design shops in **Punavuori** (p179)

4 Selecting from the city's huge range of museums and galleries; **Kiasma** (p173) is first stop for great contemporary art

5 Hire a **bike** (p182) and take advantage of the great network of cycle paths to explore on two wheels

6 Sweat out your cares in the traditional, atmospheric **Kotiharjun Sauna** (p174)

7 **Dine** (p177) on traditional Finnish comfort food such as meatballs or liver and mash, or experiment with the latest avant-garde new-Suomi cuisine at Olo or Juuri

⊙ Sights

The *kauppatori* (market square) is the heart of central Helsinki; it's where urban ferries dock and fresh fish and berries, as well as souvenirs, are sold.

Helsinki has over 50 museums, including several good galleries apart from those mentioned here. For a full list, pick up the *Museums* booklet (free) from the tourist office.

Suomenlinna
FORTRESS

(www.suomenlinna.fi) Just a 15-minute ferry ride from the kauppatori, a visit to the 'fortress of Finland' is a Helsinki must-do. Set on a tight cluster of four islands connected by bridges, it was originally built by the Swedes in the mid-18th century.

From the main quay, a walking path connects the main attractions. By the bridge leading to the main island, Susisaari, is **Suomenlinnakeskus** (www.suomenlinna.fi; walking tours €7; ⊙10am-6pm May-Sep, 10.30am-4.30pm Oct-Apr, English walking tours 11am & 2pm Jun-Aug), with tourist information, internet access, maps and guided walking tours, daily in summer and weekends only in winter. Also inside is **Suomenlinna-museo** (admission €5), a two-level museum of the fortress' history.

The most atmospheric part of Suomenlinna is at the end of the trail, the southern end of Susisaari. Explore the old bunkers, crumbling fortress walls and cannons, and relax: there are plenty of grassy picnic spots.

Several other museums dot the islands, including an old submarine. There are also several cafes and restaurants.

Ferries (15 minutes, three times hourly 6.20am to 2.20am) depart from the kauppatori in Helsinki to the main quay at Suomenlinna, also stopping at other points on the islands in summer. Tickets (single/return €2/3.80) are available at the pier.

Tuomiokirkko
CHURCH

(Lutheran cathedral; www.visithelsinki.fi; Unioninkatu 29; ⊙9am-6pm Sep-May, 9am-midnight Jun-Aug) One of CL Engel's finest creations, the chalk-white neoclassical Lutheran cathedral presides over Senate Sq though, as it was not completed until 1852, the architect, who died in 1840, never saw it. Though it was created to serve as a reminder of God's supremacy, its high flight of stairs has become a meeting place for canoodling couples and a setting for New Year's revelry. The spartan interior has little ornamentation under the lofty dome.

Uspenskin Katedraali
CHURCH

(Uspenski cathedral; www.visithelsinki.fi; Kanavakatu 1; ⊙9.30am-4pm Mon-Fri, 9.30am-2pm Sat, noon-3pm Sun, closed Mon Oct-Apr) Facing the Lutheran cathedral, the eye-catching redbrick Uspenski cathedral is equally imposing on nearby Katajanokka Island. The two buildings face off high above the city like two queens on a theological chessboard. Built as a Russian Orthodox church in 1868, it features classic onion domes and now serves the Finnish Orthodox congregation. The high, square interior has a lavish iconostasis with the Evangelists flanking panels depicting the Last Supper and the Ascension.

Kiasma
GALLERY

(www.kiasma.fi; Mannerheiminaukio 2; adult/child under 18yr €8/free; ⊙10am-8.30pm Wed-Fri, 10am-6pm Sat & Sun, 10am-5pm Tue) Now just one of a series of elegant contemporary buildings in this part of town, curvaceous and quirky metallic Kiasma, designed by American architect Steven Holl and finished in 1998, is still a symbol of the city's modernisation. It exhibits an eclectic collection of Finnish and international modern art and keeps people on their toes with its striking contemporary exhibitions.

Ateneum
GALLERY

(www.ateneum.fi; Kaivokatu 2; adult/child €8/free; ⊙10am-6pm Tue & Fri, 10am-8pm Wed & Thu, 11am-5pm Sat & Sun) The top floor of Finland's premier art gallery is an ideal crash course in the nation's art. It houses Finnish paintings and sculptures from the 'golden age' of the late 19th century through to the 1950s. Pride of place goes to the prolific Akseli Gallen-Kallela's triptych from the *Kalevala* epic. There's also a small but interesting collection of 19th- and early-20th-century foreign art.

HELSINKI AT A GLANCE

» **Area** 745 sq km (greater urban area)

» **Country code** +358

» **Departure tax** none

» **Money** euro (€)

» **Population** 1 million (greater urban area)

» **Official languages** Finnish, Swedish

» **Visa** Generally not required for stays of up to 90 days; some nationalities will need a Schengen visa

HELSINKI IN...

One Day

Finns are the world's biggest coffee drinkers so, first up, it's a caffeine shot with a *pulla* (cinnamon bun) at a classic **cafe**. Then to the **kauppatori** (market square) and the adjacent **kauppahalli** market building. Put a picnic together and boat out to the island fortress of **Suomenlinna**. Back in town, check out the **Lutheran cathedral** on Senaatintori (Senate Sq) and nearby **Uspenski cathedral**. Take the metro to legendary **Kotiharjun Sauna** for a pre-dinner sweat. Eat traditional Finnish at **Kuu** or **Sea Horse**.

Two Days

With a second day to spare, investigate the art and design scene. Head to the **Ateneum** for the golden age of Finnish painting, then see contemporary works at still-iconic **Kiasma**. Feet tired? Catch **tram 3** for a circular sightseeing trip around town, before browsing **design shops** around Punavuori. In the evening, head up to the **Ateljee Bar** for great views and on to **Tavastia** for a rock gig.

Kansallismuseo   MUSEUM
(National Museum; www.kansallismuseo.fi; Mannerheimintie 34; adult/child €7/free; ☉11am-8pm Tue, 11am-6pm Wed-Sun) The impressive National Museum, built in National Romantic style in 1916, resembles a Gothic church with its heavy stonework and tall square tower. This is Finland's premier historical museum, divided into rooms covering different periods of Finnish history, including prehistory and archaeological finds, church relics, ethnography and changing cultural exhibitions. It's a thorough, old-style museum – you might have trouble selling this one to the kids – but provides a comprehensive overview.

FREE Helsingin Kaupunginmuseo MUSEUMS
(www.helsinkicitymuseum.fi) A group of small museums scattered around the city centre constitute the Kaupunginmuseo, which all have free entry. All buildings focus on an aspect of the city's past or present through permanent and temporary exhibitions.

The must-see of the bunch is Helsinki City Museum (Sofiankatu 4; ☉9am-5pm Mon-Fri, to 7pm Thu, 11am-5pm Sat & Sun), just off Senate Sq. Its excellent collection of historical artefacts and photos is backed up by entertaining information on the history of the city, piecing together Helsinki's transition from Swedish to Russian hands and into independence.

Temppeliaukion Kirkko   CHURCH
(Lutherinkatu 3; ☉10am-8pm Mon-Fri, to 6.45pm Wed, 10am-6pm Sat, noon-1.45pm & 3.30-6pm Sun) The Temppeliaukio church, designed by Timo and Tuomo Suomalainen in 1969,

remains one of Helsinki's foremost attractions. Hewn into solid stone, it feels close to a Finnish ideal of spirituality in nature – you could be in a rocky glade were it not for the stunning 24m-diameter roof covered in 22km of copper stripping. There are regular concerts, with great acoustics.

Seurasaaren ulkomuseo   MUSEUM
(www.seurasaari.fi; adult/child €6/free; ☉11am-5pm Jun-Aug, 9am-3pm Mon-Fri, 11am-5pm Sat & Sun late May & early Sep) West of the centre, this excellent open-air island museum has a collection of historic traditional houses, manors and outbuildings transferred here from around Finland. Wandering around the wooded island is a pleasure in itself; guides dressed in traditional costume demonstrate folk dancing and crafts such as spinning, embroidery and troll-making. From central Helsinki, take bus 24, or tram 4 and walk.

🏃 Activities

One of the joys of Helsinki is grabbing a bike and taking advantage of its long waterfronts, numerous parks, and comprehensive network of cycle lanes. See p182 for bike hire.

TOP CHOICE Kotiharjun Sauna   SAUNA
(www.kotiharjunsauna.fi; Harjutorinkatu 1; adult/child €10/5; ☉2-8pm Tue-Fri, 1-7pm Sat, sauna time until 10pm) This traditional public wood-fired sauna dates back to 1928. This type of place largely disappeared with the advent of shared saunas in apartment buildings, but it's a classic experience, where you can also get a scrub down and massage. There are

separate saunas for men and women. It's a short stroll from Sörnäinen metro station.

Yrjönkadun Uimahalli SWIMMING, SAUNA
(www.hel.fi; Yrjönkatu 21; swim/swim & sauna €5/12; ☺men Tue, Thu & Sat, women Mon, Wed, Fri & Sun, closed Jun-Aug) For a sauna and swim, these art deco baths are a Helsinki institution – a fusion of soaring Nordic elegance and Roman tradition. There are separate hours for men and women. Nudity is compulsory in the saunas; bathing suits are optional in the pool.

Cruises CRUISE
Numerous summer cruises leave from the kauppatori. A 1½-hour jaunt costs €17 to €20; dinner cruises, bus–boat combinations and sunset cruises are all available. Most go past Suomenlinna and weave between other islands. Cruises run from May to September; there's no need to book, just turn up and pick the next departure.

☞ Tours

An excellent budget alternative is to catch the 3T/3B tram and pick up the free *Sightseeing on 3T/3B* brochure as your guide around the city centre and out to Kallio.

Helsinki Expert BUS
(☎2288 1600; www.helsinkiexpert.fi; adult/child €27/15, with Helsinki Card free) Based at the tourist office, runs 90-minute sightseeing tours in its bright orange bus.

✦ Festivals & Events

Helsinki Day CULTURAL
(www.hel.fi) Celebrating the city's anniversary brings many free events to Esplanadi Park (situated between Pohjoisesplanadi and Eteläesplanadi) on 12 June.

Helsinki Festival ARTS
(Helsingin Juhlaviikot; www.helsinginjuhlaviikot.fi) From late August to early September, this arts festival features chamber music, jazz, theatre, opera and more.

🛏 Sleeping

Accommodation is expensive in Helsinki. From mid-May to mid-August, bookings are strongly advised.

TOP CHOICE Hotel GLO HOTEL €€€
(☎010 344 4400; www.palacekamp.fi; Kluuvikatu 4; standard r around €200; @) There are no starched suits at reception at this laid-back designer pad, and the relaxed atmosphere continues through the comfortably modish public areas to the rooms. Beds: exceptionally inviting. Facilities: top notch and mostly free. Location: On a pedestrian street in the heart of town. Online prices are the best; if there's not much difference between the standard and the standard XL, go for the latter as you get quite a bit more space.

TOP CHOICE Hotelli Helka HOTEL €€€
(☎613 580; www.helka.fi; Pohjoinen Rautatiekatu 23A; s/d €151/189, weekends & summer €100/124; P@) One of the centre's best midrange hotels – you can nearly always get it cheaper than the listed price – the Helka has competent, friendly staff and excellent facilities, including free parking if you can bag one of the limited spots. Best are the rooms, with backlit prints of an autumn forest hanging over the beds.

Hotel Fabian HOTEL €€
(☎040-521 0356; www.hotelfabian.fi; Fabianinkatu 7; standard r €150; P@) Central, but in a quiet part without the bustle of the other designer hotels, this place hasn't been open long but is getting everything right. Elegant standard rooms with whimsical lighting and chessboard tiles are extremely comfortable; they vary substantially in size.

Hotel Finn HOTEL €€
(☎684 4360; www.hotellifinn.fi; Kalevankatu 3B; s/d with toilet from €69/79, with toilet & shower from €79/99) High in a central city building, this small, friendly hotel was under gradual refurbishment when we last passed by. The corridors were darkly done out in sexy chocolate and red, with art from young Finnish photographers on the walls, but the rooms were all bright white and blond parquet. Rates go up when it's nearly full, but if you get one of the standard rates listed here, it's great value for Helsinki.

Hostel Academica HOSTEL €
(☎1311 4334; www.hostelacademica.fi; Hietaniemenkatu 14; dm/s/d €25/57/72; ☺Jun-Aug;

SLEEPING PRICE RANGES

» **€**	up to €70 per night for the cheapest double room
» **€€**	cheapest double €70 to €160
» **€€€**	cheapest double over €160

Helsinki

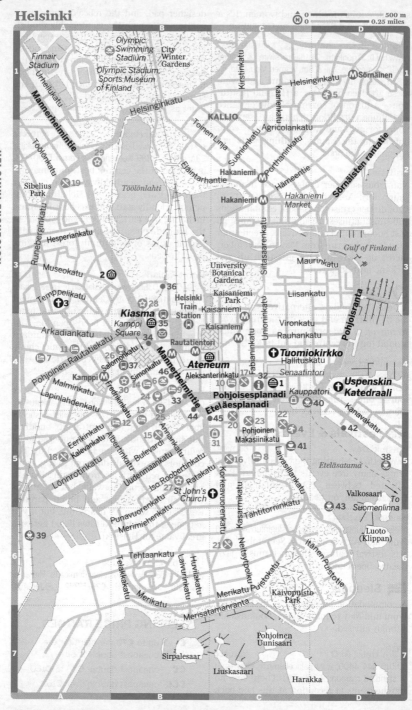

Helsinki

⊙ Top Sights

Ateneum.. B4
Kiasma.. B4
Tuomiokirkko.. C4
Uspenskin Katedraali........................ D4

⊙ Sights

1 Helsinki City Museum C4
2 Kansallismuseo.................................... A3
3 Temppeliaukion Kirkko A3

⊙ Activities, Courses & Tours

4 Cruise Boats C5
5 Kotiharjun Sauna................................. D1
6 Yrjönkadun Uimahalli.......................... B4

⊙ Sleeping

7 Hostel Academica A4
8 Hotel Fabian... C5
9 Hotel Finn B4
10 Hotel GLO... C4
11 Hotelli Helka... A4
12 Omenahotelli Eerikinkatu B5
13 Omenahotelli Lönnrotinkatu B5
14 Omenahotelli Yrjönkatu B4

⊙ Eating

15 Café Ekberg.. B5
16 Juuri.. C5
17 Karl Fazer C4
18 Konstan Möljä A5
19 Kuu.. A2
20 Olo... C5
21 Sea Horse C6
22 Vanha Kauppahalli................................ C5
23 Zucchini.. C5

⊙ Drinking

A21 Cocktail Lounge .... (see 25)
24 Ateljee Bar B4
25 Bar Loose... B4
26 Teerenpeli... B4

⊙ Entertainment

27 DTM... B5
28 Musiikkitalo.. B3
29 Oopperatalo.. A2
Semifinal................................... (see 30)
30 Tavastia... B4
Tiger .... (see 37)

⊙ Shopping

31 Design Forum Finland.......................... C5

⊙ Information

32 Tourist Office.. C4

⊙ Transport

33 Eckerö Line B4
34 Europcar... B4
35 Finnair Buses.. B4
36 Greenbike B3
37 Kamppi Bus Station B4
38 Katajanokka Ferry Terminal................. D5
39 Länsiterminaali...................................... A6
Linda Line................................... (see 41)
40 Local Ferries... C4
41 Makasiini Ferry Terminal...................... C5
42 Nordic Jet Line D5
43 Olympia Ferry Terminal........................ D5
44 Silja Line B4
45 Tallink... C5
46 Viking Line B4

HELSINKI EXCURSION EATING

$P@⊠$) Finnish students live well, so in summer take advantage of this residence, a super-clean spot packed with features (pool and sauna) and cheery staff. The modern rooms are great; all come with bar fridges and their own bathrooms. Dorms have only two or three berths so there's no crowding. HI discount.

Omenahotelli HOTELS €€
($\boxed{\square}$0600 18018; www.omena.com; r €80-99) Eerikinkatu (Eerikinkatu 24); Lönnrotinkatu (Lönnrotinkatu 13); Yrjönkatu (Yrjönkatu 30) This good-value unstaffed-hotel chain has three handy Helsinki locations. As well as a double bed, rooms have fold-out chairs that can sleep two more, plus there's a microwave and minifridge. Book online or via a terminal in the lobby. Windows don't open so rooms can be stuffy on hot days.

🍴 Eating

Helsinki has a great range of restaurants, whether for Finnish classics, new Finnish cuisine or international dining. Good budget places are in shorter supply: cafes offer good lunch options and Helsinki's famous love of coffee means there are always great places to grab a cup and a traditional pastry.

A good resource is the website www .eat.fi, which plots restaurants on a map of town: even if you can't read all the reviews, you'll soon spot which ones are the latest favourites.

EATING PRICE RANGES

For this chapter we've based the budget breakdowns on the following price ranges, according to the cheapest main meal offered.

- » €   less than €5
- » €€   €5 to €25
- » €€€ more than €25

TOP CHOICE Olo   FINNISH €€

(☎665 565, www.olo-restaurant.com; Kasarmikatu 44; lunch menus from €29, 4-course dinner €59; ⊙11.30am-1.30pm Mon-Fri, 5-10pm Tue-Sat) Casual surveys on the street repeatedly flag this up as one of the city's favourite current restaurants. It's one of ours, too. Despite the quality, Olo is refreshingly unpretentious with a dining room of muted greys and whites. All meals come with house-baked breads (try the fruity malt) and the wine list is broad enough to appeal to all palates.

Zucchini   VEGETARIAN €

(www.zucchini.fi; Fabianinkatu 4; lunches €7-11; ⊙11am-3pm Mon-Fri) One of the city's few vegetarian cafes, this is a top-notch lunchtime spot; queues out the door are not unusual. Piping-hot soups banish winter chills; fresh-baked quiche on the sunny terrace out the back is a summer treat.

Juuri   MODERN FINNISH €€

(☎635 732; www.juuri.fi; Korkeavuorenkatu 27; mains €24; ⊙11am-2pm & 4-11pm Mon-Fri, noon-11pm Sat, 4-11pm Sun) Creative takes on classic Finnish ingredients draw the crowds to this stylish modern restaurant, but the best way to eat is to sample the 'sapas', which are tapas with a Suomi twist (€4.30 a plate). You might graze on marinated fish, smoked beef or homemade sausages. There are cheap lunch specials here, but they're not as interesting.

Sea Horse   FINNISH €€

(☎010-837 5700; www.seahorse.fi; Kapteeninkatu 11; mains €14-24; ⊙10.30am-midnight) Seahorse dates back to the '30s and is as traditional a Finnish restaurant as you'll find anywhere. Locals gather in the gloriously unchanged interior to meet and drink over hefty dishes of Baltic herring, Finnish meatballs and cabbage rolls.

Konstan Mölja   FINNISH €

(☎694 7504; www.konstanmolja.fi; Hietalahdenkatu 14; lunch/dinner buffet €8/18; ⊙11am-2.30pm & 5-10pm Tue-Fri, 4-10pm Sat) The maritime interior of this old sailor's eatery hosts an impressive husband-and-wife team who turn out a great-value Finnish buffet for lunch and dinner. Though these days it sees plenty of tourists, it's solid traditional fare with salmon, soup, reindeer and friendly explanations of what goes with what. There's also à la carte available. It tends to close for a month or so in summer, so ring ahead to check it's open.

Kuu   FINNISH €€

(☎2709 0973; www.ravintolakuu.info; Töölönkatu 27; mains €14-26; ⊙11am-midnight Mon-Fri, 1pm-midnight Sat, 1-10pm Sun) Excellent choice for traditional Finnish fare. On a corner behind the Crowne Plaza hotel on Mannerheimintie.

Café Ekberg   CAFE €

(www.cafeekberg.fi; Bulevardi 9; lunches €8-10; ⊙7.30am-7pm Mon-Fri, 8.30am-5pm Sat, 10am-5pm Sun) There's been a cafe of this name in Helsinki since 1861 and today it continues to be a family-run place renowned for pastries such as the Napoleon cake. The buffet breakfasts and daily lunch specials are also popular, plus there's fresh bread to take away.

Karl Fazer   CAFE €

(www.fazer.fi; Kluuvikatu 3; lunches €8-12; ⊙7.30am-10pm Mon-Fri, 9am-10pm Sat, also 10am-6pm Sun summer) This classic cafe is the flagship for the mighty chocolate empire of the same name. The cupola famously reflects sound, so locals say it's a bad place to gossip. It is ideal, however, for buying Fazer confectionary or enjoying the towering sundaes or slabs of cake.

🍷 Drinking

Finns don't mind a drink and Helsinki has some of Scandinavia's most diverse nightlife. In winter locals gather in cosy bars, while in summer early-opening beer terraces sprout up all over town.

The centre's full of bars and clubs, with the Punavuori area around Iso-Roobertinkatu one of the most worthwhile for trendy alternative choices.

TOP CHOICE Teerenpeli   PUB

(www.teerenpeli.com; Olavinkatu 2) Get away from the Finnish lager mainstream with this excellent pub right by the bus station.

It serves very tasty ales, stouts and berry ciders from a microbrewery in Lahti in a long, split-level place with romantically low lighting, intimate tables and an indoor smokers' patio. A top spot.

A21 Cocktail Lounge   BAR
(www.a21.fi; Annankatu 21; ⊙Tue-Sat) You'll need to ring the doorbell to get into this chic club but it's worth the intrigue to swing with Helsinki's arty set. The interior is sumptuous in gold, but the real lushness is in the cocktails, particularly the Finnish blends that toss cloudberry liqueur and rhubarb to create the city's most innovative tipples.

Bar Loose   BAR
(www.barloose.com; Annankatu 21; ⊙4pm-2am Mon-Tue, 4pm-4am Wed-Sat, 6pm-4am Sun) The opulent blood-red interior and comfortably cosy seating seem too stylish for a rock bar, but that's what this is, with portraits of guitar heroes lining one wall and an eclectic mix of people filling the upstairs, served by two bars. Downstairs is a club area, with live music more nights than not.

Ateljee Bar   BAR
(Sokos Hotel Torni, Yrjönkatu 26; ⊙2pm-2am Mon-Thu, noon-2am Fri & Sat, 2pm-1am Sun) It's worth heading up to this tiny perch on the roof of the Sokos Hotel Torni for the city panorama. Take the lift to the 12th floor, then there's a narrow spiral staircase to the top.

☆ Entertainment

As the nation's big smoke, Helsinki has the hottest culture and nightlife. Music is

---

THE OLD MARKET HALL

In summer there are food stalls, fresh produce and expensive berries at the kauppatori, but the real picnic treats are in the **Vanha Kauppahalli** (Old Market Hall; Eteläranta 1; ⊙8am-6pm Mon-Fri, 8am-4pm Sat, 10am-4pm Sun summer only) nearby. Built in 1889, some of it's touristy these days (reindeer kebabs?), but it's still a traditional Finnish market, where you can get filled rolls, cheese, breads, fish and an array of typical snacks and delicacies. Here you'll also find **Soppakeittiö** (soups €7-9; ⊙lunch Mon-Fri), a great soup bar with famously good bouillabaisse, which is also open on Saturday at Vanha Kauppahalli.

---

particularly big here, from metal clubs to opera. The latest events are publicised in *Helsinki This Week*.

Helsinki has a dynamic club scene that's always changing. Some club nights have age limits (often over 20) so check event details on websites before you arrive.

For concerts and performances, see *Helsinki This Week*, enquire at the tourist office, or check the website of ticket outlet **Lippupiste** (☏0600 900 900; www.lippu.fi). Opera and ballet are at the **Oopperatalo** (Opera House; ☏4030 2211; www.opera.fi; Helsinginkatu 58). Next to Kiasma, the stunning new **Musiikkitalo** (Helsinki Music Centre; www.musiikkitalo.fi; Mannerheimintie 13) has a main auditorium and several smaller ones: a fitting venue for the city's wonderful classical concerts.

Tavastia   LIVE MUSIC
(www.tavastiaklubi.fi; Urho Kekkosenkatu 4; ⊙9pm-late) One of Helsinki's legendary rock venues, this attracts both up-and-coming local acts and bigger international groups. There's a band every night of the week. Also check out what's on at **Semifinal**, the smaller venue next door.

Tiger   CLUB
(www.thetiger.fi; Urho Kekkosenkatu 1A; ⊙10pm-4am Fri-Sun) Ascend into clubbing heaven at this super-slick club with stellar lighting and high-altitude cocktails. Music runs from chart hits to R&B; drinks are expensive and there's a €10 door charge, but the view from the terrace is stunning. Entrance via Kamppi Sq.

DTM   GAY
(www.dtm.fi; Iso Roobertinkatu 28; ⊙9am-4am Mon-Sat, noon-4am Sun) Scandinavia's biggest gay club is a multilevel complex with an early-opening cafe-bar. There are a couple of club areas opening at 9pm (with cover charge and a minimum age of 22) and regular club nights, as well as drag shows or women-only sessions.

🛍 Shopping

Known for design and art, Helsinki is an epicentre of Nordic cool, from fashion to the latest furniture and homewares. The further you wander from Pohjoisesplanadi, the main tourist street in town, the lower prices become. The hippest area is definitely Punavuori, which has several good boutiques and art galleries to explore. The whole of

HELSINKI CARD

If you plan to see a lot of sights, the **Helsinki Card** (www.helsinkicard.fi; adult for 24/48/72hr €35/45/55, child €14/17/20) gives you free travel, entry to more than 50 attractions in and around Helsinki and discounts on day tours. It's cheaper to buy it online; otherwise get it at the tourist office, hotels, the ubiquitous R-kioskis shops and transport terminals.

that side of town is bristling with design shops and studios. A couple of hundred of these are part of **Design District Helsinki** (www.designdistrict.fi), whose invaluable map you can find at the tourist office. To get some pointers, stop by central **Design Forum Finland** (www.designforum.fi; Erottajankatu 7; ☺10am-7pm Mon-Fri, 10am-6pm Sat, noon-5pm Sun), which operates a shop that hosts many designers' work. You're often better off price-wise to hunt down your own bargains, though.

 Information

Packed your phone? Helsinki has a cut-down version of its tourism website designed to be delivered to your mobile at www.helsinki.mobi.

Internet access at various public libraries is free. Large parts of the city centre have free wi-fi, as do many bars and cafes – some also have terminals for customers' use. Public telephones are non-existent.

City of Helsinki (www.hel.fi) Helsinki City website, with links to all the information you might need.

General Emergency (☎112)

Helsinki Expert (www.helsinkiexpert.fi) Site that offers sightseeing tours, accommodation bookings, tickets and events listings.

HSL/HRT (www.hsl.fi) Website for public transport information and journey planner.

Police (☎122)

Sidewalk Express (www.sidewalkexpress.com; internet per hr €2). There are several of these unstaffed stand-up internet access points around town. Buy your ticket from the machine; it's valid for all of them. Handy locations include the central railway station (far left as you look at the trains) and Kamppi bus station (outside the ticket office).

Tourist Office (☎3101 3300; www.visit helsinki.fi; Pohjoisesplanadi 19; ☺9am-6pm Mon-Fri, 9am-5pm Sat & Sun Jun-Aug, 10am-4.30pm Mon-Fri, 10am-4pm Sat Sep-May)

Busy multilingual office with a great quantity of information on the city. Also offices at the train station and the airport.

Visit Helsinki (www.visithelsinki.fi) Excellent tourist-board website full of information.

UNDERSTAND HELSINKI

Helsinki Today

From its days as a shy wallflower on the confident Nordic dance floor, Finland has positioned itself in the vanguard of nations, with Helsinki at the forefront. Its reputation as Europe's worst capital for foodies has been banished, with a raft of restaurants sourcing excellent traditional produce and presenting it in contemporary, stodge-free ways. The technology sector has suffered a dip with the global economic crisis, but the long-term outlook is more or less optimistic. The city's design studios continue to set a global benchmark, but the charm of its centenarian buildings and museums is undimmed. The rise to prominence of the anti-immigration True Finns party has raised questions about Finland's role in the euro and the EU in general but a period of introspection is a very traditional manner of decision making in this large corner of the north.

History

Founded in 1550 by the Swedish king Gustav Vasa, Helsinki was to be a rival to the Hansa trading town of Tallinn. For more than 200 years it remained a backwater, suffering from various Russian incursions until the Swedes built their fortress named Sveaborg in 1748 to protect this eastern part of their empire. Once the Russians took control of Finland in 1809, a capital closer to St Petersburg was required to keep a closer eye on Finland's domestic politics. Helsinki was chosen – in large part because of the sea fortress (now called Suomenlinna) just outside the harbour – and so in 1812 Turku lost its longstanding status as Finland's capital and premier town.

In the 19th and early 20th centuries, Helsinki grew rapidly in all directions. German architect CL Engel was called on to dignify the city centre, which resulted in the neoclassical Senaatintori (Senate Sq). The city suffered heavy Russian bombing during

WWII, but in the postwar period Helsinki recovered and went on to host the Summer Olympic Games in 1952.

These days, the capital is so much the centre of everything that goes on in Finland that its past as an obscure market town is totally forgotten.

SURVIVAL GUIDE

Getting There & Away

Small/large lockers cost €2/4 per 24 hours at the bus and train station. There are similar lockers and left-luggage counters at the ferry terminals.

Air

Helsinki's **airport** (www.helsinki-vantaa.fi) is at Vantaa, 19km north of Helsinki. There are a growing number of direct flights from European, American and Asian destinations. It's also served by various budget carriers from several European countries, especially Ryanair, Air Baltic and Blue1. Most other flights are with Finnair or Scandinavian Airlines (SAS).

Boat

International ferries link Helsinki with Stockholm (Sweden), Tallinn (Estonia; see boxed text), St Petersburg (Russia) and destinations in Germany and Poland. Ferry tickets may be purchased at the terminal, from a ferry company's office (and often its website) or, in some cases, from the city tourist office. Book well in advance during the high season (late June to mid-August) and at weekends. There is also a regular catamaran and hydrofoil service from Tallinn.

There are five main terminals, three close to the centre:

Katajanokka terminal Served by bus 13 and trams 2, 2V and 4.

Olympia and Makasiini terminals Served by trams 3B and 3T. **Länsiterminaali (West Terminal)** Served by bus 15.

Hansaterminaali (Vuosaari) Further afield; can be reached on bus 90A.

Bus

Purchase long-distance and express bus tickets at **Kamppi bus station** (Frederikinkatu; ⏰7am-7pm Mon-Fri, 7am-5pm Sat, 9am-6pm Sun) or on the bus itself. Long-distance buses also depart from here to all of Finland.

Train

Helsinki's **train station** (rautatieasema; www.vr.fi; ⏰tickets 6.30am-9pm Mon-Sat, 8am-9pm Sun) is central and easy to find your way around. It's linked by subway to the metro (Rautatientori stop), and is a short walk from the bus station.

The train is the fastest and cheapest way to get from Helsinki to major Finnish centres. There are also daily trains (buy tickets from the international counter) to the Russian cities of Vyborg, St Petersburg and Moscow.

Getting Around
To/From the Airport

Bus 615 (€4, 30 to 45 minutes, 5am to midnight) shuttles between Helsinki-Vantaa airport (platform 21) and platform 5 at Rautatientori (Railway Sq) next to the main train station. Bus stops are marked with a blue sign featuring a plane.

FERRIES TO TALLINN

» **Eckerö Line** (☎0600-04300; www.eckeroline.fi; Mannerheimintie 10) Sails daily to Tallinn year-round (adult €19-25, car €17-25, three to 3½ hours) from Länsiterminaali.

» **Linda Line** (☎0600-0668 970; www.lindaline.fi; Makasiini terminal) The fastest. Small passenger-only hydrofoil company ploughing the waters to Tallinn (from €26 to €46, day trips €35 to €45, 1½ hours) eight times daily when ice-free.

» **Tallink/Silja** (☎0600-15700; www.tallinksilja.com; Erottajankatu 19) Runs at least six Tallinn services (one way adult €26 to €44, vehicle from €25, two hours), from Länsiterminaali.

» **Viking Line** (☎12351; www.vikingline.fi; Lönnrotinkatu 2) Operates car ferries (adult €21 to €39, vehicle plus two passengers €60 to €100, 2½ hours) from Katajanokka terminal.

Faster **Finnair buses** (€6.20, 30 minutes, every 20 minutes, 5am to midnight) depart from Elielinaukio platform 30 on the other side of the train station, stopping once en route, by the top-end hotels further up Mannerheimintie. The 415 bus departs from the adjacent stand but it's slower than the other two.

There are also door-to-door **airport taxis** (☑0600-555 555; www.airporttaxi.fi), which need to be booked the previous day, before 6pm, if you're leaving Helsinki (one to two people €27). A normal cab should cost €40 to €50.

There's a new airport–city rail link due to open in 2014.

Bicycle

With a flat inner city and well-marked cycling paths, Helsinki is ideal for cycling. Get hold of a copy of the Helsinki cycling map at the tourist office.

The city of Helsinki provides distinctive green 'City Bikes' at stands within a radius of 2km from the kauppatori. The bikes are free: you deposit a €2 coin into the stand that locks them, then reclaim it when you return it to any stand.

For something more sophisticated, **Greenbike** (☑050-404 0400; www.greenbike .fi; Bulevardi 32; ⊗10am-6pm May-Sep) rents out quality bikes (per day/24 hours/week from €25/30/75) including 24-speed hybrid mountain bikes. Enter on Albertinkatu. **Ecobike** (☑040-084 4358; www.ecobike.fi; Savilankatu 1B; ⊗1-6pm, Mon-Thu) is another good option for bike hire, opposite Finnair Stadium. Call ahead to hire outside these hours.

Public Transport

The city's public transport system, **HSL** (www.hsl.fi), operates buses, metro and local trains, trams and a ferry to Suomenlinna. A one-hour flat-fare ticket for any HSL transport costs €2.50 when purchased on board, €2 when purchased in advance. The ticket allows unlimited transfers but must be validated in the stamping machine on board when you first use it. A single tram ticket is €2 full fare. And because it's Nokialand you can order any of these tickets for the same prices using your mobile: send an SMS to ☑16355 texting A1. Day or multiday tickets for up to seven days (24/48/72 hours €7/10.50/14) are the best option if you're in town for a short time.

Taxi

Hail cabs off the street or join a queue at one of the taxi stands located at the train station, bus station or Senaatintori. You can phone for a taxi on ☑010-00700.

Latvia

Includes »

Rīga 185
Jūrmala 218
Cape Kolka
(Kolkasrags) 225
Abava River Valley 227
Kuldīga 229
Ventspils 231
Pāvilosta 234
Liepāja 235
Rundāle Palace 239
Gauja National Park 245
Daugavpils 259
Latgale Lakelands 262

Best Places to Eat

» Istaba (p209)
» Aragats (p209)
» 36.Line (p221)
» Fish Restaurant @ Dome (p208)
» Dārziņš (p231)

Best Places to Stay

» Rumene Manor (p227)
» Hotel Bergs (p206)
» Radisson Blu Elizabete Hotel (p206)
» Līvkalns (p251)
» Fontaine Royal (p237)

Why Go?

Tucked between Estonia to the north and Lithuania to the south, Latvia is the meat of the Baltic sandwich. We're not implying that the neighbouring nations are slices of white bread, but Latvia is the savoury middle, loaded with colourful fixings. Thick greens take the form of Gauja Valley pines; onion-domed cathedrals sprout up above local towns; cheesy Russian pop blares along coastal beaches; and spicy Rīga adds an extra zing as the country's cosmopolitan nexus and the unofficial capital of the entire Baltic.

If that doesn't whet your appetite, hear this: the country's under-the-radar profile makes it the perfect pit stop for those seeking something a bit more authentic than the overrun tourist hubs further afield. So consider a trip here rather than the usual suspects of Eastern Europe.

When to Go

Spend the holidays in the birthplace of the Christmas tree, and try some bobsledding if you dare during the frigid weeks of December and January. The all-night solstice in June rings in the warmer months as locals flock to their coastal cottages for beach-lazing and midnight sun. Refusing to let summer go, Rīgans sip lattes under outdoor heat lamps as the cool September air blows through at the season's last alfresco cafes.

Fast Facts

» **Area** 64,589 sq km
» **Capital** Rīga
» **Population** 2.2 million
» **Telephone country code** ☎371
» **Emergency** ☎112

Exchange Rates

Australia	A$1	0.54Ls
Canada	C$1	0.52Ls
Euro zone	€1	0.71Ls
Japan	¥100	0.69Ls
New Zealand	NZ$1	0.41Ls
UK	UK£1	0.83Ls
USA	US$1	0.53Ls

» For current exchange rates see www.xe.com

Set Your Budget

» **Budget hotel room** 25Ls
» **Two-course evening meal** 10Ls
» **Museum entrance** 1.50Ls
» **Beer** 1.20Ls
» **City transport ticket** 0.70Ls

Arriving in Latvia

Latvia is the link in the Baltic chain, making Rīga a convenient connecting point between Tallinn and Vilnius. Long-distance buses and trains also connect the capital to St Petersburg, Moscow and Warsaw, and ferry services shuttle passengers to Stockholm and the German towns of Rostock and Lübeck. Rīga is the hub of airBaltic, which offers direct service to more than 50 European cities.

LANGUAGE

Hello (good day)	Labdien	*lab-dee-in*
Hi (informal)	Sveiki	*sfay-kee*
How are you?	Kā jums klājas	*kah yooms klah-yus*
Thank you	Paldies	*paul-dee-iss*
Please/you're welcome	Lūdzu	*lood-zoo*

Essential Food & Drink

» **Black Balzām** Goethe called it the 'elixir of life'. The jet-black, 45%-proof concoction is a secret recipe of more than a dozen fairy-tale ingredients including oak bark, wormwood and linden blossoms. A shot a day keeps the doctor away, so say most of Latvia's pensioners. Try mixing it with a glass of cola to take the edge off.

» **Mushrooms** A national obsession; mushroom-picking takes the country by storm during the first showers of autumn.

» **Alus** For such a tiny nation there's definitely no shortage of *alus* (beer) – each major town has its own brew. You can't go wrong with Užavas (Ventspils' contribution).

» **Smoked fish** Dozens of fish shacks dot the Kurzeme coast – look for the veritable smoke signals rising above the tree line. Grab 'em to go; they make the perfect afternoon snack.

» **Kvass** Single-handedly responsible for the decline of Coca Cola at the turn of the 21st century, Kvass is a beloved beverage made from fermented rye bread. It's surprisingly popular with kids!

RĪGA

POP 703,500

'The Paris of the North', 'The Second City that Never Sleeps' – everyone's so keen to tack on qualifying superlatives to Latvia's capital, but regal Rīga does a hell of a job of holding its own. For starters, the city has the largest and most impressive showing of art-nouveau architecture in Europe. Nightmarish gargoyles and praying goddesses adorn more than 750 buildings along the stately boulevards radiating out from Rīga's castle core. The heart of the city – Old Town – is a fairy-tale kingdom of winding, wobbly lanes and gingerbread trim that beats to the sound of a bumpin' discotheque.

History

Although some Latvians may lament the fact that they are an ethnic minority in their own capital, others will be quick to point out that Rīga was never a 'Latvian' city. Founded in 1201 by the German bishop Albert von Buxhoevden (say that fast three times) as a bridgehead for the crusade against the northern 'heathens', Rīga became a stronghold for the Knights of the Sword and the newest trading junction between Russia and the West. When Sweden snagged the city in 1621, it grew into the largest holding of the Swedish Empire (even bigger than Stockholm!). Then the Russians snatched Latvia from Sweden's grip and added an industrial element to the bustling burg. By the mid-1860s Rīga was the world's biggest timber port and Russia's third city after Moscow and St Petersburg. The 20th century also saw the birth of cafes, salons, dance clubs and a thriving intellectual culture, which was all bombed to high hell in WWI, and subsequently captured by the Nazis during WWII. Somehow, Rīga's indelible international flavour managed to rise up from the rubble, and even as a part of the USSR, Rīga was known for its forward thinking and thriving cultural life.

Today, Rīga's cosmopolitan past has enabled the city to effortlessly adjust to a global climate, making it more than just the capital of Latvia – it's the cornerstone of the Baltic.

◎ Sights

Rīga quietly sits along the Daugava River, which flows another 15km north before dumping into the Gulf of Rīga. Old Rīga (Vecrīga), the historic heart of the city, stretches 1km along the river's eastern

LATVIA AT A GLANCE

Currency Lats (Ls)

Language Latvian, Russian (unofficial)

Money ATMs are widespread; cash preferred to credit cards for small purchases.

Visas None required for stays of up to 90 days for Australian, Canadian, EU, New Zealand and US citizens.

side and 600m back from its banks. This medieval section of town is mostly pedestrian, containing a flurry of curving cobbled streets and alleys.

As Kaļķu iela continues away from the river, it turns into Brīvības bulvāris (Freedom Boulevard) when it hits the thin, picturesque ring of parkland that protects the medieval centre from the gridiron of grand boulevards just beyond. The copper-topped Freedom Monument, in the middle of Brīvības bulvāris, is the unofficial gateway into Central Rīga. This part of the city, constructed in the 19th and 20th centuries, sports wide avenues, luxurious apartment blocks and plenty of art-nouveau architecture. At the outer edges of the city centre, the European grandeur begins to fade into Soviet block housing and *microrajons* (microregions, or suburbs).

OLD RĪGA (VECRĪGA)

The curving cobbled streets of Rīga's medieval core are best explored at random. Once you're sufficiently lost amid the tangle of gabled roofs, church spires and crooked alleyways, you will begin to uncover a stunning, World Heritage–listed realm of sky-scraping cathedrals, gaping city squares and crumbling castle walls.

RĀTSLAUKUMS

Touristy Rātslaukums is a great place to start one's exploration of the old city. There's a tourist information centre stuffed to the gills with brochures and maps; it's located in Blackheads' House.

[TOP CHOICE] **Blackheads' House**   HISTORIC BUILDING

(Map p190; http://nami.riga.lv/mn; Rātslaukums 7; admission 2Ls; ☻10am-5pm Tue-Sun) Touristy Rātslaukums is home to the postcard-worthy Blackheads' House, built in 1344 as a veritable fraternity house for the Blackheads

Baltic Sea

Saaremaa

Kihnu

Rīga to Stockholm

To Nynashamn, Sweden

Lübeck to Rīga (Latvia)

③ Cape Kolka

Mazirbe

Ruhnu

Ikš

Ainaži

Salacgrīva

Lübeck to Ventspils
Rostock to Ventspils

Ovīši

Mīķeltornis

Dundaga

Kaltene

◎ **Ventspils**

Vārve

Ugāle

Valdemarpils

Gulf of Rīga

Mērsrags

Skult

Saulkrasti

KURZEME

Talsi ◎

Stende

Baltic Sea

Teranda

Sabile

Kandava

Plieņciems

Alsvanga

◎ **Kuldīga**

Kabile

Tukums ◎

Jūrmala
⑦

Old Rīga
② ①

Pāvilosta

Pedvale

Zemite

Rīga **①**

Salaspil

Kalnciems

Dzukste

Baldor

Aizpute

Skrunda

◎ **Saldus**

⑥ Liepāja

Dobele

◎ **Jelgava**

Lecava

Kiburi

Priekule

Ezere

Auce

Kalnamuiza

Pirunsdāle

Bauska

Klampji

Krumini

Mažeikiai

Alsiai

Zabare

Eleja

⑤

Rundāle Palace

Skuodas

Naujoji Akmenė

Zeimelis

Saločiai

Medininkai
Salantai

Seda

Papile

Joniškis

Linkuva

Lake Plateliai

Darbėnai

Plateliai

Plokštinė

Tryskiai

Gruzdžiai

Pasval

Palanga

Plungė

Telšiai

Čaganė

Kuršenai

Kretinga

Klaipėda ◎

Zarenai

Šiauliai ◎

Gargzdai

Rietavas

Varniai

Lake Lūkstas

Radviliškis

Smilgiai

Seduva

Panevėžys ◎

Priekule

Laukuva

Kelme

Juodkrantė

Sveksna

Kvėdarna

Pampenai

Šilalė

Grinkiskis

Latvia Highlights

① Click your camera at the nightmarish menagerie of devilish gargoyles, mythical beasts, praying goddesses and twisting vines that inhabits

the surplus of art-nouveau architecture in **Rīga** (p202)

② Lose yourself in the maze of cobblestones, church spires and gingerbread trim that is

Unesco-protected **Old Rīga** (p185)

③ Listen to the waves pound the awesomely remote **Cape Kolka** (p225), which crowns the desolate Kurzeme coast

4 Swing through **Sigulda** (p245) on a bungee cord, while chronicling its vivid history with stops at rambling Livonian castles

5 Sneak away from the capital and indulge in aristocratic decadence at **Rundāle Palace** (p239)

6 Wander past gritty Soviet tenements and gilded cathedrals in the crumbling Karosta district of **Liepāja** (p235)

7 Hobnob with Russian jetsetters in the heart of the swanky spa scene of **Jūrmala** (p218)

RĪGA IN...

Two Days

Start your adventure in the heart of the city with a stop at the much-loved **Blackheads' House** in Rātslaukums. Pick up some handy brochures at the in-house information centre, then spend the rest of the morning wandering among the twisting cobbled lanes that snake through medieval **Old Rīga**. After a leisurely lunch, wander beyond the ancient walls, passing the **Freedom Monument** as you make your way to the grand boulevards that radiate away from the city's castle core. Head to the **Quiet Centre**, where you'll find some of Rīga's finest examples of art-nouveau architecture. Don't miss the **Rīga Art Nouveau Centre**, then try our **art-nouveau walking tour**.

On your second day, fine-tune your bargaining skills (and your Russian) during a visit to the **Central Market**, where you can haggle for anything from wildberries to knock-off T-shirts. Have a walk through the small **Spīķeri district** then take a relaxing **boat ride** along the Daugava and the city's inner canals. For a late lunch, wander up to the **Miera iela** area just north of the art-nouveau district to enjoy the city's emerging hipster cafe culture near the sweet-smelling Laima chocolate factory. In the evening, if the opera is in season, treat yourself to some of the finest classical music in Europe.

Four Days

After completing the two-day itinerary above, spend day three in your swimsuit along the silky sands in **Jūrmala**, Latvia's uber-resort town. Rent a bike in the afternoon and roam around the stunning wooden cottages near the sea. End the day with a relaxing spa treatment, then return to Rīga to party all night at one of the city's notorious clubbing venues.

Your fourth day can be spent exploring some of Rīga's lesser-known nooks, or you can make tracks to **Gauja National Park** for an action-packed day of castle ogling mixed with adventure sports. Start in **Sigulda** and get the blood rushing on the Olympic bobsled track, swing through **Turaida** before making your way to the secreted Soviet bunker in **Līgatne**, then finish the day at the fortress ruins in **Cēsis** before returning to the capital.

guild of unmarried German merchants. The house was decimated in 1941, and flattened by the Soviets seven years later. Somehow the original blueprints survived and an exact replica was completed in 2001 for Rīga's 800th birthday.

FREE **Museum of the Occupation of Latvia**   MUSEUM
(Latvijas okupācijas muzejs; Map p190; ✆6721 2715; www.omf.lv; Latviešu Strēlnieku laukums 1; admission by donation; ⊙11am-6pm) The Latvian government has done an admirable job of razing all traces of Soviet oppression (ie ugly utilitarian structures), but they left one hideous reminder behind to purposefully contrast the rest of Rātslaukums' ornate architecture. The Museum of the Occupation of Latvia ironically inhabits this Soviet bunker, and carefully details Latvia's Soviet and Nazi occupations between 1940 and 1991. Some of the exhibits have been curated to shock visitors – dozens of gruesome photographs depict murdered and mangled Latvians. Captions are in a variety of languages, although they can sometimes be difficult to follow without a basic knowledge of Latvia's recent history. Audioguides are available for supplemental information. Allow a couple of hours to take it all in.

Mentzendorff's House   HISTORIC BUILDING
(Mencendorfa nams; Map p190; ✆6721 2951; www.mencendorfanams.com; Grēcinieku iela 18; admission 0.40-2Ls; ⊙10am-5pm) Once the home of a wealthy German noble, the 17th-century Mentzendorff's House offers insight into Rīga's history of shipping excess through the everyday trappings of an elite merchant family.

Town Hall   HISTORIC BUILDING
(Map p190; Rātslaukums) Facing the Blackheads' House across the square is the town hall, also rebuilt from scratch in recent years. A statue of Rīga's patron saint St

Roland stands between the two buildings. It's a replica of the original, erected in 1897, which now sits in St Peter's.

Latvian Riflemen Monument   MONUMENT
(Latviešu Strēlnieku laukums; Map p190) Latvian Riflemen Sq, on the other side of the Occupation Museum, was once home to Rīga's central market. Today the square is dominated by the imposing, dark-red Latvian Riflemen Monument, a controversial statue honouring Latvia's Red Riflemen, some of whom served as Lenin's personal bodyguards.

PĒTERBAZNĪCA LAUKUMS

St Peter's Lutheran Church   CHURCH
(Sv Pētera baznīca; Map p190; www.peterbaznica.lv; Skārņu iela 19; admission 3Ls; ⊘11am-6pm Tue-Sun) Rīga's skyline centrepiece is this Gothic church, thought to be around 800 years old. Don't miss the view from the spire, which has been rebuilt three times in the same baroque form. Legend has it that in 1667 the builders threw glass from the top to see how long the spire would last; a greater number of shards meant a very long life. The glass ended up landing on a pile of straw and didn't break – a year later the tower was incinerated. When the spire was resurrected after a bombing during WWII, the ceremonial glass chucking was repeated, and this time it was a smash hit. The spire is 123.25m, but the lift only whisks you up to 72m.

Museum of Decorative Arts & Design   MUSEUM
(Dekoratīvi lietišķās mākslas muzejs; Map p190; ☑6722 7833; www.lnmm.lv; Skārņu iela 10/20; admission 0.70Ls; ⊘11am-5pm Tue-Sun, to 7pm Wed) Behind St Peter's sits another impressive religious structure – the former St George's Church – which is now the Museum of Decorative Arts & Design. The museum highlights Latvia's impressive

collection of woodcuts, tapestries and ceramics. The building's foundations date back to 1207 when the Livonian Brothers of the Sword erected their castle here.

Rīga Porcelain Museum   MUSEUM
(Map p190; ☑6750 3769; Kalēju iela 9/11; admission 0.50Ls; ⊘11am-6pm Tue-Sun) Yet more ceramics can be viewed here, tucked away in John's Yard (Jāņa Sēta; Map p190; Skārņu iela 22), the restored courtyard of a former convent and original residence of Bishop Albert, the founder of Rīga.

St John's Church   CHURCH
(Jāņa baznīca; Map p190; Skārņu iela 24) A 13th- to 19th-century amalgam of Gothic, Renaissance and baroque styles.

KALĒJU IELA & MĀRSTAĻU IELA
Zigzagging Kalēju iela and Mārstaļu iela are dotted with poignant reminders of the city's legacy as a wealthy northern European trading centre. Several of the old merchants' manors have been transformed into museums like the Latvian Photography Museum (Latvijas fotogrāfijas muzejs; ☑6722 2713; www.fotomuzejs.lv; Mārstaļu iela 8; admission 1.50Ls; ⊘10am-5pm Wed & Fri-Sun, noon-7pm Thu), which displays unique photographs from 1920s Rīga.

Don't forget to look up at the curling vines and barking gargoyles adorning several art-nouveau facades (see also p202) including Rīga Synagogue (Peitavas iela 6/8), the only active Jewish house of worship in the capital. The structure was restored in a 'sacral art nouveau' style at the end of 2009 after a generous infusion of money from the EU.

Nearby, the one-room Latvian People's Front Museum (Latvijas tautas frontes muzejs; Map p190; ☑6722 4502; Vecpilsētas iela 13-15; admission free; ⊘2-7pm Tue, noon-5pm Wed-Fri, noon-4pm Sat) remains furnished exactly as it was when it served as the office of the Latvian People's Front prior to 1990.

LATVIA RĪGA

OH CHRISTMAS TREE

Rīga's Blackheads' House was known for its wild parties; it was, after all, a clubhouse for unmarried merchants. On a cold Christmas Eve in 1510, the squad of bachelors, full of holiday spirit (and other spirits, so to speak), hauled a great pine tree up to their clubhouse and smothered it with flowers. At the end of the evening, they burned the tree to the ground in an impressive blaze. From then on, decorating the 'Christmas tree' became an annual tradition, which eventually spread across the globe (as you probably know, the burning part never really caught on).

An octagonal commemorative plaque, inlaid in cobbled Rātslaukums, marks the spot where the original tree once stood.

Old Rīga (Vecrīga)

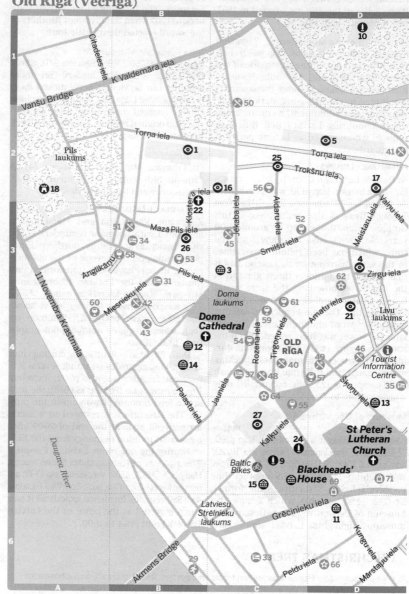

LIVU LAUKUMS

Lively Livu laukums, near the busiest entrance to Old Rīga along Kaļķu iela, features several beer gardens during summer and an outdoor **ice rink** (admission free; ⊙10am-1am Nov-Mar) in the colder months. A colourful row of 18th-century buildings lines the square – most of which have been turned into restaurants.

Cat House   HISTORIC BUILDING
(Map p190; Meistaru iela 10) The building, located at Meistaru iela 10, is known to most

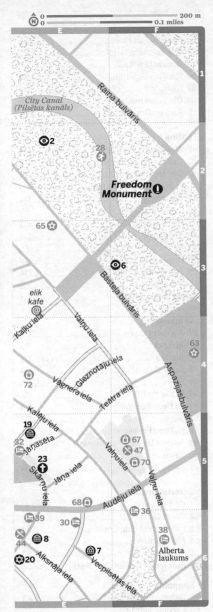

esteemed Great Guild Hall. The members of the guild were outraged, and after a lengthy court battle the merchant was admitted into the club on the condition that the cat be turned in the opposite direction.

Great & Small Guilds HISTORIC BUILDINGS
The 19th-century Gothic exterior of the **Great Guild** (Lielā gilde; Map p190; Amatu iela 6) encloses a sumptuous merchants' meeting hall, built during the height of German power in the 1330s. Today, the Great Guild houses the Latvian National Symphony Orchestra. The fairy-tale castle next door is the **Small Guild** (Mazā gilde; Map p190; Amatu iela 5), founded in the 14th century as the meeting place for local artisans.

DOMA LAUKUMS

Dome Cathedral CHURCH
(Doma baznīca; Map p190; ☎6721 3213; www .doms.lv; Doma laukums 1; admission 2Ls; ◷9am-5pm) The centrepiece of expansive Doma laukums is Rīga's enormous Dome Cathedral. Founded in 1211 as the seat of the Rīga diocese, it is still the largest church in the Baltic. The behemoth's architecture is an amalgam of styles from the 13th to the 18th centuries: the eastern end, the oldest portion, has Romanesque features; the tower is 18th-century baroque; and much of the rest dates from a 15th-century Gothic rebuilding. The floor and walls of the huge interior are dotted with old stone tombs – note the carved symbols denoting the rank or post of the occupant. Eminent citizens would pay to be buried as close to the altar as possible. In 1709 the cholera and typhoid outbreak that killed a third of Rīga's population was blamed on a flood that inundated the tombs. The cathedral's pulpit dates from 1641 and the huge 6768-pipe organ was the world's largest when it was completed in 1884 (it's now the fourth largest). During Soviet times, services were strictly forbidden and much of the cathedral's ornate interior decor was stripped away. Today, mass is held at noon on Sundays and at 8am every other day of the week.

Biržasnams Art Museum MUSEUM
(Map p190; ☎6722 6467; www.lnmm.lv; Doma laukums 6; ◷10am-6pm Tue-Sun) On the verge of opening at the time of research, Rīga's new museum will house the city's wealth of foreign art in a beautifully restored building that was once the city's stock-market centre. The clay-tinged facade features an ornate coterie of deities that dance between the

as the 'Cat House' for the spooked black cat sitting on the roof. According to legend, the owner was rejected from the local merchant's guild across the street, and exacted revenge by placing a black cat on the top of his turret with its tail raised towards the

LATVIA RĪGA

Old Rīga (Vecrīga)

◎ Top Sights
Blackheads' House C5
Dome Cathedral B4
Freedom Monument F2
St Peter's Lutheran Church D5

◎ Sights
1 Arsenāls Museum of Art B2
2 Bastion Hill E2
3 Bižasnams Art Museum C3
4 Cat House D3
Great Guild .... (see 62)
History Museum of Latvia .... (see 18)
5 Jacob's Barracks D2
John's Yard .... (see 19)
6 Laima Clock F3
Latvian National Opera .... (see 63)
7 Latvian People's Front Museum E6
8 Latvian Photography Museum E6
9 Latvian Riflemen Monument C5
10 Memorials to Victims of 20
January 1991 .... D1
11 Mentzendorff's House D6
12 Museum of Barricades of 1991 .... B4
13 Museum of Decorative Arts &
Design D5
14 Museum of the History of Rīga
& Navigation B4
15 Museum of the Occupation of
Latvia C5
16 Parliament C2
17 Powder Tower D2
18 Rīga Castle A2
Rīga Museum of Architecture ...... (see 26)
19 Rīga Porcelain Museum E5
20 Rīga Synagogue E6
21 Small Guild D4
St George's Church .... (see 13)
22 St Jacob's Cathedral B2
23 St John's Church E5
24 St Roland Statue C5
25 Swedish Gate C2
26 Three Brothers B3
27 Town Hall C5

◎ Activities, Courses & Tours
28 Riga By Canal E2
29 Riga By Canal Docks B6

◎ Sleeping
Blue Cow Barracks .... (see 5)
30 Centra E6
31 Dome Hotel B3
32 Ekes Konventas E5

33 Friendly Fun Franks C6
34 Grand Palace Hotel B3
35 Konventa Sēta D4
36 Naughty Squirrel F6
37 Neiburgs C4
38 Old Town Hostel F6
39 Radi un Draugi E6

◎ Eating
40 Alus Seta C4
41 Cadets de Gascogne D2
42 Dorian Gray B4
Fish Restaurant @ Dome .... (see 31)
43 Gutenbergs B4
44 Indian Raja E6
45 Ķiploku Krogs C3
46 Pelmeņi XL D4
47 Rimi F5
48 Rozengrāls C4
49 Šefpavārs Vilhelms D4
50 V. Ķuze C1
51 Vecmeita ar kaki B3

◎ Drinking
52 Ala Folks Clubs C3
53 Apiteka B3
Apsara .... (see 32)
54 Cuba Cafe C4
55 Egle C5
56 I Love You C2
57 La Belle Epoque D4
58 Mojo B3
59 Nekādu Problēmu C4
60 Paldies Dievam Piektdiena Ir
Klāt A4
61 Radio Bar C4

◎ Entertainment
Carpe Diem .... (see 4)
62 Great Guild D3
63 Latvian National Opera F4
64 Moon Safari C4
65 Nabaklab E3
66 Pulkvedim Neviens Neraksta D6

◎ Shopping
67 Galerija Centrs F5
68 Latvijas Balzāms E5
69 Pienene D5
Street Vendors .... (see 32)
70 Taste Latvia F5
71 Tornis D5
72 Upe E4

windows. Inside, visitors will uncover vaulted ceilings and gorgeous tilework.

Museum of the History of Rīga & Navigation   MUSEUM
(Rīgas vēstures un kuģniecības muzejs; Map p190; ☑6735 6676; www.rigamuz.lv; Palasta iela 4; admission 3Ls; ⊙11am-5pm Fri-Tue, noon-7pm Thu) The Baltics' oldest museum, is situated in the monastery's cloister at the back of the Dome Cathedral complex. Founded in 1773, the exhibition space features a permanent collection of artefacts from the Bronze Age all the way up to WWII. The three-room **Museum of Barricades of 1991** (1991 gada barikāžu muzejs; Map p190; ☑6721 3525; www .barikades.lv; admission free; ⊙10am-5pm Mon-Sat), also at the back of the Dome Cathedral, details the events that took place in Rīga in January 1991 through models, replicas and photographs.

Three Brothers   HISTORIC BUILDING
(Trīs brāļi; Map p190; Mazā Pils iela 17, 19 & 21) Located behind Doma laukums, away from the cathedral, three architectural gems neatly line up in a photogenic row. Known as the Three Brothers, these three stone houses exemplify Old Rīga's diverse collection of architectural styles (and echo Tallinn's 'Three Sisters'). No 17 is over 600 years old, making it the oldest stone dwelling in town, and No 19 (built in the 17th century) is now the **Rīga Museum of Architecture** (Map p190; Latvijas arhitektūras muzejs; www.archmuseum.lv; admission by donation; ⊙9am-5pm Mon-Fri). Note the tiny windows on the upper levels – Rīga's property taxes during the Middle Ages were based on the size of one's windows.

St Jacob's Cathedral   CHURCH
(Sv Jēkaba katedrāle; Map p190; Klostera iela) Latvia's first Lutheran services were held in St Jacob's Cathedral, which has an interior dating back to 1225. Today it is the seat of Rīga's Roman Catholic archbishopric.

PILS LAUKUMS

Rīga Castle   HISTORIC BUILDING
(Rīgas pils; Map p190; Pils laukums 3) In the far corner of Old Rīga near the Vanšu Bridge, verdant Pils laukums sits at the doorstep of Rīga Castle. Originally built as the headquarters for the Livonian Order, the foundation dates to 1330 and served as the residence of the order's grand master. The striking bastion (which doesn't look very castley when viewed from Pils laukums) is now home to Latvia's president.

The castle also houses the **History Museum of Latvia** (Latvijas vēstures muzejs; Map p190; ☑6722 3004; www.history-museum.lv; admission 1Ls, free Wed; ⊙11am-5pm Wed-Sun), which traces the history of Latvia and its people from the Stone Age to the present day. Displays are only captioned in Latvian, although English brochures can be purchased at the ticket counter.

Arsenāls Museum of Art & Parliament   MUSEUM
(Mākslas muzejs Arsenāls; Map p190; ☑6721 3695; Torņa iela 1; adult/child 0.70/0.40Ls; ⊙11am-5pm Tue, Wed & Fri-Sun, to 7pm Thu) This museum sits just east of Pils laukums and shares a block with Latvia's **Parliament** (Saeima; Map p190; Jēkaba iela 11), a Florentine Renaissance structure originally commissioned as the Knights' House of the German landlords.

TORŅA IELA

From Pils laukums, photogenic Torņa iela makes a beeline for City Canal (Pilsētas kanāls) at the other end of Old Rīga. Almost the entire north side of the street is flanked by the custard-coloured **Jacob's Barracks** (Jēkaba Kazarmas; Map p190; Torna iela 4), built as an enormous warehouse in the 16th century. Tourist-friendly cafes and boutiques now inhabit the refurbished building – at one time the American Embassy used the space for entertaining.

Swedish Gate   HISTORIC BUILDING
(Zviedru vārti; Map p190; Torņu iela 11) On the opposite side of the street from the sweeping Jacob's Barracks complex, you'll find Trokšnu iela, Old Rīga's narrowest *iela* (street), and the **Swedish Gate**, which was built onto the city's medieval walls in 1698 while under Swedish rule. When Rīga fell under Swedish rule, the city was the largest port in the entire empire. Today, this is the only remaining gate to Old Rīga.

Powder Tower   HISTORIC BUILDING
(Pulvera Tornis; Map p190; Smilšu iela 20) The cylindrical Powder Tower dates back to the 14th century and is the only survivor of the 18 original towers that punctuated the old city wall. Nine Russian cannonballs from 17th- and 18th-century assaults are embedded in the tower's walls. In the past it has served as a gunpowder warehouse, prison, torture chamber and frat house. Today it is the **Museum of War** (Kara muzejs; ☑6722 8147; www.karamuzejs.gov.lv; Smilšu iela 20; admission free; ⊙10am-6pm), which details the political

and military history of Latvia from medieval times to the present day (with a special focus on the world wars).

CENTRAL RĪGA (CENTRS)

As Kaļķu iela breaks free from the urban jumble of turrets and towers, it turns into Brīvības bulvāris (Freedom Blvd), and continues to neatly cut the city centre into two equal parts. An emerald necklace of lush parks acts as a buffer between the medieval walls and the large-scale gridiron of stately boulevards. Central Rīga's hodgepodge of memorable sights includes the flamboyant art-nouveau district, a sprawling Central Market housed in mammoth zeppelin hangars and the iconic Freedom Monument.

ESPLANADE & AROUND

Freedom Monument   MONUMENT
(Brīvības bulvāris; Map p190) Affectionately known as 'Milda', Rīga's Freedom Monument towers above the city between Old and Central Rīga. Paid for by public donations, the monument was designed by Kārlis Zāle and erected in 1935 where a statue of Russian ruler Peter the Great once stood. At the base of the monument there is an inscription that reads 'Tēvzemei un Brīvībai' (For Fatherland and Freedom), accompanied by granite friezes of Latvians singing and fighting for their freedom. A copper female Liberty tops the soaring monument, holding three gold stars in her hands. The three stars represent the three original cultural regions of Latvia: Kurzeme, Vidzeme and Latgale (Latvia's fourth cultural region, Zemgale, was initially part of Kurzeme).

Surprisingly, during the Soviet years the Freedom Monument was never demolished. The communist government reinterpreted the star-toting Liberty as 'Mother Russia' caring for its three newest members of the union: Estonia, Latvia and Lithuania. Milda was strictly off limits, and anyone seen placing flowers at the base was promptly arrested and deported to Siberia. To further decrease the monument's significance, a large statue of Lenin was erected up the street, facing the other way down Brīvības. It was removed when Latvia regained its independence.

Today, two soldiers stand guard at the monument through the day and perform a modest changing of the guards every hour on the hour from 9am to 6pm.

A second spire, the **Laima Clock** (Map p190), sits between Milda and the entrance to Old Rīga. Built in the 1920s as a gentle way to encourage Rīgans not to be late for work, the clock is now used as a meeting place for young Latvians.

Pilsētas Kanāls (City Canal)   PARK
Pilsētas kanāls, the city's old moat, once protected the medieval interior from invaders. Today, the snaking ravine has been incorporated into a thin belt of stunning parkland splitting Old and Central Rīga. Stately Raiņa bulvāris follows the rivulet on the north side, and used to be known as 'Embassy Row' during Latvia's independence between the world wars. Raiņa has once again assumed its dignified status, with the stars and stripes fluttering in front of No 7, and *bleu blanc rouge* installed at No 9. Additional diplomatic estates face the central park and moat on Kronvalda bulvāris and Kalpaka bulvāris.

Humble **Bastion Hill** (Bastejkalns; Map p190) lies along the banks of Pilsētas kanāls near Brīvības, and is the last remnant of medieval Rīga's sand bulwark fortifications. Beneath Bastejkalns, five red stone slabs lie as **memorials to the victims of 20 January 1991** (Map p190; they were killed here when Soviet troops stormed the nearby Interior Ministry).

On 18 November 1918, Latvia declared its independence at the baroque **National Theatre** (Nacionālais teātris; Map p196), at the junction of the canal and K Valdemāra iela. The beloved **Latvian National Opera** (Map p190; ☑6707 3777; www.opera.lv; Aspazijas bulvāris 3; ⊗box office 10am-7pm), which resembles Moscow's Bolshoi Theatre, sits at the other end of the park near K Barona iela.

Vērmanes dārzs (Vērmanes Garden) PARK
(Map p196) From Brīvības, pass the swirls of colour at the 24-hour **flower market** along Tērbatas iela to find the inviting Vērmanes dārzs frequented by locals. During the summer months, local bands perform in the small **outdoor amphitheatre**, and artisans set up shop along the brick walkways.

Esplanāde   PARK
An echo of Vērmanes dārzs across bustling Brīvības, the expansive Esplanāde is a large park dotted with imposing trees, wooden benches, historic statues and a couple of cafes. The **Latvian National Museum of Art** (Valsts mākslas muzejs; Map p196; ☑6732 4461; K Valdemāra iela 10a; ⊗11am-5pm Wed-Mon) sits within the leafy grounds along K Valdemāra iela. When open it predominantly features

RĪGA CARD

If you have a long list of sights and activities on your checklist, we recommend picking up a Rīga Card. Perks include free admission to most museums, 10% to 20% discounts on accommodation, a free walking tour of Old Rīga, and a complimentary copy of *Rīga in Your Pocket*. Cards are available for purchase at a variety of locations including the tourist office, the airport and several major hotels. Prices for one-/two-/three-day cards are 12/14/18Ls. Contact **Rīga Card** (☑6721 7217; www.rigacard.lv) for more information.

pre-WWII Russian and Latvian art displayed among the Soviet grandeur of ruched net curtains, marble columns and red carpets. The museum is, however, closed for massive renovations until 2014 when the city will be the European culture capital.

At the other end of the park, the stunning 19th-century **Russian Orthodox Cathedral** (Pareizticīgo katedrāle; Map p196; Brīvības bulvāris), with its rolling gilded cupolas, majestically rises off Brīvības. During the Soviet era, the church was used as a planetarium.

Natural History Museum   MUSEUM
(Dabas muzejs; Map p196; ☑6735 6024; www .dabasmuzejs.gov.lv; K Barona iela 4; admission 1Ls; ⊙10am-5pm Wed, Fri & Sat, noon-6pm Thu, 10am-4pm Sun) Sitting diagonally opposite to the garden across K Barona iela, this museum features a permanent collection that includes stuffed birds, dinosaur fossils, details about Latvia's ecosystem and information on the region's ethnic origins.

CENTRAL MARKET DISTRICT

TOP CHOICE **Central Market**   MARKET
(Centrāl tirgus; Map p196; www.centraltirgus.lv; Nēģu iela 7; ⊙7am-5pm Sun-Mon, to 6pm Tue-Sat) Visiting Rīga without seeing the Central Market is like going to Paris and not stopping by the Louvre. Although, rather than stuffy still lifes of fruit, Rīga's bustling centrepiece bursts with life as vendors peddle crates stuffed with freshly picked fruit.

A 1330 manuscript makes reference to a small market in Doma laukums being moved to what is now called Latviešu Strēlnieku laukums (Latvian Riflemen Sq). Rīga's market moved once again in 1570, this time to the banks of the Daugava to facilitate trading directly along the river. The market flourished during the mid-1600s when the city outgrew Stockholm to become the largest stronghold of the Swedish Empire.

In 1930 the market moved to its current location on the border of Central Rīga and the Russified Maskavas neighbourhood ('Little Moscow') to make use of the railway, which replaced the river as the principal trade route. Confronted with the market's ever-growing size, the city of Rīga decided to bring in five enormous zeppelin hangars from the town of Vainode in Western Latvia. At a cost of five million lats, these hangars – each 35m high – added 57,000 sq m of vending space, allowing an additional 1250 vendors to peddle their goods.

Parts of the market are closed for maintenance on the mornings of each month's first and last Monday. Check the website for additional information.

Spīķeri   NEIGHBOURHOOD
(off Map p196; www.spikeri.lv) The shipping yard behind the Central Market is the latest district to benefit from a generous dose of gentrification. These crumbling brick warehouses were once filled with swinging slabs of hanger meat; these days you'll find hip cafes and start-up companies. Stop by during the day to check out **Kim?** (☑6722 3321; www .kim.lv; Maskavas iela 12/1; admission free; ⊙2-7pm Wed-Fri, noon-7pm Sat & Sun) – an experimental art zone that dabbles with contemporary media – or come in the evening to peruse the surplus of farm produce at the **night market** (Maskavas iela 12; ⊙9pm-dawn).

Academy of Science   HISTORIC BUILDING
(Zinātņu Akadēmija; Map p196; www.lza.lv; Akadēmijas laukums 1; ⊙9am-8pm) The most interesting building adorning Rīga's eccentric skyline sits in the heart of Akadēmijas laukums. Known to most as 'Stalin's birthday cake', the Academy of Science is Rīga's own Russified 'Empire State Building'. Those with eagle eyes will spot hammers and sickles hidden in the convoluted facade. A mere 2Ls grants you admission to the sprawling observation deck on the 17th floor.

Holocaust Memorial   MONUMENT
(Map p196) Don't miss the moving Holocaust Memorial, aptly sitting a block behind Akadēmijas laukums in a quiet garden. A large synagogue once occupied this street corner until it was burned to the ground during WWII, tragically with

Central Rīga (Centrs)

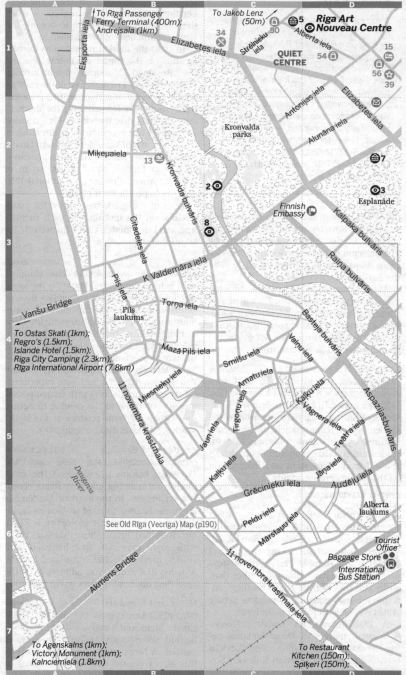

To Rīga Passenger
Ferry Terminal (400m);
Andrejsala (1km)

To Jakob Lenz
(50m)

5

**Rīga Art
Nouveau Centre**

50

Alberta iela

Elizabetes iela

Strēlnieku
iela

**QUIET
CENTRE**

54

15

56

39

34

Antonijas iela

Elizabetes iela

Eksporta iela

Alunāna iela

Miķeņaiela

13

Kronvalda
parks

Kronvalda bulvāris

7

2

Finnish
Embassy

3

Esplanāde

Kalpaka bulvāris

8

Citadeles iela

Raiņa bulvāris

Pils iela

K Valdemāra iela

Vanšu Bridge

Torņa iela

Pils
laukums

To Ostas Skati (1km);
Regro's (1.5km);
Islande Hotel (1.5km);
Riga City Camping (2.3km);
Rīga International Airport (7.8km)

Maza Pils iela

Smilšu iela

Basteja bulvāris

Valņu iela

Miesnieku iela

Amatu iela

Kaļķu iela

Vāgnera iela

Teātra iela

Aspazijas bulvāris

Jauniela

Tirgoņu iela

Jāņa iela

Audēju iela

Daugava
River

11 novembra krastmala

Grēcinieku iela

Peldu iela

Alberta
laukums

See Old Rīga (Vecrīga) Map (p190)

Tourist
Office

Baggage Store

Akmens Bridge

Mārstaļu iela

11 novembra krastmala iela

International
Bus Station

To Āgenskalns (1km);
Victory Monument (1km);
Kalnciemiela (1.8km)

To Restaurant
Kitchen (150m);
Spīķeri (150m);

LATVIA RĪGA

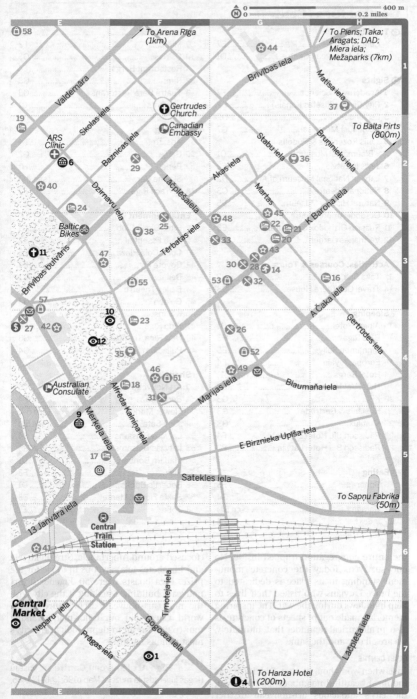

0   400 m
0   0.2 miles

58

To Arena Rīga
(1km)

To Piens; Taka;
Aragats; DAD;
Miera iela;
Mežaparks (7km)

44

Brīvības iela

Matīsa iela

Valdemāra

Gertrudes
Church

37

Skolas iela

Canadian
Embassy

To Balta Pirts
(800m)

19

Stabu iela

Baznīcas iela

ARS
Clinic

Bruņinieku iela

6

29

36

40

Akas iela

Lāčplēšaiela

Dzirnavu iela

Martas

24

45

48

K Barona iela

Baltic
Bikes

25

38

22

21

Tērbatas iela

33

20

47

43

11

Brīvības bulvāris

30

28

14

55

53

32

16

A Čaka iela

57

Gertrūdes iela

27

42

10

23

12

26

35

52

Australian
Consulate

46

49

18

51

Blaumaņa iela

31

Marijas iela

9

Alfrēda Kalniņa iela

Merķeļa iela

17

E Birznieka Upīša iela

Satekles iela

To Sapņu Fabrika
(50m)

13 Janvāra iela

Central
Train
Station

41

Central
Market

Neparu iela

Timoteja iela

Gogoļa iela

1

Prāgas iela

To Hanza Hotel
(200m)

4

Central Rīga (Centrs)

◉ Top Sights
Central Market.............................E7
Riga Art Nouveau Centre.................D1

◉ Sights
1 Academy of Science.....................F7
2 City Canal (Pilsētas Kanāls)..........C2
3 Esplanāde...............................D2
4 Holocaust Memorial.....................G7
5 Janis Rozentāls & Rūdolfs
    Blaumanis' Museum....................C1
6 Jews in Latvia..........................E2
7 Latvian National Museum of Art........D2
8 National Theatre........................C3
9 Natural History Museum.................E5
10 Outdoor Amphitheatre...................F4
11 Russian Orthodox Cathedral............E3
12 Vērmanes Garden........................E4

◔ Activities, Courses & Tours
13 Taka Spa................................B2
14 Travel Out There House................G3

◛ Sleeping
15 Albert Hotel...........................D1
16 B&B Rīga...............................H3
17 Cinnamon Sally.........................E5
18 Europa Royale..........................F4
    Hotel Bergs......................(see 51)
19 Hotel Valdemārs........................E2
20 KB.....................................G3
21 Krišjānis & Ģertrūde...................G3
22 Multilux...............................G3
23 Radisson Blu Hotel Elizabete..........F4
24 Radisson Blu Hotel Latvija............E2

◚ Eating
25 Bonēra.................................F3
26 Charlestons............................G4
    Garage...........................(see 51)
27 Index..................................E4

28 Istaba.................................G3
29 Miit...................................F2
30 Osīriss................................G3
31 Restaurant Bergs.......................F4
32 Rimi...................................G3
33 Teātra Bāra Restorāns..................G3
34 Vincents...............................C1

◕ Drinking
35 Apsara.................................F4
36 Gauja..................................G2
37 Perle..................................H1
    Skyline Bar......................(see 24)
38 Terrace Riga...........................F3

◑ Entertainment
39 Bites Blues Club.......................D1
40 Club Essential.........................E2
41 Coca-Cola Plaza........................E6
42 Coyote Fly.............................E4
43 Daile..................................G3
44 Dailes Theatre.........................G1
45 Golden.................................G3
46 K Suns.................................F4
47 Kino Rīga..............................E3
48 New Rīga Theatre.......................G3
49 Palladium..............................G4

◔ Shopping
50 Art Nouveau Riga.......................C1
51 Berga Bazārs...........................F4
    Flower Market....................(see 57)
    Jāņa Sēta........................(see 51)
52 Latvijas Balsāms.......................G4
53 Latvijas Balsāms.......................G3
54 Madam Bonbon...........................D1
55 Riija..................................F3
56 Robert's Books.........................D1
57 Sakta Flower Market....................E3
58 ZoFa...................................E1

the entire congregation trapped inside. No one survived. Today the concrete monument standing in its place is dedicated to the brave Latvians who risked their lives to help hide Jews during the war. The inspiring memorial, made out of sheets of concrete, is also an allegorical reminder that, ultimately, we are all one and the same.

QUIET CENTRE

Just when you thought that Old Rīga was the most beautiful neighbourhood in town, the city's audacious art-nouveau district (focused around Alberta iela, Strēlnieku iela and Elizabetes iela) swoops in to vie for the prize. Rīga boasts over 750 Jugendstil (art nouveau) buildings, making it the city with the most art-nouveau architecture in the world. Check out our tailor-made walking tour (p202) for an in-depth look at the city's most famous facades.

TOP CHOICE **Rīga Art Nouveau Centre** MUSEUM
(Rīgas jūgemdstila muzejs; Map p196; ☑6718 1465; www.jugendstils.riga.lv; Alberta iela 12; admission

RĪGA FOR CHILDREN

The Unesco-protected streets of Old Rīga can feel like a magical time warp for the 12-and-under bunch. For a trip into the future, try laser tag and a racing simulator at **Go Planet** (www.goplanet.lv; Gunara Astras iela 2b). During the summer months, take the tykes to the zoo in forested Mežaparks or let the little ones cool off on the beach in nearby Jūrmala. Here, between spirited sessions of wave-jumping and sandcastle-building try Līvu Akvaparks (p219), Latvia's largest indoor water park, which features a wave pool and a tangle of waterslides.

3Ls, English tour 10.50Ls; ☉10am-6pm Tue-Sun) If you're curious about what lurks behind Rīga's imaginative art-nouveau facades, then it's definitely worth stopping by here. Once the home of Constantīns Pēkšēns (a local architect responsible for over 250 of the city's buildings), the centre has been completely restored to resemble a middle-class apartment from the 1920s. Note the geometric frescos, rounded furniture, original stained glass in the dining room and the still-functioning stove in the kitchen. Don't miss the free 10-minute video detailing the city's distinct decor, and check out the centre's website for details about the art-nouveau walking routes around town. Enter from Strēlnieku iela; push No 12 on the doorbell.

Janis Rozentāls and Rūdolfs Blaumanis' Museum   MUSEUM

(Map p196; ☏6733 1641; Alberta iela 12; admission 1Ls; ☉11am-6pm Wed-Sun) Follow the wonderfully lavish stairwell up to the 5th floor to find the former apartment of Janis Rozentāls, one of Latvia's most celebrated painters. Enter from Strēlnieku iela; push No 9 on the doorbell.

FREE Jews in Latvia   MUSEUM

(Map p196; ☏6728 3484; www.jewishmuseum.lv; Skolas iela 6; admission by donation; ☉noon-5pm Sun-Thu) This small and rather informal space briefly recounts the city's history of Jewish life until 1945 through artefacts and photography. Rīga's Jewish population (unlike that of Vilnius) was very much integrated into the rest of society. You'll find a teeny kosher cafe in the basement (entrance on Dzirnavu iela) selling traditional treats like *challa* bread and gefilte fish.

MIERA IELA

Old factory meets olfactory along Miera iela, an industrial district that's home to the Laima chocolate maker just beyond the scatter of stunning art-nouveau facades in the Quiet Centre. Walk down the main street to find a charming assortment of cafes, craft shops and bookstores; sadly there are no golden tickets available to visit the chocolate factory.

OUTLYING NEIGHBOURHOODS

Those who venture beyond Rīga's inner sphere of cobbled alleyways and over-the-top art nouveau will uncover a burgeoning artists' colony, a couple of excellent museums, and a handful of other neighbourhoods that help paint a full picture of this cosmopolitan capital.

MEŽAPARKS

Woodsy Mežaparks (literally 'Forest Park' in Latvian), along Lake Ķīšezers, 7km north of the centre, is Europe's oldest planned suburb. Built by the Germans in the 20th century, this 'garden city', originally called Kaiserwald, was the go-to neighbourhood for wealthy merchants looking to escape the city's grimy industrial core. The atmosphere hasn't changed all that much over the last 100 years – tourists will find prim country homes, gorgeous art-nouveau facades, hiking trails, bike paths and lazy sailboats gliding along the lake.

Mežaparks is home to the **Rīga National Zoo** (Zoologiskais dārz; ☏6751 8669; www.rigazoo.lv; Meža prospekts 1; adult/child 4/3Ls; ☉10am-4pm). Set in a hilly pine forest, the zoo has a motley collection of animals, including a new assortment of tropical fauna, as well as the usual cast of Noah's ark.

There are also a handful of picturesque cemeteries nearby including **Brothers' Cemetery** (Brāļu kapi), which features a monument by Kārlis Zāle (the designer of the Freedom Monument) dedicated to the Latvian soldiers who died defending their country between 1915 and 1920. The **Rainis Cemetery** (Raiņa kapi) is the final resting place of Jānis Rainis, his wife (feminist poet Aspazija) and several other influential Latvians.

LATVIA RĪGA

Locals flock to **Cabo** (mains 1-4Ls; ☉Jun-Aug) a casual lakeside restaurant with plenty of outdoor seating in both beanbag and wicker form. During the day everyone queues for tasty snacks before taking a dip in the lake; evenings are more subdued as patrons sip beer and enjoy the serene scenery as dusk turns to night fairly late in the evening.

To reach Mežaparks, take tram 11 from K Barona iela to the 'Mežaparks' stop; get off at the 'Brāļu Kapi' stop for the Brothers' Cemetery.

ĀGENSKALNS & KALNCIEMIELA

Rīga's gritty working-class neighbourhood across the Daugava River is a serious throwback to earlier times, especially at Užaras Park. This sprawling green space (now mostly used as a soccer field) is home to the so-called **Victory Monument** (Užaras Piemineklis; off Map p196), which was built by the Soviets to commemorate the communist 'victory' over fascism. The monument has five stars commemorating the five years of WWII.

Unlike many of Rīga's other districts, this area was not destroyed during WWII, and it thus makes for a great place to wander around by bicycle to get a feel for how life was here many decades ago. Don't miss **Kalnciemiela**, a lovingly restored courtyard with several wooden buildings. It has become the location of a very popular weekend market during the summer months (usually on Thursday evenings in the colder months), where Rīgans hawk their local produce – fresh meats, cheeses, vegetables and even local spirits. The on-site restaurant, **Maja** (www.restoransmaja.lv/en; Kalnciema iela 5) is worth a look for those with big wallets.

Take tram 2 or 8 over the Akmens Bridge, and disembark at the 'Āgenskalna Tirgus' stop, or take tram 5 and get off at the second stop on the other side of the bridge.

ĶĪPSALA

Just a quick 10-minute walk west over Vanšu Bridge, quiet Ķīpsala is Rīga's veritable Left Bank. Over the last five years the island has seen quite a bit of gentrification – wooden houses have been completely restored, and abandoned factories turned into trendy loft apartments. Rīga Technical University and the Ķīpsala Exhibition Hall complex are also located on the island. The tree-lined riverside is a great spot for taking photos of the city centre across the Daugava River.

MUSEUMS

The following museums orbit Rīga's central core several kilometres out.

Latvian Ethnographic Open-Air Museum
MUSEUM

(Latvijas etnogrāfiskais brīvdabas muzejs; ☑6799 4510; www.brivdabasmuzejs.lv; Brīvības gatve 440; adult/child 1/0.50Ls; ☉10am-5pm mid-May–Oct) If you don't have time to visit the heart of the Latvian countryside, then a stop at this open-air museum is a must. Sitting along the shores of Lake Jugla just northeast of the city limits, this vast stretch of forest contains more than 100 wooden buildings from each of Latvia's four cultural regions. These churches, windmills and farmhouses contain myriad artefacts, which tell the story of a bygone bucolic lifestyle. Take bus 1 from the corner of Merķeļa iela and Tērbatas iela to the 'Brīvdabas muzejs' stop.

Rīga Motor Museum
MUSEUM

(Rīgas motormuzejs; ☑6709 7170; www.motormuzejs.lv; Eizenšteina iela 6; adult/child 1/0.50Ls; ☉10am-6pm) The stars of the collection at this fantastic museum are cars that once belonged to Soviet luminaries such as Gorky, Stalin, Khrushchev and Brezhnev, complete with irreverent life-sized figures of the men themselves. Stalin, pockmarked cheeks and all, sits regally in the back of his 7-tonne, 6005cc-armoured limousine. The car has 1.5cm-thick iron plating everywhere except on the 8cm-thick windows. It drank a litre of petrol every 2.5km. At the time of research, a new hall was being added to further expand the museum. The museum is 8km outside the city centre along Brīvības iela, then 2km south to the Mežciems suburb. Take bus 21 from the Russian Orthodox Cathedral to the Pansionāts stop on Šmerļa iela.

🏃 Activities

For an intense adrenalin fix, such as bungee jumping, bobsledding, mountain biking and skydiving, head to the town of Sigulda (p245) in Gauja National Park. Water-sports enthusiasts should spend the day in Jūrmala (p218). Cyclists will be glad to know that there are dozens of routes around town – check out http://liveriga .com/en/4270-cycling-paths-and-bike-routes.

You don't have to run all the way to Jūrmala to see some serious spa action. Rīga has a few standout places to get pampered in traditional Latvian style: being whipped by dried birch branches while sweating it out in temperatures beyond 40°C (over 100°F). Visit www.spa.lv for additional options and details. Sounds relaxing...

Baltā Pirts   SPA
(off Map p196; ☑6727 1733; www.baltapirts.lv; Tallinas iela 71; sauna 7Ls; ⊗8am-8pm Wed-Sun) Frequented mostly by locals rather than tourists, Baltā Pirts combines traditional Latvian relaxation techniques (the name means 'white birch') with a subtle, oriental design scheme. In the 1980s the property was mostly a front for prostitution, but the original owners of the sauna have since reclaimed the building and turned it into quite a wonderful affair. Take a tram heading north along A Čaka until you reach Tallinas iela.

Taka Spa   SPA
(Map p196; ☑6732 3150; www.takaspa.lv; Kronvalda bulvāris 3a; cleansing 'rituals' from €80; ⊗11am-9pm Mon-Wed, 9am-9pm Thu & Fri, 10am-7pm Sat, 10am-5pm Sun) High-end Taka Spa offers massages, wraps, scrubs and sauna treatments. Try the signature 'opening ritual' in which clients move between saunas and plunge pools while drinking herbal teas. Yoga classes, pilates courses and exercise facilities are also available.

Regro's   SHOOTING RANGE
(off Map p196; ☑6760 1705; Daugavgrīvas iela 31; per bullet 0.80-2Ls; ⊗10am-5pm Mon-Sat, Sun by appointment) The ambience here is reason enough to visit: a dingy Soviet fallout shelter adorned with posters of rifle-toting models wearing fur bikinis. Choose from a large selection of retro firearms (including Kalashnikovs) to aim at your paper cut-out of James Bond. You pay by the bullet, and don't forget your passport. Take Vanšu Bridge across the river, pass Ķīpsala and take your first right until you hit a petrol station. Trams 13 and 13A will take you directly to Regro's – get off at Kiņģeru iela; if you pass two petrol stations you've gone too far.

👉 Tours

Swarms of operators offer tours around Rīga as well as day trips to popular sights nearby. For more information on day trips, see p212.

Amber Way   SIGHTSEEING
(☑6727 1915; www.sightseeing.lv; tour 10Ls) A smorgasbord of city tours, either on a bus

or walking. Tours depart at 11am, noon, 1pm and 3pm. Ask about a walking-bus-lunch combo for 20Ls. Day trips depart at 11am from the Opera House to Rundāle Palace (every Saturday), to Sigulda (every Friday) and to Jūrmala (every Sunday). Most midrange and top-end hotels can book these tours.

Eat Riga   OFFBEAT
(☑2246 9888; www.eatriga.lv; tour 5Ls) No, it's not a foodie's tour; three-hour walks stop at less touristy attractions around town. Tours depart in front of St Peter's Church every day at noon.

Retro Tram   HISTORY/ARCHITECTURE
(☑6730 7900; adult/child 6/3Ls; ⊗10am-5pm) Two routes, aboard a restored tram, meander through the art-nouveau district and on to Mežaparks. Free guided walking tours of the art-nouveau district are available on weekends departing 11.40am, 1.40pm and 3.40pm from the Auseklļa tram stop.

Rīga By Canal   BOAT
(Map p190; ☑6750 9974; www.kmk.lv; Mon/Tue-Fri/Sat & Sun 4/5/6Ls; ⊗9am-11pm) Enjoy a different perspective of the city aboard the 100-year-old 'Darling', a charming wooden canal cruiser that runs on 15% solar energy (the rest diesel). There are three other boats in the fleet that paddle along the same route and operate on electrical power.

Rīga City Tour   SIGHTSEEING
(☑2665 5405; www.citytour.lv; adult/child 10/9Ls) A hop-on, hop-off double-decker bus that wends its way through Rīga stopping at 15 spots on both sides of the Daugava River. Buses leave from Rātslaukums on the hour between 10am and 3pm.

Rīga Mobile Guide   SIGHTSEEING
(☑English 9000 6102, German 9000 6104, Russian 9000 6103, Latvian 9000 6101; call 0.84Ls) A savvy, self-guided tour using your mobile phone. Dial the code for your desired attraction (21 stops in total) and learn about its history and significance.

Travel Out There   OFFBEAT
(Map p196; ☑2938 9450; www.rigaoutthere.com; tours from 10Ls) Organises loads of tours and activities for tourists including day trips to adrenalin-packed Sigulda, Soviet walking tours, spa bookings and late-night pub crawls. It also runs a comfy hostel on the same premises.

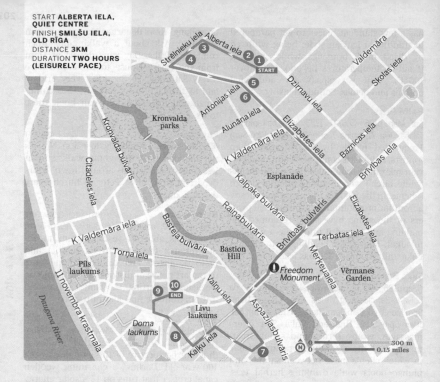

Walking Tour
Art Nouveau in Rīga

❯ If you ask any Rīgan where to find the city's world-famous art-nouveau architecture, you will always get the same answer: 'Look up!' More than 750 buildings in Rīga (more than any other city in Europe) boast this flamboyant and haunting style of decor; and the number continues to grow as myriad restoration projects get under way. Art nouveau is also known as Jugendstil, meaning 'Youth Style', named after a Munich-based magazine called *Die Jugend*, which popularised the design in its pages.

Art nouveau's early influence was Japanese print art disseminated throughout Western Europe, but as the movement gained momentum, the style became more ostentatious and freeform – design schemes started to feature mythical beasts, screaming masks, twisting flora, goddesses and goblins. The turn of the 20th century marked the height of the art-nouveau movement as it swept through every major European city from Porto to Petersburg.

The art-nouveau movement in Rīga can be divided into three pronounced phases. The first phase was called 'Eclectic Decorative Art Nouveau'; it occurred during the first five years of the 20th century. During this time, the primary focus was the facade rather than the interior, as highly ornate patterns were imported from Germany by the local architects who studied there. The intricate sculpture work was also locally designed, mostly by August Volz, who did his apprenticeship in Germany as well. This design phase is the most pronounced in Central Rīga because the prevalence of the style coincided with the opening of a local architectural faculty.

After the revolution of 1905, however, this art-nouveau style was quickly phased out as local architects furiously dabbled with the notion of establishing a design scheme with nationalistic flair. The so-called 'National Romanticism' was born out of this idea, and reflected Latvian ethnographic motifs. An affinity for natural materials flourished as urban facades were left unpainted to show the greys and browns of the building materials. Facades were meant to act as windows, so to speak, into the layout of the structure within. Although this rather un-art-nouveau style was only popular for four years, it coincided with a boom in the city's trading wealth, and thus a lot of structures exhibit this style, even today.

The final phase was known as 'Perpendicular Art Nouveau' – it flourished from around 1908 to 1912. The style was a hybrid design between the existing art-nouveau traits and a return to classical motifs (presented in a heavily stylised fashion). An accentuation on verticality was pronounced, as was the penchant for balconies and bay windows.

In Rīga, the most noted Jugendstil architect was Mikhail Eisenstein (father of Sergei Eisenstein, a noted Soviet film director) who flexed his artistic muscles on Alberta iela. At ❶ **Alberta iela 2a**, constructed in 1906, serene faces with chevalier helmets stand guard atop the facade, which noticeably extends far beyond the actual roof of the structure. Screaming masks and horrible goblins adorn the lower sections amid clean lines and surprising robot-like shapes. Most noticeable are the two stone satyr phoenix-women that stand guard at the front. The facade of the building next door is in much better condition. The three heads on ❷ **Alberta iela 4**, two doors down from 2a, will surely capture your attention. If you look carefully, you'll see a nest of snakes slithering around their heads, evoking Medusa. All six eyes seem transfixed on some unseen horror, but only two of the faces are screaming in shock and fear. Two elaborate reliefs near the entrance feature majestic griffins, and ferocious lions with erect, fist-like tails keep watch on the roof. Further down the street, the Rīga Graduate School of Law at ❸ **Alberta iela 13** epitomises Jugendstil's attention to detail. Peacocks, tangled shrubs and bare-breasted heroines abound while cheery pastoral scenes are depicted in relief on Erykah Badu-like turbans atop the giant yawning masks. The triangular summit is a mishmash of nightmarish imagery: lion heads taper off into snake tails (like Chimera), sobbing faces weep in agony and a strange futuristic mask stoically stares out over the city from the apex.

Turn the corner to find the Stockholm School of Economics at ❹ **Strēlnieku iela 4a**, filled in with sumptuous blue brick and framed by garland-wielding goddesses. More eye-candy awaits at ❺ **Elizabetes iela 33**, with muscular men balancing stacks of Corinthian columns on their shoulders. The blue-and-white facade at ❻ **Elizabetes iela 10b**, also designed by Eisenstein, is one of the city's earliest examples of art nouveau and a clear fan favourite. The enormous sullen heads squished at the top of the facade are the subjects of myriad postcards. Continue down Elizabetes iela in the direction of the towering Radisson Blu Hotel Latvija and make a right on Brīvības iela. Follow Brīvības past the Freedom Monument and make your way into medieval Old Rīga.

Most visitors don't realise that Old Rīga also offers wonderfully ornate gargoyle heads, mythical beasts and ancient gods hidden among its patchwork of gabled roofs and church spires. Enter the city's medieval core on Teātra iela and pause at ❼ **Teātra iela 9**, the Italian Embassy, to admire the facade's pantheon of Greek figures – two ragged older men (Prometheus perhaps) frantically clutch their necks while supporting the convoluted wrought-iron balcony above. Further up, reliefs of Athena and Hermes stand proud. Look way up high to spot Atlas with the world on his shoulders (literally). The stunning zinc-and-glass globe sparkles in the evening.

If you look closely at ❽ **Šķūņu iela 10/12** you'll spot a variety of 'D's hidden in the front design – the initials of the original owner. A watchdog stands guard at the top. The building at ❾ **Smilšu iela 2** is considered to be one of the finest examples of Jugendstil in Old Rīga. The exterior features a variety of hybrid creatures including intertwining vines that morph, like a mermaid's tail, into the torso of two caryatids. The home of the building's architect can be visited at Rīga Art Nouveau Centre. On the same street, at ❿ **Smilšu iela 8**, two women stand atop a protruding bay carrying an elaborate crown of leaves. A large mask of a melancholic woman with her eyes shut hovers over the entrance – a common theme early on in the art-nouveau movement. The building's lobby continues a similar ornamental theme to the exterior.

✰✰ Festivals & Events

Rīgans will find any excuse to celebrate, especially when the sun comes out during the summer months. Check out www.rigatourism.lv for a complete list of local events.

International Baltic Ballet Festival DANCE
(www.ballet-festival.lv) This three-week festival starts in late April, with performances by Latvian and international companies.

Rīga Opera Festival MUSIC
(www.music.lv/opera) The Latvian National Opera's showcase event takes place over 10 days in June and includes performances by world-renowned talents.

Midsummer Celebration PARTY
Latvians return to their pagan roots while celebrating the solstice on 23 June. Crowds gather along the embankment and public transport is free.

Rīgas Ritmi MUSIC
(www.rigasritmi.lv) 'Rīga's Rhythms' is the capital's international music festival held at the beginning of July.

Baltā Nakts CULTURE
(www.baltanakts.lv) Held at the end of August, this 'white night' event, sponsored by the Contemporary Art Forum, mirrors Paris' night-long showcase of artists and culture around the city.

Arsenāls International Film Forum FILM
(www.arsenals.lv) An annual film festival held in September showcasing more than 100 movies relating to experiential and interactive themes.

Arēna New Music Festival MUSIC
(www.arenafest.lv) Contemporary music festival held at venues throughout Rīga during the last two weeks of October.

Beaming Rīga LIGHT DISPLAY
(www.staroriga.lv) Held around National Day celebrations in November, this festival of lights lifts spirits as Rīga begins to face the long winter ahead. Myriad civic buildings and public objects are lit up during the long nights.

Christmas Tree Path HOLIDAYS
Rīga claims to be the city that originated the Christmas tree (p189), and thus at Christmas each year, locals decorate an ornate tree in Rātslaukums amid much ado.

LIVE LIKE A LOCAL

Planning on sticking around town for a while? Check out **Rent In Riga** (www.rentinriga.lv) for a detailed listing of available (and red tape–free!) apartments in town. Click on Vecrīga or Centrs to find a flat in the core of the city.

🛏 Sleeping

When considering where to stay in Rīga, your first choice will be whether you want to stay in Old Rīga or Central Rīga – both are excellent options for different reasons. The city lends itself well to pedestrians so staying in either neighbourhood will not be limiting. If you're only in town for a day it's probably best to stay in Old Rīga as you're within arm's reach of most of the city's main attractions. Those who are in town for a bit longer might find Central Rīga to be a better option. The prices are slightly lower and you'll feel more like a local. The summer months are very busy, so whatever your choice, always book a room in advance from June through to August.

Hostels dominate the budget-accommodation scene in Rīga, and the competition can be rather fierce in the summer months. Soaring real-estate prices mean that the mainstream backpacker scene is always in flux – some places close their doors for the winter and never reopen when high season rolls around. Virtually every hostel has free internet and wi-fi; you can count on price hikes (1 to 3Ls) for weekend rates.

At the opposite end of the spectrum, Rīga's crème de la crème can be sharply divided into two categories: flamboyant throwbacks to the city's aristocratic past (think sumptuous antiques and gushing drapery) or avant-garde gems ripped straight from the latest Scandinavian architectural magazine.

OLD RĪGA (VECRĪGA)

Neiburgs BOUTIQUE HOTEL €€€
(Map p190; ☎6711 5522; www.neiburgs.com; Jauniela 25/27; s/d/ste incl breakfast from 100/130/170Ls; @☎) Beautiful Neiburgs blends contemporary touches (patterned accent walls and chrome in the bathroom) with carefully preserved details (like curling crown moulding) for its signature blend of boutique-chic style. Try for a room on one of the higher floors – you'll be treated to a view of a colourful clutter of

gabled roofs and twisting medieval spires. The in-house restaurant is exceptionally popular with locals.

Grand Palace Hotel
LUXURY HOTEL €€€

(Map p190; ☑6704 4000; www.grandpalaceriga .com; Pils iela 12; d from €150; @😊) You'll find no better place to be pampered than the lavish Grand Palace. Rooms are bedecked in period furnishings that feel classy rather than cluttered, and the friendly staff wax nostalgic about the various luminaries who have stayed here, including Catherine Deneuve and REM – but it's actually more fit for royalty than rock stars.

🏷 Dome Hotel
BOUTIQUE HOTEL €€€

(Map p190; ☑6750 9010; www.domehotel.lv; Miesnieku iela 4; d/ste from 190/280Ls; @😊) An exciting addition to Old Rīga's clutch of high-end accommodation options, Dome Hotel occupies an almost-ancient structure that was once part of a row of butcheries. Today, a gorgeous wooden staircase leads guests up to the charming assortment of uniquely decorated rooms that sport eaved ceilings, wooden panelling, upholstered furniture and pictures with city views.

Naughty Squirrel
HOSTEL €€

(Map p190; ☑2646 1248; www.naughtysquirrel backpackers.com; Kalēju iela 50; dm/d 8/30Ls; @😊) Kalēju iela 50 has been the address of several hostel incarnations, and the Naughty Squirrel is by far the best yet. Brilliant slashes of bright paint and cartoon graffiti have breathed new life into the city's capital of backpacker-dom, which buzzes as travellers rattle the foosball table and chill out in the TV room. Sign up for regular pub crawls, adrenaline day trips to the countryside or summer BBQs. The owners also run the excellent **Blue Cow Barracks** (Map p190; ☑2773 6700; www.bluecowbarracks.com; Torņa iela 4-2b; dm/d 10/35Ls; @😊), a smaller and more intimate hostel in the historic Jacob's Barracks on the other side of Old Rīga.

Ekes Konventas
HISTORIC HOTEL €€€

(Map p190; ☑6735 8393; www.ekeskonvents.lv; Skārņu iela 22; d incl breakfast €57; 😊) Not to be confused with Konventa Sēta next door, the 600-year-old Ekes Konventas oozes wobbly medieval charm from every crooked nook and cranny. Curl up with a book in the adorable stone alcoves on the landing of each storey. Breakfast is served in the mod cafe down the block.

Old Town Hostel
HOSTEL €€

(Map p190; ☑6722 3406; www.rigaoldtown hostel.lv; Vaļņu iela 43; dm/d 7/30Ls; @😊) The cosy English-style pub on the ground floor doubles as the hostel's hang-out space, and if you can manage to lug your suitcase past the faux bookshelf door and up the twisting staircase, you'll find spacious dorms with chandeliers and plenty of sunlight. Private rooms are located in another building near the train station.

Friendly Fun Franks
HOSTEL €€

(Map p190; ☑2599 0612; www.franks.lv; 11 Novembra Krastmala 29; dm/d from 5.90/40Ls; @😊) If you want to party, look no further than this bright-orange stag-magnet, where every backpacker is greeted with a hearty hello and a complimentary pint of beer. The staff offer free 'What to Do' tours of Rīga, beach parties and Saturday trips to Sigulda. Bus 22 from the airport conveniently stops in front of the hostel. Accommodation must be booked in advance – walk-ins are not accepted.

Radi un Draugi
HOTEL €€€

(Map p190; ☑6782 0200; www.draugi.lv; Mārstaļu iela 1; s/d/ste 42/52/58Ls; @😊) Despite recent renovation attempts, this old-timer is starting to show its age. We're not a huge fan of puke-green shag carpeting, but if you can turn your expectations down a notch, then Radi un Draugi offers a great bang for your buck if you want to stay in the heart of Old Rīga.

Konventa Sēta
HOTEL €€€

(Map p190; ☑2708 7501; www.konventa.lv; Kalēju iela 9/11; s/d/ste 63/67/95Ls; 🅿@😊) Beyond its location in a 15th-century convent, there's nothing particularly special about this Old Rīga behemoth. Rooms are prim with white-linen drapes (ask for a nonsmoking room), but they feel small like a nun's cell. Parking is 8Ls per night.

Centra
HOTEL €€€

(Map p190; ☑6722 6441; www.centra.lv; Audēju iela 1; s/d 77/84Ls; @😊) Centra is a great choice for comfort in the heart of Old Rīga. Recently renovated rooms are spacious and sport loads of designer details such as swish LCD TVs, porcelain basin sinks and minimalist art on the walls. Rooms on the 5th and 6th floors have lower ceilings but better views of the medieval streets below.

CENTRAL RĪGA (CENTRS)

TOP CHOICE Hotel Bergs
BOUTIQUE HOTEL €€€

(Map p196; ✆6777 0900; www.hotelbergs.lv; Elizabetes iela 83/85; ste from €164; @🖥) A refurbished manor house embellished with Scandi-sleek design, Hotel Bergs embodies the term 'luxury' from the lobby's mix of sharp lines, rococo portraits and tribal reliefs, to the spacious suites lavished with high-quality monochromatic furnishings worthy of a magazine spread. Countless other treats await, like a custom-composed sleeping soundtrack in the room's CD player, and an endless supply of complimentary Acqua Panna. Our favourite – the 'pillow service' – allows guests to choose from an array of different bed pillows based on material and texture. Be sure to check out the in-house restaurant – the menu of refined Latvian fare reads like an ode to your tastebuds, and all seasonal items are locally sourced.

Radisson Blu Elizabete Hotel
HOTEL €€€

(Map p196; ✆6778 5555; www.radissonblu.com /elizabetehotel-riga; Elizabetes iela 73; d incl breakfast from €85; @🖥) The newest link in the Radisson Blu chain is a flash address designed by an up-and-coming London architectural firm. The facade is an eye-catching mix of chrome, steel and giant sheets of glass, and the interior continues to impress: stylish furnishings and clever floor plans give the rooms a cosy, yet trendy, feel.

Europa Royale
HISTORIC HOTEL €€€

(Map p196; ✆6707 9444; www.europaroyale.com; K Barona iela 12; s/d/ste incl breakfast €79/89/189; @🖥) Once the home of media mogul Emilija Benjamiņa (Latvia's version of Anna Wintour), this ornate manse retains much of its original opulence with sweeping staircases and stately bedrooms. In fact, when Latvia regained its independence, the house was initially chosen to be the president's digs but the government didn't have enough funds for the restoration. There are 60 large rooms, yet guests will feel like they're staying at their posh aunt's estate.

Albert Hotel
HOTEL €€€

(Map p196; ✆6733 1717; www.alberthotel.lv; Dzirnavu iela 33; s/d incl breakfast €64/69; @🖥) The boxy, metallic facade starkly contrasts with the surrounding art-nouveau gargoyles, but the interior design is undeniably hip and pays tribute to the hotel's namesake, Albert Einstein. The patterned carpeting features rows of atomic-energy symbols, the clocks in the lobby are set to 'imaginary time' and 'linear time', and the 'do not disturb' doorknob danglers have been replaced with red tags that say 'I'm thinking'. The complimentary buffet breakfast can be a bit of a bloodbath as 200 rooms' worth of guests battle it out for the last strip of bacon.

Radisson Blu Hotel Latvija
HOTEL €€€

(Map p196; ✆6777 2222; www.radissonblu.com /latvijahotel-riga; Elizabetes iela 55; d incl breakfast from €79; @🖥🏊) During the height of the Soviet regime, the Hotel Latvija was a drab monstrosity in which several floors were devoted to monitoring the various goings-on of the hotel's guests. The room keys weighed several kilos, as they were outfitted with conspicuous listening devices. Today, after a much-needed facelift, the era of espionage is long gone; it's all swipe-cards and smiley service now. Don't miss the views from the Skyline Bar on the 26th floor.

Hotel Valdemārs
HOTEL €€€

(Map p196; ✆6733 4462; www.valdemars.lv; Valdemāra iela 23; s/d incl half board from €50/60; @🖥) Modern Hotel Valdemārs is a great find geared towards the Scandinavian market – rooms feel efficient yet homey, in an upmarket IKEA kind of way. A partnership with the Clarion chain means that half- or full-board room rates are available at bargain prices, making it an excellent choice for those without an adventurous appetite Don't forget to give away the flower adorning the bureau in your room – it's a Latvian tradition!

Krišjānis & Ģertrūde
B&B €€

(Map p196; ✆6750 6604; www.kg.lv; K Barona iela 39; s/d/tr incl breakfast €35/45/55; @🖥) Step off the bustling intersection into this quaint, family-run B&B adorned with still-life paintings of fruit and flowers. It's best to book ahead since there are only six cosy rooms tucked around the sociable dining room with its crooked upright piano.

B&B Rīga
APARTMENT €€

(Map p196; ✆6727 8505; www.bb-riga.lv; Ģertrūdes iela 43; s/d €39/49; @🖥) Snug, apartment-style accommodation comes in different configurations (suites with lofted bedrooms are particularly charming), and are scattered throughout a residential block.

KB
B&B €

(Map p196; ✆6731 2323; www.kbhotel.lv; K Barona iela 37; s/d/tr 19/21/23Ls; @🖥) This great find in the pinch-a-penny category is located up a rather opulent marble staircase. The rooms are simple but well appointed, and there's a modern communal kitchen.

Jakob Lenz INN €€
(off Map p196; ☑6733 3343; www.guesthouse lenz.lv; Lenču iela 2; s/d from 25/35Ls, with shared bathroom 20/25Ls; @🛜) Tucked away along a random side street on the fringes of the art-nouveau district, this great find offers 25 adorable rooms and a gut-busting breakfast in the morning.

Multilux B&B €
(Map p196; ☑6731 1602; www.multilux.lv; K Barona iela 37; s/d/tr 18/24/35Ls, with shared bathroom 14/18/28Ls; @🛜) Multilux isn't brimming with character, but the spartan rooms are a good second choice if KB is full. Breakfast included.

Cinnamon Sally HOSTEL €
(Map p196; ☑2204 2280; www.cinnamonsally .com; Merķela iela 3; dm from €8; @🛜) Quickly earning a reputation as one of the better

FROM RAGS TO RICHES TO RAGS

At the beginning of WWII, after 22 years of independence, the Soviet regime forced Latvia into the USSR, setting up a puppet government in Rīga. In order to avoid dissent, the Soviets rounded up those deemed a potential threat to safeguarding the newly instated ideals. Politicians, writers, professors, bankers and many others were carted off to Siberia and forced to work in lumber camps. No one could escape the communist clutches, not even the city's wealthiest citizens – not even Emilija Benjamiņa, Latvia's unofficial First Lady.

During the 1920s and '30s, Emilija was the pinnacle of Rīga's social elite. The daughter of a widowed peasant, Emilija rose from obscurity to become the country's media queen and beloved socialite. The following details about Emilija's inspirational rags-to-riches life were recounted to us during an interview with Laima Muktupāvela, a former local columnist, who chronicled the famed Rīgan's story (with a bit of hyperbole) in a biography entitled *Mila Benjamiņa*.

At a young age, the future media mogul escaped a bucolic lifestyle to sell ads for a newspaper in Rīga. She quickly realised that she had a knack for sales and began her own journal with her soon-to-be-husband Antons Benjamiņš. Her recipe for success was simple: since most Latvians were literate but poor, she sold her newspapers for one cent. Soon after she was selling 900,000 copies per day. In the office, Emilija rewarded intelligence, offering high salaries to her staff and attracting the nation's top writers, including Vilis Lācis, a peasant who enjoyed writing about the 'common man'. Under the guidance of Emilija, Vilis quickly became one of Latvia's best-known figures.

At the height of her career, Ms Benjamiņa was a full-fledged cosmopolitan woman who travelled across Europe and dabbled in fashion and plastic surgery. She grew beyond the status of 'media queen' – her power and influence were absolute, and she would often accompany the president to formal affairs since he was a bachelor. She opened the floodgates for cultural life in Latvia, making her salon the epicentre of the intellectual avant-garde. Dozens of intriguing personalities would pass through, including foreign dignitaries, poets, opera singers and even a clairvoyant – a man by the name of Eižens Finks, who was laughed out the door when he told Emilija that she would meet her end in rags rather than surrounded by riches.

When the Soviets seized power in 1940, her sumptuous mansion, the site of so many world-class affairs, was 'nationalised'. Friends and family encouraged Emilija to leave the country after hearing rumours that she might be deported, but she could not fathom that a shift in power could mean serious trouble. After all, five of her former employees were granted the top positions in the new local Soviet government, including Vilis Lācis, who became Minister of the Interior.

On a humid June evening in 1941, armed soldiers surprised Emilija in her pink nightie while she was preparing for bed. They carried orders for her arrest, signed by none other than Vilis Lācis. She was allowed to change into an elegant black gown before being loaded onto a cattle-car bound for the Siberian gulags. She brought nothing else.

Emilija, dressed in rags, died of dysentery and starvation in her Siberian work camp on 23 September 1941...exactly as the clairvoyant Eižens Finks had predicted.

hostels in the city, Cinnamon Sally still has a long way to go to truly earn its place in backpacker-dom. Rooms are perfectly clean and the common area is cluttered with sociable characters, but there are far too few bathrooms on the premises. The manager is very friendly, but her staff can be difficult to deal with.

Islande Hotel
HOTEL €€€

(off Map p196; ☑6760 8000; www.islandehotel.lv; Ķīpsalas iela 20; s/d €74/80; @⊛) The international clocks hung above the front desk display the local time in all-important global centres of Reykjavik and Tobago (we're as confused as you are). Upstairs, guests will find modern rooms with great views of downtown Rīga across the river. Strike out at the six-lane bowling alley in the basement.

Hanza Hotel
HOTEL €€€

(off Map p196; ☑6779 6040; www.hanzahotel.lv; Elijas iela 7; d incl breakfast €55; @⊛) Just beyond the Central Market, this newer addition to Rīga's lodging scene is a former apartment building transformed into six floors of tidy rooms, some with great views of Stalin's Birthday Cake.

Riga City Camping
CAMPING €

(off Map p196; ☑6706 5000; www.rigacamping.lv; Ķīpsalas iela 8; sites per adult/child/tent 2.50/1/5Ls; ⊛mid-May–mid-Sep; @) Located on Ķīpsala across the river from Old Rīga, this large camp site is surprisingly close to the city centre and offers plenty of room for campers and campervanners. Discounts are available for those staying more than three nights.

✗ Eating

For centuries in Latvia, food equalled fuel, energising peasants as they worked the fields, and warming their bellies during bone-chilling Baltic winters. Today, the era of boiled potatoes and pork gristle has faded away as food becomes a sensorial experience rather than a necessary evil. Although it will be a while before globetrotters stop qualifying local restaurants as being 'good for Rīga', the cuisine scene has improved by leaps and bounds over the last decade. Please note, however, that as Rīga's dining scene expands, there's a great deal of turnover – especially during these uncertain economic times – and dining options can come and go with the seasons.

Lately the Slow Food movement has taken the city's high-end dining scene by storm. Seasonal menus feature carefully prepared, environmentally conscious dishes using organic produce grown across Latvia's ample farmland. Beyond the sphere of trendy eats, most local joints embrace the literal sense of the term 'slow food' with turtle-speed service.

As Rīga's dining scene continues to draw its influence from a clash of other cultures, tipping (apkalpošana) is evolving from customary to obligatory. A 10% gratuity is common in the capital, and many restaurants are now tacking the tip onto the bill.

OLD RĪGA (VECRĪGA)

If you're self-catering, there's a branch of Rimi (Map p190; www.rimi.lv; Audēju iela 16), a reputable supermarket chain, in Old Rīga's Galerija Centrs shopping mall.

TOP CHOICE Fish Restaurant @ Dome SEAFOOD €€€

(Map p190; www.domehotel.lv; Miesnieku iela 4; mains 7-18Ls; ⊛lunch & dinner) The Dome Hotel's restaurant quickly reminds diners that Rīga sits near a body of water that's full of delicious fish. Service is impeccable, and dishes are expertly prepared to reflect the eclectic assortment of recipes in the modern Latvian lexicon – this is not to be missed if you're looking for a place to splurge.

Dorian Gray
CAFE €€

(Map p190; www.doriangray.lv, in Latvian; Mazā Muzeja iela 1; mains 3.60-8Ls) With seating purchased from a car boot sale, random pillows scattered about and cracked crimson brick crumbling off the walls, Dorian Gray might just be (rather ironically) the least image-obsessed place in town. Down-to-earth wait staff serves curious concoctions like chicken stuffed with shrimp and a strange carrot cake that could more appropriately be defined as a dessert salad. Swing by for weekly movie nights and brunch-time screenings of Ugly Betty.

Indian Raja
INDIAN €€

(Sue's Indian Raja; Map p190; Skārņu iela 7; mains from 7.50Ls) Who knew the Baltic had such brilliant Indian food?! Tucked away down a medieval alley you'll find a welcome antedote to the bland ingredients that rule most Latvian fare – here it's all about savoury curries that incorporate spices directly from the subcontinent.

Pelmeņi XL
FAST FOOD €

(Map p190; Kaļķu iela 7; dumpling bowls 0.86-2.50Ls; ☺9am-4am) A Rīga institution for backpackers and undiscerning drunkards, this extra-large cafeteria stays open extra-late serving up huge bowls of *pelmeņi* (Russian-style ravioli stuffed with meat) amid Flintstones-meets-Gaudí decor (you'll see). There are a couple of secondary locations, including one in the central train station.

Alus Seta
LATVIAN €

(Map p190; www.lido.lv; Tirgoņu iela 6; mains 2-7Ls; ☺lunch & dinner) The pick of the LIDO litter – Latvia's version of locally themed fast food – Alus Seta feels like an old Latvian brew house. It's popular with locals as well as tourists – everyone flocks here for cheap-as-chips grub and homemade beer. Seating floods the cobbled streets during the warmer months.

Cadets de Gascogne
BAKERY €

(Franču Maiznīca; Map p190; Basteja bulvāris 8; baguette sandwich 2.20Ls; ☺7am-10pm Mon-Sat) Got a tummy ache from one too many *pelmeņi*? Nurse your digestive system at this French-run bakery – pick up a mug of hot chocolate and a baguette sandwich stuffed with ham and *cornichons* (gherkins). Additional seating available on the roof promenade. There's a second location in Berga Bāzars (Elizabetes iela 81/83).

V. Kuze
CONFECTIONER €

(Map p190; www.kuze.lv; Jēkaba iela 20/22; coffee & cake from 1.20Ls) Vilhelms Ķuze was a prominent entrepreneur and chocolatier while Latvia flirted with freedom between the world wars. When the Soviets barged in he was promptly deported to Siberia where he met his maker. Today, Ķuze Chocolates is up and running once more, and this charming cafe-cum-confectioner functions not only as a memoriam to dear Vilhelms, but also as a tribute to the colourful art-nouveau era when arcing furniture and geometric nature motifs were en vogue.

Gutenbergs
LATVIAN €€

(Map p190; www.gutenbergs.eu; Doma laukums 1; mains 5.90-11.90Ls; ☺May-Oct) Go one better than dining with a view – dine *in* the view! The Hotel Gutenbergs' rooftop terrace in the heart of Old Rīga squats between sky-scraping spires and gingerbread trim. Potted plants, cherubic statues and trickling fountains contribute to a decidedly Florentine vibe, although the menu focuses on local favourites.

Rozengrāls
MEDIEVAL €€€

(Map p190; www.rozengrals.lv; Rozena iela 1; mains 4.50-19.20Ls) Remember 500 years ago when potatoes weren't the heart and soul of Latvian cuisine? We don't, but Rozengrāls does – this candlelit haunt takes diners back a few centuries offering medieval game (sans spuds) served by costume-clad waiters.

Vecmeita ar kaki
LATVIAN €€

(The Spinster & Her Cat; Map p190; Mazā Pils iela 1; mains 3.10-9.90Ls) This cosy spot across from the president's palace specialises in cheap Latvian grub and meaty mains. In warmer weather patrons dine outside on converted sewing-machine tables.

Ķiploku Krogs
INTERNATIONAL €€

(Garlic Bar; Map p190; Jēkaba iela 3/5; mains 3.40-9.80Ls) Vampires beware – *everything* at this joint contains garlic, even the ice cream. The menu is pretty hit-and-miss, but no matter what, it's best to avoid the garlic pesto spread – it'll taint your breath for days (trust us). Enter from Mazā Pils.

Šefpavārs Vilhelms
FAST FOOD €

(Chef William; Map p190; Šķūņu iela 6; pancake rolls 0.65Ls) Customers of every ilk are constantly queuing for a quick nosh – three blintze-like pancakes smothered in sour cream and jam equals the perfect backpacker's breakfast.

CENTRAL RĪGA (CENTRS)

Self-caterers should try **Rimi** (Map p196; www.rimi.lv; K Barona iela 46) in the Barona Centrs shopping mall or check out the Central Market.

⬆TOP CHOICE Istaba
CAFE €€

(Map p196; ☎6728 1141; K Barona iela 31a; mains 3-10Ls; ☺Mon-Sat) Owned by local chef and TV personality Mārtiņš Sirmais, 'The Room' sits in the rafters above a like-named gallery space adorned with trend-setting bric-a-brac. In summer you can dine on the street-side veranda, though we prefer heading upstairs to grab a seat in the mob of discarded lamps and sofas. There's no set menu – you're subject to the cook's fancy – but it's all about flavourful and filling portions served on mismatched dishware. Reservations are recommended.

Aragats
GEORGIAN €€

(off Map p196; ☎6737 3445; Miera iela 15; mains 4-8Ls; ☺Tue-Sat) Ignore the plastic shrubbery – this place is all about sampling some killer cuisine from the Caucasus. Start with an appetiser of pickled vegetables – the perfect chaser for your home-brewed *chacha* (Georgian vodka). Then, make nice with the matronly owner as she dices up fresh herbs at your table to mix with the savoury lamb stew. At the end of the meal men will have to pay for the ladies at the table, as the menus handed to women don't have any of the prices listed!

Bonēra
CAFE €

(Map p196; Bonheur; Blaumaņa iela 12a; mains 3-5Ls; ⊗lunch & dinner Mon-Sat) Life is indeed good at Bonēra, whose name is a play on the word 'happiness'. The cafe doubles as a vintage-clothing store, though these days most locals come for the 5Ls all-you-can-eat buffet dinner that's stocked with an unending assortment of delicious dishes like Waldorf salads, homemade pâté and scrumptious carbonara pasta.

Osīriss
CAFE €€

(Map p196; K Barona iela 31; mains 3-9Ls; ⊗8am-midnight; 🕾) Despite Rīga's mercurial cafe culture, Osīriss continues to be a local mainstay. The green faux-marble tabletops haven't changed since the mid-'90s and neither has the clientele: angsty artsy types scribbling in their Moleskines over a glass of red wine.

Garage
CAFE €

(Demokrātisks vīna bārs; Map p196; Elizabetes iela 83/85; mains 2-7Ls; ⊗lunch & dinner) Although it bills itself more as a wine bar attached to a Latvian handicrafts shop, Garage has transformed into a trendy cafe serving brilliant snacks and light dishes after legions of local fans have encouraged its expansion into some of the retail space. Friendly staff and an eclectic assortment of secondhard chairs give it that extra *je ne sais quoi*.

Miit
CAFE €

(Map p196; www.miit.lv; Lāčplēša iela 10; mains from 2Ls; ⊗lunch & dinner) A bike shop-cum-cafe that takes its cues from Berlin's hipster culture, Miit is a wonderful addition to Rīga's student scene with plenty of space to sip a latte and blog about Nietzsche amid toppled-over IKEA bookcases, comfy couches and discarded bicycle parts. The two-course lunch is a fantastic deal for penny-pinchers – expect a soup and a main course for under 3Ls (dishes change every day).

🍴 Vincents
FINE DINING €€€

(Map p196; 🕾6733 2634; www.restorans.lv; Elizabetes iela 19; mains 13-20Ls; ⊗6-11pm Mon-Sat)

Ask any older Rīgan – they'll all tell you that Vincents is the top spot in town. So it's no surprise that it's also the most expensive. Apparently when Queen Elizabeth spent a day in town, she ate both her lunch and dinner here, and other world figures have followed suit. The head chef is a stalwart of the Slow Food movement, and crafts his ever-changing menu amid eye-catching van Gogh–inspired decor (hence the name).

LIDO Atpūtas Centrs
LATVIAN €

(LIDO Recreation Centre; www.lido.lv; Krasta iela 76; mains 2-6.50Ls) If Latvia and Disney World had a love child it would be the LIDO Atpūtas Centrs – an enormous wooden palace dedicated to the country's coronary-inducing cuisine. Servers dressed like Baltic milkmaids bounce around as patrons hit the rows of buffets for classics like pork tongue and cold beet soup. Take the free bus from Ratslaukums, or tram 3, 7 or 9 and get off at the 'LIDO' stop several kilometres beyond the city centre. There's a handful of smaller LIDO restaurants – like Alus Seta (p209) – dotted around town for those who don't have time to make it out to the mothership.

Restaurant Bergs
FINE DINING €€€

(Map p196; ✉6777 0957; Elizabetes iela 83/85; mains 8.50-16.50Ls; ⊗breakfast, lunch & dinner) The short-but-sweet menu reads like a poem: spring salmon fillet with an orange and fennel salad, rack of lamb with wholegrain mustard and minted aubergine stew. Bergs' ever-changing menu of international eats is Vincents' biggest competitor when it comes to high-end bites.

DAD
CAFE €

(off Map p196; www.dadcaferiga.blogspot.com; Miera iela 17; mains 3.50Ls; ⊗lunch & dinner; 🕾) DAD are the three initials of the owners, who proudly explain the DAD stands for so much more (you'll have to ask them what else DAD means). Couches, chairs and an upright piano are loosely tossed around the modest storefront – several tables spill out onto the street during the warmer months. It's a casual and unpretentious place to gather with friends, and maybe make some new ones.

Taka
CAFE €

(off Map p196; Miera iela 10; mains 2.50-3.50Ls; ⊗lunch & dinner Mon-Sat; 🕾🖉) This stop on the underground music scene has a flock of origami cranes dangling in the front window. Inside you'll find bright murals on the walls, extra-comfy couches, and 20- to 30-somethings gathered around during mealtimes to down some delicious vegetarian fare.

Restaurant Kitchen GOURMET €€
(off Map p196; www.restaurantkitchen.lv; Maskavas iela 12, korpuss 1; mains 3-9Ls; ⊙lunch & dinner) The little Spīķeri district is booming as of late, and Restaurant Kitchen is the current spot that's luring foodies beyond the city's central core. Dishes are overflowing with fresh ingredients from the Central Market next door – sample favourites like the self-proclaimed 'best burger in Rīga', which features an almost steak-like patty covered in thick savoury-sweet sauces (you'll need a fork).

Charlestons INTERNATIONAL €€
(Čarlstons; Map p196; www.charlestons.lv; Blaumaņa iela 38/40; mains 4.95-18.95Ls; 🛜) If you're up to your elbows in pork tongue, Charlestons is a sure bet to get rid of the meat sweats. Lounge around the terraced courtyard in the heart of a residential block and feast on delicious platters of Norwegian salmon, sautéed duck and the best Caesar salad in the Baltic.

Index SANDWICHES €
(Map p196; www.indexcafe.lv; Brīvības iela 32; sandwiches/salads from 1.85/2.19Ls; ⊙7am-10pm Mon-Fri, 10am-10pm Sat & Sun) Latvia's trendier version of Prêt a Manger is a step up from ready-made sandwiches at the grocery store. Black-and-yellow stencil art rocks the walls and large picture windows open up onto busy Brīvības – the perfect spot for some serious people-watching. There's a second (and slightly cosier) location in the heart of Old Rīga at Šķūņu iela 16.

Teātra Bāra Restorāns INTERNATIONAL €€
(Map p196; Lāčplēša iela 25; mains 5-9Ls; ⊙lunch & dinner) This hip spot, associated with the progressive theatre next door, lures artsy types with affordable prices and trendy decor that spills out into a spacious courtyard. After dinner, head to the like-named bar across the street for a round of evening cocktails while eavesdropping on local gossip.

Drinking

If you want to party like a Latvian, assemble a gang of friends and pub crawl your way through the city, stopping at colourful haunts for rounds of beer, belly laughter and, of course, Black Balzām. On summer evenings, nab a spot at one of the beer gardens in Old Rīga.

OLD RĪGA (VECRĪGA)
Nekādu Problēmu BEER GARDEN
(No Problem; Map p190; www.nekaduproblemu.lv; Doma laukums) This sea of sturdy patio ware livens Doma laukums in the warmer months as the rousing fits of live music bounce off the cathedral walls. Sample more than 20 types of draught beer, and the food's pretty darn good, too.

Cuba Cafe BAR
(Map p190; www.cubacafe.lv; Jaun iela 15; 🛜) An authentic mojito and a table overlooking Doma laukums is just what the doctor ordered after a long day of sightseeing. On colder days, swig your caipirinha inside amid dangling Cuban flags, wobbly stained-glass lamps and the murmur of trumpet jazz.

La Belle Epoque BAR
(French Bar; Map p190; Mazā Jaunavu iela 8) Students flock to this boisterous basement bar to power down its trademark 'apple pie' shots (1Ls). The Renoir mural and kitschy *Moulin Rouge* posters seem to successfully ward off stag parties.

Egle BEER GARDEN
(Map p190; www.spoguegle.lv; Kaļķu iela 1a) Old Rīga's second beer garden after No Problem recently came to life after the removal of an old Soviet office building. It's a cosier addition to the city, with tables plunked closely together and folk music in the evenings.

Ala Folks Clubs BAR/CLUB
(Map p190; Smilšu iela 16) Owned by an Australian Latvian, the heart of Ala Folks Clubs is tucked away in an interior courtyard that's stuffed with a small stage. When you enter, go under the mural, walk through the restaurant, turn left at the toilets, and go up the stairs to find a rowdy crowd listening to live beats.

Mojo LOUNGE
(Map p190; www.mojocafe.lv; Pils iela 7) Oh Mojo, how you endear us with your retro wallpaper prints, shaggy rugs and dozens of other throwbacks to the '70s, like old radios and leather couches dyed in odd colours.

Paldies Dievam Piektdiena Ir Klāt BAR
(Thank Goodness It's Friday; Map p190; www.piektdiena.lv; 11 Novembra Krastmala 9) No relation to the fried food–slinging American chain, this 'TGIF' rescues locals from bitter winter nights with loud Caribbean decor, appropriately attired barkeeps and fruity shooters.

Aptieka BAR
(Pharmacy Bar; Map p190; Mazā Miesnieku iela 1) Antique apothecary bottles confirm the subtle-but-stylish theme at this popular drinking haunt run by a Latvian American.

I Love You BAR
(Map p190; Aldaru iela 9) The three words everyone loves to hear is a chill joint tucked away down one of Old Rīga's wobbly streets. Sneak downstairs for a sea of comfy couches. DJs spin alternative beats on Thursday nights and there's plenty of outdoor seating in the warmer months.

Radio Bar BAR
(Map p190; Šķūņu iela 17, entrance on Zirgu iela) A stone's throw from Doma laukums, this happenin' bar/nightclub, decked out in radio dials and doodads, blasts mostly house and hip-hop.

CENTRAL RĪGA (CENTRS)

TOP CHOICE Piens BAR/CLUB
(Milk; Off Map p196; Brīana iela 9) Piens is, without a doubt, the most happening spot in town. Located up in the Miera iela area, this bar-club hybrid occupies a large chunk of industrial land and features a brilliant mix of decorative motifs – Soviet, I Love Lucy '50s and geometric art nouveau. The newly added Delisnack – a beloved import from Liepāja –

means that trips to the west coast are no longer necessary to devour their trademark hangover-curing hamburgers.

Pērle BAR/CAFE
(Map p196; Tērbatas iela 65) Pērle is where outmoded technology goes to die a stylish rockstar death. It's everything you'd want in a neighbourhood hipster hangout: discarded Gameboys, racks of vintage tweed, a massacre of mannequin parts, and designer lattes...with Baileys. Oh, and everything's for sale. Naturally.

Gauja BAR
(Map p196; Tērbatas iela 56) Step off the street and into time-warped Gauja – a small bar decked out in Soviet-style decor. Hunker down amid period furnishings for a rousing duel on the retro chessboard, or link together the set of wooden dominos while unique beats soar above (the owners have their own recording studio).

Terrace Riga BEER GARDEN
(Map p196; Gallerija Riga, Dzirnavu iela 67) Soaring high over the grand boulevards of Central Rīga, Terrace Riga, on the roof of the Gallerija Riga shopping mall, is an enormous open-air space that attempts to give off a Miami South Beach vibe, where umbrellas act as palm trees and heartier spirits replace

---

TOP DAY TRIPS FROM RĪGA

Leave Rīga's mess of art-nouveau goblins and swirling church spires behind and explore Latvia's other gems: flaxen shorelines, rambling palaces, quaint provincial villages and forests full of shady trees.

» **Jūrmala** (p218) The Soviet Union's ultimate beach destination still teems with the Russian elite sporting bikinis and bad haircuts. Take Rīga's suburban train bound for Skola or Tukums, get off at Majōri station, and you'll be smack in the middle of spa-land in 30 minutes flat.

» **Saulkrasti** (p244) If you're looking for a quieter stretch of sand undisturbed by the tan-hungry glitterati, try quaint Saulkrasti, only an hour by train up the Vidzeme Coast.

» **Sigulda** (p245) It's hard not to be enchanted by Turaida Castle, hidden deep within the pine forests of Gauja National Park. Adrenalin junkies will get their fix with an endless array of activities such as bobsledding and bungee jumping from a moving cable car. Sigulda is only 1¼ hours away by bus or train.

» **Rundāle Palace** (p239) Latvia's miniature version of Versailles (but without the crowds) is a stunning, 138-room homage to aristocratic ostentatiousness. Try a bus tour (around 20Ls) or rent a car to navigate the 75km trek; public buses only run to Bauska, where you must switch to a local route to complete the last 12km.

» **Abava River Valley** (p227) The quiet valley along the murmuring Abava River starkly contrasts Rīga's bustling urban core. Wander through charming three-street villages and an organic farmstead, and picnic under looming sculptures at the awesome Pedvāle Open-Air Art Museum. A rental car is the best mode of transport.

daiquiris and pina coladas. It's popular with Russian tourists but you'll find just about everyone up here on warmer, windless evenings in summer.

Skyline Bar
HOTEL BAR

(Map p196; Elizabetes iela 55; 🖀) A must for every visitor, glitzy Skyline Bar sits on the 26th floor of the Radisson Blu Hotel Latvija. The sweeping views are the city's best, and the mix of glam spirit-sippers makes for great people-watching under the retro purple lighting.

Apsara
TEA HOUSE

(Map p196; Elizabetes iela 74) A charming wooden pagoda set within Vērmanes dārzs, Apsara is a veritable library of rare teas imported from beyond the Himalaya. Daintily sip your imported brews while relaxing on the floor amid a sea of pastel pillows. There are a couple of locations around town, including Tērbatas iela 2, Elizabetes iela 74, Kristiana Barona iela 2a and Skarnu iela 22.

☆ Entertainment

Rīga in Your Pocket and *Rīga This Week* have the most up-to-date listings for opera, ballet, guest DJs, live music and other events around town. The tourist office in the Blackheads' House can help travellers book tickets at any concert venue around town. Several trip operators offer bar and club tours if you'd rather have someone else arrange your big night out. Backpackers staying at sociable digs might find hostel-organised pub crawls and parties.

Nightclubs

Rīga's nightclubs are always brimming with bouncing bodies – usually Russians. Latvians tend to prefer pub crawling across town and tossing back vodka shots with friends. Check the drinking and eating sections – after dark, a lot of establishments in Rīga transform, like a superhero, into a grittier venue with pumping beats.

Some of the city's nightspots have a bit of an edge and cater to an unsavoury clientele. Check the 'Culture & Events' chapter of *Rīga in Your Pocket* for a list of businesses blacklisted by the American Embassy.

Nabaklab
CLUB

(Map p190; www.nabaklab.lv, in Latvian; Meierovica bulvaris 12) Imagine if your favourite alternative radio station opened a nightspot that played its signature blend of experimental tunes and electronica. Well, look no further – Naba's (93.1FM) club space attracts the city's boho hobos with its DJ'd beats, vintage clothes racks, art gallery and cheap beer in a quaint Soviet-style den.

Pulkvedim Neviens Neraksta
CLUB

(No-one Writes to the Colonel; Map p190; www.pulkvedis.lv, in Latvian; Peldu iela 26/28) There's no such thing as a dull night at Pulkvedis. The atmosphere is 'warehouse chic', with pumping '80s tunes on the ground floor and trance beats down below.

Club Essential
CLUB

(Map p196; www.essential.lv; Skolas iela 2) Essential is a spectacle of beautiful people boogieing to some of Europe's top DJ talent. Overzealous security aside, this two-storey complex is your safest bet if partying till dawn is your mission.

Moon Safari
CLUB

(Map p190; www.moonsafari.lv; Krāmu iela 2) Beds in the 'VIP room' and a pet snake at the bar? It's all pretty suggestive, but the 2Ls cocktails and colourful karaoke booth lure a young Erasmus crowd for all-night shenanigans.

Golden
GAY

(Map p196; www.mygoldenclub.com; Ģertrūdes iela 33/35; admission 3-5Ls) It's all about smoke and mirrors (literally) at Rīga's most 'open' venue. However, if you're looking for a thriving gay scene, better pick another city.

Coyote Fly
CLUB

(Map p196; Vērmanes dārzs; admission 3-8Ls) An evening at Coyote Fly is more of an anthropological experiment than a night out on the town. The bouncers are notorious for only letting Latvians in – try your luck at the door and see if you can fool security.

Opera, Ballet & Theatre

Rīga's ballet, opera and theatre season breaks for summer holidays (between June and September).

New Rīga Theatre
THEATRE

(Jaunais Rīgas Teātris; Map p196; ☎6728 0765; www.jrt.lv; Lačplēša iela 25) Contemporary repertory theatre.

Dailes Theatre
THEATRE

(Map p196; ☎6727 0463; www.dailesteatris.lv; Brīvibas iela 75) Rīga's largest modern theatre; it retains a lot of its original architectural elements from the Soviet era.

Latvian National Opera
OPERA, DANCE

(Map p190; ☎6707 3777; www.opera.lv; Aspazijas bulvāris 3) Home to the Rīga Ballet, this is the pride of Latvia, boasting some of the finest opera in all of Europe (and for the fraction of the price of other countries). Mikhail Baryshnikov got his start here.

Concert Venues

Arena Rīga
LIVE MUSIC

(off Map p196; ☎6738 8200; www.arenariga.com; Skantes iela 21) Rīga's 10,000-seat venue hosts dance revues and pop concerts when it is not being used for sporting events.

Dome Cathedral
LIVE MUSIC

(Doma baznīca; Map p190; ☎6721 3213; www.doms.lv; Doma laukums 1) Twice-weekly, short organ concerts (Wednesday and Saturday evenings) and lengthier Friday-night performances are well worth attending.

Great Guild
LIVE MUSIC

(Map p190; ☎6722 4850; www.lnso.lv; Amatu iela 6) Home to the acclaimed Latvian National Symphony Orchestra. Classical music and jazz scats are often heard from the window.

Sapņu Fabrika
LIVE MUSIC

(off Map p196; ☎6728 1222; www.sapnufabrika.lv; Lāčplēša iela 101) Housed in a former industrial plant, the 'Dream Factory' hosts live bands, hip-hop and electronica.

Palladium
LIVE MUSIC

(Map p196; Marijas iela 21) The newest addition to the city's venues is built on the grounds of an old movie theatre. The Palladium is intended to attract international acts.

Carpe Diem
JAZZ

(Map p190; ☎6722 8488; Meistaru iela 10/12; mains from 10Ls; ☺10am-midnight, live music 7.30-10.30pm) Jazz is the main dish at this posh restaurant in the infamous Cat House.

Bites Blues Club
JAZZ

(Map p196; ☎6733 3123; www.bluesclub.lv; Dzirnavu iela 34a; cover 3-5Ls; ☺11am-11pm Mon-Wed, to 2am Thu-Sat) Try stopping for some grub (mostly French or Italian) an hour or two before the show – you'll skip the cover charge and catch some preconcert riffing. Friday nights see most of the live-music action during the summer; in winter expect tunes on Thursday and Saturday as well.

Cinemas

Catching a movie is a great way to spend a rainy day in Rīga (trust us, there are many). Films are generally shown in their original language – usually English – with Latvian or Russian subtitles. Tickets cost between 2Ls and 4Ls depending on the day of the week and venue. Check the cinemas' websites for show-time details. All theatres (except K Suns) have assigned seating.

Coca-Cola Plaza
CINEMA

(Map p196; ☎1189; www.forumcinemas.lv; Jaņvāra iela 13) Rīga's multiplex has stadium seating, 14 screens and a cafe on the top floor. Expect the usual Hollywood fare and the occasional Latvian film.

Daile
CINEMA

(Map p196; ☎1189; K Barona iela 31) Shows hand-me-down films from Rīga's main Cineplex at Coca-Cola Plaza.

Kino Rīga
CINEMA

(Map p196; ☎6728 9755; Elizabetes iela 61) The Baltic's first theatre to feature movies with sound now specialises in European films and hosts several film festivals including the international Future Shorts (www.futureshorts.lv).

K Suns
CINEMA

(Ka Suns; Map p196; ☎6728 5411; www.kinogalerija.lv/ksuns.php, in Latvian; Elizabetes iela 83/85, Bergs Bazārs) An artsy cinema that projects mostly indie films on its one screen. Popcorn and soft drinks available.

🛍 Shopping

Latvians love their shopping malls (a palpable marker of globalisation), but tourists will be pleased to find a wide assortment of local shops that specialise in all sorts of Latvian items – knits, crafts, spirits and fashion. You'll find a wonderful assortment at Berga Bazārs (www.bergabazars.lv; Dzirnavu iela 84), a maze of upmarket boutiques orbiting the five-star Hotel Bergs. Street sellers peddle their wares – amber trinkets, paintings and Russian dolls – outside St Peter's Church on Skārņu iela and along the southern end of Vaļņu iela. Rīga's large crafts fair, the Gadatirgus, is held in Vērmanes dārzs on the first weekend in June. Keep an eye out for the beautiful Nameju rings worn by Latvians around the world as a way to recognise one another.

Madam Bonbon
ACCESSORIES

(Map p196; www.madambonbon.lv; Alberta iela 1-7a) Carrie Bradshaw's died and gone to

ELĪNA DOBELE: THE SOLE OF LATVIAN FASHION

We had the opportunity to spend time with Elīna Dobele, one of Latvia's most celebrated new designers who specialises in custom-made shoes (check out her shop ZoFA). She was the recent winner of a countrywide entrepreneurial award, and currently sells her soles in Japan, Russia and the UK. Here are her thoughts on the growing prominence of a Latvian design aesthetic.

'Ironically in Latvia, a new generation of designers has emerged from this period of (economic) crisis. People have left their original field of work to pursue their passions. I am an architect, but when work opportunities started to dry up I changed my profile. We Latvians don't have a good educational system when it comes to fashion and design – many people study abroad, but in a way not having an organised teaching system promotes a truly unique perspective. People without a fashion background haven't been conditioned to think a certain way.

'So what exactly is Latvian design? It begins with the emphasis on handmade items. We have a long tradition of handicrafts, but mostly we don't have the resources and budget to import work from China. Everything is limited edition – nothing for the mass market. While Scandinavia has a school and confirmed thought about design, our vocabulary is very new here – there is no definition yet. No strong identity.

'Latvians who truly care about what they wear are mixing vintage items. They want to be 'hipsters'... in a positive way. If you're in your 20s and you work in Rīga, you probably can't afford to buy designer fashions, and brand names don't seem to matter anymore. Rīgans are keen to support local shops – people are moved to purchase an item because of the design, not because of the label.

'And as for the future of Latvian design? Well, there are already two designers that have opened boutiques in London. I don't know if they will be successful, but it is a good experiment.'

heaven: every surface in this old-school art-nouveau apartment features some sort of foot furniture. Squeeze into the stiletto on the baby grand piano, or go for the boot behind the teapot on the kitchen table.

Sakta Flower Market   MARKET
(Map p196; Tērbatas iela 2a) Open extra-late for those midnight *mea culpas* when you've gotta bring a gift home to your spouse after a long evening out with friends.

ZoFA   FASHION
(Map p196; www.zofa.eu; Antonijas iela 23) Uber-friendly Elīna greets customers with her uberslanty haircut in an uberchic black dress. Custom-made shoes for men and women range from 130Ls to 180Ls, which is a great deal considering that they are designed and assembled in the studio behind the storefront.

Taste Latvia   FASHION
(Map p190; www.tastelatvia.lv; Audēju iela 16) Hidden on the 4th floor of an otherwise corporate shopping centre, Taste Latvia is a stark white realm filled with the latest fashion creations of local designers.

Riija   FASHION
(Map p196; www.riija.lv; Tērbatas iela 6/8) Scandi-sleek design inhabits every polished nook and cranny at this new design enclave in the heart of Centrs. Look out Sweden, Latvian design is on the rise!

Pienene   ACCESSORIES
(Map p190; Kungu iela 7/9) 'The Dandelion' is an airy boutique in the heart of Old Rīga where visitors can sample some of the countryside's richest wellness products. Expect soaps and candles made from local wax and herbs.

Upe   MUSIC
(Map p190; www.upett.lv; Vāgnera iela 5) Classical Latvian tunes play as customers peruse traditional instruments and CDs of local folk, rock and experimental sounds.

Latvijas Balzāms   FOOD & DRINK
(Map p190; www.lb.lv; Audēju iela 8) A popular chain of liquor stores selling the trademark Latvian Black Balzām. One of myriad branches around town (others can be found at Marijas iela 25, K Barona iela 31 and Audeju iela 8).

ℹ️ LOCAL GUIDEBOOKS

It's well worth picking up the following print publications to supplement the information in this guide.

» **Rīga in Your Pocket** (www.inyourpocket.com/latvia/riga) Handy city guide published every other month. Download a PDF version or pick up a copy at most midrange or top-end hotels (free). The tourist offices and several bookshops also have copies (2Ls).

» **Riga this Week** (www.rigathisweek.lv) An excellent (and free) city guide available at virtually every sleeping option in town. Published every second month.

Robert's Books   BOOKS
(Map p196; www.robertsbooksriga.com; Antonijas iela 12) Robert used to write for the *Economist*; these days he calls Rīga home and tends to his small collection of used English books. Traditional textiles and beeswax candles are also on offer. Enter on Dzirvanu iela.

Jāņa Sēta   BOOKS
(Map p196; www.mapshop.lv; Elizabetes iela 83/85) The largest travel bookstore in the Baltic overflows with a bounty of maps, souvenir photo books and Lonely Planet guides.

Art Nouveau Riga   SOUVENIRS
(Map p196; www.artnouveauriga.lv; Strēlnieku iela 9) Purchase a variety of art nouveau–related souvenirs, from guidebooks and postcards to stone gargoyles and bits of stained glass.

Tornis   JEWELLERY
(Map p190; Grēcinieku iela 11-2) A fine assortment of jewellery depicting intriguing pagan symbols. Enter from Pēterbaznīcas laukums.

ℹ️ Information

Internet Access

Every hostel and hotel has some form of internet connection available to guests. Internet cafes are a dying breed in Rīga and they're usually filled with 12-year-old goons blasting cybermonsters.

Elik Kafe (Map p196; Merķeļa iela 1; per 30min/1hr 0.45/0.85Ls; ⏱24hr) Conveniently located near the train station above the McDonalds. Second location at Kaļķu iela 11.

Medical Services

ARS (Map p196; ☎6720 1003; www.ars-med.lv; Skola iela 5) English-speaking doctors; 24-hour consultation available.

Money

There are scores of ATMs scattered around the capital. If for some reason you are having trouble locating a bank, walk down Kaļķu iela (which turns into Brīvības bulvārīs) and within seconds you will find a bank or ATM. Withdrawing cash is easier than trying to exchange travellers cheques or foreign currencies; exchange bureaus often have lousy rates and most do not take travellers cheques. For detailed information about Latvian currency and exchange rates visit www.bank.lv.

Marika (Brīvības bulvāris 30) Offers 24-hour currency exchange services with reasonable rates. Second location at Dzirnavu 96.

Post

Those blue storefronts with 'Pasta' written on them aren't Italian restaurants – they're post offices. See www.pasts.lv for more info.

Central post office (Brīvības bulvaris 32; ⏱7.30am-8pm Mon-Fri, 8am-6pm Sat, 10am-4pm Sun) International calling and faxing services available.

Post office (Elizabetes iela 41/43; ⏱7.30am-9pm Mon-Fri, 8am-4pm Sat)

Tourist Information

Tourism information centre (☎6730 7900; www.rigatourism.com; Rātslaukums 6; ⏱9am-6pm) Gives out excellent tourist maps and walking-tour brochures. Staff can arrange accommodation and book day trips. Sells concert and opera tickets in summer, and the **Rīga Card** (www.rigacard.lv; 24hr card 10Ls), which offers discounts on sights and restaurants, and free rides on public transportation (see p195). Satellite tourism offices can be found in Livu laukums, and at the train station, bus station and airport.

Websites

www.1188.lv Lists virtually every establishment in Rīga and the rest of Latvia. The Latvian language setting yields the most search results. The search engine also provides up-to-date information on nightlife and traffic.

www.rigaoutthere.com A site managed by a locally run tour operator and featuring a handy travel planner in the right-hand column.

www.zl.lv Another excellent Latvian database offering detailed information about businesses in Rīga and the entire country.

ℹ️ Getting There & Away

See p404 for additional information regarding travel between Latvia and countries beyond the Baltic.

Air

Rīga International Airport (Lidosta Rīga; www.riga-airport.com, Marupes pagast) is in the suburb of Skulte, 13km southwest of the city centre. See p404 for info on airlines flying into the capital. At the time of writing Rīga was the only city in Latvia with a commercial airport.

Boat

Rīga's **passenger ferry terminal** (☑6732 6200; www.portofriga.lv; Eksporta iela 3a), located about 1km downstream (north) of Akmens Bridge, offers service to Stockholm aboard **Tallink** (☑6709 9700; www.tallink.lv). **DFDS Ferry Lines** (☑6735 3523; www.lisco.lv; Zivju iela 1) and **Ave Line** (☑6709 7999; www.aveline.lv; Uriekstes 3) leave from the Vecmīgrāvja cargo terminal (further down the Daugava) for Travemünde (Lübeck), Germany. Service is often suspended in the colder months.

Bus

Buses depart from Rīga's **international bus station** (Rīgas starptautiskā autoosta; www.autoosta.lv; Prāgas iela 1), located behind the railway embankment just beyond the southeastern edge of Old Rīga. International destinations include Tallinn, Vilnius, Warsaw, Pärnu, Kaunas, St Petersburg and Moscow. Try one of following companies:

Ecolines (☑6721 4512; www.ecolines.net)

Eurolines Lux Express (☑6778 1350; www.luxexpress.eu)

Nordeka (☑6746 4620; www.nordeka.lv)

Baltic services from Rīga include the following:

Aglona 5.60Ls, four hours, daily at 4pm and/or 6pm

Bauska 2Ls, 1¼ hours, every 30 minutes from 6.30am to 11pm

Cēsis 2.60Ls, two hours, every 30 minutes from 7.30am to 9.30pm

Daugavpils 5.60Ls, 3½ to 4¼ hours, 15 daily between 5.15am and midnight

Dobele 2.10Ls, 1½ hours, twice hourly between 6.45am and 9.45pm

Jelgava 1.50Ls, one hour, every 30 minutes between 6am and 11.30pm

Kandava 2.70Ls, 1½ to two hours, 10 daily between 8am and 10pm

Kaunas 9.30Ls, four to 5½ hours, three daily between 4pm and midnight

Kolka 4Ls to 5Ls, 3½ to 4½ hours, five daily from 7.20am to 5.15pm

Kuldīga 4.10Ls, 2½ to 3¼ hours, hourly from 7am to 8pm

Liepāja 5.50Ls to 6.50Ls, four hours, every 45 minutes from 6.45am to 7.30pm

Pärnu 5Ls to 5.40Ls, 2¾ hours, 15 daily between 6.20am and 2am

Pāvilosta 5.50Ls, 4½ hours, daily at 8.25pm

Sigulda 1.80Ls, one hour, every 30 minutes from 7am to 9.30pm

Tallinn 10Ls to 14Ls, 4½ hours, 16 daily between 6.40am and 11.15pm

Valmiera 3Ls to 3.30Ls, two to 2½ hours, twice hourly between 6.20am and 10.50pm

Ventspils 4.70Ls, three to four hours, hourly from 7am to 10.30pm

Vilnius 9Ls to 12Ls, four hours, 13 daily between 6.35am and 10.30pm

Train

Rīga's **central train station** (centrālā stacija; Stacijas laukums) is convenient to Old and Central Rīga, and is housed in a conspicuous glass-encased shopping centre near the Central Market. Give yourself extra time to find the ticket booths as they are scattered throughout the building and sometimes tricky to find.

Most Latvians live in the large suburban and rural ring around Rīga, and commute into the city for work. The city's network of ultrahandy suburban train lines help facilitate commuting, and make day trips to nearby towns a whole lot easier too. Rīga has six suburban lines: the oft-used Sigulda–Cēsis–Valmiera Line (regularly stopping in all three towns), the Skulte Line (which stops in Saulkrasti), the Dubulti–Sloka–Ķemeri–Tukums Line (the track to take for Jūrmala), the Orge–Krustpils Line (headed for Salaspils and Daugavpils), the Jelgava Line and the Ērgļi–Suntaži Line. Purchase tickets for Jūrmala, Sigulda and Cēsis at windows 7 to 12.

Rīga is directly linked by long-distance trains to Daugavpils (4¾ hours), Moscow (16½ hours), St Petersburg (13¼ hours) and Pskov (8½ hours). Visit www.ldz.lv to view the timetables and prices for long-haul international and domestic trains. Train service is not convenient to any destinations in western Latvia.

Check www.1188.lv for the most up-to-date prices. Amid the jumble of schedules, the following services are available:

Cēsis 2.30Ls, two hours, five daily between 6.35am and 9pm

Jūrmala (Majori) 0.95Ls, 30 minutes, two to three per hour between 5.50am and 11.40pm

Jelgava 1.35Ls, 45 minutes, two per hour between 5.30am and 10.30pm

Ķemeri 1.35Ls, one hour, hourly between 5.50am and 11.40pm

Salaspils 0.70Ls, 25 minutes, two to three per hour between 5am and 11pm

Saulkrasti 1.45Ls, one hour, one or two per hour between 5.45am and 10.30pm

Sigulda 1.55Ls, one to 1¼ hours, hourly between 6am and 9pm

Valmiera 2.80Ls, 2¼ hours, four daily between 6.35am and 9pm

ⓘ Getting Around

To/From the Airport

There are three means of transport connecting the city centre to the airport. The cheapest option is bus 22 (0.70Ls), which runs every 15 minutes and stops at several points around town including the Stockmanns complex and the Daugava River (near Friendly Fun Franks hostel). Passengers who carry luggage onto public transportation (with the exception of bus 22) need a 'luggage ticket' (0.10Ls; available from the driver). airBaltic runs lime-green minibuses (3Ls) from the airport to a selection of midrange hotels in Central Rīga. Lime-green taxis cost a flat rate of 10Ls from the airport; cabbies run the meter when heading to the airport (figure around 8Ls from Central Rīga with mild traffic).

Bicycle

Zip around town with **Baltic Bikes** (✆6778 8333; www.balticbike.lv; per hr 0.70Ls). A handful of stands are conveniently positioned around Rīga and Jūrmala; simply choose your bike, call the rental service and receive the code to unlock your wheels.

Car & Motorcycle

For information on car rentals, see p275. Motorists must pay 5Ls per hour to enter Old Rīga – tickets must be purchased in advance at Statoil stations or foreign exchange bureaux.

Public Transport

If you weren't born in Rīga, you won't have the gene that innately enables you to understand the city's horribly convoluted network of buses, trams and trolleybuses. Lucky for you, most of Rīga's main tourist attractions are within walking distance of one another, so you might never have to use the city's public transport. Tickets cost 0.70Ls (0.50Ls if you buy your ticket ahead of time from an automated machine or newsstand). A five-day unlimited transport pass can be purchased for 9Ls. City transport runs daily from 5.30am to midnight. Some routes have an hourly night service. For routes and schedules visit www.rigassatiksme.lv.

Taxi

Taxis charge 0.40Ls to 0.50Ls per kilometre (oftentimes 0.50Ls to 0.60Ls between 10pm and 6am). Insist on having the meter on before you set off. Meters usually start running at 1Ls to 1.50Ls. It shouldn't cost more than 4Ls for a short journey (like crossing the Daugava for dinner in Ķīpsala). There are taxi ranks outside the bus and train stations, at the airport and in front of a few major hotels in Central Rīga, such as Radisson Blu Hotel Latvija.

AROUND RĪGA

It's hard to believe that long stretches of flaxen beaches and shady pine forests lie just 20km from Rīga's metropolitan core. Both Jūrmala and Ķemeri National Park make excellent day trips from Rīga.

The highway connecting Rīga to Jūrmala (Latvia's only six-lane road) was known as '10 minutes in America' during Soviet times, because locally produced films set in the USA were always filmed on this busy asphalt strip.

Jūrmala

POP 56,000

The Baltic's version of the French Riviera, Jūrmala (pronounced *yoor*-muh-lah) is a long string of townships with stately wooden beach estates belonging to Russian oil tycoons and their trophy wives. Even during the height of communism, Jūrmala was always a place to *sea* and be seen. Wealthy fashionistas would flaunt their couture beachwear while worshipping the sun between spa treatments. On summer weekends, vehicles clog the roads when jetsetters and day-tripping Rīgans flock to the resort town for some serious fun in the sun.

Jūrmala's 32km strip of land consists of 14 townships. If you don't have a car or bicycle, you'll want to head straight to the heart of the action – the townships of Majori and Dzintari. A 1km-long pedestrian street, Jomas iela, connects these two districts and is considered to be Jūrmala's main drag, with loads of tourist-centric venues. Unlike many European resort towns, most of Jūrmala's restaurants and hotels are several blocks away from the beach, which keeps the seashore (somewhat) pristine.

⊙ Sights

Besides its 'Blue Flag' beach, Jūrmala's main attraction is its colourful art-nouveau **wooden houses**, distinguishable by frilly awnings, detailed facades and elaborate towers. There are over 4000 wooden structures found throughout Jūrmala (most are lavish summer cottages), but you can get your fill of wood by taking a leisurely stroll along Jūras iela, which parallels Jomas iela between Majori and Dzintari. The houses are in various states of repair; some are dilapidated and abandoned, others are beautifully renovated and some are brand-new constructions. The tourist office has a handy booklet called *The Resort Architecture of Jūrmala City,* which features several self-guided architectural walking tours – page eight highlights Majori neighbourhood.

At the other end of the architectural spectrum are several particularly gaudy beachfront Soviet-era sanatoriums. No specimen glorifies the genre quite like the Vaivari sanatorium (Asaru prospekts 61), on the main road 5km west of Majori. It resembles a giant, beached cruise ship that's been mothballed since the Brezhnev era. Surprisingly it still functions, catering to an elderly clientele who have been visiting regularly since, well, the Brezhnev era.

Jūrmala City Museum   MUSEUM
(✆6776 4746; Tirgoņu iela 29; admission 0.50Ls, free Fri; ⊙11am-6pm Wed-Sun) After a pricey renovation, this museum now features a beautiful permanent exhibit detailing Jūrmala's colourful history as *the* go-to resort town in the former USSR.

Jūrmala Open-Air Museum   MUSEUM
(✆6775 4909; Tīklu iela 1a; admission 0.50Ls, free Tue; ⊙10am-6pm Tue-Sun) Further afield in Lielupe, this museum preserves 19th-century fishers' houses and a collection of nautical equipment. If you're lucky, you'll get to try smoked fish prepared in a traditional Latvian manner.

Art Rezidence 'Inner Light'   GALLERY
(✆6787 1937; www.jermolajev.lv; Omnibusa iela 19; admission 1Ls; ⊙11am-6pm Jun-Aug, noon-5pm Sat & Sun Sep-May) A visit here will surely cure any rainy-day blues. A local Russian artist runs the studio out of his home, and dabbles with a secret recipe for glow-in-the-dark paint by creating portraits that morph when different amounts of light strike the painting. Ethereal Enya music further enhances the trippy experience as the paintings shine brilliantly in the pulsing darkness.

🏃 Activities

Jūrmala's first spa opened in 1838, and since then the area has been known far and wide as the spa capital of the Baltic. Treatments are available at a variety of big-name hotels and hulking Soviet sanatoriums further along the beach towards Ķemeri National Park. Many accommodations offer combined spa and sleeping deals.

TOP CHOICE Baltic Beach Hotel Spa Centre   SPA
(✆6777 1400; www.balticbeach.lv; Jūras iela 23-25; massage 60/90min 25/35Ls; ⊙8am-10pm) The Baltic Beach Hotel's spa is the largest treatment centre in the Baltic, with three rambling storeys full of massage rooms, saunas, yoga studios, swimming pools and Jacuzzis. The 1st floor is themed like a country barn and features invigorating hot-and-cold treatments in which one takes regular breaks from the steam room by pouring buckets of ice water over one's head à la Jennifer Beals in *Flashdance.* Try an array of organic teas on the 2nd level, and splurge on a champagne-filled couple's massage in the Egyptian-themed Cleopatra Room on the top floor. Smaller budgets can enjoy The Garden (25Ls for two people), a miniature oasis stocked with a variety of calming pools and steam rooms.

Saliena Golf Course   GOLF COURSE
(✆6716 0300; www.salienagolf.com; 18 holes weekday/weekend 22/28Ls; ⊙8.20am-6pm) For obvious reasons golfing isn't available throughout the year, but during the height of summer head here for 18 well-maintained holes (par 72). Bookings can be made at a variety of hotels in Jūrmala and Rīga.

Nemo Water Park   WATER PARK
(✆6773 2350; www.nemo.lv; Atbalss iela 1; adult/child 5/2.50Ls; ⊙11am-5pm Wed-Sun May-Sep) Vaivari township, about 5km west of central Majori, is home to the wet and wonderful Nemo Water Park, with shoelace-like waterslides, a sauna and two heated pools right on the beach. The centre also rents bicycles for 5Ls per hour.

Līvu Akvaparks   WATER PARK
(✆6775 5636; www.akvaparks.lv; Viestura iela 24; 1-day adult/child 18.50/12.95Ls; ⊙11am-10pm Mon-Fri, 10am-10pm Sat & Sun) A massive, family-friendly water park in Lielupe, located between Jūrmala and Rīga.

🎉 Festivals & Events

Jūrmala has scores of events and festivals to lure locals and tourists away from Rīga.

Joma Street Festival   CIVIC FESTIVAL
(www.jurmala.lv) Jūrmala's annual city festival held in July; 2009 marked the 50-year anniversary of the unification of Jūrmala's townships. Don't miss the sand-sculpture contest along the beach (www.magicsand.lv).

Jūrmala

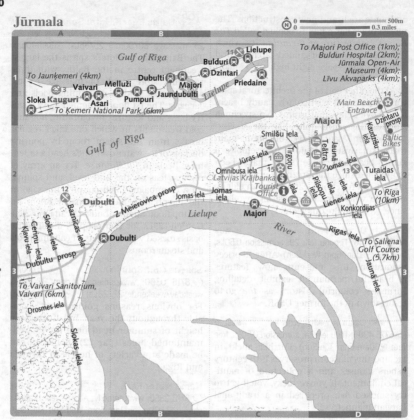

New Wave Song Festival MUSIC
(Jaunais Vilnis; www.newwavestars.com) Held in Dzintari Concert Hall at the end of July, this soloist song contest attracts competitors from around the world. This event is exceedingly popular with visiting Russians – it's best to avoid Jūrmala during the festivities if you are not taking part in the events.

Sleeping

Jūrmala has a wide selection of lodging options – very few of them offer good value. In fact, if penny-pinching's your game, do a day trip to Jūrmala and sleep in Rīga. The tourist office can assist with booking accommodation in your price bracket. It also keeps a list of locals that rent out private rooms when everything is booked. Summertime prices are listed below; room rates fall dramatically during the low-season months.

TOP CHOICE Hotel MaMa BOUTIQUE HOTEL €€
(6776 1271; www.hotelmama.lv; Tirgoņu iela 22; d 40-325Ls; @☎) The bedroom doors have thick, mattress-like padding on the interior (psycho-chic?) and the suites themselves are a veritable blizzard of white drapery. A mix of silver paint and pixie dust accents the ultramodern furnishings and amenities (plasma TVs, kitchenettes, California-king-sized beds, and suspiciously erotic floral imagery framed on the ceiling). If heaven had a bordello, it would probably look something like this. Sneak up to the widow's walk on the roof for breezy views of beach town.

Baltic Beach Hotel HOTEL €€€
(6777 1400; www.balticbeach.lv; Jūras iela 23-25; r incl breakfast 55-870Ls; @☎☎) Concrete Soviet monstrosities look especially ugly along the sea, and Baltic Beach Hotel is no exception. However, the hotel's interior ain't so

Jūrmala

◎ **Sights**
1 Art Rezidence 'Inner Light' C2
2 Jūrmala City Museum A1

● **Activities, Courses & Tours**
3 Nemo Water Park C2

● **Sleeping**
4 Baltic Beach Hotel C2
5 Baltā Pūce.......................................D2
6 Elina D2
7 Hotel Jūrmala Spa D2
8 Hotel MaMa C2
9 Sunset Hotel D2
10 Villa Joma.......................................D2
   Kempings Nemo ....(see 3)

● **Eating**
11 36. Line...C1
12 Orizzonte...B2
   Il Sole ....(see 4)
   MaMa...(see 8)
13 Sue's Asia..D2

● **Drinking**
   Seaside Bar..................................(see 7)

● **Entertainment**
14 Dzintari Concert Hall.........................D1
15 Majori Cultural House &
   Cinema...C1

shabby – the lobby sparkles with polished marble after a recent renovation, and rooms upstairs all have excellent ocean views. The top-notch spa – the Baltic's biggest – is the hotel's best feature.

Villa Joma   BOUTIQUE HOTEL €€
(✆6777 1999; www.villajoma.lv; Jomas iela 90; r 40-75Ls) This inviting boutique hotel sports 15 immaculate rooms that come in quirky configurations. Try for a room with a skylight. Although Villa Joma is several blocks from the beach, there's a lovely garden terrace in the back to catch some rays. Don't miss out on the fantastic food (lunch mains 6Ls to 8Ls, dinner mains 9Ls to 17Ls) served at the airy ground-floor restaurant.

Hotel Jūrmala Spa   HOTEL €€€
(✆6778 4415; www.hoteljurmala.com; Jomas iela 47/49; r 60-235Ls; @🖥🐾🏊) The rooms in this towering black behemoth are on the small side, but you'll hardly notice – everything sparkles after a recent renovation. Breakfast is included. Rooms on the 8th and 9th floor

have sweeping views of both the inland river and the sea. Check out the swinging cocktail lounge on the top floor.

Kempings Nemo   CAMPING €
(✆6773 2350; www.nemo.lv; Atbalss iela 1; sites from 2Ls; cottages 7.50-32Ls; P🏊) Bright yellow-and-blue banners welcome guests to this popular camp site, located right beside Nemo Water Park on the beach in Vaivari township. Pitch a tent or snag a small cottage, and don't miss the home-cooked Latvian breakfast every morning (3.90Ls). Parking is 2Ls.

Baltā Pūce   HOTEL €€
(✆6751 2722; www.baltapuce.lv; Pilsoņu iela 7/9; r 20-100Ls; 🖥) Literally 'the White Owl', this charming inn, set in a 100-year-old house, has quaint rooms and a lobby littered with toy hooters. The rooms are a smidgen nicer at Sunset Hotel next door, but Baltā Pūce has a much more sociable vibe.

Sunset Hotel   HOTEL €€
(✆6775 5311; www.sunsethotel.lv; Pilsoņu iela 7/9; r 25-125Ls; @🖥) Set in a summery, pistachio-coloured beach house, Sunset's refurbished rooms sport antique hardwood floors and hi-tech showers covered with tonnes of nozzles and buttons.

Elina   GUEST HOUSE €€
(✆6776 1665; www.elinahotel.lv; Lienes iela 43; r 25-125Ls) This mom-and-pop operation offers cheery, no-frills accommodation in a wobbly wooden house. There's a small convenience store on the ground floor and the kitchen staff whip up ubercheap eats (3Ls).

🍴 Eating & Drinking

In summer, stroll down Jomas iela and take your pick from beer tents, cafe terraces and trendy restaurants. If you're not feeling adventurous, almost all of Rīga's popular chain restaurants have a franchise in Jūrmala. Most places are open year-round, catering to beach bums in the summer and spa junkies who pass through for treatments during the winter months. Most hotels also have on-site restaurants.

36. Line 〔TOP CHOICE〕   GOURMET €€€
(✆2201 0696; www.lauris-restaurant.lv; Līnija 36; mains 4.50-21Ls; ⏱lunch & dinner) The brainchild of popular local chef Lauris Alekseyev, 36. Line has a private slice of sand in the corner of Jūrmala where diners can tailor an entire day around a meal. Enjoy the beach

LATVIA JŪRMALA

in the late afternoon and switch to casual attire while savouring modern twists on traditional Latvian dishes. In the evening it's not uncommon to find DJs spinning beats.

Orizzonte GOURMET €€
(www.orizzonte.lv; Baznīcas iela 2B; mains 5-19Ls) Located directly along the sandy shores in Jūrmala's Dubulti district, Orizzonte is a fantastic place to watch the sun dip below the Gulf of Rīga. After dark it's all out white tablecloths, candlelight and gentle strums of the guitar in the corner.

MaMa GOURMET €€
(Tirgoņu iela 22; mains 5.50-16.50Ls; ⊘lunch & dinner) At MaMa, Italian and Latvian fusion cuisine is served on crisp white-clothed tables surrounded by a mishmash of throne-like chairs. You may notice that some of the seats are particularly tiny – these are reserved for pets (the chef even created a gourmet menu for Fido). Don't miss the technicoloured bathroom with a fun surprise on the ceiling.

Sue's Asia INDIAN €€
(Jomas iela 74; mains 6-15Ls; ⊘lunch & dinner) Although it's a bit odd seeing bleach-blonde Baltic women serving pan-Asian platters in saris, Sue's is worshipped by locals for its almost-authentic cuisine. Enjoy spicy curries or tender butter chicken amid statues of praying deities.

Il Sole ITALIAN €€€
(Jūras iela 23/25; mains 8-25Ls; ⊘11am-11pm) A romantic restaurant at the Baltic Beach Hotel, Il Sole has fantastic ocean-side seating and a long list of delicious Italian dishes matched with imported wines. The Florentine decor is rather cheesy, but you'll hardly notice while staring out at the setting sun.

Seaside Bar BAR
(Jomas iela 47/49; ⊘3pm-3am) This hot dancing spot sits high above the trees on the 11th floor of Hotel Jūrmala Spa. Nurse your cocktail in a space-age bucket seat or get jiggy with it under the disco ball.

☆ Entertainment

Majori Culture House & Cinema LIVE MUSIC, CINEMA
(Majori Kultūras nams; ☑6776 2403; Jomas iela 35) Hosts films, music concerts and various arts and craft exhibitions.

Dzintari Concert Hall LIVE MUSIC
(Dzintari Koncertzāle; ☑6776 2092; Turaidas iela 1) At the northern beach end of Turaidas iela,

it features a season of summer concerts from June to August.

Information

Free internet access is available at the tourist office. The Jūrmala City Museum has free wi-fi access. Public toilets are located in Concert Garden behind the information centre.

Bulduri Hospital (Vienības prospekts 19/21)

Latvijas Krājbanka (Jomas iela 37; ⊘9am-5pm) On-site 24-hour ATM available.

Majori post office (Strēlnieku prospekts 16; ⊘7.30am-7pm Mon-Fri, 8am-4pm Sat) Located in Dubulti township, a 2km walk west from Majori.

Tourist office (☑6714 7900; www.tourism .jurmala.lv; Lienes iela 5; ⊘9am-7pm Mon-Fri, 10am-5pm Sat, 10am-3pm Sun) Located across from Majori train station, this helpful office has scores of brochures outlining walks, bike routes and attractions. Staff can assist with accommodation bookings and bike rental. A giant map outside helps orient visitors when the centre is closed.

Getting There & Around

BICYCLE Rentals are available at Kempings Nemo or arrangements can be made at the tourist office, where you'll find **Baltic Bike** (www.balticbike.lv).

CAR Motorists driving the 15km into Jūrmala must pay a 1Ls toll per day, even if you are just passing through. Keep an eye out for the self-service toll stations sitting at both ends of the resort town. Drivers caught without proof of payment will be fined 50Ls. All parking around Jūrmala is free.

MINIBUSES Also a common mode of transport between Rīga and Jūrmala; take minibuses (1Ls, 30 minutes) in the direction of Sloka, Jaunķemeri or Dubulti and ask the driver to let you off at Majori. If you go further, the ride will cost 1.40Ls. These vans depart every five to 15 minutes between 6am and midnight and leave opposite Rīga's central train station. Catch the bus at Majori train station for a lift back. These regularly running minibuses can also be used to access other townships within Jūrmala's long sandy stretch. From 9am to midnight, minibuses also connect Jūrmala to Rīga International Airport (2Ls).

SLOW BOAT (☑2923 7123; Lielais Kristaps; adult/child 5/3Ls; ⊘11am, 2.30pm, 4pm, 5.30pm & 7pm) Departs from Rīga Riflemen Square and docks in Majori near the train station. The journey takes one hour.

TRAIN Two to three trains per hour link the sandy shores of Jūrmala to Central Rīga. Take a suburban train bound for Sloka, Tukums or

Dubulti and disembark at Majori station (0.95Ls, 30 to 35 minutes). The first train departs Rīga around 5.50am and the last train leaves Majori around 10.44pm. Jūrmala-bound trains usually depart from tracks 3 and 4, and stop six or seven times within the resort's 'city limits' if you wish to get off in another neighbourhood. Visit www.1188.lv for the most up-to-date information.

Ķemeri National Park

After Jūrmala's chic stretch of celebrity homes and seaside bar huts lies a verdant hinterland called Ķemeri National Park (☼Jun-Aug). Today, the park features sleepy fishing villages tucked between protected bogs, lakes and forests, but at the end of the 1800s, Ķemeri was known for its curative mud and spring water, attracting visitors from as far away as Moscow. Note that the park's land is 'open' year-round, but the infrastructure for the park only works from June to August.

Ķemeri's **park information centre** (☎6714 6819; www.kemeri.lv; ☼10am-6pm Jun-Aug) is located in an old barnlike hotel and restaurant called the 'Funny Mosquito'. Although most of the info is in Latvian, you can rent bikes (4Ls for two hours) and sign up for lectures and programs such as bat- and bird-watching. A scenic 600m **trail** starts at the info centre and circles through a slice of flat plain forest.

The pungent smell of rotten eggs wafts through the air at the national park's spa resort, also called Ķemeri (pronounced kyeh-meh-ree or *tyeh*-meh-ree, depending on who you ask), known for its sulphurous springs. Ķemeri's first mud bath opened in the late 1800s, and until WWII the resort had a widespread reputation as a healing oasis.

The area's spring water is perfectly potable and apparently quite healthy. Try filling your water bottle at **the Lizard**, a stone sculpture at the mouth of a spring that trickles into the river. Sip your pungent brew while meandering past faded mint-green gazebos and small wrought iron bridges with romantic names like Bridge of Sighs or Bridge of Caprices – everything remains exactly as it was during the height of the resort's popularity in the 1930s.

It's hard to miss **Hotel Ķemeri**. Known as the 'White Ship', it was built during Latvia's brief period of independence in the 1930s, and has one of the most impressive facades outside of Rīga. At the moment, only the exterior can be appreciated due to a lack of renovation money. Have a wander across the park and take a look at **St Peter-Paul Orthodox Church**. Built in 1893, it is the oldest place of worship in Ķemeri and, if you look closely, you'll notice that this large wooden structure was constructed entirely without nails.

Fish smoking and canning remain traditional occupations in the villages further afield along the coastal road leading north towards Cape Kolka. Nowhere smells fishier than **Lapmežciems**, overlooking Lake Kaņieris, 3km west of Jūrmala. Sprats are canned in the factory on the right at the village's eastern entrance. The village market sells freshly smoked eel, sprat, salmon and tuna, as does the market in **Ragaciems**, 2km north.

❶ Getting There & Around

Ķemeri National Park is easily accessible from Rīga, as it sits just beyond Jūrmala along the capital's west-bound suburban rail line. Trains

THE EARTH GROANS AT SALASPILS CONCENTRATION CAMP

Between 1941 and 1944 about 45,000 Jews from Rīga and about 55,000 other people, including Jews from other Nazi-occupied countries and prisoners of war, were murdered in the Nazi concentration camp Kurtenhof at Salaspils, 20km southeast of Rīga. Giant, gaunt sculptures stand as a memorial on the site, which stretches over 40 hectares. The inscription on the huge concrete bunker, which forms the memorial's centrepiece, reads 'Behind this gate the earth groans' – a line from a poem by the Latvian writer Eizens Veveris, who was imprisoned in the camp. Inside the bunker a small exhibition recounts the horrors of the camp. In its shadow lies a 6m-long block of polished stone with a metronome inside, ticking a haunting heartbeat, which never stops.

To get there from Rīga, take a suburban train on the Ogre–Krustpils line to Dārziņi (not Salaspils) station. The path from the station to the *piemineklis* (memorial) starts on the barracks side. It's about a 15-minute walk. If you're driving from Rīga on the A6 highway, the hard-to-spot turn-off is on the left, 300m before the A5 junction.

between Rīga and Jūrmala's Majori station run 15 times per day. The park can also be accessed by bus 11 from Majori station, or directly from Rīga.

WESTERN LATVIA (KURZEME)

Just when you thought that Rīga was the only star of the show, in comes western Latvia from stage left, dazzling audiences with a whole different set of talents. While the capital wows the crowd with intricate architecture and metropolitan majesty, Kurzeme (Courland in English) takes things in the other direction: miles and miles of jaw-dropping natural beauty. The region's sandy strands of desolate coastline are tailor-made for an off-the-beaten-track adventure. A constellation of coastal towns – Kolka, Ventspils, Pāvilosta and Liepāja – provide pleasant breaks between the large stretches of awesome nothingness.

Kurzeme wasn't always so quiet; the region used to be occupied by the namesake Cours, a rebellious tribe known for teaming up with the Vikings for raids and battles. During the 13th century, German crusaders ploughed through, subjugating the Cours, alongside the other tribes living in Latvia. When the Livonian Order collapsed under assault from Russia's Ivan the Terrible in 1561, the Order's last master, Gotthard Kettler, salvaged Courland and neighbouring Zemgale as his own personal fiefdom.

Duke Jakob, Courland's ruler from 1640 to 1682, really put the region on the map when he developed a fleet of navy and merchant ships, and purchased two far-flung (and totally random) colonies: Tobago, in the Caribbean, and an island in the mouth of Africa's Gambia River. He even had plans to colonise Australia! His son continued the delusions of grandeur with plans to turn Jelgava (Mitau) into a 'northern Paris' (needless to say, this didn't quite work out...).

Tukums
POP 19,800

If you're heading west from Rīga, Tukums is Kurzeme's welcome mat, and the home of western Latvia's most-visited tourist attraction, **Cinevilla** (Kinopilsēta Cinevilla; ☎6774 4647; www.cinevilla.lv, in Latvian; admission 3Ls; ☺10am-7pm). After an unsuccessful

search across the country for an appropriate place to shoot *Rīgas sargi*, a film set in 1919, director Aigars Grauba decided to construct an entire city from scratch in 2004. When the movie was complete, savvy entrepreneurs turned the lot into a small theme park consisting of a faux 'city' and bogus 'small town'. In 2008 noted Latvian director Jānis Streičs filmed his comedy *Rudolf's Gold* on a third part of the lot – a simulated Kurzeme farmstead.

Tourists can follow guided tours (3Ls), play with movie props, try on costumes and even shoot their own movie. There's an on-site restaurant, the **Backlot Pub** (mains 2-5Ls; ☺10am-6pm Tue-Sun) run by LIDO.

ⓘ Getting There & Around

Tukums is the terminus for the suburban rail line that passes through the townships of Jūrmala. Thirteen daily trains from Rīga ply the route (1.30Ls to 1.75Ls, 1¼ hours). There are two stations in town – Tukums-1 and Tukums-2 – the former is closer to the centre and information centre. The bus station (across from Tukums-1) links Rīga (2.10Ls, 1¼ hours, seven daily), Kuldīga (2.50Ls, 1½ to two hours, four daily) and Talsi (1.70Ls to 1.90Ls, 1¼ hours, four daily).

Talsi
POP 34,500

Once a medieval war zone, peaceful Talsi, 115km from Rīga, is the commercial centre of northern Kurzeme and the gateway to western Latvia's desolate Cape Kolka. Locals are ferociously proud of the nine small hills that guard the city's cobbled lanes and nearby lakes, but there's very little that would appeal to a tourist.

Talsi is the unofficial transfer junction for those taking the bus between Latvia's western coast and Cape Kolka. If you want to break up the journey, the staff at the **tourist office** (☎6322 4165; www.talsi.lv; Lielā iela 19/21; ☺10am-5pm Mon-Fri), located in the **Talsi Folk House**, can recommend a couple of countryside gems such as **Lake Usma**, 30km west – a puddle of water polka-dotted with seven islands and backed by leafy forests. Spend a night on the lake at **Usma Spa Hotel & Camping** (☎6367 3710; www.usma.lv; Priežkalni; d from 38Ls; ☺May-Oct), the perfect get-away-from-it-all option for those who seek peace. You can fish, sail, row, swim and enjoy a full array of spa treatments at this lakeside site, 1km south of Rte A10 on the road to Usma village.

Western Latvia (Kurzeme)

ℹ Getting There & Around

From the **bus station** (📞6322 2105; Dundagas iela 15) there are buses to/from Rīga (3Ls to 3.60Ls, 1¾ to 2½ hours, hourly), Kolka (2.10Ls to 2.50Ls, 1¼ to two hours, three daily), Ventspils (2.30Ls, 1½ to two hours, six daily) and Liepāja (4.10Ls to 4.30Ls, 3¼ to four hours, three daily).

Cape Kolka (Kolkasrags)

Enchantingly desolate and hauntingly beautiful, a journey to Cape Kolka (Kolkasrags) feels like a trip to the end of the earth. During Soviet times the entire peninsula was zoned off as a high-security military base, strictly out of bounds to civilians. The region's development was subsequently stunted and today the string of desolate coastal villages has a distinctly anachronistic feel – as though they've been locked away in a time capsule.

Slītere National Park (📞6329 1066; www .slitere.gov.lv) guards the last 25km of the cape, right up until Dižjūra (the Great Sea, or Baltic Sea) meets Mazjūra (the Little Sea – the Gulf of Rīga) in a great clash full of sound and fury. The park's administrative offices are in the nearby town of **Dundaga** (the purported birthplace of the man who inspired the film *Crocodile Dundee*), although information is also available at the Slītere Lighthouse. This towering spire acts as the gatekeeper to the park's rugged, often tundra-like expanse, home to wild deer, elk, buzzards and beaver. In mid-April, during spring migration, the Kolka peninsula sings with the calls of 60,000-odd birds and, during the summer, the park's meagre human population doubles when high-profile Rīgans escape to their holiday retreats.

GULF COAST ROAD
Those with a need for speed will prefer taking the inland road through Talsi and Dundaga to reach the tip of the cape, but if you have a little extra time on your hands, try taking the slower scenic coastal road that wanders through dozens of lazy fishing villages along the Gulf of Rīga.

Break up the journey to the horn of the cape with a stop at **Lake Engure Nature Park** (www.eedp.lv), tucked away on the isthmus between Lake Engure and the sea. Birdbuffs can spy on over 180 types of avian, and lucky visitors might spot a wild horse or an elusive blue cow (see the boxed text, p228).

Roja, 36km further north, is an angler's haven, and the last real 'town' (and we use that term lightly) before the quiet ride to Kolka. If you need to spend the night in town (there's that word again), the **Roja Hotel** (☎6323 2227; Jūras iela 6; s/d 20/25Ls), just past the harbour, is a comfortable place with run-of-the-mill motel furnishings.

KOLKA
The village of Kolka is nothing to write home about, but the windswept moonscape at the waning edge of the cape (just 1km away) could have you daydreaming for days. It's here that the Gulf of Rīga meets the Baltic Sea in a very dramatic fashion. The raw, powerful effect of this desolate point was amplified by a biblical winter storm in 2005, which uprooted dozens of trees and tossed them like matchsticks onto the sandy beach, where they remain hideously entombed, roots in the air.

A **monument** to those claimed by treacherous waters marks the entrance to the beach near a small **information centre** (☎2914 9105) with varying hours. The poignant stone slab, with its haunting anthropomorphic silhouette, was erected in 2002 after three Swedes drowned in the cape's shallow but turbulent waters. One side

reads, 'For people, ships and Livian earth'; the other, 'For those the sea took away'. Locals claim the cape's waters are littered with more shipwrecks than anywhere else in the Baltic. For obvious reasons, Cape Kolka's beauty is best appreciated from the safety of the sand.

Centuries ago, bonfires were lit at the cape's tip to guide sailors around the protruding sandbar. Today, the solar-powered **Kolka Lighthouse** guides vessels to safety. The shimmering scarlet tower, built in 1884, sits on an artificial island 6km offshore.

If you plan to stay the night, **Ūši** (☎2947 5692; www.kolka.info; s/d incl breakfast 16/22Ls, camping per person 2.50Ls) has simple but prim rooms, and a spot to pitch tents in the garden. Look for the brick guesthouse, opposite the onion-domed Orthodox church near the 'Ūši' bus stop. Bike rentals are available for 7.50Ls per day. Try to track down a local fisherman for some authentic smoked fish.

BALTIC COAST ROAD
The path stretching south from Kolka towards Ventspils used to be a secret runway for Soviet aircrafts. Today, it's the widest road in Latvia, connecting a quiet row of one-street villages like a string of pearls. Time moves especially slowly here, as very little has changed over many decades. Rusty Soviet remnants occasionally dot the landscape, but they feel more like abstract art installations than reminders of harder times. The beaches' west-facing position offers unforgettable sunsets over the churning sea and stark, sandy terrain.

Elk antlers dangle from a signpost in **Vaide**, 10km southwest of Kolka, where there is little to see or do except wonder at the simple wooden houses. If the antlers spark your curiosity, there are 518 more in the **Museum of Horns & Antlers** (Ragu kolekcija; ☎6324 4217; admission 0.50Ls; ⊙9am-8pm May-Oct). The collection, creatively arranged in an attic, is the result of one man's lifetime of work as a forest warden in the region (none are hunting trophies). In summer you can **camp** (sites per person 1Ls) in the field behind the museum (there are toilets and picnic tables), although the temperature markedly drops to sweater weather in the evenings, even during the height of summer.

Eighteenth-century wooden buildings line the sand-paved streets in pleasant **Košrags**, 6km further along. Spend the night at **Pitagi** (☎2937 2728; www.pitagi.lv; sites

THE LAST OF THE LIVS

Kurzeme is home to some of the last remaining Livs, Finno-Ugric peoples who first migrated to northern Latvia 5000 years ago. Although many Latvians are descended from this fishing tribe, less than 200 Livs remain in Latvia today, clustered in 14 fishing villages along the Baltic coast south of Cape Kolka. Hungary, Finland and Estonia also have small Liv populations, but they consider this area their homeland and return every August for the Liv Festival in Mazirbe, 18km southwest of Kolka.

While the Liv language is still taught in local elementary schools and at Tartu University in Estonia, there are fewer than 20 native speakers remaining in the world. You can learn about the Livs at the small Livonian Centre (☏2327 7267; ☺9am-6pm Mon-Fri) behind the library on the main street in Kolka, and in a few other Kurzeme towns.

per person 1.50Ls, d/tr 25/30Ls), a quaint guesthouse with beautifully furnished rooms, an on-site sauna and hearty breakfasts in the morning. Rent a bike for the day (5Ls) and peddle up to the cape's tip.

The gorgeous strip of dune-backed beach in neighbouring Mazirbe, another 4km down the coast, is home to the Livonian People's House (Lībiešu tautas nams; Livlist rovkuoda in Livonian), which hosts gatherings of Liv descendants and has exhibitions on their culture. Liv ethnographical and household treasures, including a small costume display, are found at the Rundāli Museum (Muzejs Rundāli; ☏6324 8371; ☺by appointment), located inside a squat, barnlike building on your right when entering the village.

About 5km south of Mazirbe you will see a sign for Slītere Lighthouse (Slīteres bāka; ☏6329 1066; www.slitere.gov.lv; ☺10am-6pm Tue-Sun Jun-Aug), 1.4km down an even rougher track. Built in 1849, the lighthouse now functions as an information booth and lookout tower for the park. If the lighthouse is closed, have a wander down the neighbouring nature trail.

❶ Getting There & Around

The easiest way to reach Cape Kolka is by private vehicle, but buses are also available. To reach the town of Kolka, buses either follow the Gulf Coast road through Roja, or they ply the route through Talsi and Dundaga (inland). Either way, there are five buses that link Rīga and Kolka town per day between 4.30am and 5.15pm (3.85Ls to 4.85Ls, 3½ to 4¾ hours). The first and last bus of the day continues on to Vaide and Mazirbe (for an extra 0.45Ls). Note that there are two stops in the town of Kolka: 'Delfini' and 'Ūši' (in that order). The first three daily buses departing Cape Kolka for Rīga all leave before 7am. Those travelling to/from Kuldīga, Ventspils or Liepāja must switch buses in Talsi.

Abava River Valley

When the glaciers receded at the end of the last Ice Age, the crescent-shaped Abava Valley was born. Gnarled oaks and idyllic villages dot the gushing stream, luring city slickers away for a day of unhurried scenery. This area is best explored by private vehicle.

Kandava

Bucolic Kandava, 30km west of Tukums, is a good example of a typical town in rural Latvia. There's a charming collection of stone and wooden houses, a soaring church spire and traces of a fallen empire in the form of Livonian Order castle ruins. From the top of the castle mound, there is an excellent view of the fine stone bridge (1875) – one of Latvia's oldest – across the Abava River.

Kandava's tourist office (☏6318 1150; www.kandava.lv, in Latvian; Kūrortu iela 1b; ☺9am-6pm Mon-Fri, 10am-5pm Sat) is located directly along the route that connects Rīga to Kuldīga. The affable staff can help you sort out bike rental. Plosti (☏2613 0303; www.plosti .lv; Rēdnieki), further along the Abava River towards Sabile, offers bike hire, canoe hire, horse rides and guided paddles down the Abava in addition to accommodation. This is a great place to have lunch along the river.

The town's biggest draw, however, is Rumene Manor (☏6777 0966; www.rumene .lv; Rumene; ste €450; @☎), one of the most elegant manor houses in all of Latvia, if not Europe. This sumptuous manse was originally erected in the 18th century, but had fallen into disrepair until the owners of Hotel Bergs in Rīga lovingly restored the property to its former grandeur. Several new design elements (including the awe-inducing glass ceiling in the kitchen) were added by a noted local architect, and the interior design scheme is nothing short of breathtaking (think hound's-tooth wingback chairs, and ivory chessboard tables). If ever you were to consider getting married in Latvia, this would be the ideal location.

Near the village of Kukšas, 10km south of Kandava, foodies can pamper their taste-buds at **Kukšu Muiža** (☑2920 5188; www.kuksumuiza.lv; s/d from 60/80Ls), a large peach-coloured mansion serenely sitting along the banks of the Vēdzele River. The owner has poured his heart and soul into turning the once-derelict estate into one of the top rural inns in Latvia – the beds, however, are strangely uncomfortable. The rooms and salons are stuffed with gilded aristocratic heirlooms and flamboyant chandeliers, but the true *pièce de rèsistance* is the owner's made-to-order dinner menu, which caters to every guest's whim and only features locally grown organic produce.

Sabile

The sleepy, cobbled-street village of Sabile (pronounced *sah*-bee-leh), 14km downstream from Kandava, is famed for its vineyard, which is apparently listed in the *Guinness Book of Records* as the world's most northern open-air grape grower (or so say all of the locals). **Vīnakalns** (Wine Hill), located on a tiny mound, just 200m from the **tourist office** (☑6325 2344; www.sabile.lv, in Latvian; Pilskalna iela 6; ☉10am-5.30pm Mon-Fri, to 3pm Sat & Sun), started operating during the 13th century and was resurrected in the 17th century by Duke Jakob of Courland. The duke's vineyard was never very productive and fell into disuse. Although operations resumed in 1936, the vineyard's focus lay in researching hardy strains of vines rather than producing high-quality wines. The only chance to taste local wine (it's impossible to buy) is at Sabile's **wine festival** during the last weekend in July.

Across the river from Sabile the road climbs to the not-to-be-missed **Pedvāle Open-Air Art Museum** (Pedvāles brīvdabas mākslas muzejs; ☑6325 2249; www.pedvale.lv; adult/child 2Ls/free, group guide 25Ls; ☉10am-6pm May–mid-Oct, to 4pm mid-Oct–Apr), located about 1.5km south of the tourist office. Founded in 1991 by Ojars Feldbergs, a Latvian sculptor, the museum showcases over 100 jaw-dropping installations on 100 hectares of rolling hills. Many of the sculptures were created by Feldbergs himself, who often collaborates with other artists from all over the globe. Every year the pieces rotate, reflecting a prevalent theme that permeates the museum's works. Past themes have included meditations on the Earth's prime elements and time. Standout works include **Muna Muna**, a swirling sphere of TV parts; **Chair**, an enormous seat made from bright blue oil drums; and the iconic **Petriflora Pedvalensis**, a bouquet of flowers whose petals have been replaced with spiral stones. The handy orange *Pedvāle Walk* booklet plots all of the sculptures on a neatly drawn map, and provides simple captions with the artists' names. Additional pieces are on display at Sabile's former **synagogue** (Strauta iela 4), which Mr Feldbergs transformed into a contemporary art space.

Spend the night at the on-site inn, **Firkspedvāle Muiža** (☑6325 2248; r per person 10Ls), an atmospheric guesthouse with a handful of simply furnished rooms featuring wooden floors and rustic beams. Next door, **Dāre** (☑6325 2273; mains from 4Ls) dishes up satisfying food, from simple salads to hearty plates of freshly caught trout. Sit outside on the wooden terrace in summer.

BLUE MOOER

It sounds like your classic old wives' tale: blue cows delivered from the sea by mermaids. Yet at least part of this Liv legend is true – Latvia does indeed have blue cows. About 100 of them, to be exact, making it the world's rarest breed of cow.

These curious ruminants originated in Latvia's Kurzeme region. The first ones appeared in the early 1900s. No one is sure why or how they appeared, which is why the bit about mermaids can't be completely ruled out, but their star quickly waxed as they proved remarkably resistant to cold, rain and wind – three things that Latvia has in great supply.

The blue-cow population dwindled to less than 50 in Soviet times, but began to rebound in the 1990s as geneticists realised the value in cross-breeding with these hearty beasts.

For a truly unique experience, you can camp (sites per person 1Ls; ☺May–mid-Oct) anywhere within the open-air museum. Uncurl your sleeping bag and watch the midnight shadows dance along the larger-than-life sculptures – we can't think of a better place in Latvia to pitch a tent.

Other Sabile highlights include a 17th-century Lutheran church, at the western edge of town. The blazing white chapel features an arresting baroque pulpit held up by four griffon-headed snakes. Follow the trail behind the church to the summit of Castle Hill, where there's an ancient fort and excellent views of the valley.

Kuldīga

POP 27,000

If adorable Kuldīga (kool-*dee*-ga) were a tad closer to Rīga it would be crowded with legions of day-tripping camera-clickers. Fortunately, the town is located deep in the heart of rural Kurzeme, making it just far enough to be the perfect reward for more intrepid travellers. In its heyday, Kuldīga served as the capital of the Duchy of Courland (1596–1616) and was known throughout the region as the 'city where salmon fly'. Kuldīga earned its puzzling moniker due to its strategic location along Ventas Rumba – the widest waterfall in Europe. During spawning season, the salmon would swim upstream, and when they reached the waterfall they would jump through the air attempting to surpass it.

The town itself is oriented around three town squares on the west side of the waterfall. Pedestrian Liepājas iela, with its 19th-century lanterns, links Rātslaukums (home of the tourist office) to Pilsētas laukums, the town's 'new square', complete with hotel, bank and grocery store. The rather unremarkable medieval square was actually the first place in all of Latvia to trade potatoes. Kuldīga was badly damaged during the Great Northern War, and was never quite able to regain its former lustre. Today, this blast from the past is a favourite spot to shoot Latvian period-piece films – 29 movies and counting...

◉ Sights & Activities

OLD TOWN

Kuldīga's Old Town orbits three town squares: the medieval square, the town-hall square and the 'new' square. The town-hall square, known as Rātslaukums, is the most attractive and makes a good place to start your trip. The square gets its name from the 17th-century town hall (Rātslaukums 5), now home to an information centre, some souvenir shops and a charming cafe. The new town hall, built in 1860 in Italian Renaissance style, is at the southern end of the square, and Kurzeme's oldest wooden house – built in 1670, reconstructed in 1742 and renovated in 1982 – stands here on the northern corner of Pasta iela.

St Katrīna's Church   CHURCH

(Baznīcas iela) This Lutheran church isn't particularly beautiful, but it's the most important house of worship in town, since Katrina (St Catherine) is Kuldīga's patron saint and protector (she's even featured on the town's coat of arms). The first church on the site was built in the 1200s, and the current incarnation dates back to Duke Jakob's rule in the mid-1600s. During the Soviet era, the church was used as a barn for horses and cows, but today it is once again a place for prayer, with a large organ and fresh flowers adorning the pews.

Livonian Order Castle   RUIN

Cross the teeny Alekšupīte ravine to reach the site of this castle, built from 1242 to 1245, but ruined during the Great Northern War. The castle watchman's house (Pils iela 4) was built in 1735 to protect the ruins. Legend has it that the house was the site of executions and beheadings, and the stream behind the house ran red with the victims' blood. Today a lovely sculpture garden has been set up around the subtle ruins. On the grounds you'll find the mildly interesting Kuldīga Historic Museum (Kuldīgas novada muzejs; Pils iela; adult/child 0.50/0.30Ls; ☺10am-5pm), located inside a home built in Paris in 1900 to house the Russian pavilion at the World Exhibition. The museum features an exhibit on international playing cards, Viking history and an art gallery on the top floor. A cluster of Duke Jakob's cannons sits on the front lawn. From the old castle grounds you'll have a great view of Ventas Rumba (Kuldīga Waterfall), the widest waterfall in Europe stretching 275m across the river. The chute is only about 2–3ft high and is a popular spot for a quick (and frigid) swim.

Kuldīga

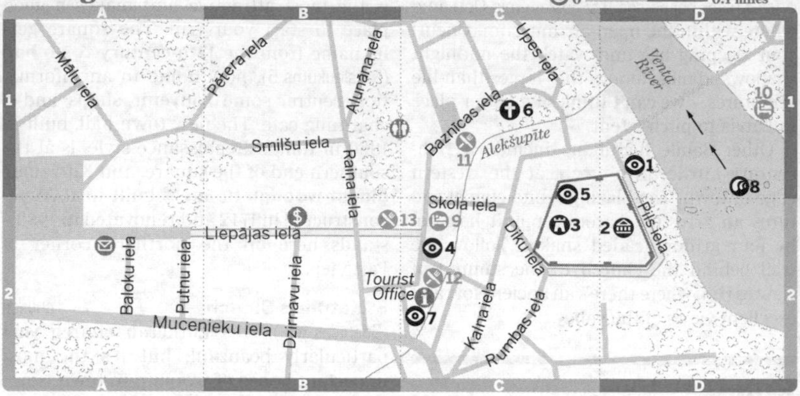

Kuldīga

Sights

1 Castle Watchman's House D1
2 Kuldīga History Museum D2
3 Livonian Order Castle......................... C2
4 Oldest Wooden House C2
5 Sculpture Garden C1
6 St Katrina's Church C1
7 Town Hall.. C2
8 Ventas Rumba (Kuldīga Waterfall).. D1

Sleeping

9 Hotel Metropole C2
10 Ventas Rumba D1

Eating

11 Dārziņš C1
12 Pagrabiņš C2
13 Stenders B2

Ventas Rumba (Kuldīga Waterfall) WATERFALL

Despite the pomp of being 'Europe's widest waterfall', Ventas rumba might not impress as much as one might think, namely because the chute is not very tall – 2ft or 3ft maximum. It is, however, a great spot for a photo op (you'll see a lot of wedding ceremonies here in summer) and most importantly it's the centrepiece of little Kuldīga's colourful history. In fact, it is said that when the city was the seat of the Duchy, locals could actually see salmon jumping over the low-lying waterfall to spawn further upstream. Needless to say, salmon was quite a popular dish.

AROUND TOWN

Several attractive **bike routes** wind their way through the dense forests around town (one of them also leads to the caves). Stop by the information centre to rent a bicycle (6Ls) and pick up one of the six brochures detailing these cycle trails.

Old Castle Hill RUIN

The large **old castle hill** *(pilskalns)*, 2.5km north of town on the western bank of the Venta, was the fortress of Lamekins, the Cour who ruled much of Kurzeme before the 13th-century German invasion. Legend has it that the castle – now ruined beyond recognition – was so staggeringly beautiful (glistening copper pendants hung from the roof) that invaders were reluctant to sack the structure. To get to the hill, follow Ventspils iela then Virkas iela north from the centre, and take a right at the fork in the road.

Riežupe Sand Caves CAVES

(Smilšu alas; ☎6332 6236; adult/child 2/1Ls; ⏰11am-5pm May-Oct) Located 5km outside of town along the unpaved Krasta iela, Riežupe Sand Caves feature 460m of labyrinthine tunnels that can be visited by candlelight. They're a chilly 8°C, so bring a warm sweater. The cave is accessible by personal vehicle – staff at the tourist office can give directions (like most places in rural Latvia, private transport is a must if you don't want to wait five or more hours for a bus).

Sleeping

Hotel Metropole BOUTIQUE HOTEL €€

(☎6335 0588; Baznīcasiela 11; d incl breakfast from 44Ls; @📶) Kuldīga's best hotel rolls out the red carpet (literally) up its mod concrete stairwell to charming double-decker bedrooms overlooking pedestrian Liepājas iela and Rātslaukums. Black-and-white photos of old Kuldīga are sprinkled throughout, even in the trendy cafe.

Ventas Rumba HOSTEL €
(☑2643 8250; www.ventasrumba.lv; Stendesiela; d from 20Ls; @) You won't get any warm hellos here, but this simple hostel has perfectly functional rooms just a stone's throw from the charming waterfall nearby.

✗ Eating

Kuldīga's hotels also offer decent places to grab grub. Several restaurants in town serve *rupjmaizes kārojums/kārtojums,* which translates as 'black bread mix'. The recipe for the popular dessert is over 1000 years old: Vikings would blend crumbled bread, cream and honey for an after-dinner treat. It tastes a bit like Black Forest gateau.

TOP CHOICE Dārziņš BAKERY €
(Baznīcas iela; snacks 0.10-2Ls; ⊘8am-6pm Mon-Fri, to 3pm Sat) This traditional bakery is such a wonderful throwback to earlier days – the cashier tallies your bill with an amber abacus. Try the *sklandu rausis* (0.22Ls), an ancient Cour Viking carrot cake made from carrot, potato, rye bread and sweet cream purée.

Pagrabiņš CAFE €
(Baznīcas iela 5; mains 4Ls; ⊘9am-11pm) Pagrabiņš lurks in the cellar beneath the information centre in what used to be the town's prison. Today, scrumptious homemade chocolates are served with your Italian coffee under low-slung alcoves lined with honey-coloured bricks. In warmer weather, enjoy your snacks on the small verandah, which sits atop the trickling Alekšupīte ravine out the back.

Stenders LATVIAN €
(Liepājas iela 3; mains 3Ls; ⊘lunch & dinner) Not to be confused with Stenders soap shop across the street, this popular joint, housed on the 2nd storey of an 18th-century storage house, specialises in warm potato pancakes and cool pints of Užavas.

ℹ Information

Public toilets are located in '1905 Park'.
Hansabanka (Liepājas iela 15) Offers currency exchange and has an ATM outside.

Post office (Liepājas iela 34) Near Pilsētas laukums.
Tourist office (☑6332 2259; www.kuldiga .lv; Baznīcas iela 5; ⊘9am-6pm Mon-Sat, 10am-2pm Sun mid-May–mid-Sep, 9am-5pm Mon-Fri mid-Sep–mid-May) Tons of informative brochures about the town and two charming souvenir shops on either side.

ℹ Getting There & Away

From the **bus station** (☑6332 2061; Stacijas iela 2), buses run to/from Rīga (4.10Ls to 4.70Ls, 2½ to 3½ hours, 12 daily), Liepāja (2.50Ls to 3.10Ls, 1¾ hours, seven daily), Ventspils (1.75Ls to 1.90Ls, 1¼ hours, seven daily) and Talsi (2.10Ls to 2.40Ls, 1½ to 2¼ hours, four daily).

Ventspils
POP 42,500
Fabulous amounts of oil and shipping money have turned Ventspils into one of Latvia's most beautiful and dynamic cities. The air is brisk and clean, and the well-kept buildings are done up in an assortment of cheery colours – even the towering industrial machinery is coated in bright paint. Latvia's biggest and busiest port wasn't always smiles and rainbows, though – Ventspils' strategic ice-free location served as the naval and industrial workhorse for the original settlement of Cours in the 12th century, the Livonian Order in the 13th century, the Hanseatic League through the 16th century and finally the USSR in recent times. Although locals coddle their Užavas beer and claim that there's not much to do, tourists will find a weekend's worth of fun in the form of brilliant beaches, interactive museums and winding Old Town streets dotted with the odd boutique and cafe.

◉ Sights

Ventspils' prime attraction is its coastline, which is laced with a sandy, dune-backed **beach** stretching south from the Venta River mouth. During the warmer months, beach bums of every ilk – from nudist to kiteboarder – line the sands to absorb the sun's rays.

A lush patch of forest south of the town centre contains an amusement park called **Aqua Park Ventspils** (Ūdens atrakciju parks; ☑6366 5853; Mednu iela 19; per hr adult/child 1/0.50Ls, per day adult/child 2/1Ls; ⊘10am-10pm Jun-Sep) and the **Open-Air Museum of the Coast** (Ventspils jūras zvejniecības brīvdabas

LATVIA VENTSPILS

Ventspils

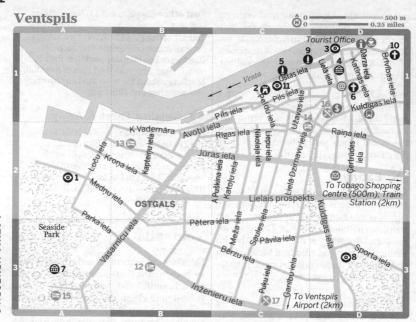

Ventspils

◉ Sights

1 Aqua Park Ventspils A2
2 Castle of the Livonian Order...............C1
3 Hecogs Jēkabs boat D1
4 House of Crafts D1
5 Monument to Krišjānis
   Valdemārs...C1
6 Nicholas Evangelical Lutheran
   Church..D1
7 Open-Air Museum of the Coast.........A3
8 Reņķa Garden....................................D3
9 Seven Mental Meteorites....................C1
10 St Nicholas Russian Orthodox
   Church..D1
11 Travelling Cow...................................C1

🛏 Sleeping

12 Hotel of the Ventspils
   University College..............................B3
13 Karlīnes Nams...................................B2
14 Kupfernams.......................................C2
15 Piejūras Kempings.............................A3

⊗ Eating

16 Buginš..D1
Melanis Sivēns ....(see 2)
17 Mūsmājas..C3

muzejs; ☎6322 4467; Riņķu iela 2; adult/child 0.60/0.30Ls; ☺11am-6pm May-Oct, 11am-5pm Wed-Sun Nov-Apr), with a collection of fishing craft, anchors and other seafaring items. On weekends between May and October you can ride around the museum's extensive grounds on a narrow-gauge railway (adult/child 0.50/0.25Ls) dating back to 1916.

The Venta River separates the Old Town from the colourful port on the opposite riverbank. From April to November the **Hecogs Jēkabs boat** (☎2635 3344; cnr Ostas iela & Tirgus iela; adult/child 1/0.50Ls) sails around the mouth of the Venta River. The 45-minute excursions depart six times daily from dock 18. Keep an eye out for Feldbergs' **Seven Mental Meteorites** and the **monument to Krišjānis Valdemārs**, founder of Latvian shipping.

Take a walk through the **Ostgals neighbourhood** for a glimpse at simpler days when the town was merely a humble fishing village dotted with wooden abodes.

Castle of the Livonian Order   RUINS
(☎6362 2031; Jāņa iela 17; adult/child 1.50/0.75Ls; ☺10am-6pm Tue-Sun) The city's 13th-century castle looks rather drab and modern from the outside, but the ancient interior hosts a cutting-edge interactive museum on the region's trade and feudal history, with digital

displays and two panoramic telescopes for visitors to enjoy an eagle's-eye view of the port and city. The museum also showcases fine pieces of amber discovered on archaeological digs in the region. During Soviet rule, the castle was used as a prison and a frightening exhibit in the stables next door recounts the horrors of the jail. An adjacent Zen rock garden will sooth your soul after looking at the nightmarish photographs and frantic claw marks on the prison doors.

House of Crafts

MUSEUM

(☑6362 0174; Skolas iela 3; adult/child 0.60/0.30Ls; ⊙11am-7pm Tue-Fri, 10am-7pm Sat, 11am-3pm Sun) Visitors can learn about the handicrafts of Kurzeme here and watch local artisans weave together colourful knits. Housed in a wooden structure built during the reign of the dukes of Courland, it was used as a boys' school during Soviet times before being converted into an exhibition hall. English is pretty scarce, so call ahead if you are interested in watching ceramics demonstrations, or if you would like a guided explanation about the history of the building (a classroom still remains intact with desks and chalk slates) and the town.

Churches

Two churches soar above the clutter of prim wooden architecture: the onion-domed St Nicholas Russian Orthodox Church (Sv Nivolaja pareizticīgo baznīca; Plosu iela 10), built near the modern ferry pier in 1901, and the Nicholas Evangelical Lutheran Church (Nikolaja luterāņu baznīca; Tirgus iela 2), built in 1835 on stately Rātslaukums. Note that the church actually isn't 'St Nicholas', because the house of worship was named for Tsar Nicholas II (who was never canonised) when he donated loads of cash to the local Lutherans in a random act of guilt-induced kindness (keep in mind that he was Russian Orthodox).

Sculptures

Amid the mix of historical structures, markets and shipping relics, tourists will delight in Ventspils' most light-hearted attraction, the omnipresent cow sculptures. In 2002, the town benefited from the International Art and Patronage Project, known locally as the Ventspils Cow Parade. Around seven of the original 26 cows remain around town including the *Travelling Cow*, which looks like a weathered leather suitcase dotted with stamps. More quirky sculptures can be found in Reņķa Garden, which features dream-inducing novelty items like a giant set of keys. During the summer months, flower sculptures also cheer the city centre.

🛏 Sleeping

Kupfernams

B&B €€

(☑6362 6999; Kārļa iela 5; s/d 26/37Ls; 🛜) Our favourite spot to spend the night, this charming sleeping spot sits in an inviting wooden house at the centre of Old Town. The cheery rooms with slanted ceilings sit above a fantastic restaurant and a trendy hair salon (which doubles as the reception desk during the day).

Karlīnes Nams

B&B €€

(☑2927 7050; www.karlinesnams.viss.lv; Karlīnes iela 28; r 25-35Ls; 🛜) Located off scenic Livu

I-SPY

The Soviets designed a mammoth 32m-diameter radio telescope in Irbene to eavesdrop on Western satellite communications during the Cold War. Today scientists use it to gaze at the stars, moon and sun.

Hidden in the forest 24km north of Ventspils, Irbene's superpowerful antenna was one of three used to spy on the world by the Soviet army at the USSR Space Communication Centre. When the last Russian troops left in 1994, they took one antenna with them but left the remaining two behind (they were too large to move).

The R-32, a 600-tonne dish mounted on a 25m-tall concrete base, was built by the USSR in the 1980s and is the world's eighth-largest parabolic antenna. Since 1994 the former military installation has belonged to the Ventspils International Radio Astronomy Centre (VIRAC; Ventspils starptautiskais radioastronomijas centrs; http://virac.venta.lv/en/; ☑2923 0818; virac@venta.lv), which is part of the Latvian Academy of Sciences (☑6755 8662; www.lza.lv; Institute of Physical Energetics, Akadēmijas laukums 1, Riga). Essentially a research centre, the antennae can be visited by guided tour (2Ls), arranged in advance by calling ☑6368 2541.

iela in the quaint Ostgals Fisherman's district, Karlīnes Nams is a newer establishment set up in a former butchery. Rooms are decorated with simple slats of wood and come with fridges and TVs.

Piejūras Kempings CAMPING €
(☑6362 7925; Vasarnicu iela 56; sites per person 2Ls, 4-person cottage 18-45Ls; @) This charming campus of grassy tent grounds and pine cottages is a full-service operation with an on-site laundrette, bicycle rental (1Ls per hour), and tennis, volleyball and basketball courts.

**Hotel of the Ventspils
University College** HOSTEL €
(☑6362 9202; studentu.viesnica@ventspils.gov.lv; Inženieru iela 101; s/d with shared bathroom from 10/14Ls; ☉Jul-Aug; @) Drab rooms and hallways from *The Shining* confirm the old adage 'you get what you pay for', but alas, these are the cheapest beds in town.

✖ Eating & Drinking

TOP
CHOICE **Melanis Sivēns** MEDIEVAL €€
(Jāṇa iela 17; meals 3-8Ls; ☉11am-11pm Mon-Wed, to midnight Thu-Sun) When archaeologists restored Ventspils' Livonian Castle, they unearthed the perfectly preserved skeletal remains of a black pig (*melanis sivēns* means 'black pig'). This was quite the conundrum as ham was a favourite dish in medieval times – in other words, no one would have ever let a pig die of natural causes. Historians believe that the castle's cook was just about to roast the poor porker when invaders suddenly attacked. The restaurant is located in the castle's dungeon and specialises in dishes that would have been served on the night of that fateful ambush.

Mūsmājas BAKERY €
(Puķu iela 33; snacks 1-4Ls; ☉8am-7pm Mon-Sat, 9am-6pm Sun) Mūsmājas, which means 'our house', is a very fitting name for this homey pastry shop and cafe covered with generous swatches of floral-printed wallpaper. On warmer days, enjoy your espresso and tasty confection in the quaint garden out back.

Buginš CAFE €
(Lielā iela 1/3; mains 3-5.50Ls; ☉lunch & dinner) The decor is absolutely idiotic – creepy taxidermic owls, neon-yellow picnic tables, checkerboard ristorante tablecloths and rusty wheels that double as chandeliers –

but Buginš remains a local fave due to the equally eclectic and nonsensical menu featuring decent Latvian and international dishes.

The **Tobago shopping centre** (Lielais prospekts 3/5; ☉9am-9pm) has a **Rimi supermarket** (☉9am-10pm).

ℹ Information

Baltijas Tranzītu Banka (cnr Liela & Kuldīgas iela) Currency exchange and ATM.
Post office (Platā iela)
Tourist office (☑6362 2263; www.tourism .ventspils.lv; Dārza iela 6; ☉8am-7pm Mon-Fri, 10am-5pm Sat, 10am-3pm Sun May-Sep, 8am-5pm Mon-Fri, 10am-3pm Sat & Sun Oct-Apr) Reams of tourist info; accommodation bookings.
Ventspils Library (☑6362 4333; Akmeṇu iela 2; ☉10am-7pm Mon-Fri, to 4pm Sat; ☎) Free internet and wi-fi.

ℹ Getting There & Away

Ventspils' **bus terminal** (☑6362 4262; Kuldīgas iela 5) is served by buses to/from Rīga (4.55Ls, 2¾ to four hours, hourly), Liepāja (3.30Ls, 2¼ to three hours, seven daily), Pāvilosta (2Ls, 1¼ hours, four daily), Kuldīga (1.85Ls, 1¼ hours, seven daily) and Jelgava (3Ls, 4¾ to 5½ hours, four daily) via Kandava and Tukums.

Scandlines (☑6779 6900; www.scandlines .lt) runs ferries five times weekly to Nynashamn, Sweden (60km from Stockholm) and twice weekly to Travemünde (Rostock), Germany. Plans are in the works to run a ferry between Ventspils and Montu harbour on the Estonian island of Saaremaa. **Finnlines** (www.finnlines.de) operates a twice-weekly ferry service between St Petersburg, Russia and Lübeck, Germany.

Pāvilosta

If we awarded 'Top Choice' symbols to entire towns, Pāvilosta would easily win the prize. This sleepy beach burg, located halfway between Ventspils and Liepāja, casually pulls off a chilled-out California surfer vibe despite its location on the black Baltic Sea. Summer days are filled with windsurfing, kiteboarding, surfing and sailing interspersed with beach naps and beers. Learn how to get involved at the friendly tourist office – the staff can also set you up with traditional boat rides and fishing equipment – and if you're lucky you might get a tutorial on how to smoke fish. Make sure to notify the weather gods when you plan on passing through – dreary weather in Pāvilosta means there's really nothing to do.

🛌 Sleeping & Eating

Vēju Paradize　　　　　　　　INN €€
(☎2644 6644; www.veju-paradize.lv; Smilšu iela
14; s/d incl breakfast 24/28Ls) 'Wind Paradise'
is Pāvilosta's largest sleeping spot, with 17
tidy rooms that are simple yet feel distinctly
beachy. The aloe plants are a clever touch,
especially after spending one too many
hours splashing around in the sea. Veju's on-
site restaurant is open during the summer
months from 9am to 10pm and specialises
in light, international dishes (4Ls to 6Ls).

Das Crocodill　　　　　　BOUTIQUE HOTEL €€
(☎2615 1333; www.crocodill.lv; Kalna iela 6; r incl
breakfast 34Ls; ☒) Crocodill oozes personality from every mosaic tile and light fixture.
The decoration is a delightful mishmash of
styles from all over the world: Aboriginal
Australia, tribal Africa and a hint of Poly-
nesia as well. Splurge for one of the suites
in the back overlooking the inviting blue
swimming pool.

Āķagals　　　　　　　　　LATVIAN €
(Dzintaru iela; mains 3-6Ls; ☉lunch & dinner) Even
if you aren't staying in Pāvilosta, a stop at
Āķagals is a great way to break up the trek
between Liepāja, Kuldīga and Ventspils.
Enjoy stacks of delicious Latvian cuisine
on varnished picnic tables made from thick
logs. There's a large swing set, windswept
dunes and a rusty lookout tower out the
back to keep you busy while you wait for
your nosh (the menu inexplicably refers to
its dishes as 'noshes').

Snack Bīčbārs　　　　　　　　　CAFE
(Illy; cnr Kalna & Smilšu iela, ☉Jun-Aug) This
modified tiki hut sells coffee and cocktails
along the dirt path leading to the beach.
Take your beverage to go, or chill-out on the
trendy wicker furniture and thumb through
a weathered copy of the latest fashion mag.
Note that the bar changes names each summer, depending on which Rīga institution
takes over for the warmer months.

ℹ️ Information

There is a 24-hour ATM right beside the tourist
office.
Post office (Tirgus iela 1; ☉9am-5pm Mon-Fri)
Tourist office (www.pavilosta.lv; Dzintaru iela
2; ☉7.30am-9pm Jun-Aug, to 7.30pm Sep-
May) Friendly, English-speaking staff can help
arrange accommodation and activities. Located
along the main road to the docks, near the bus
stop.

ℹ️ Getting There & Away

Intercity buses link Pāvilosta to Liepāja (1.80Ls
to 2.35Ls, 70 minutes, five daily between
6.30am and 6.30pm), Kuldīga (1.90Ls, 65
minutes, once daily with continued service to
Rīga), and Ventspils (2.10Ls, 1¼ hours, four daily
between 8am and 9pm). Buses usually stop in
front of the tourist office.

Liepāja

POP 83,400

Founded by the Livonian Order in the 13th
century, Latvia's third-largest city wasn't a
big hit until Tsar Alexander III deepened the
harbour and built a gargantuan naval port
at the end of the 1800s. For years the industrial town earned its spot on the map as the
home to the first Baltic fleet of Russian sub-
marines, but after WWII the Soviets occupied what was left of the bombed-out burg
and turned it into a strategic military base.

For the last decade, Liepāja (pronounced
lee-ah-*pa*-yah) has been going about search-
ing for its identity like an angsty teenager.
The city's growing pains are evident in the
visual clash of gritty warehouses stacked
next to swish hipster bars and tricked-out
nightclubs. The local tourist office often calls
Liepāja 'the place where wind is born', but
we think the city's rough-around-the-edges
vibe is undoubtedly its biggest draw.

⊙ Sights

Liepāja is light on sights, so why not head
to the **beach** for some R&R. A thin green
belt known as **Jūrmala Park** acts as a buffer
between the soft dunes and tatty urban core.

KAROSTA

Off limits to everyone during the Soviet
occupation, Karosta, 4km north of central
Liepāja, is a former Russian naval base
encompassing about one-third of Liepāja's
city limits. From ageing army barracks
to ugly Soviet-style, concrete apartment
blocks (many abandoned), evidence of the
occupation still remains.

TOP CHOICE Karosta Prison　　　　　MUSEUM
(Karostas cietums; www.karostascietums.lv;
Invalīdu 4; tour 3.50Ls, 2hr reality show 5Ls,
sleepover reality show 12Ls; ☉10am-6pm May-Sep,
by appointment only Oct-Apr) A detention facility until 1997, today grungy Karosta Prison is
a must-see for tourists. Originally designed
as an infirmary in 1900, the Soviets quickly

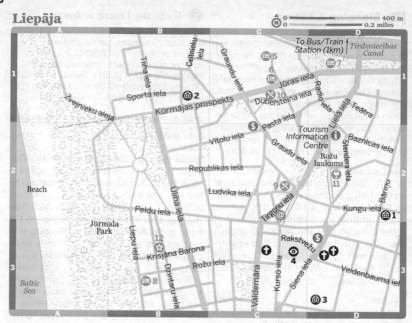

Liepāja

Liepāja

◎ Sights
1 House of Craftsmen D2
2 Liepāja History & Art Museum B1
3 Occupation & Regimes
   Department D3
4 Peter's Market C3

🛏 Sleeping
5 Fontaine Royal C1
6 Hotel Fontaine C1
7 Promenade Hotel D1
8 Roze B3

✗ Eating
Delisnack .... (see 12)
9 Pastnieka Māja C2
10 Vecais Kapteinis C1

🍷 Drinking
11 Latvia's 1st Rock Cafe D2
Prison Bar .... (see 5)

✪ Entertainment
12 Fontaine Palace B3

turned it into a military prison even before the building was completed.

Daily tours from noon to 5pm, given in a mix of Latvian, Russian and English, detail the history of the prison, which was strictly used to punish disobedient soldiers in the Russian army. Prisoners sat in their decrepit cells for six hours a day, spending the rest of their time engaged in gruelling exercises and training.

If you're craving some serious punishment, or just want to brag that you've spent the night in a Latvian jail, sign up to become a prisoner for the night. You'll be subjected to regular bed checks, verbal abuse by guards in period garb and forced to relieve yourself in the world's most disgusting latrine (seriously). Try booking the night in cell 26 – solitary confinement – you won't be bothered, but the pitch-blackness will undoubtedly drive you off the edge.

For those wanting a pinch of masochism without having to spend the night, there are two-hour 'reality shows' available for those who book ahead. Note that all shows require a quorum of participants.

TOP CHOICE St Nicholas Maritime Cathedral
CHURCH
The stunning cathedral, with its bulbous cupolas, starkly contrasts the rest of Karosta's bleak architecture. Built in 1901, its ornate architecture resembles the Russian Orthodox churches from the 17th

century, although the gilded domes are supported by four crossed arch vaults rather than columns. During WWI the church was stripped of its intricate interior decorations, and after years as a cinema and sports complex, the cathedral was restored in the 1990s.

CITY CENTRE

After tackling Karosta, Liepāja's city centre has a couple of touristy treats as well.

Peter's Market
MARKET

(Kuršu laukums) Vendors have touted their wares here since the mid-17th century. The market expanded in 1910, when a pavilion was constructed adjacent to the square. Today you'll find stalls inside and out at this bustling complex, selling everything from second-hand clothes and pirated DVDs to fresh fruit and veggies.

House of Craftsmen
MUSEUM

(☑6348 0808; cnr Kungu & Bāriņu iela; admission free; ☺10am-5pm) Check out the largest piece of amber art in the world (an enormous dangling tapestry) here plus legions of adorable old women knitting scarves, mittens and blankets available for purchase.

Liepāja History & Art Museum
MUSEUM

(Liepājas vēstures un mākslas muzejs; Kūrmājas prospekts 16/18; adult/child 0.50/0.30Ls; ☺10am-5pm Wed-Sun) Features a variety of impressive displays such as Stone and Bronze Age artefacts unearthed on local archaeological digs, and an interesting collection of old jewellery, weapons and vintage memorabilia from both world wars.

Occupation and Regimes Department
MUSEUM

(K Ukstiņa iela 79; admission free; ☺10am-5pm Wed-Sun) Traces the bloody history of the Soviet and Nazi occupations in Latvia, with an emphasis on Liepāja. Captions are in Latvian, but no words are needed to explain the powerful images of the 1939–40 deportations to Siberia (an estimated 2000 people from Liepāja were deported), the genocide committed against Latvian Jews and the 1991 fight for independence.

🛏 Sleeping

TOP CHOICE **Fontaine Royal**
BOUTIQUE HOTEL €

(☑6343 2005; www.fontaineroyal.lv; Stūrmaņu iela 1; s/d 18/25Ls, d with shared bathroom 15Ls ☎) Everything is gaudy and gilded here at Fontaine Royal, Hotel Fontaine's flashier fraternal twin. Strange knick-knacks and sculptures abound like an orphanage for unwanted objets d'arts, and the plethora of gold trimming and sparkly spray paint is blinding – as though guests were sleeping in a framed Renaissance painting. We much prefer staying here than at one of the drab cookie-cutter motels around town.

Hotel Fontaine
HOSTEL €

(☑6342 0956; www.fontaine.lv; Jūras iela 24; r from 10Ls; ☺) You'll either adore or abhor this funky hostel set in a charming 18th-century wooden house with lime-green trim. The whole place feels like a second-hand store, from the kitschy knick-knack shop used as the reception, to the 20-plus rooms stuffed to the brim with rock memorabilia, dusty oriental rugs, bright tile mosaics, Soviet propaganda and anything else deemed appropriately offbeat. There's a communal kitchen and chill-out space in the basement. Some rooms are located in a second wooden house out the back.

Roze
INN €€€

(☑6342 1155; www.parkhotel-roze.lv; Rožu iela 37; s/d from 43/52Ls; ☎) Stylish and comfortable, this pale-blue wooden guesthouse near the sea was once a summer home for the elite, and still has a certain art-nouveau styling. Rooms are spacious, and each is uniquely decorated with antique wallpaper and sheer drapery. Extras include satellite TVs, a sauna, and a gazebo-ed garden in the yard.

Promenade Hotel
LUXURY HOTEL €€€

(☑6348 8288; www.promenadehotel.lv; Vecā Ostmala 40; r from 66Ls; ☺☎) The poshest hotel in Kurzeme lives in an enormous harbour warehouse that was once used to store grain.

🍴 Eating

The city's drinking and entertainment venues also have menus with Latvian and international favourites.

Delisnack
BURGERS €

(☑6348 8523; Dzintaru iela 4; mains 1.40-7.50Ls; ☺24hr) Attached to Fontaine Palace, Liepāja's cheapest chow joint was designed with the inebriated partier in mind: the American-style burgers are a fool-proof way to soak up some of those vodka shots downed earlier in the evening. Service is notorious for being glacial-paced.

LATVIA LIEPĀJA

Vecais Kapteinis SEAFOOD €
(Old Captain; 6342 5522; Dubelsteina iela 14; mains 3-8Ls; ⏰lunch & dinner) Housed in a timber-framed building dating to 1773, the 'Old Captain' generates a romantic nautical theme with maritime curios and a lengthy seafood menu. The separate Italian menu is slightly cheaper and not half bad.

Pastnieka Māja LATVIAN €€
(🖂6340 7521; Brīvzemnieka iela 53; mains 6-12Ls; ⏰lunch & dinner) This ultraslick (for Liepāja!) two-level restaurant is housed in the city's old post office (*pastnieka māja* means 'post-office house'). The menu features traditional Latvian favourites, as well as a few very exotic offerings: chase your 'bulls' balls' (you'll see) with a pint of Līvu Alus, Liepāja's local beer.

 Drinking & Entertainment

Liepāja has a reputation throughout Latvia as the centre of the country's rock-music scene, and taking in a concert is a real treat. Even if you can't understand the lyrics, just being a part of the screaming, pulsating masses is a cultural experience you won't soon forget.

Latvia's 1st Rock Cafe CAFE, CLUB, BAR
(Stendera iela 18/20; www.pablo.lv, in Latvian; cover free-5Ls) There's no way you'll miss this massive three-storey structure with loads of shiny windows and a pseudo-industrial look. Restaurants, bars, dance floors, billiards and a rooftop beer garden are all rolled into one megacomplex. The walls are plastered with old concert posters, and Pablo, the roaring basement club, features live music every night and rave parties on the weekends. Don't forget to buy your Hard Rock Café T-shirt...er...we mean...1st Rock Cafe...

Fontaine Palace BAR
(Dzintaru iela 4) Yet another establishment of the Fontaine name fame, this never-closing rock house lures loads of live acts that jam over the crowd of sweaty fanatics.

Prison Bar BAR
(Stūrmaņu iela 1) Located on the first floor of Fontaine Royal, this local haunt is stuffed with cheesy prison-related accoutrements, and the bartender slings drinks from behind bars.

ⓘ Information

Banks with ATMs can be found along Lielā iela and Kungu iela.

Sapņu sala (🖂6348 5333; Lielā iela 12; per hr 0.60Ls; ⏰9am-9pm) Internet access.

Tourist office (🖂6348 0808; www.liepaja.lv Rožu laukums 3/5; ⏰9am-7pm Mon-Fri, to 4pm Sat, 10am-3pm Sun Jun-Aug, 9am-5pm Mon-Sat Sep-May) Loads of information and services available to tourists including bike rentals. Hertz rental car located in the coffee shop next door.

ⓘ Getting There & Away

Liepāja's **bus & train stations** (🖂6342 7552; Rīgas iela) are rolled into one, linked by tram 1 with Lielā iela in the downtown. There are convenient daily bus services to/from Rīga (5.40Ls to 6.40Ls, 3½ to 4½ hours, two or three hourly), Kuldīga (2.50Ls to 3.10Ls, 1¾ to three hours, seven daily), Pāvilosta (1.80Ls, 70 minutes, five daily) and Ventspils (3.30Ls to 4.10Ls, 2¼ to three hours, seven daily).

At the time of research, ferries were no longer operating in and out of Liepāja.

SOUTHERN LATVIA (ZEMGALE)

A long snake-like strip of land between Rīga and the Lithuanian border, southern Latvia has been dubbed the 'bread basket' of Latvia for its plethora of arable lands and mythical forests. The region is known locally as Zemgale, named after the defiant Baltic Semigallian (or Zemgallian) tribe who inhabited the region before the German conquest at the end of the 1200s. The Semigallians were a valiant bunch, warding off the impending crusaders longer than any other tribe. Before retreating to Lithuania, they burned down all of their strongholds rather than surrendering them to the invaders.

From the 16th to the 18th centuries, the region (along with Kurzeme) formed part of the semi-independent Duchy of Courland, whose rulers set up shop with two mind-boggling palaces in the town of Jelgava (also called Mitau) and in Rundāle, just outside of Bauska. Today, the summer palace at Rundāle is Zemgale's star attraction, and a must-see for art and architecture buffs.

Bauska

POP 27,000

Centuries ago, little Bauska was an important seat in the Duchy of Courland, but today it's best known as the jumping-off point for the splendid Rundāle Palace for do-it-yourself travellers. Before leaving town, swing by the **tourist office** (☑6392 3797; www.bauska.lv; Rātslaukums 1; ⊙9am-6pm Mon-Fri, to 3pm Sat). Staff will point you in the direction of a couple of interesting sights around town, including the **Bauska Castle Ruins** (Bauskas pilsdrupas; ☑6392 3793; admission 0.50Ls; ⊙9am-7pm May-Sep, to 6pm Oct). Sitting on an artificial hillock between the snaking Mēmele and Mūsa Rivers, the stone ruins were once a stronghold for Livonian knights in the 15th century, while the more modern half, known as the New Castle, was constructed as the residence for the Duke of Courland in the 16th century. Take a good look at the grey blocks along the facade of the New Castle – they appear to be bulging out of the wall, but it's actually an optical illusion – the lower left corner of each brick has been scraped with a chisel to trick the viewer into thinking that they are seeing a shadow.

The **Bauska Castle Museum**, located within the castle grounds, displays various archaeological finds and a collection of 16th- and 17th-century art.

During the 18th century, an Italian by the name of Magno Cavala moved to Bauska in search of a new business venture. He was something of a casanova (and a conman), and started collecting the water at the junction of the two rivers near the castle. He claimed that the water was a pungent love potion and made a fortune scamming the poor townspeople.

To find the castle ruins from the bus station, walk towards the central roundabout along Zaļā iela then branch left along Uzvaras iela for another 800m. Bauska's one-stop shopping mall at the roundabout along Rte A7 has a Rimi supermarket and a couple of decent spots to grab a meal. Backpackers can find cheap accommodation at the castle.

ℹ️ Getting There & Away

Bauska's **bus station** (Slimnīcas iela 11) offers two to three buses per hour between 6.10am and 10.40pm to/from Rīga (2Ls, 70 minutes to two hours).

Rundāle Palace

Built for Baron Ernst Johann Biron (1690–1772), Duke of Courland, between 1736 and 1740, **Rundāle Palace** (Rundāles pils; ☑6396 2197; www.rundale.net; garden 1Ls, long route

adult/child 3.50/2Ls, guided group tour from 10Ls; ⊙10am-6pm) is a monument to 18th-century aristocratic ostentatiousness, and rural Latvia's primo architectural highlight.

Ernst Johann had a tumultuous time as the Duke of Courland. After the death of Empress Anna Ioannovna, he was named Regent of Russia, but vying aristocratic houses quickly became threatened by his power and they banished the duke to Siberia. After he'd spent 22 years in exile, Catherine the Great restored his title and gave him back his duchy. During the greater part of his reign, Ernst Johann lived at his main palace in Jelgava – now used as a university – and summered here in Rundāle.

During court times the castle was divided into two halves; the **East Wing** was devoted to formal occasions, while the **West Wing** was the private royal residence. The **Royal Gardens**, inspired by the gardens at Versailles, were also used for public affairs. Of the palace's 138 rooms, only around a third are open to visitors. The rooms were heated by a network of 80 porcelain stoves (only six authentic stoves remain) as the castle was mostly used during the warmer months. Only three rooms in the West Wing are completely restored: the duchess' bedroom, boudoir and toilette. The **Toilette Room** is adorned with a playful colour scheme – even the chamber pot has a delightful painting of swimming salmon. The room is quite quaint compared with the rest of the castle, largely because the ceiling is noticeably low. Maid's quarters were cleverly lofted above the bathroom, which were accessed through the hidden door in the **Duchess' Bedroom** (note the slit in the wall next to the duchess' bed).

Rundāle was used in several different capacities between being a royal residence and a museum. During WWI the castle's **White Room** (the main ballroom) was turned into a hospital for wounded soldiers. If you aren't too distracted by the ornate ceiling (depicting the four seasons), look closely at the milky white walls (especially along the far wall opposite the entrance); you may notice small engravings and initials made by bored soldiers during their rehabilitation. Similarly, if you take a good look in some of the other restored rooms, you'll find the monogram 'EJ' (for Ernst Johann) incorporated into the baroque decor. After the war, the **Gold Room** (the throne room) was used as a granary and, later on, parts of the castle were turned into a makeshift

Southern Latvia (Zemgale)

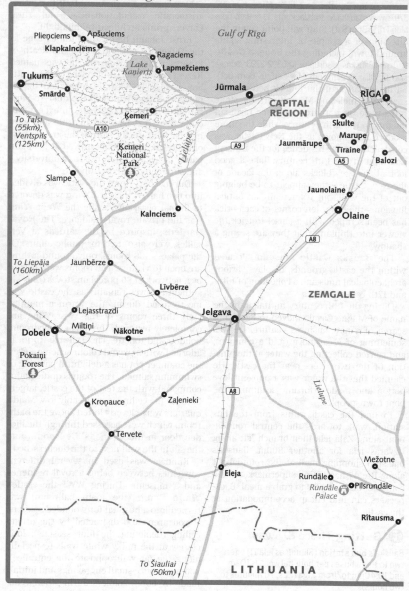

Gulf of Rīga

Plieņciems • Apšuciems
Klapkalnciems •
Ragaciems •
Lake
Kaņieris
Lapmežciems •
Tukums •
Smārde •
Jūrmala •
RĪGA •

CAPITAL REGION

To Talsi
(55km);
Ventspils
(125km)

Ķemeri •

A10

Skulte •

Marupe •
Jaunmārupe •
Tīraine •

A9

A5

Balozi •

Ķemeri
National
Park

Slampe •

Jaunolaine •

Kalnciems •

Olaine •

A8

To Liepāja
(160km)

Jaunbērze •

ZEMGALE

Lībbērze •

Lejasstrazdi •

Jelgava •

Dobele •
Miltiņi •
Nākotne •

Pokaiņi
Forest

Kroņauce •
Zaļenieki •

A8

Tērvete •

Mežotne •

Eleja •

Rundāle •
Rundāle
Palace

Pilsrundāle •

Rītausma •

To Šiauliai
(50km)

LITHUANIA

school. The **Marble Room** was the basketball court, and reliefs of Romanesque busts mark the spots where the nets used to hang.

The palace became a museum in the 1970s when a team of historians dug out the plans of the original palace layout and began the lengthy restoration process. Carefully detailed notes were left by the palace's Italian architect, Bartolomeo Rastrelli, who supposedly designed his first palace at 21 years old! After studying architecture in Paris, Rastrelli quickly

Like any good castle, Rundāle has loads of eerie ghost tales, but the most famous spectre that haunts the palace grounds is the 'White Lady'. In the 19th century, the royal doctor had a young daughter who was courted by many men, but on her 18th birthday she suddenly grew ill and died. Obsessed with her untimely demise, the doctor kept her corpse in his laboratory to study her and tried to figure out why she was ravaged by illness (or was she poisoned by a lovelorn suitor?). Unable to rest eternally, the daughter's spirit began haunting the castle and cackling wildly in the middle of the night. During Rundāle's restorations, several art historians and masons heard her wicked laughter and brought in a priest to exorcise the grounds.

Sleeping & Eating

Mežotne Palace HISTORIC HOTEL €€€
(6396 0711; www.mezotnespils.lv; Mežotne; r 50-90Ls) Live like Duke Ernst Johann and check into Mežotne Palace, about 2km from Rundāle. The palace was built in a classical style from 1797 to 1802 for Charlotte von Lieven, the governess of Russian empress Catherine II's grandchildren. After many years in disrepair, it was restored in 2001 and transformed into a hotel and restaurant. A handful of rooms are open to the public for a small fee, although a visit to Mežotne isn't worth the trek if you aren't sleeping over or eating at the popular restaurant. Rooms are stocked with aristocratic collectibles – think cast-iron bed frames, swinging chandeliers and carefully chosen antiques.

Balta Māja B&B €
(6396 2140; www.kalpumaja.lv, in Latvian; Rundāle; dm/d 10/14Ls) The 'White House' is a quaint B&B and cafe sitting in the palace's Tudor-style servants' quarters near the entrance to the grounds. Salads and meat platters are prepped in the kitchen, and the bedrooms are cluttered with wool duvets and agrarian antiques.

Rundāle Palace Restaurant CAFETERIA €
(mains 1-5Ls) Located in the palace basement, it's a convenient spot for a quick bite. Most of the food is of the Latvian persuasion.

Getting There & Away

Rundāle Palace is about 12km west of Bauska. Reaching the palace will require some planning and patience if you are not on a guided tour or

earned his reputation as a baroque genius and was appointed court architect to the Russian royal family. He would later design the palace in Jelgava and, most notably, the awe-inspiring Winter Palace in St Petersburg.

LATVIA RUNDĀLE PALACE

don't have your own set of wheels. Those taking public transport will arrive in Bauska (p238), and must switch to a Rundāle-bound bus, but make sure you get off at Pilsrundāle, the village before Rundāle. From Bauska there are hourly Pilsrundāle buses (0.40-0.80Ls) between 6am and 7.30pm.

Jelgava

POP 65,000

Jelgava was once known as the most beautiful city in Latvia – even more stunning than Rīga. Duke Ernst Johann, who summered in Rundāle, built his main castle here, and for 200 years (between the 16th and 18th centuries) it was the capital of the Duchy of Courland. During the world wars, Jelgava was bombed to high hell, and today the city is nothing more than Zemgale's biggest town and commercial centre.

Even though most of the city's aristocratic flavour was incinerated, Jelgava is a pleasant pit stop if you're travelling between Rīga and the Hill of Crosses (p334) in Lithuania. The duke's castle, the aptly named Jelgava Palace (Jelgavas pils; www.llu.lv; Leilā iela 2), miraculously still stands, and is currently the home of the Latvian Agricultural University.

❶ Getting There & Away

Buses run every 15 minutes to/from Rīga and Jelgava (1.50Ls, one hour) between 6am and 11.30pm. One or two suburban trains per hour link Rīga and Jelgava (1.35Ls, 45 minutes).

Dobele & Around

POP 27,000

Provincial Dobele, in the far western corner of Zemgale, is the gateway to a vast acreage of mythical forests and meandering rivers. The only attraction of note in the town of Dobele is the impressive Livonian Order castle ruins, which date back to the mid-1330s. This brick bastion was built over the original site of an earlier Semigallian stronghold. In 1289, the Semigallians incinerated their own castle and fled to Lithuania rather than surrendering the structure to the invading crusaders. A monument in town commemorates their departure.

POKAIŅI FOREST

Located 13km southwest of Dobele, the Pokaiņi Forest Reserve (www.mammadaba .lv; adult/child 1.20/0.60Ls, car 1Ls, camping per day 1Ls; ☺toll booth 10am-7pm) is one of Latvia's biggest unsolved mysteries. In the mid-'90s, a local historian discovered subtle stone cairns throughout the park and realised that the rocks had been transported to the forest from faraway destinations. Historians have theorised that Pokaiņi was an ancient sacred ground used in proto-pagan rituals over 2000 years ago. Volunteer efforts have helped create walking trails through the reserve, which is often visited by healers and New Age types. Ask at the toll booth for available tour guides.

TĒRVETE

The town of Tērvete, 18km south of Dobele, sits among scores of ancient Semigallian castle mounds. Tērvete Nature Park (☑6372 6212; www.latvia.travel/en/tervete-nature -park; adult/child 2/1.20Ls, car 10Ls) protects three of these ancient mounds, including the impressive Tērvete Castle Mound, which was abandoned by the Semigallians after several battles with the Livonian Order. Nearby Klosterhill was first inhabited over 3000 years ago by Semigallian ancestors, and Swedish Hill was constructed by the Livonian Order in the 13th century.

In recent years, the nature park has built a variety of family attractions such as the Fairy Tale Forest, filled with whimsical woodcarvings. A witch lives in the park during the summer, entertaining the little ones with games and potions. At the park's History Museum (☺May-Oct), visitors can learn about the history of the Semigallians through artefacts and costumes.

❶ Getting There & Away

Dobele is easily accessible by bus to/from Rīga (2.10Ls, 1½ hours), which stops in Jelgava along the way. The nearby forest reserves are best reached by car.

NORTHEASTERN LATVIA (VIDZEME)

When Rīga's urban hustle fades into a pulsing hum of chirping crickets, you've entered northeastern Latvia. Known as Vidzeme, or 'the Middle Land', to locals, the country's largest region is an excellent sampler of what Latvia has to offer. Forest folks can hike, bike or paddle through the thicketed terrain of Gauja National Park, ski bums can tackle bunny slopes

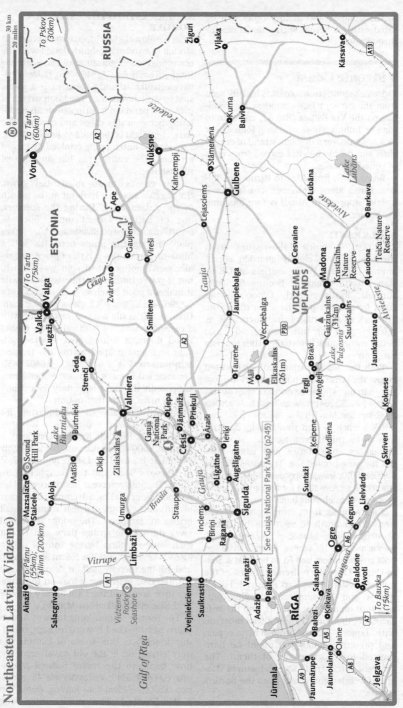

Northeastern Latvia (Vidzeme)

LATVIA NORTHEASTERN LATVIA (VIDZEME)

in the uplands and history buffs will be sated with a generous sprinkling of castles throughout.

Vidzeme Coast

Vidzeme's stone-strewn coast is usually seen from the car – or bus – window by travellers on the Via Baltica (Rte A1) en route to Rīga or Tallinn. Those who stop for a closer look will uncover a desolate strand of craggy cliffs and pebble beaches carved from eons of pounding waves.

Buses north from Rīga to Pärnu and Tallinn travel along Vidzeme's coastal road, usually stopping in Ainaži before touching the border.

SAULKRASTI

Saulkrasti, a quick 44km jaunt from the capital, is a closely guarded secret among Latvians. While tourists and Russian jetsetters make a beeline for ritzy Jūrmala, locals gingerly tiptoe up the coast for a day trip in the other direction. The lack of a tourism infrastructure is as refreshing as the salty breeze, so you'd better come quick before the other tourists catch on.

Both the bus and train stations (located across the street from one another) are just less than one kilometre north of the **tourist office** (✆6795 2641; www.saulkrasti.lv; Ainažu iela 13; ⊙9am-6pm Mon-Fri).

It's a cinch to turn your beachy day trip into an overnight extravaganza – scores of bungalows, guesthouses and camp sites dot the pine-fronted sea. Try **Jūras Priede** (✆2958 8010; www.juraspriede.lv; Ūpes iela 56a; tent sites 2Ls, cabins 10Ls) for a teeny log cabin or a spot to pitch your tent.

Take a break from jumping waves and head 16km north to visit the bodacious **Munchausen's Museum** (✆6406 5633; www.minhauzens.lv; Duntes Estate; admission 1.50Ls; ⊙10am-5pm Mon-Fri, to 6pm Sat & Sun) in Dunte. Once the retirement home of the tall tale–teller Baron Karl Friedrich Hieronymus von Munchausen (imagine putting *that* on a business card), and his wife Jacobine, the house is now a wax museum with famous figures from Latvia's past and present (though you might be hard pressed to recognise any of them). The adjacent forest trail (5.3km) features dozens of wooden characters from the Baron's stories.

SAULKRASTI TO THE ESTONIAN BORDER

After Saulkrasti, the Vidzeme coast is a silent stretch of windswept dunes dotted with the occasional lonely guesthouse. The **Vidzeme Rocky Seashore** (✆2946 4686), halfway between Saulkrasti and Salacgrīva, is a scenic spot to stretch your legs. The 14km stretch of protected parkland has rippled sands undulating between tiny capes and caverns. The park's highlight is the **Veczemju Red Cliffs**, a sandstone outcropping crinkled by jagged grottoes. The entire crag has an ethereal reddish hue.

The coast's most substantial town, **Salacgrīva** sits on a harbour at the mouth of the Salaca River. During the summer, one of Latvia's largest music festivals, **Positivus** (www.positivusfestival.lv), takes place among the pines here. It's still a blink-or-you'll-miss-it type of place, not really worth going out of your way to visit, but if you're hungry on the way to Estonia it makes a good lunch stop. **Žejnieku Sēta** (✆2962 4153; Rīgas iela 1; mains 2-6Ls; ⊙11am-11pm) is a friendly seafood restaurant with a pleasing, old-time nautical vibe – creaky wood floors, a fishing boat moored outside and nets draped across the terrace. **Minhauzen Pie Bocmaņa** (✆6407 1455; Pērmavas iela 6; mains from 2Ls; ⊙11am-11pm), supposedly the 'most legendary fisherman's pub in town', is another option.

Salacgrīva is also the headquarters for the **North Vidzeme Biosphere Reserve** (✆6407 1408; Rīgas iela 10a; ⊙8.30am-5pm), a pristine, 4500-sq-km domain that is roughly 6% of Latvia's total land share and inscribed in Unesco's 'Man and the Biosphere' program. The vast reserve is best uncovered on a canoeing or cycling adventure. Each year in autumn, visitors can fish from a small bridge for lampreys. The bridge is washed away during the spring thaw and rebuilt each summer. Stop by the **tourist office** (✆6404 1254; Rīgas iela 10a; ⊙9am-5pm Mon-Fri) and ask the friendly staff for details on local outfitters, or search for a tour on the internet (free access) at the local **library** (✆6407 1995; Silas iela 2; ⊙10am-6pm Mon-Fri).

The former shipbuilding town of **Ainaži** (derived from the Liv word *annagi,* meaning 'lonely') is 1km south of Estonia. Its only attraction is the old naval academy, now home to the **Naval School Museum** (✆6404 3349; Valdemāra iela 45; admission 0.50Ls; ⊙10am-4pm Jun-Aug, closed Sun & Mon Sep-May). This mildly interesting museum exhibits the naval academy's history and the history of shipbuilding along the Vidzeme coast.

Gauja National Park

A stunning stretch of virgin pines, this **national park** (Gaujas nacionālais parks; www.gnp.gov.lv), extends from castle-strewn Sigulda to quiet Valmiera, passing industrial Līgatne and picture-perfect Cēsis along the way. Founded in 1973, Latvia's first national park protects a very leafy hinterland popular for hiking, biking, backcountry camping, canoeing and a slew of offbeat adrenalin sports. There is no entrance fee for Gauja National Park.

SIGULDA
POP 17,800

With a name that sounds like a mythical ogress, it comes as no surprise that the gateway to the Gauja (gow-yah) is an enchanting spot with delightful surprises tucked behind every dappled tree. Locals proudly call their town the 'Switzerland of Latvia', but if you're expecting the majesty of a mountainous snow-capped realm, you'll be rather disappointed. Instead, Sigulda mixes its own brew of scenic trails, extreme sports and 800-year-old castles steeped in legends.

◉ Sights

Sigulda sprawls between its three castles with most of the action occurring on the east side of the Gauja River near New Sigulda Castle. Follow our walking tour for an abridged version of Sigulda's greatest hits, and don't forget to take a ride on the **cable car** (☑6797 2531; www.bungee.lv; Poruka iela 14; one-way ride 2Ls; ◷10am-7.30pm) across the valley for an awesome aerial perspective.

Turaida Museum Reserve CASTLE
(Turaidas muzejrezervats; ☑6797 1402; www.turaida-muzejs.lv; Turaidas iela 10; adult/child

Gauja National Park

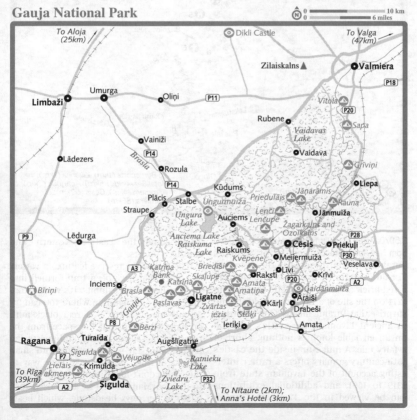

Sigulda

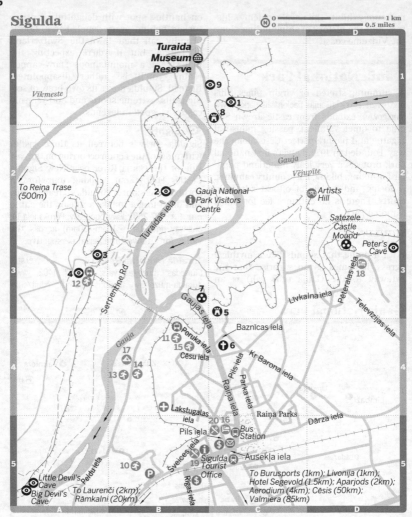

Turaida Museum Reserve

To Reiņa Trase (500m)

Gauja National Park Visitors Centre

Gauja

Vējupīte

Artists Hill

Satezele Castle Mound

Peter's Cave

Serpentīne Rd

Turaidas iela

Gaujas iela

Livkalna iela

Peterālas iela

Televīzijas iela

Baznīcas iela

Poruka iela

Cēsu iela

Kr Barona iela

Pils iela

Raiņa iela

Parka iela

Raiņa Parks

Dārza iela

Lāčplēša iela

Lakstugalas iela

Pils iela

Bus Station

Sigulda Tourist Office

Ausekļa iela

Šveices iela

Rīgas iela

Little Devil's Cave

Big Devil's Cave

To Laurenči (2km); Rāmkalni (20km)

To Burusports (1km); Livonija (1km); Hotel Segevold (1.5km); Aparjods (2km); Aerodium (4km); Cēsis (50km); Valmiera (85km)

Vikmeste

0   1 km
0   0.5 miles

3.50/0.80Ls; ⊙9am-8pm May-Oct, 10am-5pm Nov-Apr) The centrepiece of Sigulda's Turaida Museum Reserve is the stunning **Turaida Castle** (Turaidas pils; ⊙10am-6pm), a red-brick archbishop's castle founded in 1214 on the site of a Liv stronghold. It's no surprise that Turaida means 'God's Garden' in ancient Livonian; the castle's position on an enviable knoll is nothing short of a fairy tale. A **museum** inside the castle's 15th-century granary offers a rather interesting account of the Livonian state from 1319 to 1561, and additional exhibitions can be viewed in the 42m-high **Donjon Tower**, and the castle's western and southern towers.

The rest of the reserve features a variety of houses that have been transformed into small galleries and exhibits. It's worth stopping by the **smith house** where you can try forging metal. There is a real blacksmith on hand who rents out the space from the reserve – he sells his crafts, and guests can try pounding Liv pagan symbols into small chunks of iron. As you make your way to the castle, don't forget to pay your respects to ill-fated Maija Roze (see the boxed text, p249) at her onyx headstone, which bears

Sigulda

⊙ **Top Sights**

Turaida Museum Reserve.................... B1

⊙ **Sights**

1 Daina Hill Song Garden....................... C1
2 Gūtmaņa Cave....................................... B2
3 Krimulda Castle A3
4 Krimulda Manor A3
5 New Sigulda Castle.............................. C3
6 Sigulda Church..................................... C4
7 Sigulda Medieval Castle...................... B3
8 Turaida Castle C1
9 Turaida Rose Headstone..................... C1

➕ **Activities, Courses & Tours**

10 Bobsled Track B5
11 Bungee Jump B4
12 Cable Car (North Station) A3
13 Makars Tourism Bureau B4
14 Sigulda Adventure Park B4
15 Tridents... B4

🛏 **Sleeping**

16 Hotel Sigulda C5
17 Kempings Siguldas Pludmale B4
18 Līvkalns D3

❌ **Eating**

19 Elvi.. B5
20 Kaķu Māja C5

the inscription 'Turaidas Roze 1601–1620'. The hillside behind her tombstone is known as Daina Hill (Dainu kalns) and shelters the **Daina Hill Song Garden**. The *daina* (poetic folk song) is a major Latvian tradition, and the hillside is dotted with sculptures dedicated to epic Latvian heroes immortalised in the *dainas*. These sculptures were actually created during the communist times, and in order to create these distinctly Latvian pieces, the sculptors had to make one item dedicated to the Soviet regime – it's the sculpture of a strong man.

Sigulda Castles · CASTLE

Little remains of **Sigulda Medieval Castle** (Siguldas pilsdrupas; admission 0.70Ls), a knights' stronghold, built between 1207 and 1226 among woods on the northeastern edge of Sigulda. The castle hasn't been repaired since the Great Northern War, but its ruins are perhaps more evocative as a result. Recent renovation efforts are underway – a wooden path will be added through the grounds, and one of the towers will soon

be turned into a viewpoint with an elevator inside for disabled access. There's a great view through the trees to the archbishop's reconstructed Turaida Castle, on the far side of the valley.

On the way to the ruins from town, you'll pass **Sigulda Church** (Siguldas baznīca; 2 Baznīcas iela), built in 1225 and rebuilt in the 17th and 18th centuries, and also the 19th-century **New Sigulda Castle** (Siguldas jaunā pils), a sanatorium and former residence of the Russian prince Dimitri Kropotkin, who turned Sigulda into a tourist haven – it's still owned by the descendents of the prince. During Soviet times the castle was the local health ministry.

Gūtmaņa Cave · CAVE

The largest erosion cave in the Baltic is most famous for its role in the tragic legend of the Rose of Turaida (see boxed text, p249). Most tourists visit to peruse the inordinate amount of graffiti spread along the walls – some of it dates back to the 16th century – apparently eagle eyes have found the coats of arms of long-gone hunters. Some believe that the stream water flowing out of the cave has a magical blend of minerals that remove facial wrinkles (it didn't work for us).

Krimulda Castle & Manor · CASTLE

On the northern side of the valley, a track leads up from near the bridge to ruined **Krimulda Castle** (Krimuldas pilsdrupas), built between 1255 and 1273 and once used as a guesthouse for visiting dignitaries. Only one original wall remains. The big white building just west of the northern cable-car station is **Krimulda Manor** (Krimuldas muižas pils; Mednieku iela 3), confiscated by the government in 1922 and later turned into a tuberculosis hospital. Today it is a sanatorium, and it admittedly looks better from afar as a lot of paint is chipping off the facade. The building was commissioned by Baron von Lieven, a general in the Swedish army who, as it turns out, was a distant descendant of the Liv leader that ruled the area when it was invaded by German crusaders. When you visit, you can ask at the front to be let out onto the terrace for excellent views of the forested valley – this is a popular place in Latvia for newlyweds to take pictures.

🏃 **Activities**

If you're looking to test your limits with a bevy of adrenalin-pumping activities, then you've come to the right place. In fact,

DON'T MISS

PIRTS

Cast modesty aside and indulge in Latvia's most Latvian tradition, the *pirts*. A *pirts* is Latvia's version of the sauna, and while somewhat similar to the Finnish sauna, there are many elements that set this sweaty experience apart. A traditional *pirts* is run by a sauna master, who cares for her attendees while performing choreographed branch beatings that feel almost shamanistic in nature. Yes, you read that correctly – while lying down in your birthday suit, the sauna master swishes branches in the air to raise the humidity then lightly beats a variety of wildflowers and branches over your back and chest while you rest. *Pirts* also tend to be much hotter and more humid than their Finnish counterparts – a branch-beating session usually lasts around 15 minutes before one exits the sauna to jump in a nearby body of water (lake, pond or sea). The aroma of the sauna is also very important – sauna masters take great care to create a melange of herbs and spices to accent the air. In general, an afternoon at a *pirts* involves multiple sweat sessions interspersed with leaps in cool water – beer, herbal tea and snacks are a must.

All traditional saunas are in the countryside; most can be found at private cottages. If you are interested in trying out one for yourself, then head to **Hotel Sigulda** (www.hotelsigulda.lv) or **Hotel Ezeri** (www.hotelezeri.lv) – they offer private sessions at an elegantly crafted local *pirts*. An afternoon sweat (around three hours) with plenty of tea and snacks costs 50Ls for two people.

Sigulda has been Latvia's headquarters for extreme sports ever since the Russian baron created a bobsled track in the snow in the late 19th century. Those looking for something more subdued will enjoy hiking and cycling trails through the national park's shady pines, or canoeing down the lazy Gauja River.

HIGH-ADRENALIN SPORTS

Bobsled Track   EXTREME SPORT
(☑6797 3813; Sveices iela 13) Sigulda's 1200m artificial bobsled track was built for the former Soviet bobsleigh team. Today, the track hosts a portion of the European luge championships every January. In winter you can fly down the 16-bend track at 80km/h in a five-person **Vučko tourist bob** (ride per person 6Ls; ☺noon-7pm Sat & Sun Oct-Mar), or contact **Karīna** at the **Makars Tourism Bureau** (☑2924 4948; www.makars.lv; Peldu iela 1) for the real Olympian experience on the hair-raising **winter bob** (ride per person 35Ls). Summer speed fiends can ride a wheeled **summer sled** (ride per person 6Ls; ☺11am-6pm Sat & Sun May-Sep) without booking in advance.

Aerodium   EXTREME SPORT
(☑2838 4400; www.aerodium.lv; Hwy A2; 2min ride weekday/weekend 15/18Ls, additional min weekday/weekend 5/6Ls; ☺4-10pm Mon-Fri, noon-8pm Sat & Sun May-Sep) The one-of-a-kind aerodium is a giant wind tunnel that propels participants up into the sky as though they were flying. Instructors can get about 15m high,

while first-timers usually rock out at about 3m. Even though you will only be airborne for a couple of minutes, there is a brief introductory course before going skyward, so give yourself a full hour to participate and call in advance. To find the wind tunnel, look for the sign along the highway and follow a dirt road down a small hill past Sigulda Bloks warehouse.

Cable Car Bungee Jump   EXTREME SPORT
(☑2644 0660; www.bungee.lv; Poruka iela 14; Fri/weekend jump 20/25Ls; ☺7.30pm to last jump Fri-Sun May-Sep) If the bobsled wasn't enough to make you toss your cookies, take your daredevil shenanigans to the next level and try a 43m bungee jump from the bright orange cable car that glides over the Gauja River high up in the clouds. Weekday jumps can sometimes be arranged with an advance booking.

Sigulda Adventure Park   EXTREME SPORT
(Rodelis; ☑2700 1187; www.rodelis.lv; Peldu iela; toboggan track 1/6 rides 2/10Ls, ropes course adult/child 9/5Ls; ☺10am-9pm May-Oct) Across the street from the Makars Tourism Bureau, head here to swish down a toboggan track or monkey around on the 'Tarzan' ropes course.

Mežakaķis   EXTREME SPORT
(☑6797 1624; www.kakiskalns.lv; Senču iela 1; adult/child 12/6.50Ls; ☺10am-7pm May-Oct) This smaller adventure park has a ropes course with more than 80 obstacles geared towards

everyone from children to daredevils and pros. In winter, you'll find ski slopes to tackle.

HIKING & CYCLING

Sigulda is prime hiking territory, so bring your walking shoes. The surrounding Gauja National Park is currently investing €2 million in infrastructure to add better paths for trekking and cycling through the reserve. A popular (and easy) route is the 40-minute walk from Krimulda Castle to Turaida Museum Reserve via Gūtmaņa Cave and Viktors' Cave. Or you can head south from Krimulda and descend to Little Devil's Cave and Big Devil's Cave, cross the river via a footbridge, and return to Sigulda (about two hours). Note the black walls in Big Devil's Cave, which are believed to be from the fiery breath of a travelling demon that took shelter here to avoid the sunlight. Check out the handy brochure at the Sigulda Tourist Office detailing a half-day walking route linking all three castles in the region.

East of Sigulda, try the well-marked loop that joins Peter's Cave, Satezele Castle Mound and Artists' Hill; it starts from behind the Līvkalns hotel and takes about 1½ hours. The panoramic view of Turaida Castle and the Gauja River valley from Artists' Hill is spectacular.

Many outfitters around Sigulda offer bicycle and mountain-bike rentals costing somewhere between 7Ls and 10Ls per day. Try Burusports (☑6797 2051; www.burusports .lv; Mazā Gāles iela 1; ☺noon-8pm Mon, 10am-8pm Tue-Sat), Reiņa Trase (☑2927 2255; www .reinatrase.lv; Krimulda pagasts; ☺2pm-midnight Mon-Thu, to 1am Fri, 10am-1am Sat, 9am-11pm

Sun), Rāmkalni (☑6797 7277; www.ramkalni .lv; Inčukalna pagasts; ☺9am-10pm) or Makars Tourism Bureau (☑2924 4948; www.makars .lv; Peldu iela 1). Tridents (Cesu iela 14; 9am-7pm Jun-Aug), in the city centre, is the most popular option for bike rentals.

CANOEING & BOATING

Floating down the peaceful Gauja River is a great way to observe this pristine area and have a couple of wildlife encounters (if you're lucky). There are camping grounds all along the stretch of river from Sigulda to Cēsis. Team up with one of the outfitters within the national park that organises boat trips along the Gauja, or you can just head upstream, stick your arse in an innertube, and float back to town.

On the banks of the river in Sigulda, Makars Tourism Bureau (☑2924 4948; www.makars.lv; Peldu iela 1) arranges one- to three-day water tours in two- to four-person boats from Sigulda, Līgatne, Cēsis and Valmiera, ranging in length from 3km to 85km. Tours cost between 10Ls and 60Ls per boat including equipment, transport between Sigulda and the tour's starting point, and camp-site fees for up to four people. Tents, sleeping bags and life jackets can also be rented for a nominal fee. For the less intrepid paddler, Makars rents out canoes and rubber boats starting at 15Ls per day.

Both Rāmkalni (☑6797 7277; www.ramkalni .lv; Inčukalna pagasts; ☺9am-10pm) and Reiņa Trase (☑2927 2255; www.reinatrase.lv; Krimulda pagasts; ☺2pm-midnight Mon-Thu, to 1am Fri, 10am-1am Sat, 9am-11pm Sun) also rent out boating equipment.

LATVIA GAUJA NATIONAL PARK

THE ROSE OF TURAIDA

Sigulda's local beauty, Maija Roze (May Rose), was taken into Turaida Castle as a little girl when she was found among the wounded after a battle in the early 1600s. She grew into a famous beauty and was courted by men from far and wide, but her heart belonged to Viktors, a humble gardener at nearby Sigulda Medieval Castle. They would meet in secret at Gūtmaņa Cave halfway between the two castles.

One day, a particularly desperate soldier among Maija Roze's suitors lured her to the cave with a letter forged in Viktors' handwriting. When Maija Roze arrived, the soldier set his kidnapping plan in motion. Maija Roze pleaded with the soldier and offered to give him the scarf from around her neck in return for her freedom. She claimed it had magical protective powers, and to prove it, she told him to swing at her with his sword. It isn't clear whether or not she was bluffing or if she really believed in the scarf – either way, the soldier duly took his swing and killed the beauty.

The soldier was captured, convicted and hanged for his crime. Court documents have been uncovered, proving that the tale was in fact true. Today, a small stone memorial commemorates poor Maija Roze, the Rose of Turaida.

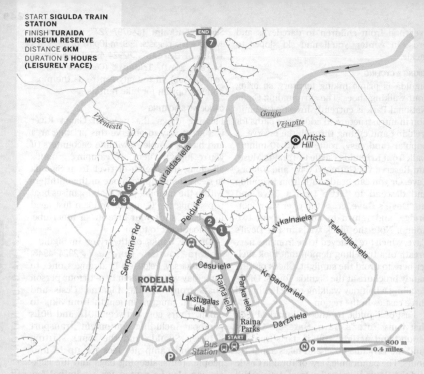

Walking Tour
Castles Day Trip

❯ If you're short on time, or visiting Sigulda on a day trip, the town's three main castle reserves and one legendary cave can be easily tackled in an afternoon.

If you just arrived from the train or bus station, walk down Raiņa iela and linden-lined Pils iela until you reach ❶ **Sigulda New Castle**, built in the 18th century during the reign of German aristocrats. Check out the ruins of ❷ **Sigulda Medieval Castle** around the back, which was constructed in 1207 by the Order of the Brethren of the Sword, but was severely damaged in the 18th century during the Great Northern War. Follow Poruka iela to the rocky precipice and take the ❸ **cable car** over the scenic river valley to ❹ **Krimulda Manor**, an elegant estate currently used as a rehabilitation clinic.

After exploring the grounds, check out the crumbling ruins of ❺ **Krimulda Medieval Castle** nearby, then follow Serpentine Rd down to ❻ **Gūtmaņa Cave**. Immortalised by the legend of the Rose of Turaida (see the boxed text, p249), it's the largest erosion cave in the Baltic. Take some time to read the myriad inscriptions carved into the walls then head up to the ❼ **Turaida Museum Reserve**. The medieval castle was erected in the 13th century for the Archbishop of Rīga over the site of an ancient Liv stronghold. Catch bus 12 back to Sigulda town when you're all castled out.

🛏 Sleeping

If all of the hotels are full, ask the tourist office about finding a room in a private home (10Ls) or renting your own apartment (25Ls to 50Ls). Check Sigulda's official website, www.tourism.sigulda.lv, for additional lodging info.

Līvkalns
INN €€

(☎6797 0916; www.livkalns.lv; Pēteralas iela; s/d from 22/30Ls; 🛜) No place is more romantically rustic than this idyllic retreat next to a pond on the forest's edge. The rooms are pine-fresh and sit among a campus of adorable thatch-roof manors. The cabin in the woods-styled restaurant is fantastic.

Aparjods
HOTEL €€

(☎6797 2230; www.aparjods.lv; Ventas iela 1; s/d 20/33Ls; @🛜) Tucked behind the glowing lights of Hesburger, Aparjods is a rather charming complex of barn-like structures with wooden doors and reed-and-shingle roofing. The rooms aren't as characterful, but are still among the cosier options in town. The hotel is located 1.5km southwest of town.

Hotel Segevold
HOTEL €€

(☎2647 6652; www.hotelsegevold.lv; Mālpils iela 4b; d 35Ls; @🛜) After entering the swankified lobby, you'll immediately forget that Segevold is bizarrely located in the heart of an industrial park – the futuristic lighting and giant tentacle-like reliefs starkly contrast the grungy Soviet tractors around the corner. Upstairs, the rooms are noticeably less glam, but they're in mint condition and kept pathologically clean.

Hotel Sigulda
HOTEL €€

(☎6797 2263; www.hotelsigulda.lv; Pils iela 6; s/d 30/35Ls; @🛜) Right in the centre of town, this is the oldest hotel in Sigulda – it was built by the Russian baron who had dreams of turning the little hamlet into an exciting tourist destination. While the old stone-and-brick facade is quite charming, the rooms are standard issue and rather plain. The friendly family that owns Hotel Sigulda also runs the more luxurious **Hotel Ezeri** (☎6797 3009; www.hotelezeri.com; s/d 45/50Ls) several kilometres outside of town. Ask about their unique sauna experience (see p248).

Kempings Siguldas Pludmale
CAMPING €

(☎2924 4948; www.makars.lv; Peldu iela 2; person/tent/car/caravan 3/1.50/1.50/6Ls; ⊙15 May-15 Sep) Pitch your tent in the grassy camping area beside the sandy beach along the Gauja. The location is perfect; however, there's only one men's and one women's bathroom for the scores of campers. Two-person tents can be hired for 4Ls per day. There's a second camping area up the river in Līgatne that's owned and operated by Makars as well. Ask at this location for directions.

Livonija
HOSTEL €

(☎6797 0916; www.livonija.viss.lv; Pulkveža Brieža iela 55; dm/s/d from 8/14/20Ls; @🛜) The eight rooms at the top of the creaky staircase vary greatly in quality, so try to look at a couple of rooms before deciding where to hang your hat. There's an inviting garden in the back with bursts of colourful petals and a droopy swing. The fully equipped kitchen is an extra bonus.

Laurenči
HOSTEL €

(☎6797 1852; Laurenču iela; dm 7-10Ls; ⊙Jun-Aug) The best deal for the backpacker crowd is only open during the summer months (when the attached school is closed) and offers spartan rooms dipped in pastels.

🍴 Eating & Drinking

Most of Sigulda's hotels and guesthouses have a small restaurant attached. Options are surprisingly dismal considering this is one of the most popular destinations in Latvia beyond Rīga.

Aparjods
INTERNATIONAL €€

(Ventas iela 1; mains 4-12Ls; ⊙lunch & dinner) Aparjods' elegant restaurant gets a special mention for its delectable assortment of cuisine served among charming clutters of household heirlooms and gold-embroidered seating. A roaring fire warms the dark-wood dining room in winter, while tables spill out onto the patio during summer. The upmarket atmosphere tends to attract an older clientele.

Kaķu Māja
CAFETERIA €

(Pils iela 8; mains from 2Ls; ⊙8am-11pm, club 10pm-4am) The 'Cat House' is the top spot around town for a cheap bite. In the bistro, point to the ready-made dishes that tickle your fancy and hunker down on one of the inviting picnic tables outside. For dessert, visit the attached bakery to try out-of-this-world pastries, pies and cakes. On Friday and Saturday nights, the restaurant in the back turns into a nightclub that busts out the disco ball until the wee hours of the morning.

MUIŽAS OF THE GAUJA

Beyond the park's four main towns, there are plenty of hidden treasures tucked deep within the Gauja region. If you have a little extra time, try checking out these gems, particularly the area's *muižas*, or manor houses.

Ungurmuiža

Beautiful **Ungurmuiža** (☑2942 4757; admission 1.50Ls; ◎10am-6pm Tue-Sun mid-May–Oct) is one of the best preserved manor houses in all of Latvia. The stately red mansion was created by Baron von Campenhousen, who served under the Swedish king and Russian tsar. Descendants of the baron lived here until WWII, when the government swiftly seized the property. It was, rather miraculously, kept in mint condition and today the delicate mural paintings and original doors are a delightful throwback to aristocratic times. Tours (20Ls per group for 30 minutes) can be easily arranged as well as evening stays in one of the quaint bedrooms (double including breakfast 35Ls).

Bīriņi Castle

Like a big pink birthday cake sitting on a verdant lawn, **Bīriņi Castle** (Bīriņu pils; ☑6402 4033; www.birinupils.lv; admission 2Ls) governs a scenic tract of land overlooking a tranquil lake. Located on the northwestern edges of the Gauja towards Saulkrasti, the baronial estate has been transformed into an opulent hotel swathed in a Renaissance style focused around the grand foyer staircase. Daytime visitors can still reap the benefits on a guided tour (8Ls), or by taking in the lovely scenery with a picnic or a boat ride (3Ls). Operating hours can be erratic (especially in the summer when there's a wedding every week). Call first and make a reservation to avoid difficulties.

Dikli Castle

It was here, in 1864, that a priest organised Latvia's first Song Festival, which gives **Dikli Castle** (Dikļu pils; ☑6402 7480; www.diklupils.lv; d/ste from 45/100Ls) an important place in the nation's history. Like at Bīriņi, this aristocratic manor has been transformed into a luxurious retreat with hotel rooms and spa services. Visitors can also enjoy strolls in the 20-hectare park and boat rides (3Ls); tours detailing the history and restoration of the manor are also available (1Ls).

Annas Hotel

Originally built in the middle of the 18th century as Annas Muiža, **Annas Hotel** (☑6418 0700; www.annashotel.com; apt 60Ls; ☜) is a modern inn that fuses historical charm with thoroughly modern motifs. There's not much to do around the property, it's all about relaxation, and the hotel provides just that – spa sessions, and lovely grounds peppered with trees and ponds.

Geidānmuiža

Not technically a *muiža*, **Geidānmuiža** (www.vesturiskiaktivs.lv, in Latvian; activities 3.50Ls per person; ◎10am-8pm) sits around the corner from Āraiši and is the project of a few young Latvian entrepreneurs. Visitors who are interested in experiencing life during 14th-century Livonia can book a variety of authentic activities from archery to feast roasts. At the time of research a crude structure was in the works.

Elvi   SUPERMARKET **€**
(☑6797 3322; Vidus iela 1; mains from 2Ls; ◎9am-10pm Mon-Sat, to 9pm Sun) Elvi is a multiservice supermarket with aisles upon aisles of groceries, a small cafeteria-style restaurant (the meats tend to be undercooked), and a

bowling alley upstairs (open until midnight) that serves up some decent grub.

ⓘ Information
Gauja National Park Visitors Centre (☑6780 0388; www.gnp.gov.lv; ◎9.30am-7pm Apr-Oct, 10am-4pm Nov-Mar) Sells maps to the park,

town and cycle routes nearby, and can arrange accommodation, guided tours, backcountry camping and other outdoor activities. Cold drinks and snacks are also available for purchase.

Hospital (Lakstugalas iela 13)

Latvijas Krājbanka (Valdemāra iela 1a; ☺9am-5pm Mon-Fri) One of several ATMs. Currently located next door to the tourist office.

Post office (Pils iela 2; ☺8am-6pm Mon, to 5pm Tue-Fri, to 2pm Sat)

Sigulda Tourist Office (☏6797 1335; www .sigulda.lv; Valdemāra iela 1a; ☺10am-7pm Jun-Sep, to 5pm Oct-May; ☎) Mountains of information about sights, activities and hotels. The friendly staff can assist with lodging bookings. There is wi-fi access and a computer terminal available to tourists.There are plans to move the information centre to the corner of Raiņa and Ausekļa iela.

Unibanka (Rīgas iela 1; ☺9am-5pm Mon-Fri) Has a currency-exchange facility.

❶ Getting There & Away

Buses trundle the 50-odd kilometers between Sigulda's bus station and Rīga (1.80Ls, one hour, every 30 minutes between 8am and 10.30pm).

One train per hour (between 6am and 9pm) travels the Rīga–Sigulda–Cēsis–Valmiera Line. Fares from Sigulda include Rīga (1.55Ls, one or 1¼ hours), Valmiera (1¼ hours), Līgatne (10 minutes) and Cēsis (40 minutes).

❶ Getting Around

Sigulda's attractions are quite spread out and after a long day of walking, bus 12 will become your new best friend. It plies the route to/from New Sigulda Castle, Turaida Castle and Krimulda Manor hourly during business hours (more on weekends). Travellers can also use the Impresso golf carts that buzz around the castle ruins as a discounted taxi service (2Ls per person).

LĪGATNE

Deep in the heart of the Gauja National Park, little Līgatne is a twilight zone of opposite extremes. The town's collection of hideous industrial relics sprouts up from a patchwork of picturesque pine forests and cool blue rivulets. Despite the unsightly Soviet reminders, it's worth stopping by for a wildlife photo shoot and a Cold War history lesson.

After entering Līgatne, the road forks in three different directions. If you follow the road as it curves to the right, you will wind your way up a small hill until you reach a dreary rehabilitation centre. This is no ordinary rehab hospital; hidden underneath the bland '60s architecture lies a top-secret Soviet bunker, known by its code name, **The Pension** (☏6416 1915, 2646 7747; www .bunkurs.lv; Skaļupes; admission per person/group from 3/30Ls; ☺3pm Mon-Fri; noon, 2pm, 4pm Sat & Sun). When Latvia was part of the USSR, 'The Pension' was one of the most important strategic hideouts during a time of nuclear threat. In fact, the bunker's location was so tightly guarded that it remained classified information until 2003. Almost all of the bunker's 2000 sq m still look as they did when it was in operation. It is interesting to note that there is only one bed in the entire bunker even though it was designed for a large crew complement (250 people) – workers were meant to sleep at their stations. Tours last up to 1½ hours and can be translated into English and German. Weekend tours include a (surprisingly tasty) Soviet-style lunch served within the bunker's cafeteria. Note the plastic flowers on the table – they've been adorning the dining hall since 1982.

Should you decide to follow Līgatne's main road straight on, rather than forking, you will reach a collection of charred crimson brick and soaring smoke stacks known as **Papīrfabrika** (Paper Factory; ☏2943 4104; Pilsoņu iela 1), Latvia's oldest industrial enterprise. In the not-so-distant past, the plant was used to print maps for the Russian army, and it also minted Estonia's paper currency. Today, the factory is still in operation and continues to use traditional paper-production machinery. Tours can be organised through the tourist information centre.

Those who decide to head left will find the **Līgatne Nature Trails** (☏6415 3313; adult/child/car 2.50/1/5Ls; ☺9.30am-5pm Mon, to 6.30pm Tue-Sun), a nature park where elk, beaver, deer, bison, lynx and wild boar roam in sizable open-air enclosures in the forest (it feels like an open-air zoo). A 5.1km motor circuit and a network of footpaths link a series of observation points, and there's a 22m lookout tower with a fine panorama. The marked footpaths include a 5.5km nature trail with wild animals, a botanical trail (1.1km), and a wild nature trail (1.3km).

Those who decide to stay the night should check out the adorable **Lāču Miga** (☏6415 3481; www.lacumiga.lv; Gaujas iela 22; s/d from 30/40Ls) near the nature trails. Built in a large log chalet, the 'Bears' Den' stays true to its moniker with a gargantuan plush teddy

LATVIA GAUJA NATIONAL PARK

bear positioned at the front entrance. Slews of stuffed bears welcome guests in their rooms – there are even ursine pillows that look like a teddy bear that's swallowed a giant Rubik's cube. The attached **restaurant** (mains from 3.50Ls; ☺lunch & dinner Sat & Sun) offers pleasant outdoor seating overlooking the scenic nature trails nearby.

Before returning to Rte A2, stop by **Vienkoču Parks** (☑2932 9065; www.vienkoci .lv; adult/child 2/1Ls; ☺10am-6pm). Rihards, a local wood carver, has filled a 10-hectare park with his unique creations. Small trails snake past bold modern art installations, a classical garden, sundials and a collection of torture instruments. Rent out the park's rustic cabin (25Ls), lit by candles in the evenings, for a 'back to nature' experience.

ℹ Getting There & Around
Public transport to Līgatne requires a bit of patience. Two buses per hour trundle along the Cēsis–Sigulda route, stopping in Līgatne along the way (1Ls). If you have your own transport, it's a quick 20-minute drive from either Sigulda or Cēsis.

CĒSIS
POP 19,500

Cēsis' unofficial moniker, 'Latvia's most Latvian town', is a bit of a chicken-and-the-egg mystery: was Cēsis (pronounced *tsay*-sis) always known by this superlative, or did it only earn the title after the government emptied their coffers while renovating the Old Town? Either way, the nickname pretty much holds true, and day trippers will be treated to a mosaic of quintessential country life – a stunning Livonian castle, soaring church spires, cobbled roads, wooden architecture and a lazy lagoon – all wrapped up in a bow like an adorable adult Disneyland.

⊙ Sights

TOP CHOICE Cēsis Castle
RUINS
(Cēsu pils; tours available for 20Ls) Founded in 1209 by the Knights of the Sword, Cēsis Castle's dominant feature is its two stout towers at the western end. To enter, visit **Cēsis History & Art Museum** (Cēsu Vēstures un mākslas muzejs; Pils laukums 9; adult/child 2/1Ls; ☺10am-6pm), in the adjoining 18th-century 'new castle'. Note the flag flying above – this was the first place in the country to fly the Latvian flag (in 1988 before the country officially broke free from the Soviet Union). The castle's western tower has a viewpoint overlooking

Castle Park, which sits along a scenic lake with lily pads. Temporary art exhibitions and chamber-music concerts are held in **Cēsis Exhibition House** (Cēsu Izstāžu nams; ☑6412 3557; Pils laukums 3; ☺10am-6pm), next to the tourist office on the same square. The yellow-and-white building housed stables and a coach house (1781) in the 18th and 19th centuries.

Old Town
NEIGHBOURHOOD

Cēsis' Old Town, surrounding Cēsis Castle, is a delightful collection of wooden houses, restored art-nouveau facades, and colourful town squares orbiting the commanding St John's Church.

🏃 Activities
In winter, skiers and snowboarders pootle down the gentle slopes and cross-country trails at **Žagarkalns** (☑2626 6266; www .zagarkalns.lv; 3hr lift pass weekday/weekend 5.50/8Ls) and **Ozolkalns** (☑2640 0200; www .ozolkalns.lv; 3hr lift pass weekday/weekend 7/9Ls), the two largest skiing areas in Vidzeme. In summer, they offer bicycle and canoe rentals, and Ozolkalns has a ropes course. Ask at the tourist office to set up a bike rental if you can't make it out to one of the hills.

🎎 Festivals & Events
There are concerts and festivals almost every weekend during the summer.

From mid-July to mid-August, Cēsis comes alive on the weekends with performances, ranging from symphonies to storytelling, held at a variety of venues around town as part of the **Mākslas Festivāls** (http://cesufestivals.lv).

🛏 Sleeping
Cēsis has loads of respectable accommodation several kilometres outside of the town centre. Check out www.tourism.cesis .lv for more information and photos.

Province
B&B €€
(☑6412 0849; www.provincecesis.viss.lv; Niniera iela 6; r 32Ls) This cute celery-green guesthouse pops out from the dreary Soviet block housing nearby. The five rooms are simple, spotless and sport funky bedspreads. The popular in-house restaurant in a glass solarium serves up a variety of tasty dishes including a few veggie options (mains start from 2.50Ls).

Hostel Putiņkrogs
HOSTEL €
(☑6412 0290; www.cdzp.lv, in Latvian; Saules iela 23; s/d with shared bathroom 9-15Ls; ☎) Find

Cēsis

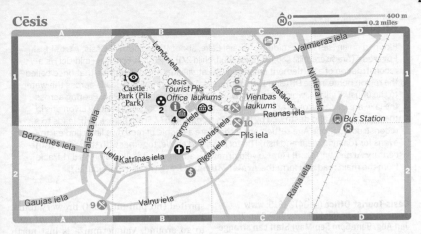

Cēsis

◎ Sights

1 Castle Park (Pils Park)	B1
2 Cēsis Castle	B1
3 Cēsis Exhibition House	B1
4 Cēsis History & Art Museum	B1
5 St John's Church	B2

🛏 Sleeping

| 6 Kolonna Hotel Cēsis | C1 |
| 7 Province | C1 |

🍴 Eating

8 Aroma	C1
9 Maxima Supermarket	A2
10 Sarunas	C1

the sign with a symbol of a fork and knife, and you've just about reached this grubby Soviet-style building. Pass the doors for the convenience store and cafe to find shockingly cheery (and tidy) rooms – even the once-sterile lobby is warmed with a mural of technicolour flowers. The hostel is located 900m west of the bus/train station.

Kolonna Hotel Cēsis HOTEL €€€
(☎6412 0122; www.hotelkolonna.com; Vienības laukums 1; r €60; @🛜) The exterior is vaguely neoclassical while the inside features rows of standard upmarket rooms. The in-house restaurant serves top-notch Latvian and European cuisine (mains 4Ls to 10Ls) in a formal setting or outdoors in the pristine garden.

🍴 Eating

Most of the accommodation in Cēsis has quality restaurants attached. Beyond that, the town has a limited amount of worthwhile eats. Consider swinging by **Maxima Supermarket** (Livu laukums; ⊙9am-10pm) to pick up some groceries for a picnic along the rambling stone steps between the castle ruins and the lake.

2 Locals CAFE €€
(Rīgas iela 24a; mains 4-10Ls; ⊙9am-midnight Sun-Thu, to 2am Fri & Sat) Cēsis' most noble attempt at savvy, locally sourced fare, 2 Locals is a new player in the town's small dining scene, and it's stirring things up with a delectable assortment of meat and fish dishes; don't miss the scrumptious homemade desserts!

Sarunas PIZZA €
(Rīgas iela 4; pizzas 2.50-4Ls; ⊙lunch & dinner) Sleek Sarunas dishes out decent pizzas to a mix of young locals and older tourists. Grab a booth on the outdoor terrace for excellent views of the central square and Cēsis' charming wooden architecture. A disco ball spins stars on the walls in the evening.

Aroma CAFE €€
(Lencu iela 4; mains 4-8Ls; ⊙8am-8pm Mon-Sat, 10am-8pm Sun) Enjoy cake and coffee on the shaded patio overflowing with colourful flowers. At night the back opens into a slick club with an industrial vibe – red walls and silver piping.

ℹ Information

There are two banks with ATMs on Raunas iela between the bus/train station and the main square (Vienības laukums).

ĀRAIŠI

Plopped on an islet in the middle of Āraiši Lake, about 10km south of Cēsis, **Āraiši Lake Fortress** (Āraišu ezerpils; ☑6419 7288; adult/child 2/1Ls; ☺10am-6pm May–mid-Oct) is a reconstruction of a settlement inhabited by Latgallians, an ancient tribe that once called the region home in the 9th and 10th centuries. A wooden walkway leads across the water to the unusual village, which was discovered by archaeologists in 1965. Peering across the lake are the ruins of **Āraiši Stone Castle** (Āraišu mūra pils), built by Livonians in the 14th century and destroyed by Ivan IV's troops in 1577. From here, a path leads to a reconstructed Stone Age settlement – there are a couple of reed dwellings and earth ovens for roasting meat and fish. The fortress and castle, together with the iconic 18th-century **Āraiši windmill** (Āraišu vējdzirnavas), are signposted 1km along a dirt track from the main road and form the **Āraiši Museum Park** (Āraišu muzejparks).

Cēsis Tourist Office (☑6412 1815; www.tourism.cesis.lv; Pils laukums 9; ☺9am-7pm Jun-Aug, 9am-6pm Sep-May) Staff can arrange bike rentals (6Ls per day), and accommodation bookings in Cēsis and rural Vidzeme. Internet available in 10-minute intervals (0.30Ls).

DnB Nord (Rigas iela 23; ☺7.30am-6.30pm Mon-Fri, to 4.30pm Sat) Bank with 24-hour outdoor ATM.

❶ Getting There & Away

Cēsis' bus and train station can be found in the same location at the roundabout connecting Raunas iela to Raiņa iela. There are up to five trains per day between 6.35am and 9pm linking Cēsis and Rīga (2.30Ls, two hours). Bikes are allowed onboard. Two or three buses per hour between 6.15am and 10.20pm ply the route from Cēsis to Rīga, stopping in Līgatne and Sigulda. Trains also run to Valmiera (0.71Ls, 30 minutes) and Sigulda (0.90Ls, 40 minutes).

VALMIERA
POP 27,000

Although less historic than Sigulda or Cēsis, as most of its Old Town burnt down in 1944, Valmiera (formerly Wolmar) dishes out its own brand of easy college-town charm. About 30km north of Cēsis, it sits at the northeastern tip of the Gauja National Park, and is the only place in Latvia where you can board a canoe in the heart of downtown.

◉ Sights

Valmiera's historic area stands on a point of land between the Gauja River and a tributary called the Ažkalna.

Valmiermuiža   BREWERY
(☑2026 4296; www.valmiermuiza.lv; Dzirnavu iela 2; admission 3.50Ls; ☺open every day by appointment) Home to Latvia's most popular ale, Valmiermuiža offers visitors a chance to see how the magic is made on their

spirited (no pun intended) brewery tours. Expect friendly guides and plenty of grog to go around. Valmiermuiža is just north of the city centre, past Hotel Wolmar and Viestura laukums.

St Simon's Church   CHURCH
(Svētā Sīmaņa Baznīca; Bruņinieku iela 2) St Simon's Church dates to 1283 and shelters a fine 19th-century organ. You can climb its church tower for a donation. Along the same street you'll find the ruins of **Valmiera Castle**, founded by the Livonian Order in the 13th century.

Valmiera Regional Museum   MUSEUM
(Valmieras Novadpētniecības muzejs; ☑6423 2733; Bruņinieku iela 3; adult/child 0.50/0.30Ls; ☺10am-5pm Mon-Fri, to 3pm Sat) This museum is of limited interest, but it's a good source of information on the district...if you read Latvian. English guides are available for 15Ls.

☘ Activities

The tourist office can assist with bike rentals. It also has pamphlets detailing biking routes throughout the region. The most popular route is the ride between Valmiera and Cēsis (42km), which is flagged by orange labels along the way. You'll need a mountain bike to tackle the trek properly. A shorter route from Valmiera to Brenguli, just 10km east, is more about the scenic journey than the destination.

Eži   ADVENTURE SPORTS
(☑6420 7263; www.ezi.lv; Valdemāra iela; ☺9am-7pm Mon-Sat, to 1pm Sun) In town, Eži, once a popular hostel, now concentrates solely on outdoor adventures. It organises all sorts of active pursuits from themed one- or two-day hiking and biking excursions to

river rafting to zip-wires through the trees (trips start at 20Ls per day). It also rents out mountain bikes (6Ls per day), helmets (2Ls per day), saddlebags and seats for kids (each 2Ls per day) along with canoes (10Ls per day). In winter the company does cross-country skiing tours across lakes and through snow-covered forests complete with picnic lunch cooked over a bonfire in the woods.

🛏 Sleeping

Elēna Guest House   GUESTHOUSE €

(☏2929 9287; www.elena.viss.lv; Garā iela 8; r 15Ls) If you ignore the particleboard floors, Elēna is great value for your money – the eight rooms above the cafe have TVs, sparkling bathrooms and comfy beds with plenty of squishy pillows. Cash only. Wi-fi available. If you're arriving into Valmiera from the south (like most visitors), cross over the river and go west down Rīgas iela.

Mēnesnīca   HOSTEL €

(☏6423 2556; menesnica@4id.lv; Vadu iela 3; dm/ s/d with shared bathroom 5/8/16Ls) The up-side: Mēnesnīca has ridiculously low prices and it's walking distance to the train station. The downside: no English is spoken here. Climb this Tower of Babel to find sun-filled rooms sprouting off rather derelict hallways. The dorm rooms are cramped, but hey, it's only 5Ls.

Wolmar   HOTEL €€

(☏6420 7301; www.hotelwolmar.lv; Tērbatas iela 16a; r 35Ls; @🛜) The town's upmarket choice features 30 rooms in a yellow and black–striped hotel. It's a testament to Valmiera's limited selection of quality accommodation.

🍴 Eating & Drinking

Those who visit little Valmiera are limited to the following dining options (in addition to the restaurants at their lodging), which are all surprisingly decent.

Rātes Vārti   INTERNATIONAL €€

(☏6428 1942; Lāčplēša iela 1; salads 1.50-4Ls, mains 3-9Ls; ⊙noon-11pm Sun-Thu, to midnight Fri & Sat) The decor leaves something to be desired – napkins are fanned out like peacocks, and the walls are blotted with sponge paint – but locals flock to this joint across from the theatre for their excellent assortment of delicious meat dishes.

Bastions Bistro   CAFETERIA €

(☏2925 8168; Bastiona iela 24; mains 1-4Ls; ⊙8am-9pm Sun-Thu, to 10pm Fri & Sat) Housed in a stately yellow manor house high on a hill overlooking the river, Bastions is Valmiera's cheapest spot to grab a bite. Locals line up at the entrance to the basement cafeteria for the standard array of hearty Latvian dishes, as well as a couple of happy surprises like a salad bar, ice cream and lemon-spritzed salmon. Outdoor seating overlooking the water is available during the summer months.

Jauna Saule   CAFE €

(☏6423 3812; Rīgas iela 10; mains from 3Ls; ⊙noon-10pm Sun-Tue, to midnight Wed-Thu, to 2am Fri & Sat) This bar and cafe dishes out a vast array of Latvian fare. There's an attached nightclub, and also a plastic jungle gym to keep the tykes busy while you have a relaxing lunch on the inviting summer terrace overlooking busy Rīgas iela.

☆ Entertainment

Valmiera Drama Theatre   THEATRE

(☏6420 7335; www.vdt.lv; Lāčplēsa iela 4; ⊙box office 10am-6.30pm Mon-Fri, 11am-2pm Sat & Sun) The Valmiera Drama Theatre began in 1919, and has garnered a lot of respect around the nation as one of the top repertory theatres. Check the website for show times and production details.

❶ Information

Pilsetas Galerija, the giant glass cube at the roundabout connecting Cēsu iela and Rīgas iela, contains an **Iki supermarket** (⊙8am-10pm), a **post office** (⊙10am-10pm) and several 24-hour ATMs among other conveniences. The Valmiera **tourist office** (☏6420 7177; www.valmiera.lv; Rīgas iela 10; ⊙9am-6pm Mon-Fri, 10am-5pm Sat, 10am-3pm Sun Jun-Aug, 9am-6pm Mon-Fri, 10am-3pm Sat Sep-May; 🛜) has maps and friendly staff who can arrange private accommodation and bike rentals. Free internet and wi-fi available.

❶ Getting There & Away

Both Valmiera **bus station** (Mazā Stacijas iela 1) and **train station** (☏6429 6203; Stacijas laukums) are on the opposite side of the river from central Valmiera. The bus station is within easy walking distance (500m) of the town centre, but the train station is further afield (1.8km) along Stacijas iela (which diverges from Cēsu iela at the bus station). Buses run twice hourly between 4.50am and 7.55pm to/from Rīga (3Ls to 3.20Ls, around 2¼ hours). Other services include 15 buses per day to/from Cēsis (1.10Ls, 45 minutes).

The train station is served by four trains daily to/from Rīga (2.80Ls, 2¼ hours) via Cēsis (0.71Ls, 30 minutes) and Sigulda (0.90Ls, 40 minutes).

Alūksne & Gulbene

Located in the far eastern corner of the country, the regions of Alūksne and Gulbene are far removed from the well-trodden tourist trail. Most visitors come to the area to take a ride on the **Gulbene–Alūksne Narrow-Gauge Railway** (☑6447 3037; www.banitis.lv; one-way ticket 2.64Ls), one of two narrow-gauge railways still operating in Latvia. There are two departures per day in either direction. The full ride takes one hour and 25 minutes.

The town of Gulbene is rundown and holds little interest for tourists. By contrast, sleepy Alūksne, the town with the largest percentage of ethnic Latvians, is a charming little village with clusters of quaint wooden houses. Ernest Glueck (1654–1705), the Lutheran clergyman who translated the Bible into Latvian, was from Alūksne, and his home has been converted into the **Ernest Glueck Bible Museum** (Ernsta Glika Bībeles muzejs; Pils iela 25a; adult/child 0.40/0.20Ls; ⊙10am-5pm Tue-Thu, 8am-5pm Fri, 10am-2pm Sat).

Stop by the **Alūksne Tourist Office** (☑6432 2804; www.aluksne.lv; Dārza iela 8a, Alūksne; ⊙8am-6pm Jun-Aug, to 5pm Sep-May) or the **Gulbene Tourist Office** (☑6449 7729; www.gulbene.lv; Ābelu iela 2-44, Gulbene; ⊙8am-6pm Jun-Aug, to 5pm Sep-May) for more info on the area's activities and accommodations.

If you are riding the narrow-gauge rail, consider getting off in the village of Stāmeriena to find the **Stāmeriena Castle** (☑6449 2054; www.stamerienaspils.lv; adult/child 0.70/0.20Ls; ⊙10am-5pm Mon-Sat). Owned by the affluent von Wolff family, the rambling manorhouse was passed down through many generations. In the 1920s, Alexandra von Wolff inherited the castle and had a largely publicised affair with noted Italian writer Giuseppe di Lampedusa, author of *The Leopard*. She later divorced her husband to marry the writer in Rīga. Visitors can tour the property grounds, and venture inside to see several interior rooms, some with dedicated exhibits about the castle's colourful history.

 Getting There & Around

Alūksne can be reached by bus from Rīga (four to 4½ hours, seven daily) and Madona (two to 2½ hours, two daily). Gulbene can also be reached from Rīga via a different bus route (3½ to 4½ hours, seven daily). There is one daily bus that connects Alūksne and Gulbene (1¼ hours).

Vidzeme Uplands

Did you know that there is no word for 'mountain' in Latvian? It's true. The word never evolved in the Latvian language for one very simple reason: there are no mountains in Latvia. The word *kalns* (hill) is used instead to describe scrubby bumps in the terrain. Latvia's biggest *kalns* is Gaiziņkalns, gradually rising to a whopping 312m (about 70m shorter than the Empire State Building). But Latvians are a resourceful bunch who appreciate the fruits of their land – even if it's vertically challenged – so little Gaiziņkalns is adored as the country's top spot for skiers and snowboarders.

Rīga's LIDO chain has opened a Latvian-themed holiday complex, **LIDO Kirsona Muiža** (☑2784 1446; Kalnadzisli), at the base of the hill, serving pints and pork tongue in a wonderfully synthetic country inn.

The uplands' economic centre is located 10km east of Gaiziņkalns in the town of **Madona** (pronounced *mah*-dwoh-nah – the emphasis is on the first syllable, unlike the pop diva). The friendly staff at the town's **tourist office** (☑6486 0573; Saieta laukums 1; ⊙8am-6pm Mon-Sat) can help get you sorted with a variety of accommodation and activities, including tours of **Teiči Nature Reserve** (Teiči reservāts; 190 sq km), the Baltic's biggest swamp, and **Krustkalni Nature Reserve** (Krustkalni rezervāts; 30 sq km), a leafy realm of indigenous vegetatian. Both parks are located south of Madona, and their fragile ecosystems require visitors to always be accompanied by a guide.

For a dose of culture, head to the former home of Latvian writer Rūdolfs Blaumanis (1863–1908) at **Braki** (adult/child 0.80/0.30Ls; ⊙10am-6pm mid-May–Nov), 30km west of Madona. The Jurjāni brothers, noted Latvian musicians, lived at **Meņģeļi** (adult/child 0.50/0.20Ls; ⊙10am-6pm mid-May–Nov), now a picturesque open-air museum and farmstead by Lake Pulgosnis.

Spa junkies should look no further than the luxurious **Marciena Manor** (☑6480 7300; www .marciena.com; d incl breakfast 80Ls; @⌗), a renovated country estate dedicated to the art of relaxation. The manor is located just outside of Sauleskalns, 11km south of Madona.

❶ Getting There & Around

Like every other region in Latvia, the Vidzeme Uplands are best explored by private vehicle. Buses link Madona to Rīga (3½ hours, 10 daily), Cēsis (three daily, 1¾ to two hours), Jēkabpils (1¾ hours, three daily) and Alūksne (2½ to three hours, two daily).

SOUTHEASTERN LATVIA (LATGALE)

Toto, I don't think we're in Rīga any more. Latvia's poorest region (and one of the poorest regions in the entire EU), southeastern Latvia sits at the far end of the mighty Daugava River along the Russian border. The area gets its name from the Latgal (Lettish) tribes who lived near the myriad lakes when German crusaders invaded in the 12th and 13th century. Evidence of great medieval battles remain in the form of haunting castle ruins that starkly contrast the hideous Soviet fossils from a much more recent era of oppression. The hushed Latgale Lakelands is the region's pearl (tucked deep within a crusty oyster), offering visitors a chance to push 'pause' on life's problems while idling through friendly lakeside villages topped with glittering steeples.

Daugava River Valley

Latvia's serpentine Daugava River, known as the 'river of fate', winds its way through Latgale, Zemgale and Vidzeme before passing Rīga and emptying out in the Gulf of Rīga. For centuries the river was Latvia's most important transport and trade corridor for clans and kingdoms further east; today goods travel via road (Rte A6) and railway following the northern bank of the river.

For those travelling to the scenic Latgale Lakelands (or gritty Daugavpils), navigating the Daugava River valley could feel like a necessary evil if not for the handful of conveniently placed attractions, which help recount the route's rich history.

From Rīga, the first worthy stopping place is **Salaspils**, just 20km southeast of the city. During WWII this town on the outskirts of the capital was the site of a Nazi concentration camp known as Kurtenhof to the Germans. See the boxed text on p223 for more information.

Lielvārde (leel-*var*-deh), 10km further east, is the hometown of Andrejs Pumpurs, a 19th-century poet best known for weaving an epic poem around the myth of Lāčplēsis, Latvia's national hero. The **Andrejs Pumpurs Museum** (Andreja Pumpura muzejs; ☑6505 3759; adult/child 0.50/0.20Ls; ☉10am-5pm Tue-Sun) has a mildly interesting collection of materials that honour the author and his epic tale. The whopping stone next to the museum was once, legend has it, the mighty Lāčplēsis' bed.

The photogenic ruins of a 13th-century knights' castle lie at the confluence of the Daugava and Perse Rivers in Koknese, 95km southeast of Rīga. Built by German crusaders in 1209, the castle ruins lost some of their dramatic cliff-top position after a hydroelectric dam increased the river's water level. Today the twisting ruins appear to be practically sitting in the river, and the sight is enchanting.

Pause in Jēkabpils, another 43km southeast; the midsized town is split in two by the roaring river. The northern half was once a separate village called Krustpils – today the towns are united and both are riddled with creaky wooden houses and a number of old churches with rusty spires. If you are travelling by train along the Daugava, get off at Krustpils station to visit Jēkabpils. Only a smidgen of English is spoken at the tourist office (☑6523 3822; Brīvības iela 140/142; ☉2-6pm Mon, 10am-6pm Tue-Fri, 10am-2pm Sat) but you'll find loads of brochures detailing activities and accommodation in the region. The small square just beyond has a couple of cafes, and down the street lies the town's best restaurant and lodging option, **Hercogs Jēkabs** (☑6523 3433; www.jnami.lv, in Latvian; Brīvības iela 182; r 35-55Ls).

The rest of the way from Jēkabpils to Daugavpils is a rather boring drive through flat lands with gnarled trees interrupted by the occasional wooden barn or crooked steeple. Those in search of Latgale's myriad lakes can veer off at Līvāni, an indus-

Southeastern Latvia (Latgale)

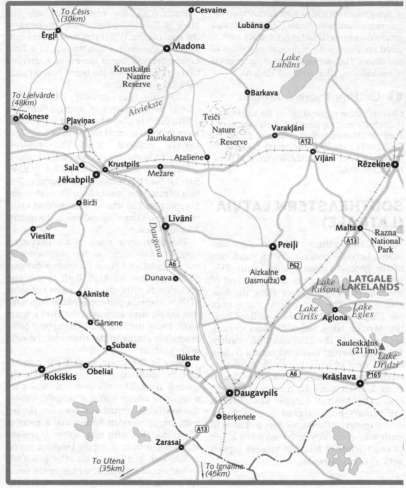

trial town famous for its traditional glass blowing, before moving on.

Daugavpils

POP 102,500

Okay, so sometimes it's hard to smile when the grey sky matches the grey tic-tac-toes of crumbling Soviet block housing – especially in a city with as many prisons as churches – but Latvia's second-largest city really isn't as scary as its reputation. Yes, Rīgans will snicker when the words 'visit' and 'Daugavpils' appear in the same sentence, so

bear in mind that most of them have never even stopped through. Those who have travelled to the heart of Latgale sing a different tune. A trip to Daugavpils will reveal a funky, friendly, energetic vibe that starkly contrasts with the drab architecture.

◉ Sights

Look up beyond the grey gridiron to find swirling church spires of numerous denominations and an impressive sculpture by Mark Rothko, born here in 1903 (he moved to the USA as a young child). The Park Hotel Latgola is the city's unsightly centrepiece,

ist through its exhibition and educational programs in local schools. Plans are in the works to turn an entire building at the city's fortress into an interactive museum dedicated to the artist.

Fortress RUINS
(☎6542 6398; adult/child 0.20/0.10Ls; ☺8am-6pm) Daugavpils' most bizarre attraction is the huge fortress built by the Russians in 1810 on the northwestern side of town. The complex, occupied by the Soviet army until 1993, doesn't fit the typical definition of a fortress – it's more a giant enclosure of uninspired architecture and decaying remains of abandoned hospitals, conference halls, artillery storage and barracks. A section has been turned into decrepit state-assisted housing.

Tickets to the inner compound are sold at the former checkpoint, which has a red-brick monument stating (in Russian and Latvian) that the Tatar poet Musa Jalil languished here from September to October 1942, in what was then the Nazi concentration camp Stalag 340.

🛏 Sleeping

Sventes Muiža MANOR HOUSE €€
(☎6542 5108; www.sventehotel.lv; Alejas iela 7, Svente; d 40Ls; @☎) Sitting in a thicket, 10km west of the city centre, this attractive country estate is a welcome retreat from the drab Soviet gridiron. Rooms are designed with a pinch of aristocratic class, and culinary treats are served up amid flamboyantly framed still lifes.

Park Hotel Latgola HOTEL €€€
(☎6540 4900; www.hotellatgola.lv; Ģimnāzijas iela 46; d 66Ls; @☎) The city's centrepiece and largest building, this Soviet monster sports modern (but overpriced) rooms behind its freshly renovated facade. Check out the views from the hotel's top-storey restaurant and bar.

🍴 Eating & Drinking
Daugavpils' new City Center complex sees most of the local action. During the warmer months, local youngsters sometimes throw parties inside the crumbling walls of Daugavpils' fortress.

Arabika CAFE €
(Viestura iela 8; mains 1-4Ls; ☺lunch & dinner) A social spot with mod furnishings, Arabika sits on the ground level of the popular

but there are intriguing views from the hotel's top-floor restaurant and bar.

Regional Studies & Art Museum MUSEUM
(Novadpētniecības un mākslas muzejs; ☎6542 4073; Rīgas iela 8; adult/child 0.40/0.20Ls; ☺11am-6pm Tue-Sat) Inside an art-nouveau house guarded by stone lions, this museum exhibits high-quality reproductions of abstract painter Mark Rothko's paintings. Although long recognised in the West, Rothko's work remained relatively anonymous in Latvia until the collapse of the Soviet Union. Today the museum is striving to awaken national interest in the art-

City Center. Try the mushroom soup, with locally picked fungi, or go for one of the international dishes; there's sushi, Greek salad and even spicy Indian curry.

Ladidas Park
LATVIAN €

(Rīgas iela 14; mains 3-5Ls; ☺lunch & dinner) Ladidas' lonely chandelier casts soft rays on patrons at this decidedly classy spot that is one taxidermic elk away from being a dimly lit, dark-wood hunting lodge.

Gliemezis
CAFE

(Rīgas iela 22; ☺3pm-1am) A top chill-out spot around town, 'The Snail' feels like a college dorm with tattered sofas, sticky floors and amateur art strung up on the walls. Friday nights are the most happenin'.

Banzai
CLUB

(www.banzai.lv; Viestura iela 8; ☺10pm-5am Fri & Sat) The grind-worthy beats at Banzai blast so loud you can feel the base tremors back in Rīga. In fact, this joint's hardcore party rep is so widespread that Rīgans are often lured down for a weekend of revelry.

❶ Information

City Center (Viestura iela 8; ☺10am-6am; 📶) Internet, wi-fi access and ATMs available.

Post office (Stacijas iela 42) Next to the train station.

Tourist office (Rīgas iela 22a; ☺9am-5pm Mon-Sat)

❶ Getting There & Away

There are four rail routes radiating out from Daugavpils' **train station** (☑6548 7261, Stacijas iela), which head to Rīga (4.70Ls to 5.20Ls, three to four hours, three daily), Vilnius (2½, one daily) and Rēzekne (1¼ hours, one daily).

From the **bus station** (☑6542 3000; www .buspark.lv; Viestura iela 10) buses run to/ from Rīga (5.60Ls, 3¾ hours, one hourly) and Rēzekne (2.50Ls, 1½ to two hours, seven daily).

Latgale Lakelands

A secret realm of greens and blues, Latvia's land of enchanting lakes has stolen the hearts of many. Hidden runes suggest that the region was first settled at the end of the Stone Age when wandering hunters, captivated by the area's serene beauty, paused along **Lake Lubāns**, Latvia's largest, covering 82 sq km. Thousands of years later, vital trade routes zigzagged between the languid lagoons connecting faraway capitals like Warsaw and St Petersburg. Today, the hushed forests and lakeside villages attract those seeking simpler times and pleasures.

RĒZEKNE & AROUND
POP 34,500

Rēzekne furtively pokes its head up from a giant muddle of derelict factories and generic block housing. The town took a heavy beating during WWII when most of its historic buildings were pulverised by artillery fire. Today, there isn't much to keep a tourist in town (even the castle ruins aren't that impressive); however, frequent trains and buses make it a convenient jumping-off point to explore the quiet lakeland further south.

The main street, Atbrīvošanas alejā, runs from Rēzekne II train station (north) to the bus station (south), and crosses the central square en route. In the square's middle stands **Māra**, a statue twice destroyed by the Soviet authorities in the 1940s and only re-erected in 1992. Its inscription 'Vienoti Latvijai' means 'United Latvia'.

Across from Māra, you'll find the town's **tourist office** (☑6460 5005; www.rezekne .lv; Atbrīvošvanas alejā 98; ☺9am-5pm Mon-Fri) tucked inside **Hotel Latgale** (☑6462 2180; www.hotellatgale.lv; Atbrīvosvanas alejā 98; s/d from 30/42Ls), a passable sleeping option in town.

Continue along Atbrīvošanas alejā and take a walk down **Latgales iela**, the town's oldest street, which is lined with dozens of charming brick facades constructed by wealthy Yiddish merchants several hundred years ago.

If you've noticed the enormous **stork nests** dotting the Latvian countryside, then head to **Untumi** (☑6463 1255; www.untumi.lv, in Latvian) a country ranch 7km northwest of town signposted off Rte A12. Here you'll find cameras and binoculars set up around a couple of stork nests allowing tourists to watch the mothers feeding their young. **Horseback riding** is available as well (9Ls for one hour).

Follow Rte P55 south of Rēzekne to find **Ezerkrasti Resort** (☑2645 0437; www.razna slicis.lv; Dukstigals, Čornajas pagasts; s from 8Ls, cottage 45Ls) along the banks of Lake Rāzna, Latvia's largest lake by volume. The lake is located within Razna National Park, a quiet preserve protecting roughly 600 sq km of Latgale's lakeland. The lush green property, dotted with charming wooden cottages, offers volleyball, paddleboats, a lake for swimming, and an indoor pool and sauna. On the other side of the lake, along Rte P56, is **Rāznas Gulbis** (☑2999 4444; www.razna.lv; d from 28Ls, townhouse from 120Ls), a spacious resort with paddleboats, an on-site **restaurant** (☺noon-11pm) and a small 'aquarium' of corralled fish in the lake.

ℹ Getting There & Around

The **bus station** (Latgales iela 17) has services to/from Daugavpils (2.50Ls, 1¾ to 2¼ hours, seven daily), Ludza (1Ls to 1.10Ls, 30 minutes to one hour, hourly), Preiļi (1.70Ls to 2Ls, one to 1¾ hours, seven daily) and Rīga (5.90Ls to 6.70Ls, four to 4½ hours, seven daily), among other destinations.

Rēzekne II train station (Stacijas iela) has one train daily each way between Rīga and St Petersburg, and Rīga and Moscow. In all, there are six trains daily to/from Rīga (3.66Ls, three to 3¾ hours). Only the St Petersburg–Vilnius train (every second day) stops at the Rēzekne I train station.

LUDZA
POP 15,000

Little Ludza, just a hop from the Russian border, was founded in 1177, making it the oldest town in all of Latvia. Located at the junction of two lakes (known as Big Ludza Lake and Little Ludza Lake), the small village and trading post grew around **Ludza Castle**, built by German crusaders in 1399 to protect the eastern front of the Livonian Order. The castle has been in ruins since 1775, and today the melange of crumbling crimson brick and smoky grey boulders is both haunting and beautiful, and makes a great place for a picnic overlooking the church spires and rivulets down the hill.

The **Ludza Craftsmen Centre** (☑2946 7925; www.ludzasamatnieki.lv; Tālavijas iela 27a; ☺9am-5pm Tue-Sat) features an excellent selection of locally made handicrafts. The centre has three attached workshops in which local artisans perfect their trade. If you ring ahead, you too can try your hand at time-honoured methods of wool spinning, pottery making and sewing. There's a collection of old tools to peruse and a traditional Latgalian costume to try on for picture taking.

ℹ Getting There & Around

Ludza is located 26km east of Rēzekne along Rte A12 as it makes its way into Russia. Traffic can often be an issue along the A12 as vehicles line up to cross the border (note the abundance of porta-potties along the side of the road for the truck drivers waiting hours on end to pass through the red tape at customs). An hourly bus connects Luzda to Rēzekne, and there's one bus per day linking Ludza to Rīga.

KRĀSLAVA
POP 19,700

Sleepy Krāslava sits 6km north of Belarus at the southern tip of the triangular Latgale lakelands region. Founded by a Polish nobleman in the 18th century, Krāslava was established as a trade centre along the Daugava River. Many craftsmen moved to the town from Poland to trade with wealthy Jewish and Russian merchants from down the river. Due to the heavy Polish influence, Krāslava is predominantly Catholic and has several white-washed houses of worship, including **St Donath Catholic Church** along the town's main drag.

For a view of the town, head to **Karņička Hill**, which is marked with a large cross – the tomb of a lovelorn soldier. According to legend, a young Polish officer was invited to Krāslava Castle for a party and fell in love with the lord's daughter. She too was struck by Cupid's arrow, but her father wouldn't allow them to get married. Crestfallen, the lovers decided that they couldn't live without each other and planned a suicide pact. At the stroke of midnight the lord's daughter would light a candle from her bedroom, meaning that she was ready to jump out of the window and plummet to her death. The officer, once having seen the candle, would shoot himself. When the young soldier saw the flickering light, he followed through with his promise, but the maiden was caught by her nurse before she had a chance to jump.

From the top of Karņička Hill, one quickly understands why Krāslava has been dubbed the 'Cucumber City' of Latvia – tonnes of small cucumber farms are peppered among the collection of humble wooden homes below.

Stop by the **pottery studio** (☑2912 8695; valdispaulins@inbox.lv; Dūmu iela 8; group demonstration 5Ls, clay 0.50Ls; ☺9am-7.30pm) run by Valdis and Olga Paulins, a husband-and-wife team who preserve the traditional Latgalian method of creating and decorating ceramics. There's a bit of a language barrier if you don't speak Latvian, Russian or German, but the friendly couple offer spirited demonstrations with big smiles and even bigger hand gestures. If you contact them in advance, they can recruit a local to swing by and translate. Although it takes quite a bit of time and talent to sculpt a vase or pot, you can learn in a matter of minutes how to make a clay duck whistle (and we guarantee you'll have a chuckle when you find out where you have to blow).

Take Rte P161 towards the village of Dagda to reach two quality lakeside resorts. Follow the signs for Konstantanova to reach **Dridži** (☑2944 1221; www.dridzi.lv; tent 4Ls, d weekday/weekend 20/25Ls, camper-van parking 7Ls, d weekday/weekend 20/25Ls, cottage weekday/weekend 50/60Ls), the perfect spot for families, featuring volleyball nets, tugboats, rafts and a lovely hillside dotted with wooden gazebos. Each cottage comes with a fully equipped kitchen. Also on Lake Dridži, **Sauleskalns** (☑2619 0186; info@skalns.lv) is popular in the winter for its gentle ski slope – the longest in Latvia. Rent a boat during the summer months and paddle around the deepest lake in the region. New motel units overlooking the water were being completed when we stopped by to have a look. Both recreation destinations are open year-round.

For those interested in horseback riding, head to **Klajumi Stables** (☑2947 2638; www .klajumi.lv; 2-/4-/7-day tours 75/189/359Ls, 1 hr trot 10Ls), 11km southwest of Krāslava near Kaplava. Ilze, the owner, comes from a long line of horse keepers and offers a variety of activities from overnight riding trips to simple countryside afternoon gallops. The adorable guest cottage (weekday/weekend 30/50Ls) looks like a gingerbread house and comes with a sauna (that doubles as a shower), kitchenette and lofted bedroom with satellite TV. The toilet is located in an outhouse nearby.

❶ Getting There & Around

To reach Krāslava, take Rte A6 east from Daugavpils, or follow Rte P62 from Aglona. There is one daily bus that plies the route from Krāslava to Aglona and on to Preiļi.

AGLONA

Believe it or not, teeny Aglona (*a*-glwo-nuh) is one of the most visited towns in all of Latvia, primarily due to the **Aglona Basilica** (☑6538 1109; Cirisu iela 8; ⊙gift shop/info booth 10am-3pm & 4-7pm Mon-Fri, 9am-3pm & 4-7pm Sat & Sun), founded over 300 years ago when a group of wandering Dominican monks discovered a healing source hidden among a thicket of spruce trees ('Aglona' means 'spruce tree' in an old dialect). Although the sulphur fount lost its apparent power a century later, pilgrims still visit the site and incorporate the spring water in their religious rituals, especially on Ascension Day (15 August).

The 18th-century church lies along the shores of Lake Egles in a vast grass courtyard, created for Pope John Paul II's visit in 1993 to bestow the title of 'Basilica Minoris' (Small Basilica) upon the holy grounds. One of the basilica's 10 altars guards a miraculous icon of the Virgin Mary, said to have saved Aglona from the plague in 1708. Mass is held at 7am and 7pm on weekdays, and at 10am, noon and 7pm on Sundays. Rosary is held at noon on weekdays and at 9.30am on Sundays.

While you're in town, consider stopping by the **Bread Museum** (Aglonas maizes muzejs; ☑2928 7044; www.latvia.travel/en/aglona-bread-museum; Daugavpils iela 7; group admission 25Ls; ⊙9am-6pm Mon-Sat) to learn about the history and traditions surrounding traditional Latgalian dark bread, a local staple. Very little English is spoken so it is best to call ahead to arrange a complimentary translator for the one-hour presentation. Even if you don't have time for the presentation, you can still stop by for fresher-than-fresh loaves of bread baked minutes before you walk in the door. Peep through the small window into the kitchen to watch the bakers hard at work.

A small **guesthouse** (☑2928 7044; Daugavpils iela 7; dm 10Ls) can be found above the Bread Museum with several cheery dorm rooms swathed in pastels. **Aglonas Cakuli** (☑6537 5465; http://aglonascakuli.lv; Ezera iela 4; s/d from 15/25Ls), another adequate sleeping option, sits one block away along Lake Ciriss.

Around 10km south of Aglona lurks **Devil's Lake** (☑6564 1332; www.lvm.lv), also called Čertoks ('little devil'). For centuries, locals have passed down the tale of a malicious demon that lives at the bottom of the oddly tranquil lagoon. Compasses and sensory equipment never seem to work when activated within the lake's vicinity, which has led scientists to speculate that a magnetic meteor sits below the crystalline surface. Some believe that a little devil never existed and that the name Čertoks is a bastardisation of the Russian word Čertog, which means 'beautiful place'. To reach Devil's Lake, take Rte P62 towards Krāslava; the turn-off to the lake is not marked (to avoid a deluge of tourists), so you will have to get directions from the friendly staff at the **Aglona Tourist**

Office (☏6532 2100; www.aglona.lv, in Latvian; Somersētas iela 34; ⊙10am-6pm Mon-Fri, to 3pm Sat Jun-Aug, 9am-5pm Mon-Fri Sep-May). To check email, head to the town's library (Daugavpils iela 37; ⊙10am-6pm Mon-Fri, to 3pm Sat; ☎), which has free internet access and wi-fi.

❶ Getting There & Around
Aglona village, wedged between Lake Egles (east) and Lake Ciriss (west), is 31km north of Krāslava along Rte P62, and 9km off the main road between Daugavpils and Rēzekne (Rte A13), which crosses the western part of the Latgale Lakelands. Several daily buses connect Aglona and Preiļi.

PREIĻI
POP 11,600
There isn't a lot to do in provincial Preiļi (*pray-* lee), but a stop at the tourist office (tic@preili.lv; Kārsavas iela 4; ⊙8.30am-5pm Mon-Sat Jun-Aug, 8.30am-5pm Mon-Fri Sep-May) is helpful if you are just arriving in the Latgale lakelands region. The English-speaking staff can offer activities suggestions and help arrange accommodation at a countryside guesthouse. The attached library (⊙10am-8pm Mon-Fri, to 5pm Sat & Sun; ☎) has free internet and wi-fi access. Note that the info office is usually closed for lunch between noon and 12.30pm.

Jānis Rainis (1865–1929), known as the Shakespeare of Latvia, wrote some of his earliest works in Aizkalne (also called Jasmuiža), 12km south of town. There, the small Rainis Museum (☏6535 4677; admission 0.30-0.70Ls; ⊙10am-5pm Tue-Sat mid-May–Nov) showcases traditional Latgalian pottery as well as changing literary exhibitions devoted to the poet.

❶ Getting There & Around
Preiļi is about halfway between Daugavpils and Rēzekne, about 16km north of the junction of Rte A13 and Rte P62. There is one daily bus that plies the route from Preiļi to Aglona and on to Krāslava.

UNDERSTAND LATVIA

Latvia Today
Oh what a ride it's been for little Latvia over the last 20 years, since the country first broke free from the Soviet Union in 1991. What was once a fledgeling post-Soviet nation has quickly become a free-thinking society that is eager to take its place on the global stage. While Estonia looks towards Scandinavia for precedents, and Lithuania seems to be looking at Poland for its modern cues, Latvia is gazing in all different directions as it assembles a brilliant kaleidoscope of ideas. The region may have thousands of years of history behind it, but modern Latvia is yet to be defined.

In the last couple of years, it seems that political machinations have taken centre stage as the country attempts to relieve itself of the economic troubles that have resulted from the global crisis. At the forefront of the parliamentary upheaval is the notion that three Russian oligarchs wield a disproportionate amount of local power and are pushing the country a bit too close towards Russia. In fact, former president Zatlers called for the dissolution of parliament when laws safeguarding the nation against oligarchical rule were not passed. The parliament was indeed dissolved towards the end of 2011 as the new president – Andris Bērziņš – took office. As it stands, the future of Latvia's political and economic relationship with Russia remains to be completely defined, although it seems quiet clear that the tie will strengthen in the upcoming years.

Although the country has been slammed by economic turmoil, a subculture of artists has emerged from the rubble. After losing their jobs in the crash, many locals sought comfort in their hobbies and transformed their pastimes into full-time careers. The sudden boom of local art – be it fashion, architecture, music, blogging or design – has ushered in Rīga's blossoming era of hipsterdom.

History
The Beginning
The first signs of modern man in the region date back to the Stone Age, although Latvians descended from tribes that migrated north from around Belarus and settled on the territory of modern Latvia around 2000 BC. These tribes settled in coastal areas to fish and take advantage of rich deposits of amber, which was more precious than gold in many places until the Middle Ages.

Eventually, four main Baltic tribes evolved: the Selonians, the Letts (or Lat-

A PRESIDENTIAL SEAL OF APPROVAL

Former president Vaira Vīķe-Freiberga made quite a name for herself in the European community as a much-needed female political presence. She was the first female Latvian president and held the position for two terms (from 1999 to 2007). The strong leader (and Canadian émigrée) was applauded for returning to her motherland to pull Latvia out of economic uncertainty and catapult the little nation towards EU membership.

We had a chance to sit down with the former president to talk about her life beyond the political spotlight. She offered her impressions of Latvia from a visitor's perspective since she had a chance to view her country with fresh eyes after spending most of her life abroad.

'There are three things in Rīga that everyone should see: the amazing Jugendstil (art-nouveau) architecture, the Blackheads' House, where I used to hold my state dinners, and finally, the Opera House, which, in my opinion, features one of the finest opera companies in the world.

'Beyond Rīga, which was, by the way, at one time a bigger port than Stockholm, I would encourage visitors to seek out the many festivals around the country, particularly during the summer. Sigulda, Bauska and Rundāle host some of my favourite music festivals. Rundāle Palace is undoubtedly the most famous castle in Latvia, but I personally enjoy the castle in Stāmeriena for its elegant architecture and interesting history. The country's wooden architecture is also of note, particularly in Kurzeme.

'Those who enjoy nature should spend some time in Jūrmala along the Bay of Rīga. I have fond memories of entertaining foreign dignitaries at the presidential estate in Jūrmala – I remember watching a beautiful sunset on my lawn during a barbecue I hosted for Boris Yeltsin. The bay is quite shallow, so it is perfect for families, and sometimes in the summer it can even be warmer than the Mediterranean Sea.'

gals), the Semigallians and the Cours. From the latter three derived the names of three of Latvia's four principal regions: Latgale, Zemgale and Kurzeme. The fourth region, Vidzeme (Livland), derived its name from the Livs, a Finno-Ugric people unrelated to the Balts (see p227).

During succeeding centuries of foreign rule these tribes merged into one Latvian identity. They were pagan until the first Christian missionaries arrived in the late 12th century.

Christianity

Arriving in Latvia in 1190, the first Christian missionaries tried to persuade the pagan population to convert. It was an uphill battle: as soon as the missionaries left, the new converts jumped into the river to wash off their baptism. In subsequent years more missionaries would arrive, and more Latvians would submit and then renounce Christianity.

In 1201, at the behest of the pope, German crusaders, led by Bishop von Buxhoevden of Bremen, conquered Latvia and founded Rīga. Von Buxhoevden also founded the Knights of the Sword, who made Rīga their base for subjugating Livonia. Colonists from northern Germany followed, and during the first period of German rule, Rīga became the major city in the German Baltic, thriving from trade between Russia and the West and joining the Hanseatic League (a medieval merchant guild) in 1282. Furs, hides, honey and wax were among the products sold westward from Russia through Rīga.

Power struggles between the Church, knights and city authorities dominated the country's history between 1253 and 1420. Rīga's bishop, elevated to archbishop in 1252, became the leader of the church in the German conquered lands, ruling a good slice of Livonia directly and further areas of Livonia and Estonia indirectly through his bishops. The Church clashed constantly with knights, who controlled most of the remainder of Livonia and Estonia, and with German merchant-dominated city authorities who managed to maintain a degree of independence during this period.

Sweden, Poland & Russia

The 15th, 16th and 17th centuries were marked with battles and disputes about how to divvy up what would one day become Latvia. The land was at the crossroads of several encroaching empires and everyone wanted to secure the area as a means of gaining a strategic upper hand. It was at this time that Martin Luther posted his theses and Lutheran ideals flooded east. Rīga quickly became a centre for the Reformation and merchant elites adopted the doctrine. Fervent religious movements spawned the emergence of written Latvian.

Western Latvia grew in influence and power under the Duchy of Courland, a semi-autonomous kingdom governed by the capable Duke Kettler, who established far-flung colonies in the Gambia and on Tobago. At this time, southeastern Latvia was grabbed by Poland, and Sweden took Rīga and the northeast. The Russians barged in at the end of the 1620s and gobbled everything up during the Great Northern War (1700–21).

National Awakening

The idea of a cohesive national identity began around the 17th century, when the peasant descendants of the original tribes started to unite under the name 'Latvia'. By the mid-19th century, the sentiment grew stronger as the first newspapers printed their issues in Latvian and the first Song and Dance Festival started up. Farmers flocked to the big city and demanded equal rights. Political parties emerged to organise worker strikes to oust the remaining German aristocracy. Democratic leaders would later call this push for freedom the 'Latvian Revolution'.

A Taste of Freedom

Out of the post-WWI confusion and turmoil arose an independent Latvian state, declared on 18 November 1918. By the 1930s Latvia had achieved one of the highest standards of living in all of Europe. In 1934 a bloodless coup, led by Kārlis Ulmanis, Latvia's first president, ended the power of parliament.

Initially, the Soviets were the first to recognise Latvia's independence, but the honeymoon didn't last long. Soviet occupation began in 1939 with the Molotov-Ribbentrop Pact. Nationalisation, killings and mass deportations to Siberia followed. Latvia was occupied partly or wholly by Nazi Germany from 1941 to 1945, when an estimated 175,000 Latvians, mostly Jews, were killed or deported.

Soviet Rule

When WWII ended, the Soviets marched back in claiming to 'save' Latvia from the Nazis. A series of deportations began anew as the nation was forced to adapt to communist ideologies. Smoke-spewing factories were swiftly erected and everyone went to work like bees in a hive. Notions of individuality were stripped away as lovely country cottages and state cosmopolitan buildings were 'nationalised', forcing everyone into drab apartment blocks.

The first public protest against Soviet occupation was on 14 June 1987, when 5000 people rallied at Rīga's Freedom Monument to commemorate the 1941 Siberia deportations. New political organisations emerged in the summer of 1988. The Popular Front of Latvia (PLF) quickly rose to the forefront of the Latvian political scene. Less than two months later, on 23 August 1989, two million Latvians, Lithuanians and Estonians formed a 650km human chain from Vilnius, through Rīga, to Tallinn, to mark the 50th anniversary of the Molotov-Ribbentrop Pact.

Looking Towards Today

Although an all-important Moscow coup failed in 1991, the attempt rocked the Soviet Union just enough so that Latvia could break free. The country declared independence on 21 August 1991 and on 17 September 1991, Latvia, along with Estonia and Lithuania, joined the UN and began taking steps to consolidate its newfound nationhood. Democratic elections were held in 1993 and the new government, headed by Guntis Ulmanis (a farmer and descendant of Kārlis Ulmanis), lurched from crisis to crisis, while a game of prime minister roulette followed the devastating crash of the country's largest commercial bank.

In 1999 Vaira Vīķe-Freiberga, a Latvian by birth but who spent most of her life in Canada, won the presidential election with her promise of propelling the country towards EU membership. It was a tough uphill battle as the nation shook off its antiquated Soviet fetters, and on 1 May 2004 the EU opened its doors to the fledgling nation. Long the Baltic laggard (and the poorest country in the EU), Latvia registered the highest economic growth in the EU in 2004, 2005, 2006 and 2007, even though thousands of Latvians left for jobs in Ireland and elsewhere.

As it turned out, however, much of Latvia's modern economy was built like a house of cards, and thus overspending and borrowing damaged the domestic economy during the global economic crisis that swept across the world at the end of 2008 and the beginning of 2009. A sudden swing towards Russia occurred as three clear oligarchs emerged from the decaying economy. While the other Baltic countries seem to be aligning themselves with other European nations, Latvia is looking east while making political and economic alliances. At the end of President Zatlers' term, he called for the dissolution of the Latvian parliament, which took place at the beginning of current president Andris Bērziņš's term towards the end of 2011. The request to dissolve the parliament was an effort by the Latvian government to put a stop to the nation's unofficial oligarchical reign.

The People

Casual hellos on the street aren't common, but Latvians are a friendly and welcoming bunch. Some will find that there is a bit of guardedness in the culture, but this caution, most likely a response to centuries of foreign rule, has helped preserve the unique language and culture through changing times. As Latvia opens up to the world, this slight xenophobia is quickly melting away. Citizens are growing secure with their nation's freedom and the younger generations have access to a more cosmopolitan culture (especially since youths are almost always trilingual and speak Latvian, Russian and English).

Latvian women were traditionally responsible for preserving the hearth and home by passing on traditional songs, recipes, legends and tales. The men, enriched by these closely kept customs, would guard the land. Today, women remain a strong presence in the household and, while gender equality is still a bit of a slippery slope, women have prominent positions in politics and business. Over 33% of the nation's CEOs are women, and Latvia's most noted president was Vaira Vīķe-Freiberga.

Latvians generally adore nature and continue to incorporate their ancient pagan traditions and customs into everyday life, despite being members of the Lutheran church (Russian citizens are mostly Roman Catholics, Orthodox or Old Believers). Superstitious beliefs are quite common and often linked to the wildlife that shares the land. In rural Latvia, families will place high wooden beams in their yard to attract storks, which are be-

GREY SKIES ARE GONNA CLEAR UP...

Over the last two decades, Latvia's environmental climate has improved by leaps and bounds, largely due to tax reforms and an infusion of EU and private money. When the little country gained its independence, the damages to the ecosystem inflicted during the Soviet era were promptly addressed. Since 1990 the amount of factory pollution has decreased by 46%, and wastewater has dropped by 44%. Latvia has more than 1300 wastewater treatment plants, which have increased the purity of river waters – the Daugava and Lielupe Rivers are now deemed 'good-quality cyprinid waters'. Pesticides and chemical farming, widely used during Soviet times, have also been monitored and addressed. Today, more than 2750 hectares of farming land (around 200 farms) refrain from using any type of artificial fertilisers, which has helped reduce the number of airborne pesticides by 1000%.

Latvia's water and sewage reforms are restoring the Baltic Sea and Gulf of Rīga to their former swimmable state. The European Blue Flag water safety and purity ranking (with its rigorous criteria) has been awarded to beaches in Jūrmala, Ventspils and Liepāja.

The Latvian Sustainable Development Strategy, a broad-reaching scheme uniting environmental, social and economic structures to increase the longevity and viability of the Latvian land, was conceived in 2002.

For additional information about environmental issues and targeted programs, check out the website for Latvia's Ministry of the Environment (www.vidm.gov.lv).

lieved to bring children. Latvians also love flowers; if you go to a birthday party or are invited into someone's home, always bring a bouquet (but make sure it's an odd number of flowers – even numbers are reserved for funerals).

The Arts

Cinema

The Fisherman's Son (Zvejnieka dēls), made in 1940, marked both the beginning and the end of an era in Latvian filmmaking. It was the nation's first full-length sound film, but it was one of the last major works before WWII and the subsequent years of oppression. At the beginning of the USSR period, the state-owned Rīga Documentary Film Studio created heaps of movies, but most were laden with propaganda. Other films had to meet ideological standards laid out by the communist government, which stifled creativity for obvious reasons. After Stalin's death in 1953, directors earned slightly more freedom, but it wasn't until the 1980s that pastiche and parody became commonplace. Most of the films up until then were adaptations of famous Latvian legends and modern novels.

Latvian director Jānis Streičs has produced a number of films pertinent to Latvia's turbulent past. *Limousine in the Colour of Summer Solstice Night* (1981) and *The Child of Man* (1991) remain popular for their blend of irony and comedy. The latter, about a boy growing up and falling in love in Soviet-occupied Latvia, won the Grand Prix at San Remo in 1992 and was nominated for an Academy Award for best foreign film in 1994. Streičs' more recent film, *The Mystery of the Old Parish Church* (2000), addresses the prickly issue of locals collaborating with Nazi and Soviet occupiers during WWII.

Other filmmakers of note include Laila Pakalnina, whose 1998 feature film *The Shoe,* about occupied Latvia, was an official selection at the Cannes 1998 film festival. Pakalnina's 1996 film *The Mail* shows the isolation of Latvia, as symbolised by the lonely delivery of the morning mail.

Rural towns such as Kuldīga are often used to stage period pieces, while other directors prefer to use the synthetic town of Cinevilla (p224), now a major tourist attraction, for filming.

Check out www.latfilma.lv, the official website for the National Film Centre in Latvia, which offers detailed information about directors, festivals, production houses and more.

Latvian Song & Dance

Traditional folk songs have always played an integral role in Latvian culture, although the recognition of music as an established art form did not come about until the mid-19th century. In 1869 Jānis Cimze started cataloguing folk tunes, some dating back 1000 years, and his collection of 20,000 melodies became the basis for Latvia's first song festival, where thousands of singers joined together in huge choirs to celebrate traditional folk music. During the Soviet occupation the song festivals were pivotal in forging a strong sense of national identity and pride, and became part of the battle cry that rallied Latvians to fight for independence. The Song and Dance Festival is held every five years (the next one will be held in July, 2013) and continues to unite myriad voices in a jaw-dropping display of patriotism.

The National Opera House, reopened in 1996 after renovation, is the home of the Rīga Ballet, which produced Mikhail Baryshnikov and Aleksander Godunov during the Soviet years. The opera itself is considered to be one of the finest in Europe and cheap seats have made it accessible to the public, who regard the theatre with the utmost respect.

Latvia struck it big when Patra Vetra, also known as Brainstorm, finished third at the Eurovision contest in 2000, and then the wee nation hit the jackpot when Marie N (Marija Naumova) took home the grand prize in 2002.

Art & Architecture

Of Latvia's spectrum of visual arts, visitors will be most awestruck by the collection of art-nouveau architecture in Rīga. The capital has more Jugendstil buildings than any other European city – 750 buildings and counting (as renovations continue). See p202 for more information and an interactive walking tour.

Jānis Rozentāls, Latvia's first major painter, lived in Rīga's art-nouveau district and his former home has since been transformed into a museum (p199). Mark

EAT YOUR WORDS

These days, most restaurants have English menus, but why not impress your waiter and order your pork gristle in Latvian. We've listed a few of the more useful eating phrases here as well.

Useful Phrases

A table for ... people, please.	*loo*-dzu *gahl*-du ... *per*-so-nahm	*Lūdzu galdu ... personām.*
Do you have a menu?	vai yums ir *eh*-dean-kar-te	*Vai jums ir ēdienkarte?*
I'm a vegetarian.	es es-mu ve-gye-tah-reah-tis/te	*Es esmu veģetārietis/ te.* (m/f)
What do you recommend?	kwo yoos *eah*-sah-kut	*Ko jūs iesakat?*
I'd like ...	es *vaa*-lwos ...	*Es vēlos ...*
The bill, please.	*loo*-dzu *reh*-kyi-nu	*Lūdzu rēķinu.*

Food Glossary

beefsteak with fried onions	*see*-po-luh see-ten-ees	*sīpolu sitenis*
beetroot soup (similar to borscht)	bee-eh-shu zoo-pa	*biešu zupa*
diced vegetable salad in sour cream and mayonnaise	*dar*-zen sa-*la*-tee	*dārzeņu salāti*
dumplings	pell-me-nee	*pelmeņi*
fish soup	zeev-yoo zoo-pah	*zivju zupa*
fresh grated cabbage	*kah*-post sa-*la*-tee	*kāpostu salāti*
fried salmon with potatoes and pickled and fresh vegetables	tsepts lah-sees ar pee-eh-dev-*am*	*cepts lasis ar piedevām*
fried pork chop with potatoes and pickled and fresh vegetables	kar-bo-*nah*-deh ar pee-eh-dev-*am*	*karbonāde ar piedevām*
grey peas with pork fat and onions	peh-*leh*-kee-eh zeer-nee ar speh-kyi	*pelēkie zirņi ar speķi*
hunter's sausages (pork)	med-nye-kuh deh-see-nyas	*mednieku desiņas*
meatballs	kot-leh-tess	*kotletes*
pickled herring with sour cream, egg and beetroot	seel-kye kah-djo-*kah*	*siļķe kažokā*
salmon in cream sauce	lah-sis *kreh*-ma mehr-tse	*lasis krējuma mērcē*
salmon in mushroom and dill sauce	lah-sis *seh*-nyu oon di-lyu mehr-tse	*lasis sēņu un diļļu mērcē*
sausage (usually smoked)	deh-sa	*desa*

Rothko, born in Daugavpils, is arguably the most famous Latvian artist around the world. Although he grew up in the USA, a recent interest in the artist and his oeuvre have inspired the construction of a new modern art space (p260), which will hopefully stimulate tourism in the otherwise quiet region of Latgale.

DO IT YOURSELF: BLACK BALZĀM COCKTAILS

A jug of Black Balzām is the perfect souvenir to bring home to your loved ones. The slender bottle has an attractive antique design, and its contents – a secret concoction of herbs and berries – are delicious. Give your family and friends a little taste of Rīga by mixing them one of the following popular Black Balzām cocktails.

» **Black Mojito:** mix one part Black Balzām with four parts lemon-lime soda, add a half of lime smashed and a drizzle of fruit syrup. Serve over crushed ice.

» **Innocent Balzām:** blend one part Black Balzām, 0.5 parts peach liqueur, three parts peach juice, three parts vanilla ice cream and one canned peach.

» **Lazybones:** add a shot of Black Balzām to a cold glass of cola (our favourite).

Food & Drink

Attention foodies: pack a sandwich if you don't want to pack an artery – traditional food in Latvia is (to put it nicely) very hearty. For centuries, eating has been but a utilitarian task rather than an art and a pleasure, and although things have changed in Rīga, one should still expect greasy menus governed by the almighty pig and ubiquitous potato.

Staples & Specialities

A walk through a Latvian market, such as Rīga's Central Market, will quickly reveal the local faves: roasted meats (including heaps of sausage), smoked fish (herring, pike, trout or salmon), fried potatoes, boiled veggies and loads of pork grease. Dairy products are also a big hit, and *biezpiens* (cottage cheese), *siers* (cheese) and *rūgušpiens* (curdled milk) are main ingredients in many dishes. In fact, during Soviet times dairy products from Latvia were considered a delicacy all over the Union.

During the summer months berry-picking is a national obsession. During autumn, fresh-picked mushrooms, cranberries and nuts replace strawberries and raspberries at the little stalls. Honey is another popular delicacy; Latvians are intrepid beekeepers and many farms have beehives and honey-production facilities.

Those with a sweet tooth won't be disappointed: berries turn into scrumptious fruit pies and *kūka* (tarts). Ancient Cour Viking dessert recipes made from sweet creams and dark breads can still be found in western Latvia. Be sure to try *rupjmaizes kārojums/kārtojums,* which tastes like Black Forest gateau.

Design Your Own Hangover

Not to be missed is Latvia's famous Black Balzām, which Goethe called 'the elixir of life'. This insidious jet-black, 45% proof concoction is a secret recipe created by Rīga druggist Abraham Kunze in the 18th century. Orange peel, oak bark, wormwood and linden blossoms are among some 14 fairy-tale ingredients known to stew in the wicked witch's cooking pot. A shot a day keeps the doctor away, so say most of Latvia's pensioners. Its name originates from *balsamon,* the ancient Greek word for a sweet-smelling medicinal balm or ointment. Its opaque ceramic bottle, labelled with a black and gold Rīga skyline, is reminiscent of the clay jars the potent liquid used to be stored in during the 18th and 19th centuries to keep it safe from sunlight.

Alus (beer) has long been a traditional favourite, and for such a small country Latvia has more than its share of breweries. Figure around 0.50Ls for a pint from a kiosk (every kiosk stocks beer) and around 1Ls to 2Ls in a bar. Try Valmiermuižas Alus, Aldaris Alus or Cēsu Alus brands, and keep an eye out for Bauskas, Piebalgas, Tērvetes and Užavas, each with a distinct taste.

Wine choices are often found on restaurant and bar menus, and tend to be a selection from the usual gamut of celebrated

EATING PRICE RANGES

For the purpose of this chapter we've based the Latvian budget breakdowns on the following price ranges, based on the average price of a main dish.

» **€**   less than 5Ls
» **€€**   5Ls to 10Ls
» **€€€**   more than 10Ls

wine-producing nations, as well as lesser regions like the Caucasus.

Where to Eat & Drink

Restorāns (restaurants) in Latvia are generally slower, sit-down affairs, while *kafejnīca* (pronounced ka-fay-*neet*-za; cafes) are multipurpose facilities where patrons enjoy a coffee, a faster meal or drinks in the evening. Bars, especially in Rīga and other major cities, often serve a full range of food. For quick, self-service choices, keep an eye out for *pelmeņi* (dumpling) and pancake shops, cafeteria-style venues such as some of the links in the LIDO restaurant chain, and supermarkets, namely Rimi, which sell to-go snacks and meals. Small towns have Latvian restaurants that often offer the occasional international dish (usually pizza).

A Latvian *brokastis* (breakfast), available from sunrise to around 11am, usually consists of bread and cheese, cold meat and smoked fish. *Pusidienās* (lunch) and *vakariņas* (dinner) are more substantial affairs, with heartier Baltic staples. Restaurants serve lunch at midday and daylight patterns often influence dinner times, which can vary from 5pm to midnight.

SURVIVAL GUIDE

Directory A–Z

The following directory contains practical information pertinent to travel in Latvia. For regional information pertaining to all three Baltic countries, see p396.

Accommodation

We highly advise booking ahead during summer. Prices listed in this chapter are for the high season; rates drop significantly in the colder months.

All rooms in this chapter are en suite unless otherwise stated. Most hotels in Latvia have a mix of smoking and non-smoking accommodation.

Visit www.hotels.lv for more info about Latvia's hospitality industry. Check out www.camping.lv for details on pitching a tent.

Activities

Latvia's miles of forested acreage are great for hiking, cycling, camping, birdwatching, berry-picking, mushrooming and canoeing during the summer months. In winter, skiing and snowshoeing are but some of the uplifting pursuits Latvia has to offer active visitors.

Don't forget to check out our Outdoor Activities chapter at the front of the book.

Customs

The **Latvian Tourism Development Agency** (www.latviatourism.lv) posts the latest customs rules on its website.

There are no customs controls at the borders with other EU countries. When travelling within Schengen, tourists (18 years and up) are only allowed to move 800 cigarettes, 200 cigars or 1kg of tobacco across the border. For alcohol, the maximum is 110L of beer, 90L of wine (not more than 60L of sparkling wine) and 10L of other alcohol products. When travelling beyond the EU, quantities of cigarettes and alcohol are reduced to 200 cigarettes, 50 cigars, 250g of smoking tobacco and 1L of distilled beverages.

Exporting documents or copies from the state archive also require permits; see www.mantojums.lv.

Embassies & Consulates

The following embassies are in Rīga. New Zealand does not have an embassy in Latvia; Australia's is an informal consulate.

Australia (Map p196; ☑6722 4251; Tomsona iela 33-1)

Belarus (☑6732 5321; www.latvia.belembassy .org; Jēzusbaznīcas 12)

Canada (Map p196; ☑6781 3945; www.latvia .gc.ca; Baznīcas iela 20/22)

Estonia (☑6781 2020; www.estemb.lv; Skolas iela 13)

France (☑6703 6600; www.ambafrance-lv.org; Raiņa bulvāris 9)

Germany (☑6708 5100; www.riga.diplo.de; Raiņa bulvāris 13)

Ireland (☑6703 9370; www.embassyofireland.lv; Alberta iela 13)

Lithuania (☑6732 1519; www.lv.mfa.lt; Rūpniecības iela 24)

Netherlands (☑6732 6147; www.netherlands embassy.lv; Torņa iela 4)

Russia (☑6733 2151; www.latvia.mid.ru; Antonijas iela 2)

Sweden (☑6768 6600; www.swedenabroad .com/riga; Pumpura iela 8)

UK (☑6777 4700; www.ukinlatvia.fco.gov.uk/en; Alunāna iela 5)

USA (☑6703 6200; http://riga.usembassy.gov; Raiņa bulvāris 7)

Festivals & Events

Latvians find any and every excuse to throw a party. Check out the events calendar (p19) for a comprehensive list of activities around Latvia and the other Baltic nations next door.

Internet Access

Almost all accommodation in Rīga offers some form of internet access. Hotels in smaller cities have been doing a good job of following suit. Internet cafes are a dying breed as many restaurants, cafes and bars now offer wireless connections.

Lattelecom (Lattelekom; www.lattelecom .lv), Latvia's main communications service provider, has set up wi-fi beacons at every payphone around the city. Users can access the internet from within a 100m radius of these phone booths. To register for a Lattelecom password and username, call ☑9000 4111, or send an SMS with the word 'WiFi' to ☑1188.

In provincial Latvia an internet cafe tends to translate as a *datorsalons,* crammed with square-eyed kids playing computer games. Make it clear you want to access the internet (rather than tangle with Lara Croft) and a kid will be kicked off to make way for you.

Internet Resources

Dear intrepid travel, meet **www.1188.lv**, your new best friend. Latvia's top search engine is like a genie that grants three wishes...and then 1000 more, answering any questions you might have about bus/train transport, postal services, business listings, traffic reports and taxis. You can even send an SMS to the website service to get listings sent to your phone.

The **Latvian Tourism Development Agency** (www.latvia.travel) and the **Latvia Institute** (www.li.lv) both have fantastic websites providing information targeted at foreign visitors.

Maps

Country, city and town maps of Latvia are available from Rīga-based **Jāņa sēta** (Map p196; ☑6724 0894; Elizabetes iela 83-85; ☺10am-7pm Mon-Sat, to 5pm Sun). Its town-plan series covers practically every town in Latvia; individual maps range in scale from 1:15,000 to 1:20,000 and cost 0.70Ls to 3Ls.

The **Latvian Tourism Development Agency** (www.latvia.travel) has a very detailed map covering each of Latvia's five regions (which correspond to the five sections of this chapter).

Money

Latvia's currency, the lats, was introduced in March 1993. The lats (Ls) is divided into 100 santīms. The national bank, **Latvijas Bankas** (Latvian Bank; www.bank.lv), posts the lats' daily exchange rate on its website. See p184 for more info. Many of Rīga's hotels publish their rack rates in euros. Although Estonia has ascended to the euro, Latvia still has quite a way to go – they are expected to join the Eurozone in 2014.

Post

The official website of Latvia's **postal service** (www.post.lv) can answer any of your mail-related questions, including shipping and stamp prices. Service is reliable; mail to North America takes 10 days, and within Europe about a week.

Public Holidays

The **Latvia Institute website** (www.li.lv) has a page devoted to special Latvian Remembrance Days under the 'About Latvia' link.

New Year's Day 1 January

Easter March/April

Labour Day 1 May

Restoration of Independence of the Republic of Latvia 4 May

Mothers' Day Second Sunday in May

Whitsunday A Sunday in May or June

Līgo Eve (Midsummer festival) 23 June

Jāņi (St John's Day and Summer Solstice) 24 June

National Day Anniversary of proclamation of Latvian Republic, 1918, on 18 November

Christmas (Ziemsvētki) 25 December

Second Holiday 26 December

New Year's Eve 31 December

Telephone

Latvian telephone numbers have eight digits; landlines start with '6' and mobile numbers start with '2'. To make any call within Latvia, simply dial the eight-digit number. To call a Latvian telephone number from abroad, dial the international access code, then the country code for Latvia (☑371) followed by the subscriber's eight-digit number.

Telephone rates are posted on the website of the partly state-owned **Lattelecom** (www.lattelecom.lv), which enjoys a monopoly on fixed-line telephone communications in Latvia.

Mobile phones are available for purchase at most shopping malls around Rīga and other major cities. If your own phone is GSM900-/1800-compatible, you can purchase a prepaid SIM-card package and top-up credit from any Narvesen superette or Rimi grocery store. The most popular plan is **ZZ by Tele2** (Tele-divi; www.tele2.lv, in Latvian; SIM-card 0.99Ls).

Calls on a public phone are made using cardphones called *telekarte,* which come in different denominations and are sold at post offices, newspaper stands and superettes.

Tourist Information

In recent years, the **Latvian Tourism Development Agency** (☑6722 9945; www.latvia.travel) has been streamlining tourist information throughout the country. Try www.tourism.*city name*.lv, or simply www.*city name*.lv for official city websites (English translations are often limited for small destinations). Every city and town in Latvia worth visiting has a tourist office, open during normal business hours (at the very least), with extended hours during the summer. Almost all of the tourist offices have English-speaking staff and oodles of pamphlets and maps.

Check out the website of the **Latvia Institute** (www.li.lv) for additional information about Latvia.

Getting There & Away

This section concentrates on travelling between Latvia and its Baltic neighbours only. For details on connections outside of the region, see p404.

Air

Rīga airport (Lidosta Rīga; ☑1187; www.riga-airport.com), about 13km southwest of the city centre, houses Latvia's national carrier, **airBaltic** (☑9000 1100; www.airbaltic.com), which offers direct flights to over 50 destinations within Europe, including Tallinn and Vilnius.

Land

In 2007 Latvia acceded to the Schengen Agreement, which removed all border control between it and both Estonia and Lithuania. We advise carrying your travel documents with you at all times, as random border checks do occur.

BUS

See p217 for further details of buses to/from Rīga.

Ecolines (www.ecolines.net) Three daily buses on the Rīga–Salacgrīva–Pärnu–Tallinn route and a daily Rīga–Valmiera–Valga–Tartu bus.

Hansabuss Business Line (www.businessline.ee) Four daily buses between Rīga and Tallinn, three of which stop in Pärnu.

Lux Express (www.luxexpress.eu) Nine daily buses between Rīga and Tallinn, some of which stop in Pärnu; two continue on to Vilnius.

CAR

Rental cars are allowed to travel around the Baltic at no extra fee. We recommend notifying your vehicle renter when you take the car off the lot.

TRAIN

Train travel is not the most convenient way to access the different destinations of the Baltic. For travel both to/from Estonia and Lithuania it is better to take buses or hire a private vehicle. See p414 for more information on train travel.

Sea

Latvia is connected to a number of destinations by sea. See p217 for details on services to/from Rīga, and p234 for details on services to/from Ventspils.

Getting Around
Bus

Buses are much more convenient than trains if you're travelling beyond the capital's clutch of suburban rail lines. Updated timetables are available at www.1188.lv. See p217 for more details.

Car & Motorcycle

Driving is on the right-hand side. Headlights must be on at all times. Be sure to ask for *'benzene'* when looking for a petrol station – *gāze* means 'air'.

You'll find the usual suspects when it comes to renting a vehicle, however several small businesses in Rīga offer cheaper options than the international companies at the airport – expect cash-only transactions and free delivery anywhere in the capital. Rentals range from €30 to €60 per day, depending on the type of car and time of year. The number of automatic cars in Latvia is limited. Companies usually allow you to drive in all three Baltic countries, but not beyond.

AddCar Rental (☑2658 9674; www.addcar rental.com)

Auto (☑2958 0448; www.carsrent.lv)

EgiCarRent (☑2953 1044; www.egi.lv)

Train

Most Latvians live in the large suburban ring around Rīga, thus the city's network of commuter rails makes it easy for tourists to reach day-tripping destinations. Latvia's further attractions are best explored by bus. All train schedule queries can be answered at www.1188.lv.

Lithuania

Includes »

Vilnius	280
Trakai	308
Aukštaitija National Park	312
Druskininkai	318
Kaunas	323
Šiauliai	334
Panevėžys	338
Klaipėda	341
Curonian Spit National Park	350
Palanga	361
Žemaitija National Park	365

Best Places to Eat

» Hotel Restaurant Labanoras (p316)

» Balzac (p300)

» Kibininė (p310)

» Nidos Seklyčia (p358)

» Sue's Indian Raja (p300)

Best Places to Stay

» Miškiniškės (p313)

» Bernardinu B&B (p297)

» Misko namas (p356)

» Litinterp Guesthouse (p346)

» Domus Maria (p297)

Why Go?

Rebellious, quirky and vibrant, Lithuania (Lietuva) is one of Europe's best-kept secrets. Though the country rarely makes it into newspapers outside its borders (and when it does, it's for some basketball exploit), the southernmost of the three Baltic countries holds a bag of treats.

Foremost among these is the country's majestic Baltic coastline and the unique sliver of white sand known as the Curonian Spit. Inland, lush forests watch over lakes that twinkle between the pine trees, and lonely coastal wetlands lure migrating birds by the tens of thousands.

The capital, Vilnius, is a beguiling artists' enclave, with mysterious courtyards, worn cobbled streets and crumbling corners, overshadowed by baroque beauty beyond belief.

Further afield, remnants of Soviet times – a disused nuclear missile site (now a museum to the Cold War) and a Soviet sculpture park – fascinate and shock. The Hill of Crosses and Orvydas stone garden are two more oddities of this awe-inspiring land.

When to Go

Lithuania is at its best in high summer, from June to August, when the days are long, the nights are short, and the Baltic Sea's waters are warm – or at least swimmable. Festival season hits high gear. One fest not to miss is Klaipėda's five-day Sea Festival in mid-July.

Spring (April and May) is cool and arrives late but is good for rafting, as the thawing snow feeds the rivers.

Autumn (September to November) can be ideal. Expect sunny days and chilly nights. Culture reaches a crescendo with classical music festivals and the annual Mama Jazz festival in Vilnius.

Arriving in Lithuania

Vilnius is the main gateway, whether you're coming by plane, train or bus. The airport is 5km from the centre, but taxis are steep (as much as 60Lt), so you're best off taking a bus or train (both 2.50Lt) into the city. The main bus and train stations are both in the centre and easily reachable by taxi or public transportation. Klaipėda in the west is the country's only ferry port, and it's possible to travel to Lithuania by boat from Germany or Sweden. If you're driving, Lithuania is a member of the EU's Schengen common border zone and there are no passport or border formalities if entering from Poland or Latvia. You'll encounter the old-school 'papers please' approach if entering from Russia or Belarus.

LANGUAGE

Hello	Sveiki	*svay*-ki
Hi (informal)	Labas	*lah*-bahs
How are you?	Kaip gyvuojate?	*kaip*-gee-vu-aw-*yah*-ta
Goodbye	Sudie	*su*-deah
Thank you	Dėkoju	deh-*kaw*-yu
I'm lost	Aš paklyd(usi/ęs)	ahsh-*pah*-kleed(usi/as)

Essential Food & Drink

» **Cepelinai** Parcels of potato dough stuffed with cheese, meat or mushrooms jokingly referred to as zeppelins, and not just for their shape – they're calorie bombs.

» **Šaltibarščiai** This cold beetroot summer soup is arguably the country's signature dish; served with a plate of boiled potatoes on the side.

» **Alus** Beer is the most widely drunk alcoholic beverage and it's pretty good stuff at that.

» **Blyneliai** Pancakes can be served sweet or savoury and eaten at any time during the day; look for Varskečiai, stuffed with sweet curd.

» **Mushrooms** Mushroom picking is especially popular in late August and September, when the forests are studded with dozens of different varieties.

RESOURCES

Bus Tickets (www.autobusubilietai.lt) Bus tickets and info.

Lithuanian Travel Information (www.travel.lt) Official tourism site.

Litrail (www.litrail.lt) Useful railway timetable and train info.

Museums of Lithuania (www.muziejai.lt) All museums, opening times and entry fees.

The Lithuania Tribune (www.lithuaniatribune.com) News and current events.

Fast Facts

» **Area** 65,303 sq km
» **Capital** Vilnius
» **Population** 3.3 million
» **Telephone country code** ☑370
» **Emergency** ☑112

Exchange Rates

Australia	A$1	2.58Lt
Canada	C$1	2.55Lt
Euro zone	€1	3.45Lt
Japan	¥100	3.31Lt
Latvia	1Ls	4.80Lt
New Zealand	NZ$1	2.07Lt
UK	UK£1	3.97Lt
USA	US$1	2.53Lt

» For current exchange rates see www.xe.com.

Set Your Budget

» **Budget hotel room** 120Lt
» **Two-course meal** 30Lt
» **Museum entrance** 6Lt
» **Bottle of beer** 6Lt
» **City transport ticket** 2Lt

Lithuania Highlights

① Wander the backstreets of the beautiful baroque capital **Vilnius** (p280) looking for that perfect bar or bistro

② Head to the **Curonian Spit** (p350) to spend time cycling, swimming in the Baltic Sea, or exploring hardy human settlements on this thin spit of sand and spruce

③ Stand in awe in front of thousands upon thousands of crosses – some tiny, others gigantic – that grace the **Hill of Crosses** (p334), a small hillock outside Šiauliai

④ Stare down the barrel of a disused nuclear missile silo

before taking a peaceful stroll through woods at **Žemaitija National Park** (p365)

5 Take time out for fishing, boating, bathing and berrying in Lithuania's beloved

lakeland, **Aukštaitija National Park** (p312)

6 Stroll, boat or take the waters at **Druskininkai** (p318), Lithuania's leading spa resort

7 Walk through **Orvydas Garden** (boxed text p366), a peaceful rock and statue garden that feels as holy as the Hill of Crosses and as quiet as a national park

VILNIUS

📱5 / POP 546,700

Vilnius (vil-nyus), the baroque beauty of the Baltic, is a city of immense allure. As stunning as it is bizarre, it easily tops the country's best-attraction bill, drawing tourists like moths to a flame with an easy, confident charm and a warm, golden glow that makes one wish for long midsummer evenings every day of the year.

The capital may be a long way north and east, but it's quintessentially continental. At its heart is Europe's largest baroque old town, so precious that Unesco added it to its World Heritage list. Viewed from a hot air balloon, the skyline – pierced by countless Orthodox and Catholic church steeples – looks like a giant bed of nails. Adding to this heady mix is a combination of cobbled alleys, crumbling corners, majestic hilltop views, breakaway states and traditional artists' workshops – all in a city so small you'd sometimes think it was a village.

It has not always been good and grand here though. There are reminders of loss and pain too, from the horror of the KGB's torture cells to the ghetto in the centre of all this beauty where the Jewish community lived before their mass wartime slaughter. Yet the spirit of freedom and resistance has prevailed, and the city is forging a new identity, combining the past with a present and future that involves world cuisine, a burgeoning nightlife and shiny new skyscrapers.

History

Legend says Vilnius was founded in the 1320s, when Lithuanian grand duke Gediminas dreamt of an iron wolf that howled with the voices of 100 wolves – a sure sign to build a city as mighty as their cry. In fact, the site had already been settled for 1000 years.

A moat, a wall and a tower on Gediminas Hill protected 14th- and 15th-century Vilnius from Teutonic attacks. Tatar attacks prompted inhabitants to build a 2.4km defensive wall (1503–22), and by the end of the 16th century Vilnius was among Eastern Europe's biggest cities. Three centuries on, industrialisation arrived: railways were laid and Vilnius became a key Jewish city. Occupied by Germany during WWI, it became an isolated pocket of Poland afterwards. WWII ushered in another German occupation and the death knoll for its Jewish population. After the war, Vilnius' skyline was filled

---

LITHUANIA AT A GLANCE

Currency lits (Lt)

Language Lithuanian

Money ATMs are widespread. Cash preferred to credit cards for small purchases.

Visas Not required for citizens of the EU, USA, Canada, Japan, New Zealand and Australia.

---

with new residential suburbs populated by Lithuanians from other parts of the country alongside immigrant Russians and Belarusians. In the late 1980s, the capital was the focus of Lithuania's push for independence from the USSR.

Vilnius has fast become a European city. In 1994 its Old Town became a Unesco World Heritage site and 15 years later shared the prestigious title of European Capital of Culture with the Austrian city Linz. In between, much of the Old Town has been restored and is now a tourist hot spot.

◉ Sights

Vilnius is a compact city, and most sights are easily reached on foot. Those visiting for a couple of days will scarcely move out of the Old Town, where souvenir stalls, folk-artist workshops and designer boutiques jostle for attention with a treasure trove of architectural gems. Stay a couple more days and the New Town beckons, with its museums, shops and riverside action.

Begin your exploration of the city at the cathedral-studded Cathedral Square, with Gediminas Hill rising behind it. Southward lies the cobbled Old Town, which has Pilies gatvė as the main pedestrian thoroughfare. Heading west, Gedimino prospektas cuts straight across the newer part of the town centre to parliament and has several sights worth taking in.

GEDIMINAS HILL

Vilnius was founded on 48m-high Gediminas Hill, topped since the 13th century by a red-brick tower. The original tower was a tier higher than the 20m structure that marks the spot today. Its walls were ruined during the Russian occupation (1655–61), but it was restored in 1930 to house the **Upper Castle Museum** (Aukštutinės pilies muziejus; Map p286; Arsenalo gatvė 5; adult/child 5/2Lt;

⏱10am-7pm daily May-Oct, 10am-5pm Tue-Sun Nov-Apr), which contains shiny armour from the 16th to 18th centuries and models of the castle in former times, as well as providing panoramic views of the city. To reach the top of the hill, clamber up some rocky steps that start from behind the cathedral on its southeastern side or take the funicular (adult/child 3/2Lt; ⏱10am-7pm May-Oct, 10am-5pm Nov-Apr). The entrance to the funicular is behind the cathedral on its northeastern side, inside a small courtyard at the rear of the Museum of Applied Arts.

CATHEDRAL SQUARE

Katedros aikštė buzzes with local life. In the 19th century markets and fairs were held here and a moat ran around what is now the square's perimeter so ships could sail to the cathedral door. Within the moat were walls and towers, the only remaining part of which is the 57m-tall belfry (Map p286) near the cathedral's western end.

Just behind the cathedral (walking right from the cathedral entrance along its southern wall) is the partly reconstructed Royal Palace, still closed to visitors at the time of research. In front of the entrance to the Royal Palace, at the square's eastern end, is an equestrian statue of Gediminas (Map p286), built on an ancient pagan site.

Behind the grand old duke, Sereikiškių Park leads to Three Crosses Hill (p292) and Kalnų Park.

Vilnius Cathedral   CATHEDRAL
(Arkikatedra bazilika; Map p286; Katredos aikštė 1; admission free; ⏱7am-7.30pm, Sun mass 9am, 10am, 11am & 7pm) This national symbol occupies the same spot that was originally used for the worship of Perkūnas, the Lithuanian thunder god; later the Soviets turned the cathedral into a picture gallery. It was reconsecrated in 1989 and mass has been celebrated daily ever since.

The first wooden cathedral was built here in 1387–88. A grander edifice was constructed under the auspices of Grand Duke Vytautas in the 15th century in Gothic style, but it has been rebuilt so often that its old form is unrecognisable. The most important restoration was carried out from 1783 to 1801, when the outside was redone in today's classical style. The statues of Sts Helene, Stanislav and Casimir are replicas of wooden versions added in 1793 but destroyed under Stalin.

The statues on the cathedral's south side facing the square are Lithuanian dukes; those on the north side are apostles and saints. The bright and expansive interior retains more of its original aspect, though the entrances to the side chapels were harmonised in the late 18th century.

St Casimir's Chapel is the showpiece. It has a baroque cupola, coloured marble and granite on the walls, white stucco sculptures, and fresco scenes from the life of St Casimir (who was canonised in 1602 and is Lithuania's patron saint). Find it at the eastern end of the south aisle.

Royal Palace   MUSEUM
(Valdovų rumai; Map p286; www.lvr.lt, in Lithuanian) Following the cathedral's southern wall brings you to the entrance of what someday will be one of the city's top attractions: the former Royal Palace of the Grand Dukes. The palace that once stood here was a modern-day wonder in the 16th and 17th centuries, with its vast courtyard and lively social calendar that included masked balls, banquets and jousting matches. Under the Russian occupation at the end of the 18th century, the palace was torn down and left a ruin. In the 2000s, the Lithuanian government came up with the great idea to rebuild the palace in its former splendour and reopen it as a museum. A decade on and an estimated 300 million euros later, the palace was still not finished at the time of research in 2011 (p368) and officials can't say when it will be ready (if ever).

LITHUANIA VILNIUS

WISH UPON A...

...star? No. Not in Vilnius. Rather, a stone tile bearing the word *stebuklas* (miracle). It marks the spot on Cathedral Sq where the human chain – formed between Tallinn and Vilnius by two million Lithuanians, Latvians and Estonians to protest Soviet occupation in 1989 – ended. To make a wish, do a clockwise 360-degree turn on the tile. Unfortunately, superstition forbids us from revealing the location of this elusive-but-lucky spot, meaning you have to search for it yourself. Hint, hint...we *did* tell you it was on Cathedral Sq...

Vilnius

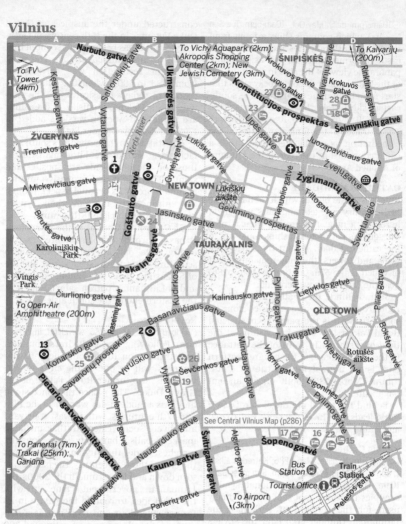

National Museum of Lithuania MUSEUM
(Lietuvos nacionalinis muziejus; Map p286; www
.lnm.lt; Arsenalo gatvė 1; adult/child 5/3Lt; ☺10am-
5pm Tue-Sat, to 3pm Sun) Following the road
that leads to the left from the cathedral
entrance brings you to two museums: the
National Museum of Lithuania and the Museum of Applied Arts. Identify the former
by the proud statue of Mindaugas, the first
and only king of Lithuania, standing out
front. Inside are exhibits looking at everyday
Lithuanian life from the 13th century until
WWII. Of particular note are some of the
country's earliest coins, dating from the 14th

century, which feature the bust of Jogaila
(p369).

Museum of Applied Arts MUSEUM
(Taikomosios dailės muziejus; Map p286; www.ldm
.lt; Arsenalo gatvė 3a; adult/child 6/3Lt; ☺11am-
6pm Tue-Sat, to 4pm Sun) Located in the old
arsenal at the foot of Gediminas Hill, this
museum has temporary exhibitions alongside a permanent collection showcasing 15th-
to 19th-century Lithuanian sacred art. Much
of it was only discovered in Vilnius Cathedral
in 1985 after being hidden in the walls by
Russian soldiers in 1655. Because of fear that

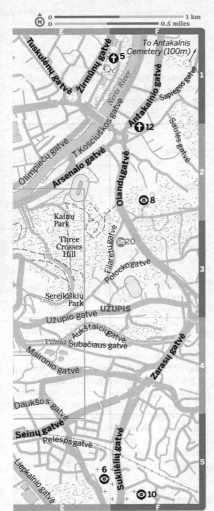

wandering Old Town backstreets. The main axis is along Pilies, Didžioji and Aušros Vartų gatvė. Its approximate boundary, starting from Katedros aikštė, runs along Stuokos-Gucevičiaus, Liejyklos, Vilniaus, Trakų, Pylimo, Bazilijonų, Šv Dvasios, Bokšto, Maironio, Radvilaitės and Šventaragio streets – an area of roughly 1 sq km.

PILIES GATVĖ

Cobbled Pilies gatvė (Castle St) – the hub of tourist action and the main entrance to Old Town from Katedros aikštė – buzzes with buskers, souvenir stalls, and the odd beggar. Until the 19th century the street was separated from the square by the lower castle wall, which ran across its northern end. Only a gate in the wall connected the two. Notice the 15th- to 17th-century brickwork of Nos 4, 12 and 16 towards the northern end of the street. The act granting Lithuania independence in 1918 was signed in No 26, the baroque **House of Signatories** (Lietuvos nepriklausomybės akto signatarų namai; Map p286; Pilies gatvė 26; admission free; 10am-5pm Tue-Sat year-round, plus 10am-3pm Sun May-Oct). This declaration of independence didn't last long; by 1920 the Poles had retaken Vilnius and the city was only returned to the Lithuanian heartland in 1939 as a 'gift' by then Soviet leader Josef Stalin (p371).

VILNIUS UNIVERSITY

Founded in 1579 during the Counter-Reformation, **Vilnius University** (Map p286; www.vu.lt; Universiteto gatvė 5) was run by Jesuits for two centuries and became one of the greatest centres of Polish learning. It produced many notable scholars but was closed by the Russians in 1832 and didn't reopen until 1919. Today it has 23,000 students and Lithuania's oldest library, shelving five million books.

The hidden but linked **13 university courtyards** (adult/child 5/1Lt; 9am-6pm Mon-Sat) are accessed by passages and gates from surrounding streets. The south gate on Šv Jono gatvė brings you into the **Grand Courtyard**. Inside is **Sts Johns' Church** (Šv Jonų bažnyčia; Map p286; 10am-5pm Mon-Sat), founded in 1387 well before the university arrived. The awkward name reflects the fact that the church is named after two St Johns: St John the Baptist and St John the apostle and evangelist. The church's 17th-century bell tower, standing on the south side of the courtyard, is a distinctive feature in

they'd be seized by the Soviets, the works, valued at €11 million, remained a secret until 1998, when they were finally displayed to the world.

OLD TOWN

Eastern Europe's largest old town deserves its Unesco status. The area, stretching 1.5km south from Katedros aikštė, was built up in the 15th and 16th centuries, and its narrow winding streets, hidden courtyards and lavish old churches retain the feel of bygone centuries. One of the purest pleasures the city has to offer is aimlessly

Vilnius

⊙ Sights

1 Church of the Saint Virgin's
  Apparition.................................... B2
  Europa Tower ....(see 27)
2 Flower Market............................. B4
3 Kenessa....................................... A2
4 Lithuanian Museum of Energy
  and Technology D2
5 Memorial Chapel............................ F1
6 Military Cemetery.........................E5
7 Municipality..................................C1
8 Old Jewish Cemetery F2
9 Parliament House........................... B2
10 Rasų Cemetery F5
11 St Raphael's Church......................C2
12 Sts Peter & Paul Church F2
  Tuskulėnų Park..........................(see 5)
13 TV & Radio Centre........................ A4

⊙ Activities, Courses & Tours

14 Oreivystės Centras.........................C2

⊙ Sleeping

15 A Hostel.. D5

16 A Hostel......................................D5
17 A Hostel......................................C5
18 Ecotel D1
19 E-Guest House B4
20 Filaretai Hostel F3
21 Old Town Hostel D5
22 Panorama Hotel D5
23 Radisson Blu Hotel Lietuva C1

⊗ Eating

24 Iki B2

⊙ Drinking

  Skybar.....................................(see 23)
  Soprano ....(see 27)

⊙ Entertainment

25 Forum Cinemas Vingis A4
26 Soho B4

⊙ Shopping

27 Europa...C1
28 Lino Kopos D1
29 Vaga B2

the Vilnius skyline. The arch through the 16th-century building opposite Sts Johns' leads to the **Astronomical Observatory Courtyard**, with an old two-domed observatory, the late 18th-century facade of which is adorned with reliefs of the zodiac.

CENTRAL OLD TOWN

Old Town is effectively bisected by Pilies gatvė, which eventually leads to Didžioji gatvė. This street then widens at its southern end into Rotušės aikštė (Town Hall Sq), the site of the former town hall and home to a branch of the tourist information office. Along this axis, worthwhile sights, museums and churches are spread out on both the eastern and western sides.

TOP CHOICE St Anne's Church   CHURCH
(Šv Onos bažnyčia; Map p286; Maironio gatvė 8; ⊙mass 6pm daily, 9am & 11am Sun) Arguably the most beautiful church in Vilnius – at least for its exterior – is the late-15th-century St Anne's Church. A graceful example of Gothic architecture, its sweeping curves and delicate pinnacles frame 33 different types of red brick. It is so fine that Napoleon reputedly wanted to take it back to Paris in the palm of his hand.

Presidential Palace   PALACE
(Map p286; ☑266 4073; www.president.lt; Daukanto gatvė 3; admission free; guided tours ⊙4.30pm Fri, 9am-2.30pm Sat) The exit from the university's Sarbievijus Courtyard to Universiteto gatvė brings you into the square opposite the former Bishops' Palace, now the Presidential Palace. It gained its current classical Russian Empire style early in the 19th century. The palace was used by Napoleon during his advance on Moscow, and by his Russian adversary General Mikhail Kutuzov when he was chasing Napoleon back to Paris. See the ceremonial changing of the guard on Sunday at noon. Visits by guided tour (in Lithuanian) must be booked in advance (call or see the website).

Mickiewicz Memorial Apartment & Museum   MUSEUM
(Mickevičiaus memorialinis butas-muziejus; Map p286; Bernardinų gatvė 11; adult/child 5/3Lt; ⊙10am-5pm Tue-Fri, to 2pm Sat & Sun) 'Lithuania, my fatherland...' is from Poland's national romantic masterpiece. It's not surprising when you realise it was Polish poet Adam Mickiewicz (1798–1855) – muse to Polish nationalists in the 19th century – who wrote the line in his poem *Pan Tadeusz*. He grew up near Vilnius and studied at the university

VILNIUS IN...

Two Days

Spend the first day exploring the Old Town, not missing the **cathedral**, **Pilies gatvė**, the **Gates of Dawn** and the **university's 13 courtyards**, followed by lunch on an Old Town terrace. At dusk, hike (or ride the funicular) up **Gediminas Hill** for a city-spire sunset. On the second day, stroll around the **Užupis Republic**, visit the **Museum of Genocide Victims**, and finish up with an aperitif and Vilnius panorama from the **TV Tower**.

Four Days

Depending on your interests, spend a day discovering **Jewish Vilnius**, marvelling at the religious jewels in the **Museum of Applied Arts**, or taking in the collections of any of a number of other museums. Finish up with a spot of **shopping**: scour the city for linen, amber and Lithuanian fashion. You can also squeeze in a day trip by train to **Trakai** and spend a leisurely few hours out on the water.

(1815–19) before being exiled for anti-Russian activities in 1824. The rooms where he wrote the well-known poem *Grażyna* (Lithuanian: *Gražia;* a Polish name for a woman with Lithuanian roots meaning 'beauty') are now filled with a few of the poet's letters.

Amber Museum-Gallery   MUSEUM

(Gintaro Muziejus-Galerija; Map p286; www .ambergallery.lt; Šv Mykolo gatvė 8; admission free; ⊙10am-7pm) The usual array of amber trinkets and jewellery to buy are displayed on the ground floor here, but it's the small but fine exhibition in the basement that warrants the most attention – not least for its archaeological excavations (the basement is set at 15th-century street level). Ceramics were fired in the two kilns in the 15th century.

Vilnius Picture Gallery   MUSEUM

(Vilniaus Galerija Paveikslų; Map p286; www.ldm.lt; Didžioji gatvė 4; adult/child 6/3Lt; ⊙noon-6pm Tue-Sat, to 5pm Sun) This museum is filled with 16th- to 20th-century Lithuanian art as well as sculpture and some decorative arts. It's housed in a 17th-century residential palace.

TOP FIVE PANORAMAS

For a breathtaking cityscape scale the following:

» Upper Castle Museum (p280) while sightseeing.
» Europa (p305) during a shopping spree.
» Tores (p300) over lunch or dinner.
» SkyBar (p302) with aperitif in hand.
» TV Tower (p294) for sunset vistas.

Kazys Varnelis Museum   MUSEUM

(Map p286; ☏279 1644; www.lnm.lt; Didžioji gatvė 26; ⊙10am-4pm Tue-Sat, arrange in advance) Near the town hall, this museum is home to the personal art collection of Lithuanian artist Kazys Varnelis. During his 50 years in the US, Varnelis earned fame and fortune with his optical and three-dimensional paintings. He collected a vast and varied array of paintings, furniture, sculptures, maps and books, including works by Dürer, Goya and Matteo Di Givanni. Visits are by appointment only, so call beforehand.

MK Čiurlionis House   MUSEUM

(Map p286; Savičiaus gatvė 11; admission free; ⊙10am-4.30pm Mon-Fri) Inside the former home of the great artist and composer are a handful of Čiurlionis reproductions, worth taking a peek at if you can't make it to the National Čiurlionis Art Museum (p328) in Kaunas.

St Casimir's   CHURCH

(Šv Kazimiero bažnyčia; Map p286; Didžioji gatvė 34; ⊙10am-6.30pm Mon-Sat, 8am-6.30pm Sun) The striking church is the city's oldest baroque place of worship. St Casimir's dome and cross-shaped ground plan defined a new style for 17th-century churches when the Jesuits built it between 1604 and 1615. It was destroyed and rebuilt several times over the centuries and has recently emerged from another bout of renovation.

AUŠROS VARTŲ GATVĖ

Vilnius' oldest street, which leads south out of Didžioji gatvė to the Gates of Dawn, is laden with churches and souvenir shops. Walking south, it's hard to miss the late-baroque

Central Vilnius

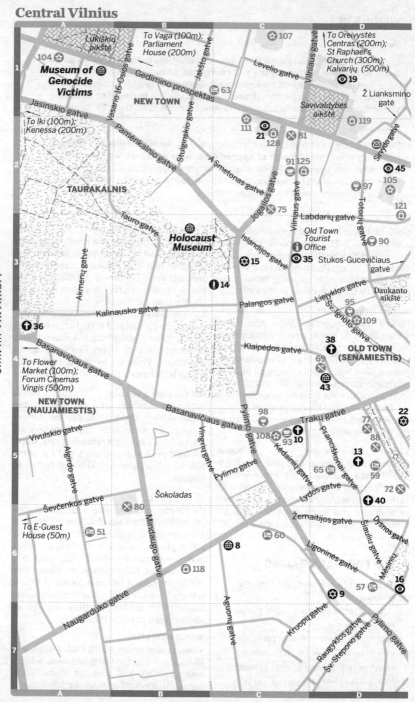

Lukiškių aikštė

To Vaga (100m);
Parliament
House (200m)

107

To Oreivystės
Centras (200m);
St Raphael's
Church (300m);
Kalvarijų (500m)

104

Museum of
Genocide
Victims

Levelio gatvė

19

Vilniaus gatvė

Jakšto gatvė

Gedimino prospektas

63

NEW TOWN

Ž Lianksmino
gatė

Jasinskio gatvė

Savivaldybės
aikštė

119

To Iki (100m);
Kenessa (200m)

111

21

128

81

Vasario 16-Osios gatvė

Stulginskio gatvė

Pamenkalnio gatvė

A Smetonas gatvė

91 125

45

TAURAKALNIS

Jogailos gatvė

97

105

121

Tauro gatvė

75

Labdarių gatvė

Totorių gatvė

Akmenų gatvė

Islandijos gatvė

Holocaust
Museum

Old Town
Tourist
Office

90

15

35

Stukos-Gucevičiaus
gatvė

14

Daukanto
aikštė

Kalinausko gatvė

Palangos gatvė

Liejyklos gatvė

95

Šv. Ignoto gatvė

109

36

Klaipėdos gatvė

38

OLD TOWN
(SENAMIESTIS)

Basanavičiaus gatvė

69

To Flower
Market (100m);
Forum Cinemas
Vingis (500m)

43

NEW TOWN
(NAUJAMIESTIS)

Basanavičiaus gatvė

98

Traku gatvė

22

Vivulskio gatvė

Pylimo gatvė

Vingrių gatvė

108 93

10

Pranciškonai gatvė

77

88

Algirdo gatvė

13

Ševčenkos gatvė

Kėdainių gatvė

65

59

Pylimo gatvė

Lydos gatvė

72

40

Šokoladas

80

Žemaitijos gatvė

Mindaugo gatvė

To E-Guest
House (50m)

51

60

Dysnos gatvė

Šiaulių gatvė

8

Ligoninės gatvė

118

Mėsinių

16

57

Naugarduko gatvė

Aguonų gatvė

9

Kruopų gatvė

Raugyklos gatvė

Pylimo gatvė

Šv. Stepono gatvė

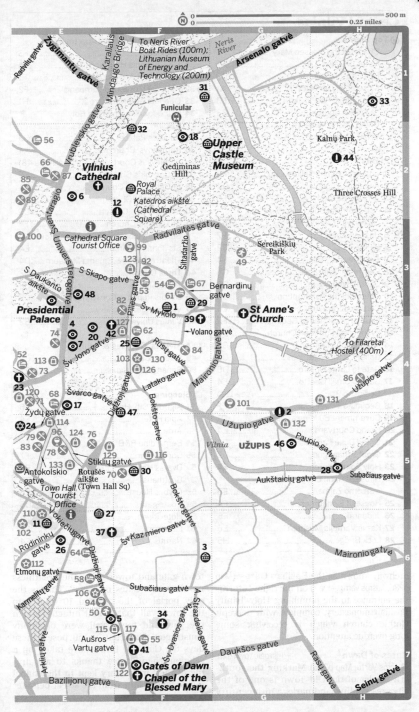

N 0 — 500 m
0 — 0.25 miles

Radvilų gatvė

Žygimantų gatvė

Karaliaus

Mindaugo Bridge

Vrublevskio gatvė

To Neris River
Boat Rides (100m);
Lithuanian Museum
of Energy and
Technology (200m)

Neris
River

Arsenalo gatvė

31

Funicular

33

Kalnų Park

32

18

Upper
Castle
Museum

44

56

Gediminas
Hill

Three Crosses Hill

66

85

87

Vilnius
Cathedral

6

Royal
Palace

12

Katedros aikštė
(Cathedral
Square)

89

S Nenaragio

Universiteto gatvė

100

Cathedral Square
Tourist Office

99

Radvilaitės gatvė

Sereikiškių
Park

49

123

92

S Daukanto
aikštė

48

S Skapo gatvė

54

67

Bernardinų
gatvė

Šiltadaržio
gatvė

Presidential
Palace

82

Pilies gatvė

53

61

Šv Mykolo

1

29

39

St Anne's
Church

4

74

20

127

42

62

Volano gatvė

Maironio gatvė

7

Šv Jono gatvė

25

84

To Filaretai
Hostel (400m)

52

113

73

103

130

126

86

Užupio gatvė

23

120

68

Švarco gatvė

Latako gatvė

131

Žydų gatvė

17

Dižioji gatvė

Bokšto gatvė

101

2

132

24

114

Užupio gatvė

79

96

124

76

Vilnia

UŽUPIS

46

Paupio gatvė

83

78

133

129

116

28

Subačiaus gatvė

Antokolskio
gatvė

Stiklių gatvė

70

30

Aukštaičių gatvė

Town Hall
Tourist
Office

Rotušės
aikštė
(Town Hall Sq)

110

11

27

102

Vokiečiu gatvė

37

Rūdininkų
gatvė

26

64

Šv Kaz miero gatvė

3

Maironio gatvė

112

Etmonų gatvė

58

106

94

Subačiaus gatvė

A Strazdelio gatvė

Karmelitų gatvė

50

5

34

115

117

55

Aušros
Vartų gatvė

41

Daukšos gatvė

Rasų gatvė

122

Gates of Dawn
Chapel of the
Blessed Mary

Bazilijonų gatvė

Arklių gatvė

Šv Dvasios gatvė

Seinų gatvė

Central Vilnius

◎ Top Sights

Chapel of the Blessed Mary F7
Gates of Dawn F7
Holocaust Museum B3
Museum of Genocide Victims...............A1
Presidential Palace...............................E3
St Anne's Church..................................G3
Upper Castle Museum F2
Vilnius Cathedral..................................E2

◎ Sights

1 Amber Museum-Gallery.........................F3
2 Angel of Užupis G4
3 Artillery Bastion F6
4 Astronomical Observatory
  Courtyard..E4
5 Basilian Gates..E7
6 Belfry...E2
7 Bell Tower E4
8 Centre for Tolerance C6
9 Choral Synagogue D6
10 Church of the Assumption C5
11 Contemporary Art Centre E6
12 Equestrian Statue of Gediminas...........F2
13 Evangelical Lutheran Church................D5
14 Frank Zappa Memorial..........................C3
15 Gallery of the Righteous C3
16 Gate to Large Ghetto............................D6
17 Gate to Small Ghetto.............................E4
  Gedimino 9 .... (see 119)
18 Gedimino Tower......................................F2
19 Government Building D1
20 Grand Courtyard.....................................E4
21 Grand Duke Palace C2
22 Great Synagogue D5
23 Holy Spirit Church E4
24 House of Gaon Elijahu Ben
  Shlomo Zalman....................................E5
25 House of Signatories..............................F4
26 Judenrat...E6
27 Kazys Varnelis Museum.........................E6
28 Lock Bridge..H5

29 Mickiewicz Memorial Apartment &
  Museum..F3
30 MK Čiurlionis House..............................F5
31 Museum of Applied Arts........................F1
32 National Museum of Lithuania F2
33 Open-air Amphitheatre H1
34 Orthodox Church of the Holy
  Spirit...F7
35 Radvilos Palace.....................................C3
36 Romanovs' Church.................................A4
  Sarbievijus Courtyard.................(see 48)
37 St Casimir's Church...............................E6
38 St Catherine's Church...........................D4
39 St Michael's Church F4
40 St Nicholas's Church.............................D5
41 St Teresa's Church.................................F7
  Strashum Library ....(see 22)
42 Sts Johns' Church..................................E4
43 Theatre, Music & Cinema Museum D4
44 Three Crosses.......................................H2
45 Three Muses..D2
46 Užupis Republic Constitution................G5
47 Vilnius Picture Gallery...........................F4
48 Vilnius University....................................E3

⊕ Activities, Courses & Tours

49 Electric Cars..G3
50 Senamiesčio Gidas................................E7

⊜ Sleeping

51 Algirdas City Hotel A6
52 Apia Hotel..E4
53 Atrium F3
54 Bernardinu B&B F3
55 Domus Maria..F7
56 Dvaras Hotel E2
57 Grotthaus D6
58 Grybas House E6
59 Hostelgate..D5
60 Hotel Rinno..C6
61 Litinterp F3
62 Narutis..F4

archway known as the **Basilian Gates** (Map p286; Aušros Vartų gatvė 7) on the right. It forms the entrance to the crumbling Holy Trinity Basilian monastery, complete with decrepit Gothic church which is receiving some long-overdue attention.

Gates of Dawn HISTORIC TOWN GATE
(Aušros Vartų; Map p286) Marking the southern border of the Old Town is one of the city's resounding landmarks, a 16th-century town gate and tower given the breathless moniker the 'Gates of Dawn'. This is the only portal of the original 10 built into the town wall that is still intact. Though the gate and town wall were originally constructed for defensive purposes, these days the Gates of Dawn have taken on a religious significance thanks to a painting of the Virgin Mary kept in the chapel inside (and visible from the street below).

63 Neringa..C1
64 Radisson Blu Astorija E6
65 Šauni Vietelė.......................................D5
66 Senatoriai Hotel E2
67 Shakespeare...F3
68 Stikliai..E4

🍴 **Eating**
69 Balti Drambliai.....................................D4
70 Balzac...F5
71 Bistro 18..E4
72 Čili Kaimas D5
73 Cozy...E4
74 Fiorentino..E4
75 Ikiukas..C2
76 Kitchen E5
77 La Provence..D5
78 Lokys...E5
79 Markus ir Ko E5
80 Maxima..B6
81 Mini Maxima C2
82 Pilies kepyklėlė.....................................F3
83 René...E5
84 Saint Germain F4
85 Sue's Indian Raja...................................E2
86 Tores..H4
87 Tres Mexicanos......................................E2
88 Žemaičiai..D5
89 Zoe's Bar & Grill E2

🍷 **Drinking**
90 Būsi Trečias D3
91 Coffee Inn..C2
92 Coffee Inn...F3
93 Coffee Inn...C5
   Coffee Inn............................... (see 119)
94 In Vino..E6
95 La Bohemė..D3
96 Notre Vie E5
97 Paparazzi...D2
98 Skonis ir Kvapas....................................C5
99 Soprano...F3

100 Tappo D'Oro...E3
101 Užupio Kavinė.......................................G4

🎭 **Entertainment**
102 Brodvėjus E6
103 Gorky...F4
104 Lithuanian Music Academy..................A1
105 Lithuanian National Drama
     Theatre D2
106 National Philharmonic...........................E6
107 Opera & Ballet Theatre.........................C1
108 Pablo Latino C5
109 Pasaka D4
110 Seacret E6
111 Small Theatre of Vilnius C2
112 Youth Theatre.......................................E6

🛍 **Shopping**
113 Akademinė Knyga E4
114 Aldona Mickuvienė's E5
115 Amber F7
116 Aukso Avis F5
117 Aušros Vartų Meno Galerija.....................F7
118 Black Ceramics Centre.........................B6
     Bronė Daškevičienė's ....(see 114)
119 Gedimino 9 ....D2
120 Humanitas..E4
121 Jjuozas Statkevičius D2
122 Jonas Bugailiškis'..................................F7
123 Lino ir Gintaro Studija F3
124 Lino ir Gintaro Studija E5
125 Lino Namai C2
126 Lino Namai F4
127 Littera...F4
128 Marks & Spencer...................................C2
129 Ramunė Piekautaitė...............................E5
130 Sauluva F4
131 Užupis Blacksmith
     Museum-Gallery H4
132 Vilnius Potters' Guild.............................G5
     Vitražo manufaktūra....................(see 78)
133 Zoraza E5

LITHUANIA VILNIUS

Chapel of the Blessed Mary
(Map p286; admission free; ⏰6am-7pm, mass 9am Mon-Sat, 9.30am Sun) Within the Gates of Dawn, a door on the street's eastern side opens onto a staircase that leads to this 18th-century chapel above the gate arch. Inside is a miracle-working painting of the Virgin Mary, known as the *Madonna of the Gates of Dawn*. The origins of the painting are unclear, though it's believed to date from the early 17th century. It is revered equally by the Catholic, Orthodox and Uniate (Greek Catholic) faiths and has evolved into one of Eastern Europe's leading pilgrimage destinations.

St Teresa's Church   CHURCH
(Šv Teresės bažnyčia; Map p286; www.ausrosvartai .lt; Aušros Vartų gatvė 14) This Catholic church is baroque through and through: early baroque outside and ornate late baroque inside. Underneath its entrance is a chamber for the

THE FORMER JEWISH QUARTER & GHETTOS

Vilnius' Old Town was once home to a sizable Jewish community that was known around the world for its piety and strength of faith; for more see the boxed text p372.

The main Jewish quarter lay in the streets west of Didžioji gatvė. Today street names like Žydų (Jews) and Gaono (Gaon) are among the few reminders of those days. The 1572 **Great Synagogue** (Map p286) and its famous 1902 **Strashun Library** stood at the western end of Žydų gatvė. The synagogue was damaged in WWII and was demolished by Soviet authorities in the 1950s. Today, a school operates where the synagogue once stood, but there's a small memorial and a sign to mark the spot. For decades before WWII, the building at Gaono gatvė 6 (today the Austrian embassy) was a Jewish house of prayer. At Žydų gatvė 3, outside the **House of Gaon Elijahu Ben Shlomo Zalman** (Map p286), is a **memorial bust**, erected in 1997 on the 200th anniversary of the death of the sage who recited the entire Talmud by heart at the age of six.

The beginning of the end of Vilnius' Jewish community began with the German invasion of Poland in 1939. Vilnius fell temporarily into Soviet hands and all of Vilnius' Jewish organisations, except communist ones, were dissolved. Many Jewish leaders were deported. Meanwhile Polish Jews fleeing the Nazis arrived in droves.

With the German invasion of the Soviet Union in the summer of 1941, Vilnius fell to the Nazis within days. In the next three months, the Germans (along with many Lithuanians, some willingly and others unwillingly) murdered around 35,000 Jews – almost half those in the city – in the Paneriai Forest (p308).

Though the murders foretold of worse to come, German policy at the time had not yet settled on the Final Solution, and a ghetto was established in a small area north of Vokiečių gatvė to hold the remaining Jews.

This first ghetto – the Small Ghetto – was liquidated 46 days later and its inhabitants killed at Paneriai; a memorial plaque outside Gaono gatvė 3 recalls the 11,000 Jews who were marched to their death from the ghetto between 6 September and 20 October 1941.

A second ghetto, known as the Large Ghetto, was created in September 1941 south of Vokiečių gatvė to hold workers whom the Germans deemed as valuable to their war effort. This ghetto lasted until September 1943, when it was liquidated on Himmler's orders dissolving all of the wartime ghettos. Some 26,000 people were killed at Paneriai and a further 10,000 were herded off to concentration camps. About 6000 Vilnius Jews escaped.

The single **gate** (Map p286) of this ghetto stood at what's now Rūdininkų gatvė 18, marked with a plaque bearing a detailed map of the ghetto. The former **Judenrat** (ghetto administration building; Map p286) was at Rūdininkų gatvė 8; its courtyard shelters a commemorative plaque to 1200 Jews selected to be sent to Paneriai.

Today the Jewish community in Lithuania numbers around 5000, 80% of whom live in Vilnius. Since independence, a number of notable events have revolved around this small community. In 1996, Germany agreed to pay €1 million to Lithuania to compensate Holocaust survivors and victims of Nazi persecution. In 2001, the **Vilnius Yiddish Institute** (www.judaicvilnius.com) was established in the History faculty at Vilnius University.

dead, which contains some fine examples of baroque tombs, but it is usually locked.

Orthodox Church of the Holy Spirit
CHURCH

(Šv Dvasios cerkvė; Map p286; Aušros Vartų gatvė 10) This pink-domed, 17th-century structure is Lithuania's chief Russian Orthodox church. In a chamber at the foot of a flight of steps in front of the altar (their feet even peep out) lie the preserved bodies of three 14th-century martyrs – Sts Anthony, Ivan and Eustachius.

Artillery Bastion
MUSEUM

(Artilerijos bastėja; Map p286; www.lnm.lt; Bokšto gatvė 20/18) From the Gates of Dawn, follow the old wall around onto Šv Dvasios gatvė, then continue north to reach the Artillery Bastion. This 17th-century fortification houses a collection of old weaponry and armour. The building was closed for long-term renovation at the time of this research and it wasn't clear when it would reopen.

VOKIEČIŲ GATVĖ & AROUND

Vokiečių gatvė, the wide boulevard running northwest from Rotušės aikštė, is lined with restaurants that sprawl out onto the green parade at its centre.

St Nicholas Church CHURCH
(Šv Mikalojaus bažnyčia; Map p286; www.mikalojus.lt; Šv Mikalojaus gatvė 4) A little south of Vokiečių on quiet Mikalojaus gatvė is Lithuania's oldest Gothic church, founded by Germans around 1320. From 1901 to 1939 it was the only church in Vilnius where mass was held in Lithuanian.

Contemporary Art Centre MUSEUM
(Šiuolaikinio meno centras; SMC; Map p286; www.cac.lt; Vokiečių gatvė 2; adult/child 8/4Lt; ☺noon-7.30pm Tue-Sun) Changing exhibitions of excellent installation art and photography by Lithuanian and foreign avant-garde artists fill the Contemporary Art Centre.

Evangelical Lutheran Church CHURCH
(Evangelikų liuteronų bažnyčia; Map p286; www.augustana.lt in Lithuanian; Vokiečių gatvė 20; ☺11am-2pm Mon-Fri) Hidden in a courtyard, this revamped church is home to Vilnius' tiny Protestant community. The church dates from 1555 but displays a mixture of Gothic, baroque and rococo elements in its architecture. Under the Soviets a concrete floor split the church into workshop and basketball court.

VILNIAUS GATVĖ & AROUND

At the confluence of Vokiečių gatvė, Vilniaus gatvė and Dominikonų gatvė stand some sizeable church and monastery complexes dating from the 17th and 18th centuries.

LEADING JEWISH HERITAGE SIGHTS

Vilnius' main Jewish and Holocaust-related sights are administered by the **Vilna Gaon State Jewish Museum** (www.jmuseum.lt). The buildings include the Holocaust Museum, the Centre for Tolerance, and the Paneriai Museum (p308) in the Paneriai Forest. A fourth building, a **Gallery of the Righteous** (Map p286; Pylimo gatvė 4), appears to be permanently closed.

Begin your exploration at the simple but fine **Holocaust Museum** (Map p286; Pamėnkalnio gatvė 12; adult/child 6/3Lt; ☺9am-5pm Mon-Thu, 10am-4pm Sun), situated in the so-called 'Green House'. The displays lack modern interactive touches but are perhaps all the more moving for it. The exhibitions document in shocking detail, with photos and paperwork, the full process of the Holocaust in Lithuania, from the German-imposed orders putting limits on Jews' freedoms, to the creation of the ghettos and ultimately the deportations to Paneriai and other places. Many of the items here were donated by survivors and victims' families.

The **Centre for Tolerance** (Map p286; Naugarduko gatvė 10; adult/child 6/3Lt; ☺10am-6pm Mon-Thu, to 4pm Sun) serves as a helpful adjunct to the Holocaust Museum. Its exhibitions focus less on the Holocaust and more on Jewish history and culture over the centuries leading up to WWII. The explanatory panels in English on the 2nd floor are long but useful guides. Each covers a theme and is balanced and informative. A small permanent exhibit on the Jewish avant-garde in Vilnius between the wars is enlightening.

Vilnius' only remaining synagogue, the **Choral Synagogue** (Map p286; Pylimo gatvė 39; entry by donation; ☺10am-2pm Sun-Fri), was built in 1894 for the wealthy and survived only because the Nazis used it as a medical store. Restored in 1995, it is used by a small Orthodox community (services 8.30am and 7.30pm).

The Soviets destroyed several Jewish cemeteries in the 1950s. The **old Jewish cemetery** (Map p282; Krivių gatvė) where Rabbi Gaon Elijahu was originally buried was ripped up in 1957 and turned into a sports stadium (Žalgiris Stadium). The tombstones were recycled as paving stones; the steps leading up Tauro Hill to the Trade Union Palace on Mykolaičio-Putino gatvė were originally built from Jewish gravestones. In 1991 the Jewish community retrieved many of these desecrated markers; a handful are now on display at the site of the old cemetery.

Gaon Elijahu is now buried in the **new Jewish cemetery** north of Vingis Park in the Virsuliskės district (entrance on Ažuolyno gatvė).

Holy Spirit Church CHURCH

(Šv Dvasios bažnyčia; Map p286; cnr Dominikonų & Šv Ignoto gatvė) Vilnius' primary Polish church (1679). Once attached to a Dominican monastery, it has a splendid gold and white interior and is hugely popular with wedding parties.

St Catherine's Church CHURCH

(Šv Kotrynos bažnyčia; Map p286; Vilniaus gatvė 30) The two towers of peach and creamy-white St Catherine's Church were once part of a Benedictine monastery; these days the church often hosts classical concerts.

Church of the Assumption CHURCH

(Map p286; Trakų gatvė 9/1) Dubbed 'Sands Church' after the quarter in which it stands, this 15th-century Franciscan church has a varied history – it was a hospital for the French army in 1812 and housed the state archives from 1864 to 1934 and 1949 to 1989. The building was returned to the Archbishopric of Vilnius in 1995 and to Franciscan friars three years later, and is currently undergoing long-term, painstaking restoration work.

Theatre, Music & Cinema Museum MUSEUM

(Teatro, muzikos ir kino muziejus; Map p286; www.ltmkm.lt; Vilniaus gatvė 41; adult/student 5/3Lt; ⊙11am-6pm Tue-Fri, 11am-4pm Sat) Memorabilia from stage and screen is the star of this museum. Of the three arts, the musical history section steals the show – the collection of traditional musical instruments, including a pūslinė (a primitive Baltic string instrument made from animal bladders) and several kanklės (plucked, fretted string instruments), will enchant anyone who has ever picked up an instrument.

Radvilos Palace MUSEUM

(Radvilų rūmai; Map p286; www.ldm.lt; Vilniaus gatvė 22; adult/student 6/3Lt; ⊙11am-5.30pm Tue-Sat, to 4.30pm Sun) A short stroll north along Vilniaus brings you to the entrance of this 17th-century palatial residence. It houses the foreign fine-arts section of the Lithuanian Art Museum above ground.

Frank Zappa Memorial MONUMENT

(Map p286; Kalinausko gatvė 1) West of Vilniaus gatvė, rock 'n' roll legend Frank Zappa is immortalised in a bronze bust atop a 4.2m-high stainless-steel pole. It was the world's first memorial to the offbeat American who died in 1993. Look carefully for it in the parking lot, as it doesn't jump out at you. Also, take a look at the graffiti on the walls surrounding the lot.

EAST OF GEDIMINAS HILL

Crossing the Vilnia River brings you into 'foreign' territory – the self-declared independent republic of Užupis (see the boxed text). The district has a few quirky attractions, including **Lock Bridge** (Map p286; Paupio gatvė), where newlyweds attach a padlock to the bridge railing to secure their marriage, but plenty more lies further east.

TOP CHOICE Antakalnis Cemetery CEMETERY

(off Karių kapų gatvė; ⊙9am-dusk) One of Eastern Europe's most peaceful graveyards lies in this leafy suburb, a short stroll east of the centre. Those killed by Soviet special forces on 13 January 1991 are buried here; a sculpture of the Madonna cradling her son memorialises them. Another memorial honours Napoleonic soldiers who died of starvation and injuries in Vilnius while retreating from the Russian army. The remains of 2000 of them were only found in 2002. Hundreds of Polish soldiers' graves, including many unknown soldiers, are also located here, which gets a mixed reception, especially on All Saints' Day (1 November). Former president Algirdas Brazauskas's grave is a bit abandoned atop a hillslope, in a newer area of the cemetery.

Rasų & Military Cemeteries CEMETERY

(Map p282; Sukilėlių gatvė) Vilnius' Rasų and Military cemeteries sit side by side in the southeastern end of the Old Town. Founded in 1801, Rasų Cemetery was the resting place for the Vilnius elite. More interesting, however, is the small military cemetery close by, where the heart of the Polish Marshal Józef Piłsudski, responsible for Poland's annexation of Vilnius in 1920, is buried. His mother shares his heart's grave (his body is buried in Kraków). Piłsudski came from this part of Lithuania and his family had an estate outside of Vilnius.

Three Crosses MONUMENT

(Trys kryžiai; Map p286) East of Gediminas Hill, three crosses stand majestically atop Three Crosses Hill (Trijų kryžių kalnas). Crosses have stood here since the 17th century in memory of three monks who were crucified on this spot. The remains of three crosses lie in the shadow of the erect ones. These are the original hill monuments, which the Soviets bulldozed after WWII. In the spirit of Lithuania the people rebuilt them but left the twisted remains of the originals as

REBELS WITH A CAUSE

The cheeky streak of rebellion pervading Lithuania flourishes in Vilnius' bohemian heart, where artists, dreamers, drunks and squatters in Užupis have declared a breakaway state.

The Užupis Republic (Užupio Republika) was officially, in an unofficial sense, born in 1998. The state has its own tongue-in-cheek president, anthem, flags and a 41-point constitution, which, among other things, gives inhabitants: the right to hot water, heating in winter and a tiled roof; and the right to be unique, to love, to be free, to be happy (or unhappy) and to be a dog. It ends 'Do not defeat. Do not fight back. Do not surrender.' Read the entire **constitution** (Map p286) in English, French, Lithuanian and several other languages on a wall on Paupio gatvė.

On April Fool's Day, citizens of the Republic of Užupis celebrate their wholly unofficial state. Border guards wearing comical outfits stamp passports at the main bridge and the Užupis president makes speeches in the quarter's small square – the intersection of Užupio, Maluno and Paupio gatvės where the republic's symbol, the **Angel of Užupis** (Map p286), stands. Increasingly hip and trendy, the neighbourhood continues to fill with art galleries and folk-artist workshops.

a historical reminder of oppression. Walk to them from Kosciuskos gatvė.

Sts Peter & Paul Church   CHURCH
(Šv Petro ir Povilo bažnyčias; Map p282; Antakalnio gatvė 1) Don't be fooled by the uninspiring exterior of this church. Its baroque interior – an orgy of thousands of ornate white sculptures created by Italian sculptors between 1675 and 1704 – is the finest icing on the cake of any church in the country. The church was founded by Lithuanian noble Mykolas Kazimieras Paca, whose tomb is on the right of the porch.

NEW TOWN
The 19th-century New Town (Naujamiestis) stretches 2km west of the cathedral and Old Town. Here the medieval charm of the Old Town is replaced by wide boulevards and pockets of lush parkland.

GEDIMINO PROSPEKTAS
Sandwiched between the Roman Catholic cathedral's dramatic skyline and the silver domes of the Russian Orthodox **Church of the Saint Virgin's Apparition** (Map p282), fashionable Gedimino is the main street of modern Vilnius. Its 1.75km length is dotted with shops, a theatre, banks, hotels, restaurants, offices, a few park squares and the seat of various official bods, including that of the Lithuanian **Government Building** (Map p286; www.lrv.lt; Gedimino prospektas 11) and Parliament House. Laid out in 1852, the sparkling street has had 11 name changes since: the tsarists named it after St George, the Poles after Mickiewicz, and

the Soviet rulers first after Stalin, then Lenin.

Striking a theatrical pose at Gedimino prospektas 4 is the **Three Muses** (Map p286) statue atop the Lithuanian National Drama Theatre. The unusual black-robed figures (representing drama, comedy and tragedy) hiding behind gold masks lean out towards an audience of tourists taking snapshots.

Some of the street's historical buildings have been turned into shopping centres that few Lithuanians can actually afford to shop in. Both **Gedimino 9** (Map p286; www.gedimino 9.lt; Gedimino prospektas 9) – the Harrods or Bloomingdale's of Vilnius – and the salmon-pink and cream **Grand Duke Palace** (Map p286; Gedimino prospektas 20/1) are worth entering simply to admire the beautiful restoration work.

A statue of Lenin once stood on **Lukiskių aikštė**, a square that used to bear the name of the levelled statue, now displayed in Druskininkai's Grūtas Park (boxed text p321).

Museum of Genocide Victims   MUSEUM
(Genocido aukų muziejus; Map p286; www.genocid .lt; Aukų gatvė 2a; adult/child 6/3Lt; ⊙10am-5pm Tue-Sat, to 3pm Sun) This former headquarters of the Soviet KGB houses a museum dedicated to the thousands of Lithuanians who were murdered, imprisoned or deported by the Soviet Union from WWII until the 1960s. Memorial plaques honouring those who perished in the harsh postwar Stalinist years tile the outside of the building.

Inside, the floors above ground cover the harsh realities of Soviet occupation, including gripping personal accounts of life as a Lithuanian deportee in Siberia. The true horror hits home on entering the basement, which contains inmate cells and an execution cell where, between 1944 and the 1960s, prisoners were shot or stabbed in the skull. In 1994 the remains of 767 victims killed here between 1944 and 1947 were found in a mass grave in Tuskulėnų Park (Map p282), north of the Neris River. In 2005 they were reburied in the park in a state-of-the-art cone-shaped memorial chapel (Map p282; Žirmūnų gatvė). During the Nazi occupation, the Gestapo was also headquartered here, giving this late-19th-century building dark karma indeed.

Parliament House GOVERNMENT BUILDING

(Seimas; Map p282; www.seimas.lt; Gedimino prospektas 53) Outside Parliament House, concrete slabs with mangled barbed wire and daubed slogans are poignant reminders of Lithuania's violent past. Barricades were erected here on 13 January 1991 to protect parliament from Soviet troops. The barricades to the north of the parliament building were left in place until December 1992, when the last Russian soldier left Vilnius.

SOUTH OF GEDIMINO PROSPEKTAS

A few blocks south of Gedimino prospektas is the Romanovs' Church (Map p286; Basanavičiaus gatvė 27), an eye-catching Russian Orthodox church with pea-green onion domes built in 1913. To the west of the church is Vilnius' flower market (off Map p286; Basanavičiaus gatvė 42; 24hr), a perfect place for those hit with a romantic streak at 3am.

West of Jasinskio gatvė across the Neris River is a kenessa (Map p282; Liubarto gatvė 6), a traditional Karaites prayer house built in 1922.

VINGIS PARK

Just over 1km southwest of parliament, at the western end of Čiurlionio gatvė, is the wooded Vingis Park (Map p282), surrounded on three sides by the Neris. The park has a large open-air amphitheatre used for the Lithuanian Song and Dance Festival. Take trolleybus 7 from the train station or 3 from the Gedimino stop on Vilniaus gatvė to the Kęstučio stop (the second after the bridge over the river), then walk over the footbridge from the end of Treniotos gatvė.

Like the more distant TV Tower, the TV & Radio Centre (Map p282; cnr Konarskio gatvė & Pietario gatvė), near the southeastern edge of the park, was stormed by Soviet tanks and troops in the early hours of 13 January 1991. Wooden crosses commemorate Lithuania's independence martyrs.

ŠNIPIŠKĖS

On the north bank of the Neris, the quarter of Šnipiškės has been transformed: the tatty Soviet concrete blocks have gone and in their place is a new skyline of skyscrapers, including the Europa Tower (Map p282) on the Europa Business & Shopping Centre (p305), which – at 129m – is the Baltic's tallest skyscraper.

This new business district, dubbed 'Sunrise Valley', continues to grow apace, with highrises and construction sites popping up like mushrooms after a rain. As part of the urban redevelopment project, two new bridges linking the Europa Tower with the centre have been built and the municipality (Map p282; Konstitucijos prospektas 3) has moved here.

It's not all glass and gleaming metal this side of the river. There are also some interesting examples of Soviet architecture, along with St Raphael's Church (Map p282; Šv Rapolo bažnyčia; 6.30-9am & 5-7.30pm) near Žaliasis tiltas (Green Bridge), sporting a classic baroque interior behind a broken facade. The power-hungry can get along to the Lithuanian Museum of Energy and Technology (Map p282; www.emuziejus.lt; Rinktinės gatvė 2; adult/child 10/5Lt; 10am-5pm Thu-Sat), which focuses on nuclear power and other Soviet (and subsequent) energy-making means. It's housed in the city's original power plant, which ceased operation in 1998.

OUTSIDE THE CENTRE

TV Tower LANDMARK

(off Map p282; www.lrtc.lt; Sausio 13-osios gatvė 10; adult/child 21/9Lt; observation deck 10am-10pm) It's hard to miss the 326m TV tower on the city's western horizon. This tall needle symbolises Lithuania's strength of spirit; on 13 January 1991, Soviet special forces killed some 14 people here. Lithuanian TV kept broadcasting until the troops came through the tower door. Wooden crosses commemorate the victims and on 13 January hundreds of people light candles here. At Christmas 6000-odd fairy lights are strung on the tower to create the world's largest Christmas tree!

VILNIUS FOR CHILDREN

Kids will love to splash around at the well-equipped Polynesian-themed water park, **Vichy Aquapark** (Vandens Parkas; www.vandensparkas.lt; Ozo gatvė 14c; adult/child 3hr 59/39Lt, 4hr from 65/45Lt; ☉noon-10pm Mon-Fri, 10am-10pm Sat & Sun). The little ones can use up their energy on the adrenalin-pumping water rides and a wave pool, while parents can recharge their batteries in the whirlpools, steam baths and massage salon.

In town, the **electric cars** in Sereikiškių Park are popular, as are pedal-powered taxis (p286) that loiter near the park entrance on Cathedral Sq. Otherwise, there's nothing like a **sky-high panorama** (boxed text p285).

In winter a nice outing for kids is the Akropolis shopping centre (p305), which has an **ice-skating rink** (☉8.30am-11pm) and a **soft play area** (☉10am-10pm) for under-12s.

From the observation deck (190m) all of Vilnius is spread out before you. Steel stomachs can eat while feasting on views at **Paukščių takas** (Milky Way; mains 20-30Lt; ☉10am-10pm), a revolving restaurant in the tower.

To get to the tower, take trolleybus 16 from the train station or 11 from Lukiskių aikštė to the Televizijos Bokstas stop on Laisvės prospektas. A trip here takes you to Vilnius' Soviet-era high-rise suburbs.

🏃 Activities

Aside from walking and cycling (p307), Vilnius isn't blessed with an immensely wild array of outdoor pursuits, but it does however offer something you don't find everywhere – hot-air ballooning.

Take a gentle ride across the Old Town rooftops (as long as the wind is in the right direction) with **Oreivystės Centras** (Map p282; ☎8-652 00510; www.ballooning.lt; Upės gatvė 5). The price is around 500Lt per person for a one-hour flight over the city.

In summer (May to September), it's possible to ride a **boat** (off Map p286; ☎8-685 01000; 1hr tour adult/child 20/10Lt; ☉11am-8pm) along the Neris River. The boat, the *Ryga*, leaves throughout the day from a small port on the southern side of the Karaliaus Mindaugo Bridge.

👉 Tours

Two-hour walking tours of the Old Town in English (35Lt), starting at 2pm on Monday, Wednesday, Friday and Sunday from mid-May to mid-September, are organised by any branch of the Vilnius **tourist office** (☎253 2115; www.vilnius-tourism.lt). They also supply audio guides (35Lt) for self-guided tours and hand out free copies of thematic walking tours, including Jewish Vilnius, Musical Vilnius, and Castles & Palaces of Vilnius.

Senamiesčio Gidas   MINIBUS TOURS
(Old Town Guides; Map p286; ☎8-699 54064; www.vilniuscitytour.com; Aušros Vartų gatvė 7) Organises half-day minibus tours of Vilnius (75Lt, two hours) and Jewish Vilnius, as well as 'Trace your Family Roots' tours and day trips to Trakai (p308; 100Lt, 3¾ hours) and Kernavė (p311), Grūtas Park (Soviet sculpture park; boxed text p321) and Europe's geographical centre (p310). Prices depend on numbers; see the website for details.

🎊 Festivals & Events

Vilnius is blessed with year-round festivals, many of which are listed online at www.vilnius-events.lt and on www.vilnius-tourism.lt. Some of the bigger events:

Užgavėnės   CARNIVAL
Pagan carnival (Mardi Gras) on Shrove Tuesday (usually February).

Kaziukas Crafts Fair   CRAFTS
(www.kaziukomuge.lt in Lithuanian) Held in the Old Town to celebrate St Casimir's Day on 4 March.

Lygiadienis   CARNIVAL
Pagan carnival marking the spring equinox in March.

New Baltic Dance   DANCE
(www.dance.lt) Contemporary dance festival in early May.

Vilnius Festival   MUSIC & DANCE
Classical music, jazz and folk-music concerts in Old Town courtyards during June.

Christopher Summer Festival   MUSIC
(www.kristupofestivaliai.lt) Music festival held in July and August.

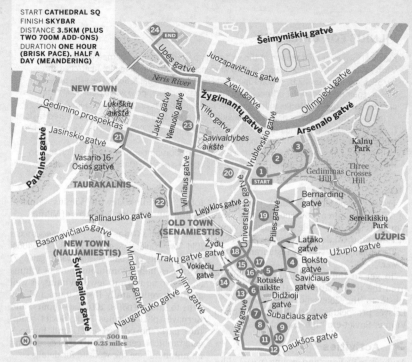

Walking Tour
The Best of Vilnius

❯ Eastern Europe's largest old town and surrounds are made for meandering. This itinerary is for those with just a few hours.

Begin on Cathedral Sq, taking in its magical tile, ❶ **cathedral** and ❷ **Royal Palace** before climbing through the park to the ❸ **Upper Castle Museum** on Gediminas Hill. From the tower survey the city then hike down into the Old Town along Pilies gatvė. To get a feel for quaint old Vilnius, cut left onto Bernardinų gatvė and zigzag along Volano gatvė, Literatu gatvė, Rusu gatvė and Lataku gatvė to Bokšto gatvė. Midway along Bokšto, turn right onto Savičiaus gatvė for the best of Lithuanian textiles at ❹ **Aukso Avis** and a taster of Lithuania's greatest artist at the ❺ **MK Čiurlionis House**. Continue along Savičiaus to Didžioji gatvė, turn left and follow the street past the ❻ **former town hall** to its southern end. Continue along Aušros Vartų, past the ❼ **National Philharmonic**, ❽ **Basilian Gates**, ❾ **Orthodox Church of the Holy Spirit**, ❿ **St Teresa's Church** and ⓫ **artist**

workshops before stopping at the sacred ⓬ **Gates of Dawn**.

Duck through the Gates of Dawn and turn west on Bazilijonų gatvė before heading north along Arklių gatvė to Rotušes aikštė where the ⓭ **Contemporary Art Centre** awaits. Quench your thirst at a ⓮ **cafe or restaurant terrace** on Vokiečių gatvė, then cut through onto Žydų gatvė for a glimpse of Jewish Vilnius. Wander north along Jewish St, and watch wedding sashes being woven at ⓯ **folk-artist workshops**. Take in design boutiques such as ⓰ **Zoraza**, ⓱ **Sufle** and ⓲ **Elementai** on Stiklių gatvė then continue south along Gaono gatvė to ⓳ **Vilnius University**.

Exhausted? Cut back onto Cathedral Sq and flop on the terrace at Zoe's Bar & Grill or ⓴ **Sue's Indian Raja**. Still raring to go? Amble west along Gedimino prospektas to the ㉑ **Museum of Genocide Victims** and return via ㉒ **Frank Zappa** or cut north along Vilniaus gatvė, past the ㉓ **Opera & Ballet Theatre**. Cross the bridge to Šnipiškės and its ㉔ **SkyBar**, where grand views await.

Capital Days

PERFORMING ARTS

Music and performing arts festival from the end of August to the beginning of September.

Sirens

THEATRE

(www.okt.lt) International theatre festival from mid-September to mid-October.

Gaida

CLASSICAL MUSIC

Showcases new music from Central and Eastern Europe in late October.

Mama Jazz

JAZZ

(www.vilniusmamajazz.lt) Mid-November festival with big-name guests.

🛏 Sleeping

For such a small capital, Vilnius has an extensive network of accommodation options. Summer season prices are quoted and include breakfast unless stated otherwise. All hotels and guesthouses listed here include private bathrooms.

TOP CHOICE Domus Maria

GUESTHOUSE €€

(Map p286; ✆264 4880; www.domusmaria.lt; Aušros Vartų gatvė 12; s 100-159Lt, d 150-221Lt, tr/q 279/299Lt; P@🛜) No guesthouse better reflects the Vilnius soul than Domus Maria. With rooms sheltered in the cells of a Carmelite monastery that was attached to St Teresa's Church and the Gates of Dawn in the 17th century, the place oozes atmosphere and charm. It's architecturally faithful to its monastic origins, with rooms off long corridors arranged around an interior courtyard. Rooms 207 and 307 – the only hotel rooms in Vilnius with a Gates of Dawn view – are booked months in advance. Breakfast is served in the vaulted refectory, original 18th-century frescos decorate the conference room and one floor is kitted out for disabled access.

TOP CHOICE Bernardinu B&B

GUESTHOUSE €€

(Map p286; ✆261 5134; www.bernardinuhouse .com; Bernardinų gatvė 5; s/d from 150/180Lt; P🛜) Charming family-owned guesthouse located on one of the most picturesque lanes in Old Town. The house dates to the 18th century, but it's been painstakingly renovated and the owners have tried hard to preserve elements like old timber flooring and ceilings. Breakfast is 15Lt and it's brought to your door on a tray at 9am.

Litinterp

GUESTHOUSE €€

(Map p286; ✆212 3850; www.litinterp.lt; Bernardinų gatvė 7-2; s/d/tr 100/160/210Lt, with shared bathroom 80/140/180Lt, apt 210Lt; ☺ office 8.30am-7pm Mon-Fri, 9am-3pm Sat; P@🛜) This bright, clean and friendly establishment has a wide range of options in the heart of Old Town. Rooms with shared bathroom can be a little cramped, but those with en suite are generously large. Guests can check in after office hours providing they give advance notice.

Ecotel

HOTEL €€

(Map p282; ✆210 2700; www.ecotel.lt; Slucko gatvė 8; s/d/tr 199/229/279Lt; P@🛜) Ecotel's ethos is to provide clean and tidy rooms at an affordable price and while it's no longer quite the steal it once was, rooms are still good value for what you get, including squeaky-clean bathrooms with heated towel racks. There is a computer with internet access in the lobby, and some rooms are designed for people with disabilities (and those who are tall); beds are 2.1m long.

Shakespeare

HOTEL €€€

(Map p286; ✆266 5885; www.shakespeare.lt; Bernardinų gatvė 8/8; s/d from 500/600Lt; P@🛜) Striving to be the best of boutique hotels, Shakespeare is a refined Old Town gem that evokes a cultured, literary feel with its abundance of books, antiques and flowers. Each room pays homage to a different writer – in name and design. The luxury suite on the upper floor has superb views that almost justify the 710Lt rack rate.

Grybas House

HOTEL €€

(Map p286; ✆264 7474; www.grybashouse.com; Aušros Vartų gatvė 3a; s 230-270Lt, d 300-340Lt, apt 420Lt; P🛜) Stase and Vladas run Grybas House – the first independent family-run hotel to crop up after independence – with grace, charm and bags of smiles. Rooms in this oasis of calm in the centre of Old Town are old-fashioned but very comfortable and some peep at the private courtyard.

Atrium

HOTEL €€€

(Map p286; ✆210 7777; www.atrium.lt; Pilies gatvė 10; s/d/ste 345/480/820Lt; P@🛜) One floor inside this 16th-century town house is kitted out for travellers with disabilities, and the cellar is equipped with a sauna and Jacuzzi. Rooms otherwise are standard midrange to top-end options in the tourist heart of Vilnius, and prices are substantially cheaper on weekends.

Grotthaus

HOTEL €€€

(Map p286; ✆266 0322; www.grotthushotel.com; Ligoninės gatvė 7; r/ste from 420/800Lt; P🛜)

LITHUANIA VILNIUS

Step through the red-canopied entrance of this buttercup-yellow townhouse boutique to find Villeroy & Boch bathtubs, 19th-century *Titanic*-style fittings, Italian-made furniture, and curtains allegedly made with the same fabric as that used by the queen of England! The Old Town location is top notch. Substantial discounts are available on weekends.

Narutis
HOTEL €€€

(Map p286; ☎212 2894; www.narutis.com; Pilies gatvė 24; s/d/ste 380/460/800Lt; P@🛜☀) Housed in a red-brick townhouse built in 1581, this classy pad has been a hotel since the 16th century. Breakfast and dinner are served in a vaulted Gothic cellar, there's wi-fi access throughout, and free apples at reception add a tasty touch. Booking over the internet can yield substantial savings.

Radisson Blu Astorija
HOTEL €€€

(Map p286; ☎212 0110; www.radissonblu.com; Didžioji gatvė 35/2; s/d/ste 610/650/1200Lt; P@🛜☀) This classical wonder – a hotel since 1901 – overlooks St Casimir's Church. Its wintertime Sunday brunches are renowned, and trouser press, safe and self-regulating heating/air-con are standard. Business-class rooms boast added luxuries, such as king-sized bed, bathrobe, slippers, iron, tea- and coffee-making facilities and free internet access.

Stikliai
HOTEL €€€

(Map p286; ☎264 9595; www.stikliaihotel.lt; Gaono gatvė 7; s/d/ste 655/828/1300Lt; P@🛜☀) The cream of the crop among Vilnius hotels, at least in terms of price, is this boutique managed by the Relais & Chateaux chain. The hotel is tucked down a picture-postcard cobbled street in the old Jewish quarter. Rooms are luxurious and the 17th-century digs are blessed with an abundance of charm.

E-Guest House
HOTEL €€

(Map p282; ☎266 0730; www.e-guesthouse.lt; Ševčenkos gatvė 16; s/d/tr/q from 150/180/230/260Lt; P@🛜) This very nice small hotel, just outside Old Town, has a philosophy of using environmentally friendly construction materials and high technology to give its mostly professional clientele a comfortable space to work. The rooms are simply but tastefully done up in a contemporary look. Breakfast is an extra 5Lt, and guests receive a 20% discount at the restaurant next door.

Šauni Vietelė
GUESTHOUSE €€

(Map p286; ☎212 4110; www.mtr.lt; Pranciškonai gatvė 3/6; s/d 90/160Lt) This three-room guesthouse above a crumbling courtyard cafe is great value for money. Its rooms are old-fashioned and filled with well-loved furniture, but they're all spacious and airy. Breakfast isn't included, but the cafe offers pancakes and such. The lovely old building was a Franciscan abbey in a previous life.

Senatoriai Hotel
HOTEL €€

(Map p286; ☎212 6491; www.senatoriai.lt; Tilto gatvė 2a; s 220Lt, d 300-350Lt; P@🛜) This small, homey hotel is so close to the cathedral you can almost hear mass. Rooms are generally spacious and feature heavy leather furniture and clean wooden floors. It offers that rarity among hotels in Lithuania: laundry service. Discounted rates over the website during slow periods.

Panorama Hotel
HOTEL €€

(Map p282; ☎233 8822; www.hotelpanorama.lt; Sodų gatvė 14; s/d from 260/290Lt; P@🛜) A Soviet-era hotel that surprises: dig beneath its kitsch, chocolate-brown tiled facade to find a bright, stylish and airy train-station hotel. Despite only being five storeys high, it has fabulous views of Old Town and the surrounding hills from its northern side. Stays of three nights or longer qualify for a 30% discount.

Hotel Rinno
HOTEL €€

(Map p286; ☎262 2828; www.rinno.lt; Vingrių gatvė 25; s/d from 260/320Lt; P@🛜) If you don't require a lift, you'll be hard pressed to find fault with Rinno. Its staff are exceptionally helpful and polite, its rooms first rate (more four-star than the three stars they're given), its location (between Old Town and the train and bus stations) handy, and its price a relative bargain. Breakfast is served in the pleasant and private back yard.

Algirdas City Hotel
HOTEL €€€

(Map p286; ☎232 6650; www.algirdashotel.lt; Algirdo gatvė 24; s/d from 210/370Lt; P🛜) Just a few years old and still feeling like a new hotel, the Algirdas pleases with simple, modern rooms, bathroom floors you could eat off and little extras, such as heated towel rails and flatscreen TVs. Deluxe rooms come with kettles and coffee.

Radisson Blu Hotel Lietuva   HOTEL €€€
(Map p282; ☑272 6272; www.radissonblu.com;
Konstitucijos prospektas 20; s/d/ste from 380/
450/800Lt; ⓟ🅐) This local representative of
the upscale Radisson Blu chain is the swankiest hotel in Vilnius' business sector and
has views of the city that are hard to beat.
Rooms are standard and businesslike, but
there are plenty of extras such as a fitness
and sauna centre and free wi-fi. The hotel
is topped by the 22nd-floor SkyBar (p302).

Neringa   HOTEL €€
(Map p286; ☑212 2288; www.neringahotel.com;
Gedimino prospektas 23; s/d from 220/270Lt;
ⓟ🅐🅢🅦) It may be a pre-independence old
girl that has retained a few fabulous 1970s
Soviet touches (take its restaurant with
mosaic floor, frescoed wall and tinkling
fountain), but everything else inside, from
the reception to the warm, spacious rooms,
has been refitted. Staff are professional and
helpful. Discounted rates can be found on
the hotel website.

Hostelgate   HOSTEL €
(Map p286; ☑8-638 32818; www.hostelgate.lt;
Mikalojaus gatvė 3; dm 33-38Lt; d/tr 110/140Lt;
ⓟ🅐🅢) Modern-style, flashpacker hostel
with a friendly vibe. The eight- to 12-bed
dorms are big, basic and cool in summer.
The hostel offers free internet access, coffee
and lockers, but no breakfast (there is a
kitchen). Location couldn't be better, just off
Vokiečių gatvė.

Dvaras Hotel   HOTEL €€
(Map p286; ☑210 7370; www.dvaras.lt; Tilto gatvė
3; s/d 260/320Lt; ⓟ🅐🅢) Opposite Senatoriai
Hotel; more like a plush country villa than a
city hotel. Each of the rooms is unique and
some have nice views over the cathedral and
Gediminas Hill.

Apia Hotel   HOTEL €€
(Map p286; ☑212 3426; www.apia.lt; Ignoto gatvė
12; d/ste from 210/280Lt; ⓟ🅐🅢) This smart,
fresh and friendly hotel occupies some
prime real estate in the heart of Old Town.
Choose from courtyard or cobbled-street
views among the hotel's 12 rooms, but if
you're after a balcony, reserve room 3 or 4.

Filaretai Hostel   HOSTEL €
(Map p282; ☑215 4627; www.filaretaihostel.lt;
Filaretų gatvė 17; dm 34Lt, s/d/tr without bathroom
70/100/120Lt; ⓟ🅐🅢) Affiliated with the
Lithuanian Hostels Association, Filaretai
occupies a quaint old villa 15 minutes' walk

(uphill) from Old Town. Dorms are five- to
eight-bedded; bed linen is provided, but
towels are an extra 1Lt, lockers 15Lt and
laundry 15Lt. Breakfast isn't included but
the hostel has a kitchen for guests to use. To
get here take bus 34 from the bus and train
stations to the seventh stop.

A Hostel   HOSTEL €
(Map p282; ☑213 9994; www.ahostel.lt; Šv Stepano
gatvė 15; 8-bed/4-bed dm 34/48Lt; 🅐🅢) Squeak-
ier than squeaky clean is the hallmark of
this modern hostel where the interior decoration screams colour. The Japanese-style
sleeping pods are adequate but not for the
claustrophobic, and there are good facilities,
including laundry (1Lt per item), internet
(first 15 minutes free) and lockers (3Lt). Two
further hostels are located at Sodų gatvė 8
and 17; breakfast isn't included.

Old Town Hostel   HOSTEL €
(Map p282; ☑262 5357; www.oldtownhostel.lt;
Aušros Vartų gatvė 20-15a; dm 35Lt, d/tr without bathroom 110/144Lt, 4-person apt 176Lt; 🅐)
This small hostel tucked away in a private
courtyard is handy to both Old Town (it's
located just *outside* the old walls) and the
bus and train stations. Rooms are basic
but accommodating, non–Hostelling International members pay 2Lt more, sheets/
laundry are 3/15Lt and internet access is free
on two computers.

✖ Eating

Whether it's *cepelinai* (zeppelins) or *kepta
duona* (deep-fried rye bread heaped with
garlic) you want, Vilnius has it covered. That
said, the Vilnius dining palate is now well
used to cuisine from around the world, and
the list of restaurants serving food from outside Lithuania's borders grows every month.
Most restaurants can be found in Old Town,
but getting a meal after midnight is more
challenging. In summer it's essential to reserve a table outside for evening dining.

TOP
CHOICE **Cozy**   INTERNATIONAL €€
(Map p286; www.cozy.lt; Dominikonų gatvė 10;
mains 10-25Lt; ⊙9am-2am Mon-Wed, to 4am Thu
& Fri, 10am-4am Sat, to 2am Sun) We can't tell
if this hip evening spot is a restaurant, bar
or club, but we do know we love the food
here. Great grilled sandwiches, served with
the best fries in Lithuania, plus salads, pastas, and imaginative soups that take their
inspiration from Asia and the Middle East.
It's also a bar, with very good cocktails, and

once they finish work on the downstairs club, they'll likely spin tunes here again too.

TOP CHOICE Sue's Indian Raja INDIAN €€
(Map p286; www.sues-lt.com; Odminių gatvė 3; mains 25-35Lt) Okay, we know it's strange to list an Indian restaurant as a top pick in the Lithuanian capital, but the food here is excellent and authentic. *After* you've had your fill of admittedly delicious local foods like potato pancakes and *cepelinai,* repair here to have your palate re-energized with spicy lentils, curries and vindaloo. The 'business lunch', served weekdays, is a steal at 20Lt.

Balzac FRENCH €€€
(Map p286; ✆8-614 89223; www.balzac.lt; Savičiaus gatvė 7; mains 30-50Lt) This classic French bistro serves what may be the best French food in Vilnius. The menu includes classics like boeuf bourguignon, stewed rabbit and duck confit. There's also a great wine list. The dining area is small, so best to phone ahead and book to avoid disappointment.

Markus ir Ko STEAKHOUSE €€€
(Map p286; http://markusirko.lt; Antokolskio gatvė 11; mains around 50Lt) Markus is a long-time favourite that remains top-notch for sweet, succulent, melt-in-your-mouth steak. Enjoy your slab of meat inside under the sultry gaze of Marilyn Monroe or outside on the fabulous terrace occupying one half of a charming Old Town street.

Pilies kepyklėlė CREPES €
(Map p286; Pilies gatvė 19; mains 10-20Lt; ⊙9am-11pm) A standout from the crowd on Vilnius' busiest tourist street, this relaxed combination creperie/bakery mixes old-world charm with a fresh, upbeat vibe. The 9am omelette here is a must-have if you're staying at a nearby guesthouse with a less-than-inspiring breakfast on offer. The savoury pancakes, stuffed with spinach or ham and cheese and topped with a dollop of mushroom sauce or sour cream, make for a filling and cheap lunch at 11Lt. The poppyseed cake is reputedly the best on this side of town.

Bistro 18 EUROPEAN €€
(Map p286; www.bistro18.lt; Stiklių gatvė 18; mains 20-40Lt) Bistro 18 is a breath of fresh air in Vilnius' restaurant scene. The service is friendly, polite and attentive, the decor is minimalist yet comfortable, the food is imaginative, international and flavoursome, and they know how to chill white wine.

The lunch menu (around 20Lt for soup and main) is an absolute bargain; dine alone and your meal will be served with a couple of books so you won't feel lonely.

Tres Mexicanos MEXICAN €€
(Map p286; www.tresmexicanos.lt; Tilto gatvė 2; mains 15-25Lt) This authentic Mexican restaurant is a nice addition to Vilnius' culinary scene. The owner, himself a happy transplant from Mexico, is trying his best to warm up the locals to spicy burritos, quesadillas and the rest – with some success. Some nights see this place overflowing to bursting.

Saint Germain FRENCH €€€
(Map p286; Literatų gatvė; mains 30-50Lt) Paris is the inspiration behind this idyllic wine-bar-cum-restaurant inside a convivial century-old house on a quiet Old Town street, making it a perfect choice for a quiet dinner for two. Of particular importance: the service is fit for the best restaurants on the continent, and advance reservations for its street terrace are essential.

Tores LITHUANIAN €€
(Map p286; www.tores.lt; Užupio gatvė 40; mains 25-50Lt) Feast your tastebuds on a plentiful mix of Lithuanian and European dishes and your eyes on a stunning Old Town panorama at this well-placed eating and drinking hang-out, atop a hill in bohemian Užupis.

Lokys LITHUANIAN €€€
(Bear; Map p286; www.lokys.lt; Stiklių gatvė 8; mains 30-60Lt) Hunt down the big wooden bear outside to find this Vilnius institution, a cellar maze going strong since 1972. Game is its mainstay, with delicacies like beaver-meat stew with plums or quail with blackberry sauce luring the culinarily curious. Folk musicians play here on summer evenings.

Zoe's Bar & Grill INTERNATIONAL €€
(Map p286; www.zoesbargrill.com; Odminių gatvė 3; mains 20-50Lt; ☎) Zoe's covers many culinary bases and manages to do it well, with the likes of fabulous homemade meatballs and sausages (26Lt), tender steaks (20Lt to 50Lt), and spicy Thai stir-fries and soups (20Lt to 30Lt). Dine outdoors with cathedral views or indoors and receive an impromptu cooking lesson.

Fiorentino ITALIAN €€
(Map p286; Universiteto gatvė 4; mains 20-40Lt; ☎) This charming Tuscan restaurant is a winner on three counts: staff who know how to

serve; chefs who know their cuisine from the boot-shaped country; and an architect who knows his Renaissance period. Pick anything on the menu then sit back and admire the colonnaded inner courtyard straight out of Rome (which backs onto the Presidential Palace, no less).

Čili Kaimas LITHUANIAN €€

(Map p286; www.cili.lt; Vokiečių gatvė 8; mains 15-30Lt; ⊙10am-midnight Sun-Thu, to 2am Fri & Sat) This is the kind of traditional chain that people love to hate, but also love to eat at. Americans might be reminded of a TGI Fridays. That said, the traditional Lithuanian food here, ranging from the ever-popular cold beetroot soup, *šaltibarščiai*, to *cepelinai*, is very good and reasonably priced. The setting is casual and family-friendly.

Žemaičiai LITHUANIAN €€

(Samogitian Tavern; Map p286; www.zemaiciai.lt; Vokiečių gatvė 24; mains 20-50Lt) Who needs veggies when you can feast on pig bits most people throw away (or throw up). Pig tongues, ears and trotters are all available here, alongside a pitchfork of assorted meat for four to five people (140Lt), 0.5m sausages, wild boar goulash and goose roast. Summertime seating is around wooden benches and cartwheels on cobbles or up top among Old Town church steeples and terracotta rooftops. Good for groups.

Kitchen INTERNATIONAL €€

(Map p286; Didžioji gatvė 11; mains 20-40Lt) We're suckers for minimalist kitchens, restaurants that focus on a few good dishes and do them well every time. Kitchen scores on this front, with a limited menu of international standards such as steak and grilled fish, done well. The smart modern decor is minimalist as well, and we like that too.

La Provence FRENCH €€€

(Map p286; ☑262 0257; Vokiečių gatvė 22; mains around 70Lt) La Provence is a silver-service restaurant that lives up to its '100% gourmet' motto. Expect to find such delicacies as boiled octopus or boneless pigeon stuffed with pheasant and goose *foie gras* filling the heavenly French menu. Book in advance in the evenings.

Balti Drambliai INTERNATIONAL €

(Map p286; Vilniaus gatvė 41; mains 10-18Lt; ☑) The 'White Elephant' whips up a vegan and veggie storm, offering pancakes, pizzas, Indian curries and tofu-based dishes to hungry non-meat eaters. Its lively courtyard (in summer) is also good for a drink, while winter dining is in its cavernous basement.

René INTERNATIONAL €€

(Map p286; Antokolskio gatvė 13; mains 20-35Lt; ☎) René bases its cuisine on beer, Belgian beer no less. Everything on the menu, from pots of mussels to homemade oven-fried sausages and chilli con carne, features the amber brew. The overall theme is a nod to surrealist painter René Magritte – serving staff don bowler hats and pencils are provided to draw on paper tablecloths. And eating here won't break the bank, if you

---

WHERE TO GO FOR WINE

Vilnius has discovered the joy of wine. Small wine bars have popped up across Old Town, and local patronage is on the rise.

» **In Vino** (Map p286; http://invino.lt; Aušros Vartų gatvė 7; ⊙4pm-2am; ☎) This wine bar has one of the loveliest courtyards in the city and is good for local celeb spotting. It features excellent wines, expensive tapas (20Lt to 30Lt) and a few mains. Arrive early in summer to secure a table and then watch the place fill to overflowing.

» **La Bohemé** (Map p286; http://laboheme.lt; Šv Ignoto gatvė 4/3; ⊙11am-midnight) Choose between wooden tables below vaulted ceilings and chandeliers, or bypass the main room and grab a comfy couch out the back. Best enjoyed in winter, when the open fire is raging.

» **Notre Vie** (Map p286; Stiklių gatvė 10; ⊙3pm-midnight; ☎) Intimate wine bar with great central Old Town location.

» **Tappo D'Oro** (Map p286; www.tempolibero.lt; Stuokos-Gucevičiaus gatvė 7; ⊙11am-11pm; ☎) Informal spot with inviting tree-shaded terrace; huge selection of Italian wines (not all are always available, though), best complemented by Italian cheeses, hams and olives.

LITHUANIA VILNIUS

time it right – lunch menus and afternoon discounts are offered on weekdays.

Self-Catering

Self-catering is a doddle with a supermarket on every second street corner. **Iki** (www.iki.lt) town (Map p282; ☎249 8340; Jasinskio gatvė 16); bus station (☎233 9162; Sodų gatvė 22) and **Maxima** (Map p286; www.maxima.lt; Mindaugo gatvė 11; ⊙24hr) are leading chains. Both run smaller corner shops: **Ikiukas** (Map p286; ☎231 3135; Jogailos gatvė 12) and **Mini Maxima** (Map p286; Gedimino prospektas 64).

 Drinking

Nightlife is a laid-back affair: most places don't hum till late evening, and many double as restaurants. In summer Vokiečių gatvė, a street lined with wooden-decking terraces in summer, is an obvious starting point; as the night wears on, Totorių gatvė, with its ever-increasing number of bars, makes for a good target. If none of these places appeal, keep Cozy (p299) in mind; it slowly morphs over the course of the evening from a casual restaurant to a rowdy bar.

TOP CHOICE Coffee Inn   CAFE
(Map p286; Vilniaus gatvė 17; ⊙7am-10pm; 🛜) Coffee Inn, a Lithuanian-owned coffee chain, is a great institution that should be replicated around the world. No cookie-cutter franchise designs here; each one is a little different. What links them, besides the name, are good coffee (5Lt), to-die-for cheesecake (6.50Lt), free wi-fi and a super chill attitude where basically anything goes and often does. Also at Trakų gatvė 7, Gedimino prospektas 9 and Pilies gatvė 10 (all on Map p286).

SkyBar   COCKTAIL BAR
(Map p282; Konstitucijos prospektas 20; ⊙4pm-1am Sun-Thu, to 2.30am Fri & Sat) It may look – and feel – like an airport lounge, but nothing can beat the panoramas of this sky-blue bar on the 22nd floor of the Radisson Blu Hotel Lietuva. DJs spin tunes on Friday and Saturday.

Paparazzi   COCKTAIL BAR
(Map p286; Totorių gatvė 3; ⊙4pm-3am Mon-Thu, to 6am Fri & Sat) Rumours come and go of this popular cocktail bar's imminent demise (cranky neighbours, rent dispute…who knows?) But on our trip here in 2011 – at least what we can remember of it – Paparazzi was alive and kicking and *the* spot to score a drink in Vilnius.

Būsi Trečias   MICROBREWERY
(Map p286; Totorių gatvė 18; ⊙11am-11pm, Sun-Fri & 11pm-3am Sat) Simple all-wood interior and 12 varieties of locally brewed beer, including lime, raspberry and caramel. No garden; best enjoyed in winter.

Užupio kavinė   CAFE
(Map p286; www.uzupiokavine.lt; Užupio gatvė 2; ⊙10am-11pm; 🛜) A legendary riverside cafe in a legendary part of town. Take a pew with the bohemian crowd that frequents the place and watch folk brave the makeshift swing under the adjacent bridge. A plaque on the wall pays homage to its soulmate – Montmartre, Paris.

Skonis ir Kvapas   CAFE
(Map p286; Trakų gatvė 8; ⊙9.30am-11pm) Heaven for tea connoisseurs, this stylish courtyard cafe knows how to make a great cup. Choose from around 100 teas from across the globe (by the cup 3Lt, per pot 6Lt to 8Lt) and a sublime array of creamy and homemade cakes, cucumber sandwiches and breakfasts. Buy some nice teas as you leave if you need to get a hostess present for someone in Lithuania.

Soprano   CAFE & ICE CREAM
(Map p286; ☎212 6042; Pilies gatvė 3; ⊙9am-10pm; 🛜) I scream, you scream, we all scream for ice cream! Get lickin' with very good fruit-topped gelato Italiano by the cone (4Lt). Also at Konstitucijos prospektas 3 (Map p282).

 Entertainment

The tourist office publishes events listings, as does the *Baltic Times*.

GAY & LESBIAN VILNIUS

The scene is low-key and underground. For general information, chat rooms and guides, contact Vilnius-based **Lithuanian Gay League** (☎233 3031; www.gay.lt), which publishes a solid online entertainment guide in English.

There are few clubs in Vilnius that cater exclusively or mostly to a gay clientele. The most popular club (as of this writing) is arguably **Soho** (Map p282; www.sohoclub.lt; Švitrigailos gatvė 7/16; admission 20Lt; ⊙10pm-4am Thu, to 7am Fri & Sat).

THE BEST OF FOLK ART IN VILNIUS

Lithuanian folk art is alive and well, as the clutch of enchanting folk-artists' workshops in and around Old Town proves.

» **Aldona Mickuvienė and Bronė Daškevičienė** (Map p286; Žydų gatvė 2-10) Two elderly women have been weaving colourful wedding sashes in their neighbouring workshops for decades. Buy a readymade sash (50Lt) or order one with your name on it (70Lt). Each sash takes a full day or more to weave.

» **Black Ceramics Centre** (BCC; Map p286; http://ceramics.w3.lt; Naugarduko gatvė 20) Ceramics as black as coal have been crafted since prehistoric times. See the result at this innovative art centre.

» **Jonas Bugailiškis** (Map p286; www.bugailiskis.com; Aušros Vartų gatvė 17-10) Angels, jumping horses, masks, birdhouses, crosses and a menagerie of other wooden creations can be seen at this creative workshop. Making traditional folk-music instruments is the artist's other love.

» **Sauluva** (Map p286; Literatų gatvė 3; ⏱10am-7pm) Learn how to make *verbos* (traditional woven dried flowers crafted to celebrate Palm Sunday) and paint traditional Lithuanian Easter eggs at this shop-cum-workshop.

» **Užupis Blacksmith Museum-Gallery** (Užupio kalvystės muziejus galerija; Map p286; Užupio gatvė 26) Forged-iron articles are sold at this traditional blacksmith's; demonstrations on Tuesday, Friday and Saturday.

» **Vilnius Potters' Guild** (Vilniaus Puodžių Cechas; Map p286; www.pottery.lt in Lithuanian; Paupio gatvė 2-20; ⏱11am-7pm Tue-Fri, noon-6pm Sat) Clay pots, mugs and vases in designs that harken back to centuries of tradition.

» **Vitražo manufaktūra** (Map p286; www.stainedglass.lt; Stiklių gatvė 6-8; ⏱10am-6pm Tue-Fri, to 4pm Sat) Exquisite stained-glass sculptures, wall murals and mobiles fill this creative stained-glass workshop; daily demonstrations noon to 4pm.

LITHUANIA VILNIUS

Nightclubs

Vilnius has a small but lively clubbing scene that occasionally sees new venues open. It doesn't get going till around midnight and is best experienced in winter, when everyone's around (in summer many go to the seashore to party).

Brodvėjus   CLUB
(Map p286; www.brodvejus.lt; Mėsinių gatvė 4; admission 5-20Lt) Live bands and cheesy tunes nightly; hugely popular with expats, students and local lookers.

Pablo Latino   CLUB
(Map p286; www.pablolatino.lt; Trakų gatvė 3; admission 15-30Lt; ⏱9pm-3am Thu-Sat) This sultry-red club specialises in sweet Latino tunes and strong cocktails. Put on your dancing shoes, fortify your liver, and be prepared for a fun night out.

Gorky   CLUB
(Map p286; Pilies gatvė 34; admission 10-20Lt; ⏱noon-3am Thu-Sat) This two-level club right in the centre of tourist Vilnius opened in 2010 to rave reviews and hasn't stopped since. On the ground floor is a bar for getting acquainted; downstairs is the dance floor playing mostly R&B, pop and some electronic.

Seacret   CLUB
(Map p286; www.seacret.lt; Vokiečių gatvė 2; ⏱9pm-3am Thu-Sat) This central dance club was just getting rolling during our visit in 2011. Expect cocktails, big crowds and jostling on the dance floor.

Cinemas

Find movie listings at www.cinema.lt (in Lithuanian only). Films are screened in English at **Forum Cinemas Vingis** (Map p282; ☎1567; www.forumcinemas.lt; Savanorių prospektas 7) and at the out-of-town **Forum Cinemas Akropolis** (off Map p282; ☎1567; www.forumcinemas.lt; Ozo gatvė 25) in the Akropolis multiplex. **Pasaka** (Map p286; ☎261 1516; www.kinopasaka.lt; Šv Ignoto gatvė 4/3) offers alternative cinema and arthouse fare, with films normally screened in their original language.

Theatre & Classical Music

Oskaras Koršunovas Theatre (OKT; Oskaro Koršuno teatro; ☎212 2099; www.okt.lt)

is Lithuania's most innovative, daring and controversial theatre company; check out the website for more details.

Resident companies perform opera and ballet at **Opera & Ballet Theatre** (Operos ir Baleto Teatras; Map p286; ☑262 0727; www.opera .lt; Vienuolio gatvė 1).

Mainstream theatre – from both Lithuania and abroad – is performed at several locations in town, including **Lithuanian National Drama Theatre** (Lietuvos nacionalinis dramos teatras; Map p286; ☑262 9771; www .teatras.lt; Gedimino prospektas 4) and **Small Theatre of Vilnius** (Vilniaus Mažasis Teatras; Map p286; ☑249 9869; www.vmt.lt; Gedimino prospektas 22). Most companies shut down for the summer season. Buy tickets at venue box offices.

Youth Theatre   DRAMA
(Jaunimo teatras; Map p286; ☑261 6126; www .jaunimoteatras.lt; Arklių gatvė 5) The country's most renowned orchestras perform concerts at several locations. The season normally starts in September and runs to June.

National Philharmonic   CLASSICAL MUSIC
(Nacionalinė filharmonija; Map p286; ☑266 5233; www.nationalphilharmonic.eu; Aušros Vartų gatvė 5) The country's foremost go-to location for classical music.

Lithuanian Music Academy   CLASSICAL MUSIC
(Lietuvos muzikos akademija; Map p286; ☑261 2691; www.lmta.lt; Gedimino prospektas 42) Stages concerts all year.

🛍 Shopping

Old Town's main thoroughfare, running from Pilies gatvė to Aušros Vartų gatvė, is something of a bustling craft market or tourist trap, depending on your perspective. Traders' stalls are laden with cheap amber trinkets, clothing and small souvenirs; painters sell their wares; and amber and linen shops are a dime a dozen. We've listed some of the best here.

Vilnius' main open-air market is the oft-disappointing **Gariūnai**, to the west, off the Kaunas road. Minibuses marked 'Gariūnai' or 'Gariūnų Turgus' ferry shoppers from the train station road to the market every morning. By car it's 11km along Savanorių prospektas from Vilnius centre. Closer to town is the food-driven **Kalvarijų** (off Map p282; Kalvarijų gatvė 61). Both markets open sunrise to noon Tuesday to Sunday.

Amber

Amber   JEWELLERY
(Map p286; www.ambergift.lt; Aušros Vartų gatvė 9) There's no shortage of shops in Vilnius selling amber, but this could arguably be called the Amber epicentre with an enormous stock of Baltic gold at reasonable prices.

Lino ir Gintaro Studija   LINEN, JEWELLERY
(Linen & Amber Studio; Map p286; www.lgstudija .lt) Stiklių (Stiklių gatvė 3); Pilies (Pilies gatvė 7 & 10) The Linen & Amber Studio stands out from the crowd of similar shops for their wide selection of quality goods at reasonable prices.

Handicrafts

Aušros Vartų Meno Galerija   HANDICRAFTS
(Map p286; Aušros Vartų gatvė 12) Good spot to look for locally made souvenirs, including paintings, lace and arts and crafts.

Fashion & Design

Juozas Statkevičius   FASHION
(Map p286; www.statkevicius.com; Odminų gatvė 11) Juozas Statkevičius is a big local name in cutting-edge fashion and has representatives in Paris, New York and Moscow, among other places.

Ramunė Piekautaitė   FASHION
(Map p286; www.ramunepiekautaite.com; Didžioji gatvė 20) This upmarket boutique of a well-regarded local designer caters to professional women with an eye for taste and quality materials.

Zoraza   FASHION
(Map p286; www.zoraza.com; Stiklių gatvė 6) Daiva Urbonavičiūtė fronts the fun and funky fashion house where a riot of colours and textures – suede, glitter, beads, felt, crystal, leather and so on – creates an urban, vintage feel.

Aukso Avis   DESIGN
(Map p286; www.auksoavis.lt; Savičiaus gatvė 10) Gallery established by Vilnius fashion designer Julija Žilėniene that sells bags, T-shirts, wall murals and jewellery (think necklaces in felt or wool) made from a rich range of material.

Linen

Lino Kopos   LINEN, FASHION
(Linen Dunes; Map p282; www.linokopos.com; Krokuvos gatvė 6) The local master of linen is Giedrius Šarkauskas. Inspired by life's natural cycle, the designer lives out his wholly naturalist philosophy with collections sewn

solely from linen. Accessories are made from amber, wood, leather and linen.

Lino Namai
LINEN
(Linen House; Map p286; ☑212 2322; www.siulas.lt) Vilniaus (Vilniaus gatvė 12); Pilies (Pilies gatvė 38) These stores sell linen from Siūlas, a company that has been producing high-quality table and bed linen for 80 years.

Shopping Centres & Department Stores

Gedimino prospektas – the main shopping street – is lined with mainstream fashion shops and department stores.

Gedimino 9
SHOPPING CENTRE
(Map p286; www.gedimino9.lt; Gedimino prospektas 9; ☺10am-7pm Mon-Sat) Centrally located and caters to an upmarket crowd with selective stores and an exclusive feel.

Marks & Spencer
DEPARTMENT STORE
(Map p286; www.marks-and-spencer.lt; Gedimino prospektas 20/1; ☺10am-9pm Mon-Sat, 11am-6pm Sun) The popular UK-based purveyor of all things useful, including a food shop with hard-to-find imported items.

Europa
SHOPPING CENTRE
(Map p282; www.pceuropa.lt; Konstitucijos prospektas 7a; ☺9am-10pm; 🛜) Large shopping centre just across the Neris River from the Old Town. Three floors of shops and a handful of restaurants and coffee joints.

Akropolis
SHOPPING CENTRE
(off Map p282; www.akropolis.lt; Ozo gatvė 25; ☺10am-10pm; 🛜) Massive shopping and entertainment complex with hundreds of stores and restaurants, a multiplex cinema, an ice-skating rink and a children's play area.

Bookshops

Akademinė Knyga
BOOKS
(Map p286; www.humanitas.lt; Universiteto gatvė 4) Translated Lithuanian prose and fiction, Lonely Planet travel guides, and maps.

Humanitas
BOOKS
(Map p286; www.humanitas.lt; Dominikonų gatvė 5) Lonely Planet guides and a staggering selection of art and design books.

Littera
BOOKS
(Map p286; Šv Jono gatvė 12) University bookshop.

Vaga
BOOKS
(Map p282; Gedimino prospektas 9 & 50/2) Great map selection and good coffee.

ⓘ Information

The tourist offices have free maps of central Vilnius that will satisfy most visitors' needs. Otherwise they, along with bookshops, some hotels and supermarkets, sell maps of Vilnius published by **Briedis** (www.briedis.lt; Parodų gatvė 4) and **Jāņa sēta** (www.kartes.lv). Jāņa sēta's *Vilnius* (1:25,000; 10Lt) covers the entire city and includes a 1:10,000 inset of the central city.

Internet Access

A growing number of cafes, restaurants and hotels have free wi-fi zones; check www.wifi.lt for more information.

Collegium (www.dora.lt; Pilies gatvė 22-1; per hr 5Lt; ☺9am-7pm Mon-Fri)

Taškas (Jasinsko gatvė; per hr 5Lt; ☺24hr)

Internet Resources

Vilnius (www.vilnius.lt) Informative city municipality website.

Vilnius Old Town Renewal Agency (www.vsaa.lt) The latest on the Old Town renovation.

Vilnius Tourism (www.vilnius-tourism.lt) Tourist office website; brilliant up-to-the-minute capital guide.

Laundry

Some Vilnius hostels have a washing machine for guests, and a handful of upmarket hotels run a laundry service.

Skalbiu sau (☑216 4689; www.skalbiusau.lt in Lithuanian; Darbiniukų gatvė 21; ☺9.30am-7.30pm) Service washes and self-service machines.

Left Luggage

Bus Station (Map p282; Sodų gatvė 22; bag per 24hr 4Lt; ☺5.30am-9.45pm Mon-Sat, 7am-8.45pm Sun)

Train Station (Map p282; Geležinkelio gatvė; central hall basement; lockers per day 6-8Lt; ☺24hr)

Libraries

American Centre (http://vilnius.usembassy.gov; Akmenų gatvė 7; ☺10am-2pm Mon, Wed-Fri, 10am-7pm Tue) Housed in the US embassy.

Centre Culturel Français (www.institut francais-lituanie.com; Didžioji gatvė 1; ☺9am-7pm Mon-Fri, 10am-3pm Sat)

Media

Vilnius in Your Pocket (www.inyourpocket.com) Quality city guide published every two months, available as PDF download or in bookshops, tourist offices and newspaper kiosks (6Lt).

Vilnius Visitor's Guide Produced by Vilnius Tourism; covers shopping, sightseeing, culture, eating out, accommodation and transport in the city. Available from tourist offices.

Medical Services

Baltic-American Medical & Surgical Clinic (☑234 2020; www.bak.lt; Nemenčinės gatvė 54a; ☉24hr)

Gedimino vaistinė (☑261 0135; Gedimino prospektas 27; ☉24hr) Pharmacy handily located on Vilnius' main commercial street.

Gintarine vaistinė (Geležinkelio gatvė 16; ☉7am-9pm Mon-Fri, 9am-6pm Sat & Sun) Pharmacy at the central hall of the train station.

Vilnius University Emergency Hospital (☑216 9069; www.vgpul.lt; Šiltnamių gatvė 29; ☉24hr)

Money

The following all have ATMs accepting Visa and MasterCard. ATMs can be found throughout the city.

Keitykla Exchange (Citadele Bankas; ☑213 5454; www.keitykla.lt; Geležinkelio gatvė 6; ☉24hr) Currency exchange with ATM. Citadele Bankas is Lithuania's Amex representative.

SEB Vilniaus Bankas Gedimino (Gedimino prospektas 12); Jogailos (Jogailos gatvė 9a); Vokiečių (Vokiečių gatvė 9)

Swedbank (www.swedbank.lt; Gedimino prospektas 56) Cashes Thomas Cook and Amex travellers cheques.

Post

Branch post office (Map p286; Vokiečių gatvė 7)

Central post office (Map p286; Gedimino prospektas 7; ☉7.30am-7pm Mon-Fri, 9am-4pm Sat)

Tourist Information

Vilnius has a string of well-run **tourist information offices** (www.vilnius-tourism.lt; ☉9am-6pm Mon-Fri, 10am-4pm Sat & Sun) that provide free maps, advice and a wealth of brochures about the city and the country. Tourist offices can make accommodation bookings (6Lt).

Cathedral Sq (Map p286; Geležinkelio gatvė 16) Information kiosk.

Old Town (Map p286; ☑262 9660; Vilniaus gatvė 22)

Town Hall (Map p286; ☑262 6470; Didžioji gatvė 31)

Train station (Map p282; ☑269 2091; Geležinkelio gatvė 16)

Travel Agencies

Baltic Travel Service (☑212 0220; www.bts.lt; Subačiaus gatvė 2) Reservations for country farmstays, bus tickets and hotels.

West Express (☑212 2500; www.westexpress.lt, in Lithuanian; Stulginskio gatvė 5) Large, nationwide travel agent.

Zigzag (☑239 7397; www.zigzag.lt, in Lithuanian; Basanavičiaus gatvė 30) Cheap fares for International Student Identity Card holders.

ℹ Getting There & Away

See p404 for details on links with countries outside the region.

Air

For international flights to/from Vilnius, see p404; at the time of research there were no domestic flights within Lithuania. Between them, **airBaltic** (www.airbaltic.com) and **Estonian Air** (www.estonian-air.ee) connect Vilnius with Tallinn up to five times daily, and Rīga up to seven times daily. Check up-to-date fares online.

Major airline offices at Vilnius airport:

airBaltic (☑235 6010; www.airbaltic.com)

Lufthansa (☑232 9290; www.lufthansa.com)

SAS (☑230 6638; www.flysas.lt)

Bus

Vilnius **bus station** (Autobusų stotis; Map p282; ☑216 2977; Sodų gatvė 22) is just south of Old Town. Inside its ticket hall, domestic tickets are sold from 6am to 7.30pm, and information is doled out at the **information office** (informacija; ☑1661; www.toks.lt, in Lithuanian; ☉6am-9pm). Timetables are displayed on a board here and on the handy website www.autobusubilietai.lt.

Tickets for international destinations, including Rīga and Tallinn, are sold by a number of companies with offices right next to the station. **Ecolines** (☑213 3300; www.ecolines.net; Sodų gatvė 24e; ☉8am-7pm Mon-Fri, 9am-5pm Sat, 9am-3pm Sun) connects Vilnius with cities in Europe and throughout the Baltic, including daily buses to Rīga and Tallinn. The budget carrier **Simple Express** (☑233 6666; www.simpleexpress.eu; Sodų gatvė 20b1) offers arguably the lowest prices to Lithuania from destinations in the Baltic, including daily buses from Vilnius to Rīga (38Lt) and Tallinn (69Lt).

Eurolines (☑233 6666; www.eurolines.lt; Sodų gatvė 24d-1; ☉8am-9pm Mon-Fri, 9am-9pm Sat & Sun) and its **Lux Express** (www.luxexpress.lt) subsidiary are additional reliable long-distance carriers. Buy tickets online or at the company's offices.

Buses to destinations within Lithuania and to Rīga and Tallinn include the following:

Druskininkai (28Lt, two hours, 8 daily)

Ignalina (15Lt, 1¾ hours, up to 10 daily)

Kaunas (22Lt, 1¾ hours, at least every 30 minutes)

Klaipėda (66Lt, four to 5½ hours, up to 15 daily)

Molėtai (17Lt, 1¼ to two hours, hourly)

Palanga (68Lt, 4¼ to six hours, seven daily)

Panevėžys (30Lt, 1¾ to three hours, hourly)

Rīga (38-65Lt, five hours, four daily)

Šiauliai (45Lt, three to 4½ hours, six daily)

Tallinn (69-110Lt, 10½ hours, up to five daily)

Visaginas (25Lt, 2½ hours, 10 daily)

Car & Motorcycle

Numerous 24-hour petrol stations selling Western-grade unleaded fuel are dotted around Vilnius. If you hire a car and intend to cross the border in a Lithuanian-registered car, check the car is insured for inter-Baltic travel.

Autobanga (☑212 7777; www.autobanga.lt) At the airport.

Avis Airport (☑232 9316); Town (☑230 6820; www.avis.lt; Laisvės prospektas 3)

Budget (☑230 6708; www.budget.lt) At the airport.

Europcar Airport (☑216 3442); Town (☑212 2739; www.europcar.lt; Stuokos-Gucevičiaus 9-1)

Hertz Airport (☑232 9301); Town (☑272 6940; www.hertz.lt; Kalvarijų gatvė14)

Sixt (☑239 5636; www.sixt.lt) At the airport.

Train

The **train station** (Geležinkelio stotis; Map p282; ☑233 0088; www.litrail.lt; Geležinkelio gatvė 16) is opposite the bus station and is equipped with ATMs, a supermarket and information desks. The domestic ticket hall is to the left as you face the central station building, and the international ticket hall is to the right. Train information and timetables (in English) are available at the information office between the two halls and online at www.litrail.lt.

There is no direct or convenient rail link between Vilnius and Rīga or Tallinn. For international trains, see p409. Direct daily services within Lithuania to/from Vilnius:

Ignalina (14Lt, two hours, seven daily)

Kaunas (16.30Lt, 1¼ to 1¾ hours, up to 17 daily)

Klaipėda (51Lt, 4½ to five hours, three daily)

Šiauliai (35Lt, 2½ to three hours, three daily)

Trakai (6.20Lt, 35 minutes, up to 10 daily)

❶ Getting Around

To/from the Airport

Vilnius International Airport (☑230 6666; www.vno.lt; Rodūnė kelias 2) lies 5km south of the centre. The airport is accessible by bus, train or taxi. Bus 1 runs between the airport and the train station; bus 2 runs between the airport and the northwestern suburb of Šeškinė via the Žaliasis bridge across the Neris and on to Lukiskių aikštė. Buy a ticket (2.50Lt) from the driver, but have small change handy.

Trains run between the airport and the train station hourly during the day (until about 9pm). Buy tickets (2.50Lt) once you're onboard. The travel time is around 10 minutes.

By taxi, rates vary depending on whether you hail a cab from one of the vehicles lined up in front of the arrivals hall (about 50Lt to 60Lt) or call a reputable firm in advance by phone (p308; 30Lt).

Bicycle

Vilnius is becoming increasingly bike-friendly and much of Old Town is criss-crossed by dedicated bike lanes heading in all directions. Outside of Old Town, bike lanes are fewer and further between, but much of the city is still possible to navigate on two wheels. In addition, the banks of the Neris River, still scruffy in spots, are accessible by bike. **Velo-city** (☑8-674 12123; www.velo-city.lt; Bernardinų gatvė 10; ◷10am-6pm) hires out bicycles for 10/40Lt per hour/day plus deposit. Pick up a free cycling map from the tourist office or go to the website of **Baltic Cycle** (www.bicycle.lt) for ideas and information.

Car & Motorcycle

Vilnius is generally easy to navigate by car, but even though the traffic burden is light compared with other capitals, it is getting heavier each year. Street parking around the centre can be hard to find and is expensive when you do nab a spot. Depending on the part of town and the desirability of the space, rates (from 8am to 8pm) run to as much as 6Lt an hour. The rate is identified by a colour code system, with blue being the most expensive. Feed coins into a parking meter and display the ticket with time stamp on the dashboard.

Avoid parking on unlit streets overnight; car break-ins are not unknown. Cars are not permitted in parts of the pedestrian Old Town.

Public Transport

The city is efficiently served by buses and trolleybuses from 5.30am or 6am to midnight; Sunday services are less frequent. Tickets cost 2Lt at news kiosks and 2.50Lt direct from the driver; punch tickets on board in a ticket machine or risk a 60Lt on-the-spot fine.

Quicker minibuses shadow most routes. They pick up/drop off passengers anywhere en route (not just at official bus stops) and can be flagged down on the street. Tickets costs 3Lt from the driver.

Note that much of Old Town is closed to traffic, meaning that very few buses and trolleybuses service this part of town. For destinations within Old Town, you'll normally have to hoof it.

For route details see www.vilniustransport.lt or pick up a transport map from tourist offices.

Taxi

Taxis rates in Vilnius can vary and are generally cheaper if ordered in advance by telephone than if hailed directly off the street or picked up at a taxi stand. Ask the hotel reception desk or restaurant waiter to call one for you. Reliable companies:

Ekipažas (☑239 5539; www.ekipazastaksi.lt)
Martono Taksi (☑240 0004; www.martonas.lt)
Mersera (☑278 8888; www.mersera.lt)

AROUND VILNIUS

The centre of Europe, a fairy-tale castle and ancient castle mounds lie within easy reach of the capital. Or there is the trip to Paneriai.

Paneriai

Here Lithuania's brutal history is starkly portrayed. As many as 100,000 people – the exact figure is not known – were murdered by the Nazis between July 1941 and July 1944 at this site, 10km southwest of central Vilnius. Around half the city's Jewish population – about 35,000 people – had been massacred here by the end of the first three months of the German occupation (June to September 1941) at the hands of Einsatzkommando 9, an SS killing unit of Nazi troops, and their Lithuanian accomplices.

The forest entrance is marked by a memorial, the **Panerių memorialas**. The text in Russian, dating from the Soviet period, commemorates the 100,000 'Soviet citizens' killed here. The memorial plaques in Lithuanian and Hebrew – erected later – honour the many Jewish victims.

A path leads to the shocking **Paneriai Museum** (Panerių muziejus; www.jmuseum.lt; Agrastų gatvė 15; ⏰11am-6pm Wed-Sat Jun-Sep, by appointment via website Oct-May). There are two monuments here: one is Jewish (marked with the Star of David), the other Soviet (an obelisk topped with a Soviet star). From here paths lead to a number of grassed-over pits where, from December 1943, the Nazis lined up the victims 10 at a time and shot them in the back of the head, allowing the corpses to simply fall into the pits. Several hundred people a day could be killed in this way. The bodies were then covered with sand to await the next layer of bodies.

The Nazis later burnt the exhumed corpses to hide the evidence of their crimes. One of the deeper pits, according to its sign, was where they eventually buried those who were forced to dig up the corpses and pulverise the bones.

There are two dozen trains daily (some terminating in Trakai or Kaunas) from Vilnius to Paneriai station (2Lt, 11 minutes). From Paneriai, make a right on leaving the station down Agrastų gatvė and it's a 1km walk southwest from here.

Trakai

☑528 / POP 5400

With its red-brick, fairy-tale castle, Karaites culture, quaint wooden houses and pretty lakeside location, Trakai is a must-see within easy reach of the capital.

Gediminas probably made Trakai, 28km west of Vilnius, his capital in the 1320s and Kęstutis certainly based his 14th-century court here. Protected by the **Trakai Historical National Park** (www.seniejitrakai .lt), spanning 82 sq km since 1991, Trakai today is a quiet town (outside summer weekends) blessed with lake views in all directions and filled with song each July during the **Trakai Festival**, which takes place at the Island Castle and features concerts and mock medieval battles.

Most of Trakai stands on a 2km-long, north-pointing tongue of land between Lake Luka (east) and Lake Totoriškių (west). Lake Galvė opens out from the northern end of the peninsula and boasts 21 islands.

◉ Sights

Island Castle   CASTLE

The centrepiece of Trakai is hard to miss. Occupying an island on Lake Galvė, the painstakingly restored Gothic red-brick Island Castle probably dates from around 1400, when Vytautas needed stronger defences than the Peninsula Castle afforded. A footbridge links it to the shore, and a moat separates the triangular outer courtyard from the main tower with its cavernous central court and a range of galleries, halls and rooms. Some house the **Trakai History Museum** (Trakų istorijos muziejus; www.trakai muziejus.lt; adult/student & child 14/7Lt; ⏰10am-7pm daily May-Sep, to 6pm Tue-Sun Oct, Mar & Apr, to 5pm Tue-Sat Nov-Feb), which charts the history of the castle and features plenty of medieval weaponry and traditional Karaite

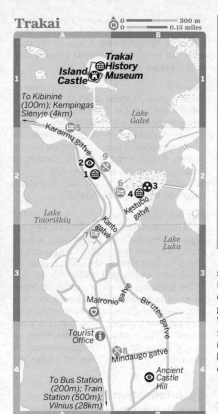

Trakai

◉ **Top Sights**
| Island Castle | A1 |
| Trakai History Musuem | A1 |

◉ **Sights**
1	Karaites Ethnographic Museum	A2
2	Kenessa	A2
3	Peninsula Castle	B2
4	Sacral Art Exhibition	B2

▣ **Sleeping**
5	Apvalaus Stalo Klubas	A1
6	Karamių 13	B2
7	Salos	A3

⊗ **Eating**
| 8 | Iki | B4 |
| 9 | Kybynlar | A2 |

smallest ethnic minority is dying out. The **Karaites Ethnographic Museum** (Karaimų etnografinė paroda; www.trakaimuziejus.lt; Karaimų gatvė 22; adult/student & child 4/2Lt; ⊙10am-6pm Wed-Sun) traces their ancestry. Their beautifully restored early-19th-century **Kenessa** (Karaite prayer house; Karaimų gatvė 30; admission by donation) can be visited but there are no set opening times.

🏃 Activities

Pick up a **pedalo** (per hr 20Lt) or **rowing boat** (per hr 15Lt) from boatmen near the footbridge leading to the Island Castle.

The tourist office can inform you about a plethora of activities, including horse riding, air ballooning and sailing. It also hires out **bicycles** (per hr/day 6/30Lt) and has information on the 14km **bicycle route** around the main sights. Kempingas Slėnyje (p310) hires out bicycles (6/25Lt per hour/day) too, along with canoes and boats (8Lt per hour). Those who prefer a quiet stroll in nature can head for the **Varnikai botanical-zoological preserve** 4km east of the Peninsula Castle. To get there, follow the signs marked 'Varnikų Gamtos Takas' across two lake bridges.

Winter guests to Trakai can expect to enjoy horse-drawn sled rides, skiing and ice-fishing.

🛏 Sleeping

Trakai is an easy day trip from Vilnius, but it's worth staying overnight to experience the place minus the weekend tourist hordes.

costumes. In summer the castle courtyard is a magical stage for concerts and plays.

Peninsula Castle & Around RUIN, MUSEUM
The peaceful ruins of Trakai's **Peninsula Castle**, built from 1362 to 1382 by Kęstutis and destroyed in the 17th century, are a little south of the Island Castle. Housed in a former Dominican chapel nearby is the **Sacral Art Exhibition** (Kestučio gatvė 4; adult/student & child 4/2Lt; ⊙10am-6pm Wed-Sun). The collection is small but fine and includes precious reliquaries and monstrances in its cellar. The peninsula itself is dotted with old wooden cottages, many built by the Karaites, a Judaic sect and Turkic minority originating in Baghdad, which adheres to the Law of Moses. Their descendants were brought to Trakai from the Crimea in around 1400 to serve as bodyguards. Only 12 families (60 Karaites) live in Trakai and their numbers – fewer than 300 in Lithuania – are dwindling, prompting fears that the country's

Apvalaus Stalo Klubas HOTEL €€
(☑55 595; www.asklubas.lt; Karaimų gatvė 53a; s/d from 300/340Lt; P@⊛≋) Upscale boutique hotel carved out of two lakeside villas across from the Island Castle. Choose a room in either the more elegant French-provincial Ežeras villa, with big comfy furnishings and bold colours on the walls, or the more workaday modern – and slightly cheaper – digs at the Karaimai villa. Rooms offer either courtyard or lakeside views, the latter being more expensive. There's a spa and an excellent restaurant in-house. Perfect for a romantic weekend.

Karamių 13 GUESTHOUSE €€
(☑51 911; www.karaimai.lt; Karaimų gatvė 13; s/d 150/200Lt; P@⊛) This lovingly renovated, simple Karaite house boasts a cafe that serves Karaite food. The wooden house was lately rebuilt in the authentic style of Karaim architecture. The rooms are all simply furnished, but have modern conveniences and internet facilities.

Salos HOTEL €€
(☑53 990; www.salos.lt; Kranto gatvė 5b; s/d/tr 120/160/220Lt; P@⊛≋) The Salos is a modern hotel on the shore of Lake Totoriškių, within walking distance of the centre and the Island Castle. There are 10 well-appointed rooms on the premises and guests have use of the Finnish sauna and pool.

Kempingas Slėnyje CAMPGROUND €
(☑53 380; www.camptrakai.lt; Slėnio gatvė 1; sites per adult/car/tent 20/10/10Lt, d/tr/q without bathroom 90/100/120Lt, cottage for 2-6 people 250-320Lt, d in guesthouse 150Lt; P) Some 5km out of Trakai in Slėnje, on the northern side of Lake Galvė off the road to Vievis, this camp site has accommodation to suit all budgets and comfort requirements. Basic bungalow accommodation is fine providing you have mosquito repellent. There are plenty of activities on offer, including a sauna and steam bath, barbecues to use, bikes to hire, folklore evenings to enjoy and a sandy beach to sprawl on.

 Eating

Buy picnic supplies at Iki (Vytauto gatvė 56).

Kibininė LITHUANIAN €
(Karaimų gatvė 65; mains 7-20Lt) This green wooden house with Karaite kitchen is *the* spot to munch on traditional Karaite pasties called *kibinai* (like a Cornish pasty). But beware that first bite – scalding-hot juices pour

out. They come with a variety of stuffings, but the traditional is pork, often served with a bowl of chicken broth. A hole in the wall doles out meat- or veg-stuffed *kibinai* (5Lt to 7Lt) to take away.

Kybynlar LITHUANIAN €€
(Karaimų gatvė 29; mains 15-30Lt;) There is a definite Turkic feel to Trakai's other Karaite-driven restaurant, where piping-hot pastries are likewise cooked up alongside predominantly meat-based fare. The writing on the wall in Arabic script is native Karaim, a language belonging to the Kipchak branch of Turkish languages and spoken as mother tongue by 535 people worldwide.

Žejų Namai FISH €€
(☑26 008; www.zvejunamai.lt; trout per kg 42Lt) If you have your own wheels and a hankering for fresh fish, travel 16km north of Trakai to Žejų Namai. On arrival, pick up a rod, bait and bucket and head for one of the pools filled with live trout. Staff are on hand to weigh, fillet and cook the fish in a choice of spices, and then bring it to your table on a platter. Žejų Namai is signposted off the road to Vievis; fish must be caught before 9pm as they take around 30 minutes to cook. Also open in winter for ice-fishing.

❶ Information

Snoras Bankas (Vytauto gatvė 56) ATM and currency exchange opposite the tourist office. Two more ATMs are next door outside Iki.

Tourist Office (☑51 934; www.trakai-visit.lt; Vytauto gatvė 69; ⊘9am-5pm Mon-Fri, 9am-3pm Sat & Sun) Sells maps and guides, and books accommodation (6Lt per booking) and proffers oodles of practical info.

❶ Getting There & Away

Up to 10 daily trains (6.20Lt, 35 minutes) travel between Trakai's **train station** (☑51 055; Vilniaus gatvė 5) and Vilnius.

Centre of Europe

Lithuania is proud of its supposed geographic *Europos centras* (centre of Europe), 25km north of Vilnius off the Molėtai highway. Despite contrary claims, the French National Geographical Institute pronounced this central position – at a latitude of 54° 54' and longitude of 25° 19' – in 1989, marking it with a boulder inscribed with the points of the compass and the words 'Geografinis Europos Centras'. In 2004 Lithuania brightened up this rather unexciting spot with 27 fluttering flags (the EU flag plus that of each member country), a wooden decking stage and a phallic white granite obelisk with a crown of gold stars. Around it the hills were landscaped and a wooden house marked 'tourist information' set up to issue 'I've been to the centre of Europe' certificates (5Lt) and sell souvenir T-shirts. Surrounding the centre is an 18-hole **golf course** (☑8-616 26366; www.golfclub.lt; club hire 80Lt, round 140Lt) and sparkling restaurant.

Most people will find the open-air museum **Europos parkas** (www.europosparkas.lt; adult/student/child 25/18/11Lt; ☉10am-sunset), some 17km from the centre of Europe off the Utena road, more appealing. Leading contemporary sculptors, including Sol LeWitt and Dennis Oppenheim, show works in wooded parkland (bring mosquito repellent in summer). The exhibitions include the largest sculpture in the world made entirely of TV sets; constructed as a maze, it consists of around 3000 TVs and is centred on a fallen statue of Lenin. The sculpture park was the brainchild of Lithuanian sculptor Gintaras Karosas in response to the 'centre of Europe' tag. Every year international workshops are held here, attracting artists from all over the world.

❶ Getting There & Away

Travelling north on the Vilnius–Molėtai road from Vilnius, the centre of Europe is to the left and marked by the sign 'Europos Centras'. Getting there by public transport requires two bus changes and plenty of patience; the Vilnius tourist offices (p306) have more information if you're dead keen.

From Vilnius, minibuses marked 'Skirgiskes' leave from the bus stop on Kalvarijų gatvė for the Europos parkas (2Lt, 30 minutes) at least three times daily. By car, head north along Kalvarijų gatvė until you reach the Santasriskių roundabout, then bear right towards Žalieji ežerai, following the signs for 'Europos parkas'.

Kernavė

Deemed an 'exceptional testimony to 10 millennia of human settlements in this region' by Unesco, which made it a World Heritage site in 2004, Kernavė (ker-na-vey) is a must-see. Thought to have been the spot where Mindaugas (responsible for uniting Lithuania for the first time) celebrated his coronation in 1253, the rural cultural reserve comprises four old castle mounds and the remains of a medieval town.

The fascinating heritage of the **Kernavė Cultural Reserve** (Kernavės kultūrinio rezervato; www.kernave.org; admission free; ☉dawn-dusk) can be explored in the **Archaeological & Historical Museum** (Archeologijos ir istorijos muziejus; ☑382-47385; Kerniaus gatvė 4a) starting in late 2011, when it reopens following multiyear, extensive renovations. Guided tours (20Lt) of the area are available by prior arrangement between 9am and 5pm Tuesday to Saturday, April to October; otherwise the area is free to explore at your leisure.

Medieval fun and frolics – axe throwing, catapulting, mead making and so on – fill Kernavė with festivity on 23 June and during the three-day **International Festival of Experimental Archaeology** (lots of fun despite the deadly name) in mid-July.

To reach Kernavė, 35km northwest of Vilnius in the Neris Valley, follow the road through Dūkštos from Maisiagala on the main road north to Ukmergė.

EASTERN & SOUTHERN LITHUANIA

The deep, magical forests of Lithuania's eastern and southern corners are a treehugger's paradise. Some of the most spectacular scenery in Lithuania is found in these wildernesses, with a lake district that extends into Belarus and Latvia.

Aukštaitija National Park is Lithuania's oldest park, framed by the 900-sq-km Labanoras-Pabradė Forest. Outdoor purists will have a ball here, pursuing canoeing, hiking, windsurfing, sailing, birdwatching and, in winter, ice-fishing and even some skiing.

Dzūkija in the far south is the biggest national park, surrounded by the 1500-sq-km Druskininkai-Varėna Forest. Both parks are blessed with an abundant berry crop in early summer, while mushrooms of all shapes and guises sprout by the bucketful from early spring until late autumn.

Close to the Dzūkija National Park is the spa resort of Druskininkai, where rich Lithuanians indulge in winter breaks and the likes of warm honey massages. The Grūtas sculpture park next door, with its busts of Lenin, Stalin and the gang, is a

Eastern Lithuania

sure nostalgia cure for anyone longing for those 'good old days'.

A few words of warning: mosquitoes are a menace so bring insect repellent; and only pick mushrooms with a local guide and be aware that the stomach of the guide – reared on mushrooms since birth – is substantially more tolerant of certain species than your own.

Aukštaitija National Park

📝386

In beloved Aukštaitija (owk-shtai-ti-ya) National Park it's clear where Lithuania's love for nature arose. The natural paradise of deep, whispering forests and blue lakes bewitched this once-pagan country.

Around 70% of the park comprises pine, spruce and deciduous forests, inhabited by elk, deer and wild boar. Its highlight is a labyrinth of 126 lakes, the deepest being **Lake**

Tauragnas (60.5m deep). A footpath leads to the top of 155m **Ice Hill** (Ledakalnis), from where a panorama of some seven lakes unfolds. Particularly pretty is **Lake Baluošas**, ensnared by woods and speckled with islands. White-tailed and golden eagles prey here and storks are rife. The **Trainiškis Wildlife Sanctuary** and **Ažvinčiai Forest Reserve**, home to 150- to 200-year-old pine trees, can only be visited with park guides.

The main jumping-off point for the park is the sleepy town of **Ignalina**, which has a supermarket, post office, hotel/ restaurant, and one of two information centres that service that park. Nearby **Palūšė**, 3km from Ignalina on the banks of Lake Lūsiai (literally 'Wild Cat Lake'), is home to the park's headquarters and main information centre.

There are around 100 settlements within the park itself: **Šuminai**, **Salos II**, **Vaišnoriškės**, **Varniškės II** and **Strazdai** are protected ethnographic centres. Ginučiai has a 19th-century **watermill** (adult/student 2/1Lt; ☉10am-6pm Tue-Sun May-Sep) with a small exhibition on its flour-and electricity-producing history. Stripeikiai's **Ancient Bee-keeping Museum** (Senorinés bitininkystés muziejus; adult/student 3/1Lt; ☉10am-7pm Tue-Sun May–mid-Oct) spins the story of beekeeping through a merry collection of carved wooden statues and hives.

The park has several ancient *piliakalnis* (fortification mounds), such as the **Taurapilio mound** on the southern shore of Lake Tauragnas, and some quaint wooden architecture, including a fine **church** and **bell tower** at Palūsė. Around Lake Lūšiai a **wooden sculpture trail** depicts Lithuanian folklore.

🏃 Activities

Boating and **trekking** are the main activities in the park. The national park office arranges treks and backpacking trips by boat, English-speaking guides (45Lt per hour), and skiing, fishing (summer and winter) and sledging. **Palūsė Tourist Information** (www.paluse.lt) has lots of information in English and is a good place to start planning.

Palūsė valtinė (☎8-686 90030; www.valtine.lt; ☉May-Oct) on the lakeshore in Palūsė hires out rowing boats (7/35Lt per hour/day), canoes and kayaks (10/60Lt per hour/day) and arranges canoeing trips, with or without guide.

Mushroom and berry picking is only permitted in designated forest areas. If you are unsure, ask at either tourist office.

🛏 Sleeping

Pick up homestay lists from the national park office and Ignalina tourist office. The **Tourism Centre Palūsė** (☎47 430) has its own very basic rooms (from 44Lt) in Palūsė village.

Miškiniškės BUNGALOW €€
(☎8-612 33577; www.miskiniskes.lt; s/d 150/250Lt, 4-person cottages from 500Lt; P) This forest hideout is a great example of ecological living. Accommodation comprises rustic log cabins with fireplaces and modern interiors, and meals served in the main house are homemade, using seasonal produce from local farmers. Activities abound: try your hand at archery, axe throwing or rock climbing; or simply wander the grounds. Miškiniškės is only practical if you have your own wheels, and even then it's not easy to find. From Ignalina, go to the village of Kazitiškis (12km) and then turn left, proceeding another 7km to see the sign for Miškiniškės. Turn left at the sign and proceed another 5km, until you reach another sign, turning right here for another 4.5km.

Žuvėdra HOTEL €€
(☎8-686 81811; www.zuvedra.com; Mokyklos gatvė 11, Ignalina; s/d/apt 90/160/250Lt; P@☎) This small hotel on the shores of Lake Paplovinis is an excellent in-town choice, within easy walking distance of the tourist office in Ignalina. The helpful staff can arrange bike and boat rental as well suggest things to see and do in the area, including playing tennis on the courts next to the hotel. The restaurant, serving

---

STORKS

Eastern Lithuania, indeed the entire country, is prime stork-sighting territory. Lithuania has approximately 13,000 pairs, giving it the highest-density stork population in Europe.

Measuring 90cm in height, this beautiful long-legged, wide-winged creature is breathtaking in flight. Equally marvellous is the catwalk stance it adopts when strutting through meadows in search of frogs to feast on. It sleeps standing on one leg.

The arrival of the stork from Africa each year marks the start of spring. Lithuanians celebrate this traditional protector of the home with Stork Day (25 March), the day farmers traditionally stir their seeds, yet to be planted, to ensure a bigger and better crop.

Storks on their return home usually settle back into the same nest they have used for years. Large and flat, the nest is balanced in a tree or atop a disused chimney or telegraph pole. Some are splayed out across wooden cartwheels, fixed on tall poles by kindly farmers keen to have their farmstead blessed by the good fortune the stork brings.

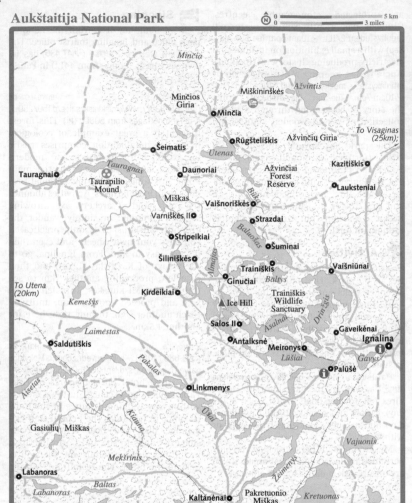

0 5 km
0 3 miles

Minčia
Mikšininškės · Ažvintis
Minčios Giria
Minčia
Rūgšteliškis · Ažvinčių Giria
To Visaginas (25km);
Šeimatis · Utenas
Daunoriai · Ažvinčiai Forest Reserve · Kazitiškis
Tauragnai · Tauragnas · Taurapilio Mound
Lauksteniai
Miškas · Vaišnoriškės · Būka
Varniškės II · Strazdai · Baluošas
Stripeikiai · Šuminai
Šiliniškės · Amatas · Vaišniūnai
Trainiškis · Baltys
To Utena (20km) · Kemešys · Kirdeikiai · Ginučiai
Ice Hill · Trainiškis Wildlife Sanctuary · Drūkšis
Salos II · Asalnai · Gaveikėnai
Laimestas · Antalksnė · Meironys · Ignalina
Saldutiškis · Pakalas · Lūšiai · Gavys
Palūšė
Aisetas · Linkmenys · Ušai
Kiauna
Gasiulių Miškas
Vajuonis
Mekšrinis · Žiemenys
Labanoras · Baltas · Kaltanėnai · Pakretuonio Miškas · Kretuonas
Labanoras

Lithuanian food (mains 15Lt to 25Lt) is arguably the best in Ignalina, and even if you're not staying here it's a convenient spot to grab a meal.

Ginučiai Watermill GUESTHOUSE €
(📞8-616 29366; Palūšė; d/apt from 130/260Lt; 🅿) Run by the Tourism Centre Palūšė, the watermill offers stripped-back rooms with clean wood interiors and as peaceful a surrounding as you'll find in Lithuania. Bring your own food to cook in the kitchen, and end the evening relaxing by the fire or in the sauna (200Lt).

Lithuanian Winter Sports Centre HOTEL €
(Lietuvos žiemos sporto centras; 📞54 102, 54 193; www.lzsc.lt in Lithuanian; Sporto gatvė 3, Ignalina; s/d/apt 60/100/240Lt; 🅿) Accommodation, which consists of presentable cottages overlooking the centre's own lake, plays second fiddle at this Soviet-era sports centre. In winter guests can hire skis (per hour/day 15/40Lt) and leap on the ski lift (per hour/day 15/40Lt). Summer activities include boating (15Lt per hour) on the lake or rollerblading along a 7.5km track. From Ignalina centre, cross the train track and follow Budrių gatvė for 2km.

ℹ Information

Both Ignalina's **tourist office** (✆52 597; www
.ignalinatic.lt; Ateites gatvė 23; ⊗8am-5pm
Mon-Fri year-round, plus 10am-3pm Sat Jun-
Aug), on the town's central square, and the
Aukštaitija National Park Office (✆53 135,
www.anp.lt or www.paluse.lt; ⊗9am-6pm Mon-
Sat), in Palūšė, have information on the park's
activities and accommodation and sell maps
(15Lt).

ℹ Getting There & Away

Hop on a bus (15Lt, 1¾ hours, eight daily) or
jump on a train (14Lt, two hours, seven daily)
from Vilnius to Ignalina; there's also at least one
bus to/from Kaunas (36Lt, four hours) via Utena
(12Lt, one hour). Several buses daily travel
between Ignalina and Palūšė (3Lt).

Visaginas & Ignalina Nuclear Power Station

✆386 / POP 28,160

The purpose-built worker-housing town
of Visaginas is as Soviet as you'll get outside the borders of Russia. Built in 1975 for
employees at the former Ignalina Nuclear
Power Station nearby, it's packed with
identical-looking blocks of flats amid forest
and circled by a ring road. Attractive it ain't;
bizarre (and fascinating) it is.

In its heyday, around 5000 shift workers
were shuttled between Visaginas and the
former plant, about 3km east of the town
centre. A Geiger counter recorded the day's
radiation level and Russian was the *lingua
franca* on the streets.

The town's future remains uncertain,
however, after the nuclear plant was shut
down at the end of 2009 as part of Lithuania's agreement to join the European Union (see boxed text). Though there's talk of
building a new plant, that won't happen
until 2018 at the earliest. In the meantime,
locals are hoping that increased tourism can
bolster the economy.

Those looking for a Soviet experience
can overnight in Hotel Aukštaitija (✆50
684; Veteranų gatvė 9; s/d from 90/150Lt; ℗),
a red-brick highrise built in the old Soviet
tradition. The rooms are not as bleak as the
exterior, and several have even been nicely
remodelled. A more welcoming affair can
be found a few hundred metres south of
the centre at the spa-hotel Gabriella (✆70
171; www.gabriella.lt; Jaunystės gatvė 21; s/d from
130/220Lt; ℗@✆). As the name suggests,
there are plenty of massage and spa options

PULLING THE PLUG AT IGNALINA

In its day the Ignalina Nuclear Power Station near Visaginas was one of the technological
wonders of the world. When the Soviets built the plant in the 1980s, its two RBMK 1500
reactors were the most powerful ones commissioned at the time and were capable of
generating around 1500MW each of electricity. Unfortunately for Ignalina, the design was
similar to the one used at the Chernobyl nuclear plant in Ukraine, which suffered a cata-
strophic meltdown in 1986. Though Ignalina's second reactor actually came online after
the Chernobyl disaster, from the start it was clear the plant's days were numbered.

After Lithuania joined the European Union in 2004, the country came under pressure
to shutter the two reactors. The EU had no intention of having a Chernobyl-like situation
on its hands. Lithuania eventually agreed and decommissioned the first reactor in 2004.
The plug was pulled on the second at the end of 2009.

Though power is no longer produced here, the plant is still the subject of some
controversy. Foremost is the question of who will bear the prohibitive decommissioning
costs, including the billions of euros needed to clean up the reactor site and dispose of
redundant radioactive material. The EU has agreed to pony up the lion's share of the costs,
though at the time of research the decommissioning fund was still hundreds of millions of
euros short. More information on the decommissioning can be found at www.iae.lt.

Adding to the controversy are plans to build another nuclear power plant here based
on a more modern, Western design. In 2006, Lithuania invited neighbours Poland, Latvia
and Estonia to collaborate in building a new reactor, and strategic investors such as
Japan's Hitachi Corp were taken on board. The project took a big PR hit in 2011 with the
Fukoshima nuclear disaster in Japan, though as of this writing officials are still saying a
new reactor could be up and running by as early as 2018. Up-to-date news on the project
can be found online at www.vae.lt.

here, though the property is not as fancy as the 'spa-hotel' tag implies. There's also a decent restaurant, which is probably the best place in town to have a meal.

In mid-August Visaginas bizarrely rocks with a bunch of cowboys – hats, boots and all – who ride into town from across Europe for the two-day international country music festival, Visagino Country (www.visagino country.lt).

From Vilnius to Visaginas there are daily trains (19.90Lt, 2½ hours, five daily) and plenty of buses (24Lt, 2½ hours).

Labanoras Regional Park

Southwest of Aukštaitija is 528 sq km of pretty parkland dotted with 285 lakes. At its heart sits lovely Labanoras, home to the Regional Park Information Centre (☑8-387 47142; www.labanoroparkas.lt in Lithuanian; ☺8am-noon & 1-5pm Mon-Fri, 8am-3.45pm Sat), where information on the park can be gathered.

Canoeing is a grand pastime in Labanoras, particularly on the Lakaja River in the southern section of the park, and the park information centre can advise on trips and rentals. Figure on a one-day kayak hire during the week/weekend costing about 40/60Lt plus extra for transportation.

Accommodation in the park is limited to a handful of homestays and one delightful hotel-restaurant in Labanoras village.

TOP CHOICE Hotel Restaurant Labanoras (☑8-655 70918; www.hotellabanoras.lt; s/d 100/150Lt; P) has a pretty terrace overlooking the village square and, in season, roosting storks. The wooden house and its six guest rooms are full of character and quirks, and jammed with all sorts of collectables. Homemade dumplings, cold beetroot soup, grilled trout, and crepes with wild berries and cream are just some of the divine choices on the menu (mains 15Lt to 30Lt). Guests can borrow a bike to explore the park.

Molėtai

☑383 / POP 6970

A small town 30km southwest of the Aukštaitija National Park, Molėtai (mo-ley-tai) is unstartling apart from its lake surrounds, about which its tourist office (☑51 187; www.infomoletai.lt; Inturkės gatvė 4; ☺8am-5pm Mon-Thu, 8am-3.45pm Fri) has information.

There are spectacular views of Molėtai's lake-studded landscape and the stars above from the Molėtai Astronomical Observatory (Molėtų astronomijos observatorija; ☑8-615 65677; www.astro.lt/mao) on Kaldiniai Hill (193m). The observatory boasts northern Europe's largest telescope; visits must be booked in advance over the phone or online. Next door, the Lithuanian Ethnocosmology Museum (Lietuvos etnokosmologijos muziejus; ☑45 424; www.cosmos.lt; adult/child 10/6Lt; ☺8am-4pm) explores the cosmos' connection to hell, heaven and earth in its bubble-shaped exhibition centre. Dwarfing it are two observation towers topped by a massive rugby ball; inside are two telescopes providing outstanding views of the surrounding lakeland. Night tours with English-speaking guides (adult/child 10/6Lt), two hours after sunset, can be arranged in advance, but note that tour schedules are shortened during the winter months (October to April).

The hourly buses from Vilnius (18Lt, 1¼ to two hours) to Molėtai normally continue onto Utena (10Lt, 35 minutes). To visit the observatory and museum, catch a bus from Molėtai to Utena and ask to be let off at the 'etnokosmologijos muziejus' turn-off (signposted 10km north of town) and follow the road to the right for another 4km.

Utena

☑389 / POP 32,480

Utena, 34km north of Molėtai, is a quiet town in the centre of Lithuania's northeastern lakeland region. Its tourist office (☑54 346; www.utenainfo.lt; Stoties gatvė 39; ☺9am-6pm Mon-Thu, 9am-5pm Fri) can provide information on accommodation and activities.

Alaušynė (☑66 045; www.abuva.lt; 4-person chalet 100-270Lt, s/d 280/350Lt; P) is a rural spot 12km northeast of Utena and immediately northeast of Sudeikiai village with a range of accommodation and leisure options, including simple log chalets sleeping up to four people and modern houses with fireplace. It offers a sauna for weary bones, boats and canoes to hire (5Lt per hour) and fishing excursions to enjoy. Alaušynė also cooks up a mean fish soup – swimming with six different fish (including eel and carp) and served in a brown loaf of bread.

Geltonasis Submarine (☑50 223; Basanavičiaus gatvė 55; small/medium/large pizza 12/14/18Lt), a Beatles-inspired pizzeria that

Southern Lithuania

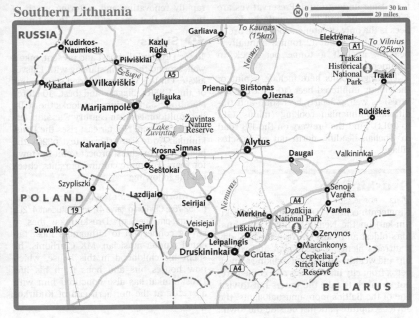

serves *pica su karka* (pizza with smoked pigs' trotters), is the cheeriest place to eat. Iki (Basanavičiaus gatvė 55) next door sells the makings of a lovely lakeside picnic.

From Utena **bus station** (✆61 740; Baranauskas gatvė 19) there is one daily bus to/ from Ignalina (12Lt, one hour), hourly buses to/from Vilnius (22Lt, 1½ to two hours), some via Molėtai (10Lt, 35 minutes), and seven daily buses to/from Kaunas (30Lt, 2½ hours).

Around Utena

Dusetos, some 34km northeast of Utena, is famous for its annual **horse race** (www .zarasai.lt) held on the first Saturday in February on frozen **Lake Sartai**. The race dates from 1865 and attracts horse enthusiasts, musicians and folk artists from all over the region, who pour into the small village to watch the race and slug local Čižo beer.

A fun spot to stay and play is **Bikėnų Uzeiga** (✆8-685 44450; www.degesa.lt; ⊗10am-10pm Apr-Sep; P) in Bikėnai on the eastern shore of **Lake Antalieptės**. The bar hires out rowing boats, canoes and kayaks for 6Lt per hour, offers a 10-person speedboat for charter (250Lt per hour) and has a water slide that snakes into the lake. The centre

also organises two-day canoeing expeditions (80Lt for a two-person canoe and tent hire) on the Šventoji River and has rooms to rent in lakeside houses for 100/200Lt per double/quad.

Bikėnų Uzeiga has a number of sister sites in the lake region, including the modern **Paukščių Sala** (✆8-685 44450; www.degesa .lt; s/d Mon-Fri 50/100Lt, Sat & Sun 100/150Lt; P) 1km east of Salakas on the shores of Lake Luodis. Rooms inside the wooden house are smallish but they're all en suite, clean and good value. The restaurant onsite will cook fish caught in the fish pond nearby (25Lt per kg), and it's activity central here, with bicycles (10/30Lt per hour/day) and canoes (10Lt per hour) for hire, plus sailing, wind surfing and, in winter, ice-fishing options.

Užeiga Prie Bravoro (✆385-56653; www .cizoalus.lt in Lithuanian; Dusetų homestead; ⊗10am-10pm Tue-Sun May-Aug) is not much to look at, but if you happen to be travelling in the area during the summer, it's worth stopping by this family-run brewery and restaurant for lunch or dinner and a pint or two.

Four generations have brewed the light, thirst-quenching Čižo *alus* (beer) here since 1863. Private brewing was strictly forbidden during Soviet times, forcing the brewery for a time underground. Preservatives are a strict no-no and honey made by forest bees is the only sweetener. Today the brewery produces about 12 tonnes annually – peaking at half a tonne per week in summer.

The high points here include a pint of the cloudy unfiltered beer (10/25Lt per 2/5 litres) as well as hearty beer soup and traditional Lithuanian cooking (mains 15Lt to 20Lt). Find the brewery on the 178 road to Obeliai, heading north out of Dusetos village.

Druskininkai

☑ 313 / POP 16,450

Nineteenth-century Druskininkai (drus-ki-nin-kai) on the Nemunas River is Lithuania's oldest and most chic spa town. Today it attracts plenty of investment and young, hip and wealthy Lithuanians seeking a quick detox from city life. Tourists also come here, not so much to take the waters but to visit one of the Baltic's more unusual sights, the Soviet sculpture park just outside the town.

During the days of the USSR, the old and ailing came to this famous health resort in search of miracle cures for all sorts of ailments. While some of these vast dinosaur sanatoriums still remain today, the town is

rapidly renovating and restoring much of the charm that was lost during those times.

◉ Sights

To see Druskininkai past and present, take a walk around the town, starting with Laisvės aikštė. On this vast tree-shaded square, one of the USSR's biggest and best, 10-storey **Nemunas Sanatorium** overlooks the striking multidomed 19th-century **Russian Orthodox church**. Not far east rises the Druskininkai **Aqua Park** (boxed text p320), the boldest and brightest project to hit the town for years. For more cultural pursuits, check out the following:

MK Čiurlionis Memorial Museum   MUSEUM
(☎52 755; Čiurlionio gatvė 41; adult/student 4/2Lt; ⊙11am-5pm Tue-Sun) Druskininkai has a strong connection to Lithuania's most talented painter-musician, MK Čiurlionis; he spent his childhood in this house, which now houses bits and bobs from his life. Druskininkai has also honoured him with a **statue** at the northern end of Kudirkos gatvė.

Museum of Armed Resistance   MUSEUM
(Vilniaus alėja 24; admission free; ⊙1-5pm Tue-Sun) On the top floor of the Cultural Centre is the small but worthwhile museum detailing the

Druskininkai

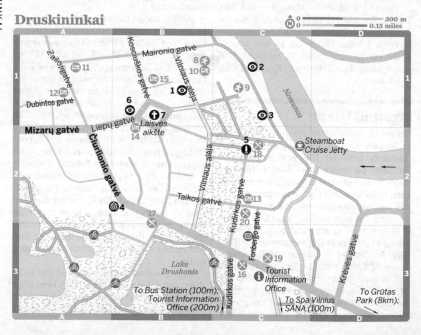

partisan movement and cultural resistance to Soviet rule. The Cultural Centre plays host to beautiful classical concerts during the Druskininkai Summer with Čiurlionis festival (June to September).

Mineralinio Vandems Biuvetė SPA
(per cup 0.40Lt or per 10/20 days 6/10Lt; ☉11.30am-1.30pm & 4-7pm Mon-Fri, 10.30am-1.30pm Sat) The magical powers of local mineral water can be tested at the Dzūkija Fountain inside the Mineralinio Vandems Biuvetė, a round green building with mosaic floor and stained-glass windows on the footpath running along the Nemunas River. Continue north to the **Fountain of Beauty** (Grožio šaltinis) – one slurp of the shockingly salty water promises eternal beauty.

Girios Aidas MUSEUM
(Echo of the Forest; Čiurlionio gatvė 102; adult/child 5/2Lt, sculpture trail 2Lt; ☉10am-6pm Wed-Sun) Heading 2km east of town, Girios Aidas is home to a pagan collection of wood carvings and a nature museum.

🏃 Activities

Spas (boxed text p320) aside, cruising around by pedal power is the way to go. Bicycle and two- or four-seater buggy **hire** (☉8am-9pm May-Oct) is available from the corner of Vilniaus and Laisvės alėjas, Vilniaus alėja 10 or opposite the tourist office at Čiurlionio gatvė 52. Expect to pay 5Lt to 6Lt per hour or up to 30Lt per day for a bicycle and 15/25Lt per 30/60 minutes for a buggy.

The tourist office sells cycling maps (5Lt) covering three local cycling trails: the southbound riverside **Sun Path** (Saulės takas; 24km) – also a footpath – goes to the windmill museum, **Stars Orbit** (Žvaigždžių orbita; 24km) snakes south into the Raigardas Valley, and the forested east-bound **Žilnas Path** (Žilvino takas; 20km) links Druskininkai with Grūtas Park (boxed text p321) 8km east – a great day trip.

Water-bound activities include **rowing boats** (per hr 15Lt) or **pedalo** (per hr 20Lt) on Lake Druskonis or taking a **steamboat cruise** (☎8-612 26982; adult/child 34/17Lt; ☉2.30pm Tue-Sun May-Oct) along the Nemunas River to Liškiava in the Dzūkija National Park (p322). Journey time is 45 minutes each way and passengers spend 1½ hours in Liškiava before sailing back to Druskininkai. Kids – both young and old – will have a ball in the Aqua Park (boxed text p320). The complex sports several water slides, a wave pool, flow pool and massive outdoor pool.

🛌 Sleeping

Prices increase on weekends and in July and August; consult the tourist offices if you need help.

Hotel Druskininkai HOTEL €€
(☎52 566; www.grandspa.lt; Kudirkos gatvė 43; s/d/ste from 220/280/420Lt; 🅿@🛜🏊) The Druskininkai is certainly one of the most stylish hotels in town. Behind its striking glass-and-wood facade are modern rooms bathed in subdued light, a Turkish bath, Jacuzzi bubbling with Druskininkai mineral water, and hotel gym. The location is excellent, close to the centre, the river and the spas.

Medūna HOTEL €
(☎58 033; www.meduna.lt; Liepų gatvė 2; s/d/apt from 100/120/290; 🅿🛜) Associated with the Aqua Park, this modern and stylish hotel represents excellent value for money. While

Druskininkai

◉ **Sights**
1 Cultural Centre	B1
2 Fountain of Beauty	C1
3 Mineralinio Vandems Biuvetė	C1
4 MK Čiurlionis Memorial Museum	B2
5 MK Čiurlionis Statue	C2
Museum of Armed Resistance	(see 1)
6 Nemunas Sanitorium	B1
7 Russian Orthodox Church	B1

⊕ **Activities, Courses & Tours**
8 Aqua Park	B1
9 Druskininkai Spa	C1
Grand Spa Lietuva	(see 13)

🛌 **Sleeping**
10 Aqua Hotel	B1
11 Galia	A1
12 Galia	A1
13 Hotel Druskininkai	C2
14 Medūna	B2
15 Regina	B1

🍴 **Eating**
16 Boulangerie	C3
17 Forto Dvaras	B2
18 Kolonada	C2
19 Mini-Maxima	C3
20 Sicilija	C2

LITHUANIA DRUSKININKAI

the prices noted here are for a 'mini-double', larger rooms are not much more expensive. There's a good onsite restaurant and the location is superb, equidistant from the lake, the river and the Aqua Park.

Aqua Hotel　　　　　　　　　HOTEL €€
(☑59 195; www.aquapark.lt; Vilniaus alėja 13-1; s/d/apt from 200/240/600Lt; P🅿🅼📶) This modern, family-friendly hotel fills one third of the Aqua Park and is the accommodation of choice if you're travelling with kids and the Aqua Park is what brought you to town in the first place. The rooms are spacious and well appointed. In addition to the water park, there are shops, spas, restaurants and a bowling alley to keep you occupied.

Galia　　　　　　　　　　　　HOTEL €€
(☑60 510; www.galia.lt; Maironio gatvė 3, Dubintos gatvė 3 & 4; s/d from 110/170Lt; P) Galia surprises with a rainbow of colours. The hotel is spread over three attractive buildings, all of which are in good condition; confirm before you check in as prices vary between the houses.

Regina　　　　　　　　　　　HOTEL €€
(☑59 060; www.regina.lt; Kosciuškos gatvė 3; s/d from 170/220Lt; P🅿📶) Solid bet for those looking for large, comfortable rooms and a broad range of facilities, such as laundry service, at a reasonable price. If you're looking for character, look somewhere else.

Druskininkai Camping　　　CAMPGROUND €
(☑60 800; camping@druskininkai.lt; Gardino gatvė 3a; site per adult/tent 10/15Lt, tepee/cabin 50/130Lt; P🅿) Large, well-organised campground near the tourist office and bus station. Tepees and cabins sleep up to two people.

✕ Eating & Drinking

Unfortunately, the dining scene leaves a little to be desired. Self-caterers can stock up at Mini-Maxima (Čiurlionio gatvė 50).

Forto Dvaras　　　　　　　LITHUANIAN €€
(www.druskininkudvaras.lt; Čiurlionio gatvė 55; mains 15-25Lt) The local branch of a Lithuanian chain of countrified restaurants serves very good traditional Lithuanian cooking, with the added benefit of sitting

---

TOP DRUSKININKAI SPAS

Druskininkai is spa-riddled. But beware, not all are swish. Step into the wrong place and you could be slapped around by a formidable babushka straight out of a horror movie. Here's a quick guide to help you make the right decision:

» **Aqua Park** (www.akvapark.lt; Vilniaus gatvė 13-2; adult/child Mon-Fri 3hr 35/31Lt, 4hr 38/35Lt, Sat & Sun 3hr 48/37Lt, 4hr 57/44Lt; ⊘noon-10pm Mon-Thu, noon-11pm Fri, 10am-11pm Sat, 10am-9pm Sun) Magnificent Soviet complex transformed into a fabulous water park, hotel and spa. The list of wellness treatments at the complex's 'East Island' spa seems endless, and includes body scrubs (70Lt), Thai and classic massages (80Lt to 250Lt) and all manner of facial and body beautifying programs. Saunas and steam baths are a dime a dozen.

» **Grand Spa Lietuva** (www.grandspa.lt; Kudirkos gatvė 43; ⊘9am-6.30pm Mon-Sat, 9am-4.30pm Sun) This spa is inside Hotel Druskininkai. Expect separate bubbling pools, filled with the likes of local mineral water or good old tap water (30Lt per hour). On the massage front (from 60Lt per hour), the body pummel with warm honey – a stronger massage than with regular or aromatic oil – wins hands down, although the massage with silky-smooth hot Hawaii stones is heavenly.

» **Spa Vilnius SANA** (www.spa-vilnius.lt; Dineikos gatvė 1; ⊘8am-10pm) Located inside an eight-storey hotel, it includes a clutch of baths, such as an indoor swimming pool (filled with local mineral water), one with seaweed (30Lt) and another with mud (25Lt). It also offers the full range of massages, including underwater body (40Lt per 20 minutes) and Shiatsu foot (60Lt per 30 minutes).

» **Druskininkai Spa** (Druskininkų gydykla; www.gydykla.lt; Vilniaus alėja 11; ⊘9am-6.30pm Mon-Sat, 9am-4.30pm Sun) Whirling, herbal, mineral, mud and even vertical (!) baths are among the wonderful watery delights on offer inside this peppermint-green riverside building. It likewise treats a mind-boggling array of diseases – cardiovascular, cutaneous, vestibular, endocrinal and more.

GRŪTAS PARK: AKA 'STALIN WORLD'

While in Druskininkai, it's worth making the 8km side trip to this ghoulish sculpture park. **Grūtas Park** (Grūto parkas; www.grutoparkas.lt; adult/6-15yr 20/10Lt, audio guide 46Lt; ☉9am-8pm), aka Stalin World, is an enormous collection of communist-era statuary that once stared down at oppressed Lithuanians in parks and squares all around the country. There are also exhibits of communist-era posters, art, newspapers and even an old reconstructed rural polling station.

It's a needed tonic for anyone with a nostalgic hankering for those 'simpler times' when Big Brother seemed to take care of everything.

The park was the idea of Viliumas Malinauskas, a former collective farm head who made a fortune canning mushrooms then won the loan of the hated objects from the Ministry of Culture. The grounds of the park form part of Malinauskas' lovely 2-sq-km estate.

Built to resemble a Siberian concentration camp, the park entrance is marked by a Soviet–Polish border crossing with barbed wire, and red-and-white (Polish) and red-and-green (USSR) striped poles. Next to it is a single carriage in which Lithuanians were deported to Siberia. Once through the turnstile, Russian tunes blast from watchtowers; in the restaurant, visitors eat vodka-doused sprats and onions with Soviet-made cutlery. Tacky souvenir stalls are rife; there is a playground with old Soviet swings and a mini children's zoo.

While there's plenty of English-language commentary on hand to help you sort through the dates, places and names, the main audience is clearly Lithuanians who suffered under the regime and their children (and grandchildren) who only have scant (if any) memory of those times. Many of the names and events will be unknown to anyone who didn't experience the system firsthand (unless they at least have a graduate degree in Soviet studies). Still, it's worthwhile for the spectacle, the trip through time, and even the artistic merit of some of the statues, which (in spite of the cause they were enlisted for) continue to mesmerise to this day.

Find Grūtas Park 8km east of Druskininkai; entering Grūtas village from the south, turn right (east) off the main road and follow the road 1km to its end. Bus 2 from the Druskininkai bus station (2Lt) regularly connects the park with the town.

right on the lake. The wood-hewn interior is tastefully done and the food is arguably the best in town.

Kolonada　　　　　　LITHUANIAN €€
(Kudirkos gatvė 22; mains around 22Lt) A diamond in the rough, this renovated late-1920s music hall combines atmosphere with fine Lithuanian cuisine, a huge patio overlooking the central park, and live music (jazz, classical, rock 'n' roll) on a regular basis.

Sicilija　　　　　　ITALIAN €
(Taikos gatvė 9; pizzas 10-20Lt, mains 12-20Lt) Pizza – over 40 varieties – is the speciality of this massively popular dining spot, which fills to overflowing at lunchtime.

Boulangerie　　　　　　CAFE €
(Čiurlionio gatvė 63; ☉9am-7pm) You'll find great coffee drinks as well as ice cream and

cakes at this French-style bakery and cafe just next to the tourist information office.

❶ Information

Post office (Kudirkos gatvė)
SEB Bankas (Čiurlionio gatvė 40) Currency exchange inside, ATM outside.
Tourist information office former train station building (☑60 800; www.info.druskininkai.lt; Gardino gatvė 3; ☉8.30am-12.15pm & 1-5.15pm Mon-Fri); town (☑51 777; Čiurlionio gatvė 65; ☉10am-1pm & 1.45-6.45pm Mon-Sat, 10am-5pm Sun)

❶ Getting There & Away

From the **bus station** (☑51 333; Gardino gatvė 1) there are up to 10 daily buses (28Lt, two hours) to/from Vilnius; hourly buses to/from Kaunas (28Lt, two to three hours); one to/from Panevėžys (50Lt, 4¼ hours) and one to/from Šiauliai (58Lt, 5¼ hours).

Dzūkija National Park

📖 310

The 555-sq-km Dzūkija (dzoo-ki-ya) National Park (Lithuania's largest) is a nature-lover's paradise. Four-fifths of it is covered by dense pine forest, and 48 lakes can be found within its borders. The Ūla and Grūda Rivers, perfect for a days' canoeing, flow through it, and an abundance of mushrooms and berries grow here during the season. Squeezed between Marcinkonys and the Belarusian border is the Čepkeliai Strict Nature Reserve, which safeguards the country's largest marsh.

Several villages, including Zervynos, between Varėna and Marcinkonys, are ethnographic reserves. Liškiava, 10km northeast of Druskininkai, has remnants of a 14th-century hilltop castle. The village church and former Dominican monastery is famous for its seven rococo-style altars and its crypt with glass coffins. Merkinė, 10km further down the Nemunas River, is the starting point for a 12km black potters' trail around workshops where pots as black as soot are made from red clay. The extraordinary colour comes from pine-wood resin fired with the pot in an outdoor kiln. Other traditions such as woodcarving, weaving, basket-making and beekeeping come to life in Marcinkonys' Ethnographic Museum (Marcinkonių etnografijos muziejus; Miškininkų gatvė 10; adult/child 2/1Lt; ⊙9am-4pm Tue-Sat May-Sep, from 10am Oct-Apr).

Two visitor centres Marcinkonys (📞44 466; www.dzukijosparkas.lt; Miškininkų gatvė 61; ⊙8am-5pm Mon-Fri, 8am-3.45pm Sat); Merkinė (📞57 245; merkine@dzukijosparkas.lt; Vilniaus gatvė 3; ⊙8am-noon & 1-5pm Mon-Thu, 8am-3.45pm Fri) advise on walking, cycling, canoeing and arranging English-speaking guides (50/200Lt per hour/day) for mushrooming or berrying. The centres also have information on the 14km Zackagiris Sightseeing Route (Zackagirio Takas), with shorter 7km and 10.5km routes, which starts outside Marcinkonys visitor centre. At Marcinkonys, staff can arrange bicycle and canoe hire, but they must be booked one day in advance.

Falling just outside the boundaries of the park, 22km northeast of Marcinkonys and 58km northeast of Druskininkai, is Varėna (www.varena.lt). Founded in the 15th century when Grand Duke Vytautas built a hunting lodge here, it is the birthplace of noted Lithuanian painter and composer MK Čiurlionis. The main road (A4) leading from Varėna to Druskininkai is lined with sculpted wooden 'totem' poles and sculptures, erected in 1975 in commemoration of the 100th anniversary of his birth.

🛏 Sleeping

Marcinkonys Visitor Centre GUESTHOUSE € (www.dzukijosparkas.lt; s/d with breakfast 100/150; ⓟ @) The visitor centre at Marcinkonys has its own simple guesthouse, with en suite rooms, along with a list of homestay ac-

---

MUSHROOMING & BERRYING

Mushrooming is a, well, mushrooming business, particularly in and around the Dzūkija National Park, which in August and September is carpeted with little white and yellow buttons. The forests lining the Varėna–Druskininkai highway (A4) and the Zervynos forests – best known for sand dunes, beehive hollows and substantial *grybas* (mushroom) populations – make rich *grybaula* (mushroom-hunting grounds) too. For mushroom addicts, there's Varėna's September **mushroom festival** (www.varena.lt).

The crinkle-topped, yellow chanterelle and stubby *boletus* are among the edible wild mushroom varieties hunted and exported to other parts of Europe. The less common *baravykas*, with its distinctive brown cap, is a stronger-tasting mushroom that ends up stuffed inside a *cepelinai* or dried and stored until Christmas Eve, when it is served as one of 12 dishes (p379). Lithuania boasts 1200 mushroom species, but only 380 are edible.

Berrying is another trade and tradition. Red bilberries only ripen in August and cranberries in September, but most other berries – wild strawberries, blueberries, buckthorn berries, sloe berries and raspberries – can be harvested whenever they are ripe.

The roadside rate for mushrooms is around 15Lt to 20Lt per kilogram. Look for locals selling at roadsides, with glass jam jars overflowing with freshly picked forest goodies lined up on car bonnets. The mushroom season runs from early spring to late autumn.

commodation (around 70Lt per person) but doesn't make bookings; camping is only allowed in designated areas.

Zervynų
BUNGALOW €

(📞8-687 50826; camping/dm 10/30Lt) A rural idyll with two wooden turn-of-the-20th-century cottages, one with wood-burning stove, the other with no heating. Both have basic bunks and no running water (bathe in the river and pee in the bushes); rough camping is in the field and meals cost 20Lt. There is a sauna (100Lt for an evening) and it organises mushrooming, berrying and canoeing expeditions on the Ūla River (50Lt per day). Call in advance and someone will meet you at Zervynos train station. By car, Zervynų is at the end of a 3km road, signposted off the main Varėna–Marcinkonys road (take the right fork at the end).

ⓘ Getting There & Away

In summer a steamboat (p319) makes trips between Druskininkai and Liškiava .

Buses to/from Druskininkai and Vilnius stop at the Merkinė intersection (Merkinės kryžkelė; 8Lt, 25 minutes), 2km east of Merkinė town centre. Three daily trains to/from Vilnius stop at Zervynos (12.90Lt, two hours) and Marcinkonys (15.70Lt, two hours).

CENTRAL LITHUANIA

Most people only give Central Lithuania a quick glance – generally from the seat of their bus or train as they're travelling from capital to coast. This flat land between the country's big attractions is often written off as dull, but such a conclusion would be foolhardy, for here resides Lithuania's most bizarre sight, along with cities of substance and bucolic splendour as far as the eye can see.

Proud Kaunas, the alternative Lithuanian capital between WWI and WWII and the country's perpetual 'number two' city, holds court in the heart of the country. Its Old Town is as intriguing as its mass of museums and art galleries, and there is no better place to base yourself for central-country forays. Within easy reach of Kaunas is Birštonas, a tiny spa town where both jazz and mud treatments are serious business.

Still in the process of reinvention is Šiauliai, once a closed city in Soviet times that sheltered the USSR's largest military base outside Russia. This northern city is full of surprises, proffering up the weird and the wonderful: not many places can boast a Bicycle Museum *and* a Museum of Cats. Yet most tourists make the pilgrimage here for the papal-blessed Hill of Crosses 10km to the north, and leave awed by the strength and devotion of the Lithuanian people.

Kaunas
📞37 / POP 353,000

Kaunas (kow-nas), a sprawling city on the banks of the Nemunas River, has a compact Old Town, a menagerie of artistic and educational museums, and a rich history all its own. Its sizeable student population provides it with plenty of vibrant, youthful energy, and its rough edges give it that extra bit of spice lacking in many of Lithuania's provincial towns and urban expanses.

History

Legend has it that Kaunas, 100km west of Vilnius at the confluence of the Nemunas and Neris Rivers, was founded by the son of tragic young lovers. Beautiful maiden Milda let the Holy Eternal Flame go out while caring for her lover Daugerutis. They were sentenced to death by vengeful gods, thus they fled to a cave, where Milda gave birth to Kaunas.

Archaeologists believe the city dates from the 13th century and until the 15th century was in the front line against the Teutonic Order in Lithuania's west. Kaunas became a successful river port in the 15th and 16th centuries. German merchants were influential here, and there was a Hanseatic League office. During the interwar period it became the capital of Lithuania as Vilnius lay in Polish hands. Its strategic position is the main reason it was destroyed 13 times before WWII – when it once again received a battering.

ⓞ Sights

Rotušės aikštė, the square wedged between the Nemunas and Neris Rivers, is the historic heart. From here pedestrianised Vilniaus gatvė runs east to meet the city's main axis, Laisvės alėja – also pedestrianised.

OLD TOWN
ROTUŠĖS AIKŠTĖ & AROUND

This large, open square at the heart of Old Town is lined with pretty 15th- and 16th-century German merchants' houses and is

Central Lithuania

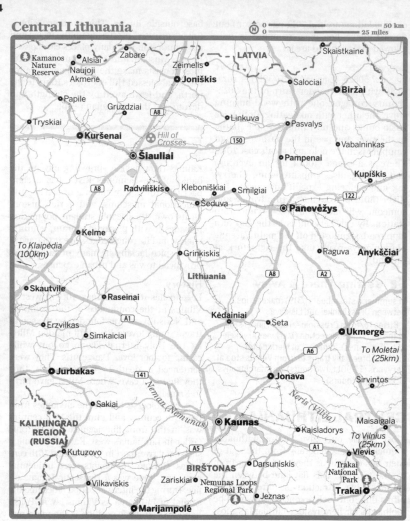

centred on the 17th-century former town hall. This is now a **Palace of Weddings**, where dozens of brides and grooms say *taip* ('I do') every Saturday in summer. In the square's southwestern corner stands a **statue of Maironis** (1862–1932), a Kaunas priest and poet named Jonas Mačiulis (Maironis was his pen name) whose writings helped to awaken the country's nationalist longings in the late 19th and early 20th centuries. Stalin banned his works.

Historic Churches
CHURCHES

The town hall square is surrounded by historic churches. The southern side is dominated by the twin-towered **St Francis Church** (Rotušės aikštė 7-9), a college and Jesuit monastery complex built between 1666 and 1720. A few steps south of the church is the curious **House of Perkūnas** (Perkūno namas; Aleksotas gatvė 6), built in red brick in the 16th century as trade offices on the site of a former temple to the Lithuanian thunder god, Perkūnas. Beyond, on the bank of the Nemunas River, the Gothic-style **Vytautas Church** (Vytauto bažnyčia; Aleksoto gatvė 5) is built of the same red brick. The western side of the square is filled by the late-Renaissance (1624–34), terracotta-roofed **Holy Trinity Church** (Rotušės aikštė 22).

Medicine & Pharmaceutical History Museum
MUSEUM

(Medicinios ir farmacijos istorijos muziejus; Rotušės aikštė 28; adult/child 3/1.50Lt; ⊘11am-6pm Wed-Sun, to 5pm Nov-May) Don't be surprised to find yourself the only visitor in this odd museum that details medical advances in Lithuania over the centuries. There are a lot of old books and bottles and a reconstructed 19th-century pharmacy. Unfortunately, there's little English commentary and what does exist is hard to follow.

Maironis Lithuanian Literary Museum
MUSEUM

(Maironio Lietuvos literatūros muziejus; www.maironiomuziejus.lt; Rotušės aikštė 13; adult/child 5/2Lt; ⊘9am-5pm Tue-Sat) This museum is dedicated to the life and works of Kaunas priest Jonas Mačiulis (aka Maironis), the poet whose words spurred the country's national stirrings in the late 19th and early 20th centuries. From 1910 to 1932 Maironis lived in this house.

Ceramics Museum
MUSEUM

(Keramikos muziejus; Rotušės aikštė 15; adult/child 4/2Lt; ⊘11am-5pm Tue-Sun) Features a nice collection of locally made decorative bricks and tiles and often houses temporary exhibitions of variable quality.

Communications Development Museum
MUSEUM

(Ryšių istorijos muziejus; www.teo.lt/en/node/1449; Rotušės aikštė 19; adult/child 5/3Lt; ⊘10am-6pm Tue-Sun) Those with a love of old telephones and big, old analogue technology should take the time to peek inside this museum, housed in the former post office.

Aleksoto funicular
FUNICULAR

(Aleksoto funikulierius; Skriaudžių gatvė 8 & Aušros gatvė 6; return ticket 0.50Lt; ⊘7am-noon & 1-4pm Mon-Fri) This historic funicular at the southern end of Aleksoto Tiltas (Aleksoto Bridge) dates from 1935 and affords great rooftop views of Old Town.

Kaunas Castle
RUIN

A reconstructed tower, sections of wall and part of a moat are all that remain of

THE HEROES OF KAUNAS

Beloved Lithuanian pilots Steponas Darius and Stanislovas Girėnas (featured on the 10Lt note) died on 15 July 1933, just 650km short of completing the longest nonstop transatlantic flight at the time. Two days after the duo set off from New York, 25,000 people gathered at Kaunas airport for their triumphant return. They never arrived. Their orange plane *Lituanica* crashed in Germany; see the wreckage in the Military Museum of Vytautas the Great (p329). After being embalmed, then hidden during Soviet occupation, the bodies came to rest at **Aukštieji Šančiai Cemetery** (Asmenos gatvė 1) in 1964.

Kaunas-based Japanese diplomat Chiune Sugihara (1900–86) – with the help of Dutch diplomat Jan Zwartendijk – saved 6000 Jewish lives between 1939 and 1940 by issuing transit visas to stranded Polish Jews who faced the advancing Nazi terror. When the Soviets annexed Lithuania and ordered that all consulates be shut he asked for a short extension. Dubbed 'Japan's Schindler', he disobeyed orders from Tokyo for some 29 days by signing 300 visas per day, and handed the stamp to a Jewish refugee when he left. **Sugihara House** (Sugiharos namai; Vaižganto gatvė 30; admission free; ⊘10am-5pm Mon-Fri, 11am-4pm Sat & Sun May-Oct, 11am-3pm Mon-Fri Nov-Apr) tells his life story, and features video installations and stories of those he managed to save.

The small **Museum of Deportation & Resistance** (Rezistencijos ir tremties muziejus; Vytauto prospektas 46; adult/child 4/2Lt; ⊘10am-4pm Tue-Fri) documents the resistance spirit embodied by the Forest Brothers, who fought the Soviet occupation from 1944 to 1953. Led by Jonas Žemaitis-Vytautas (1909–54), somewhere between 50,000 and 100,000 men and women went into Lithuania's forests to battle the regime. The museum staff estimates that one-third were killed, and the rest captured and deported (in total 150,000 Lithuanians were sent to Soviet territory during this time).

One of the most desperate anti-Soviet actions was the suicide of Kaunas student Romas Kalanta. On 14 May 1972 he doused himself in petrol and set fire to himself in protest at communist rule. A suicide note was found in his diary.

Kaunas

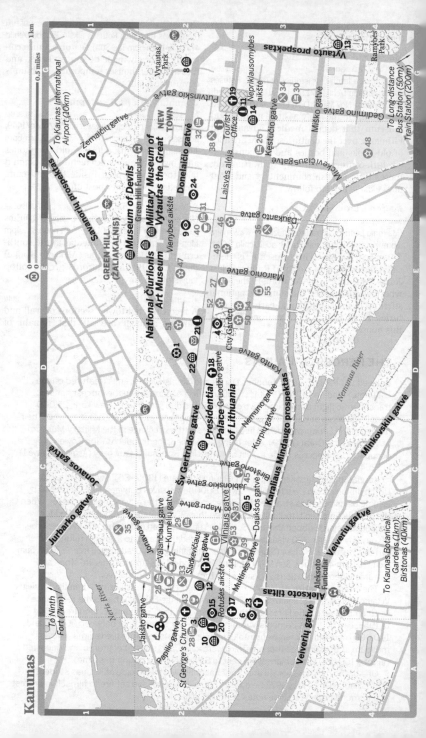

To Ninth Fort (7km)

Jakšto gatvė

St George's Church

Papilio gatvė

Jonavos gatvė

Jurbarko gatvė

Valančiaus gatvė

Kumelių gatvė

Sladkevičiaus

Vilniaus gatvė

Mapu gatvė

Jablonskio gatvė

Daukšos gatvė

Birštono gatvė

Kurpių gatvė

Nemuno gatvė

Kanto gatvė

Maironio gatvė

Daukanto gatvė

Kęstučio gatvė

Mickevičiaus gatvė

Gedimino gatvė

Miško gatvė

Muitinės gatvė

Rotušės aikštė

Sv Gertrūdos gatvė

Gruodžio gatvė

City Garden

Presidential Palace of Lithuania

National Čiurlionis Art Museum

Museum of Devils

Military Museum of Vytautas the Great

Vienybės aikštė

Donelaičio gatvė

Laisvės alėja

Putvinskio gatvė

Vytautas Park

NEW TOWN

GREEN HILL (ŽALIAKALNIS)

Green Hill Funicular

Žemaičių gatvė

Savanorių prospektas

To Kaunas International Airport (10km)

Neris River

Nemunas River

Minkovskių gatvė

Veiverių gatvė

Karaliaus Mindaugo prospektas

Aleksoto Funicular

Aleksoto tiltas

To Kaunas Botanical Gardens (1km); Birštonas (40km)

Tourist Office

Neprikalsomybės aikštė

Vytauto prospektas

Ramybės Park

To Long-distance Bus Station (50m); Train Station (200m)

0   0.5 miles
0   1 km

Kaunas

◉ Top Sights

Military Museum of Vytautas the
  Great...E2
Museum of Devils.................................E1
National Čiurlionis Art Museum...........E2
Presidential Palace of Lithuania..........C2

◉ Sights

Ceramics Museum.......................(see 15)
1 Choral Synagogue...............................D2
2 Christ's Resurrection Basilica..............F1
3 Communications Development
  Museum..A2
4 Field of Sacrifice.................................D2
5 Folk Music & Instruments
  Museum..C3
Holy Trinity Church....................(see 28)
6 House of Perkūnas..............................B3
Jesuit Monastery........................(see 17)
7 Kaunas Castle......................................A2
Kaunas Musical Theatre............(see 50)
8 Kaunas Picture Gallery.........................G2
9 Kaunas Technological University.........E2
10 Maironis Lithuanian Literary
  Museum..A2
Maironis's Tomb.........................(see 16)
11 Man Statue..G3
12 Medicine & Pharmaceutical
  History Museum................................B2
13 Museum of Deportation &
  Resistance..G4
14 Mykolas Žilinskas Art Gallery..............G3
15 Palace of Weddings.............................B2
16 SS Peter & Paul Cathedral..................B2
17 St Francis Church................................B3
18 St Gertrude's Church..........................D2
19 St Michael the Archangel
  Church...G2
20 Statue of Maironis...............................A2
21 Statue of Vytautas the Great...............D2
22 Tadas Ivanauskas Zoological
  Museum..D2
23 Vytautas Church..................................B3
24 Vytautas Magnus University................F2

◎ Sleeping

25 Apple Hotel...B2
26 Daniela..F3
27 Kaunas Hotel......................................E2
28 Kauno Arkivyskupijos Svečių
  Namai..A2
29 Kunigaikščių Menė..............................B2
30 Litinterp..G3
31 Metropolis...F2
32 Park Inn by Radisson..........................F2

◈ Eating

Avilys...(see 37)
33 Bernelių Užveiga.................................B2
34 Fu Long...G3
35 Iki..B1
36 Maxima..E3
37 Senieji Rūsiai......................................C3
38 Žalias Ratas..F2

◉ Drinking

39 BO...B3
Buon Giorno...............................(see 37)
40 Coffee Inn...E2
41 Kavos Klubas......................................B2
42 Motiejaus Kepyklėlė............................B2
43 Skliautas...B2
44 Vero Cafe..B3
45 W1640...C3

◉ Entertainment

46 Džem Pub...E2
47 Ex-it..E2
48 Forum Cinemas...................................F4
49 Kaunas Academic Drama
  Theatre..E2
50 Kaunas Musical Theatre......................D3
51 Kaunas Philharmonic..........................D2
52 Kaunas Puppet Theatre......................E2
53 Latino Baras.......................................B3
54 Youth Chamber Theatre......................E3

◉ Shopping

55 Centrinis Knygynas.............................E3
56 Humanitas...B2

Kaunas Castle, around which the town originally grew. Founded in the 13th century, it was an important bastion of Lithuania's western borders.

VILNIAUS GATVĖ & AROUND
Vilniaus gatvė is Old Town's charming main artery.

Presidential Palace of Lithuania MUSEUM, LANDMARK
(Lietuvos Respublikos prezidentūra kaune; www.istorineprezidentura.lt; Vilniaus gatvė 33; adult/student 4/2Lt; ⊙11am-5pm Tue-Sun, gardens 8am-9pm daily) The eastern end of Vilniaus gatvė is dominated by the former Presidential Palace of Lithuania from where the country

was run between 1920 and 1939. Restored to its original grandeur, the palace hosts a great exhibition on independent Lithuania. Black-and-white photographs are interspersed with gifts given to past presidents, collections of family silver and presidential awards. Statues of the former presidents stud the palace garden.

Folk Music & Instruments Museum   MUSEUM
(Lietuvos tautinės muzikos muziejus; www.muziejai.lt; Zamenhofo gatvė 12; adult/child 4/2Lt; ⊙10am-6pm Tue-Sat May-Sep, 9am-5pm Tue-Sat Oct-Apr) This museum shows that almost any raw material can be turned into a musical instrument. The wonderful collection includes wood and bone flutes, unusual reed pipes, three-string cellos, and both basic and elaborately carved *kanklės* (zithers).

SS Peter & Paul Cathedral   CHURCH
(Vilniaus gatvė 1) With its single tower, this church owes much to baroque reconstruction, especially inside, but the original 15th-century Gothic shape of its windows remains. It was probably founded by Vytautas around 1410 and now has nine altars. The tomb of Maironis stands outside the south wall.

NEW TOWN
Kaunas expanded east from Old Town in the 19th century, giving birth to the modern centre and its striking 1.7km pedestrian street, Laisvės alėja, also known as Freedom Avenue.

Independent Lithuania's first parliament convened in 1920 at the Kaunas Musical Theatre, the former State Theatre Palace overlooking City Garden (Miestos Sodas) at the western end of Laisvės alėja, which was created in 1892. The Field of Sacrifice – a name engraved on paving slabs in front of the garden – is a tragic tribute to the young Kaunas hero Romas Kalanta (boxed text p325), who set himself alight in protest at Soviet rule. Across the street is a statue of Vytautas the Great.

Tadas Ivanauskas Zoological Museum   MUSEUM
(Tado Ivanausko zoologijos muziejus; www.zoomuziejus.lt; Laisvės alėja 106; adult/child 5/3Lt; ⊙11am-7pm Tue-Sun) A little west of the Vytautas statue, a stone turtle marks the entrance to the Tadas Ivanauskas Zoological Museum. Inside, an incredible 13,000 stuffed animals jockey for attention.

St Michael the Archangel Church   CHURCH
(Šv Mykolo Arkangelo igulos bažnyčioje; Nepriklausomybės aikštė 14) The Soviets turned this blue neo-Byzantine church that fills the sky so dramatically at the eastern end of Laisvės alėja into a stained-glass museum. Built for the Russian Orthodox faith in 1895, the church was reopened to Catholic worshippers in 1991.

St Gertrude's Church   CHURCH
(Šv Gertrūdos bažnyčia; Laisvės alėja 101a) This Gothic gem of a church is tucked in a courtyard off Laisvės alėja. It was built in the late 15th century. Its red-brick crypt overflows with burning candles, prompting a separate candle shrine to be set up in a shed opposite the crypt entrance.

Choral Synagogue   SYNAGOGUE
(Choralinė sinagoga; Ožeškienės gatvė 17; admission free; ⊙5.45-6.30pm Mon-Fri, 10am-noon Sat) Not far north of the zoological museum stands one of the few remnants of Kaunas' former Jewish community. Inside this functioning synagogue is a remarkable dark-wood and gold bimah, and outside resides a memorial to 1600 children killed at the Ninth Fort. The WWII Jewish ghetto was on the western bank of the Neris, in the area bounded by Jurbarko, Panerių and Demokratų streets.

Mykolas Žilinskas Art Gallery   MUSEUM
(Mykolo Žilinsko dailės galerija; Nepriklausomybės aikštė 12; adult/child 5/2.50Lt; ⊙11am-5pm Tue-Sun) This art museum on three floors is based on the private collection of Mykolas Žilinskas, but is now operated by the National Čiurlionis Art Museum. The collection is strongest on European art from the 17th to the 20th centuries and boasts Lithuania's only Rubens. The statue of 'Man', in front of the museum, was modelled on Nike the Greek god of victory and caused a storm of controversy when its glorious 'manhood' was unveiled in 1991.

VIENYBĖS AIKŠTĖ & AROUND
Unity Sq houses Kaunas Technological University (Kauno technologijos universitetas) and the smaller Vytautas Magnus University (Vytauto didžiojo universitetas), first founded in 1922 and refounded in 1989 by an émigré Lithuanian.

TOP CHOICE National Čiurlionis Art Museum   MUSEUM
(Nacionalinis Čiurlionio dailės muziejus; www.ciurlionis.lt; Putvinskio gatvė 55; adult/child 6/3Lt; ⊙11am-5pm Tue-Sun) This museum, dedi-

cated to the work of the country's leading painter, Mikalojus Konstantinas Čiurlionis (1875–1911), is arguably the city's most important attraction. Čiurlionis was also a brilliant composer, and there's a studio here where you can sit and listen to some of his works.

TOP CHOICE **Museum of Devils**　　　　MUSEUM
(Putvinskio gatvė 64; adult/child 6/3Lt; ⊘10am-6pm Tue-Sun) Diabolical is the best word to describe the collection of 2000-odd devil statuettes in this museum, collected over the years by landscape artist Antanas Žmuidzinavičius (1876–1966). While the commentary tries to put a pseudo-intellectual sheen on things by linking the devils to Lithuanian folklore, the fun of this museum is all about the spooky masks and funny stories. Great for kids.

Military Museum of Vytautas the Great　　　　MUSEUM
(Vytauto didžiojo karo muziejus; Donelaičio gatvė 64; adult/child 4/2Lt; ⊘11am-5pm Tue-Sun) This museum covers Lithuanian history from prehistoric times to the present day with a strong emphasis on the country's military exploits. While there's little English signage around, of particular interest is the wreckage of the aircraft in which Steponas Darius and Stanislovas Girėnas died while attempting to fly nonstop from New York to Kaunas in 1933 (see the boxed text, p325).

Kaunas Picture Gallery　　　　MUSEUM
(Kauno paveikslų galerija; Donelaičio gatvė 16; adult/student 4/2Lt; ⊘11am-5pm Tue-Sun) An underrated gem, with works by late-20th-century Lithuanian artists and a room devoted to Jurgis Mačiūnas, the father of the Fluxus avant-garde movement.

Green Hill　　　　NEIGHBOURHOOD
The **Green Hill funicular** (Žaliakalnio funikulierius; Putvinskio gatvė 22; return ticket 1Lt; ⊘7am-7pm Mon-Fri, 9am-7pm Sat & Sun) to the northeast of Vienybės glides up **Green Hill** (Žaliakalnis). Above the top station towers the strikingly white **Christ's Resurrection Basilica** (Kauno paminklinė Kristhaus Prisikėlimo bašničia; Zemaicių gatvė 316; ⊘10am-7pm), a piece of history that took 70 years to build. After being used as a Nazi paper warehouse and a Soviet radio factory, the church was finally consecrated in 2004.

OUTSIDE THE CENTRE
Kaunas is a surprisingly green city, with parks around its fringes. **Vytautas Park** occupies the slope up from the end of Laisvės alėja to the stadium, behind which stretches a large majority of the lovely **Ažuolynas Park**. South along Vytauto prospektas is **Ramybės Park**, home to the Old City Cemetery until the Soviets tore up all the graves in the 1960s.

Ninth Fort　　　　JEWISH HERITAGE
(IX Fortas; www.9fortomuziejus.lt in Lithuanian; Žemaičių plentas 73; each museum adult/child 5/3Lt; ⊘10am-6pm Wed-Mon Mar-Nov, 10am-4pm Wed-Sun Dec-Feb) Lithuania's brutal history is at some of its darkest at the Ninth Fort, built on Kaunas' northwestern outskirts in the late 19th century to fortify the western frontier of the tsarist empire. During WWII the Nazis made it a death camp where 80,000 people, including most of Kaunas' Jewish population, were killed. Later it became a prison and execution site by Stalin's henchmen. The old museum covers the fort's history from its inception to the end of WWII, including exhibits on the Nazi horrors against Jews; the new museum deals with the Soviet occupation of Lithuania.

Take bus 38 from the bus station to the Mega Shopping & Leisure Centre, 7km out of town, from where it's a 1km walk west to the fort.

Kaunas Botanical Gardens　　　　GARDENS
(Kauno botanikos sodas; Žilibero gatvė 6; adult/child 7/4Lt; ⊘10am-5pm Mon-Fri, 10am-6pm Sat & Sun) Gardening buffs will enjoy these gardens, where university gardeners tend rare and wonderful plants in a 1920s manor-house garden. The gardens are around 2km south of Old Town; to get there take bus 7 or 12 from Kaunas Castle.

Pažaislis Monastery　　　　MONASTERY
(Masiulio gatvė 31; adult/child 4/2Lt; ⊘10am-5pm Tue-Sun) A fine example of 17th-century baroque architecture, Pažaislis Monastery is 9km east of the centre, near the shores of **Kaunas Sea** (Kauno marios), a large artificial lake. The monastery church, with its 50m-high cupola and luxurious Venetian interior made from pink and black Polish marble, is a sumptuous if slightly run-down affair. Passing from Catholic to Orthodox to Catholic control, the monastery has had a chequered history and was a psychiatric hospital for part of the Soviet era. The best time to visit is between June and August

during the **Pažaislis Music Festival** (www
.pazaislis.lt). Take trolleybus 5 from the
town centre to the terminus on Masiulio
gatvė, a few hundred metres before Pažaislis
Monastery.

Open-Air Museum of Lithuania MUSEUM
(Lietuvių liaudies buities muziejus; www.llbm.lt;
Nėries gatvė 6; adult/child 10/5Lt; ⊙10am-6pm
Wed-Sun May-Oct, on request via website or tourist
office Nov-Apr) Go back in time at this open-
air museum, where four villages of 18th- and
19th-century buildings represent Lithuania's
four main regions. Potters, weavers and join-
ers demonstrate their crafts in the museum
workshop. The museum is in Rumšiškės,
25km east of Kaunas, about 2km off the
Kaunas–Vilnius road. The museum is accessible by bus from Kaunas (7Lt, 30 minutes,
five daily).

✵ Festivals & Events

Kaunas' social highlights are April's four-day
International Jazz Festival (www.kaunasjazz
.lt) and the open-air **Operetta in Kaunas
Castle**, held for two weeks in the castle
ruins in late June-early July.

For classical fans, the Pažaislis Music
Festival has concerts in the courtyards and
churches of Pažaislis Monastery from June
to August.

🛏 Sleeping

Apple Hotel HOTEL €€
(✆321 404; www.applehotel.lt; Valančiaus gatvė
19; s/d/tr/q 105/150/230/270Lt; P@🖘) This
simple hotel set on the Old Town's edge in a
quiet courtyard is a highly recommendable
no-frills option. The rooms are tiny, but are
cheerful and done out in bright colours. The
bed in our room was the most comfortable
we slept on during our research in Lithuania. Some rooms have shared bath, while
others are self-contained. On the down side,
breakfast (14Lt) is hardly worth the money
and the wi-fi signal barely extends beyond
the lobby. These are minor quibbles, though,
with what remains a solid choice.

Litinterp GUESTHOUSE €
(✆228 718; www.litinterp.lt; Gedimino gatvė 28/7;
s/d/tr from 100/130/210Lt; ⊙office 8.30am-
7pm Mon-Fri, 9am-3pm Sat; P@🖘) The Litinterp empire boasts quality guesthouses in
Vilnius, Klaipėda and here in Kaunas.
There's not a lot of character here, but the
rooms are cheap, clean and highly functional. The staff could not be friendlier or

more knowledgeable. Call in advance if you
plan to arrive outside of office hours.

Kaunas Hotel HOTEL €€
(✆750 850; www.kaunashotel.lt; Laisvės alėja 79;
s/d/ste from 310/350/420Lt; P@🖘🏊) This
swanky five-floor, four-star pillow parlour
dates from 1892 and is top dog in town.
Glass fronts the top floor where room 512
sports a peek-if-you-dare glass-walled bathroom overlooking Laisvės alėja. The hotel
is a free wi-fi zone and guests can use the
business centre for 20Lt per hour.

**Kauno Arkivyskupijos
Svečių Namai** GUESTHOUSE €
(✆322 597; kaunas.lcn.lt/sveciunamai; Rotušės
aikštė 21; s/d/tr from 70/120/140Lt; P@) This
charming guesthouse, run by the Lithuanian
Catholic Church, couldn't have a better location, sitting smugly between centuries-old
churches overlooking the Old Town square.
Rooms are spartan but spacious. Breakfast
is not included. Book well in advance since
this place tends to fill up fast.

Daniela HOTEL €€
(✆321 505; www.danielahotel.lt; Mickevičiaus
gatvė 28; s/d/ste from 290/360/550Lt; P@🖘)
A retro-chic hotel owned by basketball hero
Arvydas Sabonis, Daniela is a fun and bold
place, with soft pink chairs, steely mezzanines
and extra-large bouncy sofas. Its standard
rooms are well above par, and staff do their
best to cater to guests' needs. Parking is extra.

Kunigaikščių Menė GUESTHOUSE €€
(✆320 877; www.hotelmene.lt; Daukšos gatvė 28;
s/d from 180/250Lt; P@🖘) Atmospheric,
family-run guesthouse with an excellent
Old Town location. The rooms are small, but
cuter than most at this price point. Some
have hardwood floors.

Metropolis HOTEL €
(✆205 992; www.metropolishotel.lt; Daukanto
gatvė 21; s/d/tr/q 110/145/195/240Lt) This
graceful old dame is looking a bit frayed
these days, but she still displays strong
overtones of past grandeur. Sculpted-stone
balconies overlook a leafy street; a hefty
wooden turnstile door sweeps guests into a
lobby with moulded ceiling; and age-old furnishings only add to the charm. As the sign
in Lithuanian and Russian outside says, it
was called Hotel Lietuva in the USSR.

Park Inn by Radisson HOTEL €€
(✆306 100; www.parkinn.com/hotel-kaunas;
Donelaičio gatvė 27; s/d from 260/330Lt; P@)

This smart business hotel fills eight floors of a recently renovated building in New Town. Service is slick and professional, and rooms are standard business class, with a few added extras such as heated bathroom floors and free tea and coffee. Count on the restaurant, bar and huge conference centre onsite.

✕ Eating

Dining has improved in recent years, but has yet to match the capital. Central supermarkets include Iki (Jonavos gatvė 3) and Maxima (Kęstučio gatvė 55).

Bernelių Užeiga   LITHUANIAN €€
(www.berneliuuzeiga.eu; Valančiaus gatvė 9; mains 10-30Lt) Perfect choice for an affordable, traditional Lithuanian meal with all the trimmings. The setting is rustic, but with a slightly upscale twist seen in the white linen tablecloths. The staff will patiently guide you through the long menu, and at the end of the night you'll be pleasantly surprised by the reasonable tab.

Senieji Rūsiai   LITHUANIAN €€
(Old Cellars; www.seniejirusiai.lt; Vilniaus gatvė 34; mains 18-40Lt; ⊙11am-midnight Mon-Fri, noon-2am Sat, noon-midnight Sun; 🛜) Hands down the tastiest street terrace at which to dine, drink and soak up Old Town, this fashionable spot with candlelit 17th-century cellar grills great meats and serves a wide selection, which includes frogs' legs, trout and the ubiquitous potato pancakes.

Žalias Ratas   LITHUANIAN €€
(www.zaliasratas.lt; Laisvės alėja 36b; mains 10-30Lt) Tucked away behind the tourist office, this is one of those pseudo-rustic inns where staff don traditional garb and bring out the piping-hot Lithuanian fare to eager customers. It's better than it sounds and a great choice in summer, when the terrace is buzzing with diners.

Avilys   LITHUANIAN €€
(Vilniaus gatvė 34; mains 20-40Lt; ⊙11am-midnight Mon-Thu & Sun, to 2am Fri & Sat) Sharing the same terrace as Senieji Rūsiai, Avilys is an offshoot of the award-winning brewery in Vilnius. It serves unusual beers alongside Lithuanian standards and international dishes to a discerning crowd, street-side or underground in a brick cellar.

Fu Long   CHINESE €€
(Gedmino gatvė 30; mains 10-25Lt) Decent option if you're fed up with potato dumplings, cold soup and all the rest. Good, basic Chinese cooking, with an excellent sweet-and-sour chicken, as well as friendly staff and lots of beer.

🍷 Drinking

In addition to the cafes listed here, the popular coffee chains **Coffee Inn** (Laisvės alėja 72; ⊙10am-10pm; 🛜) and **Vero Cafe** (Vilniaus gatvė 18; ⊙10am-9pm; 🛜) are represented in Kaunas and are great for quick coffee drinks, cakes and free, reliable wi-fi.

TOP CHOICE **W1640**   BAR
(Kurpių gatvė 29; ⊙5pm-1am Tue-Thu, 5pm-4am Fri & Sat; 🛜) Known locally as 'Whisky Bar', this laid-back bar does indeed have lots of different types of whisky to sample. But it's not fusty in the slightest, attracting a rowdy crowd on weekends after midnight for those who intend to keep drinking till dawn. They also serve beer and a surprisingly good Caesar salad. Go figure.

TOP CHOICE **Motiejaus Kepyklėlė**   CAFE
(Valančiaus gatvė 10; ⊙8am-8pm Mon-Fri, 9am-4pm Sat & Sun) It's hard to find the super-latives to do this tiny bakery and coffee shop justice. First there are the pastries, then there's arguably the best coffee in Lithuania. If you're staying at the Apple Hotel across the street, skip the hotel's lacklustre breakfast and gorge on croissants here instead.

Buon Giorno   WINE BAR
(Vilniaus gatvė 34; ⊙10am-midnight) Swish wine bar with a laid-back but upscale atmosphere, burning incense, chill tunes and great wine. There are some very good snacks on the menu, including our favourite: pizza topped with Parma ham and rocket.

Skliautas   BAR, CAFE
(Rotušės aikštė 26; ⊙10am-midnight Mon-Thu, to 2am Fri & Sat, 11am-11pm Sun) Skliautas bursts with energy most times of the day and night, and in summer its crowd basically takes over the small alley it occupies off Rotušės aikštė. Also good for coffee and cake.

BO   BAR
(Muitinės gatvė 9; ⊙9.30am-2am Mon-Thu, 9.30am-3am Fri, 3pm-3am Sat, 3pm-2am Sun) This laid-back bar attracts a student/ alternative set and gets rammed to over-flowing on weekends. Its own brew is a tasty offering, but rather potent.

Kavos Klubas CAFE

(Coffee Club; Valančiaus gatvė 19; ⊘9am-11pm Mon-Sat, to 7pm Sun) An excellent, classy spot for conversation, coffee and cake, plus a decent breakfast menu in case you're staying somewhere where breakfast is not part of the plan. The only hitch here is service, especially for breakfast. There's often only one cook in the kitchen and the wait for eggs can literally take an hour.

☆ Entertainment

Check daily newspaper *Kauno diena* (www .kaunodiena.lt in Lithuanian) for listings.

Nightclubs

Admission prices range between 10Lt and 40Lt for clubs.

Ex-it CLUB

(Maironio gatvė 19; ⊘10pm-5am Tue-Sat) Arguably the best club in town, with a thumping sound system, huge dance floor and quality DJs.

Latino Baras CLUB

(www.latinobaras.lt; Vilniaus gatvė 22; ⊘9pm-4am Tue-Sat) Latin music, occasional dance lessons, multiple rooms and beautiful people combine to make Latino Baras a stand-out club for many locals.

Džem Pub LIVE MUSIC

(www.dzempub.lt; Laisvės alėja 59; ⊘4pm-3am Tue-Sat) Live music venues are a dying breed, but this central option features live rock most weekends, and is a fun bar to hang out in regardless of what's on the program.

Cinemas

Catch films in their original language with Lithuanian subtitles at Forum Cinemas (www.forumcinemas.lt; Karaliaus Mindaugo prospektas 49) in the Akropolis shopping complex.

Theatre & Classical Music

Original dramas take to the stage at the innovative Kaunas Academic Drama Theatre (Akademinis dramos teatras; ☑224 064; www.dramosteatras.lt; Laisvės alėja 71) and the Youth Chamber Theatre (Jaunimo kamerinis teatras; ☑228 226; www.kamerinisteatras. lt; Kęstučio gatvė 74a). Puppets enchant at the Kaunas Puppet Theatre (Kauno valstybinis lėlių teatras; ☑221 691; www.kaunoleles .lt; Laisvės alėja 87a). All performances are in Lithuanian.

The Kaunas Philharmonic (Kauno filharmonija; ☑222 558; www.kaunofilharmonija.lt; Sapiegos gatvė 5) is the main concert hall for classical music, and operas fill the Kaunas Musical Theatre (Muzikinis teatras; ☑227 113; www.muzikinisteatras.lt; Laisvės alėja 91).

Shopping

Centrinis Knygynas BOOKS, MAPS

(Laisvės alėja 81; ⊘10am-7pm Mon-Fri, 10am-5pm Sat) Maps, English-language newspapers and magazines.

Humanitas BOOKS

(www.humanitas.lt; Vilniaus gatvė 11; ⊘10am-6pm Mon-Fri, 11am-4pm Sat) English-language books.

ⓘ Information

Banks have currency exchange inside. ATMs accepting Visa and MasterCard are located outside.

Copy (Kęstučio gatvė 54/7; per hr 5Lt; ⊘8am-7pm Mon-Fri, 9am-4pm Sat) Copy shop offers internet access.

DNB Nord (Laisvės alėja 86) Bank and ATM.

Kaunas (www.kaunas.lt) Official city website.

Kaunas in Your Pocket (www.inyourpocket .com) Annual city guide sold in hotels, art galleries and news kiosks for 6Lt; download it in PDF format at the website.

Kauno Medicinos Universiteto Klinikos (☑326 375; Eivenių gatvė 2) University medical clinic for emergencies. Approximately 2.5km north of the New Town; catch trolleybus 1 from the Old or New Town.

Post office (Laisvės alėja 102)

SEB Bankas (Laisvės alėja 82) Bank and ATM.

Tourist office (☑323 436; http://visit.kaunas .lt; Laisvės alėja 36; ⊘9am-7pm Mon-Fri, 10am-1pm & 2-6pm Sat, 10am-3pm Sun Jun-Aug, shorter hours Sep-May) Books accommodation, sells maps and guides, and arranges bicycle hire (50Lt per day plus 5Lt for lock) and guided tours of Old Town (35Lt) from mid-May to September.

ⓘ Getting There & Away

Air

Kaunas International Airport (☑399 307; www.kaunas-airport.lt; Karmėlava) is situated 10km north of the city centre. **Ryanair** (☑750 195; www.ryanair.com) handles the bulk of the airport's traffic, operating flights to/from Birmingham, Brussels, Dublin, Frankfurt, Liverpool, London (Gatwick, Luton, Stansted), Oslo, Paris and Stockholm. **airBaltic** (☑5-235 6001; www.airbaltic.com) operates a handful of flights each week from Kaunas to Rīga and return.

Bus

The **long-distance bus station** (☎409 060; Vytauto prospektas 24) handles intercity buses within Lithuania and buses further afield. Information is available from the timetable on the wall or from the helpful information desk (open 7am to 8pm).

For domestic tickets, try the Euroline's subsidiary **Kautra** (☎409 060; www.autobus ubilietai.lt; ⊙9am-6pm Mon-Fri, 10am-5pm Sat). Buy tickets inside the main bus terminal or over the company's website.

For international departures, several companies offer services, including **Eurolines** (www.eurolines.lt) and its **Lux Express** (www .luxexpress.lt) subsidiary. Buy tickets in the main hall. **Ecolines** (☎202 022; www.ecolines .net; Vytauto prospektas 23; ⊙9am-6pm Mon-Fri), across the road, also sells tickets for international destinations. **Simple Express** (☎5-233 6666; www.simpleexpress.eu) offers budget travel within the Baltic, including a daily 4.50am departure from Kaunas to Rīga for the unbeatable price of 35Lt. The company does not have a local office, so you'll have to book online.

Daily services within Lithuania and the Baltic include the following:

Birštonas (10Lt, 50 minutes, hourly)

Druskininkai (28Lt, two to three hours, hourly)

Klaipėda (50Lt, 2¾ to four hours, over 15 buses daily)

Palanga (50Lt, 3¼ hours, about eight buses daily)

Panevėžys (26Lt, two hours, 22 buses daily)

Rīga (35Lt to 100Lt, five hours, three buses daily)

Šiauliai (34Lt to 35Lt, three hours, 15 buses daily)

Tallinn (94Lt to 129Lt, nine hours, three buses daily)

Vilnius (20Lt, 1¾ hours, at least every 30 minutes)

Car

Autobanga (☎8-645 64444; www.autobanga.lt; Terminal A, Kaunas International Airport) provides car hire at the airport.

Train

From the **train station** (☎221 093; www.litrail.lt; Čiurlionio gatvė 16) there are up to 17 trains daily to/from Vilnius (16.30Lt to 18Lt, 1¼ to 1¾ hours).

❶ Getting Around

Buses and trolleybuses run from 5am to 11pm and tickets cost 1.80Lt from newspaper kiosks or 2Lt from the driver. Minibuses shadow routes and run later than regular buses; drivers sell tickets for 2.50Lt. For information on public transport, including routes and timetables, see the website **Kaunas Public Transport** (www .kvt.lt).

To get to/from the airport, take minibus 120 from the local bus station on Šv Gertrūdos gatvė or bus 29 from the stop on Vytauto prospektas. Buses depart at least once an hour between 7am and 9.30pm.

Trolleybuses 1, 5 and 7 run north from the train station along Vytauto prospektas, west along Kęstučio gatvė and Nemuno gatvė, then north on Birštono gatvė. Returning, they head east along Šv Gertrūdos gatvė, Ožeškienės gatvė and Donelaičio gatvė, then south down Vytauto prospektas to the bus and train stations.

Several taxi companies operate in Kaunas and you're always best advised to order one in advance by telephone. Try **Einesa** (☎331 533) or **Žaibiškas** (☎333 111).

Outside Old Town, driving in Kaunas is a relatively simple affair; parking is plentiful and there are only a handful of one-way streets. Old Town is a warren of small cobbled alleys, however, and can prove hard to navigate.

Birštonas

☑319 / POP 3100

Birštonas (bir-shto-nas), some 40km south of Kaunas, resides on a pretty loop of the Nemunas River. It's famous as a spa town and for hosting Birštonas Jazz (www.jazz .birstonas.lt) – arguably Lithuania's top jazz festival – in March in even-numbered years.

⊙ Sights & Activities

For Lithuanians, Birštonas is best known for its spa treatments, built around the region's mineral springs and peat bogs, which are used in applying mud baths. These are considered serious medical treatments and are used for treating a variety of ailments, including those of the circulatory system, heart, stomach and lungs. For casual visitors in good health, such treatments are not likely to be of much interest. Nevertheless, the tourist information office can offer advice on a variety of medical spas and treatments available and maintains a list of treatment centres.

For leisure travellers, most of the sights and activities are centred on the lovely Nemunas Loops Regional Park (Nemuno kilpų regioninio parko; ☑65 610; www.nemuno kilpos.lt; visitor centre, Tylioji gatvė 1; ⊙8am-5pm Mon-Thu, 8am-3.45pm Fri), which encompasses most of the surrounding countryside. The fast-flowing Verknė River provides excellent opportunities for **canoeing**, particularly in spring when the water is high. Half-day, day and two-day trips are possible, and can be arranged through the tourist office; canoes (5/25Lt per hour/day) can also be hired from the **Birštonas Sport Centre** (☑65 640; www .birstonosportas.lt in Lithuanian; Jaunimo gatvė 3; ◎9am-6pm).

River trips on the Nemunas in season include one-hour excursions (adult/child 10/20Lt) at 3pm on Sunday, on the *Vytenis*, a two-levelled pleasure boat, and more exhausting – and probably more fun – trips in **Viking ships** (☑56 360; adult/child 10/15Lt; by appointment only) used for the filming of *Elizabeth I.*

Bicycles (per hr/day 5/25Lt) can be hired from the sport centre, and the guesthouse Audenis arranges **air ballooning trips** (1/2/3 people from 400/600/800Lt).

🛏 Sleeping

Nemuno slėnis   HOTEL €€€
(☑56 493; www.nemunoslenis.lt; Verknės gatvė 8; r from 399Lt, royal ste 3500Lt; P@🛜🕹) Located on the banks of the Nemunas away from the town centre and surrounded by forest, Nemuno slėnis offers seclusion and oodles of privacy. The interior is lavish beyond belief, with rooms individually decorated in plush, antique furniture and draped in deep, warm colours, while added extras include a gourmet restaurant and fitness room. Perfect for a romantic weekend.

Sofijos Rezidencija   HOTEL €€
(☑45 200; www.sofijosrezidencija.lt; Jaunimo gatvė 6; r from 230Lt; P@🛜🕹) If you can't afford Nemuno slėnis, consider overnighting at Sofijos in the heart of Birštonas. Rooms here may border on kitsch but they win you over with pseudo-Renaissance splendour, four-poster beds, comfy couches and plenty of mod cons. There's also a small wellness centre onsite.

Audenis   GUESTHOUSE €€
(☑61 300; www.audenis.lt; Lelijų gatvė 3; s/d 150/190Lt; P@🛜) This very pleasant guesthouse has simple rooms in an array of pastel colours, friendly staff and ballooning trips. Its terraced cafe is a fine spot for a light lunch too.

ℹ Information

The extremely helpful **tourist office** (☑65 740; www.visitbirstonas.lt; Jaunimo gatvė 3; ◎9am-6pm Mon-Fri year-round, plus 10am-6pm Sat & Sun Jun-Sep) has a wealth of information on accommodation, activities, festivals and the town's spas.

ℹ Getting There & Away

From Kaunas bus station there are buses every hour or so to and from Birštonas (10Lt, 50 minutes).

Šiauliai
☑41 / POP 128,400

Lithuania's fourth-largest city, Šiauliai (show-ley), is a workaday town and not worth a special trip. That said, its central location makes it a handy stopover, whether you are moving north to south or east to west. The city's main claim to fame, at least during Soviet times, was the massive military airfield on the outskirts of town. To this day, Šiauliai retains a whiff of lingering communism.

That's not to say it's not attractive. The main drag, Vilniaus gatvė, is prime pedestrian strolling turf, lined with the usual mix of cafes and bars. The city's biggest drawcard is the incredible Hill of Crosses, 10km to the north. Outside of that, there are several offbeat museums that warrant a few hours of attention.

◎ Sights

Šiauliai is home to some of Lithuania's most unusual museums, all of which lie either on or near the main avenue, Vilniaus gatvė. In addition to those listed here, there's also the worthwhile **Photography Museum** (Fotografijos muziejus; Vilniaus gatvė 140), but this was closed for renovation in 2011 and not expected to reopen until mid-2013.

HILL OF CROSSES
Atop a small hill about 10km north of Šiauliai is a strange and inspiring sight. Here stand thousands upon thousands of crosses planted by countless pilgrims and, on Saturdays, one newlywed couple after the next.

Large and tiny, expensive and cheap, wood and metal, the crosses are devotional, to accompany prayers, or finely carved folk-art masterpieces. Others are memorials tagged with flowers, a photograph or other mementoes of the deceased, and inscribed with a sweet or sacred message. Traditional Lithuanian *koplytstulpis* (wooden sculptures of a figure topped with a little roof) intersperse

Šiauliai

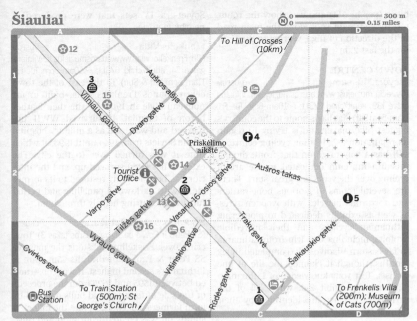

To Hill of Crosses (10km)

Priskėlimo aikštė

Tourist Office

Bus Station

To Train Station (500m); St George's Church

To Frenkelis Villa (200m); Museum of Cats (700m)

the crosses, as do magnificent sculptures of the Sorrowful Christ (Rūpintojėlis). If you wish to add your own, souvenir traders in the car park sell crosses big and small.

An alternative view of the cross-swamped hill is from inside the chapel of the modern brick **monastery**. Now home to around a dozen Franciscan monks, it was built behind the hill from 1997 to 2000. The monastery was allegedly the idea of the late Pope John Paul II, who said after visiting the hill in 1993 that he would like to see a place of prayer here. Behind the altar in the church, the striking backdrop seen through the ceiling-to-floor window of the Hill of Crosses is very moving; Italian architect Angelo Polesello designed it.

The Hill of Crosses (Kryžių kalnas) is 10km north of Šiauliai, 2km east off the road to Joniškis and Rīga, in the village of Jurgaičiai. To get here, take one of up to eight daily buses from Šiauliai bus station to Joniškis and get off at the Domantai stop, from where it is a 2km walk to the hill. Look for the sign 'Kryžių kalnas 2'. By taxi, the return taxi fare is 50Lt, with a 30-minute stop at the hill (60Lt with a one-hour stop); ask Šiauliai tourist office or your hotel/hostel to order one for you by telephone to avoid being ripped off.

Šiauliai

⊙ Sights
1	Bicycle Museum	C3
2	Photography Museum	B2
3	Radio & Television Museum	A1
4	SS Peter & Paul Cathedral	C2
5	Sundial	D2

⊜ Sleeping
6	Šaulys	B3
7	Šiauliai	C3
8	Šiauliai College Youth Hostel	C1

⊗ Eating
9	Arkos	B2
10	CanCan Pica	B2
11	Ikiukas	B2
12	Juonė Pastuogė	A1
13	Kapitonas Morganas	B2

⊛ Entertainment
14	Drama Theatre	B2
15	Laikas	A1
16	Saulė	B3

By bicycle, the Hill of Crosses makes for a gentle three-hour trip out and back, mostly along paved bicycle paths that lie to the side of the main road. The tourist office hires out bikes (per hr 5Lt) and can show the route, mostly a straight shot along the main road in the direction of Rīga, veering to the right for the last 2km.

TOWN CENTRE

Bicycle Museum
MUSEUM

(Dviračių muziejus; www.ausrosmuziejus.lt; Vilniaus gatvė 139; adult/child 6/3Lt; ☺10am-6pm Tue-Fri, 11am-5pm Sat) Šiauliai is home to the country's biggest bike maker and is trying to regain its reputation as a leading cycling centre. It still has a way to go on that front, though this fun museum dedicated to the art of cycling over the years is a great start. There are several rooms of glorious bone-rattlers and torturous bicycles with wooden tyres, as well as exhibits dedicated to pioneering Lithuanian cyclists and their incredible exploits, including one trip from Lithuania to far-eastern Vladivostok (completed in six months, though it claimed the life of one cyclist). Test your knowledge of Lithuanian language at exhibit 214, where all of the various bike parts are identified by their Lithuanian names.

Museum of Cats
MUSEUM

(Katinų muziejus; Žuvininkų gatvė 18; adult/child 4/2Lt; ☺10am-5pm Tue-Sat) Cat-lovers will certainly want to venture out to this museum southeast of the centre to see an unusual collection of feline memorabilia, including endless displays of porcelain cats and photogenic felines on the walls. There are even a couple of live cats on the premises that shadow you as you take in the various rooms. In the back room, there's a mini-zoo that will likely appeal to kids but may give animal-rights activists pause. The various animals, including possibly the most frightening-looking albino python ever locked in an aquarium, as well as a few mice, a monkey and a couple of owls, were abandoned by their owners and seem to be adequately cared for here. The problem is the small cages, which lend the site a slightly forlorn feeling.

Radio & Television Museum
MUSEUM

(Radijo ir televizijos muziejus; www.ausrosmuziejus.lt; Vilniaus gatvė 174; adult/child 2/1Lt; ☺10am-6pm Tue-Fri, 11am-5pm Sat) Šiauliai was home to some of Lithuania's first amateur radio operators in the 1920s, so it's a fitting locale for this eclectic collection of radios, TVs and phonographs. Particularly enjoyable are the big old radio receivers and some Soviet-era TV sets that were produced at nearby factories.

Frenkelis Villa
MUSEUM

(Ch Frenkelio vila; www.ausrosmuziejus.lt; Vilniaus gatvė 74; adult/child 6/3Lt; ☺10am-6pm Tue-Fri, 11am-5pm Sat & Sun) To the east of the town centre stands Frenkelis Villa, built in art nouveau style in 1908 for the then leather baron of Šiauliai. It survived WWII unscathed and was used as a military hospital by the Soviets from 1944 until 1993, at which time it was turned over to the city. The exterior has been spruced up, and the interior has been lovingly restored to its former glory, with dark-wood panelling and period furniture featuring heavily throughout.

SS Peter & Paul Cathedral
CHURCH

(Šv Petro ir Povilo bažnyčia; Aušros takas 3) Towering over Prisikėlimo aikštė is the massive SS Peter & Paul Cathedral; its 75m spire is Lithuania's second highest. It was constructed between 1595 and 1625 from the proceeds of the sale of four-year-old bulls donated by local farmers. Legend says that the hillock it stands on was created from sand and dust, which blew over a dead ox that wandered into Šiauliai, sat down and died.

Sundial
MONUMENT

(cnr Salkauskjo gatvė & Ežero gatvė) A distinctive city landmark is the mammoth sundial, topped by a shining bronze statue of an archer in what has become known as 'Sundial Square'. It was built in 1986 to commemorate the 750th anniversary of the Battle of Saulė (1236), the battle in which local Samogitians defeated the Knights of the Sword and founded the town.

St George's Church
CHURCH

(Šv Jurgio bažnyčia; Kražių gatvė 17) This is an attractive Catholic church with an onion dome – a reminder of its Russian origins.

🛏 Sleeping

The tourist office has information on homestay accommodation around Šiauliai.

Šiauliai
HOTEL €€

(✆437 333; www.hotelsiauliai.lt; Draugystės prospektas 25; s/d/ste 95/165/265Lt; 🅿@🛜) The town's old 14-storey Soviet hotel has enjoyed recent renovation both inside and out, leaving it with pleasant rooms dressed in pale yellow and brown. The views are still as great as ever. Skip breakfast and save 15Lt on the room rate; you can do much better

THE ART OF CRAFTING CROSSES

Crosses were once symbols of sacred fervour and national identity, both pagan and Catholic; cross crafting is the embodiment of Lithuanian contradiction.

Handed down from master to pupil, the crosses were carved from oak, the sacred pagan tree. They were made as offerings to gods, and were draped with food, coloured scarves (for a wedding) or aprons (for fertility). Once consecrated by priests, they became linked with Christian ceremonies, with unmistakable sacred significance. The crosses, which measure up to 5m in height, then became symbols of defiance against occupation.

When it comes to explaining the origin of the Hill of Crosses, there are almost as many myths as crosses. Some claim it was created in three days and three nights by the bereaved families of warriors killed in a great battle. Others say it was the work of a father who, in a desperate bid to cure his sick daughter, planted a cross on the hill. Pagan traditions tell stories of sacred fires being lit here and tended by celestial virgins.

Crosses first appeared here in the 14th century. They multiplied after bloody anti-tsarist uprisings to become a potent symbol of suffering and hope.

During the Soviet era planting a cross was an arrestable offence – but pilgrims kept coming to commemorate the thousands killed and deported. The hill was bulldozed at least three times. In 1961 the Red Army destroyed the 2000-odd crosses that stood on the mound, sealed off the tracks leading to the hill and dug ditches at its base, yet overnight more crosses appeared. In 1972 they were destroyed after the immolation of a Kaunas student (see the boxed text, p325) in protest at Soviet occupation. But by 1990 the Hill of Crosses comprised a staggering 40,000 crosses, spanning 4600 sq metres. Since independence, they have multiplied at least 10 times – and are multiplying still. In 1993 Pope John Paul II celebrated mass here (his pulpit still stands) and graced the hill a year later with a papal cross, adding his own message to the mountain of scribbled-on crosses: 'Thank you, Lithuanians, for this Hill of Crosses which testifies to the nations of Europe and to the whole world the faith of the people of this land'.

than the hotel's tired breakfast buffet at one of the coffee joints on nearby Vilniaus gatvė.

Šaulys HOTEL €€
(☎520 812; www.saulys.lt; Vasario 16-osios gatvė 40; s/d/tr/apt from 230/290/400/575Lt; Ⓟⓐⓖⓡ) This four-star establishment is Šiauliai's swankiest choice. Hidden behind its deep-red facade are suitably plush rooms and staff who can organise paragliding, parachuting and biplane flights.

Šiauliai College Youth Hostel HOSTEL €
(Šiaulių Kolegijos Jaunimo Navynės Namai; ☎523 764; www.jnn.siauliukolegija.lt; Tilžės gatvė 159; s/d/tr 50/70/90Lt; ⊙reception 7am-11pm; Ⓟ) This former college has been renovated with EU funds to create a spanking clean and sparkling hostel with kitchen and TV room. The reception staff don't speak much English, but they do their best to help.

✗ Eating

Most restaurants are clustered along central Vilniaus gatvė. Self-caterers can stock up at Ikiukas (Vilniaus gatvė 128).

TOP CHOICE Arkos LITHUANIAN €€
(www.arkos.lt in Lithuanian; Vilniaus gatvė 213; mains 15-30Lt; ⊙11am-11pm) Arkos is easily the nicest of several restaurants on the main pedestrian drag. This clean and warming red-brick cellar restaurant lures an office crowd for lunch and everyone else for dinner with good-value daily specials and a broad menu mixing Lithuanian and international dishes.

Kapitonas Morganas INTERNATIONAL €€
(Vilniaus gatvė 183; mains 20-40Lt) Come to Captain Morgan's jolly pirate ship to meet happy punters busily eating European fodder, drinking local beer and merrymaking on a great street terrace.

Juonė Pastuogė INTERNATIONAL €€
(www.jonis.lt/tavern.juonepastuoge.htm; Aušros 31a; mains 10-30Lt; ⊙10am-4pm Mon-Thu, 10am-midnight Fri & Sat) This restaurant and music club lures diners with an imaginative menu, including the likes of ostrich steak, hearty country stews and vegetarian pancakes. Live music is often on the cards at the weekend;

during the week, though, the club and restaurant are closed most evenings. To find it, walk down the small lane that starts beside Vilniaus gatvė 212; it's in a small cabin off to the right.

CanCan Pica   ITALIAN €€
(www.cancan.lt; Vilniaus gatvė 146; pizza 13-40Lt)
This local branch of this nationwide pizza chain has enough pizza choices (more than 40 in all) to satisfy everybody, including vegetarians. Securing an outdoor table in summer can prove difficult, however.

☆ Entertainment

Spend the evening at a Lithuanian-language performance at the Drama Theatre (Tilžės gatvė 155), watching an English-language flick at Laikas (Vilniaus gatvė 172) or Saulė (Tilžės gatvė 140), or, on weekends, catching some live music at Juonė Pastuogė (p337).

❶ Information

Left luggage (per 24hr 2Lt) bus station (◐6am-7pm Mon-Fri, 6am-6pm Sat, 8am-4pm Sun); train station (◐7am-5.30pm)
Post office (Aušros alėja 42)
Šiauliai bankas (Tilžės gatvė 149)
Snoras bankas (Vilniaus gatvė 204)
Topos Centras (Tilžės gatvė; per hr 3Lt; ◐9am-8pm) Internet access at the main information kiosk in the Saulės Miestas shopping centre.
Tourist office (☏523 110; http://tic.siauliai .lt/en; Vilniaus gatvė 213; ◐9am-6pm Mon-Fri, 10am-4pm Sat & Sun) Sells maps and guides, hires out bicycles for 5Lt per hour, and makes accommodation bookings.

❶ Getting There & Away

Bus
Services to/from Šiauliai **bus station** (☏525 058; Tilžės gatvė 109):
Kaunas (33Lt to 38Lt, three hours, 20 buses daily)
Klaipėda (33Lt, 3½ hours, six daily)
Palanga (31Lt, three hours, eight daily)
Panevėžys (17Lt, 1½ hours, 20 daily)
Rīga (30Lt, 2½ hours, four daily)
Vilnius (44Lt, three to 4½ hours, six daily)

Train
Services to/from Šiauliai **train station** (☏430 652; Dubijos gatvė 44) include Klaipėda (23Lt to 28Lt, two to three hours, five daily), Panevėžys (13Lt, 1½ hours, two daily) and Vilnius (35Lt, 2½ to three hours, three daily).

Radviliškis & Around

Grim Radviliškis (rad-vi-lish-kis; population 19,700), 22km southeast of Šiauliai, is notable only as the central hub of the rail network, but there are a couple of interesting stops on the 55km stretch of the A9 heading east towards Panevėžys.

Šeduva (she-du-va; population 3200), 15km east of Radviliškis, is a large village with a faded yellow-and-white baroque church framed by cobbled streets. Šeduvos Malūnas (www.seduvosmalunas.lt; mains 14-25Lt), a windmill that houses a kitsch but fun restaurant, sits on its western outskirts, not far from the main highway. The structure, built in 1905, still retains the original central-core cog mechanism, and nowadays serves traditional Lithuanian cuisine on its four levels. The restaurant owners also run the pleasant hotel next door, housed in a modern building (double without breakfast 110Lt, parking available).

In Kleboniškiai, signposted 5km further east along the A9 to Panevėžys, is another windmill (1884) and – 1km down a dusty road – the Kleboniškiai Rural Life Exhibition (Kleboniškių kaimo buites ekspozicija; adult/student 6/3Lt, camera 10Lt; ◐9am-6pm Tue-Sun). The beautiful farmstead, with 19th- and early-20th-century farm buildings, offers a picture-postcard peek at rural Lithuania. It is brimful with collectors' items, including wooden sleds, farming tools and a marvellous tractor dating from 1926. The exhibition is part of the Daugyvenė Cultural History Museum Reserve (Daugyvenės kultūros istorijos muziejus-draustinis), which encompasses burial grounds, mounds and other local sights.

Plenty of buses between Šiauliai and Panevėžys stop at Radviliškis. There are buses every 30 minutes to/from Radviliškis and Šeduva (4Lt, 15 minutes) and six a day to/from Vilnius (32Lt, three hours).

There are two trains daily to/from Šiauliai and Šeduva (8Lt, 50 minutes), while three run between Vilnius (32Lt, 2½ hours) and Radviliškis and five between Klaipėda (31Lt, 2½ hours) and Radviliškis.

Panevėžys
☏45 / POP 114,600
Panevėžys (pa-ne-vey-zhees) is far from a tourist hot spot, and most people who venture to the town will do so en route from

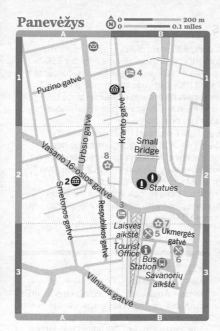

Panevėžys

Panevėžys

⊙ **Sights**
1 Oldest Building B1
2 Regional Museum..............................A2

🛏 **Sleeping**
3 Hotel Panevėžys B2
4 Hotel Romantik....................................B1

🍴 **Eating**
5 Galerija XX..B3
6 Iki B3

🎭 **Entertainment**
7 Juozas Miltinio Drama Theatre B2
8 Puppet Wagon Theatre......................A2

Vilnius to Rīga by bus. If you've got time to kill, there are a couple of sights to explore in this, Lithuania's fifth-largest city.

At the centre of town is Laisvės aikštė, bordered at its northern end by east–west Elektros gatvė and at its southern end by Vilniaus gatvė. Basanavičiaus gatvė runs north to the Rīga road and south to Kaunas and Vilnius. The train station is 2km northwest of the centre; the bus station is on Savanorių aikštė.

⊙ Sights & Activities

Triangular-shaped **Laisvės aikštė** is a central tree-lined pedestrianised spot, pleasant for two months in summer and quiet the rest of the year. It is surrounded by a few uninspiring cafes and shops and the Juozas Miltinio Drama Theatre, in action since 1940. By the river, a **small bridge** and **statues** make for a pleasant stroll.

Regional Museum
MUSEUM
(Kraštotyros muziejus; www.paneveziomuziejus.lt; Vasario 16-osios gatvė 23; adult/child 3/1.50Lt; ⊙8am-5pm Mon-Thu, 8am-3.45pm Fri) This tiny museum focuses on ethnography and also hosts temporary exhibitions in the city's oldest building, dating from 1614, at Kranto gatvė 21.

🛏 Sleeping & Eating

Hotel Panevėžys
HOTEL
(☑435 115; www.centraspanevezys.lt; Laisvės aikštė 26; s/d from 90/150Lt) If you're stuck overnight, this Soviet-style high-rise towering over the central square offers nicely remodelled rooms on the 5th floor (the rest of the complex has been converted to office space). The entrance to the reception area is located behind the building, beside the car park.

Hotel Romantik
HOTEL
(☑584 860; www.romantic.lt; Kranto gatvė 24; s/d/ste 360/380/700Lt; P@🛜🖥) Housed in a converted old mill, its rooms are suitably plush (and priced accordingly). The restaurant terrace overlooking the park – definitely the best place in town to dine – is a delight (mains 22Lt to 55Lt).

Galerija XX
LITHUANIAN
(Laisvės aikštė 7; mains 12-20Lt) With a terrace on the main square, this is as good an option as any.

Iki
SUPERMARKET
(Ukmerges gatvė 18a) Self-caterers and snackers can head to this supermarket in the shopping centre adjoining the bus station.

Entertainment

Juozas Miltinio Drama Theatre
THEATRE
(☑booking office 584 614; www.miltinio-teatras.lt; Laisvės aikštė 5) In action since 1940. Most of the performances are in Lithuanian.

Puppet Wagon Theatre
PUPPET THEATRE
(Pasakų traukinukas; ☑ booking office 511 236; www.leliuvezimoteatras.lt; Respublikos gatvė 30; admission 6Lt; ⊙8am-5pm Mon-Fri) A great

SAMPLING THE NORTHERN ALES

Northern Lithuania is the land of barley-malt beer, with ale-makers keeping to ancient recipes and rituals practised by their ancestors 1000 years ago. People here drink 160L of beer a year, say proud locals. The biggest drinkers in the world, the Czechs, consume around the same amount. The Brits down around 100L per year, the Australians 110L.

Big-name brews to glug include **Horn** (www.ragutis.lt), brewed in Kaunas since 1853; Šiauliai-made **Gubernija** (www.gubernija.lt); and **Kalnapilis** from Panevėžys, whose **brewery** (505 219; www.kalnapilis.lt; Taikos alėja 1) is open for tours.

Lakeside Biržai, 65km north of Panevėžys and the true heart of Lithuanian beer country, hosts the annual two-day **Biržai Town Festival** in August, a madcap fiesta where the town's breweries sell their wares on the street; expect plenty of beer swilling and general drunken behaviour. Its **Rinkuškiai Brewery** (www.rinkuskiai.lt; Alyvų gatvė 8) can be visited, and its beer – everything from light lager to lead-heavy stout – can be bought in bulk in its factory shop. A lesser-known label to look out for is the sweet **Butautų alaus bravoras**, an ale bottled in brown glass with a ceramic, metal-snap cap. It has been brewed in the village of Butautų since 1750.

escape for the kids are the magical dolls and puppets in the Fairytale Train of the Puppet Wagon Theatre. Lithuania's only travelling cart theatre is rarely at home (it travels most of the summer), but the characters displayed inside this old narrow-gauge train carriage are enchanting.

ℹ Information

For ATMs and currency exchange, try the banks at Laisvė aikštė 18 and Ukmerges gatvė 18a.

E-kopija (Laisvės aikštė 16; per hr 2Lt; 8.30am-6.30pm Mon-Fri, 10am-3pm Sat) Internet access.

Left luggage (per 24hr 3Lt; 5.30am-7pm Mon-Fri, 7am-12.20pm & 12.50-4pm Sat & Sun) At the bus station.

Post office (Respublikos gatvė 60)

Tourist office (508 080; www.panevezys info.lt; Laisvės aikštė 11; 9am-6pm Mon-Fri & 9am-2pm Sat Apr-Sep, 8am-5pm Mon-Fri Oct-Mar)

ℹ Getting There & Away

Bus

Services to and from the **bus station** (463 333; Savanorių aikštė 5) include the following:

Kaunas (25Lt, two hours, 22 daily)
Rīga (from 32Lt, 2½ to three hours, six daily)
Šiauliai (17Lt, 1½ hours, around 20 daily)
Vilnius (30Lt, 1¾ hours, hourly)

Train

Service to/from the **train station** (463 615; Kerbedžio gatvė 9) is limited but includes Šiauliai (13Lt, 1½ hours, two daily), from where you can connect to onward rail destinations.

Anykščiai

381 / POP 12,000

Lovely Anykščiai (a-neeksh-chey), 60km southeast of Panevėžys, sits on the confluence of the Šentoji and Anykšta Rivers. Fanning eastward are 76 lakes, the largest of which – **Lake Rubikiai** (9.68 sq km and 16m deep) – is freckled with 16 islands. There are a handful of sights here, and in winter the city transforms itself into that rarity of rarities, a Lithuanian ski resort.

◎ Sights & Activities

The chance to clamber over train cars and even to take a ride on an old narrow-gauge locomotive is arguably the town's biggest attraction, and a big draw for kids.

Narrow-Gauge Railway Museum   MUSEUM
(Siaurojo geležinkelis istorijos ekspozicija; www.baranauskas.lt; Viltis gatvė 2; adult/child 3.50/3Lt; 10am-5pm May-Oct, by appointment via website or tourist office Nov-Apr) The centre of the action, this museum is housed in Anykščiai's old station. Visitors can ride on manual rail cars and, on weekends from May to October, take a trip along the line to either Troškūnai or Rubikiai, depending on the schedule. Trains leave at 11am and return at 2.30pm; tickets cost 20Lt. More information can be found at www.siaurukas.eu or at the Anykščiai tourist information office.

Horse Museum   MUSEUM
(Arklio muziejus; www.arkliomuziejus.lt; adult/child 7/4Lt; 8am-6pm, to 5pm Sep-Jun) Horse lovers – and kids – will want to make the journey

6km north to Lithuania's only horse museum, in the tiny village of Niūronys. Set out as a traditional farmstead, the museum delves into equine matters from a Lithuanian point of view, displaying black-and-white photos of horse-drawn transport in Vilnius alongside a fine collection of horse-drawn fire engines, carriages and taxis. Horse (4Lt) and carriage (2Lt) rides are available and kids will have a ball mucking about in the big playground. As an added treat, you can even bake your own black bread here Lithuanian-style (adult/child 13/7Lt; by appointment only via the website or through the tourist office). Two buses daily (2Lt, 20 minutes) connect Niūronys with Anykščiai.

Puntukas Stone   NATURAL LANDMARK
A pine forest 10km south of Anykščiai contains the Puntakas Stone (Puntuko akmuo), a boulder 5.7m tall, 6.7m wide and 6.9m long, which legend says was put there by the devil. While he was trying to destroy Anykščiai's twin-steeple church, St Mathew's (1899–1909), a rooster crowed and the devil thundered to hell – prompting the boulder to hurtle down from the sky.

Kalitos Kalnas   SKI RESORT
(☑78 144; www.kalitoskalnas.lt; Kalno gatvė 25) In winter, Anykščiai transforms itself into one of the country's few ski resorts. This ski centre operates two ski lifts in season (December–March), has equipment for hire and offers skiing lessons. The tourist information office can help make arrangements.

🛏 Sleeping

The Anykščiai tourist information office can suggest homestays and farmstays, which are the most common accommodation options in town. Otherwise, try Keturi Kalnai (☑58 520; www.keturikalnai.lt; Liudiškių gatvė 18; s/d from 50/90Lt; ⏹), a former sports hotel that offers excellent value in unadorned but comfortable private rooms. Plus, there's a small pool onsite.

ℹ Information

Anykščiai's extremely helpful **tourist information office** (☑59 177; www.antour.lt; Gegužės gatvė 1; ⊙8am-5pm Mon-Sat, to 4pm Sun) should be your first port of call. The enthusiastic staff here will have you wondering why you didn't plan your entire holiday here. They can help book homestays as well as advise on sights and travel info.

ℹ Getting There & Away

With Anykščiai's rail line effectively transformed into a tourist attraction, that leaves just the bus. From the **bus station** (☑51 333; Vienuolio gatvė 1), opposite the tourist office, there are buses to/from Panevėžys (15Lt, 1¼ hours, two daily), Vilnius (26Lt, 2½ hours, five daily), Kaunas (26Lt, 2¼ hours, 11 daily) and Utena (11Lt, one hour, six daily).

WESTERN LITHUANIA

Lithuania's Baltic coastline is one of the country's leading tourist draws. While the season is mercilessly short (running from just mid-May to mid-September, with only July and August suitable for swimming), locals and visitors alike come here in droves to enjoy the nearly 100km stretch of glistening sea, white-sand beaches, and vibrant summertime energy.

Topping the bill is a unique gem: the Curonian Spit (Kuršių Nerija), a skinny leg of sand that stalks into Russia. So precious and extraordinary is this slice between the relentless Baltic Sea and the lapping Curonian Lagoon that Unesco added it to its World Heritage list in 2000. Its historical fishing villages and East Prussian past are fascinating backdrops to the real attraction: giant sand dunes and dense pine forests.

The gateway to the spit is Klaipėda, the country's third-largest city and only major port. This busy city with its tiny Old Town and constant flow of ferries has its own rhythms. To the north is Palanga, a party town if ever there was one; finding a room here in summer can be a challenge.

South of Klaipėda, the Nemunas Delta Regional Park is an oasis for birds and bird lovers. Inland, the Žemaitija National Park was once home to a secret Soviet nuclear base. The base has now been converted to the new Cold War Museum and is a must for history buffs.

Klaipėda

☑46 / POP 161,300
Lithuania's third-largest city is a mix of old and new. This former Prussian capital (when it was named Memel) has retained a distinct German flavour in the architecture of its heavily cobbled Old Town and one remaining tower of its red-brick castle. It's also

Western Lithuania

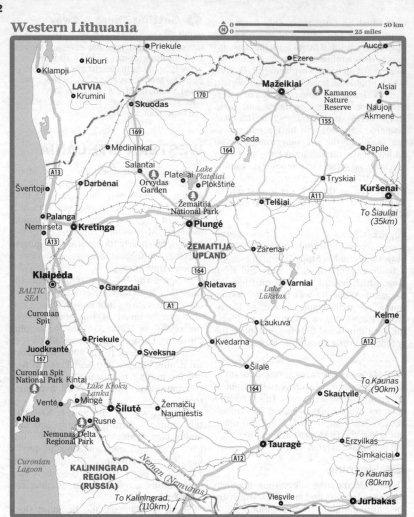

Lithuania's only port of call for *Titanic*-sized cruise ships, and a vital sea link for cargo and passenger ferries between Lithuania, Scandinavia and beyond.

Most people will only catch a glimpse of Klaipėda (klai-pey-da) as they rush head-long for the ferry to the Curonian Spit, but spend a few hours – or even better, a day – and you'll be justly rewarded.

The Danė River flows westward across the city centre and enters the Curonian Lagoon 4km from the Baltic Sea. The river cuts the city into two distinct parts. South of the river is the more modern New Town,

where you'll find some hotels, the train and bus stations, and Klaipėda University. The main axis here is Manto gatvė, which runs north–south. North of the river is the gentrifying Old Town, which has the tour-ist information office as well as shops, bars, restaurants and a smattering of hotels. The main drag here is Tiltų gatvė and Taikos prospektas.

A third district, Smiltynė, lies across the Curonian Lagoon from the rest of the city on the northern tip of Curonian Spit. It has a handful of interesting sights and is reachable only by ferry.

History

Klaipėda was Memel until 1925. Founded in 1252 by the Teutonic Order, who built the city's first castle, it was a key trading port from the 15th century until 1629, when Swedish forces destroyed it. After the Napoleonic wars of the early 19th century, it became part of Prussia and stayed in Prussian hands until WWI. The population at this time was an even split of Germans and Lithuanians.

Under the Treaty of Versailles that ended WWI, Memel town, the northern half of the Curonian Spit and a strip of land (about 150km long and 20km wide) along the eastern side of the Curonian Lagoon and the northern side of the Nemunas River were separated from Germany as an 'international territory'. It remained stateless until 1923, when Lithuanian troops marched in, annexed it, and changed the name of Memel to Klaipėda.

Germany eventually reclaimed Klaipėda during WWII and the city served as a Nazi submarine base. The city's strategic value ensured that it was all but destroyed during the war. After much rebuilding and repopulating, it has developed into an important city on the back of shipbuilding and fishing. In 1991 its university opened, followed in 2003 by a new cruise terminal. In recent years the town has begun to focus its attention on the tourist trade, building smart new hotels and restaurants.

◎ Sights

OLD TOWN

Little of German Klaipėda remains but there are some restored streets in the oldest part of town wedged between the river and Turgaus aikštė. Pretty Teatro aikštė (Theatre Sq) is the Old Town focus, dominated by the fine classical-style Drama Theatre (1857; under renovation). Hitler proclaimed the *Anschluss* (incorporation) of Memel into Germany to a crowd on the square from the theatre's balcony.

In front tinkles a fountain dedicated to Simon Dach, a Klaipėda-born German poet (1605–59) who was the focus of a circle of Königsberg writers and musicians. On a pedestal in the middle of the water stands Ännchen von Tharau (1912), a statue of Ann from Tharau sculpted by Berlin artist Alfred Kune (a replica; the original was destroyed in WWII) and inspired by a famous German wedding and love song originally written in the East Prussian dialect.

Castle   RUIN, MUSEUM

West of Pilies gatvė are the remains of Klaipėda's once mighty, moat-protected castle, the earliest parts of which date back to the 13th century. The Klaipėda Castle Museum (Klaipėdos pilies muziejus; www.mlimuziejus.lt; Pilies gatvė 4; adult/child 6/3Lt; ⊙10am-6pm Tue-Sat) inside the one remaining tower tells the castle's story through the ages until the 19th century, when most of it was pulled down. There are also some fascinating photos on display here from WWII and the immediate postwar years, when the city was rebuilt by Soviet planners. To find the museum, walk through the Klaipėda State Sea Port Authority building and a ship-repair yard.

LITHUANIA KLAIPĖDA

KLAIPĖDA'S SCULPTURE SCAPE

In true Lithuanian style, Klaipėda is studded with great sculptures, including 120-odd pieces from the late 1970s in the Martynas Mažvydas Sculpture Park (Liepų gatvė), the city's main cemetery until 1977. Not far from the park on Lietuvninkų aikštė is a monumental 3.5m sculpture in granite of the geezer the park is named after – Martynas Mažvydas, author of the first book published in Lithuanian in 1547.

The red granite pillar propping up a broken grey arch of almighty proportions at the southern end of Manto gatvė is Lithuania's biggest granite sculpture. Engraved with the quote 'We are one nation, one land, one Lithuania' by local poet Ieva Simonaitytė (1897–1978), Arka (Arch) celebrates Klaipėda joining Lithuania in 1923.

Outside the train station stands Farewell (2002), a moving statue of a mother with a headscarf, a suitcase in one hand, and the hand of a small boy clutching a teddy bear in the other. It was given by Germany to Klaipėda to remember Germans who said goodbye to their homeland after the city became part of Lithuania in 1923.

Smaller works seem to pop up overnight in Klaipėda. Inside Old Town are sculptures of a dog, cat, mouse, spider and disturbing red dragon, while on its outskirts reside an apple, a row of oversized yellow chairs, and a boy with a dog waving off the ferries. Discover them on your wanders.

Klaipėda

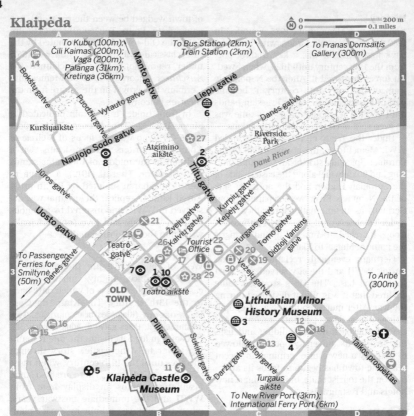

Lithuania Minor History Museum MUSEUM
(Mažosios lietuvos istorijos muziejus; www
.mlimuziejus.lt; Didžioji Vandens gatvė 2; adult/
child 5/2.50Lt; ⊘10am-6pm Tue-Sat) This
history museum traces the early origins
of 'Lithuania Minor', or *Kleinlitauen*, as
much of the Lithuanian coastal region
was referred to over the centuries as part
of Eastern Prussia. With the exception of
greater Klaipėda, which was annexed by
Lithuania after WWI, parts of the coast,
as well as Kaliningrad (Russia), remained
part of Germany until WWII.

The museum includes fascinating bits
and pieces of the German legacy, such as
Prussian maps, labour-intensive weaving
machines and traditional folk art.

Blacksmith's Museum MUSEUM
(Kalvystės muziejus; www.mlimuziejus.lt; Šžaltkalvių
gatvė 2; adult/child 5/2.50Lt; ⊘10am-6pm
Tue-Sat) The cute Blacksmith's Museum
displays ornate forged-iron works such

as elaborate crosses transferred from
the town's former cemetery (Martynas
Mažvydas Sculpture Park).

Mary Queen of Peace Church CHURCH
(Švč Mergelės Marijos Taikos Karalienės bažnyčia;
Rumpiškės gatvė 6a) Not far from the town's
scruffy market stands this church, the only
Catholic place of worship to be built in the
Baltic during the period of the Soviet Union.
Its 46.5m tower is one of the highest points
in the city. Visits can be booked through the
tourist office.

Baroti Gallery ART GALLERY
(Baroti galerija; Aukštoji gatvė 3/3; admission
free) This gallery, with its lively program of
visiting exhibitions, is partly housed in a
converted fish warehouse (1819). Its exposed-
timber style, called *Fachwerk,* is typical of
German Memel.

Klaipėda

◎ Top Sights
Klaipėda Castle Museum B4
Lithuanian Minor History
Museum C3

◎ Sights
1 Ännchen von Tharau Statue B3
2 Arka B2
3 Baroti Gallery C4
4 Blacksmith's Museum C4
5 Castle A4
6 Clock Museum B1
7 Drama Theatre B3
8 K Building A2
9 Mary Queen of Peace Church D4
10 Simon Dach Fountain B3

◆ Activities, Courses & Tours
11 Cruise Ship Terminal Entrance B4

◎ Sleeping
Amberton .... (see 8)
12 Friedricho C4
13 Hotel Euterpė C4
14 Litinterp Guesthouse A1
15 Old Port Hotel A4

16 Old Port Hotel A4
17 Preliudija Guesthouse B3

◆ Eating
18 Friedricho D4
19 Hämmerli C3
20 Ikiukas C3
Keltininko Namas .... (see 15)
21 La Terrasse B2

◆ Drinking
22 Max Coffee C3
23 Memelis B3
24 Senoji Hansa B3
25 Švyturys Brewery D4
Viva Lavita .... (see 8)

◆ Entertainment
26 Kurpiai B3
27 Musical Theatre B2
28 Relax B3

◆ Shopping
29 Parko C3
30 Pėda C3

NORTH OF THE RIVER

A riverside park skirts the northern bank of the Danė. A little further north, Liepų gatvė – called Adolf-Hitler-Strasse for a brief spell – has a few attractions of its own.

Clock Museum   MUSEUM
(Laikrodžių muziejus; www.muziejai.lt; Liepų gatvė 12; adult/child 6/3Lt; ☺noon-5.30pm Tue-Sat, to 4.30pm Sun) Adjacent to the neo-Gothic post office at No 16 is the Clock Museum, where all manner of clocks – from Gothic to nuclear – just keep ticking; its sunny back yard alone is worth the entrance fee.

Pranas Domšaitis Gallery   MUSEUM
(www.ldm.lt; Liepų gatvė 33; adult/child 6/3Lt; ☺11am-6pm Tue-Sat, noon-5pm Sun) At Liepų gatvė's northwestern end is this gallery with works by the German-Lithuanian expressionist painter Pranas Domšaitis (1880–1965).

K Building   LANDMARK BUILDING
(Naujojo Sodo gatvė 1) Back toward the lagoon is Klaipėda's tallest building, which, appropriately, is shaped like a 'K'. It houses the Amberton hotel and is topped by the Viva Lavita bar.

SMILTYNĖ

The small village of Smiltynė (Map p350) is a hop, skip and five-minute ferry ride away across the thin strait that divides Klaipėda from its beautiful coastal sister, the Curonian Spit (p350). This strait-side patch of paradise – packed on summer weekends with Klaipėda residents – has beautiful beaches, sandy dunes and sweet-smelling pine forests.

Lithuanian Sea Museum   MUSEUM
(Map p350; Lietuvos jūrų muziejus; www.juru .muziejus.lt; adult/student Jun-Aug 15/7Lt, Sep-May 12/6Lt; ☺10.30am-6.30pm Tue-Sun Jun-Aug, 10.30am-6pm Wed-Sun May & Sep–mid-Oct, 10.30am-5pm Sat & Sun mid-Oct–Apr) This popular museum, set in a former 19th-century fort about 1.5km from the passenger ferry landing (for Old Castle Port ferries), has some fascinating stuffed sea animals, aquariums and live shows that feature seals, sea lions and dolphins. Note that the dolphinarium was closed for reconstruction on our visit in 2011 but was expected to reopen in 2012.

In July and August horse-drawn carriages (70Lt for up to eight passengers) carry tourists from the ferry landing to the museum. Otherwise, catch the electric **tourist train** (adult/7-10yr 4/3Lt) that covers the same ground, hire a **bicycle** (per hr/day 8/40Lt; ☺10am-8pm May-Sep), or cover the distance on foot. The granite boulder at the start of the path honours past winners of the three- and six-nautical-mile races run around Smiltynė on the second Saturday in October.

Exposition of the National Park of the Curonian Spit
MUSEUM
(Map p350; Kursių nerijos nacionalinis parkas gamtos muziejus ekspozicija; www.nerija.lt; Smiltynė plentas 11; admission free; ☺11am-6pm Wed-Sun May-Sep) This nature museum is spread across three wooden houses. There are plenty of stuffed examples of the birds and animals that normally roam the spit, including wild pigs, badgers, beavers and elk, a large collection of insects, and information on measures being taken to protect the dunes.

Ethnographic Sea Fishermen's Farmstead
MUSEUM
(Map p350; admission free; ☺dusk-dawn) About 700m further north of the nature museum are **old fishing vessels** to explore inside and out, including three Baltic Sea fishing trawlers built in the late 1940s and a 1935 **kurėnas** (a traditional 10.8m flat-bottomed Curonian sailing boat used for fishing). Next door, the Ethnographic Sea Fishermen's Farmstead, with its collection of traditional 19th-century buildings (the granary, dwelling house, cellar, cattle shed and so on), proffers a glimpse of traditional fishing life.

🏃 Activities

Grab your Speedos and hit Smiltynė, where footpaths cut through pine forests across the spit's 1km-wide tip to a bleached-white sandy **beach**. From the ferry landing, walk straight ahead across the car park, then bear left towards Nida; on your right a large sign marks a smooth footpath that leads through pine forest to a women's beach (Moterų pliažas; 1km), mixed beach (Bendras pliažas; 700m) and men's beach (Vyrų pliažas; 900m). Nude or topless bathing is the norm on single-sex beaches.

Melnragė, 1km north of Klaipėda, has a pier and beach which city dwellers like to visit at sunset; **Giruliai Beach** is 1km further north. Buses 6 and 4 respectively link Manto gatvė with both. **Karklė**, another 1km north, is known for having amber specks

wash up on its unusually stony beach after autumn storms and for the protected **Dutch Cap**, a 24m sea cliff.

Boat trips on the lagoon are arranged through the tourist office. **Sailing excursions** (3hr trip 70Lt) on the Baltic Sea only take place during the Sea Festival in July; once again, contact the tourist office.

With its Turkish sauna, pool and masseurs, the **Sothys Spa Centras** (☎315 063; www.sothys.lt in Lithuanian; Mažoji Smilties gatvė 2; ☺8am-9pm Mon-Fri, 9am-8pm Sat) will appeal to winter visitors. The tourist office can help with **ice-fishing** contacts.

✿ Festivals & Events

Klaipėda celebrates its rich nautical heritage on the third weekend in July with a flamboyant five-day **Sea Festival** (www.juros.svente.lt).

🛌 Sleeping

Try to book in advance during the summer season, especially during the Sea Festival. The tourist office has private rooms from 70Lt and can help with country stays.

TOP CHOICE Litinterp Guesthouse GUESTHOUSE €
(☎410 644; www.litinterp.com; Puodžių gatvė 17; s/d/tr 100/160/210Lt, without bathroom 80/140/180Lt; ☺reception 8.30am-7pm Mon-Fri, 10am-3pm Sat; 🅿❷@🛜) While it's certainly not luxurious, this clean and quiet guesthouse gets our nod for offering excellent value for money. The 16 rooms are spotless and furnished in a light pinewood that creates a fresh, contemporary look. The location is excellent, north of the river but within walking distance of Old Town and the ports. One thing they might improve on is the ordinary breakfast of just a couple of pieces of bread, salami and cheese – delivered to your room in a basket. But at these prices, we're not complaining.

Preliudija Guesthouse GUESTHOUSE €€
(☎310 077; www.preliudija.com; Kepėjų gatvė 7; s/d from 180/210Lt; @🛜) Snug in an Old Town townhouse dating to 1856, this upscale guesthouse – still a relatively rare breed in Klaipėda – is charming. Despite its history, the rooms are minimalist and modern; each has a single fresh flower in a vase and a sparkling bathroom.

Friedricho GUESTHOUSE €€
(☎391 020; www.pasazas.lt; Šaltkalvių gatvė 3; r from 300Lt; 🅿🛜) This pretty six-room guesthouse is run by the same people who

operate the restaurants along Friedricho Pasažas. The rooms themselves are more like small apartments, with kitchenettes and sitting rooms, and are perfect for families. Four rooms come with their own computers. The Old Town setting is ideal.

Aribė
HOTEL €€
(☎490 940; www.aribe.lt; Bangų gatvė 17a; s/d 140/170Lt; P@☎) This three-star establishment is a 10-minute walk from Old Town and hides behind an unassuming facade in an unassuming neighbourhood. Rooms are quiet, pleasant and dressed in light, bright colours. The staff couldn't be more helpful.

Amberton
HOTEL €€
(☎404 372; www.ambertonhotels.com; Naujojo Sodo gatvė 1; s/d/ste from 200/300/600Lt; P@☎) This four-star hotel is one of the top addresses in town and occupies the unusual red-brick tower and 'K' buildings just to the north of the river. There's a good range of accommodation on offer from relatively simple singles and doubles in the older wing, at reasonable prices, all the way up to multiroom, luxury suites in the newer K building that include Jacuzzis and sea views. All guests have access to amenities like the spa, tennis courts and casino.

Hotel Euterpė
HOTEL €€
(☎474 703; www.euterpe.lt; Daržų gatvė 9; s/d from 240/320Lt; P@☎) Sidling up to former German merchant houses in Old Town is this upscale hotel. Rooms are bathed in earthy colours and have a neat, minimalist look about them. Downstairs is the hotel's courtyard cafe and (in the reception) a Renaissance-era tile of Euterpe, a Greek muse, uncovered during excavations.

Old Port Hotel
HOTEL €€
(☎474 764; www.oldporthotel.lt; Žvejų gatvė 20/22; s/d from 260/290Lt; P) Split between two renovated fishing houses on the southern bank of the Danė River, the Old Port Hotel offers small but supremely comfortable rooms with views of the docks or Klaipėda Castle. Those looking for Curonian Spit views should book rooms 46, 47 or 57.

Klaipėda Hostel
HOSTEL €
(☎211 879; www.klaipedahostel.com; Butkų Juzės gatvė 7/4; dm/d 44/88Lt; P@☎) This friendly hostel close to the bus station looks terrible from the outside but is very homey and pleasant inside. Two small dorms sleep 12 people and there's one double, as well as

a kitchen and free tea and coffee. Book in advance; no credit cards accepted.

Pajūrio Kempingas
CAMPGROUND €
(☎677 732 27; www.campingklaipeda.lt; Šlaito gatvė 3, Giruliai; per person/tent 15/15Lt; P) This quiet camping ground is around 8km north of Klaipėda's Old Town near the village of Giruliai. It's conveniently situated close to both the sea and the local train station, with regular services to and from Klaipėda.

✗ Eating

Self-caterers can head for **Iki** (Mažvydo alėja 7/11) and **Ikiukas** (Turgaus gatvė) supermarkets.

┌TOP┐ Friedricho
│CHOICE│
└─────┘
INTERNATIONAL €€
(www.pasazas.lt; Tiltų 26a; mains 20-50Lt; ⊙11am-1am Mon-Sat, noon-11pm Sun; ☎) This is not just one restaurant but a series of varied eateries that line a picturesque courtyard on the southern side of Old Town. The main restaurant, Friedricho Restoranas, wins the eating award with an attractive selection of international wines and creative Mediterranean dishes, but there are also fine pizzas (Friedricho Pizzeria) and good Lithuanian meals (Friedricho Smuklė) to be had here. The best advice is to take a stroll and check out the various menus to see what appeals. The entire passageway is covered with a free, reliable wi-fi connection.

Keltininko Namas
LITHUANIAN €€
(www.oldporthotel.lt; Žvejų 20/22; mains 20-40Lt; ☎) The house restaurant of the Old Port Hotel wins the atmosphere award for its port setting overlooking the Danė River. The chefs here really try to incorporate fresh local ingredients, including an ample amount of fish dishes. The linen and silverware lend a fancy touch, but the prices are surprisingly reasonable for the quality.

La Terrasse
ITALIAN €€
(Žvejų 10; mains 15-30Lt; ☎) This relatively new addition in a remodelled building along the Danė River focuses on well-made Italian dishes, including pizzas, pastas, salads and fish. The decor is a stripped-down contemporary that's perfect for a relaxing lunch or dinner. In nice weather, you can dine on the river.

Hämmerli
SWISS €€
(Didžioji Vandens 13/16; mains 15-40Lt; ⊙9am-11pm Mon-Sat) Hämmerli specialises in Swiss cuisine, with equal portions of French,

German and Italian flavours thrown in. It's a heavily meat-based menu but vegetarians will find something to keep them happy. Further bonuses include top-notch service, a bright and breezy atmosphere, courtyard seating and a superb lunch menu.

Čili Kaimas LITHUANIAN €

(www.cili.lt; Manto gatvė 11; mains 12-25Lt; 🛜) This local branch of the nationwide chain does one thing very well: serves very good Lithuanian food at reasonable prices. The atmosphere tends towards the cheesy, with waitresses clad in traditional peasant dress, but it's still enjoyable.

🍷 Drinking

Klaipėda is home to Švyturys, Lithuania's big beer brewed in the country's oldest operating brewery (since 1784). An alternative to slurping the stuff in a bar is to take a tour of the Švyturys brewery (www.svyturys.lt); organised by the tourist office, tours are 1½ to two hours and cost around 30Lt per person (including tastings), and leave any time between 10am and 4pm Monday to Friday. Reservations essential.

 Viva Lavita COCKTAIL BAR

(www.ambertonhotels.com; Naujojo Sodo 1; ⊘noon-3am) Occupying the 20th floor of the K building of the Amberton hotel, Viva Lavita offers up spectacular views of the swathe of docks along Klaipėda's waterfront, the spit's northern point, and the Baltic Sea beyond. To the east stretches Lithuania as far as the eye can see, and even lifts A and B provide astounding views.

Memelis MICROBREWERY

(www.memelis.lt; Žvejų gatvė 4; ⊘noon-midnight Sun-Thu, noon-2am Fri & Sat) This red-brick brewery-restaurant by the river has been in operation since 1871. The interior is an old-style beer hall; outside is industrial-feel riverside terrace. The home-brewed beer, in four varieties, is some of the best and most potent around.

Senoji Hansa BAR, CAFE

(www.senojihansa.lt; Kurpių gatvė 1; ⊘10am-midnight; 🛜) This combination bar, restaurant and cafe sits wedged just behind the Memelis microbrewery. It's a great choice for beer, coffee or even lunch or dinner (mains 15Lt to 30Lt). The terrace out back is covered and can draw a fun crowd on a weekend evening.

Kubu CAFE

(Manto gatvė 10; ⊘10am-9pm Mon-Thu, 10am-midnight Fri & Sat, noon-9pm Sun; 🛜) This is as close as it gets in Klaipėda to a Coffee Inn or a Vero Cafe – in other words to a trendy coffee bar where the emphasis is on premium coffee (served in a paper cup) and a relaxed, casual attitude where you're welcome to surf at your leisure over the cafe's free wi-fi.

Max Coffee CAFE

(www.maxcoffee.lt; Turgaus gatvė 11; ⊘9am-10pm; 🛜) This convenient coffee shop is situated just a block away from the tourist office, and makes a good place to repair to once you've obtained your handful of brochures and free maps. Decent coffee drinks, plus very good pastries and cakes.

☆ Entertainment

Catch high-brow entertainment at the Klaipėda Concert Hall (📞410 561; www.koncertusale.lt; Šaulių gatvė 36). The Klaipėda Philharmonic plays at the Musical Theatre (Muzikinis teatras; 📞397 402; www.muzikinis-teatras.lt, in Lithuanian; Danės gatvė 19).

 Kurpiai LIVE MUSIC

(www.jazzkurpiai.lt in Lithuanian; Kurpių gatvė 1a; ⊘noon-3am) This Old Town jazz club has been a Klaipėda legend for years, opening way before the postindependence bars and restaurants mushroomed. Its cobbled terrace and dark old-world interior are not only the best place in town to catch live jazz, but also to sample decent food and drink. Arrive before 9pm on weekends (entrance Friday/Saturday 10/15Lt) or you'll be fighting for standing space.

Relax NIGHTCLUB

(www.nesepb.lt; Turgaus gatvė 1) This flashy basement club is a fun night out when there's a crowd around. Men should wear a collared shirt or the bouncers may not let you in. Cover charges vary but can run as high as 25Lt depending on the night.

🛍 Shopping

Klaipėda is known for its amber (stalls selling souvenirs dot Teatro aikštė), but it's also possible to pick up fine linen and artwork in town. Galleries worth seeking out include Parko (Turgaus gatvė 9), for contemporary paintings, sculptures and etchings, and Pėda (Vežejų gatvė) for designs by contemporary jeweller Jurga Karčiauskaitė-Lago.

Pegasas (www.pegasas.lt; Taikos prospektas 61) is arguably the best bookshop in Klaipėda; it's south of Old Town in the Akropolis shopping centre. Maps, guidebooks and English-language fiction are available at Akademija (Daukanto gatvė 16). Vaga (www .vaga.lt; Manto gatvė 9) has maps, travel guides and the *Baltic Times*.

❶ Information

Jāņa sēta's *Klaipėda Neringa* map covers Klaipėda's northern beach suburbs, Smiltynė and Curonian Spit as well as central Klaipėda (1:10,000). Bookshops sell it for 8Lt.

Bankas Snoras (Manto gatvė 9) Change cash or withdraw it with Visa or MasterCard at an ATM.

Klaipėda in Your Pocket (www.inyourpocket .com) Annual city guide published locally and sold in hotels and news kiosks for 6Lt.

Krantas Travel (☑395 111; www.krantas.lt; Teatro gatvė 5) Sells Sassnitz, Kiel and Karlshamn ferry tickets.

Left luggage (lockers 12/24 hr 4/5Lt; ☺6am-10pm) At the train station.

Mėja Travel (☑310 295; www.meja.lt; Simkaus gatvė 21-8) Excursions for cruise-ship passengers and amber-fishing.

Post office (Liepų gatvė 16) Gorgeous red-brick edifice.

Tourist office (☑412 186; www.klaipedainfo.lt; Turgaus gatvė 7; ☺9am-7pm Mon-Fri, 10am-4pm Sat & Sun Jun-Aug, 9am-6pm Mon-Fri, 10am-4pm Sat May & Sep, 9am-6pm Mon-Fri Oct-Apr) Exceptionally efficient tourist office selling maps and locally published guidebooks. It arranges accommodation and English-speaking guides (140/160Lt for one/two hours), hires out bicycles (8/30Lt per hour/day plus €100/300Lt deposit), and has a pet parrot named Rico. It has a couple of computers for surfing (4Lt per hour).

Zigzag (☑314 672; www.zigzag.lt in Lithuanian; Janonio gatvė 16) Specialises in student travel.

❶ Getting There & Away
Boat

From Klaipėda's **International Ferry Port** (Klaipėdos Nafta; ☑395 051; www.dfdsseaways .lt; Perkėlos gatvė 10), **DFDS Seaways** (☑395 000; www.lisco.lt; Šaulių gatvė 19) runs big passenger and car ferries regularly to Kiel and Sassnitz (in Germany) and to Karlshamn (in Sweden); see p409.

The travel company **Jukunda** (☑300 700; www.jukunda.lt; Karklų gatvė 9) previously offered regular ferry services in summer between Klaipėda and Nida (60Lt, 4½ hours),

calling at Juodkrantė (30Lt, 1½ hours), but it suspended this service in 2011. Contact the company directly to see whether service has resumed.

Bus

Ecolines (☑310 103; www.ecolines.net; Mažvydo alėja 1; ☺9am-6pm Mon-Fri, 10am-3pm Sat) sells tickets for international destinations (p384), as does **Eurolines** (☑415 555; www.eurolines.lt; Tiakos prospektas 41; ☺9am-6pm Mon-Fri, 10am-4pm Sat).

At the **bus station** (☑411 547; www.klap.lt; Butkų Juzės gatvė 9) the **information window** (☺3.30am-7.30pm) has timetable information. Most buses to/from Juodkrantė and Nida depart from the ferry landing at Smiltynė on the Curonian Spit.

Services to/from Klaipėda bus station include the following:

Kaliningrad (36Lt, 4½ hours, two buses daily departing 6.30am and 6.20pm, the latter via Nida and departing from the Smiltynė ferry landing)

Kaunas (50Lt, 2¾ to four hours, over 20 buses a day)

Kretinga (5Lt, 30 to 50 minutes, half-hourly between 6.25am and 9.30pm)

Liepāja (18Lt, 2¾ hours, one bus departing 9am daily via Palanga)

Nida (11Lt, 1½ hours, buses depart every one to two hours from Smiltynė)

Palanga (5Lt, 45 minutes, at least half-hourly between 4.15am and 10.35pm)

Pärnu (106Lt, 8¾ hours, three buses daily via Rīga)

Rīga (60Lt, five hours, three buses daily)

Šiauliai (33Lt, 3½ hours, six buses daily)

Tallinn (from 125Lt, 10 hours, three buses daily via Rīga)

Vilnius (66Lt, four to 5½ hours, up to 15 buses daily)

Train

The **train station** (☑313 677; www.litrail.lt; Priestočio gatvė 1), 150m from the bus station, has an unusual helmeted clock tower and a moving sculpture (boxed text p343) in front.

Daily services include three trains to/from Vilnius (52Lt, 4½ to five hours) and five trains to/from Šiauliai (20Lt to 23.50Lt, two to three hours) and Kretinga (4.50Lt, 20 to 35 minutes).

❶ Getting Around
Boat

Everything about **Smiltynė ferries** (Smiltynės perkėla; ☑24hr information line 311 117; www .keltas.lt) – timetables, fares, newsflashes – is online.

The passenger ferry for Smiltynė leaves from **Old Castle Port** (Senoji perkėla; ☎311 117; Žvejų gatvė 8), just on the northern side of the Danė River. Look for signs to 'Neringa'. It docks on the eastern side of Smiltynė, at the start of the Nida road. Ferries sail at least every half-hour between 6.30am and midnight June to August (at least hourly until 11pm the rest of the year). The crossing takes 10 minutes and a return passenger fare is 2.90Lt per person; bicycles and children under the age of seven sail for free.

Year-round, vehicles can use the **New River Port** (Naujoji perkėla; ☎311 117; Nemuno gatvė 8), around 2km south of the mouth of the Danė River. Look for road signs to 'Neringa'. Ferries sail half-hourly between 5am and 2am and dock on the Curonian Spit 2.5km south of the Smiltynė ferry landing. Cars cost 40Lt to transport, motorcycles 18Lt. Bus 1 links Klaipėda city centre with the New River Port.

Bus

Buy tickets for local buses from news kiosks for 2Lt or from the driver for 2.40Lt. Bus 8 (known for pickpockets) links the train station with Manto gatvė, the city centre and the Turgaus stop, on Taikos prospektas. Bus 11 links the bus station with Manto gatvė. Minibuses, which follow the same route, can be flagged down on the street and cost 2.50Lt; pay the driver.

Curonian Spit National Park

☎469 / POP 3100

The Curonian Spit National Park (Kuršių Nerijos Nacionalinis Parkas) was established in 1991 to protect the rare ecosystems found on Curonian Spit, including the sand dunes, the Curonian Lagoon and the surrounding sea. It covers most of the Lithuanian section of the spit, running from the village of Smiltynė in the north down to Nida, 50km to the south.

The park is refreshingly wild and undeveloped. Pine forests filled with deer, elk and wild boar cover about 70% of the park. Sand dunes make up 25% of it. Just a small fraction is urban, namely four main villages – Nida, Juodkrantė, Pervalka and Preila – known collectively on maps and signs as 'Neringa'. The main industry is tourism, centred around the villages of Nida and Juodkrantė, a double-edged sword that yields both its main source of income and its biggest environmental threat.

Up until the first decades of the 20th century, most of the spit was German territory.

Curonian Spit National Park

The area used to have a hugely magnetic attraction for German exiles, and continues to attract a large number of German tourists to this day.

These days, Lithuania shares the spit with the Russian-controlled Kaliningrad Region.

Curonian Spit National Park

◉ Sights

1 Ethnographic Sea Fishermen's Farmstead..A3
2 Exposition of the National Park of the Curonian Spit (Birds & Mammals Section)..A3
3 Exposition of the National Park of the Curonian Spit (Landscape Section)........................A4
4 Exposition of the National Park of the Curonian Spit (Plants & Insects Section)...............A4
5 Lithuanian Sea Museum.....................A3

A road runs the whole length of the spit all the way to Kaliningrad and indeed, with the proper paperwork, it's possible to combine a visit to the spit with a mini-trip to Russia (p386).

✵✵ Festivals & Events

The summer season – mid-June to the end of August – is lined end to end with festivals. The highlights include the International Folk Festival, held on a weekend in late June, which swamps Nida with visitors, and the Nida Jazz Marathon (www.nidajazz.lt), two weeks of jazz performances in late July and early August.

❶ Information

Curonian Spit National Park (www.nerija.lt)
Kopos (www.kopos.lt) For accommodation.
National Park Visitors Centre Nida (Lankytojų centras; ☑51 256; infonida@nerija.lt; Naglių gatvė 8; ☺9am-noon & 1-5pm Mon-Thu, to 6pm Fri & Sat, to 4pm Sun May-Sep); Smiltynė (☑46-402 257; info@nerija.lt; Smiltynės plentas 11; ☺9am-noon & 1-6pm Mon-Fri, 9am-6pm Sat, 9am-4pm Sun Jun-Aug, 8am-noon & 1-5pm Mon-Fri Sep-May) Arranges guides (35Lt per hour, minimum 10 people) and stocks an abundance of information on walking, cycling, boating and lazy activities in the park.
Neringa Tourist Information (www.visit neringa.com)

❶ Getting There & Around

The Curonian Spit is accessible only via boat or ferry (there are no bridges linking the spit to the mainland). From Klaipėda, two ferries run regularly: a passenger ferry, known as the 'Old Ferry', goes to Smiltynė; and a vehicle ferry, the 'New Ferry', connects to a point on the spit around 2km south of Smiltynė. The New Ferry departs from a port 2km south of Klaipėda's Old Town (see p349).

Regular buses run to villages on the spit, including Nida (11Lt) and Juodkrantė (7Lt), but these depart from Smiltynė, meaning you'll

---

SHIFTING SANDS & DELICATE DUNES

Legend has it that motherly sea giantess Neringa created the spit, lovingly carrying armfuls of sand in her apron to form a protected harbour for the local fishing folk. The truth is just as enchanting. The waves and winds of the Baltic Sea let sand accumulate in its shallow waters near the coast 5000 or 6000 years ago to create an original beauty found nowhere else.

Massive deforestation in the 16th century started the sands shifting. Trees were felled for timber, leaving the sands free to roam unhindered at the whim of the strong coastal winds. At a pace of 20m a year, the sands swallowed 14 villages in the space of three centuries.

It was soon dubbed the 'Sahara of Lithuania' due to its desert state; drastic action was needed. In 1768 an international commission set about replanting. Today this remains a priority of the national park authorities. Deciduous forest (mainly birch groves) covers 20% of the national park; coniferous forest, primarily pine and mountain pine trees, constitutes a further 53%. Alder trees can be found on 2.6 sq km (3% of the park's area). Lattices of branches and wooden stakes have pinned down the sand.

But the sands are still moving – at least 1m a year. Slowly the spit is drifting into the Baltic Sea. Each tourist who scrambles and romps on Parnidis Dune – the only remaining free-drifting dune – meanwhile pushes down several tonnes of sand. With 1.5 million people visiting the dunes each year, the threat posed by them wandering off designated paths – not to mention the risk of forest fire – is high.

The dunes are also shrinking. Winds, waves and humans have reduced them by 20m in 40 years. Its precious beauty may yet be lost forever.

first have to use the passenger ferry to get to the bus. Once in Smiltynė, taxis are a viable alternative to the bus if you've got enough passengers to share the fare. The fare per person to Nida split among four works out to around 15Lt.

if you've got the weather for it, cycling (boxed text p355) is a great way to explore the spit. There is a well-marked trail that runs the entire length of the spit from Smiltynė to Nida via Juodkrantė (about 50km). Hire bikes in Klaipėda and take them across the lagoon via the passenger ferry for free.

You can also reach Kaliningrad (south) in Russia from here. The Russian border post is 3km south of Nida on the main road. Don't contemplate this without the necessary Russian visa and paperwork (see p403).

JUODKRANTĖ
✔469

The long, thin village of Juodkrantė (ywad-kran-tey) – Schwarzort to Germans – is 20km south of Smiltynė and is spread out along the lagoon. The pace of life here is slow even in the height of summer, and the sweet smell of smoked fish follows you wherever you go.

⊙ Sights

Contemporary stone sculptures and a silky-smooth promenade sidle up to the water's edge, while the main road – Liudviko Rėzos gatvė – is lined with holiday homes and quaint *žuvis* (fish) outlets.

At Juodkrantė's northern end is an area around a fishing harbour known as **Amber Bay** (Gintaro įlanka), recalling the amber excavated in the village in three separate clusters – 2250 tonnes in all – in 1854 to 1855 and 1860. The spit is about 1.5km wide at this point and the fine stretch of forest – good for spotting elk in the early morning and evening – is among the loveliest you will find on the peninsula.

A lazy stroll south from the centre brings you to the **Witches' Hill** (Raganos kalnas; Map p350), where devils, witches, ghouls and other fantastical and grotesque wooden carvings from Lithuanian folklore skulk along a sculpture trail careering from fairy tale to nightmare. It's located in the woods and signposted immediately south of Liudviko Rėzos gatvė 46.

The red-brick German **Evangelical-Lutheran church** (Liudviko Rėzos gatvė 56) built in 1885 and a **Weathervanes Gallery** (Vetrungių galerija; Liudviko Rėzos gatvė 13), selling authentic weathervanes (boxed text p352) and quality amber jewellery, mark the village's southern end.

🛏 Sleeping & Eating

Many places close down during the 'cold' season (October to April) so be sure to book in advance to avoid disappointment. Smoked fish is sold all along Liudviko Rėzos gatvė and self-caterers are limited to an expensive **store** (⊙8am-10pm) near the start of the Witches' Hill trail.

Vila Flora   GUESTHOUSE €€
(✆53 024; www.vilaflora.lt; Kalno gatvė 7a; s/d 220/280Lt; P) This well-run property is open all year and is located in an attractive rust- and wine-red building. It's filled with bright, stylish rooms, some of which sport balconies and conservatories. Its restaurant on the ground floor is the best in town, offering bog-standard Lithuanian dishes with a twist. Prices fall by half in winter.

Kurėnas   HOTEL €€
(✆53 101; kurenas@gmail.com; Liudviko Rėzos gatvė 10; r from 240Lt; P🛜) Named after a flat-bottomed Curonian boat, this busy and bright cafe-bar with streetside terrace sports large, individually decorated rooms with wooden floors and clean white walls.

SEAFARING WEATHERVANES

Nowhere are Juodkrantė's and Nida's seafaring roots better reflected than on top of the 19th-century wooden cottages that speckle these spit villages. A ruling in 1844 saw weathervanes or cocks used to identify fishing vessels. They quickly became ornamentation for rooftops. Originally made from tin and later from wood, these 60cm x 30cm plaques were fastened to the boat mast so other fishermen could see where a *kurėnas* (Neringa boat) had sailed. Each village had its own unique symbol – a black-and-white geometrical design – incorporated in the weathercock and then embellished with an eclectic assortment of mythical cut-outs; see the different designs first hand in the Neringa History Museum (p354).

SPIT RULES

» Neringa municipality entrance fee: motorbike/car July to August 7/20Lt, September to June 5/10Lt.

» Speed limit: 50km/h in villages, 70km/h on open roads.

» Don't romp in the dunes, pick flowers or stray off designated footpaths.

» Don't damage flora or fauna, mess with bird nests or light campfires.

» Don't pitch a tent or park a camper overnight anywhere in the park.

» Don't fish without a permit; purchase them at tourist offices.

» Beware of elk and wild boar crossing the road, and don't feed them!

» Break a rule and risk an on-the-spot fine of up to 500Lt.

» In case of forest fire, call ☎01, 112, Smiltyne 8-656 35025, Juodkrantė 8-656 34998, Prèila and Pervalka 8-687 27758, Nida 8-656 34992.

Reserve one with a balcony overlooking the lagoon.

Hotel Ažuolynas HOTEL €€
(☎53 310; www.hotelazuolynas.lt; Liudviko Rėzos gatvė 54; s/d/tr/q Jun-Aug 205/270/440Lt, May & Sep 160/230/380Lt; ℗⊠) This modern hotel lacks character, but has reasonable rooms and a full set of facilities, including tennis courts, a pool table, gift shop, a sauna and a swimming pool, that smaller properties lack. The hotel is open the entire year, and prices in the off-season (October to April) run to about half the high-season rate. Breakfast not included.

Kogas LITHUANIAN €€
(Liudviko Rėzos gatvė 1; mains 20-40Lt) Board this pseudo pirate ship moored at Juodkrantė's harbour and chow down on a plethora of meaty dishes or simply rock up for a swash-buckling time and a few hearty ales.

Pamario takas LITHUANIAN €€
(Liudviko Rėzos gatvė 42; mains 15-30Lt) Fun, family-run restaurant in a quaint wooden cottage with accompanying flower-filled garden.

❶ Information

The village's tiny centre is home to a pier, bus stop, post office and tourist office.

Post office (Kalno gatvė 3)

Snoras Bankas Only ATM in town; opposite Kurėnas cafe-bar.

Tourist office (☎53 490; juodkrante@visit neringa.lt; Liudviko Rėzos gatvė 8; ⊙10am-8pm Mon-Sat, 10am-3pm Sun Jun-Aug, 9am-1pm & 2-5pm Tue-Fri, 10am-3pm Sat Sep-May) Located opposite the bus stop; has accommodation and activity information.

❶ Getting There & Away

Buses to/from Nida (7Lt, 45 minutes) and Smiltynė (5Lt, 15 to 20 minutes) stop in Juodkrantė. Bicycle hire (8/30Lt per hour/day) can be found near the tourist office.

JUODKRANTĖ TO NIDA

South of Juodkrantė is Lithuania's largest colony of grey herons and cormorants, observed here since the 19th century. Wooden steps lead from the road to a **viewing platform** where the panorama of thousands of nests amid pine trees – not to mention the noise of the 6500-strong colony – is astonishing. Cormorants arrive in early February (herons a little later) to pick and rebuild their nests. By May chicks are screaming for food. Starlings, thrushes, warblers, and grey, spotted and black woodpeckers can also be seen here.

Almost immediately afterwards, the road switches from the eastern side of the peninsula to the western. The 16.8-sq-km **Naglių Strict Nature Reserve** (Naglių rezervatas) here protects the Dead or Grey Dunes (named after the greyish flora that covers them) that stretch 8km south and are 2km wide; a marked footpath leads into the reserve from the main road.

Shifting sands in the mid-19th century forced villagers here to flee to **Pervalka** and **Preila** on the east coast, accessible by side roads from the main road. Pine-forested **Vecekrugas Dune** (67.2m), the peninsula's highest dune, south of Preila, stands on a ridge called Old Inn Hill – named after an inn that stood at the foot of the dune before being buried by sand; view it from the Juodkrantė–Nida cycling path (boxed text p355).

Accommodation and eating options are limited here; don't count on cash machines. Neringos Luize (Pervalkos gatvė 29e; mains 20-40Lt), right on the lagoon at Pervalka, is a welcome respite for cyclists on the Nida–Juodkrantė trail. At the southern end of Preila is Kuršmarių vila (☑55 117, 8-685 56317; kursmariuvila@gmail.com; Preilos gatvė 93; r Jun-Sep 220Lt, Oct-May 150Lt; P), which offers both sleeping and eating year-round under its thatched roof. Run by a fishing family, it produces some of the finest smoked fish in the area in its old smokehouse in the garden. Roach and bream are the most frequent catch in the Curonian Lagoon – pike, perch, ling and eel are less common. It's also an excellent spot to try your hand at ice-fishing, if you can brave the Lithuanian winter.

NIDA
☑469

Lovely Nida (Nidden in German) is the largest settlement on the Lithuanian half of the Curonian Spit; it's also the spit's tourist hot spot. Remnants of a former life as an old-fashioned fishing village are plain to see in its pretty wooden cottages and harbour jammed with seafaring vessels, but these days Nida makes its money from holidaymakers and busloads of Germans exploring historical East Prussia.

Natural beauty abounds here, and white-sand beaches are only a 2km walk away through hazy pine forests. To the south is the most impressive dune on the peninsula, Parnidis Dune (Parnidžio kopa), which has steps up to its 52m summit from where there are stunning views of rippling, untouched dunes stretching into Russia.

From the late 19th century a colony of artists drew inspiration from the area. Nida developed as a tourist resort and there were five hotels by the 1930s, when the German writer Thomas Mann (1875–1955) had a summer home built here. In 1965 French philosopher Jean Paul Sartre and companion Simone de Beauvoir were granted special permission by Khrushchev to spend five days on the dunes, and Lithuanian photographer Antanas Sutkus was allowed to shoot the pair in the sand.

Nida is 48km from Klaipėda and 3km from the Russian border; the town stretches for 2km, but its centre is at the southern end, behind the harbour.

◉ Sights & Activities

There's plenty to keep you occupied on land and water, or you could avoid it all and simply chill out. Outside the high season, scour the beaches for speckles of amber washed up on the shores during the spring and autumn storms, and in the depths of winter brave the frozen lagoon and ice-fish for smelt and burbot.

At the harbour, opt for a one-hour boat trip aboard a handsome replica of a kurėnas (☑8-686 65242; per person 20Lt), a traditional 19th-century fishing boat operating in July and August; take a lagoon cruise on more modern boats (20Lt to 30Lt, one hour); or sail across the lagoon to the Nemunas Delta (120Lt, five hours). For more information on boat hire, organised trips and fishing expeditions in the lagoon, contact the tourist office.

There are outlets with bicycles to hire around almost every street corner in Nida centre, including a couple run by Lucijos Ratai (bicycle per hr/day/24hr 8/30/35Lt; ◎9am-sunset May-Oct) near the bus station. Lucijos also offers one-way hire between Nida, Juodkrantė and Smiltynė – a huge advantage if you don't have the legs for the return journey.

NORTH OF THE HARBOUR

Breathtaking views of Parnidis Dune can be had at the harbour; from there a pleasant waterfront lagoon promenade stretches for over 1km.

Neringa History Museum   MUSEUM
(Neringos istorijos muziejus; www.visitneringa.com; Pamario gatvė 53; adult/child 2/1Lt; ◎10am-6pm daily Jun–mid-Sep, 10am-5pm Mon-Sat mid-Sep–May) Black-and-white photographs of Nida in its more brutal spear-fishing, crow-biting days fill the thoughtfully laid-out displays in this history museum, where Nida's tale from the Stone Age to 1939 is told. Particularly brilliant are the images of local hunters biting a crow's neck to kill the bird, followed by them a taking a shot of vodka to dull the taste. Eating crows and seagulls' eggs was common on the spit in the 17th to 19th centuries, when continually drifting sands rendered previously arable land useless.

Thomas Mann Memorial Museum   MUSEUM
(Tomo Mano memorialinis muziejus; www.mann .lt; adult/child 4/2Lt; ◎10am-6pm daily Jun-Aug, 10am-5pm Tue-Sat Sep-May) A flight of steps leads up from the promenade to German writer Thomas Mann's former Baltic villa,

BY BIKE FROM NIDA TO JUODKRANTĖ

One of Lithuania's best cycling trips follows the Curonian Spit end to end, connecting in the south with a path that leads into the Kaliningrad Region and to the north with another trail that heads off eventually to Palanga and onward towards Latvia (p29). The trail forms part of Eurovelo cycling route no 10, the 'Baltic Sea Circuit'. For our money, arguably the best section of the entire trail runs the 30km from Nida to Juodkrantė.

This part of the trail passes some of the spit's greatest natural treasures, including the Vecekrugas Dune and an authentic fish smoker in Preila. Footpaths lead from the cycling path to Karvaičiai Reservation, where entire villages were buried by sand. Cycling the path also provides the perfect opportunity to spot wild boar and elk, something not so easily accomplished while seated in a car or bus.

To pick up the path in Nida, follow the red-paved cycling track north along the lagoon promenade and, after passing the Thomas Mann Memorial Museum, follow the track left around the corner onto Puvynės gatvė. On the road, turn immediately right and follow it for 3.5km until you see a dirt track forking left into pine forest: this is the start of the cycling path, complete with 0.0km marker.

Heading north, at Pervalka you can cycle through or around the village (the quicker route), arriving 4km later at the entrance to the Naglių Strict Nature Reserve. Shortly afterward, the cycling path crosses the main road to take cyclists along the opposite (western) side of the spit for the remaining 9km to Juodkrantė.

The first 5km snake beneath pine trees alongside the main road and the final 4km skirts seaside sand dunes. Once you're out of the reserve, leap into the sea for a quick cool-down before the last leg – an uphill slog through forested dunes to arrive in Juodkrantė behind the village.

which is now a museum. Mann spent three summers with his wife and children in this traditional cottage from 1930 to 1932, before he was forced to flee Germany in 1933.

Evangelical-Lutheran Church CHURCH
(⊙mass 11am Sun May-Sep) Back towards the town centre, a path leads to this 1888 red-brick church. Its peaceful woodland cemetery is pinpricked with *krikstai* – crosses carved from wood to help the deceased ascend to heaven more easily.

Amber Gallery Museum GALLERY
(Gintaro galerija muziejus; www.ambergallery.lt; Pamario gatvė 20; ⊙10am-7pm mid-Apr–Sep) Opposite the church is this museum, with a small amber garden and exceptional pieces of amber jewellery. It runs a second gallery, **Kurėnas** (Naglių gatvė 18c; ⊙9am-9pm mid-Apr–Sep), in a striking glass box encased in an old wooden boat near the harbour.

WEST OF THE HARBOUR
All westward routes lead to the beach. One way is to turn north off Taikos gatvė, opposite the post office. The street bends sharply left after 150m and climbs. A path leads up the hill to the 29.3m **Urbas Hill Lighthouse** (closed to visitors), at the highest point in the area. Continue 700m along the path

behind the lighthouse to come out on a straight path that leads back down to the main road and, 400m beyond that, to the beach.

A less adventurous option is to follow Taikos gatvė westward until it meets the main Smiltynė–Nida road, then continue in the same direction along a paved footpath (signposted) through pine forest until you hit sand.

SOUTH OF THE HARBOUR
Heading south are two or three streets of fishing cottages with pretty flower-filled gardens. The **Ethnographic Fisherman's Museum** (Žejo etnografinė sodyba; www.visitneringa.com; Naglių gatvė 4; adult/child 2/1Lt; ⊙10am-6pm daily May-Sep, 10am-5pm Tue-Sat Sep-May) is a peek at Nida in the 19th century, with original weathervanes decorating the garden, and rooms inside arranged as they were a couple of centuries ago.

Beyond Lotmiškio gatvė a path leads along the coastline and through a wooded area to a meadow at the foot of the **Parnidis Dune** (Parnidžio kopos), an unforested, 7km thread of golden sand that snakes south into Russia. In the meadow, dubbed 'Silence Valley', walkers can pick up the **Parnidis Cognitive Path** (Parnidžio pažintinis takas),

Nida

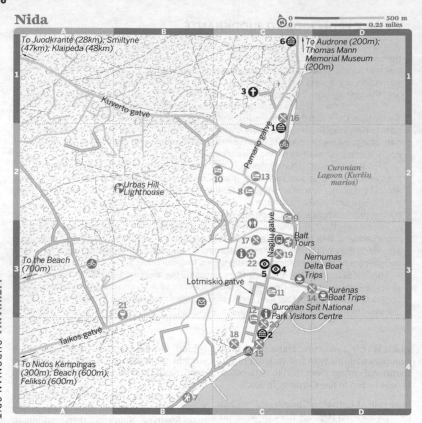

0 — 500 m
0 — 0.25 miles

To Juodkrantė (28km); Smiltynė (47km); Klaipėda (48km)

To Audrone (200m); Thomas Mann Memorial Museum (200m)

Kuverto gatvė

Urbas Hill Lighthouse

Curonian Lagoon (Kuršių marios)

Pamario gatvė

Naglių gatvė

Balt Tours

Nemumas Delta Boat Trips

To the Beach (700m)

Lotmiskio gatvė

Kurėnas Boat Trips

Curonian Spit National Park Visitors Centre

Taikos gatvė

To Nidos Kempingas (300m); Beach (600m); Felikso (600m)

a 1.8km nature trail with information panels highlighting dune flora and fauna. At the bottom of the flight of 180 steps, two dune photographs are displayed – one taken in 1960, the other in 2002. The difference in dune height – 20m in 40 years – is a warning to those keen to romp in the sand.

At the top of the spectacularly high bare dune, a panorama of sand, both coastlines, the forests to the north, and a mixture of sand and forests to the south is unforgettable. Park authorities have left the smashed remains of the granite **sundial** that stood 12m tall on the 52m dune peak until 1999, when a hurricane sent it crashing to the ground as a symbol of 'nature's uncontrollable forces' – another warning to wannabe sand rompers.

From here, the Kaliningrad border is 3km south – see the signs. If you stick to the designated wooden footpaths, you have no chance of wandering into Russia by mistake.

From the dune, the Parnidis Cognitive Path continues past the lighthouse and pine forest to Taikos gatvė.

🛏 Sleeping

Prices in Nida fluctuate wildly between winter and summer; high-season prices (June, July and August) are listed here. During the 'cold' season (October to April), rates can fall by half (and many places close down altogether). The places listed here are open year-round, but be sure to call ahead if you're travelling outside the summer season. Camping is available at Nidos Kempingas (camping in the wild can land you a 500Lt fine).

TOP
CHOICE **Misko namas**   GUESTHOUSE €€
(☎52 290; www.miskonamas.com; Pamario gatvė 11-2; r from 250Lt; 🅿) This unpretentious guesthouse is an appealing sky-blue cottage laden with flower boxes and

Nida

⊙ **Sights**
1 Amber Gallery Museum C2
2 Ethnographic Fisherman's
   Museum...C4
3 Evangelical-Lutheran Church.............C1
4 Kurėnas C3
5 Lucijos Ratai......................................C3
6 Neringa History Museum....................C1
   Pedalo Hire....................................(see 5)

⊕ **Activities, Courses & Tours**
7 Parnidis Cognitive Path.....................B4

⊜ **Sleeping**
8 Hotel Jūratė C2
9 Inkaro Kaimas....................................C2
10 Misko Namas C2
11 Naglis...C3
12 Poilsis Nidojė...................................C4
13 Vila Banga C2

⊗ **Eating**
14 Čili Pica D3
15 Ešerinė..C4
16 Laumė C1
   Market ....(see 11)
17 Maxima Supermarket C3
18 Nidos Seklyčia C4
19 Smoked Fish Outlet...........................C3
20 Užeiga Sena Sodyba C4

⊜ **Drinking**
21 In Vino..B3

⊛ **Entertainment**
22 Agila Cultural Centre.........................C3

oozing charm. Every room has a fridge, sink and kettle, and a couple have fully fledged kitchens and balconies. Guests can cook meals in a communal kitchen, hire bicycles, choose books from the small library, or laze in the garden.

Vila Banga GUESTHOUSE €€
(☑51 139; www.nidosbanga.lt; Pamario gatvė 2; d 260Lt, apt 400-500Lt) This pristine wooden house with bright-blue shutters and perfect thatched roof is a gem of a guesthouse. It has seven comfortable rooms in its pinewood interior and a sauna (100Lt per hour).

Naglis GUESTHOUSE €€
(☑51 124; www.naglis.lt; Naglių gatvė 12; d/apt 250/300Lt; ℗) This charming guesthouse in a wooden house between the market, main street and harbour is full of smiles.

Doubles comprise two rooms, and most have a door opening out to the table-dotted, tree-shaded garden. There's a dining room and kitchen for guests to share, one room has a fireplace and sauna (100Lt per hour), and the guesthouse hires out bikes (8/30Lt per hour/day).

Inkaro Kaimas GUESTHOUSE €€
(☑8-698 85003; www.inkarokaimas.lt; Naglių gatvė 26-1; d 280Lt; ℗) Blue pillars prop up this beautifully maintained red wooden house on the water's edge. Accommodation is in individual apartments, each with its own entrance. The place dates from 1901 and a couple of pine-furnished rooms boast a balcony overlooking the lagoon. Look for the giant anchor in its small but sweet garden.

Poilsis Nidojė GUESTHOUSE €€
(☑8-686 31698; www.neringahotels.lt; Naglių gatvė 11; d from 270Lt; ℗) Another wooden-house favourite, Poilsis Nidojė sports spacious yet cosy doubles with kitchenettes. Interior design is rustic, an optional breakfast (20Lt) is served in the kitchen around a shared table, and guests can cook up dinner on a barbecue in the pretty garden.

Audrone GUESTHOUSE €€
(☑52 676; r without/with balcony 200/300Lt; ℗) Located next to the Thomas Mann Memorial Museum, this guesthouse has enormous rooms, shared facilities (including a full kitchen) and really stunning views of the lagoon.

Hotel Jūratė HOTEL €€
(☑52 300; www.hotel-jurate.lt; Pamario gatvė 3; s/d from 156/225Lt; ℗) This hotel looks and feels like a sanatorium but its supremely central position and relatively cheap rooms help to balance things out. Soviet diehards will be thrilled to know that the hotel's most recent facelift didn't get rid of the kitsch glitter cement on the corridor walls.

Nidos Kempingas CAMPGROUND €
(☑52 045; www.kempingas.lt; Taikos gatvė 45a; site per tent 11-17Lt, per person 17-22Lt, car 11-17Lt, d from 250Lt, 4-/6-room studios with garden 350/490Lt; ℗⊛) Set in pine forest at the foot of a path that leads to Parnidis Dune, this spruced-up campsite has accommodation to suit all budgets. Double rooms have satellite TV and fridge, and apartments are fully equipped for self-caterers. There are also bikes for hire, and basketball and tennis courts to use.

LITHUANIA CURONIAN SPIT NATIONAL PARK

✖ Eating

Opening hours follow the Nida standard: 10am to 10pm daily mid-May to mid-September unless otherwise stated. Out of season, little is open.

Self-caterers have to make do with the **Maxima supermarket** (Taikos gatvė; ☺7am-midnight) in the centre of town. The one-stall **market** (opposite Naglių gatvė 17) sells plastic cups of wild strawberries, cranberries and other berries picked fresh from the forest, while Nida's **smoked fish outlet** (Rūkyta žuvis; Naglių gatvė 18), next to the bus station, has *ungurys* (long slippery eel), *starkis* (pikeperch), *stinta* (smelt), *ešerys* (perch) and *karšis* (bream).

TOP CHOICE Nidos Seklyčia — FISH €€
(☑50 001; www.neringaonline.lt; Lotmiškio gatvė 1; mains 30-50Lt) Lovely, lovely, lovely. With a small terrace looking directly onto the lagoon and Kaliningrad beyond, there's no better place to chow down on Curonian fish while watching the sun set behind the dune. Open all year. Worth booking ahead in summer.

Užeiga Sena Sodyba — LITHUANIAN €€
(Naglių gatvė 6; mains 16-25Lt) The selection of fish dishes at this delightful wooden cottage restaurant is impressive – and inviting – but it's the pancakes that win the day here. If you're here during berry season you'll be in gastronomic heaven.

Felikso — LITHUANIAN €
(Taikos gatvė 58; mains 10-20Lt) This simple place in among the pines is the only real spot for lunch, dinner or a drink near the beach. The smell of smoking fish is a huge enticement. Open from June to August.

Ešerinė — LITHUANIAN €€
(Naglių gatvė 2; mains 20-40Lt) With its odd Hawaiian-style construction, Ešerinė looks completely out of place. However, its vast waterfront terrace and views of the Parnidis Dune make it massively popular for dining. Choose from a variety of fish dishes or mainland Lithuanian cuisine.

Laumė — PIZZA €
(www.nidospastoge.com; Pamario gatvė 24-3a; mains 12-20Lt) Towards the north of town is this simple eatery offering standard international fodder such as pizza and pasta. Better yet are the awesome views and fresh air provided by the delightful flower-bedecked terrace. Open from June to August.

Čili Pica — PIZZA €
(www.cili.lt; Naglių gatvė 16; mains 15-30Lt; ☺9am-3am) It may be a chain but no one seems to care. Pop in for decent pizzas and Lithuanian cuisine, and take advantage of the pavement terrace overlooking bobbing boats. After sunset it transforms into a lively bar (for Nida, at least).

🍸 Drinking & Entertainment

People don't come to Nida to party. For drinking, try Čili Pica or **In Vino** (Taikos gatvė 32), the only places showing any life after dark. Both are open from about mid-May to early September.

Agila Cultural Centre (Taikos gatvė 4), adjoining the tourist office, has the occasional disco, film and art exhibition.

❶ Information

Balt Tours (☑51 190; www.balttours.lt; Naglių gatvė 18; ☺9am-7pm May-Sep, 9am-5pm Oct-Apr) Books bus and ferry tickets, has information on Nemunas Delta boat trips and organises ice-fishing in winter.

Bankas Snoras (Naglių gatvė 27) Currency exchange and ATM opposite the bus station.

Curonian Spit National Park Visitors Centre (see p351)

Laundry (Taikos gatvė 4a; per load 20Lt, soap 3Lt; ☺10am-7pm Mon-Sat) Shock, horror! A self-service laundry in Lithuania! Open from June to August.

Pharmacy (Taikos gatvė 11; ☺8.30am-8.30pm Mon-Sat May-Sep)

Police (☑52 202; Taikos gatvė 5)

Post office (Taikos gatvė 15) In the Palvė Hotel.

Tourist office (☑52 345; www.visitneringa .com; Taikos gatvė 4; ☺10am-8pm Mon-Sat, to 3pm Sun Jun-Aug, 9am-5pm Mon-Fri Sep-May) Handy office sells maps, provides info on boat trips and guides, helps book accommodation (5Lt) and stocks loads of information (including photographs) about private rooms and flats to rent.

❶ Getting There & Away

The Nida **bus station** (☑54 859; Naglių gatvė 20) has services every one or two hours to and from Smiltynė (11Lt, one hour) between 6am and 8pm, stopping en route in Juodkrantė (7Lt, 35 minutes). From Smiltynė take the passenger ferry to Klaipėda. For longer trips, there is one bus daily at 3.15pm to Vilnius (81Lt, six hours), at 4.30pm to Kaunas (67Lt, 4½ hours), and at 8.09am to Kaliningrad (30Lt, three hours).

Nemunas Delta

📖441

The low-lying, marsh-dotted eastern side of the Curonian Lagoon (Kuršių marios) could be the end of the world. Tourism has scarcely touched this remote rural and isolated landscape where summer skies offer magnificent views of the spit's white dunes across the lagoon. In winter ice-fishers sit on the frozen lagoon – up to 12km wide in places – waiting for a smelt to bite.

The gateway into the extraordinary Nemunas Delta (Nemuno Delta), where the Nemunas River ends its 937km journey from its source in neighbouring Belarus, is Šilutė (population 21,000), a sleepy town an hours' drive south of Klaipėda. The cluster of islands forms a savage but beautiful landscape protected since 1992 by the Nemunas Delta Regional Park (Nemuno Deltos Regioninis Parkas; www.nemuno delta.lt). One-fifth of the park is water – which freezes most winters, exposing hardy residents to extreme weather conditions. Rusnė Island, the largest island, covers 48 sq km and increases in size by 15cm to 20cm a year.

Boat is the main form of transport; villagers travel in and out of the park by an amphibious tractor from March to mid-May, when merciless spring floods plunge about 5% of the park under water. In 1994 floodwaters rose to 1.5m in places, although 40cm to 70cm is the norm.

From Nida there are seasonal boats (p354) across the lagoon to the delta settlement of Mingė (also called Minija after the river that forms the main 'street' through the village). No more than 100 people live in Mingė – dubbed the 'Venice of Lithuania' – and only a handful of people still speak Lietuvinkai, an ethnic dialect of Lithuanian distinct to the delta. The 19th-century riverside houses are made of wood with reed roofs and are protected architectural monuments.

A good way to explore this area is by bicycle; from Mingė a cycling track runs around Lake Krokų Lanka, the largest lake in the park at 4km long and 3.3km wide.

⊙ Sights & Activities

In the heart of the Nemunas Delta is Rusnė, on the island of the same name, 8km southwest of Šilutė, where the main stream divides into three: the Atmata, the Pakalnė and the Skirvytė. In this fishing village there's nothing to do except regret not bringing a picnic to enjoy on its pretty riverbanks and visit the tiny Ethnographic Farmstead Museum (Etnografinė Sodyba Muziejus; admission by donation; ⊙10am-6pm Fri-Sun mid-May–mid-Sep), signposted 1.8km from the village. Exhibitions of tools, furnishings and three farm buildings (in exceptional condition considering their age) reflect the harsh face of delta life centuries ago – and today.

Dike-protected polders (land reclaimed from the sea) cover the park, the first polder being built in 1840 to protect Rusnė. The red-brick water-pumping station (1907) near the lighthouse (švyturys) in Uostadvaris, 8km from the bridge in Rusnė, now houses the tiny Polder Museum (admission by donation; ⊙variable); you can swim in the river from the small beach here. Many lower polders are still flooded seasonally and serve as valuable spawning grounds for various fish species (there are some 60 in the park). Close by, on the shores of Lake Dumblė, is Lithuania's lowest point, 1.3m below sea level.

Ventės Ragas (World's Edge) is a sparsely inhabited area on the south-pointing promontory of the delta, which, with its dramatic nature and uplifting isolation, is beautifully wild. A Teutonic Order castle was built here in the 1360s to protect shipping, only for it to collapse within a couple of hundred years due to severe storms on this isolated point. The church was rebuilt, only to be storm-wrecked again in 1702. Its stones were used to build a new church at Kintai, 10km north on the regional park's northeastern boundary.

Bar a few fishers' houses and the lighthouse (1862), the main attraction here is the Ventės Ragas Ornithological Station (adult/child 4/2Lt; ⊙10am-5pm daily Jun-Sep, Mon-Fri Oct-May), 66km south of Klaipėda at the end of the Kintai–Ventė road.

The first bird-ringing station was established here in 1929, but it was not until 1959 to 1960 that large bird traps were installed. Today, around 100,000 birds pass through the station each migratory period; zigzag, snipe, cobweb and duck traps ensnare birds to be ringed. Two exhibition rooms inside the station explain the birdlife, and an observation deck encourages visitors to spot species first-hand. The station or tourist office can put you in contact with local English-speaking ornithological guides.

BIRDING IN THE NEMUNAS DELTA

This wetland is a birder's heaven. Some 270 of the 330 bird species found in Lithuania frequent the Nemunas Delta Regional Park and many rare birds breed in the lush marshes around Rusnė, including black storks, white-tailed eagles, black-tailed godwits, pintails, dunlin, ruff and great snipe. The common white stork breeds like there's no tomorrow in Ventė.

The Arctic–European–East African bird-migration flight path cuts through the park, making it a key spot for migratory waterfowl. But it's not just a stopover or feeding site – the park is a breeding ground for around 170 species of bird, and some, such as the pintail, don't breed anywhere else in Lithuania.

Rare aquatic warblers, corncrakes, black-headed gulls, white-winged black terns and great crested grebes have their biggest colonies in the delta. In autumn up to 200,000 birds – 80% of which are tits and finches – fly overhead at any one time in the sky above Ventės Ragas Ornithological Station (p359), and up to 5000 are ringed each day for research into world migration.

🛏 Sleeping & Eating

Campers can pitch tents at designated spots in the park – the regional park office can tell you where – but bring food provisions with you. Wonderful farm accommodation is spread throughout the delta and can be organised through the regional park office or the tourist office in Šilutė; many also advertise their services. Beds cost on average 50Lt a night and meals can often be arranged for a little extra; a taste of delta life, though, is priceless.

Laimutės   HOTEL €€

(☎59 690; r 150Lt; P🐾) Laimutės is an all-in-one package, offering eye-catching rooms, a wellness and sauna centre, bicycle hire, boat and farm trips, winter lake fishing, and, despite all the activities, peace and relaxation. Its restaurant only uses organic produce from local farmers, and freshly caught trout from the nearby lake. The room price includes breakfast and dinner. Find Laimutės about 15km east of Šilutė in Žemaičių Naumiestis.

Kintai   GUESTHOUSE €€

(☎47 339; www.kintai.lt; d/tr/q from 150/200/260Lt; P) This hotel-restaurant and boating complex attracts guests with comfort, seclusion and a plethora of waterbound activities. All rooms come with balcony, and some literally sit on water (located in a house boat). There are also places to pitch tents (person/tent 10/10Lt). Fishing trips can be organised, as can tours of the delta by boat. Find Kintai 6km east of Kintai village on the Minija River.

Ventainė   HOTEL, CAMPGROUND €€

(☎68 525; www.ventaine.lt in Lithuanian; Ventė; campsite per adult/car/tent 10/10/10Lt, cabins 120Lt, d from 200Lt; P@🐾) This complex, a 20-minute walk from the ringing station, sits on the lagoon shore with views of the spit's sandy dunes. Comfy villa rooms have fridge and heated bathroom floors, and campers are well catered for with wooden huts, campsites and a clean, modern shower-and-toilet block. Its restaurant serves imaginative Lithuanian cuisine (mains 20Lt to 35Lt), including very good fish soup.

ℹ Information

An influx of government and EU money to increase tourism is steadily making the region more accessible.

Regional park headquarters (☎58 154; www .nemunodelta.lt; Pakalne gatvė 40; ⊗8am-noon & 12.45-5pm Mon-Fri) In the tiny village of Rusnė; it can also help with organising itineraries, and additionally has rooms and bicycles for hire.

Šilutė tourist office (☎77 785; www.silute info.lt; Lietuvininkų gatvė 10; ⊗8am-5pm Mon-Thu, 8am-3.45pm Fri) This immensely helpful office on Šilutė's main road should be the first port of call for those seeking information on accommodation, activities and transport. Among other things, it produces a handy cycling guide to the region and the annual newspaper *Šilutės kraštas*, which covers accommodation and cultural events in the delta.

ℹ Getting There & Around

Getting to the area without your own wheels is tough. In summer Šilutė is served by several buses a day to/from Klaipėda (12Lt, one hour), as well as a handful of buses to/from Kaunas (40Lt, 3½ hours) and Vilnius (50Lt, 5¼ hours).

Boats are the best means of exploring the delta (it's 8km from Pakalnė to Kintai by boat but 45km by road). The main routes follow the three main delta tributaries – the Atmata (13km), Skirvytė (9km) and Pakalnė (9km) Rivers – which fan out westwards from Rusnė.

At Kintai, Ventainė and Laimutės you can hire out boats with a boatman-guide. The offices in Šilutė can also help.

Palanga

♪460 / POP 17,594

Palanga is a seaside resort with a split personality – peaceful pensioner paradise in winter, pounding party spot in summer. Tourists from all over Lithuania and abroad come for its idyllic 10km sandy beach backed by sand dunes and scented pines.

Despite the crowds and encroaching neon, Palanga, 25km directly north of Klaipėda, retains a semblance of its traditional charm, with wooden houses and the ting-a-ling of bicycle bells and pedal-powered taxis adding a quaint air to red-brick Basanavičiaus gatvė – the pedestrian heart of the action.

History

Palanga has often been Lithuania's only port over the centuries; however, it was destroyed by the Swedes in 1710. It was a resort in the 19th century, and a Soviet hot spot. After 1991, villas and holiday homes nationalised under the Soviets were slowly returned to their original owners, and family-run hotels and restaurants opened. In 2005 the city's main pedestrian street enjoyed a facelift befitting the sparkling reputation Palanga now enjoys.

◉ Sights & Activities

Nearly all of the action happens on Basanavičiaus gatvė, a long pedestrian-only concourse that runs perpendicular to the coast and is lined end to end with restaurants, cafes, bars and shops. South of here are the city's two leading non-beach attractions: the Botanical Park and Amber Museum.

BASANAVIČIAUS GATVĖ

A stroll along Basanavičiaus gatvė is a sight in itself – and it's the way most holidaymakers pass dusky evenings. Stalls selling amber straddle the eastern end

and amusements dot its entire length – inflatable slides, bungee-jump simulators, merry-go-rounds, electric cars, portrait artists, buskers and street performers with monkeys. A discordant note amid all this party madness is struck by the small photographic display inside the Resistance Museum (Basanavičiaus gatvė 21; admission free; ⊙4-6pm Wed, Sat & Sun), dedicated to those who struggled against Soviet oppression and the many who were exiled to Siberia for their efforts.

From the end of Basanavičiaus gatvė, a boardwalk leads across the dunes to the pier. By day, street vendors sell popcorn, *ledai* (ice cream), *dešrainiai* (hot dogs), *alus* and *gira* here. At sunset (around 10pm in July), families and lovers gather here on the sea-facing benches to watch the sunset.

From the pier end of Basanavičiaus, a walking and cycling path wends north and south through pine forest. Skinny paths cut west onto the sandy beach at several points. Follow the main path (Meilės alėja) about 500m south onto Darius ir Girėno gatvė, to reach the Botanical Park, where cycling and walking tracks are rife.

BOTANICAL PARK & AMBER MUSEUM

Lush greenery and swans gliding on still lakes make Palanga's Botanical Park a haven of peace after the frenetic-paced beach and town centre. The 1-sq-km park includes a rose garden, 18km of footpaths and Birutė Hill (Birutės kalnas), once a pagan shrine. According to legend, it was tended by vestal virgins, one of whom, Birutė, was kidnapped and married by Grand Duke Kęstutis. A 19th-century chapel tops the hill.

Amber Museum   MUSEUM
(Gintaro muziejus; www.pgm.lt; Vytauto gatvė 17; adult/child 8/4Lt; ⊙10am-8pm Tue-Sat, to 7pm Sun Jun-Aug, 11am-5pm Tue-Sat, 11am-4pm Sun Sep-May) This highly popular museum showcases what is reputedly the world's sixth-largest collection of Baltic gold – 20,000-odd examples in all. An additional highlight here is the sweeping neoclassical palace that houses the museum and was built in 1897. Visitors are welcome until one hour before closing.

NORTH OF THE BOTANICAL PARK

Amber Processing Gallery   GALLERY
(Gintaro dirbtuvės galerija; Dariaus ir Girėno gatvė 27; admission free; ⊙10am-6pm Mon-Sat) In the late 19th century Palanga was one of the largest

Palanga

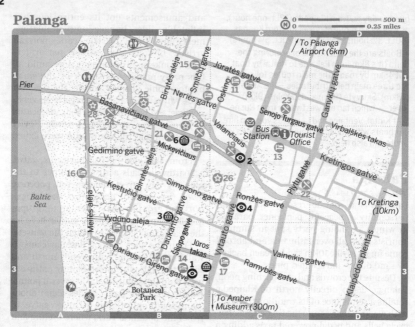

amber-processing centres in the Baltic, its amber products being transported first to Russia, from where they were sent all around the world. The town was graced with a dozen or so amber workshops, but today only this one remains. Run by the Palanga Guild of Amber Masters, the gallery sells beautiful amber pieces (jewellery, sculptures, chessboards etc). The masters ply their trade in a workshop above the gallery, where it's possible to try your hand at fashioning your own piece of amber jewellery. Exceptional works of the Baltic gold are also for sale at **Baltijos Aukas** (Vytauto gatvė 66; ⊙10am-9pm).

Antanas Mončys House Museum MUSEUM
(Antonio Mančio namai muzeijus; Daukanto gatvė 16; adult/child 4/2Lt; ⊙1-7pm Wed-Sun) This museum displays large wooden sculptures, collages and masks by Lithuanian émigré artist Antanas Mončys (1921–93).

Dr Jono Šliūpas Memorial House MUSEUM
(Jono Šliūpo memorialinė sodyba; Vytauto gatvė 23a; adult/child 2/1Lt; ⊙noon-7pm daily Jun-Aug, 11am-5pm Tue-Sun Sep-May) Fascinating black-and-white photos of old Palanga fill this house, the former home of the town's first mayor.

✿ Festivals & Events

Palanga Seals FOOD
(Palangos ruoniai) The 'seals' in question are actually smelts, the tiny fish delicacy that arrive on Palanga's shores for a short period in February. During this three-day festival in mid-February the smelts are prepared around town in all their glory. As an added attraction, hundreds of hardy souls brave the cold waters of the Baltic for a polar bear swim.

Palanga Summer Festival STREET ARTS, MUSIC
(www.palangosvasara.lt) The highlight of the summer season, the festival opens on the first Saturday of June and closes with a massive street carnival, song festival and pop concert on the last Saturday in August. It's one long merry-go-round of music concerts of all genres.

🛏 Sleeping

In season (June to August), try haggling with one of the many locals who stand at the eastern end of Kretingos gatvė touting 'Nuomojami kambariai' (rooms for rent) signs. Many houses on Nėries gatvė and Birutės alėja carry the same sign. Count on paying 50Lt to 100Lt a night, depending on room quality and facilities. Alternatively,

Palanga

◎ Sights

1	Amber Processing Gallery	B3
2	Amber Stalls	C2
3	Antanas Mončys House Museum	B2
4	Baltijos Aukas	C2
5	Dr Jono Šliūpas Memorial House	B3
6	Resistance Museum	B2

🛏 Sleeping

7	Corona Maris	A3
8	Ema	C1
9	Hotel Alanga	B1
10	Hotel Palanga	B3
11	Mama Rosa	C1
12	Palangos Vėtra	B3
13	Palbiuras	C2
14	Pusų Paunksnėje	B3
15	Seklytėlė	B1
16	Vasaros Ambasada	A2
17	Vila Ramybė	C3
18	Vila Žaigždė	B2

🍴 Eating

19	Baras 1925	C2
20	Čagino	B2
	Čili Pica	(see 28)
21	Lašas	B2
22	Maxima	C2
23	Mini Maxima	C1
24	Žuvinė	A1

⊕ Entertainment

25	Exit	B1
26	Open-air Concert Hall	C2
27	Piano	B2
28	Šachmatinė	A1

check with the tourist office or contact the apartment-rental agency **Palbiuras** (⌨51 500; www.palbiuras.lt; Kretingos gatvė 12; ☺9am-6pm Mon-Fri).

Prices listed are for the summer season, when everything gets booked up fast; winter sees rates slashed by up to 50%.

TOP CHOICE **Hotel Palanga** HOTEL €€€
(⌨41 414; www.palangahotel.lt; Birutės alėja 60; d 600-700Lt, 1-/2-room apt 1200/1600Lt; P@🛜🏊) This swish hotel of glass and wood wrapped in a grove of pine trees is a stunner. Rooms peer out on blue sky and tree trunks, treetops or sea (in the case of the top floor), while furnishings

are subtle and luxurious, with natural hues of amber, cream and sand predominating. Some even sport their own sauna or Jacuzzi. The outdoor pool is a sparkling expanse of blue between trees while the sauna complex is, as the hotel bumf phrases it, 'an oasis for body and soul'.

Vila Ramybė GUESTHOUSE €€
(⌨54 124; www.vilaramybe.lt; Vytauto gatvė 54; d 180-250Lt; P@🛜) It is tricky to snag a room at this stylish, unpretentious standout. This 1920s wooden villa is the pick of the crop as far as Vilnius trendies are concerned. Pine-clad rooms come in soothing pastel hues of blues and greens, seven of the 12 have a terrace and most have a little lounge. Its terrace restaurant is equally hip.

Mama Rosa GUESTHOUSE €€
(⌨48 581; www.mamarosa.lt; Jūratės gatvė 28a; s/d from 320/420Lt; P@🛜) The height of romance, Mama Rosa has eight sweet rooms, each cosily furnished English-style with fireplace, heated bathroom floor and wrought-iron bedheads. There is a stylish lounge and restaurant as well as a sauna complex and Jacuzzi.

Palangos Vėtra HOTEL €€
(⌨53 032; www.palangosvetra.lt; Daukanto gatvė 35; s/d from 300/400Lt; P@🛜🏊) An oasis of Scandinavian glass and wood, Palangos Vėtra accommodates every guest's need. Standouts include an excellent inhouse restaurant, the quick-service coffee bar and the spa and wellness centre, with its complex of pools and whirlpools. It's situated in a quiet area of town.

Corona Maris GUESTHOUSE €€
(⌨8-620 31535; www.coronamaris.lt; Darius ir Girėno gatvė 5; d/q 400/700Lt; P@🛜) This smart guesthouse offers accommodation in luxury apartments in two sizes, for two or four persons. All of the apartments come with efficiency kitchens, sittings rooms and extras like heated floors in the living room. The larger apartments come with fireplaces.

Vila Žaigždė PENSION €€
(⌨49 012; Daukanto gatvė 6; r 200-250Lt; P) Žaigždė may only be steps away from Basanavičiaus gatvė, but it's miles away in atmosphere. This lovingly renovated villa has massive yet cosy rooms with a touch of romance about them, and the ground

LITHUANIA PALANGA

floor is given over to a popular Ukrainian restaurant. Breakfast is an extra 20Lt.

Vasaros Ambasada
HOTEL €€

(☎8-698 08333; www.palangosambasada.lt; Meilės alėja 16; r 345Lt; P) This attractive smaller hotel enjoys one of the most enviable locations in town: right on the coast, but a few metres away from the throngs on Basanavičiaus gatvė. The rooms are plainly furnished and there's not much English spoken here, but everything is clean and well tended.

Pusų Paunksnėje
GUESTHOUSE €€

(☎49 080; www.pusupaunksneje.lt; Dariaus ir Girėno gatvė 25; d 700Lt, apt 800-1500Lt; P@☎) We love this upscale, rustic guesthouse owned by Lithuanian basketball star Arvydas Sabonis, and not just for the rooms. It's the only lodging establishment we've ever seen with a full-sized basketball court on the premises, where guests are invited to a little three-on-three action. The guesthouse has 14 luxury apartments, each with fireplace.

Hotel Alanga
HOTEL €€

(☎49 215; www.alanga.lt; Nėries gatvė 14; d/ste/apt 250/360/480Lt; P@☎☎) Families will love this hotel. It has a children's playroom, nanny care, billiard room and fitness centre alongside spotlessly clean and comfortable rooms. The decor is a bit bleak but balconies are livened up with bright-red dahlias.

Seklytėlė
GUESTHOUSE €

(☎57 415; Jūratės gatvė 18; r 100-150Lt) Above the restaurant of the same name are large rooms going for a song in summer. The furniture and bedding may not entirely match but that doesn't distract from their homey feel. The cheaper variety have shared facilities.

Ema
GUESTHOUSE €

(☎48 608; www.ema.lt; Jūratės gatvė 32; r from 150Lt) This basic guesthouse has stripped-back rooms in every pastel colour known to man. A cactus marks the spot.

✖ Eating

Basanavičiaus gatvė plays host to the majority of restaurants in town, but the focus here is on mass appeal over quality. There are, however, a few diamonds in the rough. Don't pass over your own hotel's restaurant as it could be serving some of the best food in town. For instance Seklytėlė (mains 12Lt to 30Lt) has a wonderful selection of pancakes, and granny quilts for chilly

evenings; Vila Žaigždė (mains 20Lt to 35Lt) whips up a Ukrainian storm in its kitchen; Vila Ramybė (mains 15Lt to 30Lt) has sweet service and formidable *cepelinai* (dumplings); and Pusų Paunksnėje (mains 30Lt to 50Lt) specialises in silver service.

Self-caterers should check out **Maxima** (Plytų gatvė 9; ☺7am-midnight) and **Mini Maxima** (Senojo Turgaus gatvė 1; ☺8am-midnight) supermarkets.

Baras 1925
LITHUANIAN €€

(Basanavičiaus gatvė 4; mains 20-40Lt; ☺10am-midnight) Sunk down from Basanavičiaus, this old wooden house provides relief from the main-street madness. The Lithuanian cuisine is good and simple, and the restaurant's back garden with church view is the least Disneylike you'll find.

Lašas
STEAKHOUSE €€

(www.lasashotel.com; Basanavičiaus gatvė 29; mains 20-40Lt; ☺10am-midnight) Highly recommended steaks cooked to order, as well as grilled pork and offerings like duck and venison. Eat on the terrace in nice weather.

Čagino
RUSSIAN €€

(Basanavičiaus gatvė 14a; mains 20-50Lt; ☺noon-midnight) This Russian restaurant offers something a little different from the standard Lithuanian and pizza fare, like traditional Russian pancakes.

Čili Pica
ITALIAN €

(www.cili.lt; Basanavičiaus gatvė 45; 20/50cm pizza from 12/48Lt; ☺10am-11pm) This pizzeria is the face of Palanga, with its mixed crowd of kid-clad couples, noisy families and young beauties out to party. Find it propped up on candyfloss-pink pillars.

Žuvinė
FISH €€

(http://zuvine.lt; Basanavičiaus gatvė 37a; fish 30-70Lt; ☺11am-11pm) For a seaside resort, there are not many places to get fresh fish. This overpriced eatery toward the seashore end of Basanavičiaus gatvė is arguably the best in town. There are some local fish on the menu, but the waiter will inevitably try to steer you toward more expensive international varieties.

☆ Entertainment

The tourist office knows what's on where. Concerts are often held at the **Open-air Concert Hall** (Vasaros Estrada; ☎52 210; Vytauto gatvė 43), and Vila Ramybė (p363) hosts regular live music evenings.

Clubs only kick on in summer: **Piano** (Basanavičiaus gatvė 24a) and **Šachmatinė** (Basanavičiaus gatvė 45) play standard pop; **Exit** (Neries gatvė 39) attracts international DJs.

ℹ Information

Jāņa sēta's *Palanga* town plan (1:15,000), featuring Palanga and Šventoji, costs 9Lt and is available from the tourist office.

Bankas Snoras Basanavičiaus (Basanavičiaus gatvė); Jūratės (cnr Vytauto & Jūratės gatvė) Blue booths with currency exchange and ATM.

Laukinių Vakarų Salūnas (Basanavičiaus gatvė 16; internet per hr 6Lt; ☺9am-7am) Saloon bar with internet room.

Palangos vaistinė (Vytauto gatvė 33; ☺9am-8pm Mon-Fri, 9am-6pm Sat, 9am-4pm Sun) Pharmacy in the former KGB headquarters (1944–51).

Police station (☎53 837; Vytauto gatvė 4)

Post office (Vytauto gatvė 53)

Tourist office (☎48 811; www.palangatic.lt; Kretingos gatvė 1; ☺9am-7pm Mon-Fri, 10am-4pm Sat & Sun mid-Jun–Aug, 1-5pm Mon, 10am-5pm Tue-Sat Sep–mid-Jun) Books accommodation and sells maps and guides; at Palanga bus station.

ℹ Getting There & Away

Reach Palanga by road or air; services are substantially more frequent in summer.

Air

Palanga Airport (☎52 020; www.palanga-airport.lt; Liepojos plentas 1), 6km north of the centre, has regular passenger services to Copenhagen and Oslo via **SAS** (www.flysas.com), as well as intermittent services to Oslo with **Norwegian Air Shuttle** (www.norwegian.com) and Rīga via **airBaltic** (www.airbaltic.com).

Bus

Services at the tiny **bus station** (☎53 333; Kretingos gatvė 1) include Kaunas (50Lt, 3¼ hours, about 14 daily), Klaipėda (5Lt, 45 minutes, at least half-hourly between 4.15am and 10.35pm), Šiauliai (32Lt, three hours, eight daily) and Vilnius (66Lt, 4¼ to six hours, seven daily).

ℹ Getting Around

Bus 3 runs to and from the airport (adult/child 3/1.50Lt) roughly every hour from 7am to midnight. Timetables are posted at its town centre stop on Vytauto gatvė near the bus station.

The main taxi stand is on Kretingos gatvė in front of the bus station; a taxi from the airport into town costs between 30Lt and 35Lt.

Pedal-powered taxis are at the eastern end of Basanavičius gatvė. From May to September, bicycle-hire stalls pepper the town. Hourly/daily rates are 8/30Lt for a bicycle, 25Lt per day for a four-wheel buggy for two and 25Lt for a kid's buggy.

Around Palanga

Brash **Šventoji**, 12km north, lacks the panache of Palanga but – with its inflatable fish that spit out kids, its dodgem cars and its merry-go-round of restaurant entertainers and fun-fair rides – it entertains.

Nemirseta, a couple of kilometres south of Palanga, is known for its incredible sand dunes and for being the furthest east the Prussians ever got. Five buses daily run to Šventoji from Palanga, but to reach Nemirseta you'll need your own transport.

About 10km east of Palanga, the town of **Kretinga** is a sight for plant-lovers. A crumbling winter garden attached to the **Kretinga Museum** (Kretingos muziejus; www.kretingosmuziejus.lt; Vilniaus gatvė 20; adult/student 5/2Lt; ☺museum 10am-6pm Wed-Sun, winter garden 10am-6pm Tue-Sun, cafe noon-10pm) houses a tropical mirage of 850 species of exotic plants. The museum itself is located in one of the many homes of the Tyszkiewicz family of Polish nobles.

Kretinga is connected to Palanga by frequent buses (4Lt, 15 minutes). Find the museum west of the centre in the Kretinga city park.

Žemaitija National Park

☎448 / POP 3500

After the kitsch of Palanga, arriving at Žemaitija (zhe-mai-ti-ya) National Park is equivalent to jumping into a cool and refreshing pool. The 200-sq-km park, a magical landscape of lake and forest, is as mysterious as it is beautiful, and it's easy to see why it is enshrined in fables of devils, ghosts and buried treasure.

The draw here is two-fold. You can swim, boat and bike around at your leisure, as well as pay a visit to one of the country's newest and most bizarre attractions: a museum to the Cold War, housed in what was once a Soviet nuclear missile base.

The best access point is the small town of **Plateliai**, on the western shore of the lake of the same name and home to the helpful Žemaitija National Park Visitor Centre.

WORTH A TRIP

ORVYDAS GARDEN

Within an easy drive or bus ride from Kretinga and not far from Žemaitija National Park is one of the most unusual sights in all of Lithuania; a rock and sculpture garden as firm in its faith as the Hill of Crosses (p334) but more eccentric and in its own way even more fascinating.

The **Orvydas Garden** (adult/child 6/3Lt; ⊙10am-7pm Tue-Sun) was the work of stonemason Kazys Orvydas (1905–89) and his oldest son turned Franciscan monk, Vilius (1952–92). The carvings were originally created for the village cemetery in nearby Salantai but were brought here to the Orvydas homestead after then Soviet leader Nikita Khrushchev turned his wrath on religious objects in the 1960s. The Soviets later blocked access to the house to prevent visitors getting to the persecuted Orvydas family.

Today, visitors can walk through the lovely farmstead gardens admiring literally hundreds of statues, carvings, busts and just plain oddities. It's an experience as awe-inspiring as it is confounding, but one that will linger long in the memory. A reminder of the former Soviet presence can be seen today in the form of a rusting WWII tank in the car park.

Stone and wood carvers' workshops are held at the farmstead on a regular basis, keeping the tradition alive. A traditional Samogitian roadside cross marks the farmstead entrance, 5km south of Salantai on the road to Plungė.

Three daily buses between Kretinga and Skuodas stop in Salantai and Mosėdis. For the Orvydas Garden get off at the last stop before Salantai and walk about 1km.

About 20km northeast of the park is **Samogitian Calvary** (Žemaičių Kalvarija), built on the site of 9th- to 13th-century burial grounds. Pilgrims come here during the first two weeks of July to climb the seven hills where 20 chapels form a 7km 'Stations of the Cross' route in commemoration of Christ's life, death and resurrection.

⊙ Sights

TOP CHOICE **Cold War Museum** MUSEUM
(Šaltojo Karo Muziejus; www.zemaitijosnp.lt; Plokštinė; adult/child 10/5Lt; ⊙9am-6pm Tue-Fri, 10am-5pm Sat & Sun) The end of 2011 saw the opening of this long-anticipated museum on the site of a former Soviet nuclear missile base built in the early 1960s that once packed enough power to destroy most of Europe. The base is situated deep in the heart of the Žemaitija National Park and was kept secret from the Lithuanian people for decades. There's a small exhibition on the history of the Cold War, particularly on how it played out in the Baltic countries, and on the construction and role of the base. The highlight, however, is the chance to poke around inside one of the former missile bunkers.

The museum is situated about 8km from the national park's information centre in Plateliai and is reachable by car or bike following signs along the main road to Plokštinė and then 5km along a gravel road. Note the museum was preparing to open as we were going to press and the operating hours and admission prices listed here are indicative only and not confirmed. Visit the Žemaitija National Park website for further details. See the boxed text p361 for a history of the base and its possible role in the Cuban missile crisis of 1962.

Plateliai Manor Museum Complex MUSEUM
(www.zemaitijosnp.lt; Plateliai; adult/child 6/3Lt; ⊙9am-5pm Tue-Fri, 10am-5pm Sat & Sun Jun-Aug) A short walk from the national park's information centre brings you to the old granary and stable of the former **Plateliai Manor**, which now house a highly worthwhile museum complex. The granary holds a multistorey exhibition dedicated to the nature, history and ethnography of the area, as well as archaeological findings from Sventrokalnis and Pilies islands on the lake. The stable houses a fascinating exhibition of local Shrove Tuesday Carnival customs, complete with around 250 (scary) masks.

Žemaitija Art Museum MUSEUM
(Žemaičių dailės muziejus; Parko gatvė 1; adult/child 4/2Lt; ⊙10am-6pm Wed-Sun mid-May–Nov, till 5pm Nov–mid-May) The 19th-century Oginski Palace in the nearby city of Plungė, holds an interesting collection of modern Samogitian art (carvings and metal works).

🏃 Activities

Most activities centre around **Lake Plateliai** (Platelių ežeras), renowned for its seven islets and seven ancient shore terraces. It's the park's most stunning natural feature, and the site of midsummer celebrations on 23 and 24 June, when bonfires are lit and traditional songs sung. Legend says the lake was swept into the sky by a storm before being dropped where it lies now after the magic words 'Ale plate lej' (the rain goes wide) were uttered.

If it gets warm enough, swim in the lake. Otherwise, boats for excursions on the lake can be hired from the **Yacht Club** (🕿8-682 42062; Ežero gatvė 40).

Many traditional Samogitian festivals are celebrated in the small town of Plateliai on the lake's western shore, including the amazingly colourful **Shrove Tuesday Carnival** (Mardi Gras; the Tuesday before Ash Wednesday in the Christian calendar).

The national park visitor centre can assist in bike rentals and hands out cycling maps. One of the easiest and most enjoyable rides is to remote Plokštinė (8km), the site of the former missile base and now home to the Cold War Museum.

🛏️ Sleeping & Eating

In July and August diehards can kip the night in the former military barracks: around 15Lt gets you a bed (no hot water, no shower, one loo between everyone); the national park visitor centre can book you in.

Otherwise the visitor centre has a list of B&Bs (around 50Lt to 70Lt per person) in some fabulous farms and private homes in the park, including the flowery lakeside home of **Marija Striaukienė** (🕿49 152, 8-698 03485) in the village of Beržoras.

In Plateliai, **Julija and Bronius Staponkai** (🕿8-617 03418; jb@zebra.lt; Ežero gatvė 38; r 70-120Lt; 🅿) rent out cosy apartments and are located a short walk from the lake. For more facilities, try **Hotel Linelis** (🕿8-655 77666; www.linelis.lt; Paplatelės; s/d/tr 120/140 /160Lt; 🅿🖳), which has a fine restaurant and spa centre on the lake's eastern edge. Breakfast costs an additional 15Lt.

Eating options in Plateliai are limited, but you could do worse than dine in its **Yacht Club** (mains 15-30Lt) right on the lake, which has a limited menu but breathtaking lake views.

ℹ️ Information

National Park Visitor Centre (🕿49 231; www.zemaitijosnp.lt; Didžioji gatvė 8; ☺8am-5pm Mon-Thu, 8am-3.45pm Fri, 10am-5pm Sat Jun-Aug) In Plateliai. Issues fishing permits (1/3Lt per day/month), arranges guides (30Lt an hour, must be booked in advance), has information

FROM RUSSIA WITH LOVE

Deep in the forests of Žemaitija National Park resides a former secret Soviet underground missile base that once housed nuclear missiles with enough firepower to destroy most of Europe.

Now home to the country's only Cold War Museum (p366), this terrifying arsenal – which consisted of 22m R12 rockets with 3m warheads – lay hidden from the Lithuanian people for at least two decades.

The base, a circular underground centre, was flanked by four missile silos, only visible from the ground by their domed tops. The James Bond–style pad, which lies in Plokštinė, just a few kilometres east of the idyllic rural village of Plateliai, was equipped with electrical and radio stations, and control rooms.

Ten thousand soldiers were secretly brought in from USSR satellite states to construct the base in 1960, taking eight months to dig out the enormous 25m-deep silos. It was home to the 79th Rocket Regiment until 1978 – when the missiles mysteriously disappeared and the base was left to rot.

During its history the base deployed rockets to Cuba during the crisis in September 1962 and was put on red alert during the 1968 Warsaw Pact invasion of Czechoslovakia. The military town of Plokštinė, once home to 320 soldiers, stands nearby: travellers can sleep in its barracks (p367).

The museum is situated about 8km from the national park visitor centre in Plateliai and is reachable by car or bike following signs along the main road to Plokštinė and then 5km along a gravel road.

on yacht, windsurfer and boat hire, and can direct you to the workshops of local folk artists. It also hosts a small exhibition on park flora and fauna and provides internet access (5Lt per hour).

ⓘ Getting There & Away

Plungė, the nearest city, is best reached by train from Klaipėda (12-14.40Lt, one hour, up to five daily) and from Vilnius (46Lt, four hours, three daily). There are several buses daily from Kaunas (46Lt, four hours) and from Palanga (12Lt, 1¼ hours). From Plungė, there are limited buses onward to Plateliai.

UNDERSTAND LITHUANIA

Lithuania Today

Linguistic Tensions with Poland

Lithuania's relations with Poland have always been important, given the two countries' long bilateral history that includes, for a period in the Middle Ages, co-presiding over the largest political entity at the time on the European continent.

These days, the two EU neighbours find themselves at loggerheads over language, specifically the right of Polish students (part of the country's Polish minority of more than 200,000) to receive most of their education in the Polish language. A new Lithuanian law (passed in 2011 and due to enter into force in 2013) would make Lithuanian the language of instruction for most classes and mandate that standardised school-leaving exams be administered only in Lithuanian. The Polish minority called the law discriminatory, while the Lithuanians, for their part, argued that any student, regardless of ethnicity, would need good Lithuanian in order to succeed after graduation.

The Polish government in Warsaw cried foul, accusing the Lithuanian government of oppressing the rights of ethnic Poles. Poland's pleas assumed extra oomph by virtue of the fact the country held the EU's rotating presidency in the second half of 2011. September of that year brought thousands of Poles onto the streets in Vilnius to protest the law. The dispute was still ongoing as we went to press, but there were signs that Lithuania was ready to relent, at least in part. One compromise proposal called for gradually phasing in the law until 2018,

while another would ease the law's restrictions to allow for more classes to be taught in Polish.

How Much do You Want for that Royal Palace?

At one time several centuries ago, Vilnius' Royal Palace of the Grand Dukes (p281) was Lithuania's pride and joy. In the 17th century, the Renaissance-era structure, and especially its vast 10,000-sq-metre courtyard, buzzed with masked balls, banquets and operas. Around 1800, with the Russian occupation of Lithuania, the palace was demolished.

What better way, then, to celebrate the rebirth of a revitalised Lithuania than to rebuild the Royal Palace in all of its former splendour? At least that was the argument a decade ago, when ambitious plans were laid to reconstruct the palace, brick by brick, in its former location next to the cathedral. Instead of a banquet hall, this time around the palace would function as a museum, with displays detailing the reconstruction work and the treasure trove of Gothic and baroque archaeological finds discovered during the excavation.

The project was not without its sceptics. Many argued the rebuilding would transform the palace into a Disney-esque folly and waste hard-won government revenue that could be better put to other purposes. The naysayers were scoffed at and the project commenced in earnest. And then it stopped.

The original timetable was to reopen the palace on 6 July 2009 to mark the millennial anniversary of the first mention of Lithuania in writing, but that date was never met. Instead, delays, cost-overruns running to hundreds of millions of euros, and the inevitable whiff of corruption forced construction to grind to a halt in 2011. As of this writing, the palace is around 90% finished, and wrapped all around by high metal fencing.

The future remains unclear, though ultimately the Lithuanian government has gone too far to turn back and will have to finish the palace someday. With luck, the gala might even coincide with your visit. Check in with the Vilnius tourist information offices (p306).

Watch where You Park Your Car!

Every big city around the world has to deal with the problem of illegally parked cars that block sidewalks and cycling routes and generally pose a nuisance to the pedestrian public. The problem is especially acute – and galling – when it's millionaires who park their Mercedes and Ferraris wherever they want. After all, what's the price of a parking ticket – or even a towing fee – if you've got millions in the bank?

That was essentially the problem facing Vilnius mayor Artūras Zuokas. His pet bugbear was illegal parking on the city's main artery, Gedimino prospektas.

That's when he came up with a plan to solve the problem once and for all. His solution was to commandeer a tank from the Lithuanian army, drive it down the street, and, yes, run right over an illegally parked Mercedes.

Not surprisingly, the stunt attracted attention from around the world. As of this writing, the YouTube clip of the event (search for 'Vilius Mayor'!) had more than 3 million hits. Harvard University even awarded the mayor one of its coveted 'anti-Nobel' prizes.

Quickly, however, rumours began to surface that the whole act was staged, a stunt to bolster the mayor's sagging popularity and divert attention from corruption allegations that have dogged him most of his career.

For his part, Zuokas has stayed coy. It might have been a stunt or maybe not. He's not saying. Either way, the lesson for drivers is clear: watch where you park you car (or if it's a rental, at least have good insurance!).

History

A powerful state in its own right at its peak in the 14th to 16th centuries, Lithuania subsequently disappeared from the map in the 18th century, only to reappear briefly during the interwar period. Lithuania regained its independence in 1991 after decades of Soviet rule. Kaunas' Military Museum of Vytautas the Great (p329) and Vilnius' National Museum of Lithuania (p282) cover the whole span of Lithuania's history.

Tribal Testosterone

Human habitation in the wedge of land that makes up present-day Lithuania goes back to at least 9000 BC. Trade in amber started during the Neolithic period (6000 to 4500 years ago), providing the Balts – the ancestors of modern Lithuanians – with a readymade source of wealth when they arrived

on the scene from the southeast some time around 2000 BC.

Two millennia on, it was this fossilised pine resin and the far-flung routes across the globe its trade had forged – all brilliantly explained in Palanga's Amber Museum (p361) – that prompted a mention of the amber-gathering *aesti* on the shores of the Baltic Sea in *Germania,* a beast of a book about Germanic tribes outside the Roman Empire written in AD 98. It wasn't until AD 1009 that Litae (Latin for Lithuania) was mentioned for the first time in written sources (the *Kvedlinburgh Chronicle*) as the place where an archbishop called Brunonus was struck on the head by pagans.

By the 12th century Lithuania's peoples had split into two tribal groups: the Samogitians (lowlanders) in the west and the Aukštaitija (highlanders) in the east and southeast. Around this time, some sources say, a wooden castle was built on the top of Gediminas Hill in Vilnius.

Medieval Mayhem

In the mid-13th century Aukštaitija leader Mindaugas unified Lithuanian tribes to create the Grand Duchy of Lithuania, of which he was crowned king in 1253 at Kernavė. Mindaugas accepted Catholicism in a bid to defuse the threat from the Teutonic Order – Germanic crusaders who conquered various Prussian territories, including Memel (present-day Klaipėda). Unfortunately, neither conversion nor unity lasted very long: Mindaugas was assassinated in 1263 by nobles keen to keep Lithuania pagan and reject Christianity.

Under Grand Duke Gediminas (1316–41), Lithuania's borders extended south and east into modern-day Belarus and Ukraine, and even included Kiev for a time. After Gediminas' death, two of his sons shared the realm: in Vilnius, Algirdas pushed the southern borders of Lithuania past Kyiv, while Kęstutis – who plumped for a pretty lake island in Trakai as a site for his castle – fought off the Teutonic Order.

Algirdas' son Jogaila took control of the country in 1382, but the rising Teutonic threat forced him to make a watershed decision in the history of Europe. In 1386 he wed Jadwiga, crown princess of Poland, to become Władysław II Jagiełło of Poland and forge a Lithuanian-Polish alliance that would last 400 years. The Aukštaitija were

LATE TO THE CHURCH

While today Lithuanians are staunchly Roman Catholic (a short stroll through steeple-rich Vilnius is enough to convince any doubters), it wasn't always this way. In fact, Lithuania is considered to be the last pagan country in Europe. It wasn't fully baptised into Roman Catholicism until 1413.

There are lots of reasons for this: foremost among them was the Lithuanians' fierce independence streak that managed to repel any and every attempt to convert them.

The country's relatively recent experience (if you can call the 15th century 'recent') with paganism explains why so much of its religious art, national culture and traditions have pagan roots.

During the Soviet years, Catholicism was persecuted and hence became a symbol of nationalistic fervour. Churches were seized, closed and turned into 'museums of atheism' or used for other secular purposes (such as a radio station in the case of Christ's Resurrection Basilica in Kaunas, open for business as usual today) by the state.

After independence in 1991, the Catholic Church quickly began the process, continuing today, of reacquiring church property and reconsecrating places of worship.

These days, around 80% of Lithuanians consider themselves to be Catholics. There are small minorities of other sects and faiths, including Russian Orthodox (4%) and Protestant Christians (2%).

baptised in 1387 and the Samogitians in 1413, making Lithuania the last European country to accept Christianity.

Glory Days

Jogaila spent most of his time in Kraków, but trouble was brewing at home. In 1390 his cousin Vytautas revolted, forcing Jogaila's hand. In 1392 he named Vytautas Grand Duke of Lithuania on condition that he and Jogaila share a common policy. The decisive defeat of the Teutonic Order by their combined armies at Grünwald (in modern-day Poland) in 1410 ushered in a golden period of prosperity, particularly for the Lithuanian capital Vilnius, which saw its legendary Old Town born.

Vytautas ('the Great') extended Lithuanian control further south and east. By 1430, when he died, Lithuania stretched beyond Kursk in the east and almost to the Black Sea in the south, creating one of Europe's largest empires. Nowhere was its grandeur and clout better reflected than in 16th-century Vilnius, which, with a population of 25,000-odd, was one of eastern Europe's biggest cities. Fine late-Gothic and Renaissance buildings sprung up, and Lithuanians such as Žygimantas I and II occupied the Polish-Lithuanian throne inside the sumptuous Royal Palace.

In 1579 Polish Jesuits founded Vilnius University and made the city a bastion of the Catholic Counter Reformation. Under Jesuit influence, baroque architecture also arrived.

Polonisation & Partitions

Lithuania gradually sank into a junior role in its partnership with Poland, climaxing with the formal union of the two states (instead of just their crowns) at the Union of Lublin in 1569 during the Livonian War with Muscovy.

Under the so-called Rzeczpospolita (Commonwealth), Lithuania played second fiddle to Poland. Its gentry adopted Polish culture and language, its peasants became serfs and Warsaw usurped Vilnius as political and social hub.

A century on it was Russia's turn to play tough. In 1654 Russia invaded the Rzeczpospolita and temporarily snatched significant territory from it. By 1772 the Rzeczpospolita was so weakened that the states of Russia, Austria and Prussia simply carved it up in the Partitions of Poland (1772, 1793 and 1795). Most of Lithuania went to Russia, while a small chunk in the southwest was annexed by Prussia, but passed into Russian hands after the Napoleonic wars.

Russification & Nationalism

While neighbouring Estonia and Latvia were governed as separate provinces, Russian rule took a different stance with rebellious Lithuania.

Vilnius had quickly become a refuge for Polish and Lithuanian gentry dispossessed by the region's new Russian rulers and a focus of the Polish national revival, in which

Vilnius-bred poet Adam Mickiewicz was a leading inspiration. When Lithuanians joined a failed Polish rebellion against Russian rule in 1830, Tsarist authorities clamped down extra hard. They shut Vilnius University, closed Catholic churches and monasteries and imposed Russian Orthodoxy. Russian law was introduced in 1840 and the Russian language was used for teaching. A year after a second rebellion in 1863, books could only be published in Lithuanian if they used the Cyrillic alphabet, while publications in Polish (spoken by the Lithuanian gentry) were banned altogether.

National revival gained some momentum in the 19th and early 20th centuries. While most Lithuanians continued to live in rural areas and villages, the rapid industrialisation of Vilnius and other towns gave nationalist drives more clout. Vilnius became an important Jewish centre during this period, with Jews making up around 75,000 of its 160,000-strong population in the early 20th century to earn it the nickname 'Jerusalem of the North'.

Independence

Ideas of Baltic national autonomy and independence had been voiced during the 1905 Russian revolution, but it was not until 1918 that the restoration of the Independent State of Lithuania was declared. During WWI Lithuania was occupied by Germany and it was still under German occupation on 16 February 1918 when a Lithuanian national council, the Taryba, declared independence in Vilnius in the House of Signatories. In November, Germany signed an armistice with the Western Allies, and the same day a Lithuanian republican government was set up.

With the re-emergence of an independent Poland eager to see Lithuania reunited with it or to cede the Vilnius area, which had a heavily Polish and/or Polonised population, things turned nasty. On 31 December 1918 the Lithuanian government fled to Kaunas, and days later the Red Army installed a communist government in Vilnius. Over the next two years the Poles and Bolsheviks played a game of tug-of-war with the city, until the Poles annexed Vilnius once and for all on 10 October 1920. Thus from 1920 until 1939 Vilnius and its surrounds formed a corner of Poland, while the rest of Lithuania was ruled from Kaunas under the authoritarian rule (1926–40) of Lithuania's first president, Antanas Smetona (1874–1944).

In 1923 Lithuania annexed Memel (present-day Klaipėda), much to the displeasure of its former ruler, a much-weakened Germany.

WWII & Soviet Rule

With the signing of the Nazi-Soviet non-aggression pact in 1939 and the German invasion of Poland in September of that year, Lithuania fell into Soviet hands. The USSR insisted on signing a 'mutual-assistance pact' with Lithuania in October and returned Vilnius to the Lithuanian motherland as part of the inducement. But this was little consolation for the terror Lithuania experienced as a USSR republic – Soviet purges saw thousands upon thousands of people killed or deported.

LITHUANIA HISTORY

TOP FIVE HISTORICAL READS

» **The Last Girl** (Stephan Collishaw) Absolutely spellbinding, this superb historical novel set in Vilnius flits between WWII and the 1990s.

» **Lithuania Awakening** (Alfred Senn) From 'new winds' (the birth of the independence movement in the 1980s) to a 'new era' (independence), Senn's look at how the Lithuanians achieved independence remains the best in its field; read the entire thing free online at http://ark.cdlib.org/ark:/13030/ft3x0nb2m8.

» **And Kovno Wept** (Waldemar Ginsburg) Life in the Kovno ghetto is powerfully retold by one of its survivors.

» **Lithuania – Independent Again: The Autobiography of Vytautas Landsbergis** The scene outside parliament on 13 January 1991 is among the dramatic moments Landsbergis brings vividly to life in his autobiography.

» **Forest of the Gods** (Balys Sruoga) The author's powerful account of his time spent in the Stutthof Nazi concentration camp in the early 1940s was censored, and hence not published until 1957. It was transferred onto celluloid by Algimantas Puipa in 2005.

VILNIUS: THE 'JERUSALEM OF THE NORTH'

One of Europe's most prominent Jewish communities flourished in prewar Vilnius (Vilne in Yiddish), but Nazi (and later Soviet) brutality virtually wiped it out.

The city's Jewish roots go back some eight centuries when 3000 Jews settled in Vilnius at the invitation of Grand Duke Gediminas (1316–41). In the 19th century, Vilnius became a centre for the European Jewish language, Yiddish. Famous Jews from the city's community include rabbi and scholar Gaon Elijahu ben Shlomo Zalman (1720–97), who led opposition to the widespread Jewish mystical movement Hassidism, and landscape artist Isaak Levitan (1860–1900).

The city's Jewish population peaked on the eve of WWI at almost 100,000 (out of 240,000 in Lithuania). However, plagued by discrimination and poverty, the Jewish community diminished in the interwar years when Vilnius was an outpost of Poland.

Despite this, Vilnius blossomed into the Jewish cultural hub of Eastern Europe, and was chosen ahead of the other Yiddish centres, Warsaw and New York, as the headquarters of the Yiddish-language scientific research institute YIVO in 1925 (the institute stood on Vivulskio gatvė). Jewish schools, libraries, literature and theatre flourished. There were 100 synagogues and prayer houses, and six daily Jewish newspapers.

By the end of WWII Lithuania's Jewish community was all but destroyed and during the mid-1980s *perestroika* (restructuring) years an estimated 6000 Jews left for Israel.

Following Hitler's invasion of the USSR and the German occupation of the region in 1941, nearly all of Lithuania's Jewish population – more than 90% of the country's 200,000 Jews – was killed; most Vilnius Jews died in its ghetto or in the nearby Paneriai Forest (p308). Ethnic Lithuanians suffered proportionately much less, but thousands of Lithuanians were killed and some 80,000 were forced to escape to the West between 1944 and 1945 to avoid the Red Army's reconquest of the Baltic countries.

Immediate resistance to the reoccupation of Lithuania by the USSR, in the form of the partisan movement 'Forest Brothers', began in 1944. Discover their story in museums across the country, including the Museum of Deportation & Resistance (boxed text p325) in Kaunas.

Between 1944 and 1952 under Soviet rule, a further 250,000 Lithuanians were killed, arrested or deported, suppression of spirit and free thought being the order of the day. Nowhere is this dark period explained more powerfully than at the Museum of Genocide Victims (p293) in the old KGB headquarters in Vilnius.

Finally Free

A yearning for independence had simmered during the *glasnost* years of the mid-1980s, but it was with the storming success of Lithuania's popular front, Sajūdis, in the March 1989 elections for the USSR Congress of People's Deputies (Sajūdis won 36 of the 42 directly elected Lithuanian seats) that Lithuania surged ahead in the Baltic push for independence. The pan-Baltic human chain, which was formed to mark the 50th anniversary of the Nazi-Soviet nonaggression pact a few months later, confirmed public opinion and, in December that year, the Lithuanian Communist Party left the Communist Party of the Soviet Union.

Vast pro-independence crowds met then Soviet leader Mikhail Gorbachev when he visited Vilnius in January 1990. Sajūdis won a majority in the elections to Lithuania's supreme Soviet in February, and on 11 March the assembly declared Lithuania an independent republic. In response, Moscow carried out weeks of troop manoeuvres around Vilnius and clamped an economic blockade on Lithuania, cutting off fuel supplies.

Soviet hardliners gained the ascendancy in Moscow in the winter of 1990–91, and in January 1991 Soviet troops and paramilitary police stormed and occupied Vilnius' TV tower and TV centre, killing 14 people. Some of the barricades put up around the parliament remain. On 6 September 1991 the USSR recognised the independence of Lithuania.

Towards Europe

Lithuanians have a sense of irony: they led the Baltic push for independence then, at their first democratic parliamentary elections in 1992, raised eyebrows by voting in the ex-communist Lithuanian Democratic

Labour Party (LDDP). Presidential elections followed in 1993, the year the last Soviet soldier left the country, with former Communist Party first secretary Algirdas Brazauskas winning 60% of the vote.

It was a painful time for the country. Corruption scandals dogged Brazauskas' term in office and inflation ran wild, peaking around 1000%. Thousands of jobs were lost and the country's banking system collapsed in 1995–96.

But change was under way that would eventually fuel economic growth. The litas replaced the *talonas* (coupon), the transitional currency used during the phasing out of the Soviet rouble in Lithuania, and a stock exchange opened.

Presidential elections in 1998 ushered in wild card Valdas Adamkus (b 1926), a Lithuanian émigré and US citizen who had come to the US after WWII when his parents fled the Soviet advance.

Adamkus appointed a member of the ruling Conservative Party, 43-year-old Rolandas Paksas, prime minister in 1999. The popular Vilnius mayor and champion stunt pilot won instant approval as 'the people's choice' – so much so that he challenged Adamkus for the presidency in 2003 and won.

Large-scale privatisation took place in 1997–98, but a deep recession struck following the 1998 economic crisis in Russia. Nevertheless, Lithuania managed to claw its way back and by 2001 its economy was being praised by the International Monetary Fund as one of the world's fastest growing.

Lithuania joined the World Trade Organization in 2000, and in 2002 – in a bid to make exports competitive and show a determination to join Europe – pegged its currency to the euro instead of the US dollar.

True to his Lithuanian heritage, Adamkus battled hard in the political ring and regained the presidency in 2004 following the impeachment of Paksas for granting Lithuanian citizenship to a shady Russian businessman who was a major financial supporter. Adamkus finished his five-year term in office in 2009 and was replaced by current president Dalia Grybauskaitė, who became the country's first female head of state.

In 2004, Lithuania joined the EU and NATO and has been a staunch supporter of both ever since. In November 2004 it became the first EU member to ratify the EU constitution. The former USSR military base outside Šiauliai is now home to NATO F-16 fighter jets that protect the air space of all three Baltic countries.

The People

The Lithuanian population is predominantly urban: two-thirds of people live in urban areas, with the five largest cities – Vilnius, Kaunas, Klaipėda, Šiauliai and Panevėžys – accounting for nearly half the population.

Lithuania is also the most ethnically homogeneous population of the three Baltic countries; indigenous Lithuanians count for almost 85% of the total population, making multiculturalism less of a hot potato than in Latvia or Estonia. Poles form the second-biggest grouping, making up around 6% of the population, or slightly more than 200,000 people. Russians form around 5% of the population, while Jews make up just 0.1%.

The country's smallest ethnic community, numbering just 280, are the Karaites. An early-19th-century prayer house and ethnographic museum in Trakai provide insight into the culture and beliefs of this tiny Turkic minority.

Lithuanian Roma officially number around 2800. Vilnius' **Human Rights Monitoring Institute** (www.hrmi.lt) reckons some 46% are aged under 20 and many, unlike the Roma elders they live with, don't speak Lithuanian.

Net migration has been negative for the past several years, with literally hundreds of thousands of Lithuanians emigrating to countries where they can earn salaries two to three times higher than available locally for cleaning homes and tending bars. For years, the destinations of choice have been Ireland and the UK, but with the ongoing

---

DOS & DON'TS

» When visiting a Lithuanian bring an odd number of flowers: even-numbered bouquets are for dead-solemn occasions – and the dead!

» Don't shake hands across the threshold; it brings bad luck.

» Always maintain eye contact when toasting your host or they'll think you're shifty.

economic crisis, more and more Lithuanians are choosing to live in Scandinavia. Indeed, Norwegian and Danish language classes are very popular.

More than three million Lithuanians live abroad, including an estimated 800,000 in the USA. Other large communities exist in Canada, South America and Australia.

Rural vs Urban

The contrast between life in Vilnius and elsewhere is stark. Citizens of the capital enjoy a lifestyle similar to those in Western Europe, living in nice apartments, often working in professional jobs and often owning a car. Many have gained a cosmopolitan view of the world and consumerism has become a way of life.

In provincial towns and rural areas poverty is still prevalent – urban dwellers have around a third more income at their disposal than their rural counterparts, and about a third of homes in farming communities are below the poverty line, compared to about 20% in built-up areas.

Life expectancy for males is relatively low compared with other European countries – around 70 years (2011 estimate). The life expectancy for women is around 80 years.

Until 1998 there were only a handful of places in Lithuania to offer a university degree. Since then, several dozen colleges and universities have sprung up. Almost 90% of Lithuanians complete secondary school, and the majority of pupils go on to some form of further education; many students work full time alongside studying and live in university dorms or with friends rather than remaining in the parental nest.

Family ties remain strong, however, and married couples often choose to live with elderly parents who are no longer able to live alone. Despite increased career prospects, especially for women, Lithuanians tend to marry relatively young – the majority of women who marry do so between the ages of 20 and 24. A high number of marriages – almost half – end in divorce, but this figure is falling. This is partly due to the fact that many couples choose cohabitation over marriage and thus don't figure in the official divorce statistics.

The Arts

Lithuania is Baltic queen of contemporary jazz, theatre and the avant-garde, while its arts scene is young, fresh and dynamic.

LITHUANIA'S HOOP DREAMS

Though Lithuanians traditionally excel at many sports, including recent Olympic medals in events as disparate as the discus throw, the modern pentathlon and the decathlon, there's really only one sport that gets their blood pumping: basketball.

For Lithuanians, b-ball is more than a sport; it's a religion. During Soviet times, success at basketball within the Soviet National League was one of the few acceptable ways for Lithuanians to express their national identity. Since independence, Lithuanians have looked to basketball to help put them on the world map. The worshipped national team scooped bronze in three successive Olympic Games (1992, 1996 and 2000), only to be nosed out for bronze in both 2004 and 2008. The team also took the bronze in the FIBA World Basketball Championship in Istanbul in 2010.

Lithuanians have been a global basketball power since the 1930s, but the glory years came in the mid-1980s with the unparalleled success of the leading Lithuanian team at the time, Žalgiris Kaunas. Led by phenom centre Arvydas Sabonis, Žalgiris won the Soviet national championship three years running in 1985, '86 and '87 – each time defeating the dreaded Red Army superpower CSKA Moscow. Lithuanians made up the core of the Soviet team that won Olympic gold in Seoul in 1988.

Lithuanians' success at the time did more than prove their dominance on the basketball court, it helped to spark a national revival that ultimately led to the country's independence in 1991.

In 2011, Lithuania hosted the FIBA Eurobasket 2011 championship, the most prestigious basketball tournament in Europe, for the first time since 1939. Though the home team didn't win, the event was deemed a big success in the main host cities of Vilnius and Kaunas. As a consolation prize, Lithuania managed to beat a scrappy Slovenian team to secure a spot in the qualifying tournament for the 2012 Olympic Games in London.

and cultures, that couldn't be addressed in Lithuanian literature until after 1989 and the collapse of communism throughout Eastern Europe.

Herkus Kunčius (b 1965) has gained a reputation for scandalous novels that tear at the fabric of cultural norms; his *The Tumulus of Cocks* (2004) introduced gay and lesbian scenes to Lithuanian literature. Marius Ivaškevičius (b 1973), on the other hand, has distinguished himself by looking at historical themes through a modern lens. *The Greens* (2002), detailing the partisan movement after WWII, has proven to be Ivaškevičius' best seller to date.

Cinema & TV

Lithuania has a long cinematic history – the first short films were shot way back in 1909 – but it wasn't until the late 1980s that independent film truly began to flourish.

The grim reality of the post-Soviet experience is the focus for talented film director Šarūnas Bartas (b 1964), whose silent black-and-white movie *Koridorius* (*The Corridor;* 1994) – set in a dilapidated apartment block in a Vilnius suburb – received international recognition. Bartas opened Lithuania's first independent film studio in 1987.

The 11 documentaries and one short film made by Audrius Stonys are acclaimed Europe-wide: *510 Seconds of Silence* (2000) – an angel's flight over Vilnius' Old Town, the lake-studded Aukštaitija National Park and Neringa – is awesome; watch it at www.stonys.lt.

Stonys codirected *Baltic Way* (1990) – which landed best European documentary in 1992 – with director-producer and European Film Academy member Arūnas Matelis (b 1961). Matelis won critical acclaim and a heap of awards for *Before Flying Back to the Earth* (2005), a documentary on children with leukaemia. Find him and his film crew at www.nominum.lt.

Algimantas Puipa became prominent with *Vilko dantu karoliai* (T*he Necklace of Wolf's Teeth*; 1998) and *Elze is Gilijos* (*Elsie from Gilija*; 1999), and hit the headlines again with both *Forest of the Gods* (2005) and *Whisper of Sin* (2007).

Lithuania has been the location for a number of big-budget TV series, due to its reputation as a low-cost film location. They include *The New Adventures of Robin Hood* (1995–96) and *Elizabeth I* (filmed 2005), starring Jeremy Irons and Helen Mirren.

The Lithuanian Film Studios (www.lfs.lt), founded in Kaunas in 1948 and now located in Vilnius, has had a hand in all major foreign productions in the country.

More information on Lithuania's cinema and TV heritage can be gleaned at the Theatre, Music & Cinema Museum (p292) in Vilnius.

Music

Dainos – the Lithuanian name for songs – form the basis of the country's folk music. Their lyrics deal with every aspect of life, from birth to death, and more often than not they are sung by women, alone or in a group. Instruments include the *kanklė*, a Baltic version of the zither, a variety of flutes, and reed instruments. Kaunas' Folk Music & Instruments Museum (p328) has a fine collection to peer at.

Romantic folk-influenced Mikalojus Konstantinas Čiurlionis (1875–1911) is Lithuania's leading composer from earlier periods. Two of his major works are the symphonic poems *Miske* (*In the Forest*) and *Jūra* (*The Sea;* 1900–07), but Čiurlionis also wrote many piano pieces.

Bronius Kutavičius (b 1932) is heralded as the harbinger of minimalism in Lithuanian music, while Rytis Mažulis (b 1961) represents a new generation of composers with his neo-avant-garde stance expressed in minimalist compositions for voice. Country-and-western icon Virgis Stakėnas is the larger-than-life force behind the country's cult country music festival, the Visagano Country, in the eastern city of Visaginas.

Lithuania is the Baltic jazz giant. Two noteworthy musicians are sparkling pianist Gintautas Abarius and cerebral saxophonist Petras Vysniauskas. As famed is the Ganelin Trio, whose avant-garde jazz stunned the West when discovered in the 1980s. The club Kurpiai in Klaipėda and the Birštonas and the Kaunas jazz festivals are *the* spots to catch Lithuanian jazz.

Lithuania has yet to break into the international rock and pop scene, but that doesn't mean there aren't any local heroes. Andrius Mamontovas has been a household name for almost two decades; Amberlife, Mango, and Auguestė dominate the boy- and girl-band genre; and Skamp is an interesting mix of hip-hop, R'n'B, and funk. The biggest bands to explode onto the scene in recent years are Inculto, an eclectic group whose creative output reflects diverse world influences, and Gravel, a Brit-pop-esque four-piece with talent and attitude.

Music Export Lithuania (www.mxl.lt) is a helpful online information source on Lithuania's various music genres.

Visual Arts

Lithuania's finest painter and musician is Varėna-born Mikalojus Konstantinas Čiurlionis, who spent his childhood in Druskininkai, where his home is now a museum. He produced romantic masterpieces in gentle, lyrical tones, theatre backdrops and some exquisite stained glass. The best collection of these works is in the National Čiurlionis Art Museum in Kaunas. Depression dogged Čiurlionis, although when he died aged 35 it was of pneumonia.

Lithuania has a thriving contemporary art scene. Vilnius artists created the tongue-in-cheek Republic of Užupis (boxed text p293), which hosts alternative art festivals, fashion shows and exhibitions in its 'breakaway' state. Some 19km north, Lithuanian sculptor Gintaras Karosas heads up a sculpture park, Europos parkas (p311).

From Lenin to rock legend, Konstantinas Bogdanas was famed for his bronzes of communist heroes (see some in Druskininkai's Grūtas Park; boxed text p321) and for his bust of American musician and composer Frank Zappa (p292).

Lithuanian photography has achieved international recognition. Vytautas Stanionis (1917–66) was the leading postwar figure, while artist Antanas Sutkus (b 1939) stunned the photographic world with his legendary shots of French philosopher Jean-Paul Sartre and novelist Simone de Beauvoir cavorting in the sand on the Curonian Spit. Vitalijus Butyrinas's (b 1947) famous series *Tales of the Sea* uses abstract expressionism to make powerful images. For more on these and others, visit the **Union of Lithuanian Art Photographers** (www.photography.lt).

Theatre

Lithuanian theatre has become an international force, with several young experimental directors turning European heads left, right and centre.

The superstar of Lithuanian theatre directors is arguably Eimuntas Nekrošius, who has won many international awards. Another well-known name, Vilnius-based Oskaras Koršunovas (b 1969), has done Europe's theatre-festival circuit with *Old Woman, Shopping and Fucking, PS Files OK* and his 2003 adaptation of *Romeo and Juliet*. In 1998 he established his own theatre company in Vilnius, the Oskaras Koršunovas Theatre (OKT), albeit one with no fixed stage.

Other big names include Gintaras Varnas (b 1961), artistic director at the Kaunas Academic Drama Theatre, voted Lithuania's best director of the year five times; and Rimas Tuminas (b 1952), who heads the Small Theatre of Vilnius.

A key online information source on Lithuanian theatre is www.theatre.lt.

Food & Drink

Long, miserable winters are to blame for Lithuania's hearty, waist-widening diet based on potatoes, meat and dairy products. Cuisine between regions does not vary enormously, although certain traits become noticeable as you eat your way around: mushrooms, berries and game dishes dominate in heavily forested eastern and southern Lithuania; beer sneaks its way into northern cooking pots; while fish reigns on the coast and in lake districts like Trakai. Bread everywhere tends to be black and rye.

Staples, Specialities & 'Zeppelins'

Lithuanian food is epitomised in the formidable *cepelinai* (tsep-e-lin-ay), sometimes jokingly called zeppelins. These are parcels of thick potato dough stuffed with cheese, *mesa* (meat) or *grybai* (gree-bai; mushrooms). They come topped with a rich sauce made from onions, butter, sour cream and bacon bits.

Another favourite is sour cream–topped *kugelis* – a 'cannon ball' dish borrowed from German cuisine that bakes grated potatoes and carrots in the oven. *Koldūnai* (kol-doon-ay) are hearty ravioli stuffed with meat or mushrooms and *virtiniai* are stodgy dumplings.

Lithuanians tend to like the less popular bits of animals: *liežuvis* (lea-zhu-vis; cow's tongue) and *alionių skilandis* (a-lyo-nyoo ski-lan-dis; minced meat smoked in pork bladders) are delicacies, and Lithuanians pork out on *vėdarai* (fried pork innards).

EAT YOUR WORDS

Caught in a restaurant without a phrasebook? Here are a few useful sentences to get by. For other words and phrases see p419.

Useful Phrases

A table for ..., please.	*stah*-lah ... prah-*show*	*Stalą ..., prašau.*
May I see the menu, please?	ahr gah-*leh*-chow gow-ti man-*yew* prah-*show*	*Ar galėčiau gauti meniu prašau?*
Do you have the menu in English?	ahr yoos *tu*-ri-ta man-*yew* ahn-glish-kai	*Ar jūs turite meniu angliеškai?*
I'd like to try that.	ahsh naw-*reh*-chow ish bahn-*dee*-ti taw	*Aš norėčau išbandyti to.*
I don't eat ...	ahsh na-*vahl*-gow	*Aš nevalgau ...*
meat	*meh*-sish-kaw	*mėsiško*

Food Glossary

beef	*yoh*-tien-a	*jautiena*
beer	*ah*-lus	*alus*
boiled potato dumplings stuffed with meat	tsep-e-*lin*-ay	*cepelinai*
breaded pork chop	kar-bo-*na*-das	*karbonadas*
butter	*svie*-stas	*sviestas*
cheese	*soo*-ris	*sūris*
chicken	vi-*shtie*-na	*vištiena*
coffee	ka-*va*	*kava*
cold beetroot soup	shal-*ti*-barshi-ay	*šaltibarščiai*
eggs	(ki-o)-*shin*-i-ay	*kiaušiniai*
Lithuanian dumplings	kol-*doon*-ay	*koldūnai*
milk	*pien*-as	*pienas*
mushrooms	*gree*-bay	*grybai*
pancakes	blee-*nyal*-i-ay	*blyneliai*
pork	ki-ow-*lie*-na	*kiauliena*
tea	ar-ba-*ta*	*arbata*

Hodgepodge or *šiupinys* (shyu-pi-nees) – often mistakenly assumed to be hedgehog – is pork snout stewed with pork tail, trotter, peas and beans (try it in Vilnius at Žemaičiai, p301). Smoked pigs' ears, trotters and tails are popular beer snacks alongside *kepta duona* (kep-ta dwa-na) – sticks of black rye bread heaped with garlic and deep-fried. Order them with or without a gooey cheese topping.

Wild boar, rabbit and venison are popular in the Aukštaitija National Park, where hunted birds and animals were traditionally fried in a clay coating or on a spit over an open fire in the 18th century. When perpetually drifting sands on the Curonian Spit on the Baltic Sea in the 17th to 19th centuries made growing crops impossible, locals took to hunting and eating migrating crows in winter: one bite (followed by a generous slug of vodka) at the crow's neck killed the bird, after which its meat was eaten fresh, smoked or salted.

Blyneliai (blee-nyal-i-ay; pancakes) – a real favourite – are sweet or savoury and eaten any time of the day. *Varskečiai* (vars-ko-chyai) are stuffed with sweet curd, and *bulviniai blyneliai* are made with grated potato and stuffed with meat, *varske* (cheese curd) or fruit and chocolate.

Cold Pink Soup & Other Starters

Lithuanians love soup and no self-respecting chef would plan a meal without one, but one soup rises above all others (maybe for its shocking pink colour, or maybe simply because it's delicious). *Šaltibarsčiai* (shal-ti-barshi-ay) is a cold beetroot soup popular in summer and served with dill-sprinkled boiled potatoes and sour cream.

Other soups to look out for include nettle, sorrel, cabbage and bread soup (not to mention blood soup, which does indeed have goose, duck or chicken blood in it). Eel soup is specific to the Curonian Spit, where eel also comes as a main course. In Aukštaitija, fish soup served in a loaf of brown bread is the dish to try.

Popular starters include *silkė* (herring), *sprotai* (sprats) and salads. *Lietuviškos salotos* (lea-tu-vish-kos sa-lo-tos; Lithuanian salad) is a mayonnaise-coated mix of diced gherkins, boiled carrots, meat and anything else that happens to be in the fridge.

Mushrooms are popular, especially in August and September when forests are studded with dozens of different varieties – some edible, some deadly. Mushrooms are particularly abundant in the Aukštaitija and Dzūkija national parks; see the boxed text p322 for advice on picking mushrooms. In spring and early summer the same forests buzz with berry pickers; locals stand at road-sides in the region selling glass jam jars of wild strawberries, blueberries, blackberries and so on.

Beer & Other Beverages

Alus (beer) is the most widespread drink, local brands being Švyturys, Utenos, and Kalnapilis (boxed text p340). Brewing traditions are oldest in the northern part of Lithuania, where small family-run breweries treat lucky palates to natural beer free of preservatives.

Midus (mead) – honey boiled with water, berries and spices, then fermented with hops to produce an alcoholic drink of 10% to 15% proof – is Lithuania's oldest and most noble drink. It was popular until the decline of beekeeping in the 18th century, but made a comeback in 1959 when **Lietuviškas midus** (www.midus.lt) in Stakliškės in central Lithuania started making authentic mead; it produces several varieties today.

Vynas (wine) has made inroads into the drinking habits of Vilnius locals (boxed text p301), but provincial Lithuania is still in two minds about it. *Degtinė* (vodka) is widely consumed and best enjoyed neat, chilled and with company.

The more sober-minded might enjoy the honey liqueur *stakliskes* or *starka,* made from apple-tree and pear-tree leaves. Herbal and fruit teas and brews made from linden, thyme, caraway, ginger, mint, rhubarb and

---

THE TWELVE DISHES OF CHRISTMAS

Christmas is the major culinary feast of the year. On 24 December families sit down to dinner in the evening around a candlelit hay-covered table topped with a white linen cloth; the hay anticipates Jesus' birth and serves as a place for the souls of dead family members to rest. (Indeed, one place around the table is always laid for someone who died that year.)

The Christmas Eve feast that unfolds comprises 12 dishes – one for each month of the coming year to ensure year-long happiness and plenty. Dishes are fish and vegetable based, and often include festive *kučiukai* (koo-chiu-kai) – small cubed poppy-seed biscuits served in a bowl of poppy-seed milk; others like herrings, pike, mushrooms and various soups are not necessarily seasonal.

Šakotis (sha-ko-tis) – 'egg cake' – is a large tree-shaped cake covered with long spikes (made from a rather dry, spongecake mixture of flour, margarine, sugar, sour cream and dozens and dozens of eggs), which is served at weddings and other special occasions.

EATING PRICE RANGES

For the purpose of this chapter we've based the Lithuanian budget break-downs on the following price ranges, according to the cheapest main meal offered.

» €   less than 15Lt
» €€   15-40Lt
» €€€   more than 40Lt

a bounty of other sweet ingredients are age-old; Skonis ir Kvapas (p302) in Vilnius provides a unique opportunity to taste some.

Gira, another nonalcoholic drink, is a cloudy liquid made from bread. It's available across the country.

Where to Eat & Drink

Dining Lithuanian-style can mean spending anything from 20Lt for a three-course meal in a self-service cafe in a provincial town well off the tourist trail to 100Lt or more in a swish upmarket restaurant in the capital.

In Vilnius, the choice of cuisine and price range covers the whole gamut, and an English-language menu is usually available (likewise along the coast); elsewhere the choice is limited and menus are not always translated. Service is at its best in the capital – and generally average to poor everywhere else.

Eating Habits & Customs

A traditional dose of hospitality means loosening your belt several notches and skipping breakfast. Feasting is lengthy and plentiful, punctuated by many choruses of *Išgeriam!* (ish-ge-ryam; Let's drink!) and *Iki dugno!* (Bottoms up!). Starter dishes can be deceptively generous, leading unsuspecting guests to think they're the main meal. To decline further helpings may offend and be taken to mean that you don't like the food or the hospitality.

The family meal is a ceremonious affair and one that is taken very seriously, albeit one increasingly reserved for feast days, birthdays and other occasions in urban Lithuania's quicker-paced society. Each member of the family has a set place at the table – father at the head, mother opposite. If you arrive at someone's home while the family is seated, be sure to say *skanaus* (enjoy your meal!).

SURVIVAL GUIDE

Directory A–Z

For regional information pertaining to all three countries, see p396.

Accommodation

Lithuania has a wide choice of accommodation options to suit most budgets, including hotels, guesthouses, farmstays, hostels and campgrounds. Prices across these categories have risen in recent years but are generally lower than comparable facilities in Western Europe. For more on accommodation see p396.

This book divides accommodation options into three categories based on price: budget, midrange and top end. Budget properties include hostels, cheaper guesthouses, farmsteads and campgrounds. Midrange accommodation includes most hotels and better guesthouses. Top end means corporate chains, luxury hotels and high-end boutiques.

» Vilnius is the most expensive place to stay, followed by Kaunas and the resort areas on the Baltic coast during the summer season.

» Watch for seasonal fluctuations on rates. Summer resorts, particularly on the Baltic coast, have much higher prices in season (June to August). Rates fall by as much as half during the 'cold season' (October to May). Many resort properties close for the winter.

» Prices do not always include breakfast. This is particularly true for guesthouses, which sometimes reckon a fee of 10Lt to 20Lt for breakfast.

» Parking may or may not be included in the room rate. Paid parking usually adds another 10Lt to 20Lt per night to the tab.

Hotels

A stay in a *viešbutis* (hotel) is the most common type of accommodation offering. The term encompasses a variety of old and new places, ranging from very basic to ultra-plush.

At the top end are the international hotel chains that offer high-standard accommodation to a mostly business-oriented clientele, usually at prices aimed at expense accounts. Going down the line, there are plenty of smaller, privately owned hotels that cater to the midrange market. While rates at these

SLEEPING PRICE RANGES

» € up to 150Lt per night for the cheapest double room

» €€ cheapest double 150–350Lt

» €€€ cheapest double over 350Lt

places vary, expect to pay around 150Lt for a single and from 180Lt for a double room.

Guesthouses

Svečių namai (guesthouses) can be found all around Lithuania, particularly in the larger cities. They can run the gamut from simple rooms in private houses to near-luxury level boutiques but usually represent better value than hotels, and are often much more atmospheric. While prices vary depending on the location and comfort level, expect to pay around 120/160Lt for a single/double, usually not including breakfast.

Homestays & Farmstays

Staying on a farm or rural homestead is a popular and highly recommended way of seeing the country. Homestays and farmstays are far more common in rural areas and small towns, and in the central and eastern parts of Lithuania, particularly in small cities like Utena or Anykščiai or around national parks, may be the only game in town.

The local tourist offices will generally keep a list of homestays on hand and can make recommendations based on your needs. Otherwise, check the helpful website of the **Lithuanian Countryside Tourism Association** (www.countryside.lt), which maintains a list of properties by region and has lots of good info on what to expect.

Rates vary greatly depending on the facilities and the season, but expect to pay around 120Lt per room in season (June to August), and half that out of season. Rates do not normally include breakfast.

Hostels

Lithuania does not have a particularly well-developed infrastructure of youth hostels, and what does exist is usually of the old-school variety, often in a school dormitory or very basic sport hotel. Most hostels are located in large cities; and outside of these you're better off choosing guesthouses or farmstays.

The **Lithuanian Hostel Association** (www.lha.lt) provides a directory of youth hostels, with links to individual properties.

Expect to pay around 30Lt to 35Lt per bed in dorm accommodation, depending on the property, location and time of year.

Campgrounds

Lithuania is dotted with campgrounds; some are in highly scenic areas such as along the Baltic coast or occupying desirable spots in national parks. Most campgrounds are equipped to handle both tent camping and caravans. Some also offer basic accommodation in bungalows or similar.

The **Lithuanian Camp Site Association** (www.camping.lt) maintains a helpful website that lists campgrounds and provides contact info and photos. The association also publishes the very helpful brochure *Kempingai Lietuvoje (Campsites in Lithuania)*, usually available at tourist offices or as a download from the association website.

Rates vary but expect to pay around 15Lt per person to camp and another 15Lt or so for a tent site. You will likely have to pay extra for parking a car or access to electricity. Some campgrounds operate only in season (May to September), so be sure to contact the campground in advance to ensure that it will be open during your visit.

Activities

Lithuanians love nature. People were still worshipping ancient oak trees a mere six centuries ago, and these days in their free time they make regular pilgrimages to their country's many luscious lakes and forests and its long, sandy coastline. Boating, berrying, mushrooming, birdwatching and ballooning are uplifting pursuits. Travellers can walk and cycle into the wilderness, sweat in traditional lakeside saunas and enjoy ice-fishing in winter. For more details see p28 and individual destinations.

Customs

For pointers on customs regulations, see p398. The **Lithuanian Customs Department** (www.cust.lt) in Vilnius has online updates.

From outside the EU you can import duty-free into Lithuania: 1L of spirits, 2L of wine or champagne, and 200 cigarettes or 250g of tobacco. Meat and dairy products cannot be brought in as hand luggage from outside the EU. Upon entering, you must declare foreign currency in cash above €10,000, and the same amount when exiting.

When travelling within the EU, there are no restrictions on what you can take in and out of Lithuania providing it's for personal use.

Lithuania limits amber exports, but a few souvenirs should be OK providing the value doesn't exceed 3500Lt. You need a Culture Ministry permit, and to pay 10% to 20% duty, to export artworks over 50 years old. Contact the **Committee of Cultural Heritage** (www .kpd.lt) for info.

Embassies & Consulates

The website http://embassy-finder.com maintains an up-to-date list of consulate and embassies around the world. Embassies are located in Vilnius. For Lithuanian embassies abroad, see the website of the **Lithuanian Foreign Affairs Ministry** (www.urm.lt).

Australia (☑5-212 3369; www.sweden.embassy .gov.au; Vilniaus gatvė 23)

Belarus (☑5-225 1666; www.belarus.lt; Muitinės gatvė 41)

Canada (☑5-249 0950; http://Baltictates.gc.ca; Jogailos gatvė 4)

Denmark (☑5-264 8760; www.ambvilnius.um .dk; Kosciuškos gatvė 36)

Estonia (☑5-278 0200; www.estemb.lt; Mickevičiaus gatvė 4a)

Finland (☑5-266 8010; www.finland.lt; Kalinausko gatvė 24, 2nd fl)

France (☑5-212 2979; www.ambafrance-lt.org; Švarco gatvė 1)

Germany (☑5-210 6400; www.wilna.diplo.de; Sierakausko gatvė 24/8)

Latvia (☑5-213 1260; www.mfa.gov.lv/vilnius; Čiurlionio gatvė 76)

Netherlands (☑5-269 0072; www.netherlands embassy.lt; Jogailos gatvė 4)

Poland (☑5-270 9001; www.polembassy.lt; Smėlio gatvė 20a)

Russia (☑5-272 1763; www.lithuania.mid.ru; Latvių gatvė 53/54)

UK (☑5-246 2900; http://ukinlithuania.fco.gov .uk; Antakalnio gatvė 2)

USA (☑5-266 5500; http://vilnius.usembassy .gov; Akmenų gatvė 6)

Public Holidays

New Year's Day 1 January

Independence Day (Nepriklausomybės diena) 16 February; anniversary of 1918 independence declaration

Lithuanian Independence Restoration Day 11 March

Easter Sunday March/April

Easter Monday March/April

International Labour Day 1 May

Mothers' Day First Sunday in May

Feast of St John (Midsummer) 24 June

Statehood Day 6 July; commemoration of coronation of Grand Duke Mindaugas in the 13th century

Assumption of Blessed Virgin 15 August

All Saints' Day 1 November

Christmas (Kalėdos) 25 and 26 December

Lithuania also celebrates such days as the Day of the Lithuanian Flag (1 January), St Casimir's Day (4 March), Earth Day (20 March), Partisans' Day (fourth Sunday in May), Black Ribbon Day (23 August) and the Genocide Day of Lithuanian Jews (23 September). People still work on these days, but the national flag flutters outside most public buildings and private homes.

Internet Access

Internet use has developed at a staggering pace in Lithuania (at least in the country's larger urban centres), outstripping much of Western Europe. With the introduction of wireless technology, and more affordable PCs and laptops, an ever-increasing number of Lithuanians are becoming internet savvy. What this means for travellers is a decrease in the number of internet cafes and an increase in wi-fi hotspots. Most major cities still sport a cafe dedicated to internet access (on average 5Lt per hour) but in rural areas you'll be hard-pressed to find one. Occasionally, the tourist information office will have a computer available for a few minutes of gratis surfing. Big coffee chains, like **Coffee Inn** or **Vero Cafe** (www.verocafe.lt), in large cities have free and reliable wi-fi for customers. For a listing of other wi-fi hot spots in Lithuania, check www.wifi.lt.

Almost all hotels, including even most budget options, advertise internet access in rooms. This usually means wi-fi (often free but occasionally charged for), but there are a few hotels that still use LAN connections (and have Ethernet cables to borrow at the reception desk). Of course, you'll need your laptop or wi-fi enabled smartphone to use such services. The quality of the wi-fi connection can vary considerably depending on how far your room is from the wi-fi router. If an internet connection is important, be sure to make this clear at the reception desk and request a room with a strong signal.

A couple of top-end hotels in Vilnius and Kaunas have computer-equipped business centres for guests to use at a fairly substantial fee. Many budget and midrange places, meanwhile, have a computer terminal in the lobby, on which guests can surf for free. Another option is to ask to use the hotel's computer to check email (sometimes possible, sometimes not).

Maps

For regional maps, see p401. For Lithuania nothing can beat the interactive and searchable maps covering the entire country at Maps.lt (www.maps.lt).

In print, Lithuania is best covered by the *Lietuva* (1:400,000) road map, published by Vilnius-based map publisher Briedis (www .briedis.lt; Parodu gatvė 4) and sold by the publisher online. Bookshops, tourist offices and supermarkets in Lithuania sell it for 12Lt. Jāņa sēta's *Lietuva* (1:500,000) is also worth recommending, and is available for around the same price.

For stress-free navigation buy Jāņa sēta's *miesto planas* (city maps) covering Vilnius, Kaunas and Klaipėda at a scale of 1:25,000, with a 1:10,000 inset of the centre, and Palanga (1:15,000), Šiauliai and Panevėžys (1:20,000). They cost 6Lt to 12Lt apiece in bookshops and some tourist offices.

Note too that most international SatNav and GPS systems (including TomTom and Garmin) offer Lithuanian maps as part of

their European downloads. If you're planning on renting a car, pack your home GPS and use it on the road here just like you do at home.

Money

The Lithuanian litas (Lt) will remain firmly in place until at least 2015, when Lithuania could possibly trade in its litas for the euro. Some hotels and restaurants list prices in euros as well as litų, but payment is still in litų only.

The litas (plural: litų or litai) is divided into 100 centai (singular: centas). It comes in note denominations of 10Lt, 20Lt, 50Lt, 100Lt, 200Lt and 500Lt and coins of 1Lt, 2Lt and 5Lt alongside virtually worthless centai coins. Since 2002 the litas has been pegged to the euro at a fixed rate of 3.45Lt.

For practical matters, always try to keep a few 1Lt, 2Lt and 5Lt coins handy for small purchases and ticket machines.

ATMs are ubiquitous in cities and towns, and even the smallest hamlet is likely to have at least one. The majority accept Visa and MasterCard. Change money at banks, though the easiest way to carry money is in the form of a debit card, and withdraw cash as needed from an ATM.

Visa and MasterCard are widely accepted for goods and services. The only place you may experience a problem is at a very small establishment or for a very small transaction. American Express cards are typically accepted at larger hotels and restaurants, though they are not as widely recognised as other cards.

Post

Lithuania's postal system (www.post.lt) is quick and cheap. Posting letters/postcards costs 2.80/2.45Lt to other EU countries, 2.90/2.60Lt outside the EU and 1.55/1.45Lt domestically. Mail to the USA takes about 10 days, to Europe about a week. State-run EMS

LITHUANIA DIRECTORY A–Z

TIPPING TIPS

» In restaurants, tip 10% of the bill to reward good service. Leave the tip in the pouch that the bill is delivered in or hand the money directly to the waiter.

» Tip hairdressers and other personal services around 10% of the total.

» Taxis drivers won't expect a tip, but it's fine to round the fare up to the nearest 5Lt or 10Lt increment to reward special service.

» Tipping in hotels is essentially restricted to the top-end establishments, which usually have decent room service and porters, who all expect to be tipped.

is the cheapest express mail service; find it in Vilnius at the central post office (p306).

Telephone

Lithuania's digitised telephone network, run by **TEO** (www.teo.lt), is quick and efficient, although knowing what code to dial can be confusing.

To call other cities from a landline within Lithuania, dial ✑8, wait for the tone, then dial the area code and telephone number.

To make an international call from Lithuania, dial ✑00 followed by the country code.

To call Lithuania from abroad, dial Lithuania's country code (✑370), the area code and telephone number.

Then of course there are mobile telephones. No self-respecting Lithuanian would be seen without a mobile surgically attached to their ear, and indeed, many a hotel and restaurant – especially in more rural parts – lists a mobile telephone as its main number. Mobile numbers comprise a three-digit code and a five-digit number.

To call a mobile within Lithuania, dial ✑8 followed by the eight-digit mobile number. To call a mobile from abroad, dial ✑370 followed by the eight-digit mobile number. This guide lists full mobile numbers; i.e. ✑8-xxx xxxxx.

Mobile companies **Bitė** (www.bite.lt), **Omnitel** (www.omnitel.lt) and **Tele 2** (www.tele2.lt) sell prepaid SIM cards; Tele2 offers free roaming with its prepaid cards, making it the best choice for those travelling in Estonia, Latvia and Poland too. It also offers the cheapest rates.

Public telephones – increasingly rare given the widespread use of mobiles – are blue and only accept phone cards, sold in denominations of 50/200 units for 9/30Lt at newspaper kiosks.

Tourist Information

Most towns have a tourist office with staff who usually speak at least some English. Tourist offices range from the superbly helpful, useful and obliging to the downright useless and are coordinated by the Vilnius-based **State Department of Tourism** (www.tourism.lt). Tourist offices will often help in finding a room, sometimes accompanied by a fee of 5Lt or 6Lt per booking. Among the best tourist offices in the country are those in Vilnius, Kaunas, Klaipėda and Trakai, all of which stock a wealth of highly useful brochures. Details of tourist offices in cities and towns are given in the Information sections throughout the chapter.

For more info on Lithuania's four Unesco World Heritage sites – Neringa, Vilnius' Old Town, Kernavė and Struve Geodetic Arcs – visit the Vilnius-based **Lithuanian National Commission for Unesco** (✑5-210 7340; www.unesco.lt; Šv Jono gatvė 11, Vilnius).

Getting There & Away

This section concentrates on travelling to Lithuania from Latvia and Estonia only. For details on connections outside of the region, see p404.

Air

airBaltic (BT; ✑1825; www.airbaltic.com) Flies to Vilnius from Rīga several times daily and from Tallinn on most days. Also offers scheduled if sporadic service from Rīga to both Kaunas and Palanga. These flights are more common in summer (May to September).

Estonian Air (OV; ✑00372-640 1162; www.estonian-air.ee) Flies between Tallinn and Vilnius twice each weekday.

Bus

See each city's transport section for the frequency and cost of these services.

Ecolines (✑5-213 3300; www.ecolines.net) Runs two daily buses each to Kaunas and Vilnius from Rīga, and two daily buses to Vilnius and Kaunas from Tallinn.

Lux Express (✑5-233 6666; www.luxexpress.lt) Operates three daily buses between Rīga and Vilnius via Panevėžys. Some of these call at Rīga airport.

Simple Express (✑5-233 6666; www.simpleexpress.eu) Budget bus carrier offering arguably the lowest prices to Lithuania from destinations in the Baltic, including daily buses to Vilnius from Rīga (38Lt) and Tallinn (69Lt) and to Kaunas from Rīga for 35Lt.

Car & Motorcycle

The three Baltic countries are all part of the EU's common-border Schengen Agreement, so there are no border checks when driving between Lithuania and Latvia. There's usually no problem taking hire cars across the border but it pays to let the rental company know at the time of hire if you intend to do so.

Train

At the time of research there was no longer a direct train from Vilnius to Rīga. There is one daily departure for Rīga (at 6.18pm), but that requires a change of train and six-hour layover at the Rēzekne 2 station in Latvia. The bus is a much better option.

Train service from Vilnius to Tallinn is simply impractical. The comically circuitous route requires two changes and some 36 hours of travel time. Here again, the bus is a better option.

Getting Around
Bike, Car & Motorcycle

Lithuanian roads are generally very good and driving is easy. Four-lane highways link the main cities of Vilnius, Kaunas and Klaipėda and the drive from Vilnius all the way to the Baltic coast (330km) generally takes three to four hours.

Touring cyclists will find Lithuania mercifully flat. In rural areas, some roads are unsealed but they're usually kept in good condition. Winter poses particular problems for those not used to driving in ice and snow. Car and bike hire is offered in all the major cities.

Bus

The national bus network is extensive, linking all the major cities to each other and the smaller towns to their regional hubs. Most services are summarised on the extremely handy website **Bus Tickets** (www .autobusubilietai.lt).

Train

Local services are operated by **Lithuanian Rail** (www.litrail.lt), with regional hubs in Vilnius, Kaunas and Klaipėda. The Lithuanian Rail website is a model of user-friendliness and has routes, times and prices in English. Whether you take the bus or the train depends very much on the route. For common train journeys like Vilnius to Kaunas or to Klaipėda, the train is often more comfortable and better value than the bus. For other routes, the opposite might be true.

Kaliningrad Excursion

Includes »

Sights 387

Sleeping 389

Eating 391

Entertainment 392

Understand
Kaliningrad 393

Survival Guide 394

Best Places to Stay

» Chaika (p389)

» Radisson Hotel Kaliningrad (p389)

» Amigos Hostel (p389)

Best Places to Eat

» Dolce Vita (p391)

» Little Buddha (p391)

» Zarya (p391)

Why Go?

Inside Russia's smallest territory you'll find all the traditions of the big parent, alongside plenty of fine hotels and restaurants, welcoming locals, beautiful countryside, splendid beaches and fascinating historical sights.

The Teutonic Knights ruled the Baltic in the Middle Ages from Königsberg (now the region's capital, Kaliningrad) in a land once known as Prussia. Although little remains to indicate that Königsberg was once a Middle European architectural gem equal to Prague or Krakow, there are attractive residential suburbs and remnants of the city's old fortifications that evoke the Prussian past. Interesting museums, slick shopping centres and a multitude of leafy parks also soften the vast swaths of brutal Soviet-era architecture.

Plentiful transport options make Kaliningrad an ideal base from which to see the rest of the region – nothing is more than a few hours' drive away. If you plan to visit areas outside the region's capital, pick up a copy of Lonely Planet's *Russia* guide.

When to Go

In mid-May there's free entry to Kaliningrad's museums on Museum Night, plus special events including music and dance performances and fire and body-art shows. Russian Navy Day at the start of the fourth week of July offers a rare chance to visit the nearby naval port of Baltiysk, which is usually off-limits to tourists unless they are on pre-organised tours. The Don Chento Jazz Festival is held in Kaliningrad every August, the main shows taking place in the city's Central Park.

KALININGRAD AT A GLANCE

» **Area** 15,100 sq km (region)

» **Country code** ⌧2 within the region, 4012 from elsewhere

» **Departure tax** none

» **Money** rouble; €1 = R41.40; US$1 = R29.1; UK£1 = R47.2

» **Population** 423,000

» **Official language** Russian

» **Visa** You need a Russian visa to enter Kaliningrad (see p403). Citizens of Schengen countries, the UK, Switzerland and Japan can enter with an on-demand 72-hour tourist visa. These need to be arranged via local private travel agencies.

◉ Sights

KANT ISLAND & AROUND

This once densely populated island – now all parkland dotted with sculptures – is dominated by the reconstructed Gothic cathedral. A few nearby buildings – the former stock exchange from the 1870s (now housing various community clubs) and the neo-traditional row of shops, restaurants and hotels known as Fish Village – just hint at what this riverside area looked like pre-WWII.

Kaliningrad Cathedral   MUSEUM

(⌧631 705; www.sobor-kaliningrad.ru; adult/student R150/75; ⊘9am-5pm) Photos displayed inside this Unesco World Heritage cathedral show how thoroughly in ruins it was until the early 1990s when German donations helped it to be rebuilt; the original dates back to 1333. The lofty interior is dominated by an ornate organ used for regular concerts that are worth attending; the Russian version of the website has the schedule. Upstairs is the carved-wood Wallenrodt Library, interesting displays of old Königsberg and objects from archaeological digs. On the top floor is an exhibition devoted to Immanuel Kant, including his death mask. The philosopher's rose-marble tomb can be found on the outer north side of the building.

Museum of the World Ocean   MARITIME MUSEUM

(http://world-ocean.ru/en/; nab Petra Velikogo 1; adult/student R250/170, individual vessels R120/80; ⊘10am-6pm Wed-Sun) Strung along the banks of the Pregolya River are several ships, a sub, maritime machinery and a couple of exhibition halls that make up this excellent museum. Explore the handsome former expedition vessel *Vityaz,* which, during its heyday, conducted many scientific studies around the world. It's moored alongside the *Viktor Patsaev,* named after one of Kaliningrad's famous cosmonauts; its exhibits relate to space research. Inside the B-413 submarine, sample what life was like for the 300 submariners who once lived and worked aboard.

A restored old storehouse building houses interesting displays on fishing and the sea-connected history of Kaliningrad, as well as a rare archaeological find of the remains of a 19th-century wooden fishing boat. There's also a pavilion with the skeleton of a 16.8m-long sperm whale, and halls with small aquariums and general information about the ocean.

CITY FORTIFICATIONS & GATES

Scattered around the city are the remains of Königsberg's red-brick fortification walls, bastions and gates, built in stages between the 17th and 19th centuries. Sections have been rescued from ruin and turned into museums.

Amber Museum   MUSEUM

(www.ambermuseum.ru; pl Marshala Vasilevskogo 1; adult/student R120/90; ⊘10am-6pm Tue-Sun) Housed in the Dohna Tower this museum has some 6000 examples of amber artworks, the most impressive being from the Soviet period. In addition to enormous pieces of jewellery containing suspended prehistoric insects, one of the more fascinating works is a four-panelled amber and ivory chalice depicting Columbus, the *Niña,* the *Pinta* and the *Santa Maria.* You can buy amber jewellery in the museum or from the vendors outside. Adjacent to the museum the Rossgarten Gate now houses a restaurant.

Friedland Gate   MUSEUM

(www.fvmuseum.ru; ul Dzerzhinskogo 30; museum, adult/student R50/20; ⊘10am-6pm Tue-Sun) The best way to see what pre-WWII Königsberg looked like is to attend the 40-minute multimedia show (R30; ⊘on the hour, noon-5pm) screened in the halls of this well-put-together museum occupying one of the 13 original city gates. The evocative show is made up of projections of photos taken in the city

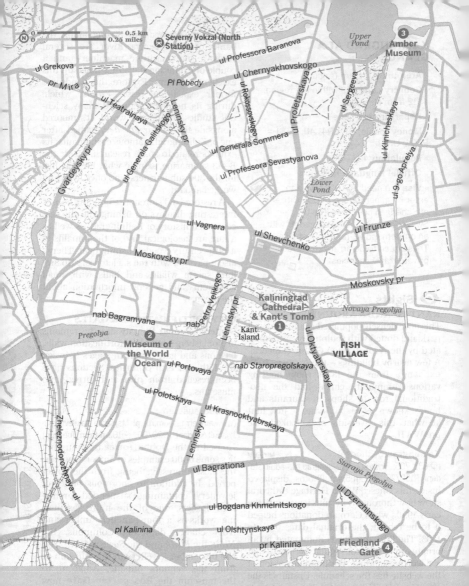

Kaliningrad Highlights

1 Visit the grave of philosopher Immanuel Kant and listen to an organ concert in **Kaliningrad Cathedral** (p387)

2 Learn about Russian maritime history at

Kaliningrad's fascinating **Museum of the World Ocean** (p387)

3 Admire beautiful pieces of jewellery and art made from petrified pine resin at the **Amber Museum** (p387)

4 Be transported back to old Königsberg at the **Friedland Gate** (p387)

between 1908 and 1913 and some grainy footage shot in 1937 around the castle.

King's Gate
MUSEUM

(ul Frunze 112; adult/student R50/30; ⊘11am-7pm Wed-Sun) Focusing on Peter the Great's Royal Embassy to the city in 1697, this revamped gate also has good models of old Königsberg and exhibits on the personalities who shaped the region's history. A little south of here, where Moskovsky pr meets Litovsky val, is the twin-towered Sackheim Gate.

OTHER SIGHTS

Amalienau & Maraunenhof
NEIGHBOURHOODS

Casual strolls through the linden-scented, tree-lined neighbourhoods of Amalienau (to the city's west along pr Mira) and Maraunenhof (at the north end of the Prud Verkhny) provide a further glimpse of genteel pre-WWII Königsberg. Amalienau is particularly lovely, with an eclectic range of villas, many designed by the architect Friedrich Heitmann along ul Kutuzova and the streets connecting prs Pobedy and Mira. There are several appealing small hotels in Marannenhof.

History & Arts Museum
MUSEUM

(⏱453 844; ul Klinicheskaya 21; adult/student R80/70; ⊘10am-6pm Tue-Sun) Housed in a reconstructed 1912 concert hall by the banks of the pretty Lower Pond (Prud Nizhny), this museum mainly focuses on events since Russia's takeover of the region, though the German past is not ignored in the many interesting displays.

Bunker Museum
MUSEUM

(Universitetskaya ul 3; adult/student R80/70; ⊘10am-6pm Tue-Sun) The city's last German commander, Otto van Lasch, capitulated to the Soviets from this buried German command post in 1945. It now houses interesting displays about the events of WWII in the region.

Kaliningrad Art Gallery
GALLERY

(Moskovsky pr 60-62; adult/student R120/60; ⊘10am-6pm Tue-Sun) View contemporary works by local artists and some striking pieces from the Soviet decades, as well as various temporary exhibitions, in this large municipal gallery.

Ploshchad Pobedy
SQUARE

The city's centre is surrounded by shopping malls and the Russo-Byzantine-style Cathedral of Christ the Saviour (Kafedralny Sobor Khrista Spasitelya), built in 2006, its gold domes visible from many points in the city.

KALININGRAD IN...

One Day

If your time is limited to a day, see the cathedral, Museum of the World Ocean and Amber Museum and stroll around Kaliningrad's leafy parks. End the day with a meal at Don Chento.

Two Days

With more time, visit the Kurshskaya Kosa National Park on the coast and perhaps the seaside resorts of Svetlagorsk and Yantarny – for full details of these two, see Lonely Planet's Russia. Also drop by the cafe-bar arty hang-out Kvartira in Kaliningrad city.

Kaliningradsky Zoopark
ZOO

(http://kldzoo.ru; pr Mira 26; adult/child R100/50; ⊘9am-7pm) Bears, hippos, seals and flamingos are among the creatures that call this city-centre zoo home.

Central Park
PARK

(main entrance pr Mira 1) The forested grounds here, dotted with statuary and amusement rides, are pleasant for a stroll.

🛏 Sleeping

Kaliningrad is well served with midrange and top-end hotels, but budget accommodation is thin on the ground. Unless noted, rates include breakfast.

TOP CHOICE Chaika
HOTEL €€€

(⏱210 729; www.hotelchaika.ru; ul Pugacheva 13; s/d from R3500/4450; @🛜) On a leafy street near the picturesque Amalienau area, 'Seagull' is a delightful 28-room property decorated with classy heritage touches. It also has a restaurant, comfy lounge and fitness room.

Radisson Hotel Kaliningrad
HOTEL €€€

(⏱593 344; www.radisson.ru/hotel-kaliningrad; pl Pobedy 10; s/d from R5900/6350; @🛜) This international chain hotel keeps up top standards, offering spacious and stylishly decorated rooms, some with views of the nearby cathedral. The rates drop by R2000 per night from Friday to Sunday.

Amigos Hostel
HOSTEL €

(⏱911 485 2157; http://amigoshostel.ru; Epronovskaya ul 20-102; dm R500-600; 🛜) On the

Kaliningrad

13th floor of a modern apartment block overlooking the cathedral and Fish Village, this welcoming place offers three mixed dorms – one with six beds, the others with eight. All share one bathroom and a well-equipped kitchen.

Heliopark Kaiserhof HOTEL €€€
(☎592 222; www.heliopark.ru; ul Oktyabrskaya 6a; s/d from R4500/4950; @🛜🏊) An anchor of the Fish Village development, this nicely designed and furnished hotel has pleasant, light-filled rooms and a full-service spa and sauna. Rates are almost halved Friday to Sunday.

Hotel Kaliningrad HOTEL €€
(☎350 500; www.hotel.kaliningrad.ru; Leninsky pr 81; s/d from R1900/2100; 🛜) Much improved following a recent facelift, and the Kaliningrad's location is ace, with many of its functional rooms offering views across to the cathedral.

Villa Severin GUESTHOUSE €€
(☎365 373; www.villa-severin.ru; ul Leningradskaya 9a; s/d from R1600/1850; @🛜) There's a homely atmosphere at this pretty villa, set back from the Upper Pond, with 10 comfortably furnished rooms including one simple student room (R1000 without

Kaliningrad

◎ Sights

1 Amber Museum	D2
2 Bunker Museum	C3
3 Cathedral of Christ the Saviour	C2
Dohna Tower	(see 1)
4 Former Stock Exchange	C4
5 Friedland Gate	D5
6 History & Arts Museum	D3
7 Kaliningrad Art Gallery	D3
8 Kaliningrad Cathedral	D4
9 Kaliningradsky Zoopark	B2
Kant's Tomb	(see 8)
10 Museum of the World Ocean	C4
Rossgarten Gate	(see 1)

◎ Sleeping

11 Amigos Hostel	D4
12 Chaika	A1
13 Heliopark Kaiserhof	D4
14 Hotel Kaliningrad	C3
15 Komnaty Otdykha	C5
16 Radisson Hotel Kaliningrad	C2
17 Villa Severin	D1

◎ Eating

18 Central Market	C2
19 Croissant Café	B2
20 Croissant Café	C2
21 Croissant Café	D2
22 Dolce Vita	D2
23 Don Chento	C2
24 La Plas Cafe	C2
25 Little Buddha	C2
26 Viktoriya	C5
27 Viktoriya	C3
28 Viktoriya	D4
29 Zarya	B2

◎ Drinking

30 Bar Verf	D4
31 Kaputsin	C1
Kmel	(see 25)
32 Untsiya	C3

◎ Entertainment

33 Kvartira	B2
34 Philharmonic Hall	C5
35 Reporter	C1
Universal	(see 29)
36 Vagonka	A3

◎ Information

37 Baltma Tours	A2
King's Castle	(see 14)
38 Regional Tourism Information Centre	B2

◎ Transport

39 Buses to Svetlogorsk & Zelenogradsk	C2
40 Yuzhny Bus Station	C5

breakfast). It also has a small sauna and cafe.

Komnaty Otdykha HOSTEL €
(☎586 447; pl Kalinina; s R500, r without breakfast R1500) Inside the south train station, these single 'resting rooms', which come in blocks of two or three that share a bathroom, are quiet and clean. Find them by turning right down the corridor after the ticket hall and walking up to the 3rd floor.

✕ Eating

TOP CHOICE Dolce Vita RUSSIAN, INTERNATIONAL €€€
(☎351 612; http://dolcevita.kaliningrad.ru; pl Marshala Vasilevskogo 2; meals R1000-1500; ☻noon-midnight; ☎☼) Dishes that appear overly fussy on the menu, for the most part, deliver the goods in reality. There's an excellent selection for vegetarians and luxurious takes on old Russian standards such as *pelmeni*

and borscht. The main dining room is plush and there's a lovely garden patio.

Little Buddha ASIAN €€€
(☎593 395; www.littlebuddhakaliningrad.com; Clover City Centre, pl Pobedy 10; meals R800-1500; ☻noon-1am Tue-Thu, until 4am Fri & Sat; ☎) This swanky Asian-fusion restaurant, sushi bar and nightclub has spectacular interior design, dominated by a far from little Buddha. The food is well prepared and the cocktails are inventive. Major DJs play the upstairs club section at weekends, when there may be a cover charge if you're not dining.

Zarya RUSSIAN, INTERNATIONAL €
(☎213 929; pr Mira 43; meals R300-400; ☻10am-3am; ☎) This fashionable brasserie in the lobby of the Scala cinema is beautifully decorated and also has an attractive outdoor area. The reasonably priced food is reliable – try the potato pancakes

KURSHSKAYA KOSA NATIONAL PARK

Over half of the 98km-long Curonian Spit (see p350) lies in Russian territory and is protected within the **Kurshskaya Kosa National Park** (www.kurshskayakosa.ru; admission per person/car R30/200). Easily accessible in a day from Kaliningrad city, it's a fascinating place to explore, go wildlife- and bird-spotting or simply relax on pristine beaches. Highlights include the spectacular views of the dunes from raised platforms at **Vistota Efa** (42km mark; admission free), and the **Dancing Forest** (Tantsuyushchiy Les; 37km mark; admission free) where wind-sculpted pines do indeed appear to be frozen mid-boogie.

Buses from Kaliningrad head up the spit (R101; two hours; four daily); all stop in the coastal resort of Zelenogradsk on the way there and back. Kaliningrad's Regional Tourism Centre has the current timetable. Alternatively, hire a car (from around R1500) or arrange a tour (around R700) in either Kaliningrad or Zelenogradsk.

with salmon caviar or the excellent locally reared steaks.

La Plas Cafe RUSSIAN, INTERNATIONAL €
(pl Pobedy 1; meals R300-400; ⊘24hr) Offering big window views onto pl Pobedy and tasty food that actually looks as good as it does on the photo menu, this round-the-clock place is a good fit for whatever meal or snack you desire.

Croissant Café BAKERY, CAFE €
(pr Lenina 63; meals R100-300; ⊘8am-11pm; 🛜)
Branches of this chic baked-goods heaven have proliferated around the city; you'll find others at ul Mira 23, ul Proletarskaya 79 and in the Evropa mall. Indulge in flaky pastries, quiches, muffins, biscuits and cakes, as well as omelettes and blini for breakfast. It does a business lunch for R190 from noon to 4pm.

Don Chento PIZZA €
(Sovetsky pr 9-11; meals R200-300) Dig in at the self-serve salad bar or pick a slice of pizza at this stylish chain with several branches across the city.

Self-caterers should visit the lively **central market** (ul Chernyakhovskogo; ⊘8am-6pm) or the supermarket **Viktoriya** (Kaliningrad Plaza, Leninsky pr 30; ⊘10am-10pm) with branches also opposite the southern bus and train station and near Fish Village.

🍷 Drinking

The following also serve food and are often good alternatives to the restaurants and cafes above.

Untsiya TEAHOUSE €€
(ul Zhitomirskaya 22) This elegant, old-world teashop serves all manner of black, green, white and fruit-flavoured teas and infusions,

as well as tasty snacks such as quiche, salads and cakes.

Kmel PUB €€
(Clover City Centre, pl Pobedy 10; meals R350-500; ⊘10am-2am) Four types of beer are brewed at this appealing multilevel gastro-pub overlooking pl Pobedy. An interesting range of Russian and Siberian dishes are on the menu, including unusual ingredients such as reindeer and *omul*, a fish from Lake Baikal.

Bar Verf CAFE-BAR €
(Fish Village, ul Oktyabrskaya 4A; ⊘11am-midnight; 🛜) The ambience is pleasant at this relaxed wine bar that also has outdoor tables overlooking the cathedral. It screens movies and provides coloured pencils and paper for you to doodle with.

Kaputsin CAFE €
(ul Kirova 3/5; ⊘9am-10pm Mon-Sat, 10am-5pm Sun) Looking like an arts student's living room, plastered with books, maps and other knick-knacks (some for sale), this laid-back place serves nicely brewed coffee and DIY noodle and rice dishes – choose your starch, topping and sauce for around R150 a plate.

☆ Entertainment

Classical concerts are occasionally held at the cathedral. Major DJs from Russia and Western Europe jet in for gigs at Kaliningrad's clubs, which open around 9pm but typically don't get going until well after midnight.

Reporter LIVE MUSIC
(📞571 601; www.reporter-club.ru; ul Ozerova 18; ⊘11am-1am) Live music in a wide range of genres – from Spanish to jazz and Afro-beat – kicks off at this industrial, cool club space

most nights at 9pm. It also occasionally screens films and it serves food; set lunches are R130.

Philharmonic Hall CLASSICAL MUSIC
(☑643 451; www.kenigfil.ru; ul Bogdana Khmelnitskogo 61a) This beautifully restored neo-Gothic church, which has excellent acoustics, stages organ concerts, chamber-music recitals and the occasional symphony orchestra.

Universal CLUB
(☑952 996; pr Mira 43) Kaliningrad's classiest club is also the location of the Scala cinema.

Vagonka CLUB
(☑956 677; www.vagonka.net; Stanochnaya ul 12) Attracts a wide-ranging crowd with its mix of events, from live music to theme parties and top DJs.

ℹ Information

Baltma Tours (☑931 931; www.baltma.ru; pr Mira 94, 4th fl) The multilingual staff can arrange visas, hotel accommodation, tailored city tours and local excursions.

Emergency Hospital (☑534 556; ul A. Nevskogo 90; ⏰24hr)

King's Castle (☑350 782; www.kaliningrad info.ru; Hotel Kaliningrad, Leninskiy pr 81; ⏰8am-8pm Mon-Fri; 9am-4pm Sat) Access the internet here and book tours, including ones to the Kurshskaya Kosa.

KVARTIRA

On the ground floor of an apartment block, about 200m south of Croissant Café, Kvartira (☑216 736; ul Serzhanta Koloskova 13; 🛜) is tricky to classify but unquestionably one of Kaliningrad's coolest hang-outs. Lined with a fascinating range of pop culture books, CDs, records and DVDs, all for sale or rent (as is everything else in the space, including the stylish furniture), Kvartira – which means 'apartment' – also serves drinks and snacks, but there's no menu. Movies are screened for free on several nights while on others there may be a party or an art event; whatever's happening you're sure to make friends with locals. Opening hours are erratic, so call before setting off for this place.

Königsberg (www.konigsberg.ru) Web-based tour agency through which you can arrange visas and book hotels.

Post office (ul Chernyakhovskogo 32; per hr R50; ⏰post office 10am-2pm & 3-7pm Mon-Fri, 10am-2pm & 3-6pm Sat, internet room 10am-2pm & 3-10pm Mon-Sat) Internet access and postal services.

Regional Tourism Information Centre (☑555 200; www.visit-kaliningrad.ru; pr Mira 4; ⏰9am-8pm Mon-Fri, 11am-6pm Sat Jun-Sep, 9am-6pm Mon-Fri, 11am-4pm Sat Oct-May) Helpful English-speaking staff and lots of information on the region.

Telekom (ul Teatralnaya 13; internet per hr R50; ⏰9am-7pm) For long-distance calls, fax and internet access.

UNDERSTAND KALININGRAD

Kaliningrad Today

Like much of Russia, Kaliningrad struggled through extreme economic difficulties in the early 1990s. The discovery of oil off the coast and the granting of special economic zone status has helped it turn the corner. One of the venues for the 2018 FIFA World Cup, Kaliningrad is also among a handful of Russian regions permitted to develop a casino; the proposed location is near Yantarny.

History

Founded in 1255, Königsberg joined the Hanseatic League in 1340, and from 1457 to 1618 was the residence of the grand masters of the Teutonic order and their successors, the dukes of Prussia. Prussia's first king, Frederick I, was crowned in 1701 in the city's castle. For the next couple of centuries Königsberg flourished, producing citizens such as the 18th-century philosopher Immanuel Kant.

The city centre was flattened by British air raids in August 1944 and the Red Army assault from 6 to 9 April 1945. Renamed Kaliningrad on 4 July 1946, the city was rebuilt in grand Soviet concrete style, albeit tempered by parks, a network of ponds and waterways and Kaliningrad Lagoon.

The remains of the castle were destroyed and replaced by the outstandingly ugly Dom Sovetov (House of Soviets) in the 1960s.

During the eyesore's construction it was discovered that the land below it was hollow, with a (now flooded) four-level underground passage connecting to the cathedral. The decaying half-finished building has never been used.

SURVIVAL GUIDE

Getting There & Away

Air

Khrabrovo airport (☎610 358; http://kgd-airport.org/en) is 24km north of the city. There are daily flights to Rīga, Moscow, and St Petersburg; see website for other connections.

Bus

Mainly local buses depart from the **Yuzhny bus station** (ul Zheleznodorozhnaya 7) as well as international bus services run by **Ecolines** (☎656 501; www.ecolines.ru) to Warsaw and several German cities. **König Avto** (☎999 199; www.kenigavto.ru) international services to the Baltic countries leave from

the **international bus station** (Moskovsky pr 184).

Train

All long-distance and most local trains go from **Yuzhny Vokzal** (South Station; pl Kalinina), some passing through, but not always stopping at, **Severny Vokzal** (North Station; pl Pobedy).

Long-distance destinations include Moscow, St Petersburg and Minsk; local services are to Svetlogorsk and Zelenogradsk.

Getting Around

Trams (R10), trolleybuses (R10), buses (R12) and minibuses (R12 to R17) will get you most places. For the airport, take bus 144 from the bus station (R30, 30 minutes). A taxi to/from the airport is R450 with **Taxi Kaliningrad** (☎585 858; www.taxi-kaliningrad.ru).

Car hire is available from **City-Rent** (☎509 191; http://city-rent39.com; Moskovsky pr 182a; per day from €26), which also has a branch at the airport.

Survival Guide

DIRECTORY A–Z 396

Accommodation........ 396
Business Hours 397
Climate................ 398
Customs Regulations ... 398
Discount Cards........ 398
Electricity 399
Embassies &
Consulates 399
Gay & Lesbian
Travellers 399
Health................. 400
Insurance.............. 400
Internet Access........ 400
Legal Matters 400
Maps...................401
Money..................401
Post....................401
Telephone 402
Time 402
Toilets................. 402
Tourist Information 402
Travellers with
Disabilities............ 402
Visas.................. 403
Volunteering 403
Women Travellers....... 403
Work 403

TRANSPORT 404

GETTING THERE
& AWAY 404
Entering Estonia, Latvia
& Lithuania 404
Air 404
Land 407
Sea 409
Tours...................410
GETTING AROUND.......410
Air 410
Bicycle 411
Boat 411
Bus 411
Car & Motorcycle........413
Hitching 413
Local Transport.........414
Tours..................414
Train 414

LANGUAGE 416

GLOSSARY.............. 421

Directory A–Z

This chapter contains the nuts and bolts of travelling in the Baltic. Country-specific information can be found in the directories for Estonia (p167), Latvia (p272) and Lithuania (p380).

Accommodation

In the Baltic, the Eastern Bloc bedtime blues are now largely a thing of the past. There are still a few grey Soviet monsters lurking about (mostly in Latvia), but many have been renovated and nowadays there are plenty of other options available. The capitals tend to have the best range – from hostels to international hotel chains – but things can get tight on summer weekends.

In this book, accommodation is ordered according to the author's preference, with their favourite options listed first under each town or neighbourhood heading. Beside each property name you'll find a price indicator, enabling you to quickly locate budget (€), midrange (€€) or top-end (€€€) options. The price bands for each country differ slightly,

due to the disparity in currencies and prices (Estonia tends to be more expensive than the others), so you'll need to refer to the individual country chapters for the breakdowns. Generally speaking, hostels, camp sites and cheaper guesthouses fall into the budget category; most of the guesthouses and the less expensive hotels are rated midrange; while top-end places include the ritzier hotels and boutique properties.

The peak tourist season is from June to August (the ski resorts have a second peak in winter). If you come then, you should book well in advance. This is essential in Tallinn, Vilnius and Rīga – and in popular summer-lovin' destinations, including the Estonian islands and all the coastal resorts.

Rates published in this guide reflect high-season prices. From October to April (and to a lesser extent September and May), room prices typically drop by about 30% – sometimes substantially more, depending on your powers of persuasion. Also keep in mind that popular seaside spots and other weekend getaway destinations (including Tallinn) are pricier on Friday and Saturday than during the week.

Camping

Many Baltic campgrounds are beautifully located by lakes or within forests, but most are difficult to reach unless you have a private vehicle. Some have permanent wooden cottages or, occasionally, brick bungalows. Cabins vary in shape and size but are usually small one-room affairs with three or four beds. Showers and toilets are nearly always communal and vary dramatically in cleanliness.

Campgrounds usually open in May or June and close in mid- to late September. A night in a wooden cottage typically costs €7 to €30 per person, while tent sites range from €2 to €10 per person.

Estonia, in particular, has an extremely well-organised outfit overseeing camping. RMK (☑676 7500; www .rmk.ee) maintains dozens of free basic camp sites in forests all over the country.

Farmstays

The term 'farmstay' can vary widely and isn't always the

BOOK YOUR STAY ONLINE

For more accommodation reviews and recommendations by Lonely Planet authors, check out lonelyplanet.com/hotels. You'll find the true, insider lowdown on the best places to stay. Reviews are thorough and independent. Best of all, you can book online.

COTTAGE RENTAL

Baltcott (www.baltcott.com); is an Estonian company with dozens of cottages and apartments on its books, throughout Estonia (☎648 5788) and Latvia (☎6756 9435). Scour its website for a log cabin in Lahemaa National Park, a farmstead on Saaremaa, a beachside apartment in Pärnu or Jūrmala, or a city base in Tallinn or Rīga.

farm-based homestay experience you might be expecting. Many 'tourist farms' are set up as small guesthouses, while others offer self-contained apartments or whole cottages. Regardless, farmstays can prove to be a memorable choice. For a fee, host families will often provide home-cooked meals and arrange fishing, boating, horse riding, mushrooming, berry-gathering and other activities.

Baltic Country Holidays (Lauku Ceļotājs; ☎6761 7600; www.traveller.lv) Latvia-based but books accommodation in rural settings all over the Baltic. Options include B&B and guesthouse rooms, whole cottages and camp sites.

Countryside Tourism Association of Lithuania (☎37-400 354; www .countryside.lt) Arranges accommodation in farmhouses and rural cottages throughout Lithuania.

Estonian Rural Tourism (☎600 9999; www.maa turism.ee) The full range of accommodation – from camping and farm-based B&B to palaces and castle hotels – can be booked through this umbrella organisation.

Guesthouses

Somewhat bigger than B&Bs but smaller than hotels, private guesthouses are a good bet for affordable travel in the Baltic and often offer a cosy, informal setting. Typically they have less than a dozen rooms but beyond that there are no rules. Some

have en-suite bathrooms while others have communal bathrooms; some offer breakfast and others don't; and, these days, free wi-fi is more common than not. Standards of cleanliness can also vary but generally the quality is high. Prices range from around €20 to €90 per room.

Hostels

There are a growing number of hostels scattered throughout the Baltic, mostly concentrated in the capitals and larger cities. Dorm beds in the capital cities in high season range from about €10 to €15. Book your bed well in advance if you come in the summer.

You'll find **Hostelling International** (www.hihostels .com) hostels in all of the Baltic countries. For backpacker recommendations, check out **Hostelworld** (www .hostelworld.com). Websites with a (noncomprehensive) list of hostels in each country:

Estonia www.hostels.ee

Latvia www.hostellinglatvia .com

Lithuania www.lha.lt

Hotels

The Baltic has hotels to suit every price range, although

budget hotel accommodation in the increasingly glam capitals has become dishearteningly scarce. As more cheap hotels make the effort to brighten up their image, nightly rates are being yanked up too.

But delightfully horrible relics from the Soviet era still exist – though they may retain that blocky, twilight-zone exterior, the interior is usually (but not always) modernised.

The midrange option – both in and outside the capitals – includes small, family-run hotels whose only downside is that they have few rooms so get booked up quickly.

Top hotels are a dime a dozen. Many are under Western management or are part of a recognised international hotel chain, while others – such as Europa Royale in Rīga, the Radisson SAS Astorija in Vilnius and the Three Sisters in Tallinn – are housed in exquisitely renovated, historic buildings dating from the 13th to 19th centuries.

Spa Hotels

Spa hotels are both an excellent place to be pampered and, in the case of those with waterparks attached, to take the kids. Even if you don't stay, you can pop in for treatments: mud baths, massages, herbal baths, and dozens of other options. Estonia and Latvia have the most selections, with Jūrmala in Latvia known as the spa centre of the Baltic. Druskininkai is Lithuania's premier spa connection, with Birštonas also popular.

Business Hours

In this book we've only listed hours in individual reviews if they vary significantly from the following standard hours.

Banks 9am to 4pm or 5pm Monday to Friday.

WHICH FLOOR?

Before you start traipsing up the stairs, note that in the Baltic countries the ground floor is referred to as the 1st floor.

Bars 11am or noon to midnight from Sunday to Thursday, until 2am or 3am Friday and Saturday.

Cafes 8am or 9am to 10pm or 11pm daily.

Clubs 10pm to 4am or 5am Thursday to Saturday. In Latvia they start filling up at 11pm and close around 6am, Wednesday to Saturday; in warmer months they often open Sunday to Tuesday as well.

Post offices 8am to 6pm or 7pm Monday to Friday, 8am or 9am to 2pm or 3pm Saturday.

Restaurants Noon to 11pm or midnight daily.

Shops 10am to 6pm or 7pm Monday to Friday, 10am to 3pm or 4pm Saturday.

Supermarkets 8am or 9am to 10pm daily.

THINGS CHANGE...

While prices quoted in this guide were correct at the time of research, visitors should be aware that the economic situation in the region is as volatile as it is in the rest of the world. Changes can also occur depending on season, demand, competition, big events and so on; some places listed may not be able to ride out the economic storm and may well be closed when you visit. Our best advice when it comes to accommodation: check the hotel website for up-to-date prices, ask the hotel for its best rates, and do some hunting around for internet bookings to find good deals.

Customs Regulations

If you think that a painting or other cultural object you want to buy in one of the Baltic countries might attract customs duty or require special permission to export, check with the seller before purchasing. You may have to get permission from a government office before it can be exported. For country-specific customs information, see Estonia (p167), Latvia (p272) and Lithuania (p381).

Discount Cards

City Discount Cards

Both Tallinn (p76) and Rīga (p195) offer discount cards to visitors. See the relevant sections for details.

Hostel Cards

A HI (Hostelling International) card yields discounts of up to 20% at affiliated hostels (though there are many non-HI hostels throughout the Baltic). You can buy one at participating hostels en route or purchase it before you go, via your national **Youth Hostel Association** (YHA; www.hihostels.com).

Seniors Cards

There are some discounts available to older people – museums often reduce the entrance fee, and concert and performance tickets may also be reduced, so it's always worth asking. Ferries and long-distance buses will often have seniors' fares (discounts of around 10%). To take advantage of discounts it would pay to carry ID providing proof of your age.

Climate

Rīga

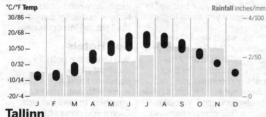

Tallinn

Vilnius

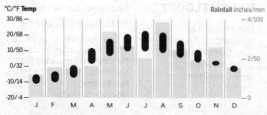

Student & Youth Cards

Carrying a student card entitles you to a wide variety of discounts throughout the Baltic. The most common card is the **International Student Identity Card** (ISIC; www.isic.org), which is issued to full-time students aged 12 years and over, and gives the bearer discounts on accommodation, transport and admission to some attractions. It's available from student unions, hostelling organisations and some travel agencies; for more information, see the website of the **International Student Travel Confederation** (ISTC; www.istc.org).

The ISTC is also the body behind the **International Youth Travel Card** (IYTC or Go25), which is issued to people who are between 12 and 26 years of age and not full-time students, and gives equivalent benefits to the ISIC. A similar ISTC brainchild is the **International Teacher Identity Card** (ITIC), available to teaching professionals.

Electricity

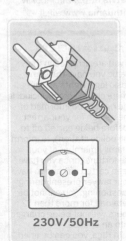

230V/50Hz

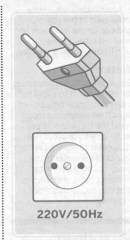

220V/50Hz

Embassies & Consulates

Estonia, Latvia and Lithuania each have numerous diplomatic missions overseas. Likewise, many countries have their own embassies or missions in the Baltic capitals. See Estonia (p167), Latvia (p272) and Lithuania (p382) for details.

It's important to realise what your own embassy can and can't do for you if you get into trouble. Remember that you are bound by the laws of the country you are in. Your embassy will not be sympathetic if you end up in jail after committing a crime locally, even if such actions are legal in your own country.

Some countries opt to have only one diplomatic mission for the entire Baltic region (usually in Rīga), while others may be served out of embassies in Stockholm or Berlin.

Gay & Lesbian Travellers

Following independence, all three Baltic States decriminalised homosexual acts and today there is an equal age of consent for sexual acts for all citizens (set at 14 in Estonia and 16 in Latvia and Lithuania). Yet not all is as rosy as it seems. Of the three, secular Estonia is the most tolerant (see p168), while life is considerably harder for gays and lesbians in Catholic Lithuania and arguably worse still in Latvia. Being 'out' is largely out of the question, as small displays of public affection can provoke some nasty responses. In the International Lesbian and Gay Association (ILGA) of Europe's 2011 *Rainbow Europe Map*, which ranks each nation according to the legal protection offered to its lesbian, gay, bisexual and transgender (LGBT) citizens (with 17 being full equality), Estonia scored 2, Lithuania 1 and Latvia zero (which is not as bad as Russia's -2 and the Ukraine's -4).

While there is a small gay scene in Tallinn, Rīga and Vilnius, there's almost nothing elsewhere. Baltic Pride has become an annual festival, with a successful, problem-free celebration held in Tallinn in 2011 – the same can't be said for previous events held in the other capitals. Refusing to be cowed, it's Rīga's turn again in 2012 and Vilnius' in 2013.

If reading all this has you yearning for a drink, you'll find gay and lesbian venues listed under Entertainment in Tallinn (p73), Rīga (p213) and Vilnius (p302).

Resources

Estonian LGBT portal (www.gay.ee)

ILGA Europe (www.ilga-europe .org) Excellent country-by-country information on gay life and acceptance in all of Europe, including the Baltic countries.

Latvian LGBT portal (www .gay.lv)

Lithuanian LGBT portal (www.gay.lt)

Health

The Baltic region is, on the whole, a pretty healthy place to travel in, though medical facilities outside of the capital cities may not be entirely up to Western standards. Practically all pharmacies in the capitals and larger towns stock imported Western medicines. In the capitals, private clinics offer Western-standard, English-speaking medical care but they are often expensive. In an emergency, seek your hotel's help first (if you're in one); the bigger hotels may have doctors on call. Emergency care is free in all three countries.

If you're an EU citizen, a European Health Insurance Card (EHIC, which replaced the E111 form in 2006) covers you for most medical care, but not for non-emergencies or the cost of repatriation. You can apply for one online in many EU countries via your government health department's website.

Insect Bites & Stings

Spread by tick bites, tick-borne encephalitis is a serious infection of the brain. If you intend to spend a lot of time in forested areas, including by the coast where pine forest prevails, vaccination is advised. Two doses of vaccine will give a year's protection, three doses give up to three years'. You should always check all over your body if you have been walking through a potentially tick-infested area. Signs along the Lithuanian coast alert walkers and beachgoers to particularly rampant tick areas. If you find an attached tick, press down around its head with tweezers, grab the head and gently pull upwards. Avoid pulling the rear of the body as this may squeeze the tick's gut contents through the attached mouth parts into the skin, increasing the risk of infection and disease.

Mosquitoes are a voracious pest in the region, and can cause irritation and infected bites. Use a DEET-based insect repellent.

Water

Some official travel advisories detail the need to avoid tap water and drink only boiled or bottled water, but locals insist the tap water is perfectly safe to drink (if not altogether pleasant-tasting). Do not drink water from rivers or lakes as it may contain bacteria or viruses that can cause diarrhoea or vomiting.

Insurance

A travel insurance policy to cover theft, loss of property and medical problems is a good idea. Worldwide travel insurance is available at www.lonelyplanet.com/travel_services. You can buy, extend and claim online anytime – even if you're already on the road.

Some policies offer lower and higher medical expense options. Policies can vary widely, so be sure to check the fine print. Some insurance policies will specifically exclude 'dangerous activities', which can include hiking.

You may prefer a policy that pays doctors or hospitals rather than requiring you to pay on the spot and claim later. If you have to claim later make sure you keep all documentation. Some policies ask you to call back (reverse charges) to a centre in your home country where an immediate assessment of your problem is made. Check that the policy covers ambulances and an emergency flight home.

Internet Access

Internet use has developed at a staggering pace in the Baltic, outstripping much of Western Europe. With the introduction of wireless technology and more affordable laptops and smartphones, an ever-increasing number of locals are becoming internet savvy. What this means for travellers is a decrease in the number of internet cafes and an increase in wi-fi hotspots – Estonia in particular is virtually blanketed in wi-fi. Most major cities still sport a cafe or two dedicated to internet access, but in rural areas you'll be hard pressed to find one; in these parts tourist offices or libraries are your best bet.

Almost all top-end hotels, an ever-expanding number of midrange places and even many budget options advertise internet access in rooms. What is actually meant by this varies enormously, though. Some simply have a telephone plug in the room or provide you with a cable, while many others are covered by wi-fi (often free). A small number of places rent laptops or have computers in each room. Many places have a computer terminal in the lobby for guest use.

Each of the countries maintains lists of hotspots you can tap into. For details:
Estonia www.wifi.ee
Latvia http://wifi.inbox.lv
Lithuania www.wifi.lt

Legal Matters

If you are arrested in the Baltic you have the same basic legal rights as anywhere else in Europe, including the right to be informed of the reason for your arrest (before being carted off to the police station), to inform a family member of your misfortune (once you have been carted off) and to have your lawyer present during questioning. You cannot be detained for more than 72 hours without being charged with an offence.

In Rīga, you can be fined on the spot for straying from public footpaths onto the neatly mowed grass lawns in city parks. In Vilnius, you can sit/lie/sunbathe on the grass in city parks but you can't sleep; police patrol on horseback to check that your eyes aren't shut.

Smoking is not permitted in restaurants, bars, nightclubs and cafes in all three countries, although it is permitted on outdoor terraces or in closed-off smoking rooms (with proper ventilation).

See also p413 for information on road rules.

Maps

Decent regional and country maps are widely available outside the region, as are quality city maps in each country. A map covering the region is useful for planning: *Estonia, Latvia, Lithuania* (Cartographia; www.cartographia.hu) has a 1:700,000-scale map of the three countries, and many publishers produce something similar. Insight Travel Maps has a useful 1:800,000 *Baltic States* map, with city plans of Tallinn and Rīga.

Good maps to look for in the region include *Eesti Latvija Lietuva* (1:700,000) published by Vilnius-based Briedis (www.briedis.eu). In Estonia, EO Map (www.eomap.ee) does a pretty mean *Baltimaad* (Baltic States, 1:800,000), which is widely available in Estonian bookshops.

In Latvia, map publisher Jāņa sēta (www.kartes.lv) is the market leader, with its pocket-sized, spiral-bound, 152-page *Baltic Countries & Kaliningrad Region* (1:500,000) containing 72 city and town plans as well as road maps covering the entire region. Its *Baltic Countries* (1:700,000) road map is equally good.

The website www.maps.com is a decent digital map resource. See also p168 for Estonia, p273 for Latvia and p383 for Lithuania.

Money

ATMs

ATMs accepting Cirrus, Visa and MasterCard are widespread in cities and larger towns, enabling you to get cash 24 hours a day. Most ATMs are multilingual, using the main European languages.

Credit Cards

Credit cards are widely accepted in hotels, restaurants and shops, especially at the upper end of the market. Visa and MasterCard are the most commonly accepted but Diners Club and Amex also crop up. They are essential for hiring a car. It's generally easiest to use an ATM for a Visa or MasterCard cash advance.

Moneychangers

Every town has somewhere you can change cash: usually a bank, exchange office or currency-exchange kiosk. The latter crop up in all sorts of places, particularly transport terminals, airports, bus stations and train stations. Rates vary from one outlet to another. Exchange places are generally open during usual business hours.

Tipping & Bargaining

It's fairly common, though not compulsory, to tip waiters 5% to 10% by rounding up the bill. Some bargaining (but not a lot) goes on at flea markets. Savings are not likely to be more than 10% to 20% of the initial asking price.

Travellers Cheques

Given the explosion of ATMs accepting international cards, travellers cheques are going the way of the dinosaurs, but you should still be able to exchange them (for a hefty commission) at banks in major cities.

Post

Letters and postcards from any of the three countries take about two to four days to Western Europe, seven to 10 days to North America and two weeks to Australia, New Zealand and South Africa. Occasionally, as in any other country, a letter or parcel might go astray for a couple of weeks, but generally everything arrives.

You can buy your stamps at a post office (Estonian: *postkontor;* Latvian: *pasts;* Lithuanian: *paštas*) and post your mail there. In Estonia, you can bypass the post office, buy stamps in shops and slip the envelope in any post box.

For postal rates and other information, take a look at the websites of the postal companies:

Eesti Post (www.post.ee) Estonia.
Latvijas Pasts (www.pasts.lv/en/) Latvia.
Lietuvos Paštas (www.post.lt) Lithuania.

Expensive international express-mail services are available in the capital cities.

The way addresses are written conforms to Western norms, for example:

Kazimiera Jones
Veidenbauma iela 35-17
LV-5432 Ventspils
Latvia

Veidenbauma iela 35-17 means Veidenbaum Street, building No 35, flat No 17. Postcodes in Estonia are the letters EE plus five digits, in Latvia LV- plus four digits, and in Lithuania LT- plus five digits (although the LT isn't essential). For people wanting to receive mail on the move, there are poste-restante services in the main post offices in Tallinn and Vilnius, and at the post office next to Rīga train station. All three keep mail for a month. Address letters to poste restante as follows, preceded by the full name of the recipient:

ANSWERING THE CALL OF NATURE

We hope you're not busting for a pee, as working out which toilet door to enter may require some thinking time. The letter 'M' marks a men's toilet in Estonian, 'V' in Latvian or Lithuanian. 'N' indicates a women's toilet in Estonian, 'S' in Latvian and 'M' in Lithuanian. Some toilets sport the triangle system: a skirtlike triangle for women and a broad-shouldered, upside-down triangle for men. To add even more confusion, in Lithuania (as in neighbouring Poland), male toilets may be indicated by a triangle and female toilets by a circle.

Estonia Poste Restante, Narva maantee 1, EE10101 Tallinn, Estonia

Latvia Poste Restante, Rīga, LV-1050 Latvia

Lithuania Poste Restante, Vilnius ACP, Gedimino prospektas 7, LT-01001 Vilnius, Lithuania

Telephone

City codes are a thing of the past in little Estonia and Latvia, meaning if you're calling from abroad you just dial the country code then the listed number. In Lithuania things are a little more complicated. Precise details on calling as well as the low-down on the local phone scene (hint: it's mobile-centric in all three countries) can be found in the country directories (see Estonia, p169; Latvia, p273; and Lithuania, p384).

Speaking of mobile phones, Estonia, Latvia and Lithuania all use GSM 900/1800 – compatible with the rest of Europe and Australia, but not with the North American GSM 1900 or the totally different system in Japan. Assuming your phone is GSM 900/1800-compatible, you can buy a cheap SIM-card package from a choice of mobile-phone providers in all three countries, and get dialling. Again, see the country directories for more details.

Time

Estonia, Latvia and Lithuania are on Eastern European Time (GMT/UTC + 2). All three countries adhere to daylight savings, which runs from the last Sunday in March to the last Sunday in October. At this time it's GMT + 3.

The 24-hour clock is used for train, bus and flight timetables, while letters (the initial letter of each day) or numerals (I or 1 = Monday; VII or 7 = Sunday) may indicate the days of the week in posted opening hours or timetables. Dates may be listed the American way: the month first, followed by the day and the year; ie 01/06/74 referring to 6 January 1974, not 1 June 1974. If you're in any doubt, it's best to ask.

Toilets

Public toilets in the Baltic countries are wondrous things compared to the stinking black holes of the past. Today you'll find mostly clean, modern systems (no grubby baskets in the corner, just flush the paper). That isn't to say that we recommend spending much time in the public restrooms of train or bus stations; they aren't the most inviting of places – but you should've been here 15 years ago! Although there are public toilets in some places, you can also stroll into large hotels in major cities and use the toilets without upsetting the staff too much. Or do what everyone else does and pop into the nearest McDonald's.

Tourist Information

All three capitals, plus most cities, towns and seaside resorts, sport an efficient tourist office of sorts that doles out accommodation lists and information brochures, many in English and usually delivered with a smile. These tourist offices are coordinated by each country's national tourist board, listed in the country directories (Estonia, p169; Latvia, p274; and Lithuania, p384).

Travellers with Disabilities

With its cobbled streets, rickety pavements and old buildings (often without elevators), the Baltic presents challenges for travellers with disabilities. That said, many city hotels have rooms equipped for disabled travellers; your first port of call for this information should be the tourist information centres of the capitals. Some beaches on the western Lithuanian coast in Nida and Palanga have ramps to allow wheelchair access to the sand.

Useful resources:

Able Travel (www.able-travel .com) Has information on Estonia on its website (sadly there's no information for either Latvia or Lithuania).

Apeirons (☑6729 9277; www .apeirons.lv) This organisation of people with disabilities and their friends is a good first contact in Latvia.

Freedom of Movement (Liikumisvabadus; http:// liikumisvabadus.invainfo.ee) This fantastic resource provides detailed information (in English) about accessibility in Estonia for wheelchair-users and those with limited movement, split into regions, towns and places of interest.

Visas

Your number-one document is your passport. Make sure it's valid for at least three months after the end of your Baltic travels. Only some nationalities need visas. Citizens from the EU, Australia, Canada, Japan, New Zealand and the US do not require visas for entry into Estonia, Latvia or Lithuania.

Other nationalities should check the websites of the relevant Ministries of Foreign Affairs:

Estonia Välisministeerium; www.vm.ee

Latvia www.pmlp.gov.lv

Lithuania www.migracija.lt

Visa Extensions

Single-entry visas can sometimes be extended in the Baltic. In Latvia visit the foreigners' service centre of the **Office of Citizenship & Migration Affairs** (Pilsonības un migrācijas lietu pārvalde; ☎6721 9656; www.pmlp.gov.lv; Alunāna iela 1, Rīga). In Lithuania your first port of call should probably be the migration department inside the **Ministry of Interior** (Migracijos Departamentas; ☎52-717 112; www.migracija.lt; L. Sapiegos 1, Vilnius).

Belarusian Visas

You will need a Belarusian visa, arranged in advance, even to transit the country. Visas are not issued at road borders. Belarusian embassies in all three Baltic capitals issue visas – see www.belembassy.org for contact details. For the low-down, see the **Ministry of Foreign Affairs of the Republic of Belarus** (www.mfa.gov.by).

Russian Visas

All foreign visitors need a visa to enter Russia. Getting the visa can be time-consuming, and our strongest advice is that you obtain one before you leave home. A tourist visa requires an invitation, which can be issued from a hotel or some hostels in Russia or from online visa specialists (eg www.visatorussia.com). You then present your invitation and application to a Russian consulate and receive your visa a few weeks later (or an agency can do that step too, for a fee – this is recommended, as they're experts in dealing with the bureaucracy).

If you didn't get the urge to enter Russia until arriving in the Baltic, you can try your luck in obtaining a Russian visa from one of the embassies in Tallinn (p167), Rīga (p272) or Vilnius (p382). There you'll get a heavy dose of bureaucracy and perhaps a visa – there are no guarantees, and this might come down to your nationality. You might also consider asking a local travel agency for help.

A special Kaliningrad 72 Hour Express Visa is available for Russia's Kaliningrad region for citizens of Schengen countries (ie most countries of the EU, excluding the UK and Ireland), the UK and Japan, but you'll still need to apply in advance and it's only available for those arriving by plane or crossing from Poland. It's probably best to plan on obtaining a regular Russian visa, arranged in advance.

Volunteering

Estonia has an established WWOOF (World Wide Opportunities on Organic Farms) organisation (p139), facilitating volunteer work on organic farms in exchange for accommodation and meals.

Lithuania's branch is just starting out (www.wwoof.lt) and Latvia has only a couple of farms listed with WWOOF Independents (www.wwoof.org/wwind/). Occasionally volunteer opportunities for English speakers are advertised locally in the *Baltic Times* (www.baltictimes.com) newspaper.

Women Travellers

The Balts have some fairly traditional ideas about gender roles, but on the other hand they're pretty reserved and rarely impose themselves upon other people in an annoying way. Women are not likely to receive aggravation from men in the Baltic, although unaccompanied women may want to avoid a few of the sleazier bars and beer cellars. Many women travel on overnight buses and trains alone, but if you're travelling on a train at night, play safe and use the hefty metal lock on the inside of the carriage door.

Work

The Baltic region has enough difficulty keeping its own people employed, meaning there's little temporary work for visitors. Most Westerners working here have been posted by companies back home. However, these are times of change, and there is some scope for people who want to stay a while and carve themselves a new niche – though, in Western terms, you shouldn't expect to get rich doing so. The English language is certainly in demand and you might be able to earn your keep (or part of it) teaching it in one of the main cities. For teaching and other postings, try www.goabroad.com.

Transport

GETTING THERE & AWAY

There are numerous ways to enter the Baltic countries, either directly or via a close neighbour. For example, it's feasible to fly or take a bus to Warsaw and then enter Lithuania by train, or fly to Helsinki and sail from there to Estonia. Within the Baltic, distances are relatively small.

This section focuses on getting to Estonia, Latvia and Lithuania from outside the region. For travel within the region see p410. Flights, tours and rail tickets can be booked online at www.lonelyplanet.com/bookings.

Entering Estonia, Latvia & Lithuania

Whether you arrive by bus, boat, plane or train, entry procedures are fairly quick and painless. If you're travelling from within the Schengen zone (ie most countries of the EU, excluding the UK and Ireland), there are no longer any arrival formalities.

THINGS CHANGE

The information in this chapter is particularly vulnerable to change: prices for international travel are volatile, routes are introduced and cancelled, schedules change, special deals come and go, and rules and visa requirements are amended.

Airlines and governments seem to take a perverse pleasure in making price structures and regulations as complicated as possible. You should check directly with the airline or a travel agent to make sure you understand how a fare (and ticket you may buy) works. In addition, the travel industry is highly competitive and there are many lurks and perks.

The details given in this chapter should be regarded as pointers and are not a substitute for your own careful, up-to-date research.

Passport

Travellers arriving from outside the Schengen border zone need a passport, valid for three months beyond the planned stay. Very few nationalities need a visa for entering Estonia, Latvia or Lithuania. See p403 for more information.

Air

Airports & Airlines

Estonia's national carrier is Estonian Air, while Latvia's is airBaltic. Lithuania's former national carrier is now defunct. International airports within the region:

Kaunas Airport (KUN; ☎37-399 396; www.kaunasair.lt) Lithuania.

Palanga Airport (PLQ; ☎3460-52 020; www.palanga-airport.lt) Lithuania.

Rīga International Airport (RIX; ☎2931 1187; www.riga-airport.com) Latvia.

Tallinn Airport (TLL; ☎605 8888; www.tallinn-airport.ee) Estonia.

Tartu Airport (TAY; ☎605 8888; www.tartu-airport.ee) Estonia.

Vilnius Airport (VNO; ☎5-230 6666; www.vilnius-airport.lt) Lithuania.

AIRLINES FLYING TO & FROM ESTONIA, LATVIA & LITHUANIA

Aer Lingus (EI; ☎Lithuania 5-206 0728; www.aerlingus.com) Flies from Dublin to Vilnius.

Aeroflot (SU; ☎Latvia 6778 0770; www.aeroflot.com) Flies from Moscow (Sheremetjevo) to Rīga.

Aerosvit Airlines (☎Latvia 6720 7502, Lithuania 5-219 2055; www.aerosvit.com) Flies from Kiev to Rīga and Vilnius.

AirBaltic (BT; ☎Estonia 17107, Latvia 6700 6006, Lithuania 1825; www.airbaltic.com) From Ålesund, Almaty, Amman, Amsterdam, Antalya, Athens, Baku, Barcelona, Bari, Beirut,

Belgrade, Bergen, Berlin (Tegel), Billund, Brussels, Budapest, Chisinau, Copenhagen, Dushanbe, Dusseldorf, Gdansk, Hamburg, Helsinki, Heraklion, Istanbul (Ataturk), Kaliningrad, Kiev, Kuopio, Lappeenranta, London (Gatwick), Madrid (Barajas), Milan (Linate), Minsk, Moscow (Sheremetjevo), Munich, Nice, Odessa, Oslo, Paris (Charles-de-Gaulle), Rome (Fiumicino), Simferopol, Stockholm (Arlanda), St Petersburg (Pulkovo), Stavanger, Tampere, Tashkent, Tel Aviv, Tenerife, Tbilisi, Tromso, Turku, Umea, Vaasa, Venice, Vienna, Visby, Warsaw, Yerevan and Zurich to Rīga.

Austrian Airlines (OS; ☑Lithuania 5-210 5030; www .aua.com) Flies from Vienna to Vilnius.

Belavia (B2; ☑Estonia 6732 0314; http://en.belavia.by) Flies from Minsk to Rīga.

Brussels Airlines (SN; ☑Lithuania 5-252 5555; www .brusselsairlines.com) Flies from Brussels to Vilnius.

City Airline (CF; ☑Sweden 3160 0385; www.cityairline.com)

Flies from Gothenburg to Tallinn.

ČSA (Czech Airlines; OK; ☑Estonia 630 9397, Latvia 6720 7636, Lithuania 5-215 1511; www.czechairlines.com) Flies from Prague to Rīga, Tallinn and Vilnius.

easyJet (U2; ☑UK 870 600 0000; www.easyjet.com) Flies from Liverpool and London (Stansted) to Tallinn.

Estonian Air (OV; ☑Estonia 640 1160; www.estonian-air.ee) Flies from Amsterdam, Barcelona, Berlin, Brussels, Copenhagen, Kiev, London (Gatwick), Moscow (Sheremetjevo), Oslo, Paris (Charles-de-Gaulle), St Petersburg, Stockholm and Trondheim to Tallinn.

Flybe (FC; ☑UK 01392-268 529; www.flybe.com) Flies from Helsinki to Tallinn and Tartu.

Finnair (AY; ☑Estonia 626 6309, Latvia 6720 7010, Lithuania 5-261 9339; www .finnair.com) Flies from Helsinki to Rīga, Tallinn and Vilnius.

LOT (LO; ☑Estonia 668 1008, Latvia 6720 7113, Lithuania 5-273 9000; www.lot.com)

Flies from Warsaw to Rīga, Tallinn and Vilnius.

Lufthansa (LO; ☑Latvia 6728 5901, Lithuania 5-212 0220; www.lufthansa.com) Flies from Frankfurt to Rīga, Tallinn and Vilnius, and from Munich to Tallinn.

Norwegian Air Shuttle (DY; ☑Norway 2149 0015; www .norwegian.no) Flies from Oslo to Palanga, Rīga, Tallinn and Vilnius, and from Trondheim to Rīga.

Ryanair (FR; www.ryanair .com) Flies to **Kaunas** from Alicante, Birmingham, Bristol, Charleroi, Dublin, Edinburgh, Eindhoven, Frankfurt (Hahn), Gothenburg, Kos, Leeds Bradford, Liverpool, London (Gatwick, Luton and Stansted), Paris (Beauvais), Rhodes, Rygge, Skavsta and Tampere. Flies to **Rīga** from Bergamo, Bremen, Bristol (Lulsgate), Charleroi, Dublin, East Midlands, Frankfurt (Hahn), Liverpool, London (Stansted), Niederrhein, Prestwick, Rome (Ciampino), Rygge, Skavsta and Tampere. Flies to **Tallinn** from Bergamo, Bremen,

CLIMATE CHANGE & TRAVEL

Climate change is a serious threat to the ecosystems that humans rely upon, and air travel is the fastest-growing contributor to the problem. Lonely Planet regards travel, overall, as a global benefit, but believes we all have a responsibility to limit our personal impact on global warming.

Flying & Climate Change

Pretty much every form of motorised travel generates CO_2 (the main cause of human-induced climate change) but planes are far and away the worst offenders, not just because of the sheer distances they allow us to travel, but because they release greenhouse gases high into the atmosphere. The statistics are frightening: two people taking a return flight between Europe and the US will contribute as much to climate change as an average household's gas and electricity consumption over a whole year.

Carbon Offset Schemes

Climatecare.org and other websites use 'carbon calculators' that allow travellers to off-set the level of greenhouse gases they are responsible for with financial contributions to sustainable travel schemes that reduce global warming – including projects in India, Honduras, Kazakhstan and Uganda.

Lonely Planet, together with Rough Guides and other concerned partners in the travel industry, support the carbon offset scheme run by climatecare.org. Lonely Planet offsets all of its staff and author travel.

For more information check out our website: www.lonelyplanet.com.

Dublin, East Midlands, Edinburgh, Girona, London (Luton), Manchester, Niederrhein, Rygge and Skavsta. Flies to **Vilnius** from Barcelona (El Prat), Bergamo, Bremen, Dublin, Girona, London (Stansted) and Rome.

SAS Scandinavian Airlines (SK; ☎ Lithuania 5-230 6638; www.scandinavian.net) Flies from Copenhagen and Oslo to Palanga, and from Copenhagen to Vilnius.

Skyways Express (JZ; ☎ Sweden 771-95 95 00; www.skyways.se) Flies from Gothenburg to Rīga, and from Berlin and Stockholm to Vilnius.

Transaero (UN; www.transaero.ru) Flies from Moscow (Domodedovo) to Rīga.

Turkish Airlines (TK; ☎ Latvia 6735 9440; www.turkishairlines.com) Flies from Istanbul to Rīga.

UTair Aviation (UT; ☎ Estonia 622 5660; www.utair.ru) Flies from Moscow (Vnukovoto) to Rīga, Tallinn and Vilnius.

Uzbekistan Airways (HY; www.uzairways.com) Flies from New York (JFK) and Tashkent to Rīga.

Wizz Air (W6; ☎ Latvia 9020 0905; www.wizzair.com) Flies from London (Luton), Eindhoven and Oslo (Torp) to Rīga; from Barcelona, Bergen, Cork, Doncaster, Dortmund, Eindhoven, Liverpool, London (Luton), Milan, Oslo (Torp), Paris and Rome to Vilnius.

Tickets

Automated online ticket sales work well if you're planning a simple one-way or return trip on specified dates, but for complicated routing they are no substitute for a travel agent with the low-down on specials deals, strategies for avoiding stopovers and other useful advice.

Paying by credit card offers some protection if you end up dealing with a rogue fly-by-night agency, as most card issuers provide refunds if you can prove you didn't get what you paid for. Even better, buy a ticket from a bonded agent, such as one covered by the **Air Travel Organiser's Licence** (ATOL; www.atol.org.uk) scheme in the UK. If you have doubts about the service provider, at the very least call the airline and confirm that your booking has been made.

Australia & New Zealand

If you're coming from Australasia, a trip to the Baltic will necessitate at least three separate flights and there's no one airline that services the entire route. **Star Alliance** (www.staralliance.com) has the most partner airlines serving the Baltic states (Austrian Airlines, Brussels Airlines, LOT, Lufthansa, SAS and Turkish Airlines) making an Air New Zealand or Thai Airways codeshare the most flexible choice. Qantas is a member of **One World** (www.oneworld.com) but Finnair is the only One World member that flies directly to the Baltic.

The cheapest fares to Europe tend to be for routes through Asia, although you can sometimes get a good deal through the USA from New Zealand. If you're considering a route via London, note that no Baltic flights leave from Heathrow, which is where most Australian and New Zealand flights land.

Caucasus & Central Asia

Armenia AirBaltic flies from Yerevan to Rīga.

Azerbaijan AirBaltic flies from Baku to Rīga.

Georgia AirBaltic flies from Tbilisi to Rīga.

Kazakhstan AirBaltic flies from Almaty to Rīga.

Tajikistan AirBaltic flies from Dushanbe to Rīga.

Uzbekistan AirBaltic and Uzbekistan Airways fly from Tashkent to Rīga.

Continental Europe

Budget airlines have revolutionised European air transport in the past decade and the Baltic countries are well connected by both premium and budget carriers.

Austria From Vienna you can fly AirBaltic to Rīga or Austrian to Vilnius.

Belarus AirBaltic and Belavia fly from Minsk to Rīga.

Belgium From Brussels you can fly AirBaltic to Rīga, Brussels Airlines to Vilnius or Estonian Air to Tallinn. Ryanair flies from Charleroi to Kaunas and Rīga.

Czech Republic ČSA flies from Prague to Rīga, Tallinn and Vilnius.

France AirBaltic flies from Nice and Paris to Rīga. Estonian Air flies from Paris to Tallinn. Ryanair flies from Paris (Beauvais) to Kaunas. Wizz Air flies from Paris to Vilnius.

Germany AirBaltic flies from Berlin, Dusseldorf, Hamburg and Munich to Rīga. Lufthansa flies from Frankfurt to Rīga, Tallinn and Vilnius, and from Munich to Tallinn. Estonian Air flies from Berlin to Tallinn. Ryanair flies from Frankfurt (Hahn) to Kaunas and Rīga; from Niederrhein to Rīga and Tallinn; and from Bremen to Rīga, Tallinn and Vilnius. Skyways Express flies from Berlin to Vilnius. Wizz Air flies from Dortmund to Vilnius.

Greece AirBaltic flies from Athens and Heraklion to Rīga. Ryanair flies from Rhodes and Kos to Kaunas.

Hungary AirBaltic flies from Budapest to Rīga.

Italy AirBaltic flies from Bari, Milan, Rome and Venice to Rīga. Ryanair flies from Bergamo to Rīga, Tallinn and Vilnius; and from Rome (Ciampino) to Rīga and Vilnius. Wizz Air flies from Milan and Rome to Vilnius.

Netherlands From Amsterdam, take AirBaltic to Rīga or Estonian Air to Tallinn. From Eindhoven, take Ryanair to Kaunas or Wizz Air to Rīga and Vilnius.

Moldova AirBaltic flies from Chisinau to Rīga.

Poland AirBaltic flies from Gdansk and Warsaw to Rīga. LOT flies from Warsaw to Rīga, Tallinn and Vilnius.

Serbia AirBaltic flies from Belgrade to Rīga.

Spain AirBaltic flies from Barcelona, Madrid and Tenerife to Rīga. Estonian Air flies from Barcelona to Tallinn. Ryanair flies from Alicante to Kaunas; from Girona to Tallinn and Vilnius; and from Barcelona to Vilnius. Wizz Air flies from Barcelona to Vilnius.

Switzerland AirBaltic flies from Zurich to Rīga.

Ukraine Aerosvit flies from Kiev to Rīga and Vilnius. AirBaltic flies from Kiev, Odessa and Simferopol to Rīga. Estonian Air flies from Kiev to Tallinn.

Middle East

Israel AirBaltic flies from Tel Aviv to Rīga.

Jordan AirBaltic flies from Amman to Rīga.

Lebanon AirBaltic flies from Beirut to Rīga.

Turkey AirBaltic flies from Antalya and Istanbul to Rīga. Turkish Airlines flies from Istanbul to Rīga.

Nordic Countries

Denmark AirBaltic flies from Billund and Copenhagen to Rīga. Estonian Air flies from Copenhagen to Tallinn. SAS flies from Copenhagen to Palanga and Vilnius.

Finland AirBaltic flies from Helsinki, Kuopio, Lappeenranta, Tampere, Turku and Vaasa to Rīga. Flybe flies from Helsinki to Tallinn and Tartu. Finnair flies from Helsinki to Rīga, Tallinn and Vilnius. Ryanair flies from Tampere to Kaunas and Rīga.

Norway AirBaltic flies from Ålesund, Bergen, Oslo, Stavanger and Tromso to Rīga. Estonian Air flies from Oslo and Trondheim to Tallinn. Norwegian Air Shuttle flies from Oslo to Palanga, Rīga, Tallinn and Vilnius, and from Trondheim to Rīga. Ryanair flies from Rygge to Kaunas, Rīga and Tallinn. SAS flies from Oslo to Palanga. Wizz Air flies from Torp to Rīga and Vilnius and from Bergen to Vilnius.

Sweden AirBaltic flies from Stockholm, Umea and Visby to Rīga. City Airline flies from Gothenburg to Tallinn. Estonian Air flies from Stockholm to Tallinn. Ryanair flies from Gothenburg to Kaunas and from Skavsta to Kaunas, Rīga and Tallinn. Skyways Express flies from Gothenberg to Rīga and from Stockholm to Vilnius.

North America

There is a direct flight from New York (JFK) to Rīga on Uzbekistan Airways. Otherwise, book a codeshare flight through **Star Alliance** (www.staralliance.com) on Austrian Airlines, Brussels Airlines, LOT, Lufthansa, SAS or Turkish Airlines; through **One World** (www.oneworld .com) on Finnair; or through **SkyTeam** (www.skyteam.com) on Aeroflot or ČSA.

Russia

Kaliningrad AirBaltic flies to Rīga.

Moscow Aeroflot, AirBaltic and Transaero fly to Rīga. Estonian Air flies to Tallinn. UTair flies to Rīga, Tallinn and Vilnius.

St Petersburg AirBaltic flies to Rīga. Estonian Air flies to Tallinn.

UK & Ireland

Budget airlines Ryanair, easyJet and Wizz Air fly numerous routes from Ireland and the UK to the Baltic, including departures from many small regional airports. If considering connecting flights via London, allow several hours to travel between airports as 'London' airports are a long way from the city and from each other.

Birmingham Ryanair flies to Kaunas.

Bristol Ryanair flies to Kaunas and Rīga.

Cork Wizz Air flies to Vilnius.

Doncaster Wizz Air flies to Vilnius.

Dublin AerLingus flies to Vilnius. Ryanair flies to Kaunas, Rīga, Tallinn and Vilnius.

East Midlands Ryanair flies to Rīga and Tallinn.

Edinburgh Ryanair flies to Kaunas and Tallinn.

Leeds Bradford Ryanair flies to Kaunas.

London AirBaltic flies from Gatwick to Rīga. easyJet flies from Stansted to Tallinn. Ryanair flies to Kaunas, Rīga, Tallinn and Vilnius from various airports. Wizz Air flies from Luton to Rīga and Vilnius.

Liverpool Take easyJet to Tallinn, Ryanair to Kaunas and Rīga, or Wizz Air to Vilnius.

Manchester Ryanair flies to Tallinn.

Prestwick Ryanair flies to Rīga.

Land

Bicycle

Bicycles can be carried cheaply (or free) on ferries from the Nordic countries and Germany to the Baltic; see p409 for ferry routes. Pedallers through Poland face the same choice of routes as drivers; see p408 for more information.

Border Crossings

Travelling from north to south, Estonia shares borders with Russia and Latvia; Latvia shares borders with Estonia, Russia, Belarus, and Lithuania; while Lithuania borders Latvia,

Belarus, Poland and the Kaliningrad Region (part of Russia).

Now that the Baltic countries are part of the EU and part of the Schengen Agreement, border checkpoints between Estonia, Lithuania, Latvia and Poland have disappeared.

Travel to Belarus and Russia is another matter entirely. These borders continue to be rigorously controlled, and you'll need to get a visa in advance. Expect to wait up to an hour regardless. Entering Russia (including the Kaliningrad Region) or Belarus, you must fill in a declaration form, specifying how much cash (in any currency) and what valuables you are taking into the country.

At Narva-Ivangorod, on the Estonian–Russian border, particularly long queues form. The Kaliningrad Region enjoys quieter road borders with Lithuania at Panemunė–Sovietsk, between Kybartai (Lithuania) and Nesterov, and on the Curonian Spit along the Klaipėda–Zelenogradsk road. Only Belarus' road borders with Lithuania at Salčininkai, Medininkai and Lavoriškės are open to Westerners.

Bus

With a few exceptions, buses are the cheapest but least comfortable method of reaching the Baltic from within Europe. Direct buses arrive from as far north as St Petersburg, as far west as Paris, as far south as Sofia and as far east as Moscow. From much of the rest of Europe you can reach the Baltic with a single change of bus in Warsaw.

See the following bus company websites for route maps, prices, schedules, ticketing agents and more; you can also purchase tickets online. There are 10% discounts for passengers under 26 or over 60. Return tickets cost about 20% less than two one-way tickets.

MAJOR BUS ROUTES

Major routes for **Ecolines** (www.ecolines.net) include the following:

Tallinn-Narva-St Petersburg (twice daily)

Tallinn-Tartu-Pskov-Moscow (weekly)

Rīga-Valmiera-Narva-Ivangorod-St Petersburg (daily)

Rīga-Moscow (daily)

Rīga-Kiev (daily)

Rīga-Vilnius-Warsaw-Berlin-Aalborg (twice weekly)

Rīga-Vilnius-Warsaw-Krakow-Bratislava-Vienna-Budapest-Sofia (weekly)

Rīga-Vilnius-Warsaw-Dresden-Munich-Zurich (weekly)

Rīga-Vilnius-Warsaw-Antwerp-Brussels-Paris (twice weekly)

Rīga-Šiauliai-Kaliningrad (daily)

Rīga-Pskov-St Petersburg (daily)

Vilnius-Moscow (daily)

Major routes for **Lux Express** (www.luxexpress.eu) and its associated budget line **Simple Express** (www.simpleexpress.eu) include the following:

Tallinn-Narva-St Petersburg (five daily)

Rīga-Valga-Tartu-Narva-St Petersburg (twice daily)

Vilnius-Kaunas-Warsaw (twice daily)

Car & Motorcycle

If you take your own vehicle to the Baltic, get it in good condition before you leave home.

It's worth contacting motoring clubs, as well as Estonian, Latvian and Lithuanian embassies, for information on regulations, border crossing and so on.

AA (www.aa.co.nz) New Zealand.

AA (www.theaa.com) UK.

AAA (www.aaa.com) USA.

AAA (www.aaa.asn.au) Australia.

RAC (www.rac.co.uk) UK.

DOCUMENTS

Bring your vehicle's registration document, preferably in the form of an international motor vehicle certificate, which is a translation of the basic registration document. Motoring associations should be able to provide one. An International Driving Permit (IDP; also obtainable from motoring associations) is recommended but your own licence will suffice in most situations. All three Baltic countries demand compulsory accident insurance for drivers.

Insurance policies with limited compensation rates can be bought at the Estonian, Latvian and Lithuanian borders. Remember that you'll also need appropriate documentation for all the countries you pass through on the way to or from the Baltics; motoring associations can advise you.

FROM BELARUS

Suckers for punishment opt for the hellish (albeit fascinating) trip through Belarus. Do not attempt to approach the border or set foot in the country without a Belarusian transit visa, only available at Belarusian embassies. No visas are sold at any Belarus border. Even with a visa, expect to wait several hours, at least, at the border. A possible route is from Białystok, Poland, to Grodno in northwestern Belarus, then on to Merkinė in Lithuania; other routes include Brest–Lida-Vilnius or Brest–Minsk–Vilnius.

FROM FINLAND

The quickest and best-served car ferry connection is from Helsinki to Tallinn. Alternatively, from Finland you can drive through Russia; from the Finnish–Russian border at Vaalimaa–Torfyanovka it's 360km to Narva (Estonia). You could do it in a day but there's little point coming this way unless you want to look at St Petersburg on the way through. Don't delay on the road from the border to St Petersburg: it's said to be plagued by bandits.

FROM GERMANY

Bringing a vehicle into the Baltic from the south entails either a ferry trip from the German ports of Kiel, Sassnitz or Lübeck, to Klaipėda (Lithuania) or to Ventspils or Liepāja (Latvia). For ferry route details, see p410.

FROM POLAND

There's a hassle-free crossing of the Polish–Lithuanian border at Ogrodniki–Lazdijai, or on the road from Suwałki, Szypliszki and Budzisko (Poland) to Kalvarija and Marijampolė. Now that Lithuania and Poland are both part of the Schengen agreement, border formalities are minimal to nonexistent.

FROM RUSSIA

From St Petersburg the drive to the Estonian border at Ivangorod–Narva is only 140km.

SWEDEN

Vehicle ferries run from Stockholm to Tallinn or Rīga, from Nynäshamn to Venstpils (Latvia) and from Karlshamn to Klaipėda.

Train

Train travel can be an interesting way of reaching the region – usually (not always) cheaper than flying and less boring than bus. Services both to and within the region have been cut back markedly in recent years but the **Rail Baltica Project** (www.rail-baltica.net) envisages an upgraded rail link connecting Tallinn with Rīga, Kaunas and Warsaw. The first stage won't be completed until at least 2013, while the entire project looks set to drag out to 2020.

The *Thomas Cook European Timetable* is the rail-lover's bible, giving a complete listing of train schedules, supplements and reservations information. It is updated monthly and is available from Thomas Cook

outlets or from www.thomas cookpublishing.com. An independent website, with loads of excellent up-to-date tips on rail travel throughout Europe, is the brilliant **Man in Seat Sixty-One** (www.seat61 .com).

See p414 for details on train travel within Estonia, Latvia and Lithuania.

POLAND

Surprisingly, there is no longer a direct train route operating between Warsaw and Vilnius. You can make a daytime journey on local trains from Warsaw to Kaunas or Vilnius, changing trains in Šeštokai, in Lithuania (close to the Poland-Lithuania border). Timetables are designed to give a 15-minute window to transfer. Total journey time is about 9½ hours. Note, too, that this option doesn't pass through Belarus.

RUSSIA & BELARUS

The old Soviet rail network still functions over most of the former USSR. Trains linking Moscow with all the main Baltic cities enable you to combine the Baltics with a Trans-Siberian trip or other Russian or Central Asian travels. If you can make sense of it, the website www .poezda.net allows you to search timetables for trains within the former USSR, but we prefer the simpler http:// bahn.hafas.de for European train schedules, although prices aren't given.

Estonia's only rail link to Russia is the **Go Rail** (☎ in Estonia 631 0044; www.gorail.ee) overnight sleeper service between Moscow and Tallinn (€64 to €247, 964km, 16 hours, daily), via Ivangorod, Narva and Rakvere.

An overnight train trundles daily between Rīga and Moscow (16 hours), while the overnight *Baltija* links the Latvian capital with St Petersburg (12½ hours). Neither train passes through Belarus.

From Vilnius, there are two daily trains to Moscow's

Belarus train station (about 15 hours). These pass through Belarus, however, so you'll need a Belarusian visa (p403). There is also an overnight train from Vilnius to St Petersburg, which doesn't transit Belarus (about 14 hours). From Vilnius, about three daily trains travel west to Kaliningrad (a journey of about seven hours).

Sea

Numerous seafaring options offer a slower but more relaxed journey. You can sail directly from Finland to Estonia (a distance of only 85km); from Germany to Latvia and Lithuania; from Denmark to Lithuania; and from Sweden to all three Baltic countries. The Tallinn–Helsinki route has so many competing services that you should have no difficulty in getting a passage any day, but some of the other services – notably Tallinn from Stockholm and the cargo ferries to Denmark – can get booked up far in advance.

Schedules and fares change frequently – double-check both when you are planning your trip. Ferry and hydrofoil operators' websites have up-to-date schedules and fares.

Denmark

DFDS Seaways (☎ in Denmark 7620 6700, in Lithuania 4639 5088; http://freight. dfdsseaways.com) operates a cargo service connecting Fredericia (Denmark) and Klaipėda (Lithuania) via Aarhus and Copenhagen, twice a week. There is limited cabin capacity for passengers – book ahead.

Finland

A fleet of ferries now carries well over two million people each year across the 85km Gulf of Finland separating Helsinki and Tallinn. There are dozens of crossings each way every day (ships two to 3½ hours year-round; hydrofoils approximately 1½ hours). Note that in high winds or bad weather, hydrofoils are often cancelled; they operate only when the sea is free from ice (generally around late March/April to late December); larger ferries sail year-round.

Shop around: the best deals are often for advance tickets purchased on the internet. Fares vary widely, depending on season, day and time of travel, and other factors (check if the company has a fuel surcharge that's included – or not – in the advertised price). Fares are generally higher at high-demand times such as Friday evening, Saturday morning and Sunday afternoon. On most ferry lines, students and seniors get a 10% to 15% discount, children between ages six and 17 pay half price and those under six sail for free. Most operators offer special deals for families and serial tickets for frequent passengers.

See the boxed text p181 for details of services.

Germany
TO/FROM LATVIA
Scandlines (☑in Latvia 4631 0561; www.scandlines.lt) ferries sail twice weekly in each direction from Travemünde (Lübeck) to both Ventspils (car/motorbike/bicycle/seat/berth from €60/20/5/40/55, 27½ hours) and Liepāja (car/motorbike/bicycle/berth from €60/20/5/70, 32½ hours).

TO/FROM LITHUANIA
DFDS Seaways (☑in Germany 4312 0976, in Lithuania 4632 3232; www.dfds seaways.com) has ferries to Klaipēda (car/motorbike/bicycle/seat/berth 220/104/35/122/242Lt) from Kiel (22 hours, six weekly) and Sassnitz (18 hours, three weekly).

Sweden
TO/FROM ESTONIA
Tallink Silja (☑in Estonia 640 9808, in Sweden 8222 140; www.tallinksilja.com) sails every night between Tallinn and Stockholm (car/motorbike/bicycle/cabin from €52/30/10/146), stopping at Mariehamn on the Åland Islands (Finland) en route. Ferries make the 17-hour crossing year-round, leaving from Terminal D in Tallinn and the Värtahamnen Terminal in Stockholm. This service gets heavily booked, so make your reservation a month or two ahead.

TO/FROM LATVIA
Scandlines (☑in Latvia 4631 0561; www.scandlines.lt) has a ferry connecting Ventspils and Nynäshamn (about 60km from Stockholm), departing five times weekly (car/motorbike/bicycle/adult from €50/25/10/30, 11 hours) from both ports.

Tallink Silja (☑in Latvia 6709 9700, in Sweden 8222 140; www.tallinksilja.com) operates overnight services daily between Rīga and Stockholm (car/motorbike/bicycle/cabin from €66/30/10/105, 19 hours).

TO/FROM LITHUANIA
DFDS Seaways (☑in Sweden 4543 3680, in Lithuania 4632 3232; www.dfdsseaways.com) has daily ferries from Karlshamn to Klaipēda (car/motorbike/bicycle/seat/berth 110/100/35/180/270Lt; 14 hours).

Yacht
The Baltics – particularly Estonia with its islands and indented coast – attract hundreds of yachts a year, mainly from Finland and Scandinavia. Good online resources:

http://marinas.nautilus.ee Information on entry regulations, a database of all the local marinas and details for ordering the *Estonian Cruising Guide*.

www.balticyachting.com Covers southern Finland as well as western Estonia.

It's also possible to rent yachts throughout the region; see opposite for more information.

Tours
Several international travel operators specialise in the Baltic region. See also p414 for operators based in the Baltic.

Baltic Holidays (☑in the UK 0845 070 5711; www.baltic holidays.com) This UK operator offers spa or city breaks, beach, family or countryside holidays and tailor-made themed holidays. Can help with genealogy research.

Baltics and Beyond (☑in UK 0845 094 2125; www.baltics andbeyond.com) A UK-based company offering regular tours, self-guided options and tailor-made trips to the three Baltic countries and some of their neighbours (including Belarus, Russia and Poland).

Regent Holidays (☑in the UK 0117 921 1711; www.regent -holidays.co.uk) A UK company with an array of Baltic options, including fly-drive and city breaks.

Vytis Tours (☑in the US 718-423-6161; www.vytistours.com) A US company offering a range of tours, from an economical eight-day jaunt round the region's capitals to a more extensive 17-day 'Grand Tour'.

GETTING AROUND

Air
There are plenty of scheduled flights between the three Baltic capitals, but domestic flights within each country are minimal.

Airlines flying within Estonia, Latvia & Lithuania

airBaltic (BT; ☎17107; www .airbaltic.com) Flies from **Rīga** to Kaunas (most days), Palanga (daily), Tallinn (seven daily) and Vilnius (six daily); and from **Vilnius** to Tallinn (most days).

Avies (U3; ☎680 3501; www .avies.ee) Flies to/from Tallinn and Kärdla (Hiiumaa) at least daily.

Estonian Air (OV; ☎640 1160; www.estonian-air.ee) Flies from Tallinn to Kuressaare (most days), Tartu (most days) and Vilnius (twice each weekday)

LFH (☎512 4013; www .lendame.ee) Winter flights from Pärnu to the islands of Kihnu and Ruhnu, and from Kuressaare to Ruhnu.

Bicycle

The flatness and small scale of Estonia, Latvia and Lithuania, and the light traffic on most roads, make them good cycling territory. On the Estonian islands particularly, you will see cyclists galore in summer. Most bring their own bicycles but there are plenty of places where you can hire one, including each of the capitals and most major towns. See p29 for more information.

Cyclists should bring waterproof clothing, and perhaps a tent if touring: you may not find accommodation in some out-of-the-way places. Travel agencies and organisations both within and outside the region organise cycling tours.

Boat

Ferry

At the time of writing there were no ferry links between the Baltic countries. Estonia has ferry connections to many of its islands, although smaller boats don't run in winter once the seas ice up;

these services are covered in detail within the Estonia chapter. Ferries within Latvia are few, although you can catch a slow boat between Rīga and Jūrmala.

Yacht

Private yachting is a popular way to get around the Baltic Coast, particularly Estonia's coast with its many islands and bays. **Sailing.ee** (☎Estonia 5333 1117; www .sailing.ee; Regati puiestee 1, Tallinn) rents out yachts with or without a skipper.

http://marinas.nautilus.ee For information and advice on Estonia's dozens of marinas.

www.marinaslatvia.lv Details of Latvia's marinas.

Bus

The region is well served by buses, although services to off-the-beaten-track villages are infrequent. Direct bus services link the three capitals and there are other cross-border services between main towns.

Buses are generally faster than trains and often slightly cheaper. Those used for local journeys, up to about two hours long, offer few comforts. Avoid window seats in rainy, snowy or very cold weather; travel with someone you're prepared to snuggle up to for body warmth; and sit in the seat allocated to you, to avoid tangling with a merciless *babushka* who wants *her* seat that *you're* in.

Some shorter routes are serviced by nippier and more modern microbuses, holding about 15 passengers and officially making fewer stops than their big-bus counterparts.

By contrast, buses travelling between the Baltic countries are equal to long-distance coaches anywhere else in Europe. Most are clean and have a heating system, a toilet, hot drinks dispenser and TV on board. Many scheduled buses to/

from Tallinn, Rīga and Vilnius run overnight; a convenient and safe way of travelling, even for solo female travellers.

Buses operating within Estonia, Latvia & Lithuania

BussiReisid (www.bussireisid .ee) Umbrella for all Estonian services.

Ecolines (www.ecolines.net) Major routes include: Rīga–Salacgrīva–Pärnu–Tallinn; Rīga–Valmiera–Valga–Tartu–Narva; Rīga–Panevėžys–Vilnius–Kaunas; Liepāja–Palanga–Klaipėda; Rēzekne–Daugavpils–Utena–Vilnius–Kaunas.

Hansabuss Business Line (www.businessline.ee) Four daily buses between Rīga and Tallinn, three of which stop in Pärnu.

Lux Express (☎680 0909; www.luxexpress.eu) With its associated budget line **Simple Express** (www .simpleexpress.eu), major routes include: Tallinn–Pärnu–Rīga–Vilnius; Narva–Tartu–Valga–Rīga; Rīga–Vilnius; Rīga–Kaunas; Rīga–Šiauliai; Vilnius–Kaunas.

Tickets & Information

Ticket offices/windows selling national and international tickets are clearly marked in the local language and occasionally in English too. Tickets are always printed in the local language and easy to understand once you know the words for 'seat', 'bus stop' etc (see p416).

For long-distance buses, tickets are sold in advance from the station at which they begin their journey. For local buses to nearby towns or villages, or for long-distance buses that are midroute ('in transit'), you normally pay on board. This may mean a bit of a scrum for seats if there are a lot of people waiting.

Most bus and train stations in towns and cities

Railway & Ferry Routes

RUSSIA

FINLAND

HELSINKI

Hanko

Mariehamn

Kapellskär

Uppsala

STOCKHOLM

Nynäshamn

Narva

TALLINN

Paldiski

ESTONIA

Tartu

Pärnu

Kihnu

Ruhnu

Hiiumaa

Muhu

Saaremaa

Roomassaare

Mõntu

Ventspils

Pskov

Valga/
Valka

Rēzekne

Daugavpils

LATVIA

RIGA

Jelgava

Šiauliai

Liepāja

Klaipėda

LITHUANIA

VILNIUS

Kaunas

BELARUS

KALININGRAD
REGION
(RUSSIA)

Kaliningrad

Elbląg

Gdynia

Gdańsk

POLAND

Gotland

Visby

Slite

Oskarshamn

Öland

Norrköping

Linköping

Jönköping

Nässjö

Västervik

Kalmar

Växjö

Karlskrona

Karlshamn

SWEDEN

Bornholm

Sässnitz

Mukran

Rostock

Travemünde

Lübeck

Kiel

GERMANY

Aabenraa

Odense

Fredericia

Herning

Århus

Aalborg

Hirtshals

Grenå

DENMARK

COPENHAGEN

Helsingør

Malmö

Helsingborg

Trelleborg

Ystad

Halmstad

Varberg

Borås

Gothenburg

Frederikshavn

Vänersborg

Strömstad

Moss

OSLO

NORWAY

BALTIC SEA

Ruhnu

Kihnu

0   100 miles
0   200 km

have information windows with staff who generally speak some English.

Timetables & Fares

See timetables on bus company websites before leaving home or, upon arrival in the region, check schedules at the local tourist office. The offices in Tallinn, Rīga and Vilnius in particular maintain up-to-the-minute transport schedules. The **In Your Pocket** (www.inyour pocket.com) city guides to the capitals include fairly comprehensive domestic and pan-Baltic bus schedules, updated every two months.

Comprehensive time-tables are posted in bus stations' main ticket halls. A rare few need careful decoding. Most simply list the departure time and the days (using either Roman or Arabic numerals, the number 1 being Monday) on which the service runs.

Fares vary slightly between the three countries, and between bus companies, reflecting the speed of the bus, comfort levels and time of day it arrives/ departs.

Car & Motorcycle

For flexibility and access to out-of-the-way destinations, you can't beat driving. For documentation, including licences, see p408; for tips, see p36.

Fuel & Spare Parts

Petrol stations run by major companies are open 24 hours along all the major roads; many are self-service with an automated pay system accepting notes or cards with PINs. Western-grade fuel, including unleaded, is readily available.

Road Rules

The whole region drives on the right. The legal maximum blood alcohol limit varies in each country (Latvia 0.05%; Lithuania 0.04%; Estonia 0.02%). Seat belts are compulsory and headlights must be on at all times while driving. The speed limit in built-up areas is 50km/h; limits outside urban areas vary from 70km/h to 110km/h – look out for signs, as these limits are often strictly enforced. Fines may be collected on the spot –

only way to ensure officers don't also add a little pocket money for themselves is to ask for a receipt.

It is illegal to use a mobile phone while operating a vehicle (hands-free kits are allowed). Winter tyres are a legal requirement, usually from December to March every year, but if there are severe weather conditions outside these dates (likely in most years), the dates will change accordingly, so check local conditions if driving between October and April.

Traditional coin-fed parking meters are still found in some parts of the Baltics, though both Tallinn and Vilnius have moved towards electronic systems. Here drivers pay for parking via SMS, dialling a number and inputting the car's licence plate and location number (posted nearby).

There is an hourly fee to drive into the Old Town of Rīga, and you'll need to buy a *viedkarte* (a reusable card permit) for the privilege. Driving into the old towns in Tallinn, Vilnius and Kaunas is free, but parking is pricey, and often involves confusing regulations – ask at your hotel or the tourist office to avoid being fined. Motorists must pay a small entrance fee to drive into Latvia's prime seaside resort, Jūrmala, and to enter Curonian Spit National Park.

Take care driving near trams, trolleybuses and buses in towns. Passengers may run across the road to catch a tram that's still in motion. Traffic behind a tram must stop when it opens its doors to let people in and out. Trolleybuses often swing far out into the road when leaving a stop.

Hitching

Hitching is never entirely safe in any country in the world, and we don't recommend it. Travellers who decide to hitch should understand that

ROAD DISTANCES (KM)

	Tallinn	Tartu	Pärnu	Narva	Valka/Valga	Rīga	Liepāja	Daugavpils	Ventspils	Vilnius	Kaunas	Klaipėda	Panevėžys
Tartu	190												
Pärnu	130	205											
Narva	210	194	304										
Valka/Valga	276	86	140	268									
Rīga	310	253	180	435	167								
Liepāja	530	473	400	655	387	220							
Daugavpils	540	377	410	559	291	230	450						
Ventspils	510	453	380	635	367	200	119	430					
Vilnius	600	543	470	725	457	290	465	167	584				
Kaunas	575	523	460	715	447	280	230	267	349	100			
Klaipėda	620	538	490	745	477	310	155	477	274	310	210		
Panevėžys	460	403	330	585	317	150	270	168	350	140	110	235	
Šiauliai	465	383	310	565	297	130	192	387	330	220	140	155	80

they are taking a small but potentially serious risk. People who do choose to hitch will be safer if they travel in pairs and let someone know where they are planning to go.

Locally, hitching is a popular means of getting around. The **Vilnius Hitchhiking Club** (VHHC; www.autostop.lt) provides practical information and contacts to travellers hoping to hitch a ride in all three Baltic countries. Hostel notice boards in capital cities are a good place to find or offer a ride-share; the website www.digihitch.com might also be helpful.

Local Transport

Bus, Tram & Trolleybus

A mix of trams, buses and trolleybuses (buses run by electricity from overhead wires) provides thorough public transport around towns and cities in all three countries. All three types of transport get crowded, especially during the early-morning and early-evening rush hours.

Trams, trolleybuses and buses all run from about 5.30am to 12.30am, but services get pretty thin in outlying areas after about 7pm. In Tallinn and Vilnius, the same ticket is good for all types of transport (but not minibuses); in Rīga a bus ticket must be purchased on board, but trolleybus and tram tickets are interchangeable. In all three countries, you validate by punching a flat-fare ticket in one of the ticket punches fixed inside the vehicle. Tickets are sold from news kiosks displaying them in the window and by some drivers (who are easier to find but charge a little more for tickets). Multi-trip, weekly and monthly tickets are available. The system depends on honesty and lends itself to cheating but there are regular inspections, with on-the-spot

fines if you're caught riding without a punched ticket.

Travelling on all trams, trolleybuses and buses involves a particular etiquette. If you are young, fit and capable of standing for the duration of your journey, do not sit in the seats at the front – these are only for *babushkas* and small children. Secondly, plan getting off well ahead of time. The moment the bus/tram rolls away from the stop before the one you want to get off at, start making your way to the door. Pushing, shoving, stamping on toes and elbowing are, of course, allowed.

All airports are served by regular city transport as well as by taxis.

Taxi

Taxis are plentiful and usually cheap. Night-time tariffs, which generally apply between 10pm and 6am, are higher. To avoid rip-offs, insist on the meter running. In any of the cities, it's always cheaper and safer to order a cab by phone.

Train

Suburban trains serve the outskirts of the main cities and some surrounding towns and villages. They're of limited use as city transport for visitors, as they mostly go to residential or industrial areas where there's little to see. But some are useful for day trips to destinations outside the cities.

Tours

Numerous local travel operators specialise in travel around the Baltic region and can help you organise a trip. Useful local contacts are listed in the regional chapters, and tour operators originating from outside the Baltic countries can be found on p410.

City Bike (☑Estonia 511 1819; www.citybike.ee) Reputable and longstanding Tallinn-

based company, which arranges multiday cycling tours through Estonia, Latvia and Lithuania.

Scanbalt Experience (☑Estonia 5301 9139; www .scanbaltexperience.com) A backpacker-focused company offering adventure bus trips through Scandinavia and the Baltic region.

TrekBaltics (☑Estonia 5623 3255; www.trekbaltics.com) An Estonian-based operator with a great range of camping treks, adventure and activities packages (eg cycling tours) and spa breaks, taking in the three Baltic countries. The comprehensive 19-day Grand Baltics Trek can be done as a camper, or in more comfort (overnighting in cabins, farmhouses and hostels).

Train

Estonia, Latvia and Lithuania have railways, although services have been scaled back significantly in recent years and most long-distance travel within the Baltics is done by bus or plane. A planned intracountry rail network is in the pipeline (see the Rail Baltica Project, p409) but it's still some years away.

In the meantime, Baltic trains are slow and cheap, and not terribly comfortable. You can almost never open the windows, so it can be stuffy (and smelly, depending on your travelling companions), while you stand equal chances of freezing or baking, depending on whether the heating is turned on or not. Local trains, known as suburban or electric, are substantially slower and make more frequent stops than long-distance trains.

Routes

There are no direct train services running between the Baltic capitals, although you can travel from Tallinn to

Rīga by train with a stop at Valga (on the Estonia-Latvia border). From Rīga there are services to Daugavpils, where you can change for a train to Vilnius (this may involve an overnight stop in Daugavpils).

Route information for each country's network can be found in the Getting Around section at the end of each country chapter.

Tickets & Information

In Latvia and Lithuania, tickets can be purchased in advance and right before departure at train stations. In larger stations, such as Rīga, you can only buy tickets for certain types of trains or destinations at certain windows.

Except for Tallinn, Estonia's train stations are deserted places with no ticket offices or other services of any kind. You buy your tickets on the train, and don't head to the train station (which is usually quite far from the city centre) unless you know the exact departure time.

On long-distance trains between the Baltics and other countries, tickets must be surrendered to the carriage attendant, who will safeguard it for the journey's duration and return it to you 15 minutes before arrival at your final destination (a handy 'alarm clock' if you're on an overnight train).

Timetables

The railways of Latvia (www .ldz.lv) and Lithuania (www .litrail.lt) maintain updated train schedules on their websites, as does Estonia (www.edel.ee), though it's only in Estonian (click on *Sõiduplannid ja hinnad* to access the timetables and prices). Those displayed at train stations generally list the number of the train, departure and arrival times, and the platform from which it leaves. Some list return journey schedules, the number of minutes a train waits in your station or the time a train left the place it began its journey. Always study the small print on timetables, as many trains only run on certain days or between certain dates.

Language

ESTONIAN

Estonian belongs to the Baltic-Finnic branch of the Finno-Ugric languages. It's closely related to Finnish and distantly related to Hungarian. Most Estonians, especially the younger generations, understand some English and Finnish, but you'll find that people are welcoming of visitors who make an effort to speak their language.

Most Estonian consonants are the same as in English. If you read our pronunciation guides as if they were English, you'll be understood. Note that p is pronounced between the English 'p' and 'b', d between the English 't' and 'd', rr is trilled and zh sounds like the 's' in 'treasure'. As for vowels, aeh is pronounced as the 'ae' in 'aesthetic', err as the 'yrr' in 'myrrh' (rounding the lips) and ū as the 'oo' in 'too' (rounding the lips).

Stressed syllables are indicated with italics, and stress generally falls on the first syllable.

Basics

Hello.	Tere.	te·rre
Goodbye.	Head aega.	head ae·gah
Yes.	Jah.	yah
No.	Ei.	ay
Thank you.	Tänan.	ta·nahn
You're welcome.	Palun.	pah·lun
Excuse me./ Sorry.	Vabandage.	vah·bahn·dah·ge
How are you?	Kuidas läheb?	kuy·dahs la·heb
Fine.	Hästi.	has·ti

WANT MORE?
For in-depth language information and handy phrases, check out Lonely Planet's *Baltic Phrasebook*. You'll find it at **shop .lonelyplanet.com**, or you can buy Lonely Planet's iPhone phrasebooks at the Apple App Store.

What's your name?
| Mis te nimi on? | mis te ni·mi on |

My name is ...
| Mu nimi on ... | mu ni·mi on ... |

Do you speak English?
| Kas te räägite inglise keelt? | kahs te rraa·gi·te ing·li·se kehlt |

I don't understand.
| Ma ei saa aru. | mah ay saah ah·rru |

Accommodation

Where's a ...?	Kus asub ...?	kus ah·sub ...
campsite	kämping	kam·ping
hotel	hotell	ho·tell
pension	võõras-temaja	vyy·rrahs-te·mah·yah

I'd like a single/double room.
| Ma tahaksin ühe/ kahe voodiga tuba. | mah tah·hak·sin ü·he/ kah·he vaw·di·gah tu·bah |

How much is it per person/night?
| Kui palju maksab voodikoht/ööpäev? | kui pahl·yu mahk·sab vaw·di·koht/err·paehv |

Directions

Where is ...?
| Kus on ...? | kus on ... |

How far is it?
| Kui kaugel see on? | kuy kau·gel seh on |

Please show me on the map.
| Palun näidake mulle seda kaardil. | pah·lun nai·dah·ke mul·le se·dah kaahrr·dil |

Signs – Estonian

Sissepääs	Entrance
Väljapääs	Exit
Avatud/Lahti	Open
Suletud/Kinni	Closed
WC	Toilets
Meestele	Men
Naistele	Women

Eating & Drinking

Can I have a menu?
Kas ma saaksin menüü? — kas mah saahk·sin me·nüü

I'd like ...
Ma sooviksin ... — ma saw·vik·sin ...

I'm a vegetarian.
Ma olen taimetoitlane. — mah o·len tai·me·toyt·lah·ne

Bon appetit!
Head isu! — head i·su

To your health! (Cheers!)
Terviseks! — ter·vi·seks

The bill, please.
Palun arve. — pah·lun ahrr·ve

Emergencies

Help! Appi! — ahp·pi
Go away! Minge ära! — min·ge a·rrah
Call a doctor! Kutsuge arst! — kut·su·ge ahrrst
I'm ill. Ma olen haige. — mah o·len hai·ge
I'm lost. Ma olen eksinud. — mah o·len ek·si·nud

Shopping & Services

What time does it open/close?
Mis kell see avatakse/ suletakse? — mis kell seh ah·vah·tahk·se/ su·le·tahk·se

How much does it cost?
Kui palju see maksab? — kui pahl·yu seh mahk·sahb

bank	pank	pahnk
chemist/ pharmacy	apteek	ahp·tehk
market	turg	turrg
police	politsei	po·lit·say
post office	postkontor	post·kon·torr
toilet	tualett	tua·lett
tourist office	turismi-büroo	tu·rris·mi-bü·rroo

Time & Numbers

What time is it? Mis kell on? — mis kell on
It's one o'clock. Kell on üks. — kell on üks
in the morning hommikul — hom·mi·kul
in the evening õhtul — yh·tul

1	üks	üks
2	kaks	kahks
3	kolm	kolm
4	neli	ne·li
5	viis	vees
6	kuus	koos
7	seitse	sayt·se
8	kaheksa	kah·hek·sah
9	üheksa	ü·hek·sah
10	kümme	küm·me

Transport

Where's the ...? Kus on ...? — kus on ...
airport	lennujaam	len·nu·yaahm
bus station	bussijaam	bus·si·yaahm
ferry terminal	sadam	sah·dahm
train station	rongijaam	rron·gi·yaahm

Which ... goes there? Mis ... ma sinna saan? — mis ... mah sin·nah saahn
bus	bussiga	bus·si·gah
tram	trammiga	trrahm·mi·gah
trolleybus	trolliga	trrol·li·gah

What time is the next bus/train?
Mis kell on järgmine buss/rong ? — mis kell on yarrg·mi·ne buss/rrong

Please give me a one-way/return ticket.
Palun üks/ edasi-tagasi pilet. — pah·lun üks/ e·dah·si·tah·gah·si pi·let

LATVIAN

Latvian belongs to the Baltic language family. Only about 55% of the population, and just over 45% of the inhabitants of Rīga speak it as their first language. Latvian and Lithuanian have a lot of vocabulary in common, but are not mutually intelligible.

In our pronunciation guides, a line above a vowel indicates that it is a long sound. Note that uh is pronounced as the 'u' in 'fund', eh as the 'ai' in 'fair', ea as in 'fear', dz as the 'ds' in 'beds', zh as the 's' in 'pleasure' and jy is similar to the 'dy' sound in British 'duty'. Word stress is indicated with italics. The markers (m) and (f) indicate the options for male and female speakers respectively.

Basics

Hello.	Sveiks. (m)	svayks
	Sveika. (f)	svay·kuh
Goodbye.	Uz redzēšanos.	uz redz·eh·shuhn·aws
Yes.	Jā.	yah
No.	Nē.	neh
Please.	Lūdzu.	loo·dzu
Thank you.	Paldies.	puhl·deas
You're welcome.	Lūdzu.	loo·dzu
Excuse me.	Atvainojiet.	uht·vai·naw·yeat
Sorry.	Piedodiet.	pea·doad·eat

How are you?
Kā jums klājas? — kah yums klah·yuhs

Fine, thank you.
Labi, paldies. — luh·bi puhl·deas

What's your name?
Kā jūs sauc? — kah yoos sowts

My name is ...
Mani sauc ... — muhn·i sowts ...

Do you speak English?
Vai jūs runājat angliski? — vai yoos run·ah·yuht uhn·gli·ski

I don't understand.
Es nesaprotu. — es ne·suh·praw·tu

Accommodation

I'm looking for a ...
Es meklēju ... — es mek·leh·yu ...

| hotel | viesnīcu | veas·neets·u |
| youth hostel | jauniešu mītni | yow·nea·shu meet·ni |

I'd like a single/double room.
Es vēlos vienvietīgu/ divvietīgu istabu. — es vaa·laws vean·vea·tee·gu/ div·vea·tee·gu is·tuh·bu

How much is it per night?
Cik maksā diennaktī? — tsik muhk·sah dean·nuhk·tee

Directions

How do I get to ...?
Kā es tieku līdz ...? — kah es tea·ku leedz ...

Is it far from here?
Vai tas atrodas tālu? — vai tuhs uht·raw·duhs tah·lu

Could you show me (on the map), please?
Lūdzu parādiet man (uz kartes)? — loo·dzu puhr·ah·deat muhn (uz kuhrt·es)

Eating & Drinking

A table for ... people, please.
Lūdzu galdu ... personām. — loo·dzu gahl·du ... per·so·nahm

Do you have a menu?
Vai jums ir ēdienkarte? — vai yums ir eh·dean·kar te

What do you recommend?
Ko jūs iesakat? — kwo yoos eah·sah·kut

I'm a vegetarian.
Es esmu veģetārietis/te. (m/f) — es es·mu ve·gye·tah·reah·tis/te

I'd like ...
Es vēlos ... — es vaa·lwos ...

The bill, please.
Lūdzu rēķinu. — loo·dzu reh·kyi·nu

Emergencies

| Help! | Palīgā! | puh·lee·gah |
| Go away! | Ejiet projam! | ay·eat praw·yam |

Call a doctor!
Izsauciet ārstu! — iz·sowts·eat ahr·stu

I'm ill.
Es esmu slims/ slima. (m/f) — es as·mu slims/ slim·uh

I'm lost.
Es esmu apmaldījies/ apmaldījusies. (m/f) — es as·mu uhp·muhl·dee·yeas uhp·muhl·dee·yu·seas

Shopping & Services

What time does it open?
No cikiem ir atvērts? — naw tsik·eam ir uht·vaarts

What time does it close?
Cikos slēdz? — tsik·aws slaadz

How much is it?
Cik tas maksā? — tsik tuhs muhk·sah

Where are the toilets?
Kur ir tualetes? — kur ir tu·uh·le·tes

Signs – Latvian	
Ieeja	Entrance
Izeja	Exit
Atvērts	Open
Slēgts	Closed
Tualetes	Toilets
Vīriešu	Men
Sieviešu	Women

bank	banka	buhn·kuh
chemist/ pharmacy	aptieka	uhp·tea·kuh
currency exchange booth	valūtas maiņa	vuh·loo·tuhs mai·nyuh
market	tirgus	tir·gus
post office	pasts	puhsts

Time & Numbers

What time (is it)?
Cik (ir) pulkstenis?   tsik (ir) *pulk*·sten·is

It's five o'clock.
Ir pieci.   ir *peats*·i

morning	rīts	reets
afternoon	pēcpus-diena	*pehts*·pus·dea·nuh
night	nakts	nuhkts

1	viens	veans
2	divi	*di*·vi
3	trīs	trees
4	četri	*chet*·ri
5	pieci	*peats*·i
6	seši	*sesh*·i
7	septiņi	*sep*·ti·nyi
8	astoņi	*uhs*·taw·nyi
9	deviņi	*de*·vi·nyi
10	desmit	*des*·mit

Transport

Where's the ...?	Kur atrodas ...?	kur *uht*·raw·duhs ...
airport	lidosta	*lid*·aw·stuh
bus station	autoosta	*ow*·to·aws·tuh
ferry terminal	pasažieru osta	puh·suh·*zhea*·ru *aw*·stuh
train station	dzelzceļa stacija	*dzelz*·tse·lyuh *stuhts*·i·ya
tram stop	tramvaja pietura	*truhm*·vuh·yuh *pea*·tu·ruh

I want to buy a ... ticket.	Es vēlos nopirkt ... biļeti.	es *vaa*·laws *naw*·pirkt ... *bi*·lyet·i
one-way	vien-virziena	*vean*·virz·ean·uh
return	turp-atpakaļ	*turp*·uht·puh·kuhly

LITHUANIAN

Lithuanian belongs to the Baltic language family, along with Latvian. Low Lithuanian (*Žemaičiai*), spoken in the west, is a separate dialect from High Lithuanian (*Aukštaičiai*), spoken in the rest of the country and considered the standard dialect.

Note that in our pronunciation guides eah sounds as the 'ea' in 'ear', ew as in 'new', uaw as the 'wa' in 'wander', dz as the 'ds' in 'roads', zh as the 's' in 'treasure', and the r sound is trilled. Stressed syllables are in italics.

Basics

Hello.	Sveiki.	*svay*·ki
Goodbye.	Sudie.	su·*deah*
Yes./No.	Taip./Ne.	tayp/na
Please.	Prašau.	prah·*show*
Thank you.	Dėkoju.	deh·*kaw*·yu
You're welcome.	Prašau.	prah·*show*
Excuse me.	Atsiprašau.	aht·si·prah·*show*
Sorry.	Atleiskite.	aht·*lays*·ki·ta

How are you?
Kaip gyvuojate?   kaip gee·*vuaw*·yah·ta

What's your name?
Kaip jūsų vardas?   kaip yoo·soo *vahr*·dahs

My name is ...
Mano vardas yra ...   mah·naw *vahr*·dahs ee·*rah* ...

Do you speak English?
Ar kalbate angliškai?   ahr *kahl*·bah·ta *ahn*·glish·kai

I don't understand.
Aš jūsų nesuprantu.   ahsh yoo·soo na·su·prahn·*tu*

Accommodation

I'm looking for a hotel.
Aš ieškau   ahsh *yeash*·kow
viešbučio.   *veash*·bu·chaw

I'd like a single/double room.
Aš noriu   ahsh *nawr*·yu
vienviečio/   veahn·*veah*·chaw/
dviviečio   dvi·*veah*·chaw
kambario.   *kahm*·bahr·yaw

How much is it per night, per person?
Kiek kainuoja   keahk kai·*nuaw*·yah
apsistoti nakčiai   ahp·si·*staw*·ti nahk·chay
asmeniui?   ahs·man·wi

Directions

How do I get to the ...?
Prašom pasakyti,   *prah*·shom pah·sah·*kee*·ti
kaip patekti į ...?   kaip pah·*tak*·ti i ...

Is it far?
Ar toli? — ahr taw·li

Can you show me (on the map)?
Galėtumėt man — gah·leh·tu·met mahn
parodyti — pah·raw·dee·ti
(žemėlapyje)? — (zham·eh·lah·pee·ya)

Eating & Drinking

A table for ..., please.
Stalą ..., prašau. — stah·lah ... prah·show

Can I see the menu, please?
Ar galėčiau gauti — ahr gah·leh·chow gow·ti
meniu prašau? — man·yew prah·show

Do you have the menu in English?
Ar jūs turite meniu — ahr yoos tu·ri·ta man·yew
anglieškai? — ahn·glish·kai

I'd like to try that.
Aš norėčau — ahsh naw·reh·chow
išbandyti to. — ish·bahn·dee·ti taw

I don't eat (meat).
Aš nevalgau — ahsh na·vahl·gow
(mėsiško). — (meh·sish·kaw)

Emergencies

Help!	Gelbėkite!	gal·beh·ki·te
Go away!	Eik šalin!	ayk shah·lin
I'm ill.	Aš sergu.	ahsh sar·gu

Call a doctor!
Išsaukite — ish·show·ki·ta
gydytoją! — gee·dee·taw·yah

I'm lost.
Aš paklydusi/ — ahsh pah·klee·du·si/
paklydęs. (m/f) — pah·klee·das

Shopping & Services

What time does it open/close?
Kelintą valandą — kal·in·tah vah·lahn·dah
atsidaro/ — aht·si·dah·raw/
užsidaro? — uzh·si·dah·raw

How much is it?
Kiek kainuoja? — keahk kai·nu aw·yah

I'm looking for the ...	Aš ieškau ...	ahsh yeahsh·kow ...
bank	bankas	ban·kas
chemist/ pharmacy	vaistinė	vais·ti·neh
currency exchange	valiutos	vah·lyu·taws
market	turgus	tur·gows
police	policijos	paw·lit·si·yaws
post office	pašto	pahsh·taw
public toilet	tualeto	tu ah·lat·aw

Signs – Lithuanian

Įėjimas	Entrance
Išėjimas	Exit
Atidara	Open
Uždara	Closed
Dėmesio	Caution
Patogumai	Public Toilets

Time & Numbers

What time is it?
Kiek dabar laiko? — keahk dah·bahr lai·kaw

It's two o'clock.
Dabar antra — dah·bahr ahn·trah
valanda. — vah·lahn·dah

morning	rytas	ree·tahs
afternoon	popietė	paw·peah·teh
night	naktis	nahk·tis

1	vienas	veah·nahs
2	du	du
3	trys	trees
4	keturi	kat·u·ri
5	penki	pan·ki
6	šeši	shash·i
7	septyni	sap·tee·ni
8	aštuoni	ahsh·tu aw·ni
9	devyni	dav·ee·ni
10	dešimt	dash·imt

Transport

Where's the ...? Kur yra ...? — kur ee·rah ...

airport	oro uostas	aw·raw u aws·tahs
bus stop	autobuso stotelė	ow·taw·bu·saw staw·ta·leh
ferry terminal	kelto stotis	kal·taw staw·tis
train station	geležinkelio stotis	gal·azh·in·kal·yaw staw·tis

I'd like (a) ... ticket.	Aš norėčiau bilietą į ...	ahsh naw·reh·chow bil·eah·tah i ...
one-way	vieną galą	veah·nah gah·lah
return	abu galus	ah·bu gah·lus

GLOSSARY

See the individual destination chapters for some useful words and phrases dealing with food and dining; see the Language chapter (p416) for other useful words and phrases. This glossary is a list of Estonian (Est), Finnish (Fin), German (Ger), Latvian (Lat), Lithuanian (Lith), and Russian (Rus) terms you might come across during your time in the Baltic.

aikštė (Lith) – square
aludė (Lith) – beer cellar
alus (Lat, Lith) – beer
apteek (Est) – pharmacy
aptieka (Lat) – pharmacy
Aukštaitija (Lith) – Upper Lithuania
autobusų stotis (Lith) – bus station
autoosta (Lat) – bus station
autostrāde (Lat) – highway

baar (Est) – pub, bar
babushka (Rus) – grandmother/pensioner in headscarf
bagāžas glabātava (Lat) – left-luggage room
bagažinė (Lith) – left-luggage room
bāka (Lat) – lighthouse
Baltic glint – raised limestone bank stretching from Sweden across the north of Estonia into Russia
baras (Lith) – pub, bar
baznīca (Lat) – church
bažnyčia (Lith) – church
brokastis (Lat) – breakfast
bulvāris (Lat) – boulevard
bussijaam (Est) – bus station

ceļš (Lat) – railway track, road
centras (Lith) – town centre
centrs (Lat) – town centre
Chudkoye Ozero (Rus) – Lake Peipsi
Courland – Kurzeme

daina (Lat) – short, poetic oral song or verse
datorsalons (Lat) – internet cafe
dzintars (Lat) – amber

ebreji (Lat) – Jews
Eesti (Est) – Estonia
ežeras (Lith) – lake
ezerpils (Lat) – lake fortress
ezers (Lat) – lake

gatvė (Lith) – street
geležinkelio stotis (Lith) – train station
gintarinė/gintarinis (Lith) – amber

hinnakiri (Est) – price list
hommikusöök (Est) – breakfast

iela (Lat) – street
iezis (Lat) – rock
informacija (Lith) – information centre
internetas kavinė (Lith) – internet cafe
interneti kohvik (Est) – internet cafe

järv (Est) – lake

kafejnīca (Lat) – cafe
kalnas (Lith) – mountain, hill
kalns (Lat) – mountain, hill
kämping (Est) – camp site
katedra (Lith) – cathedral
katedrāle (Lat) – cathedral
kauplus (Est) – shop
kavinė (Lith) – cafe
kelias (Lith) – road
kempingas (Lith) – camp site
kempings (Lat) – camp site
kesklinn (Est) – town centre
kino (Est, Lat, Lith) – cinema
kirik (Est) – church
kohvik (Est) – cafe
kõrts (Est) – inn, tavern
krogs (Lat) – pub, bar

Kurshskaya Kosa (Rus) – Curonian Spit
Kursių marios (Lith) – Curonian Lagoon
Kursių Nerija (Lith) – Curonian Spit

laht (Est) – bay
Latvija (Lat) – Latvia
laukums (Lat) – square
lennujaam (Est) – airport
lidosta (Lat) – airport
Lietuva (Lith) – Lithuania
looduskaitseala (Est) – nature/landscape reserve
loss (Est) – castle, palace

maantee (Est) – highway
mägi (Est) – mountain, hill
Metsavennad (Est) – Forest Brothers resistance movement
midus (Lith) – mead
mõis (Est) – manor
muuseum (Est) – museum
muzejs (Lat) – museum
muziejus (Lith) – museum

nacionālais parks (Lat) – national park

õlu (Est) – beer
oro uostas (Lith) – airport
osta (Lat) – port/harbour

pakihoid (Est) – left luggage
parkas (Lith) – park
parks (Lat) – park
paštas (Lith) – post office
pasts (Lat) – post office
Peko (Est) – pagan god of fertility in Seto traditions
perkėla (Lith) – port
piletid (Est) – tickets
pilies (Lith) – castle
pils (Lat) – castle, palace
pilsdrupas (Lat) – knights' castle
pilskalns (Lat) – castle mound
plats (Est) – square

plentas (Lith) – highway, motorway

pliažas (Lith) – beach

pludmale (Lat) – beach

pood (Est) – shop

postkontor (Est) – post office

prospektas (Lith) – boulevard

prospekts (Lat) – boulevard

pubi (Est) – pub

puhketalu (Est) – tourist farm (ie a farm offering accommodation)

puiestee (Est) – boulevard

pusryčiai (Lith) – breakfast

raekoda (Est) – town/city hall

rahvuspark (Est) – national park

rand (Est) – beach

rātsnams (Lat) – town hall

raudteejaam (Est) – train station

Reval (Ger) – old German name for Tallinn

rezervāts (Lat) – reserve

Riigikogu (Est) – Parliament

rotušė (Lith)- town/city hall

rūmai (Lith) – palace

saar (Est) – island

sadam (Est) – harbour/port

Saeima (Lat) – Parliament

Seimas (Lith) – Parliament

Seto (Est) – ethnic group of mixed Estonian and Orthodox traditions

Setomaa (Est) – territory of the Seto people in southeastern Estonia and Russia

sild (Est) – bridge

smuklė (Lith) – tavern

stacija (Lat) – station

švyturys (Lith) – lighthouse

Tallinna (Fin) – Tallinn

talu (Est) – farm

tänav (Est) – street

tee (Est) – road

tiltas (Lith) – bridge

tilts (Lat) – bridge

tirgus (Lat) – market

toomkirik (Est) – cathedral

trahter (Est) – tavern

tuletorn (Est) – lighthouse

turg (Est) – market

turgus (Lith) – market

turismitalu (Est) – tourist farm (ie a farm offering accommodation)

vanalinn (Est) – old town

vaistinė (Lith) – pharmacy

väljak (Est) – square

Vecrīga (Lat) – Old Rīga

via Baltica – international road (the E67) linking Estonia with Poland

žydų (Lith) – Jews

behind the scenes

SEND US YOUR FEEDBACK

We love to hear from travellers – your comments keep us on our toes and help make our books better. Our well-travelled team reads every word on what you loved or loathed about this book. Although we cannot reply individually to postal submissions, we always guarantee that your feedback goes straight to the appropriate authors, in time for the next edition. Each person who sends us information is thanked in the next edition – and the most useful submissions are rewarded with a free book.

Visit **lonelyplanet.com/contact** to submit your updates and suggestions or to ask for help. Our award-winning website also features inspirational travel stories, news and discussions.

Note: We may edit, reproduce and incorporate your comments in Lonely Planet products such as guidebooks, websites and digital products, so let us know if you don't want your comments reproduced or your name acknowledged. For a copy of our privacy policy visit lonelyplanet.com/privacy.

OUR READERS

Many thanks to the travellers who used the last edition and wrote to us with helpful hints, useful advice and interesting anecdotes:

Hamish John Appleby, Liz Bissett, Richard Bristow, Itaru Dekio, Erica Enwall, Pierre Gaspart, Bettina Gilbert, Gina Green, Mieke Haveman, Jānis, Eric Kol, Richard Lemon, Robin Little, Mark McConnell, Lynn Miller, Gustavo Orlando-Zon, Julia Ossena, Leo Paton, Sue Pon, Paul Ravensbergen, Karlis Rozenkrons, Andreas Stueckjuergen, Dionisia Tzovandaropoulou, Claire Venema, Wing Ling Lai

AUTHOR THANKS

Brandon Presser

A massive thank you goes first and foremost to Aleksis Karlsons – this book would not be possible if it weren't for your hospitality and friendship. Thanks also to Rihards Kalnins, Jānis Jenzis, Iveta Sprudža, Agnese Kleina, Elīna Dobele, Richard Baerug, Agrita Tipane, the Latvian Institue, Live Rīga, Karlis, Ieva, Aggie, and everyone else that had a hand in making this edition a great one. At Lonely Planet, thanks to Katie, Tasmin, my capable co-authors, Mark and Peter, and a special shout out to Carolyn.

Mark Baker

Special thanks to the friendly people at Lithuania's tourist information offices, especially Natalia Tatarchuk at Žemaitija National Park. My friend Letitia Rydjeski, a Polish American with a love for Lithuania, vetted part of the manuscript and offered many critical suggestions. Vilnius-based Simona Dambauskas knows all things Vilnius and was very helpful in compiling listings. Thanks to my friends Eva and Kristina for adopting me in Kaunas, and to my co-authors, Brandon Presser and Peter Dragicevich, for making this edition a smooth ride.

Peter Dragicevich

Special thanks to Vanessa Irvine, Mark Elliott, Tracy Moyes and Kaspars Zalitis for making my time in Tallinn so enjoyable, and to Mika Keränen for entertaining me in Tartu.

Simon Richmond

For their help and company in Kaliningrad I'd like to thank Ksenia, Irina and Artyem Ryzkov.

Andy Symington

My time researching Helsinki was helped along for a few days by the excellent company of my parents, to whom thanks for the visit! As ever, a large *kiitos* to Gustav, Marja, Mirjam and recent arrival Meri Schulman for their unfailingly generous

Helsinki hospitality; thanks also to Fran Parnell for an excellent authors' evening in the capital. Lastly, I especially owe a big *igracias amor!* to Elena Vázquez Rodríguez for help, love and understanding.

ACKNOWLEDGMENTS

Climate map data adapted from Peel MC, Finlayson BL & McMahon TA (2007) 'Updated World Map of the Köppen-Geiger Climate Classification', *Hydrology and Earth System Sciences*, 11, 163344.

Cover photograph: Island Castle, Trakai, Lithuania, Stefano Cellai/Corbis

Many of the images in this guide are available for licensing from Lonely Planet Images: www.lonelyplanetimages.com.

THIS BOOK

This 6th edition of Lonely Planet's Estonia, Latvia & Lithuania guidebook was researched and written by Brandon Presser, Peter Dragicevich and Mark Baker. The Kaliningrad Excursion chapter was written by Simon Richmond and the Helsinki Excursion chapter was written by Andy Symington. The previous edition was written by Carolyn Bain, Neal Bedford, Brandon Presser and George Dunford. This guidebook was commissioned in Lonely Planet's London office, laid out by Cambridge Publishing Management, UK, and produced by the following:

Commissioning Editors Jo Cooke, Katie O'Connell, Glenn van der Knijff

Coordinating Editors Karen Beaulah, Kate James

Coordinating Cartographer Marc Milincovic

Coordinating Layout Designer Paul Queripel

Managing Editors Kirsten Rawlings, Angela Tinson, Tasmin Waby

Managing Cartographers Adrian Persoglia, Shahara Ahmed

Managing Layout Designer Chris Girdler

Assisting Editors Janice Bird, Kathryn Glendenning, Michala Green, Emma Sangster, Ceinwen Sinclair, Fionnuala Twomey

Assisting Layout Designer Julie Crane

Cover Research Naomi Parker

Internal Image Research Jessica Boland

Indexer Marie Lorimer

Language Content Branislava Vladisavljevic

Thanks to Imogen Bannister, Catherine Craddock, Ryan Evans, Yvonne Kirk, Korina Miller, Susan Paterson, Trent Paton, Martine Power, Gerard Walker

index

ABBREVIATIONS
Est   Estonia
Hel   Helsinki
Kal   Kaliningrad
Lat   Latvia
Lith   Lithuania
Rus   Russia

A
A Le Coq Beer Museum 100
Abava River Valley 212, 227-9
Academy of Science 195
accommodation 396-7, *see also* camping, *individual locations*
    apartments & rooms 66, 204
    farmstays 381, 386-7
    guesthouses 381, 397
    homestays 381
    hostels 381, 397, 398
    hotels 380, 397
    internet resources 396
activities 28-33, *see also individual activities, locations*
    children, for 35
aerodium (Lat) 248
Ägenskalns (Lat) 200
Aglona (Lat) 264-5
Ainaži (Lat) 244-5
air travel 15, 404-7
    airlines 404-6, 410-11
    climate change 405
    tickets 406
    to/from Helsinki 181
    to/from Kaliningrad 394
    to/from the Baltic 406-7
    within the Baltic 15, 169, 274, 384, 410-11
Aizkalne 265
Alajõe 91
Alatskivi Castle 92-3
alcohol, *see* drinks
Altja 83

000 Map pages
000 Photo pages

Alūksne 258
amber 369
    Amber Gallery Museum 355
    Amber Museum 387
    Amber Museum 361
    Amber Museum-Gallery 285
    Amber Processing Gallery 361-2
    House of Craftsmen 237
Angla Windmill Hill 140
animals 82, 121, *see also* birds, birdwatching, zoos, *individual species*
Antakalnis Cemetery 292
Anykščiai 340-1
Āraiši Lake Fortress 256
Araisi 256
architecture 18, *see also* art nouveau
    Architecture Museum 56
    Rīga Museum of Architecture 193
    Soviet era 56, 87, 219
area codes 15
Art by Night 22
art galleries, *see* museums & galleries
art nouveau
    Jūrmala 218-19
    Rīga 9, 18, 189, 198-9, 202-3, 269, 9
    Šiauliai 336
Artillery Bastion 290
arts, *see also individual arts*
    Estonia 161-4
    Latvia 268-9
    Lithuania 374-7
astronomical observatories 233, 284, 316
ATMs 15, 401
Aukštaitija National Park 33, 311, 312-15, **314**
Ažvinčiai Forest Reserve 312

B
Baltic Coast Road 226-7
Baltic Pride 399
banks 397
bargaining 401
bars 397, *see also individual locations*
Bartas, Šarūnas 376
basketball 74, 374
bats 107
Bauska 238-9
beaches (Estonia)
    Kärdla 149
    Käsmu 82
    Kassari 153
    Kuressaare 136
    Lake Peipsi 91
    Loksa 81
    Narva-Jõesuu 90

Pärnu 17, 123
Pirita 58
Pühajärv 113
Stroomi 59
Tahkuna 17, 140
Tartu 100
Viljandi 119
Võru 108
Võsu 82
beaches (Latvia)
    Blue Flag beaches 268
    Jūrmala 17, 218
    Liepāja 235
    Mazirbe 227
    Pāvilosta 234
    Saulkrasti 244
    Ventspils 231
beaches (Lithuania)
    Nida 17, 354
    Palanga 361
    Smiltynė 346
Beauvoir, Simone de 354
beavers 61, 82, 83, 122, 253
beer, *see also* brewery tours
    A Le Coq Beer Museum 100
    Estonia 140, 166-7
    festivals 340
    Latvia 184, 256, 271
    Lithuania 317-18, 340, 379
    Õllesummer 20, 61
    Õlletoober 20, 136
Belarus 408, 409
    visas 403, 408
Benjamiņa, Emīlija 207
berrying 31, 271, 313, 322
bicycling, *see* cycling
birds 82, *see also* birdwatching
    barn swallows 82
    cormorants 353
    herons 353
    storks 31, 82, 262, 313
birdwatching 31-2
    Aukštaitija National Park 312
    Cape Kolka 226
    Curonian Spit National Park 32, 353
    Gauja National Park 32
    Haapsalu 145
    Kassari 153
    Ķemeri National Park 32
    Lahemaa National Park 81
    Lake Engure Nature Park 32
    Matsalu National Park 31-2, 143
    Nemunas Delta 32, 359, 360
    Rēzekne 161
    Soomaa National Park 120
    Teiči Nature Reserve 32
    tours 143

birdwatching *continued*
  Ventės Ragas Ornithological
    Station 359
  Vilsandi National Park 32, 141
Bīriņi Castle 252
Birštonas 333-4
Black Balzām 184, 271
Blackheads' House 185, 188, 189
Blaumanis, Rūdolfs 258
blue cows 228
boat tours
  Birštonas 334
  Curonian Spit National Park 354
  Druskininkai 319
  Helsinki 175
  Klaipėda 346
  Matsalu National Park 143
  Nida 354
  Tartu 100
  Ventspils 232
  Vilsandi 141
boat travel, *see also* boat tours
  ferry routes **412**
  to/from Helsinki 181
  to/from the Baltic 409-10
  within the Baltic 411
boating, *see also* canoeing, kayaking,
    sailing, yachting
  Aukštaitija National Park 313, 314
  Bikėnai 317
  Birštonas 334
  Druskininkai 319
  Haapsalu 145
  Klaipėda 346
  Kuressaare 135
  Lake Peipsi 92
  Lake Plateliai 367
  Lake Usma 224
  Otepää 114
  Saaremaa 143
  Sigulda 249
  Tallinn 60
  Trakai 309
  Vilnius 295
bobsledding 33, 248
bogs 120-1, 122
bog-walking
  Lahemaa National Park 83
  Soomaa National Park 122
  Tallinn 61
books, *see also* literature
  cookery 379
  history 371
border crossings 107, 111, 407-8

boulders 81, 82, 84
bowling 146
Braki 258
brewery tours 256, 340
Brotherhood of the Blackheads 63
brown bears 81, 82, 110
budget 14, *see also individual regions*
bungee jumping 248
bus travel
  Estonia 170
  Helsinki 181
  Lithuania 385
  local transport 414
  to/from the Baltic 169, 408
  within the Baltic 37, 169, 274, 384,
    411, 413
business hours 397-8

C
cable cars 245
cafes 397, *see also individual
    locations*
camping 381, 396
  Cape Kolka 226
  Curonian Spit National Park 357
  Dobele 242
  Druskininkai 320
  Jūrmala 221
  Kassari 153
  Kihnu 129
  Klaipėda 347
  Lahemaa National Park 83, 84
  Lake Peipsi 94
  Nemunas Delta 360
  Ontika Landscape Reserve 87
  Pärnu 126
  Rīga 208
  Saaremaa 141, 142-3
  Sabile 229
  Sigulda 251
  Soomaa National Park 122
  Trakai 310
  Vidzeme Coast 244
canoeing 31
  Abava River Valley 227
  Aukštaitija National Park 313
  Bikėnai 317
  Birštonas 334
  Cēsis 254
  Haanja Nature Park 110
  Labanoras Regional Park 316
  Matsalu National Park 143
  North Vidzeme Biosphere Reserve
    244
  Otepää 113, 114
  Saaremaa 143
  Sigulda 249
  Soomaa National Park 122

Cape Kolka (Kolkasrags) 225-7
car travel 15, 36-7
  day trips 36
  hazards 15, 37
  insurance 408
  rental 15, 37, 275
  road rules 37, 413
  to/from the Baltic 408-9
  within the Baltic 413
carbon offset schemes 405
castles (Estonia)
  Alatskivi Castle 92-3
  Haapsalu Episcopal Castle 143-4
  Hermann Castle 89
  Kuressaare Castle 17, 134-5
  Maasilinnus 140
  Rakvere Castle 86
  Sangaste Castle 112
  Vastseliina Castle 108
  Viljandi Teutonic Order Castle 118
castles (Latvia) 8
  Āraiši Stone Castle 256
  Bauska Castle 239
  Bīriņi Castle 252
  Castle of the Livonian Order 232-3
  Cēsis Castle 254
  Dikli Castle 252
  Koknese Castle 259
  Krimulda Castle 247
  Livonian Order Castle (Dobele)
    242
  Livonian Order Castle (Kuldīga)
    229
  Ludza Castle 263
  Rīga Castle 193
  Sigulda castles 247, 250
  Stāmeriena Castle 258
  Turaida Castle 246-7
  Valmiera Castle 256
castles (Lithuania)
  Kaunas Castle 325-6
  Klaipėda Castle 343
  Peninsula Castle 309
  Trakai Island Castle 17, 308-9, 2
cathedrals, *see* churches &
    cathedrals
Catherine the Great 61, 109, 150,
    157, 239
Catholicism 370
caves
  Estonia 107
  Latvia 230, 247, 249
cell phones 15, 402
  Estonia 129
  Latvia 274
  Lithuania 384
cemeteries
  Jewish cemeteries 291
  Rīga 199

Valga 111
Vilnius 291, 292
Central Lithuania 323-41, **324**
Central Market 195
Centre of Europe 310-11
cepelinai 277
Čepkeliai Strict Nature Reserve 322
Cēsis 254-6, **255**
children, travel with 34-5, *see also*
    waterparks, zoos, *individual
    locations*
  Ilon's Wonderland 145
  puppet theatres 60, 332, 339-40
  Toy Museum 98
Choral Synagogue 291
Christianity 266
Christmas 23, 379
  Christmas Tree 189, 204
  markets 23
churches & cathedrals (Estonia)
  Cathedral of the Resurrection 89
  Dome Church (Haapsalu) 144
  Dome Church (Tallinn) 55
  Holy Spirit Church 50-1
  Karja Church 140
  Kassari Chapel 153
  Pühalepa Church 149
  Ruhnu wooden church 129
  St Alexander Nevsky Cathedral 54
  St Catherine's Church (Pärnu) 123
  St Catherine's Church & Cloister
      (Tallinn) 51
  St Catherine's Churches (Voru) 109
  St Elizabeth's Church 123
  St John's Church (Tartu) 98
  St John's Church (Valga) 111
  St John's Church (Viljandi) 118-19
  St Mary's Church (Saaremaa)
      139-40
  St Mary's Lutheran Church
      (Otepää) 113
  St Michael's Church 141
  St Nicholas Orthodox Church 51
  St Olaf's Church (Tallinn) 51
  St Olaf's Church (Vormsi) 154
  Sts Peter & Paul's Cathedral 51
  Tartu Cathedral 99
  Trinity Church 86
churches & cathedrals (Helsinki)
  Temppeliaukion Kirkko 174
  Tuomiokirkko 173
  Uspenskin Katedraali 173
churches & cathedrals (Latvia)
  Aglona Basilica 264
  Dome Cathedral 191
  Nicholas Evangelical Lutheran
      Church 233
  Russian Orthodox Cathedral 195
  Sabile Lutheran Church 229

Sigulda Church 247
St Jacob's Cathedral 193
St John's Church 189
St Katrīna's Church 229
St Nicholas Maritime Cathedral
    236-7
St Nicholas Russian Orthodox
    Church 233
St Peter-Paul Orthodox Church 223
St Peter's Lutheran Church 189
St Simon's Church 256
churches & cathedrals (Lithuania)
  Chapel of the Blessed Mary 289
  Christ's Resurrection Basilica 329
  Church of the Assumption 292
  Church of the Saint Virgin's
      Apparition 293
  Evangelical Lutheran Church
      (Nida) 355
  Evangelical Lutheran Church
      (Vilnius) 291
  Holy Spirit Church 292
  Mary Queen of Peace Church 344
  Orthodox Church of the Holy
      Spirit 290
  Romanovs' Church 294
  St Anne's Church 284
  St Casimir's Chapel 281
  St Casimir's Church 285
  St Catherine's Church 292
  St Gertrude's Church 328
  St Michael the Archangel Church
      328
  St Nicholas Church 291
  St Raphael's Church 294
  St Teresa's Church 289-90
  Sts Johns' Church 283-4
  Sts Peter & Paul Cathedral
      (Kaunas) 328
  Sts Peter & Paul Cathedral
      (Šiauliai) 336
  Sts Peter & Paul Church 293
  Vilnius Cathedral 281
cinema, *see also* film festivals
  Estonia 163
  Latvia 268-9
  Lithuania 376
Cinevilla 224
citizenship 88, 161
Čiurlionis, Mikalojus Konstantinas
    285, 318, 322, 328-9, 376, 377
climate 14, *see also individual
    regions*
climate change 405
climbing wall 113
clubs 398, *see also individual
    locations*
Cold War Museum 16
concentration camps
  Estonia 111

Latvia 223
Lithuania 329
consulates 399
  Estonia 167-8
  Latvia 272
  Lithuania 382
convents, *see* monasteries &
    convents
costs 14, *see also* money
  accommodation 167, 272, 381
  camping 396
  food 164, 271, 380
cottage rental 397
courses
  cooking 131
  language 64
  soap-making 139
cow sculptures 233
crafts
  cross crafting 337
  Heltermaa Crafts House 147
  House of Crafts 233
  House of Craftsmen 237
  Kaziukas Crafts Fair 295
  Kihnu Cultural Space
      Foundation 129
  Ludza Craftsmen Centre 263
  Orvydas Garden 366
  Vilnius 303
  Wool Factory 147
credit cards 15, 401
cross crafting 337
cucumber farms 263
culture, *see also* arts, crafts,
    etiquette, folk culture
  Estonia 160-1
  Latvia 268
  Lithuania 373-4
Curonian Spit National Park 8, 32, 34,
    341, 350-8, **350**, **8**
currencies 14
currency exchange, *see* exchange
    rates
customs regulations 398
  Estonia 167
  Latvia 272
  Lithuania 381-2
cycling 16, 29, 407, 411
  Altja 83
  Bicycle Museum 336
  Curonian Spit National Park 354,
      355
  Druskininkai 319
  Dzūkija National Park 322
  Haanja Nature Park 110
  Helsinki 182
  internet resources 29
  Kuldīga 230
  Lahemaa National Park 83

INDEX C-F

cycling *continued*
Matsalu National Park 143
Nemunas Delta 359
North Vidzeme Biosphere Reserve 244
Otepää 113
Palanga 361
Saaremaa 142
Sigulda 249
Tallinn 61
tour operators 29
Trakai 309
Valmiera 256

D
Daina Hill Song Garden 247
dance festivals 20, 21, 61, 295
Darius, Steponas 325
Daugava River Valley 259
Daugavpils 259-62
Daugavpils fortress 261
Devil's Lake 264
diarrhoea 400
Dikli Castle 252
disabilities, travellers with 402
discount cards 398
diving 61, 141, 152
Dobele 242
Dobele, Elīna 215
dolphinarium 345
Domšaitis, Pranas 345
Dridži 263-4
drinks, *see also* beer, wine
Black Balzām 184, 271
cocktails 271
Estonia 43, 166-7
Latvia 271
Lithuania 277, 379-80
mead 379
vodka 140, 167
water 400
driving, *see* car travel
driving licences 408
Druskininkai 29, 311-12, 318-21, **318**
Druskininkai-Varėna Forest 311
Dudayev, Dzhokhar 160
Dundaga 225-6
Dusetos 317
Dzūkija National Park 311, 322-3

E
Eastern Lithuania 311-23, **312**
electricity 398

embassies 399
Estonia 167-8
Latvia 272
Lithuania 382
emergencies
Estonia 169
medical care 400
Enlightenment 157-8
environmental issues
climate change 405
Estonia 88
Latvia 268
Lithuania 315, 351
erratic boulders 81, 82, 154
Estonia 38, 42-170, **44-5**, **79**, **92**, **116-17**, **130**
accommodation 42, 167
arts 161-4
birdwatching 31-2
budget 43
children, travel with 34, 35
citizenship laws 88, 161
climate 42
consulates 167-8
customs regulations 167
drinks 43, 166-7
economy 155, 160
education 155
embassies 167-8
emergency services 169
Estonian–Russian relations 88, 155-6
ethnic minorities 88, 105-6, 128, 155-6, 160-1
EU membership 155, 160
exchange rates 43
food 42, 43, 164-6, 167
gay & lesbian travellers 168
highlights 44-5
history 156-60
internet access 168
internet resources 15, 43
itineraries 27, **27**
language 43, 416-17
maps 168
money 43, 168
planning 42-3, 46
politics 155, 160
population 160-1
public holidays 168-9
religion 128, 161
telephone services 169
tourist information 169
travel seasons 42
travel to/from 43, 169-70
travel within 170
visas 46, 403
Estonia ferry disaster 109, 151
Estonian flag 95

Estonian History Museum 49, 58
Estonian islands 128-55
Estonian Literary Museum 160
Estonian Maritime Museum 51
Estonian National Library 56
Estonian National Museum 99
Estonian Open Air Museum 59
Estonian Sports Museum 98
Estonian Traditional Music Centre 119
ethnic minorities
Estonia 88, 105-6, 128, 155-6, 160-1
Latvia 227
Lithuania 309, 368, 373
etiquette
Estonia 167
Lithuania 373, 380
EU membership
Estonia 155, 160
Latvia 267
Lithuania 315, 373
Europa Tower 294
Europas parkas 311
European Health Insurance Card (EHIC) 400
Europos centras 310-11
events, *see* festivals & events
exchange rates 15
Estonia 43
Latvia 184
Lithuania 277

F
Fairy Tale Forest 242
farmstays 381, 396-7
fashion 16, 215
ferry travel, *see* boat travel
festivals & events (Estonia) 19-23, *see also* dance festivals, film festivals, folk festivals, food festivals, music festivals, singing festivals
Hansa Days Festival 21, 101
Hanseatic Days 119
Maritime Festival 22, 136
Medieval Festival 61
Midsummer 6, 20, 32, **7**
Old Town Days 20, 61
Õllesummer 20, 61
Õlletoober 20, 136
Tartu Ski Marathon 19, 101
Tartu Student Days 19, 101
White Lady Festival 21, 146
festivals & events (Latvia) 19-23, *see also* dance festivals, film festivals, folk festivals, food festivals, music festivals, singing festivals
Art by Night 22
Baltā Nakts 204

000 Map pages
000 Photo pages

Beaming Rīga 204
Christmas Tree Path 204
International Baltic Ballet Festival 20
Joma Street Festival 219
Makslas Festivals 254
Midsummer 6, 20, 32, 204, **7**
Piens Fest 22
Sabile Wine Festival 21
festivals & events (Lithuania) 19-23,
   see also dance festivals, film
   festivals, folk festivals, food
   festivals, music festivals, singing
   festivals
International Festival of
   Experimental Archaeology 311
Kaziukas Crafts Fair 295
Lygiadienis 295
Midsummer 6, 20, 32, **7**
Palanga Summer Festival 362
Sea Festival 20, 346
Shrove Tuesday Carnival 367
Sirenas International Theatre
   Festival 22, 297
Trakai Festival 308
Užgavėnės 295
film festivals
Arsenāls 22, 204
Black Nights 22, 64
Future Shorts 22
Horror & Fantasy Film Festival
   19, 146
Pärnu International Film Festival
   20, 124
tARTuFF 21, 101
fishing 31
Curonian Lagoon 359
Ethnographic Sea Fishermen's
   Farmstead 346
ice-fishing 309, 346, 354, 359
Lake Usma 224
North Vidzeme Biosphere Reserve
   244
Pidula Trout 141
Roja 226
Trakai 309
Utena 316
flower markets 215, 294
folk culture, *see also* crafts, folk
   festivals
Estonia 106
Estonian Traditional Music Centre
   119
Folk Music & Instruments Museum
   (Lith) 328
Latvia 269
Lithuania 376
folk festivals
Baltica International Folklore
   Festival 61
International Folk Festival 20, 351

Lithuanian Folk Art 19
Liv Festival 227
Viljandi Folk Music Festival 20, 119
Vōru Folklore Festival 21, 109
food, *see also* berrying, mushrooming
Christmas 379
cooking courses 131
Estonia 43, 164-6, 167
language 43, 166, 270, 378
Latvia 183, 184, 269-72
Lithuania 276, 277, 377-9, 380
restaurant opening hours 398
food festivals
Fish & Dips 19
Mushroom Festival 322
Palanga Seals 362
football 74
Forest Brothers 121, 159, 325, 372
Frank Zappa Memorial 292
Freedom Monument 194
Frenkelis Villa 336
funiculars 35, 281

G
Gaiziņkalns 258
galleries, *see* museums & galleries
gardens, *see* parks & gardens
gas stations 37, 413
Gates of Dawn 288
Gauja National Park 11, 32, 33, 34,
   245-57, **245**, **11**
gay travellers 399
Estonia 168
internet resources 399
Tallinn 73
Vilnius 302
Gediminas Hill 280-1
Girēnas, Stanislovas 325
Girios Aidas 319
golfing 136, 219, 311
Gorbachev, Mikhail 159, 372
Great Northern War 95, 143, 157
Grūtas Park 321
guesthouses 381, 397, *see also*
   individual locations
Gulbene 258
Gulbene–Aluksne Narrow-Gauge
   Railway 258
Gulf Coast Road 226
Gūtmaņa Cave 247

H
haabja 122
Haanja Nature Park 110-11
Haapsalu 143-7, **144**
handicrafts, *see* crafts
Hanseatic League 46, 117, 266
Hara Island 81

hazards
car travel 15, 37
insect bites & stings 400
mushrooming 312
health 400
Helsinki 171-82, **172**, **176**
accommodation 171, 175, 177
activities 174-5
drinking 178-9
entertainment 179
festivals & events 175
food 171, 177-8
Helsinki Card 180
highlights 172
history 180-1
information 180
itineraries 174
shopping 179-80
sights 173-4
travel seasons 171
travel to/from 181
travel within 181-2
Hermann Castle 89
Hiiumaa 147-53, **148**
hiking 30
Aukštaitija National Park 313
Haanja Nature Park 110
Lahemaa National Park 83
Luhasoo Nature Reserve 110
Otepää 113
Parnidis Cognitive Path 355-6
Saaremaa 142
Sigulda 249
Soomaa National Park 122
Valmiera 256
Hill of Crosses (Est) 150
Hill of Crosses (Lith) 11, 334-6,
   337, **11**
history, *see also* Soviet era, WWI,
   WWII, *individual locations*
books 371
Estonia 156-60
Helsinki 180-1
Latvia 265-8
Lithuania 369-73
hitching 413-14
holidays, *see* public holidays
Holocaust Memorial 195, 198
homestays 381
horse racing 317
horse riding 32-3
Abava River Valley 227
Hiiumaa 153
Horse Museum 340-1
Kassari 153
Krāslava 264
Lahemaa National Park 83
Latgale Lakelands 262, 264

horse riding *continued*
　Rēzekne 262
　Saaremaa 140
hostels 381, 397, *see also individual
　locations*
cards 398
hot-air ballooning 295, 309, 334
Hotel Viru KGB Museum 16
hotels 380, 397, *see also individual
　locations*
House of Perkūnas 324
House of Peter I 57
House of Signatories 283
houses, *see manor houses*
hunting 82, 165

I
ice-fishing 309, 346, 354, 359, *see
　also fishing*
ice skating
　Kuressaare 135
　Otepää 114
　Rīga 190
　Tallinn 60
　Vilnius 295
Ignalina 312
Ignalina Nuclear Power Station 315
Ilon's Wonderland 145
independence
　Estonia 150, 158-9, 372
　Latvia 267
　Lithuania 371, 372
insect bites & stings 400
insurance 400-1
　car 408
　health 400
internet access 400, *see also
　individual locations*
　Estonia 168
　Latvia 273
　Lithuania 382-3
internet resources
　accommodation 396
　cycling 29
　disabilities, travellers with 402
　Estonia 15, 143
　gay & lesbian travellers 399
　Latvia 15, 184, 273
　Lithuania 15, 277
　planning 15
　visas 403
itineraries 24-7, **24**, **25**, **26**, **27**, *see
　also individual locations*
　Estonia 27, **27**

000 Map pages
000 Photo pages

Latvia 26, **26**
Lithuania 27, **27**
Ivanauskaitė, Jurga 375-6

J
Jacob's Barracks 193
jazz 376
jazz festivals
　Birštonas Jazz 333
　Jazzkaar 19, 61
　Kaunas International Jazz Festival
　　19-20, 330
　Mama Jazz Festival 22
　Nida Jazz Marathon 21, 351
Jēkabpils 259
Jelgava 242
jet-skiing 152
Jews, *see also synagogues*
　cemeteries 291
　Estonia 161
　ghettos 290
　Jewish Quarter 290
　Latvia 199, 223
　Lithuania 290, 291, 308, 329,
　　371, 372
　Vilna Gaon State Jewish Museum
　　291
Johann, Ernst (Duke of Courland)
　239, 242
John Paul II, Pope 264, 335, 337
Jugendstil, *see art nouveau*
Juminda Peninsula 81
Juodkrantė 352-3
Jūrmala 13, 17, 29, 212, 218-23, **220**, **13**

K
Kaali Crater 139
Kadriorg 56-8, **57**
Kadriorg Art Museum 56
Käina 152-3
Kalanta, Romas 325, 328
Kaliningrad 386-94, **388**, **390**
　accommodation 386, 389-91
　drinking 392
　entertainment 392-3
　food 386, 391-2
　sights 387-9
　travel seasons 386
　travel to/from 394
　travel within 394
　visas 387
Kaliningrad Cathedral 387
Kallaste 92
Kalnciemiela 200
Kandava 227-8
Kant, Immanuel 387
Kaplinski, Jaan 163
Karaites people 294, 309, 373

Kärdla 149-50
Karņička Hill 263
Karosta 18, 235-6
Karula National Park 111
Käsmu 82
Kassari 153
Kauksi 91
Kaunas 323-33, **326**
Kaunas Botanical Gardens 329
Kaunas International Jazz Festival
　19-20, 330
kayaking
　Aukštaitija National Park 313
　Hiiumaa 152
　Otepää 114
　Tallinn 60, 61
Ķemeri National Park 32, 223-4
Keränen, Mika 100
Kernavė 311
KGB Headquarters, former 63
kicksledding 33, 122
Kihnu 128-9
Kihnu Jõnn 128
kiiking 164
Kiipsaare lighthouse 141
Kipsala 200
kite surfing 31, 152
kiteboarding 234
Klaipėda 341-50, **344**
KlebonNiškiai 338
Klosterhill 242
Koguva 18, 131
Koidula, Lydia 123-4, 162, 164
Koknese 259
Kolka 226
Kolkasrags, *see Cape Kolka*
Kolkja 93
Košrags 226
Krāslava 263-4
Kretinga 365
Kreutzwald, Friedrich Reinhold
　109, 162
Kross, Jaan 163
Krustkalni Nature Reserve 258
Krustpils 259
Kuldīga 18, 229-31, **230**
Kumu 57
Kunčius, Herkus 376
Kuressaare 132, 133-9, **136**
Kuressaare Castle 17, 134-5
Kurshskaya Kosa National Park
　(Rus) 392
Kurzeme 12, 224-38, **225**, **12**
Kutavičius, Bronius 376

L
Labanoras 18, 316
Labanoras Regional Park 316

Lahemaa National Park 13, 79, 81-5, **80**, 13
Lake Engure Nature Park 32, 226
Lake Lubāns 262
Lake Peipsi 91-4
Lake Plateliai 367
Lake Rubikiai 340
Lake Sartai 317
Lake Tauragnas 312
Lake Usma 224
language 416-20
  courses 64
  Estonian 162, 416-17
  food vocabulary (Est) 43, 166
  food vocabulary (Lat) 270
  food vocabulary (Lith) 378
  glossary 421-2
  Latvian 184, 417-19
  Lithuanian 277, 419-20
  Liv 227
  Russian 79
  Võro-Seto 105
Lapmežciems 223
Latgale (Southeastern Latvia) 259-65
Latgale Lakelands 262-5
Latvia 39, 183-275, **186-7, 225, 240-1, 243, 260-1**
  accommodation 183, 272
  activities 272
  arts 268-9
  birdwatching 32
  budget 184
  children, travel with 35
  consulates 272
  customs regulations 272
  drinks 271
  economy 265, 267
  embassies 272
  environmental programs 268
  ethnic minorities 227
  EU membership 267
  exchange rates 184
  food 183, 184, 269-72
  highlights 186-7
  history 265-8
  internet access 273
  internet resources 15, 184, 273
  itineraries 26, **26**
  language 184, 417-19
  Latvian–Russian relations 265
  maps 273
  money 184, 185, 273
  planning 183-4
  politics 267-8
  population 268
  postal services 273
  public holidays 273
  telephone services 273-4

tourist information 274
travel seasons 183
travel to/from 184, 274
travel within 274-5
visas 185, 403
Latvian Ethnographic Open-Air Museum 200
Latvian National Museum of Art 194-5
Latvian National Opera 194
Latvian People's Front Museum 189
legal matters 400-1
Leisi 140
lesbian travellers 399
  Estonia 73, 168
  Vilnius 302
Lielvārde 259
Liepāja 235-8, **236**
Līgatne 18, 253-4
lighthouses
  Estonia 81, 141, 142, 151, 152, 154
  Latvia 226, 227
  Lithuania 355
Liškiava 322
literature, see also books
  Estonia 162-3
  Lithuania 371, 375-6
Lithuania 39, 276-385, **278-9, 312, 317, 324, 342**
  accommodation 276, 380-1
  activities 381
  arts 374-7
  birdwatching 32
  budget 277
  children, travel with 35
  consulates 382
  customs regulations 381-2
  drinks 277, 379-80
  economy 373
  education 374
  embassies 382
  ethnic minorities 309, 368, 373
  EU membership 315, 373
  exchange rates 277
  food 276, 277, 377-9, 380
  highlights 278-9
  history 369-73
  internet access 382-3
  internet resources 15, 277
  itineraries 27, **27**
  language 277, 419-20
  Lithuanian–Polish relations 368
  maps 383
  migration 373-4
  money 280, 383
  planning 276-7, 280
  politics 372-3
  population 373-4
  postal services 383

public holidays 382
religion 370
telephone services 384
tourist information 384
travel seasons 276
travel to/from 277, 384-5
travel within 385
visas 280, 403
Lithuanian Ethnocosmology Museum 316
Lithuanian Minor History Museum 344
Lithuanian Museum of Energy and Technology 294
Lithuanian Sea Museum 345-6
Liv people 227
Livonian People's House 227
Livonian War 157
Ludza 263
Luhasoo Nature Reserve 110
Lutheranism 161
lynx 81, 82, 110, 253

M
Maarjamäe Manor 58
Maarjamäe War Memorial 58
Mačiulis, Jonas 375
Madona 258
Maija Roze 249
Mairionis 325, 375
Majakivi Nature Trail 81
Mann, Thomas 354-5
manor houses 8
  Geidānmuiža 252
  Krimulda Manor 247
  Maarjamäe Manor 58
  Marciena Manor 258
  Pädaste Manor 131
  Palmse Manor 82
  Rumene Manor 16, 227-8
  Sagadi Manor 83, 84
  Ungurmuiža 252
mansions, see manor houses
maps 401
  Estonia 168
  Latvia 273
  Lithuania 383
Marcinkonys 322
markets
  Central Market 195
  Christmas markets 23
  Flower Market (Lat) 215
  Flower Market (Lith) 294
  Helsinki 179
  Peter's Market 237
  Tallinn 75
Matelis, Arūnas 376
Matsalu National Park 31-2, 143
Mazirbe 227

Mažvydas, Martynas 375

mead 379

medical services 400, *see also* health, *individual locations*

Mentzendorff's House 188

Merkinė 322

meteorite craters 139, 149

Mežaparks 199-200

Mežotne Palace 241

Mickiewicz, Adam 284-5, 371, 375

Midsummer 6, 20, 32, 204, **7**

migration 373-4

Military Cemetery 292

Miłosz, Czesław 375

Mingė 359

minigolf 108

mobile phones 15, 402
- Estonia 169
- Latvia 274
- Lithuania 384

Molėtai 316

monasteries & convents
- Dominican Monastery (Est) 51
- Dominican Monastery (Lith) 322
- Pažaislis Monastery 329-40
- Pühtitsa Convent 90
- Šiauliai 335
- St Bridget's Convent 58

money 15, 401
- currencies 14
- discount cards 398
- Estonia 43, 168
- Latvia 184, 185, 273
- Lithuania 280, 383

moneychangers 401, *see also* exchange rates

mosquitoes 312, 400

motorcycle travel 408-9

motoring organisations 408

mountain-biking
- Otepää 113
- Sigulda 249
- Valmiera 257

mud baths 123, 145, 223

Muhu 130-2, **134-5**

Muhu Ostrich Farm 131

Muhu Stronghold 131

Munchausen, Baron Karl Friedrich Hieronymus von 244

museums & galleries (Estonia)
- A Le Coq Beer Museum 100
- Aaviks Museum 135-6
- Architecture Museum 56
- Citizen's Home Museum 98-9

Citizen's House Museum 86

City Museum 17, 49

Draakoni Gallery 51

Estonian Art Museum 50

Estonian History Museum 49, 58

Estonian Literary Museum 160

Estonian Maritime Museum 51

Estonian National Museum 99

Estonian Open Air Museum 59

Estonian Printing Museum 100

Estonian Railway Museum Haapsalu 145

Estonian Sports Museum 98

Hiiumaa Museum 153

Hotel Viru KGB Museum 16, 56

Ilon's Wonderland 145

Kadriorg Art Museum 56

KGB Cells Museum 99-100

Kihnu Museum 129

Koguva Open-Air Museum 131

Kolga Museum 81

Kondas Centre 118

Kreutzwald Memorial Museum 109

Kumu 18, 57

Kunstigalerii 89

Läänemaa Museum 145

Liiv Museum 93

Lydia Koidula Memorial Museum 123-4

Mihkli Farm Museum (Hiiumaa) 150-1

Mihkli Farm Museum (Saaremaa) 141

Mikkel Museum 57

Military Museum 151

Mine Museum 51

Museum of New Art 123

Museum of Occupations 17, 49-50

Museum of the Estonian Swedes 145

Museum of University History 99

Narva Museum 89

Old Believers' Museum 93

Paper Museum 100

Pärnu Museum 123

Pearsgarden Farmstead Museum 154

Photo Museum 51

Pikk Maja 149

Postal Museum 98

Rakvere Museum 86

Rudolf Tobias Museum 152

Saaremaa Museum 135

Sagadi Manor & Forest Museum 83

Sea Museum 82

Seto Farm Museum 107

Seto Museum House 107

Sillamäe Museum 88

St Nicholas' Church Museum 50

Tartu Art Museum 98

Toy Museum 98

University Art Museum 97

Valga Museum 111-12

Viinistu Art Museum 81-2

Viljandi Museum 119

Võrumaa Regional Museum 109

Winter Sports Museum 113

museums & galleries (Helsinki)
- Ateneum 173
- Helsinki City Museum 174
- Kansallismuseo 174
- Kiasma 173
- Seurasaaren ulkomuseo 174

museums & galleries (Kaliningrad)
- Amber Museum 387
- Bunker Museum 389
- Friedland Gate 387, 389
- History & Arts Museum 389
- Kaliningrad Art Gallery 389
- King's Gate 389
- Museum of the World Ocean 387

museums & galleries (Latvia)
- Andrejs Pumpurs Museum 259
- Āraiši Museum Park 256
- Arsenāls Museum of Art 193
- Art Rezidence 'Inner Light' 219
- Bauska Castle Museum 239
- Biržasnams Art Museum 191, 193
- Bread Museum 264
- Cēsis History & Art Museum 254
- Ernest Glueck Bible Museum 258
- History Museum of Latvia 193
- Janis Rozentāls & Rūdolfs Blaumanis' Museum 199
- Jews in Latvia 199
- Jūrmala City Museum 219
- Jūrmala Open-Air Museum 219
- Kuldīga Historic Museum 229
- Latvian Ethnographic Open-Air Museum 200
- Latvian National Museum of Art 194-5
- Latvian People's Front Museum 189
- Latvian Photography Museum 189
- Liepāja History & Art Museum 237
- Meņģeļi Open-Air Museum 258
- Munchausen's Museum 244
- Museum of Barricades of 1991 193
- Museum of Decorative Arts & Design 189
- Museum of Horns & Antlers 226
- Museum of the History of Rīga & Navigation 193
- Museum of the Occupation of Latvia 188
- Museum of War 193-4
- Natural History Museum 195
- Naval School Museum 244-5

Occupation & Regimes Department 237
Open-Air Museum of the Coast 231-2
Pedvāle Open-Air Art Museum 17, 228
Rainis Museum 265
Regional Studies & Art Museum 260-1
Rīga Art Nouveau Centre 198-9
Rīga Motor Museum 200
Rīga Museum of Architecture 193
Rīga Porcelain Museum 189
Rundāli Museum 227
Turaida Museum Reserve 245-7
Valmeira Regional Museum 256
museums & galleries (Lithuania)
Amber Gallery Museum 355
Amber Museum 361
Amber Museum-Gallery 285
Ancient Bee-keeping Museum 313
Antanas Mončys House Museum 362
Archaeological & Historical Museum 311
Baroti Gallery 344
Bicycle Museum 336
Blacksmith's Museum 344
Centre for Tolerance 291
Ceramics Museum 325
Clock Museum 345
Cold War Museum 16, 366, 367
Communications Development Museum 325
Contemporary Art Centre 291
Daugyvenė Cultural History Museum Reserve 338
Dr Jono Šliūpas Memorial House 362
Ethnographic Farmstead Museum 359
Ethnographic Fisherman's Museum 355
Ethnographic Museum 322
Ethnographic Sea Fishermen's Farmstead 346
Europas parkas 311
Exposition of the National Park of the Curonian Spit 346
Folk Music & Instruments Museum 328
Holocaust Museum 291
Horse Museum 340-1
Karaites Ethnographic Museum 309
Kaunas Picture Gallery 329
Kazys Varnelis Museum 285
Klaipėda Castle Museum 343
Kleboniškiai Rural Life Exhibition 338

Kretinga Museum 365
Lithuanian Ethnocosmology Museum 316
Lithuanian Minor History Museum 344
Lithuanian Museum of Energy and Technology 294
Lithuanian Sea Museum 345-6
Maironis Lithuanian Literary Museum 325
Medicine & Pharmaceutical History Museum 325
Mickiewicz Memorial Apartment & Museum 284-5
Military Museum of Vytautas the Great 329
MK Čiurlionis House 285
MK Čiurlionis Memorial Museum 318
Museum of Applied Arts 282-3
Museum of Armed Resistance 318-19
Museum of Cats 336
Museum of Deportation & Resistance 325
Museum of Devils 17, 329
Museum of Genocide Victims 293-4
Mykolas Žilinskas Art Gallery 328
Narrow-Gauge Railway Museum 340
National Čiurlionis Art Museum 328-9
National Museum of Lithuania 282
Neringa History Museum 354
Open-Air Museum of Lithuania 330
Paneriai Museum 308
Photography Museum 334
Plateliai Manor Museum Complex 366
Polder Museum 359
Pranas Domšaitis Gallery 345
Radio & Television Museum 336
Resistance Museum 361
Sacral Art Exhibition 309
Tadas Ivanauskas Zoological Museum 328
Theatre, Music & Cinema Museum 292
Thomas Mann Memorial Museum 354-5
Trakai History Museum 308-9
Upper Castle Museum 280-1
Vilna Gaon State Jewish Museum 291
Vilnius Picture Gallery 285
Žemaitija Art Museum 366
mushrooming 10, 31, 122, 312, 313, 322, **10**
music, see also jazz, music festivals
Estonia 161-2

Estonian Traditional Music Centre 119
Latvia 269
Lithuania 376-7
opera 20, 21, 136, 194, 204, 269
Seto singing 106
music festivals, see also jazz festivals, singing festivals
Arena New Music Festival 22, 204
August Blues 146
Capital Days 297
Christopher Summer Festival 21, 295
Devil's Stone Music 20-1
Early Music Festival 146
Gaida Music Festival 22, 297
MJR Alternative Music Festival 21
Old Music Festival 119
Opera Days 136
Operetta in Kaunas Castle 330
Positivus 21, 244
Riga Opera Festival 20, 204
Riga's Rhythms 21, 204
Summer Sound 21
Tallinn International Organ Festival 61
Viljandi Folk Music Festival 20, 117, 119
Vilnius Festival 295
Visagino Country 316
Mustvee 91-2
myths & legends
Estonia 106, 122, 142, 146
Latvia 241, 263
Lithuania 280, 323, 367

N

Naglių Strict Nature Reserve 353
narrow-gauge railways 232, 258, 340
Narva 88-90
Narva-Jõesuu 90-1
national & regional parks & reserves (Estonia)
Haanja Nature Park 110-11
Karula National Park 111
Lahemaa National Park 13, 79, 81-5, **80, 13**
Matsalu National Park 31-2, 143
Soomaa National Park 33, 120-2
Viidumäe Nature Reserve 142
Vilsandi National Park 32, 141
Vormsi Landscape Reserve 154
national & regional parks & reserves (Latvia)
Gauja National Park 11, 32, 33, 34, 245-57, **245, 11**
Ķemeri National Park 32, 223-4
Krustkalni Nature Reserve 258
Lake Engure Nature Park 32, 336

national & regional parks & reserves (Latvia) *continued*
Līgatne Nature Trails 253
North Vidzeme Biosphere Reserve 244
Pokaiņi Forest Reserve 242
Razna National Park 262
Slītere National Park 225-6
Teiči Nature Reserve 32, 258
Tērvete Nature Park 242
national & regional parks & reserves (Lithuania)
Aukštaitija National Park 33, 311, 312-15, **314**
Čepkeliai Strict Nature Reserve 322
Curonian Spit National Park 8, 32, 34, 341, 350-8, **350**, 8
Dzūkija National Park 311, 322-3
Labanoras Regional Park 316
Naglių Strict Nature Reserve 353
Nemuman Loops Regional Park 333-4
Nemunas Delta Regional Park 359
Trakai Historical National Park 308
Varnikai Botanical-Zoological Preserve 309
Žemaitija National Park 18, 365-8
National Awakening 95, 158, 267
National Museum of Lithuania 282
nature parks, *see* national & regional parks & reserves
Nemirseta 365
Nemunas Delta 32, 359-61
Nemunas Loops Regional Park 333-4
New Year's Day 19
New Year's Eve 23
Nida 17, 354-8, **356**
nightingales 110
nightlife, *see individual locations*
Ninth Fort 329
North Vidzeme Biosphere Reserve 244
Northeastern Estonia 79-91, **79**
Northeastern Latvia (Vidzeme) 242-59, **243**

O
Obinitsa 107-8
Okansen, Sofi 163
Old Believers 91, 92, 93
Old Rīga (Vecrīga) 185, 188-91, 193-4, **190-1**

Old Town (Tallinn) 6, 18, 47, 49-51, 54, 62-3, **62**, 6-7
Old Town (Vilnius) 9, 18, 283-5, 288-93, 9
Ontika Landscape Reserve 87
opening hours 397-8
opera 20, 21, 136, 194, 204, 269
organic farming 139
Orissaare 140
Orvydas Garden 366
ostrich farm 131
Otepää 33, 35, 112-16, **114**

P
Pädaste Manor 131
paganism 265, 266, 370
palaces, *see also* castles, manor houses
Grand Duke Palace 293
Jelgava Palace 242
Kadriorg Palace 56-7
Mežotne Palace 241
Presidential Palace (Kaunas) 327-8
Presidential Palace (Vilnius) 284
Radvilos Palace 292
Royal Palace 281, 368
Rundāle Palace 17, 212, 239-42, 8
Palanga 361-5, **362**
Palmse Manor 82
Paneriai 18, 308
Panevėžys 338-90, **339**
Panga pank 140
Papīrfabrika 253
Pärispea Peninsula 81
parks & gardens (Estonia)
Castle Park 118
Kadriorg Park 47
Paralepa Forest Park 145
Raadi Manor Park 99
Tallinn Botanic Gardens 58-9
Tartu Botanical Gardens 98
parks & gardens (Latvia)
Āraiši Museum Park 256
Castle Park 254
Daina Hill Song Garden 247
Renka Garden 233
Vērmanes darzs 194
Vienkoču Parks 254
parks & gardens (Lithuania)
Europas parkas 311
Grūtas Park 321
Kaunas Botanical Gardens 329
Martynas Mažvydas Sculpture Park 343
Orvydas Garden 366
Palanga Botanical Park 361
Vingis Park 294

Parliament (Lat) 193
Parliament House (Lith) 294
Parnidis Dune 354, 355-6
Pärnu 12, 17, 35, 122-8, **124**, 12
Pärnu International Film Festival 20, 124
Pärt, Arvo 85, 161
passports 404, *see also* visas
Pāvilosta 234-5
Pažaislis Monastery 329-40
Peko 106
Pension, The 35, 253
Peter the Great 57, 95
Peter's Market 237
Peterson, Kristjan Jaak 162
petrol stations 37, 413
Piłsudski, Jósef 292
Pirita Beach 58
pirts 29, 201, 248
Piusa Caves 107
planning 14-35, *see also individual regions*
activities 28-33
budget 14
calendar of events 19-23
children, travel with 34-5
highlights 6-13
internet resources 15
itineraries 24-7
regions 38-9
repeat visitors 16
road trips 36-7
travel seasons 14
Plateliai 365
Podmotsa 107
Pokaiņi Forest Reserve 242
polders 359
Polish–Lithuanian relations 368
population
Estonia 160-1
Latvia 268
Lithuania 373-4
Positivus (Lat) 21, 244
postal services 401
Latvia 273
Lithuania 383
opening hours 398
pottery 263, 303, 322
Preiļi 265
public holidays
Estonia 168-9
Latvia 273
Lithuania 382
Pühajärv 112-13
Pühtitsa Convent 90
Pumpurs, Andrejs 259
Puntukas Stone 341
puppet theatres 60, 332, 339-40

R
Radviliškis 338
rafting 31
　Haanja Nature Park 110
　Otepää 113
　Tallinn 61
　Valmiera 256
Rainis, Jānis 199, 265
Rakvere 85-7
Rastrelli, Bartolomeo 240-1
Rasų Cemetery 292
Razna National Park 262
regional parks, see national &
　regional parks & reserves
religion, see also Christianity,
　Catholicism, Russian Orthodoxy
　Estonia 128, 161
　Lithuania 370
　Old Believers 91, 92, 93
reserves, see national & regional
　parks & reserves
responsible travel
　climate change 405
　Curonian Spit National Park 353
Rēzekne 262-3
Riežupe Sand Caves 230
Rīga 9, 16, 185-218, **190-1**, **196-7**,
　202, **9**
　accommodation 204-8
　activities 200-1
　children, travel with 199
　day trips 212
　drinking 211-13
　entertainment 213-14
　festivals & events 204
　food 208-11
　history 185
　information 216-18
　internet access 216
　itineraries 188
　local guidebooks 216
　medical services 216
　Old Riga (Vecrīga) 185, 188-91,
　　193-4, **190-1**
　Rīga Card 195
　shopping 214-16
　sights 185, 188-200
　tourist information 216
　tours 201
　travel to/from 216-17
　travel within 218
　walking tour 202-3, **202**
Rīga Castle 193
Rīga Motor Museum 200
Rīga Museum of Architecture 193
Rīga National Zoo 199
Rīga Porcelain Museum 189
road distance chart 413
road rules 37, 413

Roja 226
rollerblading 314
Roma 373
ropes courses 248-9
Rose of Turaida 249
Rotermann Quarter 16, 56
Rothko, Mark 260-1, 269
Rõuge 18, 110
Rozentāls, Janis 199, 269
Ruhnu 129
Rumene Manor 16, 227-8
Rummo, Paul-Eerik 162-3, 164
Rundāle Palace 17, 212, 239-42, **8**
Rusnė Island 359
Russia, rail links with 409
Russian border 107
Russian–Estonian relations 88, 155-6
Russian–Latvian relations 265
Russian Orthodoxy 93, 128, 161
Russian visas 403

S
Saar, Mart 161
Sääre Tirp 153
Saaremaa 9, 132-43, **134-5**, **9**
Sabile 228-9
sacrificial stones 99
safe travel, see also emergencies,
　hazards
　hitching 413
　road 15, 37, 413
Sagadi Manor & Forest Museum 83, 84
sailing 30, 58, 234, 309, 311, 317, 346
Salacgrīva 244
Salaspils 259
Salaspils concentration camp 223
Samogitian Calvary 366
Sangaste Rye House 112
Sartre, Jean Paul 354
Sauleskalns 264
Saulkrasti 212, 244
saunas & spas 10, 29-30, **10**, see also
　individual locations
　Birštonas 333
　Druskininkai 29, 318-19, 320
　Helsinki 174-5
　Kuressaare 133
　pirts 29, 201, 248
　smoke saunas 30, 108, 150-1
Schengen Agreement 169, 407
scuba diving, see diving
sculptures
　cows 233
　Daina Hill Song Garden 247
　Europas parkas 311
　Klaipėda 343
　Martynas Mažvydas Sculpture
　　Park 343

Orvydas Garden 366
Pedvāle Open-Air Art Museum
　17, 228
　Tartu 98
seals 141
Šeduva 338
seniors cards 398
Seto people 105-6, 160-1
Setomaa 105-8
shopping, see crafts, markets,
　individual locations
Šiauliai 334-8, **335**
Sigulda 11, 35, 212, 245-53, **246**, **11**
　walking tour 250, **250**
Sillamäe 87-8
Šilutė 359
SIM cards 15, 169
singing festivals
　Birgitta Festival 22, 64
　Estonian Punk Song Festival 85
　Estonian Song & Dance
　　Celebration 61
　New Wave Song Festival 21, 220
　Song & Dance Festival 21, 269
Singing Revolution 57-8, 159
skateboarding 62
Škėma, Antanas 375
skiing 33
　Anykščiai 341
　Aukštaitija National Park 33, 314
　Cēsis 254
　Gauja National Park 33
　Haanja Nature Park 110
　Otepää 33, 113-14
　Sauleskalns 264
　Soomaa National Park 33, 122
　Tartu Ski Marathon 19, 101
　Trakai 309
　Valmiera 257
　Vidzeme Uplands 33, 258
sledding 309
sleigh rides 114
Slītere National Park 225-6
Smiltynė 345-6
smoking 401
Šnipiškės 294
snowboarding 33
　Cēsis 254
　Otepää 113, 114
　Vidzeme Uplands 33, 258
snowmobiling 114
snowshoeing
　Soomaa National Park 122
　Tallinn 61
soap-making courses 139
soccer 74
Soomaa National Park 33, 120-2
Sõrve Peninsula 142
Southeastern Estonia 91-116, **92**

Southeastern Latvia (Latgale) 259-65, **260-1**

Southern Latvia (Zemgale) 238-42, **240-1**

Southern Lithuania 311-23, **317**

Southwestern Estonia 116-29, **116-17**

Soviet era 13
Cold War Museum 366, 367
Estonia 46-7, 81, 87-8, 95, 121, 159-60
Hotel Viru KGB Museum 16, 56
KGB Cells Museum 99-100
Latvia 194, 233, 235-6, 253, 267
Lithuania 281, 293-4, 315, 325, 367, 372
Museum of Deportation & Resistance 325
Museum of Genocide Victims 293-4
Museum of the Occupation of Latvia 188
Occupation & Regimes Department 237

Soviet spy telescope 233

Soviet underground missile base 367

spa hotels 397

spas, see also saunas & spas

sports, see also activities
basketball 74, 374
Estonian Sports Museum 98
extreme sports 248-9
football 74
Winter Sports Museum 113

St Alexander Nevsky Cathedral 54

St Bridget's Convent 58

Stameriena Castle 258

stamps 401

Stonys, Audrius 376

storks 31, 82, 262, 313

Streičs, Jānis 224, 269

Stroomi beach 59

student & youth cards 398

Sugihara, Chiune 325

Sugihara House 325

Suomenlinna 173

Surf Paradiis 152

surfing
Hiiumaa 150, 152
Pāvilosta 234

Suur Munamägi 110

Suuremõisa 149

Suurjärv Lake 110

Šventoji 365

Swedish Hill 242

swimming 60, 91, 107, 119, 175, 229, 262, 359, 365, see also beaches

synagogues
Kaunas 328
Rīga 189
Vilnius 291

T

Tacitus 157

Tagamõisa Peninsula 141

Takhuna 17, 140

Tallinn 16, 34, 46-79, **48-9**, **52-3**, **62**
accommodation 64-7
activities 59-60
children, travel with 60
drinking 71-2
entertainment 72-4
festivals & events 61, 64
food 67-71
gay travellers 73
history 46-7
information 76-9
itineraries 47
language courses 64
lesbian travellers 73
medical services 76
Old Town 6, 18, 47, 49-51, 54, 62-3, **62**, **6-7**
shopping 74-6
sights 47, 49-51, 54-9
Tallinn Card 76
tourist information 76-7
tours 60-1
travel to/from 77
travel within 77-9
walking tour 62-3, **62**

Tallinn Botanic Gardens 58-9

Tallinn Song Festival Grounds 57-8

Tallinn Zoological Gardens 59

Talsi 224-5

Tammsaare, Anton Hansen 162

Tartu 10, 16, 94-105, **96**, **10**

Tartu Art Museum 98

Tartu Student Days 19, 101

Tartu University 96-7

taxis 414

Teiči Nature Reserve 32, 258

telephone services 15, 402
Estonia 169
Latvia 273-4
Lithuania 384

television, Lithuanian 376

Tērvete 242

Tērvete Nature Park 242

theatre, see also puppet theatre, individual locations
Estonia 163-4
Lithuania 377

Sirenas International Theatre Festival 22, 297

theft 199

Three Crosses 292-3

time 402

tipping 167, 383, 401

Tobias, Rudolf 152, 161

tobogganing 248

Toila 87

toilets 402

Tonja 106-7

tourist information 402, see also individual locations
Estonia 169
Latvia 274
Lithuania 384

tours 410, 414, see also boat tours, walking tours, individual locations

train travel
Estonia 170
Helsinki 181
Latvia 275
Lithuania 385
narrow-gauge railways 232, 258, 340
railway routes **412**
to/from the Baltic 409
within the Baltic 169-70, 385, 414-15

Trainiškis Wildlife Sanctuary 312-13

Trakai 308-10, **2-3**

Trakai Historical National Park 308

trams 414

travel insurance 400

travel seasons 14, see also individual locations

travel to/from the Baltic 15, 404-10

travel within the Baltic 410-15

travellers cheques 401

trolleybuses 414

Tubin, Eduard 93, 161

tubing 141, 152

Tukums 224

Tüür, Erkki-Sven 161

TV & Radio Centre 294

TV Tower (Est) 59

TV Tower (Lith) 294-5

U

Unesco World Heritage sites
Curonian Spit National Park 8, 32, 34, 341, **350**, **8**
Kaliningrad Cathedral 387
Kernave 311
Old Town (Vilnius) 9, 18, 283-5, 288-93, **9**
Suomenlinna 273

Ungurmuiža 252

Unt, Mati 163

Utena 316-17
Užupis Republic 293

V
Vabarna, Anne 106, 107
vaccinations 400
Vaide 226
Vaivari sanatorium 219
Valaste 87
Valga 111-12
Valmiera 256-7
Varėna 322
Varnelis, Kazys 285
Varnikai Botanical-Zoological
    Preserve 309
Värska 107
Vasknarva 91
Vastseliina Castle 108
Vecekrugas Dune 353
Veczemju Red Cliffs 244
Ventas Rumba 230
Ventės Ragas 359
Ventės Ragas Ornithological Station
    359, 360
Ventspils 231-4, **232**
Ventspils International Radio
    Astronomy Centre 233
Vidzeme (Northeastern Latvia)
    242-59, **243**
Vidzeme Coast 244-5
Vidzeme Rocky Seashore 244
Vidzeme Uplands 33, 258-9
Viidumäe Nature Reserve 142
Viķe-Freiberga, Vaira 266, 267
Viking ship tours 334
Vilde, Eduard 162
Viljandi 117-20, **118**
Viljandi Folk Music Festival 20,
    117
Vilnius 9, 280-308, **282-3**, **286-7**,
    296, 9
    accommodation 297-9
    activities 295
    children, travel with 295
    drinking 301, 302
    entertainment 302-4
    festivals & events 295, 297
    food 299-302
    gay & lesbian travellers 302
    history 280, 372
    information 305-8
    internet access 305
    itineraries 285
    medical services 306
    Old Town 9, 18, 283-5, 288-93, 9

    shopping 304-5
    sights 280-5, 288-95
    tourist information 306
    tours 295
    travel to/from 306-7
    travel within 307-8
    walking tour 296-7, **296**
Vilnius University 283-4
Vilnius Yiddish Institute 290
Vilsandi 141
Vilsandi National Park 32, 141
Vinakalns 228
Vingis Park 294
Virve 81
Visaginas 315-16
visas 15, 403, see also passports
    Belarus 403, 408
    Estonia 46, 403
    Kaliningrad 387
    Latvia 185, 403
    Lithuania 280, 403
    Russia 403
volunteering 139, 403
Võpolsova 106-7
Vormsi 154-5, **148**
Võro-Seto language 105
Võru 108-10
Voru Folklore Festival 21
Vosu 82

W
walking, see hiking
walking tours
    Rīga 202-3, **202**
    Sigulda 250, **250**
    Tallinn 62-3, **62**
    Vilnius 296-7, **296**
water, drinking 400
water sports 30-1, see also individual
    activities
waterfalls
    Estonia 87
    Latvia 230
waterparks
    Jūrmala 219
    Kuressaare 136
    Pärnu 123
    Rīga 199
    Tartu 100
    Ventspils 231
    Vilnius 295
waterskiing 141, 152
weather 14, see also individual
    regions
weathervanes 352

Western Estonia & the Islands
    129-55, **130**
Western Hiiumaa 150-2
Western Latvia (Kurzeme) 224-38,
    225
Western Lithuania 341-68, **342**
White Lady Festival 21, 146
wi-fi 400
    Estonia 168
    Latvia 273
    Lithuania 382-3
wife-carrying championships 98
wild boar 253, 312
wildlife, see animals
windmills
    Estonia 131, 140, 141
    Latvia 256
    Lithuania 338
windsurfing 152, 234
wine
    Estonia 167
    festivals 21, 228
    Latvia 228, 271
    Lithuania 301, 379
Witches' Hill 352
wolves 81, 82, 110
women
    Latvian 268
    Lithuanian 374
women travellers 403
wool factory 147
work opportunities 403
World Heritage sites, see Unesco
    World Heritage sites
WWI 158, 185, 239, 343, 371
WWII, see also concentration camps
    Estonia 46, 142, 150, 151, 159
    Latvia 207, 267
    Lithuania 290, 308, 329, 371

Y
yachting 91, 410, 411

Z
Zappa, Frank 292
Žemaitija National Park 18, 365-8
Zemgale (Southern Latvia) 238-42,
    240-1
Zervynos 322
zip-wiring 256
zoos
    Kaliningradsky Zoopark 389
    Mini Zoo 123
    Rīga National Zoo 199
    Tallinn Zoological Gardens 59

how to use this book

These symbols will help you find the listings you want:

- 👁 Sights
- 🐬 Beaches
- 🏃 Activities
- 🎓 Courses
- 🐘 Tours
- 🎊 Festivals & Events
- 🛏 Sleeping
- 🍴 Eating
- 🍷 Drinking
- ⭐ Entertainment
- 🛍 Shopping
- ℹ Information/Transport

Look out for these icons:

- **TOP CHOICE** Our author's recommendation
- **FREE** No payment required
- 🌱 A green or sustainable option

Our authors have nominated these places as demonstrating a strong commitment to sustainability – for example by supporting local communities and producers, operating in an environmentally friendly way, or supporting conservation projects.

These symbols give you the vital information for each listing:

- 📞 Telephone Numbers
- 🕐 Opening Hours
- Ⓟ Parking
- 🚭 Nonsmoking
- ❄ Air-Conditioning
- @ Internet Access
- 📶 Wi-Fi Access
- 🏊 Swimming Pool
- ✅ Vegetarian Selection
- 📋 English-Language Menu
- 👪 Family-Friendly
- 🐾 Pet-Friendly
- 🚌 Bus
- ⛴ Ferry
- Ⓜ Metro
- Ⓢ Subway
- 🚇 London Tube
- 🚊 Tram
- 🚉 Train

Reviews are organised by author preference.

Map Legend

Sights
- Beach
- Buddhist
- Castle
- Christian
- Hindu
- Islamic
- Jewish
- Monument
- Museum/Gallery
- Ruin
- Winery/Vineyard
- Zoo
- Other Sight

Activities, Courses & Tours
- Diving/Snorkelling
- Canoeing/Kayaking
- Skiing
- Surfing
- Swimming/Pool
- Walking
- Windsurfing
- Other Activity/Course/Tour

Sleeping
- Sleeping
- Camping

Eating
- Eating

Drinking
- Drinking
- Cafe

Entertainment
- Entertainment

Shopping
- Shopping

Information
- Bank
- Embassy/Consulate
- Hospital/Medical
- Internet
- Police
- Post Office
- Telephone
- Toilet
- Tourist Information
- Other Information

Transport
- Airport
- Border Crossing
- Bus
- Cable Car/Funicular
- Cycling
- Ferry
- Metro
- Monorail
- Parking
- Petrol Station
- Taxi
- Train/Railway
- Tram
- Other Transport

Routes
- Tollway
- Freeway
- Primary
- Secondary
- Tertiary
- Lane
- Unsealed Road
- Plaza/Mall
- Steps
- Tunnel
- Pedestrian Overpass
- Walking Tour
- Walking Tour Detour
- Path

Geographic
- Hut/Shelter
- Lighthouse
- Lookout
- Mountain/Volcano
- Oasis
- Park
- Pass
- Picnic Area
- Waterfall

Population
- Capital (National)
- Capital (State/Province)
- City/Large Town
- Town/Village

Boundaries
- International
- State/Province
- Disputed
- Regional/Suburb
- Marine Park
- Cliff
- Wall

Hydrography
- River, Creek
- Intermittent River
- Swamp/Mangrove
- Reef
- Canal
- Water
- Dry/Salt/Intermittent Lake
- Glacier

Areas
- Beach/Desert
- Cemetery (Christian)
- Cemetery (Other)
- Park/Forest
- Sportsground
- Sight (Building)
- Top Sight (Building)

Andy Symington

Helsinki Excursion Andy has covered Finland for Lonely Planet several times, having first visited Helsinki many years ago more or less by accident. Walking on frozen lakes with the midday sun low in the sky made a quick and deep impression on him, even as fingers froze in the -30°C temperatures. Since then they can't keep him away, fuelled by a love of the *Kalevala*, huskies, saunas, Finnish mustard, moody Suomi rock and metal, but above all of Finnish people and their beautiful country.

Read more about Andy Symington at:
lonelyplanet.com/members/andysymington

OUR STORY

A beat-up old car, a few dollars in the pocket and a sense of adventure. In 1972 that's all Tony and Maureen Wheeler needed for the trip of a lifetime – across Europe and Asia overland to Australia. It took several months, and at the end – broke but inspired – they sat at their kitchen table writing and stapling together their first travel guide, *Across Asia on the Cheap*. Within a week they'd sold 1500 copies. Lonely Planet was born.

Today, Lonely Planet has offices in Melbourne, London and Oakland, with more than 600 staff and writers. We share Tony's belief that 'a great guidebook should do three things: inform, educate and amuse'.

OUR WRITERS

Brandon Presser

Coordinating Author, Latvia His wanderlust always bigger than his wallet, Brandon earned his backpacker stripes after an epic overland adventure from Morocco to Finland. He then joined the glamorous ranks of eternal nomadism as a fulltime travel writer, and has since contributed to more than 40 guidebooks. He co-authored *Estonia, Latvia & Lithuania 5* and was delighted to return to the Baltic where he put his Harvard art history degree to good use while checking out Rīga's surplus of evocative art nouveau architecture.

Read more about Brandon Presser at:
lonelyplanet.com/members/brandonpresser

Mark Baker

Lithuania Though this was Mark's first foray into Lithuania, he'd been intrigued by the country since the mid-1980s when he was a grad student in Eastern European studies at New York's Columbia University. Mark is the co-author of Lonely Planet's *Poland* and was keen to see what Polish influence, if any, remained from the long period when the two nations formed a united country. In addition to Lithuania and Poland, Mark has also written for the Lonely Planet *Prague* and *Romania* guides. When he's not on the road, he teaches Central European History at Anglo-American University in his home city of Prague.

Read more about Mark Baker at:
lonelyplanet.com/members/markbaker

Peter Dragicevich

Estonia It's been 20 years since Peter first started writing reviews for a variety of publications. Among the two dozen or so books that he's co-authored for Lonely Planet are the last three editions of the *Eastern Europe* guide. He rates Tallinn as one of his favourite European cities and strongly suggests you allocate ample time for eating your way around the restaurants lurking in forgotten corners of the Old Town.

Read more about Peter Dragicevich at:
lonelyplanet.com/members/peterdragicevich

Simon Richmond

Kaliningrad Excursion Simon's first visit to Russia was in 1994 when he wandered goggle-eyed around gorgeous St Petersburg, and peeked at Lenin's mummified corpse in Red Sq. He's since travelled the breadth of the nation on many trips, visiting Kaliningrad three times in recent years. An award-winning writer and photographer, Simon is the co-author of Lonely Planet's *Trans-Siberian Railway* (editions 1–3) and *Russia* (editions 3–6). Read more about his travels at www.simonrichmond.com.

Read more about Simon Richmond at:
lonelyplanet.com/members/simonrichmond

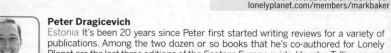

> MORE
> WRITERS

Published by Lonely Planet Publications Pty Ltd
ABN 36 005 607 983
6th edition – June 2012
ISBN 978 1 74179 581 3
© Lonely Planet 2012   Photographs © as indicated 2012
10 9 8 7 6 5 4 3 2 1
Printed in China

Although the authors and Lonely Planet have taken all reasonable care in preparing this book, we make no warranty about the accuracy or completeness of its content and, to the maximum extent permitted, disclaim all liability arising from its use.